Maui

10th Edition

The Most Complete
Guide to Family Fun
and Adventure!

CHRISTIE STILSON

Ulysses Press

Copyright Text © 2003 Paradise Publications. Copyright Maps © 2003 Ulysses Press. All rights reserved, including the right to reproduce this book or portions thereof in any form or by any means, electronic or mechanical, including photocopying, recording, or by any information storage or retrieval system, without written permission from the publisher, except for use by a reviewer in connection with a review.

Published by: Ulysses Press
P.O. Box 3440
Berkeley, CA 94703
www.ulyssespress.com

ISSN 1544-1377
ISBN 1-56975-363-6

Printed in Canada by Transcontinental Printing

10 9 8 7 6 5 4 3 2 1

Managing Editor: Claire Chun
Editor: Lily Chou
Editorial and Production: Kate Allen, Laura Brancella, Lisa Kester, Sarisa Nelson
Cartography: Pease Press
Cover Design: Leslie Henriques, Sarah Levin
Indexer: Sayre Van Young
Cover Photography: Ron Dahlquist (Surfer with boy)
Contributing Editors: Dona Early, Jody Van Aalst, Mark Halvorson

Distributed in the United States by Publishers Group West and in Canada by Raincoast Books

Ulysses Press is a federally registered trademark of BookPack, Inc.

The author and publisher have made every effort to ensure the accuracy of information contained in *Paradise Family Guides: Maui*, but can accept no liability for any loss, injury, or inconvenience sustained by any traveler as a result of information or advice contained in this guide.

Maui No Ka Oi
(Maui is the Best)

*Dedicated to Maren and Jeffrey,
the best kids and two terrific travelers.*

Write to Us!

If in your travels you discover a spot that captures the spirit of Maui, or if you live in the region and have a favorite place to share, or if you just feel like expressing your views, write to us and we'll pass your note along to the author.

Ulysses Press
P.O. Box 3440
Berkeley, CA 94703
E-mail: readermail@ulyssespress.com

Table of Contents

Introduction xv

CHAPTER 1: FAMILY PARADISE 1

Maui's Best Bets 1
The Valley Isle 6
History of Maui 6
Hawaiian Language 11
Island Ecology 13
Traveling with Children 14
Especially for Seniors 26
Travel Tips for the Physically Impaired 27
What to Pack 29
Weddings & Honeymoons 30
Helpful Information 36
Communications 36
Medical Information 39
Hazards 39
Getting There 40
Cruise Lines 46
Getting Around 47
Grocery Shopping 52
Calendar of Annual Events 54
Weather 58
Helpful Phone Numbers 61

CHAPTER 2: WHAT TO SEE, WHERE TO SHOP 63

Lahaina 63
Ka'anapali–Kapalua Area 76
    Ka'anapali 76
    Kapalua 80
Ma'alaea–Kihei–Wailea–Makena Area 84
    Ma'alaea 84
    Kihei 86
    Wailea 89
Kahului–Wailuku Area 91
Upcountry 98
Hana Highway 104

CHAPTER 3: WHERE TO STAY 119

Lodging Best Bets 124
Lahaina 127

Ka'anapali–Kapalua Area	132
Ka'anapali	132
Honokowai	138
Kahana	144
Napili	146
Kapalua	150
Ma'alaea–Kihei–Wailea–Makena Area	152
Ma'alaea	152
Kihei	155
Wailea	167
Makena	175
Kahului–Wailuku Area	176
Upcountry	178
Hana Highway	181
Rental Agents	186

CHAPTER 4: WHERE TO DINE — 191

Ethnic Foods	193
Dining Best Bets	197
Lahaina	200
Ka'anapali–Kapalua Area	218
Ma'alaea–Kihei–Wailea–Makena Area	238
Kahului–Wailuku Area	267
Upcountry	280
Hana Highway	286
Luaus and Dinner Shows	293

CHAPTER 5: BEACHES — 302

Beach Precautions	304
Best Bets	309
Using This Chapter	309
Lahaina	310
Ka'anapali–Kapalua Area	314
Ma'alaea–Kihei–Wailea–Makena Area	319
Kahului–Wailuku Area	326
Hana Highway	327

CHAPTER 6: RECREATION AND TOURS — 330

Best Bets	332
Adventures and Tours	332
Airplane Tours	332
All-Terrain Vehicles	333
Aquarium	334
Archery	334

Art Classes and Art Tours	334
Astronomy	334
Biking	335
Body Surfing	338
Bowling	339
Camping	339
Canoeing (Outrigger)	341
Cruises	342
Dance	345
Fishing	345
Golf	347
Golf—Miniature	352
Hang Gliding	352
Helicopter Tours	352
Hiking	354
Horseback Riding	359
Hunting/Sporting Clays	362
Jet Skiing	363
Kayaking	363
Kiteboarding	365
Land Tours	365
Museums/Gardens	370
Parasailing	375
Polo	376
Running	376
Scuba Diving	376
Sea Excursions, Sailing	381
Snorkeling	394
Snuba	397
Spas/Fitness Centers/Health Retreats	397
Spelunking	399
Surfing	400
Swimming	402
Tennis	402
Theater, Movies and The Arts	403
Waterskiing	405
Whale Watching	405
Windsurfing	406

CHAPTER 7: LANA'I   408

Lana'i Best Bets	408
The Pineapple Isle	408
History	410
Geography and Climate	415

Island Ecology	417
Traveling with Children	417
Weddings & Honeymoons	418
Getting There	419
Getting Around	419
What to See, Where to Shop	420
Where to Stay	425
Camping on Lana'i	425
Private Homes	425
Bed and Breakfasts	425
Hotels and Resorts	425
Where to Dine	430
Beaches	434
Recreation and Tours	435
Archery	436
Art & Culture	436
Biking	437
Fishing	437
Golf	437
Hiking	439
Horseback Riding	439
Hunting	440
Kayaking	441
Off Roading	441
Scuba Diving	441
Snorkeling	442
Spas & Fitness Centers	443
Surfing	444
Tennis	444
Theater	444
Recommended Reading	446
Index	449
Lodging Index	456
Dining Index	459
Dining Index by Cuisine	464
About the Author	475

MAPS

Hawaiian Islands	xiv
Maui	xviii
Lahaina	65
Ka'anapali–Kapalua Area	77
Ma'alaea–Kihei–Wailea–Makena Area	85
Kahului–Wailuku Area	93
Upcountry	99
Haleakala National Park	101
Hana Highway	107
Maui Beaches	311
Lana'i	411

Kawaipunahele

Nou e Kawaipunahele
Ku'u leu aloha mae'ole
Pili hemo'ole, pili pa'a pono
E huli ho'i kaua
E Kawaipunahele

Ku 'oe me ke ki'eki'e
I ka nani a'o Wailuku
Ku'u ipo henoheno,
Ku'u wehi o ka po
E huli ho'i kaua
E Kawaipunahele

Eia ho'i 'o Keali'i
Kali'ana i ka mehameha
Mehameha ho'i au, 'eha'eha ho'i au
E huli ho'i kaua
E Kawaipunahele

Puana 'ia ke aloha
Ku'u lei aloha mae 'ole
Pili hemo'ole, pili pa'a pono
Ke pono ho'i kaua
E Kawaipunahele

For you Kawaipunahele
My never-fading lei
Never separated, firmly united
Come, let's go back
O Kawaipunahele

You stand majestically
In the splendor of Wailuku
My cherished sweetheart
My adornment of the night
Come, let's go back
O Kawaipunahele

Here is Keali'i
Waiting in loneliness
I am lonely, I hurt
Come, let's go back
O Kawaipunahele

Tell of the love
Of my never-fading lei
Never separated, firmly united
When it's right, we'll go back
O Kawaipunahele

Music and lyrics by Keali'i Reichel, arrangement by Moon Kauakahi. Used with the permission of Punahele Productions, Wailuku, Maui. From Keali'i Reichel's CD recording, *Kawaipunahele*.

Although the islands have changed greatly during the century since Mark Twain visited the islands, there remains much to fall in love with. Despite the influences of what may seem to some like rampant commercialism, the physical beauty and seductiveness of the land remains ... and the true aloha spirit does survive. I am confident that as you explore these islands, you too will be charmed by their magic. Keep in mind the expressive words used by Twain over 100 years ago when he fell in love with the islands of Hawai'i.

> *"No alien land in all the world has any deep strong charm for me but that one, no other land could so longingly and so beseechingly haunt me, sleeping and waking, through half a lifetime, as that one has done. Other things leave me, but it abides; other things change, but it remains the same. For me its balmy airs are always blowing, its summer seas flashing in the sun; the pulsing of its surfbeat is in my ear; I can see its garlanded crags, its leaping cascades, its plumy palms drowsing by the shore, its remote summits floating like islands above the cloud wrack; I can feel the spirit of its woodland solitudes, I can hear the splash of its brooks; in my nostrils still lives the breath of flowers..."*

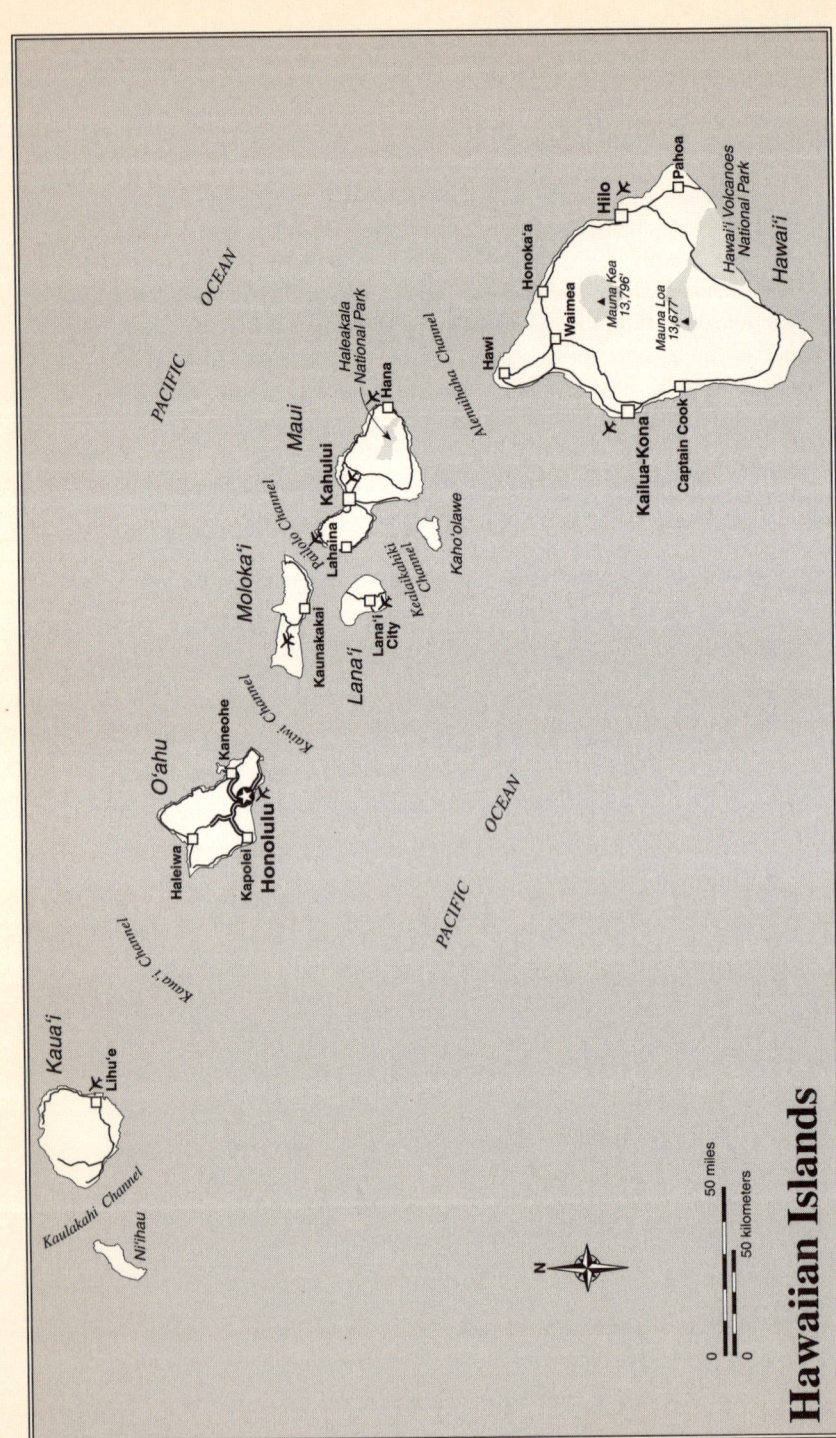

Introduction

Aloha! Congratulations on choosing Maui as the site of your vacation. You will soon see why it has the deserved slogan, Maui No Ka Oi (Maui is the Best). The sun, the sand and the lush tropicalness, combined with some of the finest restaurants and accommodations, blend sublimely together to create a perfect holiday paradise—a place both magical and beautiful. While this guide is dubbed a Family Travel Guide, it is designed for any kind of family, from a single traveler to a family reunion. It is for you, the traveler, who wishes to be in control of his/her vacation plans. From the family values buzz words of the 1990s we all know that "family" can mean anything. *Ohana*, the Hawaiian word for relative or family, is also used for an extended family of friends, neighbors, or coworkers. Even visitors who share a common love and respect for the islands are often described as "part of the *ohana*." I began visiting the islands in 1978 and quickly discovered the spirit of *ohana*. And, as did Mark Twain, became infatuated with this tropical paradise.

This book provides island experiences from different "family" viewpoints. Maui offers a perfect location for a romantic interlude, a vacation with family, or a wonderful destination to spend time relaxing with friends. There is plenty of information on traveling with children, as well as older adults who might be a part of your family. (If you don't have children or seniors to travel with, you might want to consider renting one after you read up on some of the freebies and discounts they get!)

It's difficult for me to believe this is now the 10th edition of this work! This has not been a "job" (albeit it is a lot of work) but a labor of love and a passion for me these past 20 years. Since the first edition of this book was published back in 1984, it has been an ongoing effort to continually attempt to update information, discover new things, rediscover old things and to thoroughly enjoy the tropical energy and seductive charm of Maui. While first-time visitors will delight in the diversity of activities that Maui has to offer, those making a return visit can enjoy discovering new sights and adventures on this magnificent island.

The chapters on accommodations, sights, restaurants and beaches are conveniently divided into logical areas and indexes are provided at the end of the book. This allows a better feel for, and access to, the information on the area in which you are staying, as well as greater confidence in exploring other areas. Remember that, except for Hana, most of the areas are only a short drive from each other and worth a day of sightseeing, beach exploring, or a meal at a fine restaurant.

Maui can be relatively inexpensive or extravagantly expensive depending on your preference in lodgings, activities and eating arrangements. Therefore, I have endeavored to give complete and detailed information covering the full range of budgets. The opinions expressed are based on personal experiences, and while the positive is emphasized, it is your right to know, in certain cases, a bad experience. To aid you, a "Best Bets" summary is included at the beginning of the first chapter. Refer to individual chapters for additional Best Bets and check for ★s, which identify special recommendations.

This guide is as accurate as possible at the time of publication; however, changes seem extremely rapid for an island operating on "Maui time." Ownerships, managements, names and menus do change frequently, as do prices. For the latest information on the island, Paradise Publications has available *The Maui Update*, a quarterly newsletter. You are invited to receive a complimentary issue by sending a self-addressed stamped envelope to: Paradise Publications, 8110 SW Wareham, Portland, OR 97223. Or send your request by e-mail to paradyse@att.net if you'd like to receive your sample via the internet. A yearly subscription is $10. If your itinerary includes visits to the other islands, the Paradise Family Guide Series includes *Paradise Family Guides: Kaua'i* and *Paradise Family Guides: Big Island of Hawai'i*. These essential travel accessories not only contain details on all the condos, hotels and restaurants (along with specific recreational activity information), but also inside tips and advice that most visitors never receive, shared by authors who know and love the islands. The Kaua'i book also offers an Update newsletter.

I'm delighted to be working with the folks at Ulysses Press. They have been pioneers in writing about travel to Hawai'i with their Hidden Travel series. You'll instantly notice the new and improved look of the book. The covers are vibrant and exciting and the interior has been totally redesigned for easy use. One of the major changes is that the indexes have all been moved to the back of the book and the "Accommodations" chapter is now divided into two chapters: "Where to Stay" and "What to See, Where to Shop."

A special *mahalo* to Maren Stilson for editorial consultation. And to Dona Early, Jody Van Aalst, Francine Abolofia, Kathi Langford and Mark Halvorson for their unending support and stress therapy. For editing, for phone calling, for letting me vent and just being great friends. Thanks also to all of you who have written sharing your trip experiences. (Yes, they are read and enjoyed!) It is a delight to be invited to share your trip through your letters.

> Aloha and happy travels to you!
> Christie

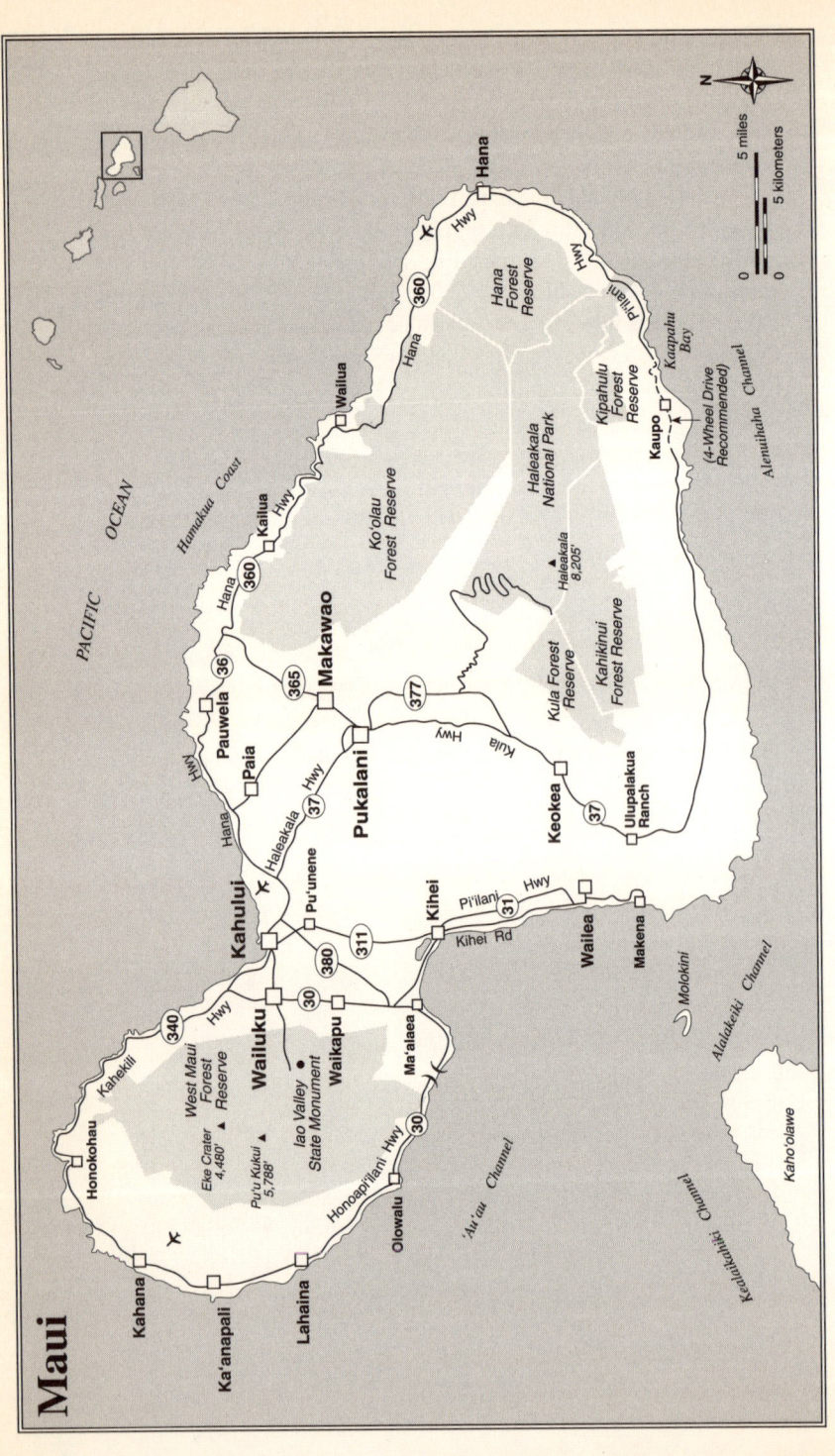

CHAPTER 1

Family Paradise

Maui's Best Bets

Aloha Wear Traditional tourist garb is available in greatest supply at the 17,000-square-foot Hilo Hattie factory in the Lahaina Center. They also have a location in Kihei at the Pi'ilani Shopping Center.

Cheap Aloha Wear While not for every traveler, the Salvation Army can be a great place to pick up some Hawaiian clothes to wear on your vacation. A muumuu for less than $5 is great for a beach cover-up or for wearing to a luau. Their Thrift Stores are located in Lahaina, Kihei and Kahului. There is also a Savers located in Kahului.

Shopping • *Affordable and fun*: Kahului Swap Meet each Saturday and Lahaina's Front Street at any time. • *Practical*: Queen Ka'ahumanu Center in Kahului. • *Extravagant*: Any of the gift shops at the fine resorts on Maui and the beautiful Shops of Wailea with many designer boutiques. • *Odds and Ends*: Longs Drug Store (Kahului, Lahaina and Kihei) and Costco (near the airport) to stock up on vacation food, supplies and even snorkel gear. Walmart or Big Kmart in Kahului are also in Kahului.

Most Spectacular Resort Grounds The Hyatt Regency Maui at Ka'anapali and the Grand Wailea Resort Hotel & Spa in Wailea tie for first place. The Westin Maui is a close second.

Excursions • *Most spectacular*: a helicopter tour. • *Best adventure on foot*: a personalized hike with Hike Maui. • *Best sailing*: a day-long snorkel and picnic to Lana'i with the congenial crew of the Trilogy.

New Sport Beyond windsurfing, beyond skiing, you can now kite surf. This craze meshes the best of a board and a kite for an aquatic thrill.

Aquatic Activity My new passion is outrigger canoeing. (See "Canoeing" in Chapter 6.)

Beaches • *Beautiful and safe*: Kapalua Bay and Ulua Beach. • *Unspoiled*: Oneloa (Makena) and Mokuleʻia (Slaughterhouse) beaches. • *For young kids*: try Puʻunoa Beach near Lahaina.

Body Surfing Slaughterhouse in winter (only for experienced surfers and strong swimmers).

Surfing Honolua Bay in winter (for experienced surfers only).

Snorkeling • *North end:* Honolua Bay in summer. • *Kapalua area:* Kapalua Bay and Namalu Bay. • *Kaʻanapali:* Black Rock at the Sheraton. Olowalu at mile-marker 14. • *Wailea:* Ulua Beach. • *Makena:* ʻAhihi-Kinaʻu Natural Reserve. • *Island of Lanaʻi:* Hulopoʻe Beach Park and Molokini Crater.

Whale Watching From the shore it is definitely the Pali on the road to West Maui and Lahaina. You won't believe your eyes! I have also found that off Makena Beach seems to be a good location in the early evening. (But then maybe that was just a "fluke") While whale-watching boat excursions are great, you'll be in for a real thrill if you can view them from a helicopter. Sign up for a helicopter excursion to Molokaʻi crosses the Pailolo Channel.

Windsurfing Hoʻokipa Beach Park (for experienced windsurfers).

Postcard Home Write your personal greetings on a coconut, mail it and surprise someone back home. They are available at various stores; the more expensive ones have been painted.

PINEAPPLES

Pineapples *are* better when you bring them home with you. However, save a bundle and pick them yourself. Take a short drive to Maui Fresh located in Haliʻimaile. Not only are the prices worth the drive, it is quite a delightful experience as well. The 1,000-square-foot shop is Maui Pineapple Company's retail outlet and offers three varieties of fresh pineapple: hybrid Hawaiian Gold extra sweet, organic hybrid and "jet-fresh" (the variety you might find in grocery stores at home) as well as salsa, cookies, jam, sauces, syrup and other Maui-made products. The pineapples are packed and agriculturally inspected for mainland travelers. They come in a two-pack ($10), 5/6 pack ($20) and a 40-pound box that holds 8-12 ($30). It is suggested you call ahead to place your order so it will be boxed and inspected prior to your arrival. The store hours are 10 a.m. to 6 p.m. Monday through Friday; 9 a.m. to 5 p.m. Saturday. They also hold twice monthly craft fairs and the Maui Pineapple Picnic in September. 808-573-5129

Unusual Gift Ideas • For the green thumb, be sure to try Dan's Green House in Lahaina for a Fuku-Bonsai planted on a lava rock. They are specially sprayed and sealed for either shipping or carrying home. • Big Kmart (and other stores) have mouse pads with Hawaiian designs—the perfect gift for all your internet friends. • Maui Crafts Guild in Paia has unusual handcrafted gifts. • Antique maps and prints make an unusual and prized gift for yourself or a family member or friend. Visit Lahaina Printsellers galleries for a piece of history. • If you'd like to share a little Hawai'i with friends back home, consider a CD of Hawaiian music. A good selection and the best prices in town are at Costco in Kahului. I'd recommend any of Keali'i Reichel's albums; Hapa and Israel Kamakawiwo'ole are fabulous. • *The Maui Onion Cookbook* is a great little book, die-cut in the shape of an onion and filled with recipes from Maui chefs and residents. It's unusual, inexpensive and easy to pack—or mail! (Tip: Bring home a few Kula onions to go with it.)

T-shirts Favorites are Crazy Shirts (regular or "flavored"), more expensive than the run of the mill variety, but excellent quality and great designs. The coffee, chocolate and *li hing mui* (preserved Chinese plum) colored tees look and smell yummy. The swap meet in Kahului on Saturday has a huge selection of T-shirts and prices are usually half of what they are in the mall shops.

Take-home Food Products • Tropical fruit, macadamia nuts (they have flavored nuts only available in Hawai'i: Kona coffee glazed, onion, etc.). • Maui chips and Maui onions.

Flowers For best flower values visit the Maui Swap Meet in Kahului. Leis are sometimes available here also. Check Ooka Supermarket in Wailuku (en route to the airport). Safeway in Lahaina and Kihei also has a fair selection. For shipping flowers home, check the phone book for a number of florists that can airship to you or your family and friends. One is Maui Floral: 888-826-1444; e-mail: floral@maui.net; www.mauifloral.com.

French Toast Castaway Cafe at Maui Ka'anapali Villas made with "Jeannie's bread."

Luau Old Lahaina Luau.

Hawaiian Food Hana Hou in Haiku.

Indulgence Select from a bath menu at The Ritz-Carlton, Kapalua and luxuriate in a butler-drawn bath. Your choice of oils or scents along with music, chocolate truffles, a chilled carafe of mai tais with "The Kapalua Bath," a split of champagne with "The Romance Bath," or a plate of sliced fruits and freshly squeezed juice for "The Travelers Relief Bath."

Free (or Almost Free) Stuff

Around the island: Free introductory scuba instruction offered poolside at many of the major resorts.
- A self-guided tour of the Grand Wailea or Hyatt Regency Maui.
- Public beaches with their free parking.
- Free snorkel guide from Maui Dive Shops.
- Free hikes with Sierra Club.
- Go to church. Churches in Hawai'i have less to do with "religion" than with fellowship, celebration, wonderful music and aloha. (See "Calendar of Annual Events" for more free stuff.)

Lahaina: • Free "Maui Historical Walking Guide" can be picked up at displays around that town. • First- and third- weekend arts-and-crafts fairs at Banyan Tree Park. • Friday night "art night" in Lahaina. You may have an opportunity to meet the artists and possibly get some free refreshment. • Front Street's Halloween Parade, Kamehameha Day Parade (June) or the Holiday Lighting of the Banyan Tree & Festival (December). • Visit Pioneer Inn, now an official U.S. Historic Landmark. • Canoe races held at Honoka'o'o Park. • The shuttle bus in West Maui is $1 and travels between Lahaina, Ka'anapali and The Ritz-Carlton. • Free admission to Wo Hing Temple in Lahaina. • The Crazy Shirts shop located on the north end of Lahaina town has a display of whaling memorabilia and a big cannon sits out behind the shop. • Gift and Craft Fair, Sunday 9 a.m. to 4 p.m. at Lahaina Civic Center. $1 admission benefits non-profit organizations (808-879-7594). • Every Tuesday and Friday at 11:30 a.m. enjoy "Hula Maui" at the Maui Theatre (808-661-9914) at Old Lahaina Center. • Hale Kahiko is a replica of a Hawaiian village located at Lahaina Center and open daily with free guided tours and weekly hula shows (see Chapter 2 for more information). • The Lahaina Cannery Mall has *keiki* hula shows Saturday and Sunday at 1 p.m. and Polynesian dancing 7 p.m. Tuesday and Thursday. • Na Mea Hawai'i's Story Time for children is on Saturday at 10:30 a.m.; yo-yo demonstrations Sunday at 2:30 p.m.; country line dancing lessons Monday 7 to 8:30 p.m.

Ka'anapali–Kapalua Area: • There is a lot happening at Whalers Village. Most evenings from 7 to 8 p.m. enjoy a rich blend of cultural entertainment. You never know what you might see but one thing's for sure, it's always free. • Check out the free tour of the artwork at the Westin Maui at Ka'anapali. • Enjoy the free hula show at the Ka'anapali Beach Hotel, held nightly at 6:30 p.m. with Hawaiian arts and crafts on display each Monday, Wednesday and Friday. • Pacific Whale Foundation's Coral Reef Information

Throughout the week, the Whalers Village "Director of Fun" leads a family program that features a variety of free activities. *Keikis* and adults can take part in hands-on activities such as sand prints, palm frond weaving and lei making, or peek through a *puka* (hole) in a large mural and snap your photo as you become a part of a fantasy underwater scene. And of course there's the free Whalers Village Museum, where you can see artifacts from the heyday of Lahaina's whaling industry, view a new selection of movies on whales and whaling in an air-conditioned theater, or take a free self-guided audio tour. 808-661-4567

Station (808-249-8811) offers a free guided morning reef tour at Kahekili Park in Ka'anapali Friday through Sunday. • Craft fair at Napili Plaza every Wednesday and Saturday. • The Kapalua Shops hosts a number of free cultural activities and performances daily. • Whalers Village offers hula performances and daily activities for the whole family.

Ma'alaea–Kihei–Wailea–Makena Area: • Pacific Whale Foundation's Coral Reef Information Station (808-249-8811) offers a free guided morning reef tour at Ulua Beach in Wailea. • Kihei Fine Art Show at Keoaloha Congregational Hawaiian Church Thursday 9 a.m. to 2 p.m. (808-879-9337). • Free hula show every Tuesday and Friday in the Molokini Lounge at the Maui Prince Resort. • The walk along the Wailea waterfront is wonderful.

Kahului–Wailuku Area: • Visit the Iao Needle located near Wailuku. • Watch windsurfing at Ho'okipa Beach on Maui's windward shore. • See the Maui Botanical Gardens in Wailuku. • Ooka Supermarket in Wailuku is worth a visit just to see the varied island foods available, from breadfruit to flying fish eggs. • The Maui Tropical Plantation has free admission to their marketplace. • Free behind-the-scenes tour of the Maui Arts & Cultural Center. Call for reservations (808-242-2787 ext. 228). • Free Hawaiian entertainment at Queen Ka'ahumanu Center (808-877-3369) every Saturday at 11 a.m.

Upcountry: • Visit Hui No'eau Visual Arts Center in Makawao or take a guided tour. • Visit Hot Island Glass Studio in Makawao to see glass blowing and tour their art shops. • Makawao Parade held the Fourth of July weekend. • Free natural and cultural history programs and guided hikes at Haleakala (808-572-4400). • Free country dance lessons Thursday 7 to 7:30 p.m. at Tavares Community Center in Pukalani (808-661-8639). • Free admission to Sunrise Protea. • Free tour and sampling at Tedeschi Winery. (Stay and star gaze: the elevation at Kula makes the stars seem bigger and clearer.)

Gift for Friends Traveling to Maui   A copy of *Paradise Family Guides: Maui* and, of course, a subscription to the quarterly *Maui Update* newsletter.

The Valley Isle

This chapter of the book is aimed at highlighting the basics for your travel plans to Maui: background on the islands and the language, what to pack, weather conditions, discounts for the traveling "seniors" in your family. Whatever the ages of your traveling family, there are lots of options to make this vacation a memorable one. Enjoy my "best bets," which highlight some of my family's favorite things to do, places to eat and locations to shop. If you have tips of your own and would like to share them, my e-mail address is located at the back of the guide. Happy travels and see you on the beach!

History of Maui

THE ISLAND   Far beneath the warm waters of the Pacific Ocean is the Pacific Plate, which moves constantly in a northwesternly direction. Each Hawaiian island was formed as it passed over a hot vent in this plate. Kaua'i, the oldest of the major islands in the Hawai'i chain, was formed first and has since moved away from the plume (the source of the lava) and is no longer growing. Some of the older islands even farther to the northwest have been gradually reduced to sandbars and atolls. The Big Island is the youngest in the chain and is continuing to grow. A new island called Lo'ihi (which means "prolonged in time"), southeast of the Big Island, is growing and expected to emerge from the oceanic depths in about a million years.

It was explosions of hot lava from two volcanoes that created the island of Maui. Mauna Kahalawai is the oldest and created the westerly section with the highest point (elevation 5,788 feet) known as Pu'u Kukui. The great Haleakala, the world's largest dormant volcano, created the southeastern portion of the island. (The last eruption on Maui took place around 1789 and flowed over to the Makena area.) A valley connects these two volcanic peaks, hence the source of Maui's nickname, "The Valley Isle."

POLYNESIANS   The first Hawaiians came from the Marquesa and Society Islands in the central Pacific. (Findings suggest that their ancestors came from the western Pacific, perhaps as far away as Madagascar.) The Polynesians left the Marquesas around the 8th century and were followed by natives from the Society Islands sometime between the 11th and 14th centuries. The Hawaiian population may well have been as high as 300,000 by the 1700s, spread throughout the chain of islands. Fish and poi were diet basics, supplemented by various fruits and occasionally meat from chickens, pigs and even dogs.

Four principal gods formed the basis of their religion until the missionaries arrived. The stone foundations of *heiaus*, ancient religious temples, can still be visited on Maui.

The major islands had a history of independent rule with, at times, open warfare. On Maui, Kahului and Hana were both sites of combat between the Maui islanders and the warriors from neighboring islands.

CAPTAIN COOK The islands were left undisturbed by Western influence until the 1778 arrival of Captain James Cook. He spotted and visited Kaua'i and O'ahu first and is believed to have arrived at Maui on November 25 or 26, 1778. He was later killed in a brawl on the Big Island of Hawai'i.

KAMEHAMEHA Kamehameha the First was born on the Big Island of Hawai'i around 1758. He was the nephew of Kalaiopi, who ruled the Big Island. Following the king's death, Kalaiopi's son came to power, only to be subsequently defeated by Kamehameha in 1794. The great chieftain Kahekili was Kamehameha's greatest rival. He ruled not only Maui, but Lana'i and Moloka'i, and also had kinship with the governing royalty of O'ahu and Kaua'i. King Kahekili died in 1794 and left control of the island to his son. A bloody battle (more like a massacre since Kamehameha used Western technology, strategy and two English advisors) in the Iao Valley resulted in the defeat of Kahekili's son, Kalanikupule, in 1795. Kamehameha united all the islands and made Lahaina the capital of Hawai'i in 1802. (It remained the capital until the 1840s, when Honolulu became the center for gov-

Visit the **Maui Friends of the Library Used Bookstore** located behind Pu'unene School, open Monday through Saturday from 8 a.m. to 4 p.m. Forget to bring some paperbacks? Pick them up here for a dime! (If you're coming from Kahului, get on Pu'unene Avenue heading for Kihei. Where the road veers to the right, by the Pu'unene Sugar Mill, keep going straight and then follow the signs on the dirt roads that will take you left, then right and then right again.) 808-871-6563

ernment affairs.) Lahaina was a popular resort for Hawaiian royalty who favored the beaches in the area. Ka'ahumanu, the favorite wife of Kamehameha was born in Hana, Maui, and spent much of her time there. (Quiet Hana was another popular spot for vacationing royalty.)

Liholiho, the heir of Kamehameha the Great, ruled as Kamehameha II from 1819 to 1824. Liholiho was not a strong ruler so Ka'ahumanu proclaimed herself prime minister during his reign. She ended many of the *kapus* of the old religion, thus creating a fortuitous vacuum that the soon-to-arrive missionaries would fill.

MISSIONARIES These New England missionaries and their families arrived in Lahaina in the spring of 1823 at the invitation of Queen Keopuolani. They brought drastic changes to the island with the education of the natives both spiritually and scholastically. The first high school and printing press west of the Rockies was established at Lahainaluna. Built just outside of Lahaina, it now houses a museum and is open to the public. Liholiho and his wife were the first Hawaiian royalty to visit the United States. When their travels continued to Europe, they succumbed to the measles while in London. Liholiho was succeeded by Kauikeaouli (the youngest son of Kamehameha the Great), who ruled under the title of Kamehameha the III from 1824 to 1854. The last monarch was Liliuokalani, who ruled from 1891 to 1893. Hawai'i became a territory of the United States in 1900 and achieved statehood in 1959.

WHALERS Beginning in 1819 and continuing for nearly 40 years, whaling ships became a frequent sight, anchored in the waters off Lahaina. The whalers hunted their prey north and south of the islands, off the Japanese coast and in the Arctic. Fifty ships were sometimes anchored off Lahaina, and during the peak year of whaling, over 400 ships visited Lahaina, with an additional 167 in Honolulu's harbor. Allowing 25 to 30 seamen per ship you can quickly see the enormous number of sailors who flooded the area. While missionaries brought their Christian beliefs, the whaling men lived under their own belief that there was "No God West of the Horn." This presented a tremendous conflict between the sailors and missionaries, with the islanders caught right in the middle.

An interesting fact is reported in the 1846 Lahaina census. The count included 3,445 Hawaiians, 112 foreigners, 600 seamen, 155 adobe houses, 822 grass houses, 59 stone and wooden houses, as well as 528 dogs!

After months at sea, sailors arrived in Lahaina anxious for the grog shops and native women. It was the missionaries who set up guidelines that forbade the island girls to visit the ships in the harbor. Horrified by the bare-breasted Hawaiian women, the missionary wives quickly set about to more thoroughly clothe the native ladies. The missionary women realized that their dresses would not be appropriate for these more robust woman and using their nightwear as a guideline, fashioned garments from these by cutting the sleeves off and enlarging the armholes. The muumuu was the result, and translated means "to amputate or to cut short."

In 1832, a coral fort was erected near the Lahaina harbor following an incident with the unhappy crew of one vessel. The story goes that a captain, disgruntled when he was detained in Lahaina for enticing "base women," ordered his crew to fire shots at the homes of some Lahaina area missionaries. Although the fort was demolished in 1854, remnants of the coral were re-excavated and a corner of the old fort reconstructed. It is located harborside by the Banyan Tree.

The whaling era strengthened Hawai'i's ties with the United States economically, and the presence of the missionaries further strengthened this bond. A combination of events brought the downfall of the whaling industry: The onset of the Civil War depleted men and ships, (one Confederate warship reportedly set 24 whaling vessels ablaze), and the growth of the petroleum industry lessened the need for whale oil. Lastly, the Arctic freezes of 1871 and 1876 resulted in many ships being crushed by the ice. Lahaina, however, continues to maintain the charm and history of those bygone whaling days. (Ironically, Maui is now the headquarters for the Hawaiian Island Humpback Whale National Marine Sanctuary, the nation's twelfth, and the only one dedicated to this species. Encompassing waters from Kaua'i to the Big Island, the Sanctuary was designated in 1998.)

AGRICULTURE Sugar cane brought by the first Hawaiians was developed into a major industry on Maui. Two sons of missionaries, Henry P. Baldwin and Samuel T. Alexander, as well as Claus Spreckels played notable roles in the expansion of the industry with their construction of a water pipeline to irrigate the arid central isthmus of Maui. This act secured the future of other agricultural development on the island.

Pineapple, another major agricultural industry, has played an important role in the history of Maui. Historians believe that pineapple may have originated in Brazil and was introduced to the modern world by Christopher Columbus on return from his second visit to the Americas. When it arrived in the islands is uncertain, but Don Francisco de Paula y Marin writes in his diary on January 21, 1813, that "This day I planted pineapples and an orange tree." The first successful report of pineapple agriculture in Hawai'i is attributed to Captain James Kidwell, an English horticulturist. He brought the smooth cayenne variety of pineapple from Jamaica and began successfully cultivating and harvesting the fruit on O'ahu in 1886.

Since the fresh fruits perished too quickly to reach the mainland, Captain Kidwell also began the first cannery, called Hawaiian Fruit and Packing Company, which operated until 1892 when it was sold to Pearl City Fruit Company. James Dole, a young Harvard graduate, arrived on O'ahu from Boston in 1899, and by 1901 had established what has today become known as the Dole Pineapple Company.

Grove Ranch and Haleakala Ranch Company both began pineapple cultivation on Maui in 1906. Baldwin Packers began as Honolua Ranch and was owned by Henry Baldwin who started it in 1912. The Grove Ranch hired David T. Fleming as company manager and began with several acres in Haiku that soon increased to 450 acres. W. A. Clark succeeded Fleming as Grove Ranch manager and while the acreage increased, for some unknown reason the pineapples failed. For ten years the fields were leased to Japanese growers who were successful.

During these early years Haleakala Ranch Company continued to expand their acreage and to successfully produce pineapples. J. Walter Cameron arrived from Honolulu to become manager of Haleakala Ranch Company around 1925. In 1929 the ranch division was separated from the pineapple division and the company became Haleakala Pineapple Company. In 1932 the Company and Grove Ranch merged, forming Maui Pineapple Company Limited; 30 years later in 1962, Baldwin Packers merged with Maui Pineapple Company to form what we know today as Maui Land and Pineapple. Maui Land and Pineapple continues to grow pineapples as well as develop land into the fine resort area known as Kapalua. The company owns 29,800 acres of land and uses 8,400 acres for company operations while employing approximately 1,870 people on a year-round or seasonal basis. While competition from abroad (particularly Thailand) has been fierce, Maui Land and Pineapple has chosen to maintain its market by supplying a quality product. Maui Land and Pineapple Company is the only 100 percent Hawaiian producer of canned pineapple in the world.

It was about 100 years ago that the first macadamia nut trees arrived from Australia. They were intended to be an ornamental tree since they had nuts that were extremely difficult to crack. It was not until the 1950s that the development of the trees began to take a commercial course. Today, some sugar cane fields are being converted to macadamia. It is a slow process, taking seven years for the grafted root (they do not grow from seed) to become a producing tree. While delicious, beware of their hazards: a half ounce of nuts contains 100 calories!

The Kula area of Maui has become the center for many delicious fruits and vegetables as well as the unusual Protea flower, a native of South Africa. Wineries have also made a comeback with the success of the Tedeschi Winery at Ulupalakua. Tedeschi started by producing an unusual pineapple wine followed by a champagne in 1984 and a red table wine in 1985. Be sure to also sample the very sweet Kula onions raised in this area (these are not the same as "Maui onions" that can be grown anywhere in Maui County) that are available to ship home.

Hawaiian Language

The Hawaiian language is an interesting one. Each letter is pronounced, which can produce some tongue-tangling challenges. Older children might enjoy the *New Pocket Hawaiian Dictionary* by Mary Kawena Pukui and Samuel Elbert. They also co-authored *Pocket Place Names of Hawai'i*. We've listed some of the common place names and their meanings along with a number of fun Hawaiian words that kids will love using on Maui and back home.

The following are some of the more commonly used words that you may hear or see:

ali'i—(ah-lee-ee)—chief
aloha—(ah-loh-hah)—greetings
hale—(hah-lay)—house
hana—(HA-nah)—work
hana hou—(ha-nah HO)—to do it again, encore
heiau—(heh-ow)—temple
haole—(how-lee)—a caucasian
ipo—(ee-po)—sweetheart
kai—(kye)—ocean
kahuna—(kah-HOO-nah)—teacher, priest
kama'aina—(kah-mah-ai-nuh)—native born
kane—(kah-nay)—man
kapu—(kah-poo)—keep out, forbidden
keiki—(kay-kee)—child
lanai—(lah-nah-ee)—porch or patio
lomi lomi—(loh-mee LOH-mee)—to rub or massage
luau—(loo-ow)—party with entertainment and imu-cooked food
mahalo—(mah-ha-low)—praise, thanks
makai—(mah-kye)—toward the ocean
malihini—(mah-lee-hee-nee)—a newcomer or visitor
mana—(mah-nah)—supernatural or divine power
mauka—(mau—*rhymes with cow*—kah)—toward the mountain
mauna—(MAU-nah)—mountain
mele—(MAY-leh)—Hawaiian song or chant
menehune—(may-nay-hoo-nee)—Hawaiian dwarf or elf
moana—(moh-ah-nah)—ocean
nani—(NAH-nee)—beautiful

ono—(oh-no)—delicious
pali—(PAH-lee)—cliff, precipice
paniolo—(pah-nee-o-low)—Hawaiian cowboy
pau—(pow)—finished
poi—(poy)—a paste made from the taro root
pua—(POO-ah)—flower
puka—(POO-ka)—a hole
pupus—(poo-poos)—appetizers
wahine—(wah-hee-nay)—woman
wiki wiki—(wee-kee wee-kee)—hurry

MAUI'S NAMES AND PLACES

Haiku—abrupt break
Haleakala—house of the sun
Hali'imaile—maile vines spread
Hana—rainy land
Honoapi'ilani—bays of Pi'ilani
Honolua—double bay
Ho'okipa—welcome
Iao—cloud supreme, name of star
Ka'anapali—land divided by cliffs
Kahana—meaning unknown, of Tahitian origin
Kaho'olawe—taking away by currents
Kahului—winning
Kapalua—two borders
Kaupo—night landing
Ke'anae—the mullet
Keawakapu—sacred harbor
Kihei—shoulder cape
Kula—open country, school
Lahaina—unmerciful sun
Lana'i—meaning lost
Ma'alaea—area of red dirt
Makawao—forest beginning
Makena—abundance
Napili—pili grass
Olowalu—many hills
Paia—noisy
Pukalani—sky opening
Ulupalakua—ripe breadfruit
Wai'anapanapa—glistening water
Wailea—water Lea (Lea was the canoe maker's goddess)
Wailua—two waters
Wailuku—water of slaughter

Island Ecology

Flashlights can turn the balmy Hawaiian evenings into adventures. One of the most friendly island residents is the Bufo. In 1932 this frog was brought from Puerto Rico to assist with insect control in the cane fields. Today this large toad still emerges at night to feed or mate and seems to be easier to spot during the winter months, especially after rain showers. While they can be found around most condominiums, Kawiliki Park (the area behind the Luana Kai, Laule'a and several other condominium complexes with access from Waipulani Road off South Kihei Road) seems to be an especially popular gathering spot. I suggest you don't touch them, however. The secretions may cause skin irritation. My family also enjoys searching for beach crabs and the African snails that have shells that may grow to a hefty five inches. Find a beach with near-shore coral reef and no waves (e.g., Pu'unoa Beach in Lahaina), shine your flashlight into the water and see marine life—even eels—feeding.

The other Hawaiian creature that cannot go without mention is the gecko. They are finding their way into the suitcases of many an island visitor, in the form of T-shirts, sun visors and jewelry. This small lizard is a relative of the chameleon and grows to a length of three or four inches. They dine on roaches, termites, mosquitoes, ants, moths and other pesky insects.

While there are nearly 800 species of geckos found in warm climates around the world, there are only about five varieties found in Hawai'i. The house gecko is the most commonly found, with tiny rows of spines that encircle its tail, while the mourning gecko has smooth, satiny skin and sports pale stripes and pairs of dark spots. The mourning gecko species is parthenogenic: there are only females that produce fertile eggs—no need for a mate! The stump-toed variety is distinguished by its thick flattened tail. The tree gecko enjoys the solitude of the forests, and the fox gecko, with a long snout and spines along its tail, prefers to hide around rocks or tree trunks. The first geckos may have reached Hawai'i with early voyagers from Polynesia, but the house gecko may have arrived as recently as the 1940s, along with military shipments to Hawai'i.

Geckos are most easily spotted at night, when they seem to enjoy the warm lights outside your door. I have heard they each establish little territories where they live and breed so you will no doubt see them around the same area each night. They are very shy and will scurry off quickly. Sometimes you may find one living in your hotel or condo. They are friendly and beneficial animals and are said to bring good luck, so make them welcome.

As for snakes, there are only two male specimens on display in the Honolulu Zoo. Hawai'i has no snakes—and they hope to keep it that way!

Traveling with Children

Traveling with children can be an exhausting experience for parents and children alike. There are a number of direct flights to Maui out of Portland, Seattle, San Francisco, Los Angeles, Chicago and Dallas, which saves stopping over in Honolulu. These flights are very popular and fill up well in advance.

ON THE PLANE WITH KIDS

Many people don't realize that cabins are pressurized to approximately the 6,000-foot level during flight. Young children may have difficulty clearing their ears when the plane lands. To help relieve the pressure of descent, have infants nurse or drink from a bottle, and older children may benefit from chewing gum. If this is a concern of yours, consult with your pediatrician about the use of a decongestant prior to descent.

Packing a child's goody bag for the long flight is a must. A few new activity books or toys that can be pulled out en route can be sanity-saving. Snacks (boxes of juice or Capri Sun) can tide over the little ones at the airport or on the plane while awaiting your food/drink service. A thermos with a drinking spout works well and is handy for use during vacations. A change of clothes and a swimsuit for the kids can be tucked into your carry-on bag. (Suitcases have been known to be lost or delayed.) Another handy addition is a small nightlight since unfamiliar accommodations can be somewhat confusing for children during the bedtime hours. And don't forget a strong sunscreen.

TRAVELING IN THE ISLANDS WITH KIDS

CAR SEATS   By law, children under 4 must travel in child safety seats in Hawai'i. While most rental agencies do have car seats for rent, you need to request them well in advance as they have a limited number. Prices run about $5 per day. You may wish to bring your own with you. Several styles are permitted by the airlines for use in flight, or it may be checked as a piece of baggage.

BABYSITTING   Most hotels have some form of babysitting service that runs $12 and up per hour. Check with your condo office as they sometimes have the numbers of local sitters. As you can easily figure from the rates, spending much time away from your children can be costly. Consider the feasibility of bringing your own sitter: it may actually be less expensive, and certainly much more convenient (and your sitter will love you forever). This has worked well for us on numerous occasions.

With any of these agencies, or through your hotel, at least a 24-hour notice for a sitter is requested. I suggest phoning them *as soon* as you have set up your plans. At certain times of the year, with the limited number of sitters available, it can be nearly impossible to get one. If you can plan out your entire vacation babysitting needs, it might also be possible to schedule the same sitter for each occasion.

There are only a couple of independent childcare services on Maui. One reason might be the increased number of resorts and hotels that are now offering half-, full-day and evening childcare programs year round. Previously, many of the resorts had only offered programs during holidays and summer months. Also, beware that most programs don't accept children younger than four or five years.

Our recommendation for your childcare needs is the **Nanny Connection**. They began serving Maui in 1991. Owner is Christine Taylor. I was told that all nannies have CPR and First Aid certification. Rates are $12 per hour for one or two children with a three-hour minimum. Extra child from the same family is an additional $2 per hour, from a different family $4 per hour per child. No travel fee, although there is a parking fee when applicable. Extra charge past midnight or holidays. Credit card is required to make and hold a reservation, but cash at the end of each service. P.O. Box 477, Pu'unene, Maui, HI 96784. 808-875-4777 in Kihei or 808-667-5777 in Lahaina; www.thenannyconnection.com.

Happy Kids owner Sue Sargent has been providing childcare services on Maui for almost a decade. They are licensed, bonded and insured, and have their sitters undergo CPR certification. They can go to guest rooms and condos and have service early, late and even overnight with a three-hour minimum. Sitters can also travel on location with guests (such as on boat tours) to help out with the kids. They can also provide a day camp itinerary for children. All sitters are 25 to 55 years of age and can travel anywhere on the island. Rates are $12 per hour for 1 or 2 children in the same family. Service from midnight to 6 a.m. is $14 per hour. Rates are higher if there are multiple families. 808-667-5437, or from the mainland 888-669-1991.

CRIBS Most condos and hotels offer cribs for a rental fee that may vary from $5 to $10 per night. For an extended stay you might consider purchasing one of the wonderful folding cribs that pack up conveniently. There are several varieties that fold up into a large duffel bag. At around $60, depending on the length of your stay, they might be worth bringing along.

FOR EMERGENCIES There are several clinics around the island that take emergencies or walk-in patients. Your condominium or hotel desk can provide you with suggestions, or check the phone book. Kaiser Permanente Medical Care Facilities are located in Wailuku (808-243-6000), Lahaina (808-662-6900) and Kihei (808-891-6800). Doctors on Call (Hyatt, Westin or Ritz: 808-667-7676) open seven days a week from 8 a.m. to 9 p.m. for house or hotel calls or office visits. Dr. Ben Azman at West Maui Health Care Center (Whalers Village: 808-667-9721) specializes in visitor care. See "Helpful Phone Numbers" at the end of this chapter. Calling 911 will put you in contact with local fire, police and ambulances.

DINING You'll find *keiki* (children's) menus at restaurants as diverse as Kimo's, Canoe's, Kobe Streak House, Sea House, Tony Roma's and Café Kiowai. Stop by the very kid-friendly Ruby's Diner in Kahului filled with memorabilia from Hawai'i's early aviation days. If any restaurant doesn't offer you a menu then ask if they have children's prices and portions for their regular menu items. Look for the little girl with a hat in Chapter 4 for family-friendly restaurants.

BEACHES—POOLS

Among the best beaches for fairly young children are the Lahaina and Pu'unoa beaches in Lahaina, where the water is shallow and calm. Kapalua Bay is also well protected and has fairly gentle wave action. Remember to have children well supervised and wearing flotation devices because even the calmest beaches can have a surprise wave. Several of the island's beaches offer lifeguards, among them the

Kama'ole I, II and III beaches in Kihei. Kama'ole III Park also has large open areas and playground equipment. In the Ma'alaea area, follow the road down past the condominiums to the public access for the beach area. A short walk down the *kiawe*-lined beach—to the small rock jetty with the large pipe—is a seawater pool on either side that is well protected and ideal for the younger child. Look for the shovel and pail picture in Chapter 5 for child-friendly beaches.

A number of complexes have small shallow pools designed with the young ones in mind. These include the Ka'anapali Ali'i, Hyatt Regency (with a sand pool), Sands of Kahana, Grand Wailea Resort and the Kahana Sunset. I recommend taking a life jacket or water wings (floaties). Packing a small inflatable pool for use on your lanai or courtyard may provide a cool and safe retreat for your little one. Typically, Maui resorts and hotels do not offer lifeguard services;

never leave your child unattended near any body of water. Older children will be astounded by the labyrinth of pools and rivers at the Grand Wailea Resort. The Hyatt Regency has a great waterslide; the Westin Maui also has one. The Outrigger Wailea has a fun children's pool with slides and spray. To inquire about public pools (e.g., Lahaina's Aquatic Center and the Kihei community pool), or lifeguard status and information on county beaches, call 808-270-7383; www.co.maui.hi.us/departments/parks.

CHILDCARE PROGRAMS

During the summer, Christmas holidays and Easter, many of the resort hotels offer partial- or full-day activities for children. Rates range from free to $65 per day. Some of these children's programs are available to non-hotel or resort guests. Camp Grande at the Grand Wailea Resort Hotel will take non-resort guests. Most properties have half- or full-day programs. Each resort generally has a theme and since these change very often, we'll summarize what might be offered: lei making, hula lessons and other Hawaiiana arts and crafts, sandcastle building, nature walks, picnics, swimming, Olympic-like games and scavenger hunts. Some even provide tours to places such as the Whalers Museum at Ka'anapali or take the kids for a ride on the Sugar Cane Train. Most properties tend to center their operations outside, but a few, like the Grand Wailea, have very impressive indoor facilities. Many include lunch and a few give the kids a free T-shirt.

The following are properties that offer children's programs on a regular basis. Please be sure to check with the resort for the current schedules, availability and prices for their children's programs. Check with your resort concierge for additional youth activities. In Chapter 3, look for the girl in the bathing suit. She indicates a childcare program.

Aston Ka'anapali Shores features a year-round program for children 5 to 12 years. Camp Ka'anapali is offered from 8 a.m. to 3 p.m. Monday through Friday. A $10 initial registration covers you regardless of the length of your stay and includes a camp T-shirt and a button. They have two sessions daily: 8 a.m. to 12:30 p.m. for $20 includes lunch; 12:30 to 3 p.m. for $15 has no lunch. The program is available for resort guests only but they will accept all sister Aston property guests as well. Limit of 6 hours per week per child. 808-667-2211.

Embassy Vacation Resort's children's program, "Beach Buddies," operates year round from 8:30 a.m. to 2:30 p.m. This program is for resort guests only. Activities (hula, lei making, coconut weaving and crafts) are designed to keep children 5 to 12 years entertained as well as acquainting them with the Hawaiian way of life. Daily rate of $30 includes a T-shirt and lunch. Evening program is 6 p.m. to 9 p.m. Fridays during spring, summer and winter breaks. 808-661-2000.

Fairmont Kea Lani Hotel, Suites & Villas offers "Keiki Lani" (Heavenly Kids) for kids 5 to 11 years. This program emphasizes Hawaiian culture and the island's ecosystems and is available year round from 9 a.m. to 3 p.m. to registered hotel guests only. Charge is $55 for first child, $40 for each additional child in the same family. 808-659-4100; www.kealani.com.

Camp Grande–Grand Wailea Resort Hotel offers the most incredible 20,000-square-foot space devoted to youthful guests 5 to 12 years. The camp facility has a video room, arts-and-crafts center, special kiddie pool and movie theater. A huge area is designed with crafts in mind. Adjacent is a 1950s-style soda fountain. The program is also available to non-resort guests for an additional fee. Day camp from 9 a.m. to 4 p.m. includes lunch, $75. A half day is 9 a.m. to 12:30 p.m. (including lunch) or 12:30 p.m. to 4 p.m., $45. There is an evening camp from 5 p.m. to 10 p.m. including dinner for $55, one to three times each week, depending on the season. Guests of the resort may accompany (and stay) with their children and enjoy the facilities of Camp Grande, but you still pay the child's camp fees. Ask about one-hour workshops on authentic lei making, computer graphics, pottery, tile painting and more for $15 kids, $20 adults. Nanny services can be arranged. The Camp Video Arcade and Escapades are for all guests, not just kids. Candy, chips, juice and ice cream can be purchased.

The **Four Seasons Resort Wailea** features "Kids for all Seasons," a daily complimentary program for youths 5 to 12 with year-round supervised activities from 9 a.m. to 5 p.m. The program has great indoor and outdoor activities including swimming and beach games. "Ricky and Lucy, the parrot mascots, often stop by for a visit. The "Season's Club" is just for teens. Reservations are required for events that might include a night at the movies, beach volleyball, an inline skate party, or a sail and snorkel. Some events are complimentary, others have a fee. They also have night events for 3 hours (6 p.m. to 9 p.m.) at $45. For "children" 12 and over, they have a free scuba clinic to help you decide if you want more than just the pool. If you do, then you get to go to the dive spot just off the resort, but you pay for the shore dive. 808-874-8000; www.fourseasons.com/maui.

Parental supervision is required for children under 10 years of age. The arcade is complimentary to hotel guests. The whale wading pool, playground and kiddieland are complimentary to hotel guests, accompanied by their children. 808-875-1234; www.grandwailea.com.

Hyatt Regency Maui operates Camp Hyatt for kids 5 to 12 years. At presstime, the Hyatt is going through license renewal with the state. So until they get re-licensed, they are limited by law to have a child for only 6 total hours in a 7-day period. The program is daily from 9 a.m. to 3 p.m. for $60, but on Monday and Thursday it is $75 when they have off-site excursions. They offer half-day sessions (except on Monday and Thursday) 9 a.m. to 12:30 p.m. or 12:30 p.m. to 3 p.m., $35 with lunch, $30 without. Camp is also offered nightly from 6 p.m. to 10 p.m. Evening activities include table games, movies, video games and light snacks, $12 per hour per child. 808-661-1234; www.maui.hyatt.com.

Ka'anapali Beach Hotel has a fun program called "Aloha Passport for Kids." Children 12 and under can participate to learn more about Hawaiian culture and receive a stamp on their "passport." They receive a free gift when they reach their destination. The program was implemented because they found that parents preferred spending time with their children while on vacation, rather than sending them off to camp. So all of the activities can be done with parents and older siblings. Destinations include flower lei making, hula lessons, cultural garden tour, *lau* (leaf) printing, pineapple cutting and ti leaf skirt making. 808-661-0011; www.kbhmaui.com.

Kapalua Bay Hotel and Ocean Villas offers Kamp Kapalua (808-669-5656) for kids 5 to 12 years. The full-day (9 a.m. to 3 p.m.) program runs daily year round for Kapalua guests. The price is $45 per child, and $35 for second child in the same family. Kapalua Art School (808-665-0007) is a summer option for kids 9 to 12 years. The program runs $45 per day for students is available Monday through Friday from 8 a.m. to 5 p.m. www.kapaluabayhotel.com.

Maui Prince Hotel offers a year-round program called the "Prince Keiki Club." Children 5 to 12 years can have hours of fun with activities such as bamboo pole fishing, sand castle building, pool swims, Hawaiian arts and crafts, and treasure hunts. Three sessions are offered to hotel guests throughout the day. The morning session (9 a.m. to noon) and the afternoon session (noon to 3 p.m.) are each $25. Or combine the two sessions for a full day for $50. If there is only one child in the session, you can have a private session for double the cost. 808-874-1111; www.mauiprincehotel.com.

Napili Kai Beach Resort offers a Keiki Club for youth 6 to 12 years during Easter break, mid-June through August and Christmas holidays. The complimentary camp is two hours daily except Sunday, 10 a.m. to 12 p.m. Activities include Hawaiian games, hula, lei making and nature walks. Wednesday evening is a movie and snack, beginning at 5:30 p.m. 808-669-6271; www.napilikai.com.

Renaissance Wailea Beach Resort provides Camp Wailea for in-house guests 5 to 12 years. Offered Tuesday, Thursday and Saturday from 9 a.m. to 1 p.m. Lunch included. 800-468-3571; 808-879-4900; www.renaissance hotels.com.

The Ritz-Carlton, Kapalua's Ritz-Kids program is a half- or full-day program that explores the wonders of Maui. Theme programs focus on nature, culture, art and ecology with daily trips to D.T. Fleming Beach and the swimming pool. Other activities that highlight the day are playing on the nine-hole putting green and the croquet lawn. Hotel guests will be delighted at the $15 fee for kids 5 to 12 years for a full-day program 9 a.m. to 4 p.m., including lunch. Half-day programs—9 a.m. until noon or 1 to 4 p.m.—are complimentary for hotel guests. One night each week is Kids Night Out with games, dinner, a movie and popcorn ($40/child). 808-669-6200; www.ritz carlton.com.

Sheraton Maui works with another Starwood Property, the Westin Maui, and offers a program at that location. (See Westin below for details.) 808-661-0031.

Wailea Marriott, An Outrigger Resort offers Cowabunga Kids Club for children 5 to 13 years. Available Monday through Saturday 9 a.m. to 2 p.m. Cost is $50 per child per day and available only to registered guests. Lunch is included along with a free T-shirt. Reservation must be made by 2 p.m. the day before. 808-879-1922; www.outrigger.com.

Westin Maui offers Keiki Kamp Ka'anapali for kids 5 to 12 years. The program runs daily from 9 a.m. to 3 p.m., $45 for guests of the Westin or Sheraton Resorts ($60 for non-guests) and includes lunch as well as a T-shirt on the first day. An evening program is available 6:30 to 9:30 p.m. for $20. A half-day program goes from 9 a.m. to 12:45 p.m., with lunch $25.50, without lunch $22.50. Discount for siblings. The Sheraton, another Starwood property, combines their childcare system with the Westin. This is one of the few programs that is available for non-Westin guests. Cost is $60 for the first child and $40 for each sibling. Half day with lunch $30 for each child. Non-guest evening program is $30 for the first child and $20 for each sibling. 808-667-2525; www.westinmaui.com.

The Whaler on Ka'anapali Beach provides a program during summer, Christmas and spring break sessions. Call for current information. 808-661-4861.

SPORTS INSTRUCTORS AND PROGRAMS

Wailea Resort Company offers junior tennis clinics and golf lessons during various weeks in the summer. 808-879-1958.

Wailea Golf Course offers year-round programs for junior golfers. 808-875-7450.

Play the 18-hole **miniature golf course** on the roof of the Embassy Vacation Resort in Honokowai. Open 11 a.m. to 9 p.m. daily. Adults $5; $2.50 12 and under. 808-661-2000.

The island's only bowling alley is **Maui Bowling Center** on Vineyard Street in Wailuku. 808-244-4596.

Kalama Park, Kihei's in-line hockey rink, is open to the public for rollerblading from 4 to 8 p.m. on weekends. 808-874-6834.

Maui Raceway has drag races on Friday and Saturday nights from February through November. Tickets are $7 adults, $6 kids and seniors. Mokulele Highway, just above Kihei. 808-281-1273; www.mrp.org.

Using the "Discover" technique (so kids can learn on their own), Ron Bass offers special **kayaking classes** with appropriately smaller-sized equipment. He also coordinates special drug-free trips for youth to pick up litter and plant trees. Call for schedule and prices. 808-572-6299; fax 808-572-6151; www.maui.net/~kayaking.

Kids (and their parents) will love learning to surf with **Goofy Foot Surf School**. An easy land lesson prepares you before you get wet. The dry lessons are done in front of 505 Front Street and the wet lessons are just off shore in the gentle waves of the Lahaina Harbor. Two-hour group lessons are offered at 8 a.m., 11 a.m. and 2 p.m. at $55 for one person or $110 for two. They guarantee that you will learn to surf or the lesson is free! Private lessons available. 808-244-WAVE; www.goofyfootsurfschool.com.

> **Maui Sports Unlimited** has three-day Kid's Windsurfing Camps ($150) offered Wednesday through Friday, June through August, for kids 6 to 12 years. Six hours of instruction. 1001 Kauhikoa Road, Haiku; 808-575-2266; e-mail: stottie@maui.net

ENTERTAINMENT

The 112-acre **Maui Tropical Plantation** has become one of the top visitor attractions in the state. I find it touristy, but an interesting stop anyway. Surrounding the visitor center are acres planted in sugar cane, macadamia, guava, mango, banana, papaya, pineapple, passion fruit, star fruit and coffee in addition to an array of flowers. There are also displays of Hawai'i's agricultural history throughout the grounds. Admission to the plantation market and restaurant are free, but there is a charge for the tram that takes visitors through the functioning mini-plantation. Hours are 9 a.m. to 5 p.m. daily. 808-244-7643; www.mauitropicalplantation.com.

Warren & Annabelle's in Lahaina has a family magic show seasonally on Tuesday and Thursday beginning at 4:45 p.m.; arrive by 4:30 to check in. Each show is approximately 1 hour and 15 minutes. Children must be at least 6 years of age. 808-667-MAGIC; www.hawaiimagic.com.

Kupanaha: Maui Magic for All Ages is a dinner show extravaganza at the Ka'anapali Beach Hotel. Shows are Tuesday through Saturday; $69 adults, $49 children 13 to 20, $29 children 6 to 12. 808-667-0128; 800-262-8450.

The Napili Kai Beach Resort's Sea House restaurant has for years been involved with local performers. They offer a Friday-evening dinner show where children perform Hawaiian songs and dances. The **Napili Kai Foundation Dinner Show** costs $50 adults and $25 children, seating at 6 p.m., show at 7:30 p.m. 800-367-5030; 808-669-6271; www.napilikai.com.

MOVIES AND THEATERS

Always a great option on the occasional rainy day. There is a six-plex cinema at the Ka'ahumanu Center and a four-plex in Kihei's Kukui Mall. In Lahaina, there is a tri-cinema at The Wharf Cinema (Shopping) Center and another set of four theaters at the Lahaina Center. The Maui Mall offers 12 theaters with stadium seating in what was once Woolworth's. The Castle Theater at the Maui Arts & Cultural Center has one screen.

The Front Street Cinemas at Lahaina Center and the Wharf Cinemas both offer a matinee discount of $5 (before 6 p.m. weekdays and before 3:30 p.m. on weekends and holidays), $4 senior and children. The same rates and times apply for the other Wallace Theater at Maui Mall. The Queen Ka'ahumanu Center theaters and the Kukui Theaters are owned by Consolidated and their matinees are, at least for now, $5, except the Kukui Mall Theater, which charges $5.25. There are also special showings hosted by the Maui Film Festival both in Kahului and in Lahaina.

> Check out this website for more information on Maui resorts: www.hotelfun4kids.com/hotelandresort/ushotels/hawaii/maui.htm.

There are also a number of video stores that rent movies and equipment, and the major resorts have video rentals for guests. www.mauigateway.com/~rw/movie.

Maui has some great theater. **Maui On Stage** produces a full season of professional quality plays and musicals performed almost every weekend from October through June. They are located in the Historic Iao Theatre on Market Street in Wailuku. 808-242-6969.

The **Maui Academy of Performing Arts** clearly has it all when it comes to entertainment. An educational and performing arts organization for kids and adults, it's located in Wailuku. 808-244-8760. **Maui Myth and Magic Theatre** presents 'Ulalena (which means "Wind From the North"), one of the most exciting theatrical presentations on the island. Tickets are $25 to $45 kids 10 and under, $45 to $65 adults. 877-688-4800; 808-661-9913; www.mauitheatre.com. The **Maui Arts & Cultural Center** offers everything from local community events to concert performances by internationally known performers. 808-242-SHOW; www.mauiarts.org.

EXCURSIONS AND ADVENTURES

Upcountry Maui—Traveling up the slopes of Haleakala will bring you to Upcountry Maui. Upcountry Maui features astounding views of central Maui and guided walking tours of the Enchanted Flower Garden. Visit Maui's upcountry petting zoo (reservations required), lots of fun with picnic facilities for small groups. Shop in the rustic town of Makawao, Maui's "Old West" cowboy town. Travel to Paia and visit Ho'okipa Park, one of the world's best windsurfing locations.

Central Maui—Visit the historic Iao Valley and Bailey House Museum for a view of Maui's ancient Hawaiian ancestry. Travel to the Maui Tropical Plantation and experience one of Maui's most popular attractions or take a shopping tour of Maui's largest mall, the Queen Ka'ahumanu Shopping Center. In addition to baseball and mini-soccer fields, the 110-acre **Maui Central Park** (Keopuolani) in Kahului offers playgrounds and picnic tables throughout, and a skateboard park. Adjoining are the **Maui Botanical Gardens** (formerly a zoo). In 2000, the nonprofit Maui Botanical Gardens received a five-year lease on this property; they are in the midst of creating an environmental and education garden. Though it's no longer a zoo, it's a great stop-off so bring along a picnic lunch.

Keiki Zoo Maui offers one- to one-and-a-half-hour tours by appointment at their Kula facility. Interact eyelash to eyelash with a Hawaiian hawk or nene, a cow, owl or Belgian horse, but watch out for Louie De Llama—he loves to kiss the ladies! Admission is $5 (discounts for larger groups). Appointments Tuesday, Thursday and Friday; no appointment is necessary on Saturday, when they are open from noon to 2 p.m. 808-878-2189; www.keikizoo.com.

The **Hawai'i Nature Center** at Iao Valley offers an interactive nature museum and gift shop. There are more than 30 exhibits focusing on Hawai'i's natural history. A towering glass solarium presents an ever-changing view of the valley, rushing water flowing over impressive rock formations into touch pools, and aquariums of native streamlife. Rainforest explorations as well as live insect and stream animal exhibits provide adventuresome and educational attractions. They also offer weekly guided "themed" hikes for children where they can go worm hunting, learn about forest plants, make a tree rubbing, have a bug bash, recycle with "garbage games and trash tricks," get wet, sing bird songs, make a mask or just play in the mud. Hours are 10 a.m. to 4 p.m. daily (subject to change). Admission to the interactive center is $6 adults, $4 children. Call for schedule on other events. 808-244-6500; fax 808-244-6525.

Allow a minimum of two hours to visit the **Maui Ocean Center**, located in Ma'alaea, which offers tours, films and classes on their exhibits, which include an aquarium (the only one of its kind in Hawai'i); reef, turtle and ray pools (plus an outdoor "touch pool"); a shark tank; and whale center. See Chapter 6 for more information. Open 9 a.m. to 5 p.m. Admission $18.50 adults, $12.50 children. 808-270-7000.

Maui Golf and Sports Park is located at the Ma'alaea Triangle and open 10 a.m. to 10 p.m. seven days a week. Featuring two 18-hole miniature golf courses and a bumper boat lagoon with waterfalls. In my opinion this park isn't worth the time or trouble. It is a very uninteresting golf course and the wind in the afternoon at Ma'alaea is sure to provide an annoyance. The ocean aquarium is a much better option for time and money.

Take a self-guided tour of the coastal wetlands and sand dunes of the **Kealia Pond National Wildlife Refuge**. There will be (we hope) by late 2003 interpretive signs along the boardwalk (.75 mile) on the tour trail to explain the features and the wildlife here. 808-875-1582. Or for a guided tour, check with Arnold DeClercq of Hidden Adventures, 808-264-1423, who specializes in family adventures.

The **Whaling Museum** at Whalers Village is a most informative stop. And even better that it is free and open daily from 9:30 a.m. to 10 p.m.

Check to see if there are any sand sculptures being built in the lower courtyard area of the shopping center. They used to be a regular feature but it is unclear if they will continue. Very elaborate and amazing works of art!

See "Calendar of Annual Events" later in this chapter for special Christmas activities.

Keiki Ocean Discovery Time is held at the Pacific Whale Foundations Marine Resource Center at The Harbor Shops at Ma'alaea on the second, third and fourth of each month at 10 a.m. for kids 4 to 10 years. Kids receive a free junior naturalist bag for participating. 808-249-8811; e-mail: programs@pacificwhale.org.

ALL ABOARD

In the Lahaina–Ka'anapali area, the colorful **Sugar Cane Train** runs a course several times a day along Honoapi'ilani Highway from Ka'anapali to Lahaina. Transportation can be purchased alone or in combination with one of several excursions in Lahaina. After arrival in Lahaina, you will board a red double-decker bus for the short drive to the Lahaina Harbor. (See "Land Tours" in Chapter 6 for more information.) Take some time for a stroll, stop by the Baldwin Missionary Home, and have lunch at one of the oceanfront eateries before returning to the train for the trip home. The Sugar Cane Train also has an evening activity, the Paniolo Express is the first scheduled evening train in the history of the railway: departing from the Pu'ukoli'i Station in Ka'anapali each Tuesday and Thursday at 5 p.m. for a stop at the Ka'anapali Station for a *paniolo*-style |barbecue. The kids will love the hearty dinner of chicken, ribs, hot dogs, hamburgers and a salad bar. Top it off with smoothies to drink and mix with a little cowboy-hula entertainment. Reservations required for the Paniolo Express, $59 adult, $39 children 3 to 12. Daytime trains run 363 days a year (closed Thanksgiving and Christmas) from 10:15 a.m. to 4 p.m. from Pu'ukoli'i, Ka'anapali and Lahaina. The prices are children 3 to 12 $9.95 round trip. For adults it's $15.95 round trip. 808-499-2307 or 808-667-6851; e-mail: mail@sugarcanetrain.com; www.sugarcanetrain.com.

The **Power of Art** is a children's exhibit in the Old Jail Gallery in the courthouse building in Lahaina. Sponsored by the Lahaina Arts Society it offers year-round classes at no charge to children of all ages. Display open daily 9 a.m. to 5 p.m.

Maui Marine C.O.R.E. has monthly recreational outings designed to inspire youth about the natural environment. Held the first and third Saturday of each month and is free for kids in grades 8 through 12. Most outings meet at the Pacific Whale Foundation's office at The Harbor Shops at Ma'alaea; call to confirm. 808-249-8811; e-mail: programs@pacificwhale.org.

Borders bookstore in Kahului has an outstanding selection for children with a special area and "Kidstaff" to provide storytelling, arrange book character visits and present special programs. It's on Dairy Road as you leave the airport and go to the main road towards Kihei/Lahaina. 808-877-6160.

The **Paper Airplane Museum** in the Maui Mall features the unique juice-can creations of the Tin Can Man along with aviation model exhibits and pictures depicting the history of aviation in the Hawaiian islands. They have 2,500 paper airplane kits that you can buy. Tin can and paper airplane demonstrations, too. 808-877-8916; www.hawaiiweb.com.

You can't walk by **Kite Fantasy** in the Lahaina Cannery Mall without stopping to watch the swimming frog or the weasel ball. Display tables in front have a great selection of puzzles, activity books, magic tricks and other keep-'em-occupied-on-the-way-to-Hana ideas; inside are Beanie Babies (complete with hula shirts and aloha wear), water and beach toys, dolls and, of course, kites. Open 9:30 a.m. to 9 p.m. 808-661-4766.

Camp Trilogy is a program from Trilogy Excursions. This eco-enrichment kids program is in addition to the original Discover Lana'i Adventure. It is offered June through August and during major holidays. The program begins with a snorkel lesson from Camp Trilogy's counselors who are certified Hawai'i Wildlife Fund marine naturalists. Then, a guided reef tour enables kids to learn about and view all kinds of marine wildlife. Organized beach games and activities teach team-building skills as well as respect for the environment. Camp Trilogy kids receive a special T-shirt and enjoy their own barbecue. Cost is $152.50 plus tax ($63 per person in addition to the regular child's fare of $89.50). It's an all-day trip to Lana'i, and the children need to be 3 to 15 years old and able to swim. 808-661-4743.

Especially for Seniors

More and more businesses are beginning to offer special savings to seniors. RSVP booking agency offers special rates for seniors who book their accommodations through them. They are listed in the Rental Agents section of Chapter 3. Whether it is a boating activity, an airline ticket or a condominium, be sure to ask about special senior rates. And be sure to travel with identification showing your date of birth.

SENIOR DISCOUNTS Many properties and rental agents offer senior programs or senior discounts. Mention you are a senior (some as low as age 50) and receive incredible discounts or bonuses. For example, Pleasant Hawaiian Holidays features a "Makua Club" with special rates for seniors. Outrigger offers a "Fifty-Plus Program"; Aston calls theirs the "Senior Sun Club."

A number of airlines have special discounts for seniors. Some have a wonderful feature that provides a discount for the traveling companion who is accompanying the senior. Coupon books for senior discounts are also available from a number of airline carriers.

All Maui movie theaters offer senior discounts (many for those over 52) anytime, and most also have assisted listening devices to pump up the volume—or turn it down if it's too loud. Remember that

AARP members get many travel discounts for rooms, cars and tours. Check the Yellow Pages when you arrive on Maui for the senior discount program logo. Look for a black circle with a white star in the ads.

MAUI SENIOR SERVICES Check out the Kaunoa Senior Services at 401 Ala Kapa Place, Paia, 808-270-7308, which offers volunteer opportunities and classes for folks 55 years and up, and a dining program for those 60 years and older.

Elderhostel Hawai'i arranges inexpensive housing in college dorms during summer months along with special interest classes and sports activities. Call 808-262-8942 on O'ahu for information on Maui accommodations. For kayaking and snorkeling, Ron Bass on Maui (808-572-6299) works with Elderhostel to provide senior excursions addressing their special needs.

Travel Tips for the Physically Impaired

Make your travel plans well in advance and inform hotels and airlines when making your reservations that you are a person with a disability. Bring along your medical records in the event of an emergency. It is recommended that you bring your own wheelchair and notify the airlines in advance that you will be transporting it. There are no battery rentals available on Maui.

Additional information can be obtained from the State Commission on Persons with Disabilities, c/o State Department of Health, 54 High Street, Wailuku, Maui, HI 96793 (808-984-8219 V-TT; fax 808-984-8222). Or call the State Commission on Persons with Disabilities on O'ahu: 808-586-8121 V-TT; fax 808-586-8129. They offer a book entitled *Aloha Guide to Accessibility*, which is divided into sections that provide services and information for persons with disabilities on the accessibility of hotels, beaches, parks, shopping centers, theaters and auditoriums, and visitor attractions. They will send specific sections or the entire guide for the cost of postage ($3 to $5 per section; $15 complete).

ARRIVAL AND DEPARTURE On arrival at the Kahului airport terminal, you will find the building easily accessible for mobility impaired persons. Parking areas are located in front of the main terminal for disabled persons. Restrooms with handicapped stalls (male and female) are also found in the main terminal.

TRANSPORTATION There is no public transportation on Maui (although there is an airport shuttle) and taxi service can be expensive. For short hops, the Lahaina–Ka'anapali route of the "West Maui Shopping Express" has a wheelchair-accessible bus. See "Getting Around: Rental Cars and Trucks" section later in the chapter for phone numbers of rental agencies. They need some advance notice to install the equipment. Accessible Vans of Hawai'i offers wheelchair-accessible van rentals with hand controls, and delivery and pick up of island visitors. They can also assist you if you'd like to rent a specific car and require special needs such as hand controls. 800-303-3750; 808-871-7536; fax 808-871-7536. Also check Wheelchair Get-Aways, 800-638-1912.

ACCOMMODATIONS   Each of the major island hotels offers one or more handicapped rooms including bathroom entries of at least 29" to allow for wheelchairs. Due to the limited number of rooms, reservations should be made well in advance. Information on condominium accessibility is available from the Commission on Persons with Disabilities (see above). Accessible Vans of Hawai'i also has condo listings as well as additional information on the availability of roll-in showers and wheelchair-accessible bathrooms.

ACTIVITIES   Accessible Vans of Hawai'i and Hawai'i Care Van Shuttle and Tour offer wheelchair-accessible touring and can provide information on recreational activities for the traveler. Among the options are wheelchair tennis or basketball, bowling and swimming. Contact them in advance of your arrival. Wheelchair access to some of the tourist attractions may be limited. One of a few boats to offer access for the handicapped is *The Pride of Maui*.

Maui County continues to make the beaches more accessible for disabled travelers with handicapped designations at beach parking lots, sidewalks and curb cuts, comfort stations, picnic tables, showers and an accessible pathway onto the beach. Currently beaches that have been made accessible include Kama'ole I, II and III, Hanaka'o'o Beach and Kanaha Beach.

Ron Bass is an independent tour guide who specializes in kayaking and snorkeling for the disabled. His special equipment includes three-person kayaks, view boards and beach-access wheelchairs. Ron also operates "Wilderness Wish," a non-profit organization that assists disabled folks to experience new adventures by discovering and exploring out-of-the-way places. P.O. Box 106, Pu'unene, HI 96784. 808-572-6299; fax 808-572-6151; www.maui.net/~kayaking.

MEDICAL SERVICES AND EQUIPMENT   Maui Memorial Hospital is located in Wailuku and there are also good clinics in all areas of the island. Check the local directory.

Several agencies can assist in providing personal care attendants, companions and nursing aides while on your visit. **Hale Mahaolu** at 808-872-4130, www.maui.net/~hmahaolu provides personal care attendants, as do **Aloha International Employment Service** 808-871-6373, and **Interim Health Care** 808-877-2676.

Lahaina Pharmacy (Old Lahaina Center) has wheelchairs, crutches, canes and walkers. 808-661-3119.

Gammie Home Care, Kahului Industrial Center, 292 Alamaha Place, Kahului, HI 96732, can provide medical equipment rentals, from walking aides to bathroom accessories or wheelchairs as well as oxygen services. 808-877-4032; fax 808-877-3359; www.gammie.com; e-mail: gammie@maui.net. Or go to www.thestateofhawaii.com/home health.html#maui for a listing of home health care specialists.

Accessible Vans of Hawai'i is the only travel, tour and activity agency on Maui that specializes in assisting the disabled traveler. "Imagination is your limit," they report when it comes to the activities they offer. They can assist in making reservations at a condominium or hotel to fit the needs of the traveler, make airport arrangements including ticketing and arranging for a wheelchair. They can make arrangements for personal care such as attendants, pharmacists or interpreters as well as arrange for rental cars or vans with hand controls. Accessible Vans of Hawai'i is a one-stop shopping connection for the disabled traveler and the Maui (and State of Hawaii) Representative for Accessible Vans of America. And as your personal Hawaiian concierge, travel consultant Carol Miller is happy to make recommendations (no charge). Inquire about island recreation such as snorkeling, scuba diving, helicopter tours, bowling, golf, horseback riding, boating, luaus, tennis (disabled opponent available), tours, jet skiing or ocean kayaking. Wedding and honeymoon arrangements, too. Accessible Vans of Hawai'i can also provide sand/beach wheelchairs with big inflatable rubber tires. Carol Miller: 296 Alamaha, Suite C, Kahului, HI 96732. 808-871-7785; fax 808-871-7536; www.accessiblevanshawaii.com; e-mail: carol@accessiblevanshawaii.com.

HEARING IMPAIRED   Both the Wallace and Consolidated movie theater chains have assisted listening devices available at their Lahaina, Kihei and Kahului theaters. The headsets increase the volume (or decrease the noise) on an individual basis. The Maui Arts & Cultural Center also provides headsets for plays and concerts and, as one of Maui's newer constructions, is completely ADA accessible.

VISION IMPAIRED   Legislation allows seeing-eye dogs to travel to Hawai'i without quarantine, providing that current proof of vaccinations is provided.

What to Pack

When traveling to paradise, you won't need too much. Comfortable shoes are important for all the sightseeing and shopping. Sandals are the norm for footwear. Dress is casual for dining. Many restaurants require men to wear sport shirts with collars, but only one or two require a tie. Clothes should be lightweight and easy care. Cotton and cotton blends are more comfortable for the tropical climate than polyesters. Shorts and bathing suits are the dress code here. A lightweight jacket with a hood or sweater is advisable for evenings and occasional rain showers.

The only need for warmer clothes is if your plans should include a stay Upcountry, hiking/camping in Haleakala Crater or seeing the sunrise. While it may start out warm and sunny, the weather can change very quickly Upcountry. Even during the daytime, a sweater or light jacket is a good idea when touring the area. (The cooler weather here is evidenced on the roofs of the homes where chimney stacks can be spotted.) Tennis shoes or hiking shoes are a good idea for the rougher volcanic terrain of Haleakala or hiking elsewhere as well. Sunscreens are a must. A camera, of course, needs to be tucked in. Binoculars are an option and may be well used if you are traveling between December and May when the whales arrive for their winter vacation. Special needs for traveling with children are discussed above. Anything that you need can probably be purchased once you arrive. Don't forget to leave some extra space in those suitcases for goodies that you will want to take back home.

Weddings & Honeymoons

If a Hawaiian wedding (or a renewal of vows) is in your dreams, Maui can make them all come true. While the requirements are simple, here are a few tips, based on current requirements at time of publication, for making your wedding plans run more smoothly. I advise you to double check the requirements as things change.

REGULATIONS Both bride and groom must be over 18 years of age (16 years old with written consent from parents or legal guardians). Birth certificates are not required, but you do need proof of age such as a driver's license or passport. You do not need proof of citizenship or residence. If either partner has been divorced, the date, county and state of finalization for each divorce must be verbally provided to the licensing agent. If a divorce was finalized within the last three months, then a decree must be provided to the licensing agent. One wedding agency informed us that your personal vows for a Catholic wedding require special arrangements between your home priest and the Maui priest. If both bride and groom are practicing Catholics, the Church requires that you marry within the church building, unless you are granted special permission from the Bishop in Honolulu.

A license must be purchased in person in the state of Hawai'i. Call the Department of Health in Maui (808-984-8210) for the name of a licensing agent in the area where you will be staying. Both bride and groom must appear in person before the agent. The fee is currently $60. There is no waiting period once you have the license, but the license is valid for only 30 days. Check with the Chamber of Commerce in Kahului (808-871-7711) for information regarding a pastor. Many island pastors are very flexible in meeting your needs, such as an outdoor location. (For $8 you can buy a package with a booklet and information on planning a wedding.)

For copies of current requirements and forms, write in advance to the State of Hawaii, Department of Health, Marriage License Section, P.O. Box 3378, Honolulu, HI 96801; 808-586-4545. You can also call the Maui Visitors Bureau (808-244-3530) for a copy of the requirements as well as information on free public wedding locations at Hawai'i state and national parks and how to book a marriage ceremony with a judge. (The Courthouse is at 2145 Main Street in Wailuku.) You can also go online to obtain Department of Health forms and information at www.state.hi.us/doh/records/vr_marri.html or e-mail them at yr-info@maui.health.state.hi.us.

There are a couple (at least!) of websites devoted to getting married, renewing vows and/or honeymooning on Maui: www.mauiweddingnetwork.com or www.visitmaui.com. See below for a list of wedding providers or www.mauichamber.com under "Weddings."

WEDDING BASICS
Formal Wear Rentals
Formal wear rentals for the gents in your party can be obtained from **Gilbert's Formal Wear**. 104 North Market Street, Old Wailuku Town. 808-244-4017; www.gilbertsformalwear.com.

Limousines
Arthur's Limousine Service is at 296A Alamaha Street, Kahului; 808-871-5555; 877-408-9559; fax 808-877-3333; www.arthurslimo.com. **Classy Taxi** (808-871-5555) has "gangster-style" limos (circa 1929) and a 1933 Rolls Royce. Also try **Carey Limousine Hawaii** (aka Town & Country Limousine) (808-572-3400) or **Star Maui Limousine** (808-875-6900; www.limohawaii.com; e-mail: info@limohawaii.com).

Video Tape Services
Hawai'i **Video Memories** will capture your special day on video tape. 230 Hana Highway, Suite 11. 888-255-7080; 808-871-5788.

Wedding Coordinators
Over 125 members of the Hawai'i Wedding Professionals Association are listed in their attractive, informative 12-page booklet, the *Maui Wedding Planner*. Features on island locations, leis/flowers and planning

> Arrange for a private sunset dinner cruise for your reception! See "Cruises" in Chapter 6 regarding scheduled or private charters.

timelines are offered along with advice on choosing everything from ministers to photographers. For a free copy of the booklet and a brochure, call 800-291-0110 or 808-891-1616; fax 800-368-6933 (U.S. & Canada), 808-891-1717; e-mail: married@maui.net; www.simply married.com.

Basic packages run $195 to $3,000. Although each company varies the package slightly, it will probably include assistance in choosing a location and getting your marriage license, a minister and an assortment of extras such as champagne, limited photography, cake, leis and a bridal garter. Videotaping, witnesses and music are usually extra.

A Dream Wedding Maui Style—One-on-one service, from simple ($395) to exotic ($2,400). Vow renewals. Tracy Flanagan, Consultant. And they have a really cool custom arrangement form online. 143 Dickenson Street #201, Lahaina, HI 96761; 808-661-1777; 800-743-2777; fax 808-661-0072; www.adreamwedding.net; e-mail: dreamwed@maui.net.

A Romantic Maui Wedding—Private oceanfront wedding location. Video available. Full-service wedding consulting available. P.O. Box 13232, Lahaina, HI 96761; 808-661-3990; 800-808-4144; fax 808-665-1412; www.justmauied.com.

A Wedding Just for Two—Prices begin at $150. A spiritual wedding experience sponsored by The Living Ministry. Begin with a Hawaiian lei exchange; close with a blessing. Contact Reverend Beverly Powers. P.O. Box 10937, Lahaina, HI 96761; 808-669-4400; 888-JUS-4-TWO; fax 808-669-0794.

A Wedding Made in Paradise—Custom weddings with the assistance of Alicia Bay Laurel, the "Martha Stewart of wedding planners." P.O. Box 880340, Pukalani, HI 96788; 808-879-3444; 800-453-3440 U.S. mainland; fax 808-572-6649; www.wedinparadise.com; e-mail: wedmaui@maui.net.

A White Orchid Wedding—Have your wedding "Aloha Ea Oi" (I Love You) at a "Historic Hawaiian Church," or where the "Lava Meets the Sea." Packages start at $250 to $4,100. They can also arrange travel, activities and vow renewals. They also have an a la carte shopping system. Contact Carolee Higashino. P.O. Box 2696, Wailuku, HI 9679; 808-242-VOWS; 800-240-9336; fax 808-242-6853; www.whiteorchidwedding.net or www.whiteorchidwedding.com; e-mail: awow@maui.net.

All Ways Maui'd Weddings & Ceremonies—They specialize in smaller, more intimate weddings, vow renewals, holy unions and blessings, and also offer digital and 35mm photography services. Packages for ceremonies range $125 to $750 and are usually held at Maui's public beaches or parks, but private tropical and oceanfront gardens or a Hawaiian wedding chapel are also options. Owned and operated by Rev. Kolleen O'Flaherty Wheeler, a non-denominational, state-licensed minister, and Bruce Wheeler, coordinator and photographer. They tell me they don't mind short notice. P.O. Box 817, Puʻunene, HI 96784-0817; 808-244-3167; 877-906-2843; fax 808-242-8019; cell phone 808-385-1195; www.maui-angels.com; e-mail: weddings@maui-angels.com.

Aloha Hawaii Weddings—Signa and Alberto Abreu can help plan and coordinate your wedding and vow renewals on Maui. From simple weddings on the beach ("Sweet and Simple" for $249) to extraordinary weddings with all the special touches ("Royal Poinciana" at $2,849), they'll take care of you from beginning to end. Choose a beach or private location. 1680 South Alanui Place, Kihei, HI 96753; 808-874-9393; fax 808-874-8230; e-mail: info@alohahawaiiweddings.com; www.alohahawaiiweddings.com.

John Pierre's Photographic Studio—Providing wedding photo packages since 1977. 143 Dickenson Street, Lahaina, Maui, HI 96761; 808-667-7988; www.maui.net/~jpsm; e-mail: jpsm@maui.net.

Now and Forever Maui Weddings—Owner Theresa Tuipelehake can assist with everything—even hair and makeup. Packages from "Basic" at $385 to "Just Married the Hawaiian Way" at $1,975. P.O. Box 12380, Lahaina, HI 96761; 808-661-5583; 800-327-2436; fax 808-661-5597; www.mauiweddings4unow.com; e-mail information@mauiweddings4unow.com.

Royal Hawaiian Carriage Co.—Has two carriages (one white, one black), four passengers each with two Clydesdales, one Belgian and one Percheron horse. The company does wedding transportation to and from the ceremony and/or reception and provides pick up island-wide. They are based at the Kapalua Resort. Rates for the Kapalua area are $300 for the first hour, $175 each additional hour. Extra charge for carriage rides out of the Kapalua area. They also provide restaurant transportation, horse-drawn picnics and other romantic excursions such as sunset tours. The can provide private locations such as a tropical valley or an oceanview gazebo for your wedding location. P.O. Box 10066, Lahaina, HI, 96761; 808-669-1100.

Royal Hawaiian Weddings—Janet Renoir can assist you with your most special occasion. Packages start $239 for the "Just Maui Me" to luxury with a limousine at $1,689. Choose from dazzling beachside sunsets, private oceanfront settings, tropical gardens, a Hawaiian luau, and enchanted waterfall, or remote helicopter landings. Vow renewals from $239 to $908. Name your dream. 808-875-8569; 800-659-1866 U.S. & Canada; fax 808-875-0623; www.royalhawaiianweddings.com; e-mail: info@royalhawaiianweddings.com.

Simply Married Maui Style—Owners Ken and Judy Grimes offer a choice of being "Simply Married" ($195) or taking a helicopter to a secluded waterfall ($3,000), plus plenty of options in between. Both are ordained ministers: Ken (Lutheran), Judy (Unity). P.O. Box 512, Makawao, HI 96768; 808-572-7898; www.simplemarried.com; e-mail: married@maui.net.

Tropical Gardens of Maui—They provide a garden area with waterfalls and a gazebo in the Iao Valley, $150 for up to 10 people and $200 for 11 to 20 people. 200 Iao Valley Road, Wailuku, HI 96793; 808-244-3085; fax 808-242-6152; www.tropicalgardensofmaui.com; e-mail: info@tropicalgardensofmaui.com.

Trilogy Excursions—Trilogy Excursions can make the most memorable day of your life an ocean adventure! Imagine crossing the channel to the island Lana'i while exchanging vows. They offer one to three catamarans on Saturday and Sunday. They can accommodate large or small groups ranging from 25 to 160 guests. Once on Lana'i the bride and groom will enjoy the exclusive Hale O Manele pavilion for their Hawaiian-style luau celebration. The captain and crew will prepare dinner while you enjoy live entertainment. A starlit sail back to Lahaina will be the perfect ending. Trilogy does not supply a minister or wedding cake. 888-MAUI800; 808-661-4743.

Honeymoon Holidays are available from Pleasant Hawaiian Holidays. They include special amenities such as champagne, room upgrade, fresh flower lei greeting, hotel accommodations and rental car. 808-242-9244.

The social directors of the major resorts can assist you with your wedding plans and there are a variety of locations on the grounds of these resorts to set the scene for your very special wedding:

Diamond Resort Hawaii—Has a wedding gazebo with a view of the ocean and the mountains. Great for smaller, intimate weddings. Packages from $900 to $4,500. 555 Kaukahi Street, Wailea, HI 96753; 808-874-0500; 800-800-0720; fax 808-874-8778; www.diamondresort.com; e-mail: info@diamondresort.com.

Four Seasons—This luxury Wailea property features three destination wedding packages. Amenities include musician(s), champagne and cake, floral decor, clergy, photography and use of a wedding location. Services include assistance by their wedding coordinator and a 20 percent discount on accommodations. Wedding packages run $2,500 to $12,000. The Ku'uipo Point Gazebo on the third level of the sculpture gardens with ocean and mountain vistas can accommodate 40 guests. The oceanfront lawn overlooking Wailea Beach is enhanced with floral archway and white aisle runner. It can accommodate up to 100 guests. The Seasons Lawn is a secluded garden for private ceremonies for 2 to 10. Seasons Point is set atop a gushing waterfall with bougainvillea and koi ponds and is a perfect spot for a Maui sunset as a backdrop. 3900 Wailea Alanui, Wailea, HI 96753. 808-874-8000; 800-334-MAUI; fax 808-874-2244; www.fourseasons.com/maui.

Grand Wailea—The extraordinary Grand Wailea has constructed a New England wedding chapel on their grounds. The picturesque white chapel features stained-glass windows, designed by artist Yvonne Cheng, that depict a royal Hawaiian wedding. Woods of red oak, teak and cherry dominate the interior, which is accented by three hand-crafted chandeliers from Murano, Italy. Outside the chapel is a flower-filled garden with brass-topped gazebos. A beautiful indoor location for your wedding. They also offer weddings in their chapel gardens or on Wailea Beach. Wedding packages are $2,700 to $4,300. Sunset weddings are $500 or more than the day-time weddings. A la carte package price for the chapel and gardens for 90 minutes is $2,700 and $3,200 for a sunset package. You can also add butterflies or doves. Packages for renewal of wedding vows are $1,600 to $2,000 ($500 more for sunset renewals). The Grand Wailea also gives a 20 percent discount for rooms for the bride and groom only. 3850 Wailea Alanui, Wailea, HI 96753; 808-875-1234 ext. 2804; www.grandwaileaweddings.com.

Hyatt Regency—A wedding and catering coordinator can assist with your special day plans. A wedding gazebo, designed from ohia wood from the Big Island, is set amid tropical Hawaiian gardens and waterways. Packages from $995 to $9,995. Check out their wedding planning guide online. Very helpful! 200 Nohea Kai Drive, Lahaina, HI 96761; 808-661-1234; 800-55HYATT; fax 808-667-4497; www.maui.hyatt.com.

Lana'i Wedding—The Manele Bay Resort or Lodge at Koele on the island of Lana'i offers the assistance of a wedding coordinator. The site can be either the gazebo at the Lodge at Koele or the Hawaiian or Bromeliad garden at the Manele Bay Hotel. Weddings starting from $2,500. Honeymoon and Romance packages are also available and include amenities such as aromatic bath salts and oils, massage or an intimate breakfast in bed. P.O. Box 630310, Lana'i City, HI 96763; 800-321-4666; fax 808-565-3868; www.lanairesorts.com; e-mail: reservations@lanai-resorts.com.

Royal Lahaina Resort—Rows of pink and white hibiscus line the walkways leading to the cottage courtyard and wedding gazebo that features six open-air windows. Packages begin at $650. The Royal Lahaina Resort has also introduced a unique wedding custom. They provide stepping stones engraved with the bride and groom's name and wedding date. Contact their wedding consult, ext. 2211. 2780 Keka'a Drive, Lahaina, HI 96761; 808-661-3611; 800-222-5642; fax 808-661-6150; www.hawaiianhotels.com.

Westin Maui—Ka'anapali Beach has its own resident Director of Romance who will assist you with your wedding and honeymoon plans—even if you want to be married while parasailing or scuba diving. For more traditional romantics, they offer the release of 2 to 40 white wedding doves from white wicker baskets. Packages $625 to

$2,250. 808-667-2525; www.westinmaui.com; e-mail: westinmauiweddings@westin.com.

Ritz-Carlton, Kapalua—Wedding packages can be arranged to include the use of the historic Kumulani Chapel. Construction on the 60-seat New England–style plantation church began in the late 1930s, but due to the war, it was not completed until 1951. Weddings can also be arranged at the gazebo on the lawn of the chapel, at Lava Point, or on the Beach House lawn. Wedding packages range from $3,800 to $10,500.

Helpful Information

INFORMATION BOOTHS Booths located at the shopping areas can provide helpful information and lots of brochures! (Look for the new wallet-size mini-brochures that are purse and pocket friendly.)

Maui Visitors Bureau: 1727 Wili Pa Loop, P.O. Box 580, Wailuku, HI 96793; 808-244-3530; 800-525-MAUI; fax 808-244-1337; www.visitmaui.com.

BANKS Basic hours are 8:30 a.m. to 3 p.m., but some are open until 4 or 5 p.m. Most will cash U.S. traveler's checks with a picture ID.

CREDIT CARDS A few small condominiums still do not accept any form of credit card payment, but stores and hotels almost always do. For lost or stolen credit cards phone: American Express 800-992-3404; VISA 800-847-2911.

SALES TAX A sales tax of 4.167 is added to all purchases made in Hawai'i. There is an additional room-use tax added to your hotel or condominium bill.

HOLIDAYS Holidays unique to the state of Hawai'i: March 26 is Prince Kuhio Day, June 11 is Kamehameha Day and August 21 is Admissions Day.

Communications

TELEVISION The Paradise Network, shown island-wide on Channel 7, is designed especially with visitors in mind. Information is provided on recreation, real estate, shopping, restaurants, history, culture and art.

RADIO KPOA 93.5FM/92.7FM plays great old and new Hawaiian music. KLHI ("The Point") at 101.1FM has adult alternative rock; KHPR (90.7FM) is Hawai'i Public Radio with classical music; and KDLX 94.3FM offers all country. KJMD 98.3FM is rhythmic/hip hop; KONI 104.7FM plays oldies; KAOI ("I")

FM on either 95.1 or 96.7 (Upcountry) has soft rock. KNUI 99.9FM features adult contemporary; KNUQ ("Q") 103.7 offers contemporary island music and KPMW 105.5FM ("Wild 105") has top 40 and contemporary hits with ethnic programming on the weekends. Manaʻo Radio at 91.5 KEAO-LPFM is a new listener-supported, non-profit station that offers an eclectic mix of music and information. On the AM dial, KMVI has sports talk at 550; KNUI 900AM plays traditional Hawaiian; and KAOI 1110AM has news, talk and sports.

PERIODICALS   Some of Maui's free visitor publications have self-explanatory titles: *MENU*, *Maui Menus*, *Lahaina Historical Guide*, *101 Things To Do on Maui*, *Driving Magazine of Maui*, *Drive Guide—the Map Magazine*, *Maui Activities & Attractions*, *Maui Gold Coast* (emphasis on art), *Maui Golf Review*, *Golfer's Guide*, *Homes & Land*, *Real Estate Maui Style*, "The Best" Guidebook (along with full-size publications titled by area), and the regional "Beach Resort Guides." Peruse the others (*This Week*, *Maui Gold*, *Maui Quick Guide*, *Maui Magazine*, *VIP* and *Maui Visitor*) to find maps, shuttle schedules, entertainment calendars, shopping tips, activity directories, etc. They all have lots of advertising, but most offer coupons that will give you discounts on everything from meals to sporting activities to clothing. It may save you a bit to search through these before making your purchases. *Maui No Ka Oi* is Maui's only "real" magazine—a glossy quarterly ($3.25) with columns and features on people, politics, business, lifestyles, current events, environment, history and culture.

There are also a number of newspaper-style publications that offer helpful and interesting information. The *Maui Bulletin* is a free newsprint booklet with classified ads and television listings. The free *Maui Weekly* is less touristy with more local stories. *Haleakala Times/Kihei Times* are free regional newspapers serving Upcountry and Kihei areas respectively. *Maui Time* is a free bi-weekly on music, sports and art (surfing and live entertainment are highlighted, dude). *Lahaina News* is a small weekly newspaper containing local and West Maui news, columns and lots of advertisements. Fee is 25¢. *Maui News* is the primary Maui newspaper, published Monday through Saturday for 50¢; $1.50 for the larger Sunday edition. This is a great source of local information. The Thurs-

> **TIME**
> You'll find that Hawaiʻi has not discovered daylight-saving time. They are also in a different time zone. During "standard time" in the continental U.S. (November through March) Hawaiʻi is two hours behind the Pacific time zone. Because they don't switch to daylight-saving time, from April through October they are three hours behind Pacific time. You may hear references to "Hawaiian Time" or "Maui Time"—these local phrases often refer not to the hour, but the lack of punctuality!

day Scene supplement has entertainment and dining news. (Hint: You can pick up free copies of both the *Lahaina News* and *Scene* from the Lahaina Visitor Center.)

WEBSITES As cyberspace continues to boom, this is an ever-growing category for guides. I have intermingled some websites and e-mail addresses throughout the text as space allows. If there is no e-mail address, you can probably contact them through their websites. For rental agents, check "Rental Agents" at the end of Chapter 3 for websites of those that offer them. Following are some general websites that might be of interest to you. These will have links to assist you with other information. (One that I know will be helpful is www.infomaui.com, a website directory with detailed descriptions and over 500 links to Maui web pages. It's kind of an online guidebook that includes Things To Do, Places to See, Shopping, and an interactive Q&A section.)

Haddon Holidays is one of many companies that offers packages to Hawaii. You can visit their website at www.haddon.com. Pleasant Hawaiian Holidays has a site at www.2hawaii.com, Hawaiian Hotels & Resorts at www.hawaiihotels.com. You can reach Marc Resorts at www.marcresorts.com. See "Cruise Lines" below for information and websites of companies.

Concierge Connection is an excellent resource and offers complimentary advice, information and recommendations on all aspects of your Maui vacation. 808-875-9366; 888-875-9366; e-mail: info@mauiconcierge.net; www.mauiconcierge.net.

Here are some additional Maui-related websites:

Maui On-Line: www.mauionline.com
Maui Net: www.maui.net
Tom Barefoot's Tours: www.tombarefoot.com
Jon's Maui web page: www.mauihawaii.org
AskaboutMaui: www.askaboutmaui.com
Activity Owners Association of Hawaii: www.maui.org

INTERNET ACCESS Looking to get connected? Here are some locations with internet. *West Side*: Ashley's Internet Café at Kahana Gateway Center (25¢/minute). Maui Swiss Café located between

---

FOR YOUR PROTECTION

Do not leave valuables in your car, even in your trunk. Many rental car companies urge you to not lock your car as vandals cause extensive and expensive damage breaking the locks. Many companies also warn not to drive on certain roads (Ulupalakua to Hana and the unpaved portion of Hwy. 34) unless you are willing to accept liability for all damages.

Burger King and Wharf Center in Lahaina. Westside Copy and Graphics in Honokowai by Star Market and Westside Natural Foods & Deli in Lahaina. And check out Buns of Maui at Old Lahaina Center. *South Side*: Cyberbean Internet Café at 1881 South Kihei Road by Foodland. Hale Imua Internet shop at 2463 South Kihei Road near Denny's Restaurant. *Central*: Hale Imua on Main Street in Wailuku. Café Marc Aurel on North Market Street in Wailuku.

Most of the major hotels and resorts have business centers that are available for guests but most also allow non-guest use. Rates can really run away with you! Some charge a minimum and a maximum per hour, but others charge as much as 25¢/minute and that's $21 an hour! Café Imua is $2 for the first 10 minutes and then 10¢/minute after that, which is a much better deal.

Medical Information

EMERGENCIES There are several clinics around the island that take emergencies or walk-in patients. Your condominium or hotel desk can provide you with suggestions, or check the phone book. **Kaiser Permanente Medical Care Facilities** are located in Wailuku (808-243-6000); Lahaina (808-669-6900) and Kihei (808-891-3000). **Doctors on Call** (Hyatt, Westin or Ritz-Carlton: 808-667-7676) and **Dr. Ben Azman** (Whalers Village: 808-667-9721) all specialize in visitor care. See "Helpful Phone Numbers" at the end of the chapter for more numbers. Calling 911 will put you in contact with local fire, police and ambulances.

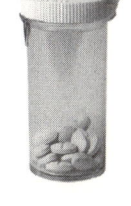

Hazards

SUN SAFETY The sunshine is stronger in Hawai'i than on the mainland, so a few basic guidelines will ensure that you return home with a tan, not a burn. Use a good lotion with a sunscreen, reapply after swimming and don't forget the lips. Be sure to moisturize after a day in the sun and wear a hat to protect your face. Exercise self-control and stay out a limited time the first few days, remembering that a gradual tan will last longer. It is best to avoid being out between the hours of noon and three when it is the hottest. Be cautious of overcast days when it is very easy to become burned unknowingly. Don't forget that the ocean acts as a reflector and time spent in it equals time spent on the beach.

Getting There

Arrival and departure tips: During your flight to Honolulu, the airline staff will provide you with a visitor information sheet. This is used by the Hawai'i Visitors Bureau to track the number of visitors and their island destinations. This is also where you must report any animals, fruits, vegetables or plants that will need to be inspected upon arrival in Honolulu.

AIRLINE INFORMATION

The best prices on major air carriers can generally be arranged through a reputable travel agent who can often secure air or air-with-car packages at good prices by volume purchasing. Prices can vary considerably so comparison shopping is a wise idea. Be sure to ask about senior citizen and companion fare discounts. It is good to be an informed traveler so check on websites even if you are dealing with a travel agent or an airline. www.orbitz.com or www.travelocity.com are just a couple of my favorites. You can register with Travelocity and they will send you an e-mail notice when airfare drops whatever dollar amount you specify. Orbitz gives you the price for airlines departing from your home city. It's a quick way to help you begin your air travel options. Keep in mind that these websites don't necessarily post all airline schedules. If you don't care what carrier you travel on and are flexible with your travel plans, check out www.hotwire.com. With Hotwire, you aren't advised you of your carrier or travel time until you have booked so you have to like surprises.

"Airfare Only" is available through **Sun Trips** (on their Sun Country Charters). These prices are incredibly good values, but on the downside you have to depart from their West Coast gateway, Oakland. See information below. **Pleasant Hawaiian Holidays** also offers air only (see information below).

Creative Leisure High-end accommodations with packages that include airfare and car if you choose. On Maui they currently have packages for Four Seasons, Grand Wailea Resort, Napili Kai, Ritz-Carlton Kapalua, Fairmont Kea Lani, Westin Maui, Hyatt Regency Maui, Kapalua Bay Hotel and Ocean Villas, Sheraton Maui, Wailea Marriott, Renaissance Wailea, Maui Prince and Hotel Hana-Maui; they also have many condominium packages available. On Lana'i, they have packages for Manele Bay Hotel and The Lodge at Koele. They work in association with United Airlines. TravelGuard insurance is also available so if there is some chance you might have to change your travel plans you won't lose what you've paid for airlines and accommodations. 800-413-1000; www.creativeleisure.com.

Pleasant Hawaiian Holidays Founded in 1959 as Pleasant Travel Service in Point Pleasant, New Jersey, Edward Hogan and his company have grown and expanded to provide a range of airfare, air only and land only options. People seem to be very pleased by the Pleasant Hawaiian service. Their non-stop scheduled "Air Cruise" is available from Los Angeles and San Francisco to Honolulu and Maui. Currently they operate six days a week (no flights on Tuesday), which means 24 non-stop flights each week. During the summer season they increase the schedule to 14 daily non-stop flights. They can also arrange for rental cars and they work with many properties on Maui and offer some of the best air/land packages to be found. Check their "Last Minute Desk" for those of you trying to find space on short notice. 800-242-9212; www.pleasantholidays.com.

Hawaiian Hotels & Resorts manages Royal Lahaina Resort on Maui. They often have special vacation packages. 800-22-ALOHA or 800-280-8155; 808-661-3611; www.hawaiihotels.com.

Sun Trips has now been serving Hawai'i-bound vacationers for several years. If you are from the Midwest, you might be familiar with Sun Country, which began in 1983 and has been flying to exotic Caribbean destinations. In 1997 they added Hawai'i. Currently they

AGRICULTURAL INSPECTION

On your return to the mainland, you will have to take your checked as well as carry-on baggage through agricultural inspection. Where your luggage will be inspected will depend upon your travel plans. If you are checking baggage at the Kahului airport, which will be transferred directly to your connecting flight in Honolulu, you will need to go through the agricultural inspection at the main entrance of the airport before proceeding to the airline ticketing counter to check in. When you arrive in Honolulu and begin trekking from your interisland flight to your mainland carrier, you'll pass through an agricultural inspection center. (In case this is your first trip, they look like regular airport baggage security centers.) At this point you will need to have your carry-on baggage inspected. You'll be amazed to see the apples, oranges and other fruits stacked up on the agricultural inspection centers. Even though they may have originally come from the mainland U.S., they will not pass inspection to get back there. Pre-inspected Maui onions, pineapples and protea, anthurium starts, ti plants and orchids are allowed. Fruit can be purchased in inspected and sealed cartons from reputable island retailers. Generally, you will not have trouble with most flowers and/or leis. If you are unsure of what is transportable, contact the U.S. Department of Agricultural at 808-877-8757 or 808-877-5261.

> **AIRLINE TIPS**
>
> The direct flights available on United, Delta and American Airlines save time and energy by avoiding the otherwise necessary stopover on O'ahu. Travel agents schedule at least an hour and a half between arrival on O'ahu and departure for Maui to account for any delays, baggage transfers and the time required to reach the interisland terminal. If you do arrive early, check with the interisland carrier. Very often you can get an earlier flight that will arrive on Maui in time to get your car, and maybe some groceries, before returning to pick up your luggage when it arrives on your scheduled flight.

are using Oakland, California, as their gateway to the Pacific. This means that if you live in California you might get a great deal, but the rest of us have to make our own travel arrangements to the Oakland airport. As we go to press they have flights 6 days each week (with two on Saturday) out of Oakland. (During the winter/fall season they only have 3 flights a week direct to Maui.) This flexibility allows you to customize the length of your vacation stay. Fly/drive, air only and combination packages including rental cars are available for O'ahu, Maui, Kaua'i and the Big Island. They also offer some unique and intriguing incentives. They also offers free children's holidays for youngsters 2 to 18 years old. You get one free child's-room accommodations if you have two full-fare adults and you share the room (and at some places, kids can also eat free!) Travel protection insurance, in the event you have to cancel at the last minute, is available, as is travel insurance. Alamo Rent a Car handles the ground transportation (Hawai'i Rental Vehicle Surcharge of $3 per day, as well as the Fleet & Road tax of 19¢ per day, the Airport tax of 8.1 percent and Hawai'i State tax of 4.167 percent are *not* included in the prices.) Aloha Airlines is the carrier for the interisland flights. Single- or multiple-island packages are available. For airfare only, rates are staggered based on the day of the week you depart and the time of the year. Call for free catalog or request one online. 800-357-2400; www.suntrips.com.

Remember: Be sure to check all the air carriers. Experience has taught us that a little leg work pays off. Sometimes the best deals are through one of these agencies, but if you have the time, it may be worth a thorough investigation. I have discovered that United Airlines may offer promotional specials that far and away beat these packages and even the charters. Always make sure you let the airline know if you are flexible on your arrival and departure days. You may be able to squeeze into some price-cut promotion window that offers an even better value on your flight dollar. Also during these times, you may want to check that the airline you are interested in is still in business, and still flies to Hawai'i. And the schedules for flights to Hawai'i change greatly with the seasons. More flights are added during the summer months.

FLIGHTS TO THE ISLANDS

Most of the airlines have their own websites. These are especially handy for getting an idea of flight schedules and prices; you can even book your reservation. The major American carriers that fly from the mainland to the Honolulu International Airport on O'ahu or to Kahului Airport on Maui are:

Aloha Airlines—Aloha Airlines makes two round-trip daily flights: one between Honolulu and Las Vegas and the other between Kahului and Las Vegas. Both flights include a connecting stopover in Oakland, California. 800-367-5250; 808-484-1111; www.alohaairlines.com.

American Airlines—Direct to Maui from Los Angeles, San Jose and St. Louis, and from Chicago and Dallas direct to Honolulu. 800-433-7300; 808-833-7600 in Honolulu; 808-244-5522 on Maui; www.aa.com.

Air Canada—Direct to Maui and Honolulu from Vancouver, B.C. www.aircanada.com.

Continental Airlines—Direct flights from Newark, Los Angeles and Houston to Honolulu with connecting service to Maui via Hawaiian Airlines. 800-525-0280; 800-523-3273; www.continental.com.

Delta Air Lines—Their flights out of Atlanta stop in Los Angeles, then fly direct to Maui. They also have one direct flight from Atlanta and one from Dallas–Fort Worth to Honolulu. 800-221-1212; flight information 800-325-1999; www.delta.com.

Hawaiian Airlines—They have direct flights from Los Angeles, Seattle, San Francisco and Portland to Maui and flights from Seattle, Portland, San Francisco and Las Vegas to Honolulu. Hawaiian Airlines also has Frequent Flyer miles, and is partnered with Alaska, American, Northwest, Continental and even Virgin Atlantic Airlines. 800-367-5320; in Honolulu 808-838-1555; www.hawaiianair.com.

Northwest Airlines—Flies into Honolulu direct from Minneapolis, Los Angeles and Seattle. 800-225-2525; 808-955-2255; www.nwa.com.

Pleasant Hawaiian Holidays—People seem to be very pleased by the Pleasant Hawaiian service. Their non-stop scheduled "Air Cruise" is available from Los Angeles and San Francisco to Honolulu and Maui. Their "Air Only" flights are through American Trans Air. 800-242-9144; www.pleasantholidays.com.

United Airlines—United has more flights to Hawai'i from more U.S. cities than any other airline. They have a number of direct flights to Maui from Los Angeles and San Francisco as well as through (but not direct) flights from Denver, Chicago and Philadelphia. United Airlines offers a free round-trip interisland ticket on Aloha Airlines for 5,000 Mileage Plus miles. If you have miles to use, check United for the price of their Oʻahu flight. Reservations 800-241-6522; flight information 800-824-6200; www.ual.com or www.united.com.

INTERISLAND FLIGHTS

Hawaiʻi is unique in that its intrastate roads are actually water or sky. For your travel by sky, there are several interisland carriers that operate between Honolulu and Maui. If you plan on doing frequent interisland excursions, some allow you to purchase a coupon book of six or so tickets that work out to being a small discount per ticket over a single ticket purchase.

The flight time from Oʻahu to Kahului on Maui is just 35 minutes. When returning from Maui to Honolulu, make sure you have plenty of time before your connecting flight to the mainland. Otherwise you might make your flight, but your baggage won't! Traveling from the main carrier to the interisland terminal can be rather exhausting and confusing. You will probably need to take one Wiki Wiki bus to a drop-off point and then pick up another to take you to the interisland terminal. If you do arrive early, check with the interisland carrier.

If you are traveling light and have only brought carry-on luggage with you, be advised that what is carry-on for the major airlines may *not* be carry-on for the interisland carriers. For example, those small suitcases with wheels and long handles that extend out to pull along behind you *must* be checked by many of the interisland carriers. Knowing this in advance, you may be able to pack those items that are more fragile in a smaller tote bag.

Most visitors arrive at the **Kahului Airport** via direct or interisland flights. The Kahului Airport is convenient with accessible parking, an on-site rental car area and even a restaurant that offers runway views (although the walk from the United Airlines gate to the baggage claim area can be quite a distance). From the airport it is only a 20- to 30-minute drive to the Kihei–Wailea–Makena areas, but a 45- to 60-minute drive to the Kaʻanapali/Kapalua areas. If your destination is West Maui from Oʻahu, Kauaʻi or Hawaiʻi, it might be more convenient to fly into the **Kapalua West Maui Airport**. This small, uncrowded airport is serviced by Island Air.

INTERISLAND CARRIERS

Aloha Airlines—Aloha offers first-class service, Drive-Thru Check-In at Honolulu and daily non-stop service between Honolulu–Maui,

Maui–Kaua'i and Maui–Hilo. This airline keeps on schedule and has always had one of the lowest passenger complaint records of all U.S. airlines. They fly over 1,200 flights weekly with their fleet of 17 Boeing 737s. They also provide weekly charter service to Midway, Johnson and Christmas Islands, and long-range charters upon request. When making your reservations, you might inquire about any special promotions, AAA membership discounts, AARP discounts or passes. Current rates are $75 for one-way unrestricted tickets, $70 for a three-day advance purchase and $66 for a seven-day advance purchase. You can also purchase a seven-day pass that allows unlimited travel on both Aloha Airlines and Island Air to all islands. If you are an AAA member and have your membership card, you can purchase a ticket for less. For 5,000 United Mileage Plus miles, you can receive a free round-trip interisland ticket. Be sure to check into their Fly/Drive packages for rental cars—especially during the slow season. 800-367-5250; in Honolulu 808-484-1111; on Maui 808-244-9071; www.alohaairlines.com.

Island Air—The sister airline to Aloha specializes in serving Hawai'i's smaller community and resort destinations. Their fleet consists of twin-engine De Havilland Dash 6 Twin Otters (turbo-prop) aircraft and 37 passenger DH Dash 8s. They fly 80 flights daily servicing Kahului and Hana and are the only airlines that currently fly in and out of the Kapalua West Maui Airport to Lana'i City, Moloka'i and Honolulu. Charters available. In Hawai'i 800-652-6541; on the mainland 800-323-3345; in Honolulu 808-484-2222; www.alohairlines.com or www.islandair.com.

Hawaiian Airlines—They fly Boeing/McDonnell Douglas DC9s between Honolulu and Maui. If you plan to do a lot of island hopping, check for specials on unlimited travel passes for varying lengths of travel. Coupon books are available through your travel agent. Cost is about $84 for a one-way ticket. Mainland 800-882-8811; Maui 808-872-4400; www.hawaiianair.com.

Pacific Wings—Pacific Wings offers scheduled flights, charter service and scenic air tours. They service Kahului to Hana (Maui), Moloka'i and Kamuela (Big Island) in their eight-passenger, twin-engine Cessna 402C. 888-575-4546; 808-873-0877; e-mail: info@pacificwings.com; www.pacificwings.com.

If you are traveling to Lana'i, you can take an interisland commuter flight or you can also shuttle there by water: **Expeditions** departs from Lahaina five times daily. Cost is $50 round trip adults, $40 children. 877-464-6284; 808-661-3756; www.mauibound.com/lanaitours_expeditions.html.

Cruise Lines

Norwegian Cruise Lines (NCL) and parent company, Star Cruises, have enlisted the *Norwegian Star* to cruise the Hawaiian waters. The cruise line began service in the islands in 2001. The *Norwegian Star* is 971 feet in length and double occupancy can accommodate 2,240 guests along with 1,100 crew. The ship offers 10 restaurants including the Versailles Main Restaurant, Aqua Main Restaurant, Le Bistro French Restaurant, Ginza, Las Ramblas Tapas Bar & Restaurant, Endless Summer Restaurant, the SoHo Room, Market Café and Kids Café, La Trattoria and Blue Lagoon, as well as 13 bars and lounges. Other amenities include two swimming pools, six hot tubs, a fitness center, basketball, volleyball and soccer court, Planet Kids and a themed kid's pool, video arcade, cinema and auditorium. Inside staterooms offer comfort and value, with a sitting area, two lower beds that convert to a double, TV and refrigerator. Oceanview staterooms with balconies feature two lower beds, a sitting area, a floor-to-ceiling glass door that opens onto private balcony. Also available are mini-suites and top-end suites and villas. Handicapped facilities are also available. The rack rates are listed below but there are generous discounts for early booking (20 to 40 percent off posted rack rate). All rates are based on double occupancy. The *Norwegian Star* cruises the Hawaiian islands, departing in Honolulu with stops at Nawiliwili, Kahului, Lahaina, Hilo and Kona. Inside staterooms run $1,629 to $1,779. Oceanview staterooms run $1,849 to $2,179. Mini-suites are $2,279 to $2,299 and other suites and penthouses are $2,999 to $4,399. The Garden Villa with two bedrooms and private whirlpool tub with butler service runs $15,999. Extra guests (3rd and 4th) are $699, but early-book discounts bring that additional guest price down to $299.

The *Norwegian Wind* is the second of the Norwegian Cruise Line ships to operate in Hawaiian waters. This vessel is 754 feet and double occupancy can accommodate 1,748 passengers along with 700 crew. All staterooms have a TV, and bathroom with shower and hair dryer. The amenities include six restaurants: Four Seasons Main Restaurant, The Terraces Main Restaurant, Sun Terrace Italian Trattoria, Le Bistro French Restaurant, Pizzeria and Sports Bar & Grill, along with 10 bars and lounges. Guests can enjoy Broadway-style theater, Monte Carlo casino, library and card room, Kid's Korner and video arcade, fitness center, spa and salon, two hot tubs and two swimming pools. The rack rates are listed below but there are generous discounts for an early book (25 to 40 percent off posted rack rate). All rates are based on double occupancy. The *Norwegian Wind* currently has a fall trip that departs from Vancouver, B.C., for an 11-day cruise to the Hawaiian islands with stops at all the Hawaiian islands. Their standard fall and spring trip is a 10-day round-trip through the Hawaiian islands. In the spring they offer a 10-day trip that departs from Honolulu and travels to Vancouver, B.C. Rack rates for 10-day cruises: inside staterooms $1,779 to $1,909; oceanview staterooms $1,979 to $2,799. A penthouse runs $5,499 and owner's suite is $6,399. Third and fourth guests additional $529. Early booking reduces that to $379.

Pre- and post-cruise packages, air add-ons and Hawaiian shore excursions are available. For information contact your travel agent or go online to Norwegian Cruise Lines at www.ncl.com or Star Cruises at www.starcruises.com. 800-327-7030 from the U.S. and Canada.

Getting Around

FROM THE AIRPORT   After arriving, there are several options. Taxi cabs, because of the distances between areas, can be very costly (i.e., $57 from Kahului to Ka'anapali). But there are also several bus and limo services available. There are some local area shuttles, and even though Maui has around-the-island public transportation, it is still very limited. The best option may be a rental car unless your resort provides transportation.

PUBLIC TRANSPORTATION   "If you don't choose a rental car, you will find Maui offers no public transportation." Well, that is what I have been saying for years. Now I am happy to report some Maui Mass Transit options. MEO (Maui Economic Opportunity, Inc.) and Akina Aloha Tours have teamed together to offer island transportation.

MEO is more of a shuttle, a free county bus service (although donations are appreciated) that travels within the Kahului–Wailuku area, making stops at shopping areas, grocery stores, theaters, post offices and government buildings. **Akina** is a privately owned service that is linked with MEO, but primarily travels between South and West Maui (from The Shops at Wailea to the Ritz-Carlton), stopping at the condominiums, hotels and shopping areas in between: Kihei, Lahaina, Ka'anapali, Honokowai, Kahana and Napili. It connects with the MEO system at Ma'alaea.

Point-to-point Akina fares run from $1 to $5 one way (depending on distance) or $10 for an all-day pass. Weekly, monthly and senior passes available. The primary buses run from approximately 7 a.m. to 10:30 p.m. (MEO hours are between 6:30 a.m. and 7 p.m.), with express options between Wailea and Ma'alaea, Lahaina or Ka'anapali. To find out more detailed information or get a bus schedule, contact Akina at 808-879-2828, www.akinatours.com or MEO at 808-877-7651, www.meoinc.com. (As this is a new service, the buses sometimes run on Maui time so be sure to check connecting schedules and allow plenty of time. And they are still working on coordinating benches and signs at the bus stops so in the meantime, just wave!)

LIMOUSINE SERVICES Travel in style with one of the limousine services. Rates between them are competitive: $79 and up per hour plus tax and gratuity, minimum two hours. (They also do tours and weddings.) **Arthur's Limousine Service** currently commutes to most resorts from the Kahului airport (877-408-9559, 808-871-5555, fax 808-877-3333). Also try **Carey Limousine Hawaii** (aka Town & Country Limousine) 808-572-3400, **Star Maui Limousine** 808-875-6900, **Wailea Limousine** 808-875-4114, **Kapalua Executive Limousine** 808-669-2300 or **ABC Rider/Coastline Limousine** 808-877-5466. **Classy Taxi** (808-665-0003) has "gangster-style" limos (circa 1929) and a 1933 Rolls Royce.

TAXIS/SHUTTLES For cab service, try **Alii Cab** 808-661-3688 or **Executive Cab** 808-667-7770. **Airport/SpeediShuttle** offers door-to-door airport service that fits your schedule. Individual fares—from $20 (Kihei) to $38 (Ka'anapali)—are far less expensive than a cab and an even better deal if there are two or more of you. Especially economical for a family! Mainland 800-977-2605; 808-661-6667 or 808-875-8070 on Maui; or just press #65 from the airport courtesy phone board; www.speedishuttle.com. (In addition to airport service, they also offer transportation to or from anywhere on the island.)

FREE SHUTTLES The free Ka'anapali **Trolley** services hotels, golf courses and Whalers Village, with stops at the Sheraton and Ka'anapali Beach hotels, Whalers Village and the Westin, Ka'anapali Golf Course, Maui Marriott, Hyatt, Maui Ka'anapali Villas and Royal Lahaina beginning at 10 a.m. and continuing until 10 p.m. Pick up times are about every 20 minutes, except for lunch and dinner breaks for the driver. You can pick up a schedule at your hotel.

Kapalua has a shuttle running 6 a.m. to 11 p.m. between the condos and the hotel. Call the front desk to request it.

There is a free shuttle in Wailea that offers transportation between hotels, restaurants and shops. Check with the front desk or concierge at the property where you stay.

Most van tours offer pick up at your hotel or condo.

RENTAL CARS AND TRUCKS It has been said that Maui has more rental cars per mile of road than anywhere else in the nation. This is not surprising when you realize that Maui has a population of well over 100,000, more than two million visitors per year and limited mass transit. So, given the status of public transportation on Maui, a rental car is still the best bet—sometimes the only way to get around the island and, for your dollar, a very good buy.

A choice of more than 20 car rental companies offers luxury or economy and new or used models. Some are local island operators, others are nation-wide chains, but all are very competitive. The rates vary, not only between high and low season, but from week to weekend and even day to day. The best values are during price wars, or super summer discount specials. Prices vary as much within the same company as they do between companies and are approximated as follows: Vans, Jeeps and Convertibles are all in the high-end range from $50 to $90, Full-size $35 to $50, Mid-size $30 to $45, Compacts $25 to $40. The least expensive choice is a late-model compact or economy. Often these cars are only two to three years old and in very good condition.

Rental car discounts are few and far between. You might be able to use some airline award coupons, but they are often very restrictive. If you are a member of AAA you can receive a discount with some rental companies. Check with Aloha Airlines for some great slow-season rates with their interisland fly and drive packages. Also available from specialty car rental agencies are a variety of luxury cars. Vans are available from a number of agencies, but camping in them is not allowed. (If camping is on your agenda consider bringing your own camping equipment.)

Many of the rental companies have booths next to the main terminal building at the Kahului Airport. This free phone is for those rental agencies that don't have an airport booth or regular shuttle service so that you can call for a pick up. A few agencies will take your flight information when your car reservation is made and will meet you and your luggage at the airport with your car.

The policies of all the rental car agencies are basically the same. Most require the driver to be a minimum of 21 to 25 years of age. And those that do allow rentals to the under-25 group will make you pay extra. Some require a major credit card. All feature unlimited mileage with you buying the gas ($2.40 to $2.50 per gallon at press time) so check for "discount days" in Wailuku/Kahului. Be sure to fill up before you return your car; the rental companies charge a lot more to do it for you.

Insurance is an option you may wish to purchase and can run an additional $15 to $25 a day. A few agencies will require insurance for those under 25. Most of the car rental agencies strongly encourage you buy the optional collision damage waiver (CDW), which provides coverage for most cars in case of loss or damage. I suggest you check with your own insurance company before you leave to verify exactly what your policy covers. Some credit cards now provide CDW coverage for rental cars if you use that credit card to charge your rental fees. This does not include liability insurance, so you need to check to see if your own policy will cover you for liability in a rental car. Add to the rental price a 4 percent sales tax and a $2 per day highway road tax. A few of Maui's roadways are rough and rugged. The rental agencies recommend that cars not traverse these areas (shown on the map they distribute) and that if these roads are attempted, you are responsible for any damage. Some restrict driving to Haleakala due to drivers riding the brakes down the steep road. In addition to the rental agency's *Maui Drive Guide* magazine and maps, you can pick up a free *Maui Driving Map* at most brochure racks. The front section of the phone book also has some excellent detailed street maps.

See "Traveling with Children" above for information on car seats for kids.

RENTAL CAR LISTINGS Dollar is the only car rental company on the island of Lana'i.

Accessible Vans of Hawaii (handicapped accessible), 800-303-3750; 808-871-7785; www.accessiblevanshawaii.com; e-mail: david@accessiblevanshawaii.com

Adventures Rent a Jeep has both new and used Jeep Wranglers and Cherokees. 800-701-JEEP; 808-877-6626; www.mauijeep.com; e-mail: mauijeeps@shaka.com

Al West's Maui Windsurfing Vans provides airport pick up. They have full-size Ford vans and multiple-passenger vans with interior or exterior racks. 808-877-0090; www.mauivans.com

Alamo, 800-327-9633; Kahului 808-871-6235; Lahaina 808-661-7181; www.goalamo.com

I recommend checking these folks out, especially if you can book over the internet. I regularly find their rates far better than other dealers and an extra percentage off if you book online.

Aloha Windsurf Vans, 808-893-2111

Avis, 800-321-3712, Kahului 808-871-7575, Ka'anapali 808-661-4588, Kihei 808-874-4077, Wailea 808-879-7601; www.avis.com

Budget, 800-527-0700, Ka'anapali 808-661-8721, Wailea 808-874-2831, Kahului 808-871-8811; www.budget.com

Dollar, 800-800-4000, Kahului 808-877-2731, Ka'anapali 808-667-2651, Interisland 800-342-7398; www.dollar.com

Rates for the island of Lana'i are two to three times higher than Maui. Lana'i rates currently are $129 for a Jeep Wrangler, $145 for a Jeep Cherokee and for paved road only they have a compact $59.99, intermediate $79.99 and mini-van $129.

Enterprise, 800-736-8222, Kahului 808-871-1511, Lahaina-Ka'anapali 808-661-8804; www.enterprise.com

Hawaii Discount Car Rentals has discounted car rental rates valid at all locations in the State of Hawaii except Lana'i and Hana. All types of cars available. Mention Paradise Family Guides to get the best rate. 800-882-9006. Car rates are posted at mywaii.com/car_rentals.html.

Hertz, 800-654-3011, Kahului 808-877-5167, Westin 808-667-5381, Kapalua Villas 808-669-8088

Hummer Rentals offers airport or resort pickup. 808-873-8448; www.hummtours.com

Island Riders rents exotic cars and Jeeps, as well as Harleys. Lahaina 808-661-4386, Kihei 808-891-0889

Kihei Rent-a-car, 800-251-5288, Kihei 808-879-7257, fax 808-875-1372; www.kiheirentacar.com

Maui Cruisers in Wailuku has more than 4 dozen cars in their fleet. All 10 years or newer. Toyota Tercels, Nissan Sentras and Geo Prisms. 808-249-2319; 877-749-7889 U.S.; 800-488-9083 Canada; www.mauicruisers.net

National, 800-227-7368, Kahului 808-871-8851; www.national.com

Surf Truck Rental (flat beds, pick-ups, vans), Wailuku 808-244-5544

Thrifty Car Rental, 800-367-2277, Kahului 808-871-2860; www.thrifty.com

The Toy Store has exotic cars, jeeps, electric cars, mopeds, scooters and Harleys. 604 Front Street, Lahaina; 808-661-1212, 808-662-0888; www.alohatoystore.com

Word of Mouth Rent a Car, 800-533-5929, Kahului 808-877-2436; www.mauirentacar.com; e-mail: word@maui.net

MOTORCYCLE RENTALS There is no helmet requirement, but you do need to show a valid motorcycle endorsement from your state of residence. (You must be 21 to rent a motorcycle or jeep; 25 to rent an exotic car. Scooter rentals: 18 with driver's license *and* experience) **Aloha Toy Store** rents Harley-Davidsons, exotic cars, jeeps. Motorcycles are $110/5 hours, $120/8 hours, $135/24 hours. Mopeds run $35/4 hours, $45/8 hours, $50/24 hours—2 or more days at $45/day; 5 days or more at $35/day. 640 Front Street, 808-662-0888; Fairway Shops in Ka'anapali, 808-661-9000; www.alohatoystore.com.

Hawaiian Riders has Harley-Davidsons as well as mopeds, bikes, jeeps and exotic cars. Fat Boys, Heritages and Dyna Glides: $69/3 hours, $99/6 hours, $135/first 24 hours. Road Kings run $79/3 hours, $109/6 hours, $145/first 24 hours. The 2003 V-Rod runs $99/3 hours, $149/6 hours, $199/24 hours. (All have discounts for multiple days.) Jeeps $89/24 hours; Isuzu Amigos $59; Miatas or vans $79. Mopeds: $29 flat rate anytime between 8 a.m. to 5 p.m. or $50/24 hours. Lahaina/Ka'anapali 808-662-4FUN or Kihei/Wailea 808-891-0889; www.hawaiianriders.com.

Hula Hogs Motorcycle Rentals offers Harley-Davidson motorcycles for daily or weekly rentals. Although there is no helmet law in the state of Hawaii, Hula Hogs offers helmets, raingear and accessories at no charge. Hotel and airport shuttle provided. Big Twins $100/6 hours, $130/24 hours; Sportster $85/6 hours, $105/24 hours. Weekend special (Saturday morning through Monday morning) Big Twin $230; Sportster $185. Group rates available. Currently the only company that lets you bike to Hana. 1279 South Kihei Road; 808-875-7433; 877-464-7433 for reservations; www.hulahogs.com. **Island Riders** has Harley-Davidson bikes for $139/24 hours. Kihei 808-874-0311, Lahaina 808-661-9966; 800-529-2925; www.islandriders.com.

Grocery Shopping

Grocery store prices may be one of the biggest surprises of your trip. While there are some locally grown foods and dairies, most of the products must be flown or shipped to the islands. The local folks can shop the advertisements and use the coupons, but it isn't so easy when traveling.

Longs Drug Stores carry some food items as do **Big Kmart** and **Costco**. Seems like half the tourist pull into Costco, conveniently located just outside the airport, and stock up on the supplies for the week. So be sure to pack your Costco card.

There is also **Grocery Outlet**, located near the airport at 380 Dairy Road in Kahului. They have an assortment of tropical candies and coffees that make great take-home gifts plus those everyday items that you may need for your stay. Obviously as an outlet store they don't have a full selection of grocery items, but check them out, keeping an eye for outdated items. Open Monday through Saturday 8 a.m. to 8 p.m. and Sunday until 5 p.m.

The three major grocery stores in Kahului are **Foodland**, **Safeway** and **Star Market**.

In Lahaina you can choose between the **Foodland** at Lahaina Square or the **Safeway** (open 24 hours) at Lahaina Cannery Mall. There is a **Star Market** in Honokowai, and Napili has a smallish grocery store.

In Kihei, there is a **Foodland** and a **Star Market**. On the Pi'ilani Highway in Kihei you'll find a 24-hour **Safeway**. It is currently the largest Safeway in the state. You'll find the same variety as your hometown store and the prices are better than at the small grocery outlets.

In Hana there is **Hasegawa's** and the **Hana Ranch Store**, both open limited hours.

Azeka's Market (Kihei) is now only a memory, but there is a take-out window on the outside of the Ace Hardware where you can still get their famous ribs—as well as teriyaki beef and chicken. 808-879-0611.

The **Maui Swap Meet**, held Saturday and Wednesday mornings in Kahului, also has some good food values, although not always a very diverse selection. Usually you can pick up papayas, pineapple and coconuts as well as some vegetable items. Lots of flowers here, too. Small admission fee charged for adults.

The Farmers' Market of Maui is a group of people that brings produce down from the Kula area. They set up roadside shopping, and you can't find it fresher. Their locations seem to change periodically, but currently the Honokowai Market is open Monday, Wednesday and Friday 7 a.m. to 11 a.m. You'll find them located in the parking lot of the Honokowai Beach Center at 3636 Lower Honoapi'ilani Highway. By summer 2003 they hope to have a permanent store in a building that will be open daily. For more information contact 808-875-0949. In Kihei (in front of Suda's Store) on Monday, Wednesday and Friday from 1:30 to 5:30 p.m. Just look for the green sandwich board signs that are set up roadside. **Ohana Farmers & Crafters Market** meets at Kahului Shopping Center every Wednesday 9 a.m. to 1 p.m., offering fresh produce plus everything from malasadas to massage. You can find them also on Friday at the Queen Ka'ahumanu Center (center stage) from 9 a.m. to 5 p.m. **Farmer's Market** next to the Iao Theater in Wailuku also offers farm-fresh produce daily from 7 a.m. to 7 p.m.

Maui Fresh Fruit Store and Farmer's Market is located in Hali'imaile, sandwiched between the Hali'imaile General Store and the plantation office. This is *the* place to pick up pineapples ready to take back to the mainland. They have history on the 100-year Maui Pineapple Company's plantation with photos and memorabilia. Local Maui growers offer their fresh fruits and vegetables here. Monday through Saturday 10 a.m. to 6 p.m. 808-573-5129; e-mail: mauipineapplestore@maui.net.

Take Home Maui is located just off Front Street in Lahaina and offers a selection of fruits and vegetables for shipment home. 808-661-8067.

Local grocery shopping is a little more adventuresome. The largest local stores are in Wailuku and Kahului. In addition to the regular food staples they often have deli sections that feature local favorites and plate lunches. **Takamiya's** at 359 North Market Street in Wailuku has a huge deli section with perhaps more than 50 cooked foods and salads as well as very fresh meats. **Ah Fook's** at the older Kahului Mall has a smaller deli section with plate lunches running about $3. **Ooka** is the largest of the three. The packed parking lot and crowded aisles prove its popularity and low prices. Besides the usual sundry items, they have a fascinating and unusual array of foods. How about a tasty fresh pig ear, pig blood, tripe, calf hoof or tongue? In the seafood aisle check out the opihi, cuttlefish, *tobiko*, *lomi* salmon, a great variety of ahi *poke* (tuna), and whole or filets of fresh island fish like catfish or *onaga*. They even have some reef fish, such as parrot fish (which I've heard is fabulous but have never tried.)

For those looking for health foods there's **West Side Natural Foods** in Lahaina, **Hawaiian Moons** in Kihei, and **Down to Earth** (with the largest selection) in Kahului. (Each has a hot food buffet and salad bar.)

Calendar of Annual Events

For the exact dates of many of these events, write to the Hawai'i Visitor & Convention Bureau, 2270 Kalakaua Avenue #801, Honolulu, HI 96815, and request the Hawai'i Special Events Calendar. The calendar also gives non-annual information and the contact person for each event. A more complete listing for Maui events can be obtained from the Maui Visitors Bureau, P.O. Box 580, Wailuku, HI 96793. Check the local papers for dates of additional events.

January/February

"Whales Alive" Celebration of the Whales—Four Seasons Resort Wailea

Chinese New Year celebrations—Lahaina and Wailea (many restaurants offer special holiday meals)

Professional **surfing**—Honolua Bay

Hula Bowl—Wailuku War Memorial Complex

Mercedes Champions—PGA Tour—Kapalua

Maui Film Festival First Light Academy Screenings—www.mauifilmfestival.com

Whale Fest—Locations around the island

March

WhaleFest—Week-long events and activities in Lahaina Town and West Maui

Maui Marathon—From Kahului to Lahaina

Kukini Run—Along the Kahakuloa Valley Trail

Prince Kuhio Day (March 26)—State holiday

East Maui Taro Festival—Entertainment, exhibits and demonstrations in Hana

St. Patrick's Day Parade—Ka'anapali Parkway

Whale Regatta/Whale Day

Just Desserts—Fundraiser for Maui Humane Society

April

David Malo Day—Hawaiian entertainment and local food at Lahainaluna High School

"Art Maui"—Free juried show with works by island artists at Hui No'eau Visual Arts Center

Budlight Triple Crown Softball Tournament—Mainland and Hawaiian teams compete in Wailuku and Kihei

Maui Marathon—10K run in Iao Valley

"Celebration of the Arts"—Music and art festival at The Ritz-Carlton, Kapalua

Ulupalakua Thing—Agricultural trade show at Ulupalakua Ranch/Tedeschi Winery with Maui product booths, entertainment, cooking contests, chef's demonstrations and lots of free samples

Kihei Sea Fest—Kama'ole Beach Park

May

Lei Day—Celebrations in Lahaina and Wailea (check with hotels for their events)

Pineapple Jam—Two-day festival on Lana'i with arts, crafts, entertainment, cooking contests and samplings

Seabury Hall annual craft fair—Held in Makawao the Saturday prior to Mother's Day

Lei Festival—Wailea Marriott, an Outrigger Resort

Hard Rock Cafe World Cup of Windsurfing—Ho'okipa Beach Park

Ka Hula Piko—Celebration of the birth of hula on Moloka'i

Tedeschi Vineyard 10K run—Through Upcountry Maui

Bankoh Kayak Challenge—Moloka'i to O'ahu 41-mile kayak race

Maui Music Festival—Memorial Day weekend celebration of jazz and contemporary music in Ka'anapali

"In Celebration of Canoes"—Parade, booths and canoe displays on Front Street

June

Maui Chamber Music Festival—Week of Hawaiian and classical music at Sacred Hearts Mission Church in Kapalua

Obon Season (late June through August)—Bon Odori festivals are held at the many Buddhist temples around the island. They are announced in the local newspapers and the public is invited

King Kamehameha Day Celebration—Front Street parade with *pa'u* riders and floral floats

Maui Upcountry Fair—Eddie Tam Center, Makawao

Hard Rock Cafe Rock N Roll—10K run

Makeke Fair—Hawaiian music, hula, crafts, food and games at the Hana Ballpark

Kapalua Wine and Food Symposium—Seminars and tastings culminating in the Kapalua Seafood Festival (sometimes in July), an event featuring goodies prepared by the best chefs from the best restaurants in the islands

Taste of South Maui—Kihei and Wailea chefs offer their best at this food festival to raise money for the Kihei Youth Center

Earth Maui Nature Summit Environmental Festival—Four days of seminars, films and exhibits, plus a 5K run, wildlife tours, hikes, golf tournament, swim challenge, *hukilau* and Harvest Festival in Kapalua

Celestial Cinema—Film festival in Wailea

July

Fourth of July celebrations with fireworks—Wailea Marriott, an Outrigger Resort, over Black Rock at Ka'anapali Beach

4th of July Rodeo & Parade—Makawao

Pineapple Festival—Queen Ka'ahumanu Center, free tastings, games, entertainment and historic photo and label displays from Maui Pineapple Co.

Canoe races—Ho'okipa Beach Park

Maui Jaycees Carnival—Wailuku War Memorial Complex

Sausa Cup races—Lahaina

Victoria to Maui Yacht Race

Wailea Open Tennis Championships—Wailea Tennis Club

August

"Maui Calls"—Celebration of Hawai'i's "boat days" at the Maui Arts & Cultural Center

Run to the Sun Marathon—Grueling trek from sea level up to the 10,000-foot level of Haleakala Crater

Ice Cream Festival—Wailuku War Memorial Complex

Maui Onion Festival—Whalers Village, Ka'anapali

August 21 is **Admissions Day**—State holiday

September

Maui County Rodeo—Makawao

Aloha Festivals—Events stretch into October

Maui Writers Conference and Retreat—Labor Day weekend at various resorts in Wailea

Garden Party—Maui Academy of Performing Arts

"Taste of Lahaina"—Maui's biggest food event with over 30 participating restaurants

Haku Mele O Hana—Traditional song and dance at Hotel Hana-Maui

Terry Fox Run and **"Under the Stars"**—Fundraising dinner sponsored by the Four Seasons Resort Wailea

Maui Pineapple Picnic—Tours, pony rides, crafts fair, farmer's market and live music in front of the Maui Fresh fruit store at Hali'imaile

October

Hawaiian Sailing Canoe Regatta—Wailea Marriott, an Outrigger Resort

Maui County Fair—Wailuku War Memorial Complex

Invitational Pro-Am Golf Championship

Polo Season—Begins at the Olinda Polo Field (808-572-2790)

"The Mardi Gras of the Pacific"—Parade and Halloween festivities in Lahaina

Lahaina Coolers Historic Fun Run—5K run/walk through Lahaina's history with entertainment and re-enactments at each landmark

Hawai'i Winter League Season opens—Wailuku Baseball Stadium (808-242-2950)

November

Queen Ka'ahumanu Festival—Maui High School

Hawai'i International Film Festival—Maui Arts & Cultural Center

Moloka'i Ranch Rodeo—Statewide event combined with the **Great Moloka'i Stew Cook Off** held on the island of Moloka'i over Thanksgiving weekend

Santa arrives—Queen Ka'ahumanu Center

La Hoomaikai—Thanksgiving luau celebration at Wailea Marriott, an Outrigger Resort

Christmas House—Hui No'eau, near Makawao, a non-profit organization featuring pottery, wreaths and other holiday artwork and gifts

Ice Carving contest—Held at the end of the month or first part of December at Lahaina Cannery Mall

December

"Heart 'n Hearth"—Craft fair at Hannibal Tavarres Cultural Center in Makawao (808-244-7185)

Santa arrives by outrigger canoe—Wailea Beach

Santa visit via helicopter—Special treat for Maui Hill guests on Christmas Eve

Maui's Largest Gala Treelighting Ceremony—The Ritz-Carlton, Kapalua honors people around the world and raises funds for the homeless during the first part of December

Boar's Head Feast—Elizabethan Madrigal Dinner with Renaissance costumes and food (808-242-7469)

Kapalua/Betsy Nagelsen Pro-Am Tennis Invitational

Bridges Family/Whales Alive Pro-Celebrity Tennis Tournament—Wailea Tennis Club

Na Mele O Maui Festival—Children's song contest, hula festival, arts and crafts fair celebrating Hawai'i's music heritage throughout the Ka'anapali Resort

Old Fashioned Holiday Celebration—Santa Claus, carolers, holiday treats on Front Street

First Night Maui—Alcohol-free, family festival at Maui Arts & Cultural Center to celebrate the New Year

Treelighting—Historic Banyan Tree, Lahaina

Weather

When thinking of Hawai'i, and especially Maui, one visualizes bright sunny days cooled by refreshing trade winds, and this is the weather at least 300 days a year. But what about the other 65 days? Most aren't really bad—just not perfect. Although there are only two seasons, summer and winter, temperatures remain quite constant.

Average Highs and Lows

January	80°F/64°F	July	86°F/70°F
February	79°F/64°F	August	87°F/71°F
March	80°F/64°F	September	87°F/70°F
April	82°F/66°F	October	86°F/69°F
May	84°F/67°F	November	83°F/68°F
June	86°F/69°F	December	80°F/66°F

Spring and winter: Mid-October through April, 75 to 80 degrees during the day, 60 to 70 degrees at night. Tradewinds are more erratic, vigorous to none. Kona winds are more frequent causing widespread cloudiness, rain showers, mugginess and even an occasional thunderstorm. Eleven hours of daylight.

Summer and fall: May through mid-October, 80 to 85 degrees during the day, 70 to 80 degrees at night. Tradewinds are more consistent, keeping the temperatures tolerable. When the trades stop, however, the weather becomes hot and sticky. Kona winds are less frequent. Thirteen hours of daylight.

Summer-type wear is suitable year round. However, a warm sweater or light-weight jacket is a good idea for evenings and trips to cooler spots like Haleakala. If you are interested in the types of weather you may encounter, or are confused by some of the terms you hear, read on. For further reference consult *Weather in Hawaiian Waters*, by Paul Haraguchi, available at island bookstores.

Trade Winds Hawai'i's weather is greatly affected by the prevailing northeast trade winds, which are an almost constant wind from the northeast through the east and are caused by the Pacific anticyclone, a high pressure area. This high pressure area is well developed and remains semi-stationary in the summer, causing the trades to remain steady over 90 percent of the time. Interruptions are much more frequent in the winter when they blow only 40 to 60 percent of the time.

Kona Winds The Kona wind is a stormy, rain-bearing wind blowing from the southwest, or basically from the opposite direction of the trades. These conditions are caused by low pressure areas northwest of the islands. Kona winds strong enough to cause property damage have occurred only twice since 1970. Lighter non-damaging Kona winds are much more common, occurring 2 to 5 times every winter (November to April).

Kona Weather Windless, hot and humid weather is referred to as Kona weather. The interruption of the normal trade wind pattern brings this on. The trades are replaced by light and variable winds and, although this may occur any time of the year, it is most noticeable during summer when the temperature is generally hotter and more humid, with fewer localized breezes.

Kona Low A Kona low is a slow-moving, meandering, extensive low pressure area that forms near the islands. This causes continuous rain, with thunderstorms over an extensive area, and lasts for several days. This usually occurs from November through May.

Rain Rainfall can be drastically different from one part of Maui to another. Kihei and Wailea are almost deserts, with minimal rain each year. Lahaina tends to receive fewer showers than Napili and Kapalua to the north. And, of course, Hana and the northern coastline lead off each month with the highest average rainfall. No wonder the coast is so lush and green. January is the wettest month with Lahaina averaging 3.49 inches, Hana 9.45 and Kahului 4.14. December is not far behind. June typically has the lowest average amount of rainfall per year, with Lahaina getting less than one inch, Kahului only a quarter inch and Hana four inches. (Fortunately for Hana visitors, the rainfall is often at night!) For more weather-related information as well as daily forecasts check out www.hawaiiweathertoday.com.

Hurricanes Hurricanes (called typhoons when they are west of 180 degrees longitude) have damaged the Hawaiian islands on several occasions. The storms that affect Hawai'i usually originate off Central America or Mexico. Most of the threatening tropical storms weaken before reaching the islands, or pass harmlessly to the west.

Their effects are usually minimal, causing only high surf on the eastern and southern shores of some of the islands. At least 21 hurricanes or tropical storms have passed within 300 miles of the islands in the last several years, but most did little or no damage. Hurricane season is considered to be May through November. Hurricanes are given Hawaiian names when they pass within 1,000 miles of the islands.

Hurricane Dot in 1959, Hurricane Iwa in 1982 and Hurricane Iniki in 1992 caused extensive damage. In each case, the island of Kaua'i was hit hardest, with lesser damage to southeast O'ahu and very little damage to Maui, except for the beaches.

Tsunamis   A tsunami is an ocean wave produced by an undersea earthquake, volcanic eruption or landslide. Tsunamis are usually generated along the coasts of South America, the Aleutian Islands, the Kamchatka Peninsula or Japan and travel through the ocean at 400 to 500 miles an hour. It takes at least four-and-a-half hours for a tsunami to reach the Hawaiian islands, unless it is caused by an earthquake on the Big Island—in which case less than 30 minutes warning is likely. A 24-hour Tsunami Warning System was established in Hawai'i in 1946. When the possibility exists of a tsunami reaching Hawaiian waters, the public is informed by the sound of the attention alert signal sirens. This particular signal is a steady one-minute siren, followed by one minute of silence, repeating as long as necessary.

What do you do when you hear the siren? Immediately turn on a TV or radio; all stations will carry CIV-Alert emergency information and instructions, including the arrival time of the first waves. Do not take chances, false alarms are not issued! Move quickly out of low-lying coastal areas that are subject to possible inundation.

The warning sirens are tested throughout the state on the first working Monday of every month at noon, so don't be alarmed when you hear the siren blare! The test lasts only a few minutes and CIV-Alert announces on all stations that the test is underway. Since 1813, there have been 112 tsunamis observed in Hawai'i, with only 16 causing significant damage.

Tsunamis may also be generated by local volcanic earthquakes. In the last 100 years there have been only six, with the last one, November 29, 1975, affecting the southeast coast of the Big Island. The Hawaiian Civil Defense has placed earthquake sensors on all the islands and, if a violent local earthquake occurs, an urgent tsunami warning will be broadcast and the tsunami sirens will sound. A locally generated tsunami will reach the other islands very quickly. Therefore, there may not be time for an attention alert signal to sound. Any violent earthquake that causes you to fall or hold onto something to prevent falling is an urgent warning, and you should immediately evacuate beaches and coastal low-lying areas.

For additional information on warnings and procedures in the event of a hurricane, tsunami, earthquake or flash flood, read the civil defense section in the foreword of the Maui phone book.

Tides The average tidal range is about two feet or less. Tide tables are available daily in the *Maui News* or by calling the marine weather number, 808-877-3477.

Sunrise and Sunset In Hawai'i, day length and the altitude of the noon sun above the horizon do not vary much throughout the year. This is because the temperate regions of the island's low latitude lie within the sub-tropics. The longest day is 13 hours 26 minutes (sunrise 5:53 a.m., sunset 7:18 p.m.) at the end of June, and the shortest day is 10 hours 50 minutes (sunrise 7:09 a.m. and sunset 6:01 p.m.) at the end of December. Daylight for outdoor activities without artificial lighting lasts about 45 minutes past sunset.

Helpful Phone Numbers

The area code for the entire state is (808). Calls anywhere on Maui are considered local calls. At a pay phone it will cost you 25¢. If you are calling another island, you must do so by dialing 1-808-plus the phone number and it is long distance. Note that most resorts charge between 75¢ and $1 for each local call you make and an additional surcharge for long distance.

EMERGENCY: Police, Ambulance, Fire: **911**
Police Non-emergency:
    Lahaina 808-661-4441
    Hana 808-248-8311
    Wailuku 808-244-6340
    Kihei 808-244-6400
Civil Defense Agency: 808-270-7285
Poison Control (on O'ahu): 800-362-3585
Helpline (suicide & crisis center): 808-244-7407
Red Cross: 808-244-0051
Consumer Protection: 808-984-8244
Concierge Connection: 808-875-9366
Visitor Complaint Hotline (Activity Owners Association): 808-891-1991
Directory Assistance:
    Local (1) 411
    interisland 808-555-1212
    Mainland 1-(area code)-555-1212

Hospital (Maui Memorial):
  Information 808-242-2036
  Switchboard 808-244-9056
Camping Permits:
  State Parks 808-984-8109
  County Parks 808-270-7230
Maui Visitors Bureau: 808-244-3530
Time of Day: 808-242-0212
Information—County of Maui (Gov't info & complaint): 808-270-7587
Haleakala National Park information (recording): 808-572-4400
'Ohe'o Headquarters Ranger Station (10 a.m. to 4 p.m.): 808-248-7375
Lahaina Town Action Committee: 808-667-9175
Baldwin Home (9 a.m. to 5 p.m.): 808-661-3262
Weather:
  Maui 808-877-5111
  Marine (also tides, sunrises, sunsets) 808-877-3477
  Recreational Area (Haleakala) 808-871-5054

For toll-free access to state agencies on O'ahu (numbers beginning with 586), dial 984-2400 then the last 5 digits of the O'ahu number (beginning with 6), followed by the # sign.

Check the Aloha Pages in the front of the phone book for various hotline numbers to call for community events, entertainment, etc., on Maui. While the call is free, the companies pay to be included, so information is biased.

CHAPTER 2

What to See, Where to Shop

Lahaina

No matter where on the island you stay, you should pencil in at least part of a day to tour the historical and cultural aspects of this quaint town and spend some time strolling through shops or enjoying a fine meal.

Lahaina is the bustling tourist center of Maui. There is much to see and do in busy Lahaina Town, which has maintained the aura of more than a century ago when it was the whaling capital of the world. Located about a 45-minute drive from the Kahului Airport (depending on traffic), this coastal port is noted for its Front Street, which is a multiblock strip of shops and restaurants along the waterfront. Lahaina Harbor is filled with boats of varying shapes and sizes, eager to take the visitor aboard for a variety of sea excursions. The word *Lahaina* means "merciless sun," and it does tend to become quite warm, especially in the afternoon, with little relief from the tropical tradewinds.

Historical memorabilia abounds in Lahaina. The Lahaina Restoration Foundation (808-661-3262) has done an admirable job restoring and maintaining many historical landmarks. These are all identified by numbered markers. A free walking tour map of Lahaina can be found in the *Lahaina Historical Walking Guide*. Look for free copies of this pocket-size guide on corner display racks in Lahaina Town. Then enjoy your walking tour of the Baldwin House, the *Brig Carthaginian*, Masters' Reading Room and Wo Hing Temple. The Lahaina Town Action Committee offers a "Walking Museum," featuring building plaques with photos and historical descriptions. You can pick up a brochure to identify the sites as you walk along.

The **Banyan Tree** is very easy to spot at the south end of Lahaina adjacent to Pioneer Inn on Front Street. It was planted on April 24, 1873, by Sheriff William Owen Smith, to commemorate the 50th anniversary of Lahaina's first Protestant Christian mission. You may find art shows or other events happening under the cool, shady boughs of this veritable arbor. With its long, heavy limbs, supported by wood braces and 12 solid trunks that have re-rooted themselves over a 200-foot area, visitors find it hard to believe that this is all one tree!

The stone ruins of **The Old Fort** can be found harborside near the Banyan Tree. The fort was constructed in the 1830s to protect the missionaries' homes from the whaling ships and the occasional cannonball that would be shot off when the sailors were too rowdy. The fort was later torn down and the coral blocks reused elsewhere. A few blocks were excavated and the corner of the fort was rebuilt as a landmark in 1964.

On the corner near the Pioneer Inn is a plaque marking the site of the **1987 Lahaina Reunion Time Capsule**, which contains newspapers, photos and other memorabilia.

Pioneer Inn is the distinguished green-and-white structure just north of the Banyan Tree. It was a haven for interisland travelers during the early days of the 20th century. Built back in 1901, it managed to survive the dry years of Prohibition, later adding a new wing, center garden and pool area in 1966. Two restaurants operate here and accommodations are available.

The history of Pioneer Inn is an interesting one. George Freeland, a robust 300-pound, 6-foot-5-inch Englishman, had relocated to Vancouver, Canada, and become a Royal Canadian Mountie. He was sent to Hawai'i in 1900 to capture a suspect, but failing to do so, chose to make Maui his home. He formed the Pioneer Hotel Co., Ltd., and sold $50 shares of stock. In October 1901 he constructed the hotel as accommodations for interisland travelers. Similar to the plantation house of the Maunalei Sugar Company on Lana'i, the total cost of constructing the hotel was $6,000. (Note: On Lana'i I heard a report that the Maunalei Plantation House was transported to Maui and became Pioneer Inn, but this was not accurate. Apparently, years ago, the *Honolulu Star-Bulletin* printed an article to this effect. George Alan Freeland, son of Pioneer Inn's founder George Freeland, spoke with Lawrence Gay, the owner of most of Lana'i at the turn of the 20th century, and was told that when the construction of Pioneer Hotel was completed, the similar-designed building on the island of Lana'i was still standing.)

Soon George Freeland opened the Pioneer Saloon, the Pioneer Grange, the Pioneer Wholesale Liquor Company and, in 1913, the

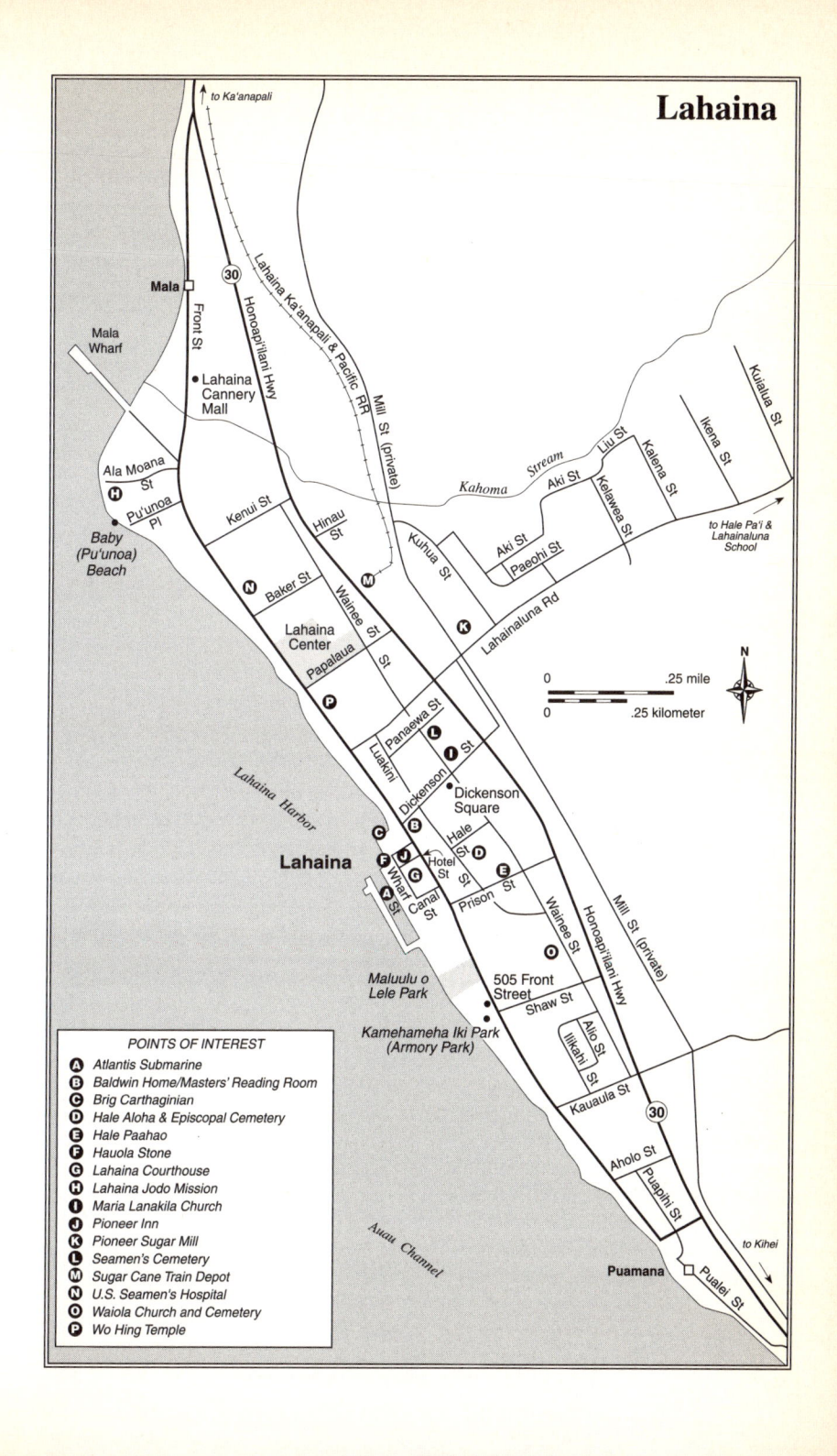

Lahaina

POINTS OF INTEREST
- **A** Atlantis Submarine
- **B** Baldwin Home/Masters' Reading Room
- **C** Brig Carthaginian
- **D** Hale Aloha & Episcopal Cemetery
- **E** Hale Paahao
- **F** Hauola Stone
- **G** Lahaina Courthouse
- **H** Lahaina Jodo Mission
- **I** Maria Lanakila Church
- **J** Pioneer Inn
- **K** Pioneer Sugar Mill
- **L** Seamen's Cemetery
- **M** Sugar Cane Train Depot
- **N** U.S. Seamen's Hospital
- **O** Waiola Church and Cemetery
- **P** Wo Hing Temple

Pioneer Theater. The Pioneer Theater ran silent movies to packed crowds and stage shows and plays were held in the theater as well. George Freeland died on July 25, 1925, survived by his wife, a Hawaiian woman, three sons and four daughters. His eldest son, George Alan Freeland, ran the business until the early 1960s. His grandson, George "Keoki" Freeland, is now the Director of the Lahaina Restoration Foundation. In the late 1960s the inn was expanded and at that time the theater was torn down. A complete history of the Pioneer Inn is available along with their brochure.

A guest in 1901 would have been required to adhere to the following "house rules," which are still posted in the lobby of the hotel:

"You must pay you rent in advance. You must not let you room go one day back. Women is not allow in you room. If you wet or burn you bed you going out. You are not allow to gamble in you room. You are not allow to give you bed to you freand. If you freand stay overnight you must see the mgr. You must leave you room at 11 am so the women can clean you room. Only on Sunday you can sleep all day. You are not allow in the down stears in the seating room or in the dinering room or in the kitchen when you are drunk. You are not allow to drink on the front porch. You must use a shirt when you come to the seating room. If you can't keep this rules please dont take the room."

You'll find the **Lahaina Courthouse** nearby, across from the Lahaina Harbor. It was built in 1859, at a cost of $7,000, from wood and stone taken from the palace of Kamehameha II. In 1925 the building was extensively remodeled to serve as courthouse, post office, police station and tax office. In 1999 work was completed on its second ren-

PARKING IN PARADISE

Parking can be somewhat irksome. Several all-day lots are located near the corner of Wainee and Dickenson (only a couple of blocks off Front Street). The farther away you get, the cheaper the lots. The prices also change seasonally and can be anywhere from $4 to $10 per day. The inexpensive lots fill up early in the day with folks going out on the tour boats. The Old Lahaina Center has a lot that is free with validation. The "new" Lahaina Center across the street has pay parking, validated with a movie ticket or purchase from one of the stores. If you don't mind a short walk, parking is available across the road from the 505 Front Street shops. Other paid parking lots are primarily on side streets off Front Street. On-street parking is limited and if you are fortunate enough to find a spot, many are only for one hour. *Beware*: The police here are quite prompt and efficient at towing.

ovation. Tenants include a **Courthouse Museum** operated by the Lahaina Restoration Foundation and located in the old courtroom upstairs. It's open daily from 10 a.m. to 4 p.m., with a docent to explain the history of the courthouse. Two art galleries, one on the main floor and another in the basement, are operated by the Lahaina Arts Society. A visitor center is located on the *makai* side of the main floor and serviced by volunteers as a part of the LahainaTown Action Committee. A meeting and video room is open to the public for community meetings and public ADA restrooms are located on the main floor and upstairs.

The **Lahaina Harbor** is in front of the Pioneer Inn and the Courthouse. You can stroll down and see the boats and visit stalls where a wide variety of water sports and tours can be arranged. (See Chapter 6.)

The **Brig Carthaginian**, anchored just outside the harbor, is a replica of a 19th-century square-rigger, typical of the ships that brought the first missionaries and whalers to these shores. The first *Carthaginian* sank on Easter Sunday, April 2, 1972. The 130-foot vessel had been built in 1921 in Denmark as a schooner and had sailed the world as a cargo ship. She was purchased by Tucker Thompson and sailed to Hawai'i in 1964. Her original name was *Wandia*, but was re-christened *Carthaginian* in Honolulu with a bottle of passion fruit juice. The ship was used in the South Pacific for a time and later restored to resemble a whaling vessel for the movie version of Michener's *Hawai'i*. The Lahaina Restoration Foundation worked to acquire the *Carthaginian* for $75,000. The ship found a home at the Lahaina wharf, becoming its definitive exhibit of the whaling era. On June 20, 1971, the ship's skipper, Don Bell, discovered that the vessel was sinking. The ship was pumped and a large hole was patched, the cause seeming to be dry rot. It was decided the following year to tow her to Honolulu for repairs in dry dock. However, 150 yards from dock she became lodged on the reef and valiant efforts to save her were not successful. An immediate search began for a replacement and it was found in the Danish port of Soby. The ship was a 97-foot steel-hulled freighter that had originally been a schooner, but had been de-masted. The ship called *Komet* had been built in the shipyards in Germany in 1920 and was purchased for $20,500. An all-Lahaina crew sailed via the Panama Canal and arrived in Hawai'i in September 1973. Volunteers set to work transforming the ship into the proud vessel it is today and it was christened Brig *Carthaginian* on April 26, 1980. The Lahaina Restoration Foundation, which operates the vessel, is uncertain of its future. At this time you can only look at it from afar moored at the harbor.

Adjacent to the *Carthaginian* is the **Lahaina Lighthouse**—adopted by the Lahaina Restoration Foundation, which added new railings and a connecting ramp—which predates any along the Pacific. "It was on this site in 1840 that King Kamehameha III ordered a nine-foot wooden tower built as an aid to navigation for the whaling ships. It was equipped with whale oil lamps kept burning at night by a Hawaiian caretaker who was paid $20 a year." In 1866 it increased to 26 feet in size and was rebuilt again in 1905. The present structure of concrete was dedicated in 1916. (Information is from an engraved plaque placed on the lighthouse by the Lahaina Restoration Foundation.)

The **Hauola Stone**, or Healing Rock, can be found in front of the Lahaina Library next to the harbor. Look for the cluster of rocks marked with a Visitors Bureau "warrior" sign. The rock, resembling a chair, was believed to have healing properties that could be obtained by merely sitting in it with feet dangling in the surf. Here you will also find remnants of the **Brick Palace** of Kamehameha the Great.

The **Baldwin Home** is across Front Street from Pioneer Inn. Built from 1834 to 1835, it was once the home of Reverend Dwight Baldwin and his family from 1837 to the mid-1800s. The residence of this medical missionary has been restored and contains many original pieces of furniture. Tours available 10 a.m. and 4 p.m. Adults $3, seniors $2, family rate of $5. 695 Front Street. 808-661-3262.

Village Gifts & Fine Arts is housed here with a lovely selection of blown glass, art and jewelry. They feature international hand-crafted gifts such as hollowed coconut shells, rounded and intricately carved in lace-like patterns, and some unique handmade Hawaiian greeting cards. Open 9 a.m. to 7:30 p.m.

The empty lot adjacent was once the home of Reverend William Richards, and a target of attack by cannonballs from angry sailors during the heyday of whaling. On the other side of the Baldwin Home is the **Masters' Reading Room**. Built in 1833, it is the oldest structure on Maui. Its original purpose was to provide a place of leisure for visiting sea captains. It is not open to the public at this time.

Hale Paahao (Old Prison) on Prison Street just off Wainee is only a short trek from Front Street. Upon entry you'll notice the large gatehouse that the Lahaina Restoration Foundation reconstructed to its original state in 1988. Nearby is a 60-year-old Royal Palm and, in the courtyard, an enormous 150-year-old breadfruit tree. The cell block was built in 1852 to house the unruly sailors from the whaling vessels and to replace the old fort; it was reconstructed in 1959. In 1854 coral walls (the blocks taken from the old fort) were constructed. The jail was used until the 1920s, when it was relocated to the basement of the Lahaina Courthouse next to the Harbor. While you're at Hale Paahao be sure to say hello to the jail's only tenant, George. He is a wax replica of a sailor who is reported to have had a few too many brews at Uncle Henry's Front Street Beer House back in the 1850s, then missed his ship's curfew and was tossed into jail by Sheriff William

O. Smith. George will briefly converse with you by means of a taped recording. The grounds are open to the public daily.

The construction of the **Waiola Church** began in 1828. The original church was called the Wainee Church, and was made of stone and was large enough to accommodate 3,000 people. **Hale Aloha** was built in 1858 as a branch of the church and was used as a school. It's name, "House of Love," was a way of giving thanks that the citizens of Lahaina did not suffer in a smallpox epidemic that ravaged the island of Oʻahu in 1853. The Waiola Church is now a United Church of Christ with worship in Hawaiian and English. In 1951 a fierce wind, called a Kauaʻula wind, seriously damaged the church and Hale Aloha. (The wind is named for a narrow valley in the mountains above Lahaina, called Kauaʻula, through which it blows and gains force. Legend has it that the wind blows when the *aliʻi* die.) Among the damage incurred during the wind of 1951 was the loss of the Hale Aloha belfry. Hale Aloha and the church were both sold to the county in the 1960s. In 1996 the belfry was restored as a result of efforts of the Lahaina Restoration Foundation. (But they're still looking for a bell!) Hale Aloha is now fully restored. In the neighboring **cemetery** you will find tombs of several notable members of Hawaiian royalty, including Queen Keopuolani, wife of Kamehameha the Great and mother of Kamehameha II and III. The church is located on Wainee and Shaw streets.

The **Maria Lanakila Church** is on the corner of Wainee and Dickenson. Built in 1928, it is a replica of the 1858 church. Next door is the **Seamen's Cemetery**.

The **Wo Hing Temple** on Front Street opened following restoration in late 1984. Built in 1912, it now houses a museum that features the influence of the Chinese population on Maui. Hours are 10 a.m. to 4 p.m. Admission $1. The adjacent cookhouse has become a theater that runs movies filmed by Thomas Edison during his trips to Hawaiʻi in 1898 and 1906. In 1993 a Koban information booth was added near the Wo Hing Temple.

A small but interesting **Whaling Museum** is located in the Crazy Shirts shop on Front Street.

Follow Front Street towards Kaʻanapali to find the **U.S. Seamen's Hospital**. This classic two-story coral structure was built by King Kamehameha III and is well removed from town and for a reason. The king wanted to have some privacy away from the eyes of the missionaries who reproached him for his drinking and gambling ways. In 1844 it was leased to the state to provide care for sick and injured seamen. In 1973 the building was purchased by the Lahaina Restoration Foundation and renovations were completed by 1982. An interesting fact was the discovery of a human skeleton on the northwest side of the building. The LRF reports, "During the ancient times, when an *ali'i* had a building constructed that would house the royal family, a commoner was put to death with a blow of an adz to his head. The victim was then buried under the northwest support so that his spirit would be bound to the house and become the 'permanent guardian.' This finding underscores the cultural upheaval that was occurring at this time, for even though the king and his charges were raised as Christians, the old ways were still strong enough for this ritual to be carried out." The remains of this guardian were restored to his resting place in the northwest corner. Businesses now occupy space in this structure located on the Ka'anapali side of Front Street.

Hale Pa'i is a former printing press on the campus of Lahainaluna school. Founded in 1831, Lahainaluna is the oldest school west of the Rockies. You will find it located just outside of Lahaina at the top of Lahainaluna Road. The hours fluctuate depending on volunteers, so call the Lahaina Restoration office at 808-661-3262 for current schedule. Their general hours are Monday through Friday 10 a.m. to 3 p.m.

The **Lahaina Jodo Mission** is located on the Ka'anapali side of Lahaina, on Ala Moana Street near the Mala Wharf. The great Buddha commemorated the 100th anniversary of the Japanese immigration to the islands at the mission in 1968. The grounds, but not the buildings, are open to the public. The public is welcome to attend their summer O'Bon festivals, usually in late June and early July. Check the papers for dates and times.

Shopping is a prime fascination in Lahaina and is such a major business that it breeds volatility. Shops change frequently, sometimes seemingly overnight, with a definite trendiness to their merchandise. It was a few years back that visitors could view artisans creating scrimshaw in numerous stores. The next few years saw the transformation to T-shirt stores. (There still are plenty of clothing stores and a little price comparison can be worthwhile.) The next theme was art, art and more art. Galleries sprang up on every corner. It was a wonderful opportunity to view the fine work of many local artists and international ones as well. Original oils, watercolors, acrylics, carvings and even pottery were all on display. Rather like a museum without any admission fee! There are still plenty of galleries where you can enjoy fine artwork. Unfortunately, one transition in the last few years was the eruption of numerous tour and activity booking agents. I find that they have infiltrated every nook and cranny, even a corner of one ice cream shop. While some are pleasant enough, others are obnoxious and extremely pushy in their attempts to sell you a visit to a timeshare in exchange for a discounted activity. More editorial opinion on this appears in Chapter 6. In thinking back, only one or two shops have remained the same along Front Street since I began this book more than 20 years ago!

Here are a few shops that I feel are worth honorable mention:

Stop by **World Gallery** at 1816 Front Street. They offer some out-of-the-ordinary gift items. Wonderful table-size waterfalls, jewelry, artwork, usable art (furniture). Say "aloha" to their wonderful life-size residents. These silicon creations are amazingly life-like.

Environmental awareness has arrived at the **Endangered Species Store** at 707 Front Street. It's filled with T-shirts, collectibles, books and toys that all focus on endangered wildlife worldwide. Next door is **The Gecko Store**, a fun store with a novel idea that certainly makes this shop stand out from the many others that line Front Street. Step through the portal and take a look at what is under your feet. We'll let you be surprised.

A newcomer to Lahaina is Yvette Barton-Weinstein (and four-legged associate Jett) at **Best in Show**. The retail shop at 628 Front Street offers a designer collection of dog collars and leashes, along with canine items like jewelry and art. They describe themselves as "fine furnishing for home and hound."

Some of the best representation of local artists may be found at **Lahaina Galleries** located at 728 Front Street in Lahaina and at the **Kapalua Shops** at 123 Bay Drive. Begun in 1976, their art falls in the $500 to $30,000 (and up) range.

Also check the galleries located in the renovated Lahaina Courthouse next to the Banyan Tree. A number of retired movie and television stars have turned artist and you'll see the work of Tony Curtis, Red Skelton, Anthony Quinn, Buddy Ebsen and Richard Chamberlain at some of the larger galleries in town.

Rock stars like Ron Wood, Miles Davis, John Lennon, Jerry Garcia and Bob Dylan are represented at **Celebrités Gallery of Fine Art** at 764 Front Street.

> Friday night in Lahaina is **Art Night**. Participating galleries feature a special event between 6 and 9 p.m. that might include guest artists.

Originals, numbered lithographs and poster prints by popular Hawaiian artists Pegge Hopper, Diana Hansen-Young and others can be found at **The Village Galleries**. **David Lee Galleries**, **Galerie Lassen**, **Robert Lyn Nelson Studio** and **Kingwell Island Arts Collection** feature the works of their namesake artists. The **Lahaina Arts Society** is a nonprofit organization featuring work by local Maui artists. You'll find an open air exhibition under the Banyan at their "Art Mart" from 8 a.m. to 5 p.m. weekends. Some weekends there are Hawaiian arts and crafts on display.

The circa-1916 **Lahaina Store** is located in the middle of Lahaina Town. You'll find **Billabong** (a surf and skateboard shop), **Vintage European Posters**, **Na Hoku** (jewelry store), and a blues, jazz and comedy club called **Paradice Blues**.

Island Sandals is tucked away in a niche of the Wharf Cinema Center near the postal center at 658 Front Street, Space #125, in Lahaina. Michael Mahnensmith is the proprietor and creator of custom-made sandals. He learned his craft in Santa Monica from David Webb, who made sandals for the Greek and Roman movies of the late '50s and early '60s. Webb rediscovered his sandal design from the sandals used 3,000 years ago by the desert warriors of Ethiopia. He developed the idea while living in Catalina in the 1960s and copyrighted it in 1978. The sandals are all leather, which is porous and keeps the feet cool and dry, with the exception of a non-skid synthetic heel. The sandals feature a single strap that laces around the big toe, then over and under the foot, and around the heel, providing comfort and good arch support. As the sandal breaks in, the strap stretches and you simply adjust the entire strap to maintain proper fit (which makes them feel more like a shoe than a sandal). They are clever and functional. His sandals have been copied by others, but never duplicated. So beware of other sandals that appear the same but don't offer the fit, comfort or function of Michael's. Last we checked, the charge for ladies is $135 for the right shoe (the left shoe is free). Men's sizes are $155 (slightly higher for sizes over 13). Anyone who gets shoes from Island Sandals becomes an agent and is authorized to trace foot prints of others. Commissions are automatic when your sales reach the "high range." (However, you must like coconuts and bananas.) Michael stresses the importance of good footwear, so stop in upon your arrival. Sandals can also be ordered by sending a tracing of both feet and both big toes, including the spaces in between (or by having an "authorized agent" do so), along with the purchase price and shipping charge of $10 (U.S.) or $20 (international) to Island Sandals. Michael can also assist with leather repair of your shoes, purses, bags or suitcases. 808-661-5110; www.islandsandals.com.

The **Fun Factory** is located in the lower level of the Wharf Cinema Center with video games and prize-oriented games. Watch artists at work and buy all Maui-made gifts at **Hawaiiana Arts & Crafts**. **Island Swimwear** has stood the test of time (although half the size it originally was).

Although built nearly a century later, **Dickenson Square** on Dickenson Street off Front Street bears a strong resemblance to the Pioneer Inn. The Contemporary Village Gallery, Whalers General Store, Lahaina Coolers restaurant and Penne Pasta Café are located here.

Dan's Green House at 133 Prison Street has a variety of beautiful tropical birds for sale as well as an array of plants for shipping home. Their specialty is Fuku-Bonsai "Lava Rock" plants. These bonsai are well packaged to tolerate the trip home. 808-661-8412.

Walking south on Front Street you'll pass the Banyan Tree and Kamehameha III School before you come to **Kamehameha Iki Park** (also known as Armory Park) on your right. Hui O Waʻa Kaulua (the assembly of the double-hulled canoe) is a nonprofit organization that is working with the County of Maui to develop and maintain it as a Hawaiian cultural park that offers both exhibits and hands-on experiences. The focus will be the design, construction, sailing and maintenance of Hawaiian double-hulled sailing canoes constructed along traditional lines. Two *Hale Waʻa*, or canoe houses, will be constructed. They will be 37 feet tall, 41 feet wide and 100 feet long. The two *Hale Waʻa* will house three double-hulled canoes on the ground floor, with room in the ceiling for smaller or lighter canoes. A 62-foot double-hulled canoe of traditional design with a single sail has already been constructed. The canoe is named *Moʻokiha*, which means sacred lizard/dragon. They also have a 42.5-foot canoe called *Moʻolele*. Plans also include the construction of a kitchen as well as a covered picnic area with space for working, teaching and demonstrating Hawaiian crafts. Landscaping of the park will include vegetation that will serve Hawaiian activities such as ti, taro, bamboo, Hawaiian medicinal plants and bananas. Completion of these projects is anticipated within the next **five** years. If you would like more information or are interested in membership, contact Hui O Waʻa Kaulua, 505 Front Street, Suite 224B Lahaina, HI 96761.

Across the street (at what is now an unassuming baseball field and parking lot) is **Mokuʻula**, a sacred place for Hawaiian royalty and home to the Maui chiefs. It was placed on the National Register of Historic Places by the U.S. Department of the Interior in 1997. Beneath the flying dust of a baseball field was once a residence and a mausoleum to generations of rulers of Hawaii. "Legend says this moated island was also home to *Kihawahine,* a fearful lizard goddess who served as the guardian of the royal family." Once a *kapu* (forbidden) island in the center of an 11-acre fishpond (*Loko o Mokuhinia*), Mokuʻula was part of the region known as *Kalua O Kiha*—the center of *aliʻi* residence when Lahaina was capital of the kingdom. *Mokuʻula* was a favored residence of King Kamehameha III where he could enjoy a quiet retreat upon the island in the midst of a freshwater pond. Carbon dating and some preliminary archaeological excavation have revealed some of the oldest Hawaiian habitation in the islands. Many years ago the swampy area was filled in after complaints about mosquitoes. It was fortunate that no grading was done and preliminary excavation shows that the remains of this once-important royal residence from the 16th to the 19th century might well remain intact beneath the earth. You can read more about it at www.mokuula.com and view a painting created by Ed Kayton of this sacred island home based on archaeological and historical documentation.

I had the opportunity for a tour with **Maui Nei**, a company devoted to cultural tourism in partnership with the Friends of *Moku'ula*, a non-profit organization aimed at restoring the site. Maui Nei offers a walking tour through Lahaina's past. Tour side streets with your *kumu* (teacher) and even local gardens to envision how the town known as "Lele" once looked. Local guides begin their discussion with the arrival of the early Polynesians and follow the history of the area through the times of the missionaries and up to the present. Over 20 sites are visited during the two-hour tour, including the oceanfront workshop of **Hui O Wa'a**, where they demonstrate to the public the legacy of the early Hawaiians and their sailing canoes. This is a not-to-be-missed tour for those who are fascinated by the rich history and culture of the islands and yearn to learn more. The tour begins at the Old Lahaina Courthouse, includes a short, shady respite with beverage midway, and ends on the beach near 505 Front Street. Tours are Tuesday and Thursday 9 to 11 a.m. Cost is $32.50 adults, $22.50 kids 8 to 16. Maui Nei, 505 Front Street, Suite 234; 808-661-9494; e-mail: mauinei@attglobal.net; www.mauinei.com.

505 Front Street (across the street and next door to the park) was originally developed as a shopping center, unsuccessfully converted into condominiums, shops and restaurants. Bamboo Bar & Grill, Gaby's Pizzeria, Hecocks and Pacific 'O offer some options for your dining pleasure. The Feast of Lele luau takes place on the beach in front. Stop by the **Lahaina Book Emporium**, which offers "beach reads," rare collectible books and vintage videos.

Lahaina Center, on the Ka'anapali end of Lahaina, is composed of two parts. The Lahaina Shopping Center is the newest of the two and the other is aptly called Old Lahaina Center. You'll find the Broadway-style Maui Theater production of *'Ulalena*, plus eating establishments. The "new" old center is anchored by Foodland supermarket. A longtime *kama'aina* family still operates the Wiki Wiki Mart. The "New Lahaina Center," located across the street, is a low-level structure with pioneer-type architecture and a validated parking lot.

A free exhibit housed here is the **Hale Kahiko** Hawaiian village, which depicts the living quarters of ancient Hawai'i with thatched *hale* (houses) on display. There is also a Japanese garden with seating by a bridge-covered pond. Open daily with free activities Monday through Friday. There's a *keiki* Tahitian show Wednesday at 2:30 p.m. and a *keiki* hula show at 6 p.m. on Friday (808-667-9216). You can also learn a Hawaiian craft Monday, Tuesday, Thursday and Saturday, or enjoy "Sunset Serenading" 5:30 to 7:30 p.m. Tuesday and Thursday.

The 17,000-square-foot **Hilo Hattie** is famous around the islands for its aloha wear. I would recommend it for its good selection of touristy souvenirs, including key chains, jams and jellies, tropical candy and macadamia nuts. (Hilo Hattie is the only retail establishment ever to win the Kahili "Keep it Hawaiian" Award for Best Attraction from the Hawai'i Visitors Bureau.) **Dive Maui**, **Banana Republic** and **Gap** are a just a few of the other shopping opportunities.

An area slightly removed from Lahaina's Front Street is termed the industrial area. Follow Honoapi'ilani Highway and turn by the Pizza Hut to the main depot of the **Lahaina Ka'anapali & Pacific Railroad**, affectionately referred to as the Sugar Cane Train. In Lahaina in 1862, the harvesting of sugar cane was one of the island's biggest industries. More than 45,000 tons were produced from 5,000 acres. The Lahaina Ka'anapali & Pacific Railroad began in 1882, replacing the slower method (mules and steers) of hauling sugar cane between the harvest area and the Pioneer Sugar Mill. This allowed a greater area of cane to be planted as well. By the 1900s the railroad was also transporting an ever-increasing number of workers to their jobs. In 1970, the Sugar Cane Train was once again restored, but financial difficulties silenced the train whistle once more. In 1973, Mr. Willes B. Kyele purchased the railroad and brought life back to its engines. Currently two trains operate on a three-foot narrow-gauge railroad with eight departures daily between 10:15 a.m. and 4 p.m. The singing conductor will guide you through history as you wind through the cane fields of Lahaina. The trains are pulled by two steam locomotives, Anaka and Myrtle. The locomotives were built in 1943 and were restored to resemble those that were used in Hawai'i at the beginning of the 20th century. The Ka'anapali Station is located across the highway from the resort area. The Pu'ukoli'i boarding platform and parking lot are located on the Kapalua side of Ka'anapali. Adults $15.95 round trip, children 3 to 12 $9.95. Reservations needed for groups of 12 or more.)

There is also an evening activity. Board the Paniolo Express at 5 p.m. for a train ride to Lahaina just in time for sunset and then back to the Ka'anapali Station in time for the dinner bell. The kids will love the hearty dinner of chicken, ribs, hot dogs, hamburgers and a salad bar, topped off with smoothies to drink and a little cowboy-hula entertainment. Reservations required for the Paniolo Express, $65 adult,

$39 children 3 to 12. Currently offered Thursday nights, but additional nights may be added. 808-661-0080 or 808-667-6851; 800-499-2307; www.sugarcanetrain.com.

Also in the industrial area, The Bakery has some fine pastries and breads. **MGM, Maui Gold Manufacturing** (808-661-8981) not only does standard repairs, but designs outstanding jewelry pieces. They can design something to your specifications, or choose a piece from one of their many photograph books. A limited number of pieces are ready-made for sale as well. And be sure to visit **Lahaina Printsellers**, where you can purchase originals and reproductions of fine old maps and artwork.

Just on the Ka'anapali side of Lahaina (a drive of less than a mile) is the **Lahaina Cannery Mall**, which opened in 1987. The original structure, built in 1920, was used as a pineapple cannery until 1963. The current facility was built to resemble its predecessor and is easy to spot as you leave Lahaina heading for Ka'anapali. A large parking area makes for convenient access. This enclosed air-conditioned mall is anchored by Safeway and Longs Drug Store. Within the mall are several fast-food eateries in their Pineapple Court, which are excellent for a family with varied tastes. There is also sit-down dining at Compadres restaurant and a soon-to-open Chinese restaurant. Shops include **Sir Wilfred's** for coffee and cigars, **Maui Dive Shop**, along with jewelry, clothing and sporting goods stores plus **Waldenbooks**. Kids might enjoy checking out the **Play to Learn Toys**, with a variety of classic toys, puzzles and educational toys. Also lots of nostalgic toys that adults will reminisce over. The Old Lahaina Luau is held across the street (ocean side of the center) at Moa'li'i. The Lahaina Cannery Mall has *keiki* hula shows Saturday and Sunday at 1 p.m. and Polynesian dancing 7 p.m. Tuesday and Thursday.

Shoppers be forewarned: If you have time, do a lot of window shopping before you buy. Prices can vary significantly on some items from one store to another.

Ka'anapali-Kapalua Area

KA'ANAPALI

The drive from Lahaina to Ka'anapali is quick (unless it's rush hour—or "luau time"). All that is really visible from the highway are a couple of gas stations, the old mill, a few nondescript commercial buildings and a Pizza Hut. The large shopping center on the left is the Lahaina Cannery Mall. As you leave Lahaina, the vista opens up with views of the Hyatt Regency and the beginning of the Kaʻanapali Beach Resort a mile off in the distance. The resort is beautifully framed by the West Maui Mountains on the right, the peaks of Molokaʻi (appearing to be another part of Maui in the background), the island of Lanaʻi off to the left and, of course, the ocean. The name Kaʻanapali means "rolling cliffs" or "land divided by cliffs" and refers to the wide, open ridges that stretch up behind the resort toward Puʻu Kukui, West Maui's highest peak. The beaches and plush resorts here are what many come to Hawaiʻi to find.

Kaʻanapali began in the early 1960s as an Amfac Development, with the first hotels, the Royal Lahaina and the Sheraton Maui, opening in late 1962 and early 1963, respectively. The Kaʻanapali Beach Resort, 500 acres along three miles of prime beachfront, is reputed to be the first large-scale planned resort in the world. There are six beachfront hotels and seven condominiums that total more than 5,000 rooms and units, 2 golf courses, 37 tennis courts and a shopping village.

The **Hyatt Regency Maui Resort and Spa** and the **Westin Maui** must be put at the top of everyone's list of things to see. Few hotels can boast that they need their own wildlife manager, but upon entry you'll see why these two do. Without spoiling the surprises too much, just envision the Hyatt with palm trees growing through the lobby,

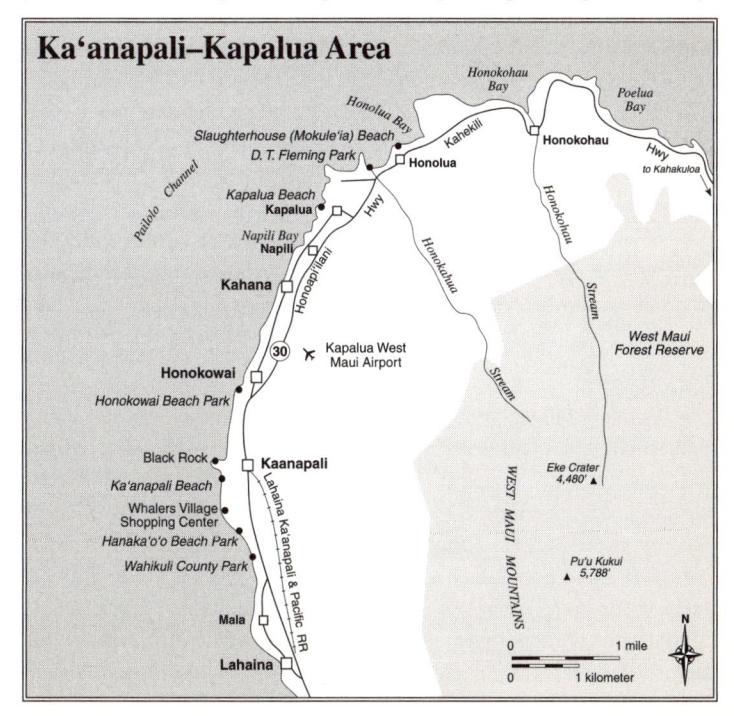

Kaʻanapali–Kapalua Area

- Honokohau Bay
- Honolua Bay
- Poelua Bay
- Slaughterhouse (Mokuleʻia) Beach
- D. T. Fleming Park
- Kahekili Hwy
- Honokohau
- Honolua
- Hwy to Kahakuloa
- Pailolo Channel
- Kapalua Beach
- Kapalua
- Napili Bay
- Napili
- Honoapiʻilani Hwy
- Honokohau Stream
- Kahana
- West Maui Forest Reserve
- Honokowai
- Kapalua West Maui Airport (30)
- Honokowai Beach Park
- Black Rock
- Kaanapali
- Kaʻanapali Beach
- Whalers Village Shopping Center
- Hanakaʻoʻo Beach Park
- Lahaina Kaʻanapali & Pacific RR
- WEST MAUI MOUNTAINS
- Eke Crater 4,480'
- Puʻu Kukui 5,788'
- Wahikuli County Park
- Mala
- Lahaina
- 0 – 1 mile
- 0 – 1 kilometer
- N

> **Hale Kohola** (House of the Whale) is a free museum located on the upper level of Whalers Village Shopping Center. A self-guided audio tour is available in both English and Japanese. Short films on whales and whaling are also offered throughout the day. The museum opened in 1984 under the directorship of curator and whale expert Lewis Eisenberg. It is dedicated to Lahaina's golden whaling era (1825–1860), with hundreds of artifacts and graphics telling the story through the eyes of the ordinary whaleman. Guided tours by marine naturalist available on pre-arranged basis. Open 9:30 a.m. to 10 p.m. daily. 808-661-5992

flamingos strolling by, and parrots perched amid extraordinary pieces of Oriental art. The lagoon and black swans are spectacular. And did I mention there are penguins, too? The spacious pool area occupies two acres and features two swim-through waterfalls and a cavern in the middle with a swim-up bar. A swinging bridge is suspended over one of the two pools and a water slide offers added thrills, particularly for the young traveler. There are exotic birds afloat on the lagoons that greet you upon your arrival and glide gracefully by two of the hotel's restaurants. The Westin is lovely and elegant but with less wildlife. Both developments were designed (or redesigned in the case of the Westin) by the remarkable, champion hotel builder of Hawai'i, Chris Hemmeter.

Be sure to take advantage of the lovely **beach walkway** that travels from the Hyatt Regency all the way to the Sheraton. A post-dinner stroll in the twilight is a perfect way to close a perfect day in Paradise. You can walk beyond to the other side of Black Rock but it requires a bit of maneuvering through the Sheraton Resort to connect with the walkway on the opposite side. **Black Rock** is, of course, the premier snorkeling spot on this stretch of beach. Enjoy an afternoon swimming with the brightly colored fish. (See "Snorkeling" in Chapter 6 for more information.)

Whalers Village Shopping Center is located in the heart of Ka'anapali. It offers a small grocery store, restaurants and a food court, art galleries and very high-end specialty and boutique shops. Designer clothing stores include Chanel, Gucci and Versace as well as Coach. Jewelry stores include Tiffany's, Maui Dive and Island Pearls. Waikiki Aloe kiosk is a good place to pick up tanning products. Other shops include the Body Shop, Del Sol (very cool products that change color in the sun), Blue Ginger, Cinnamon Girl (one of my favorites for ladies' island fashions), Lahaina Scrimshaw, Vintage European Posters and Lahaina Printsellers. Also here are Maui Toy Works, T-shirt Factory, White House/Black Market, Brighton Collectibles and Lids. Restaurants include The Rusty Harpoon, Leilani's and Hula Grill. All are beachfront and good options for breakfast, lunch or dinner. The Food Court offers several additional dining options.

From 2 to 3 p.m. on Wednesdays and Fridays **Billy Bones** entertains with sea tales, historical facts, whale lore and some tunes on an English concertina (sailor's button accordion), a 100-year-old fiddle, an Irish 10-penny flute or guitar. Billy Sayles is named after Captain William Bones from Robert Louis Stevenson's *Treasure Island*. However, Billy is a true descendant of a merchant marine captain who was a master of tall ships from 1860 to 1881. www.captain billbones.com.

The mall is a pleasant place for an evening stroll and browsing before or after dinner, followed by a seaside walk back to your accommodations on the paved beachfront sidewalk. A multilevel parking structure is adjacent to the mall. Parking is free for the first three hours with a $10 validation from shops/restaurants; $2.50/hour thereafter. You can find two-hours-free coupons in many of the visitor publications. Open daily 9:30 a.m. to 10 p.m. www.whalersvillage.com.

The **Honokowai Marketplace** is a Hawaiiana-styled shopping center with green-tile roofing anchored by the 37,500-square-foot Star Market. This shopping complex also offers Leola's Funwear, Maui Dive Shop, a video store and Maui's first Martinizing dry cleaning outlet. Subway, Java Jaza, Pizza Paradiso and Hula Scoops are among the eateries here. Just up the road don't miss Honokowai Okazuya (see Chapter 4) for one of the best deals and best plate lunches in West Maui.

To the north of Honokowai—and about seven miles north of Lahaina—is a prominent island of high-rise condos with a handful of two-story complexes strung along the coast in its lee. This is **Kahana**. The beach adjacent to the high-rises is fairly wide, but tapers off quickly after this point. Several of the larger complexes offer very nice grounds and spacious living quarters with more resort type activities than in Honokowai. The prices are lower than Ka'anapali, but higher than Honokowai. I haven't ever found any great values in this area and the beaches here simply aren't as fine as those to the north at Napili and Kapalua or south at Ka'anapali. In the past I have reported a continuing algae problem in the Honokowai to Kapalua areas. The algae bloom that clusters in the ocean offshore seems to come and go for reasons yet unknown. State officials continue their investigation but a cause or reason for this condition has not yet been determined.

Of late, the problem seems to have improved. The algae doesn't appear to be any health risk, just an annoyance for swimming and snorkeling.

There isn't much to see here in Kahana. There are several shops on the lower level of the **Kahana Manor**. Nearby, **Kahana Gateway**'s outlets include gift and dive shops, a gas station and Whalers General Store, a beauty salon, a children's fashion store, a laundry and eateries.

Napili's focal point is beautiful **Napili Bay** with good swimming, snorkeling and boogie boarding, and it even has tidepools for children to explore. Take time to stroll the beach or have a meal at the Napili Kai's Sea House restaurant. An eight-acre park is located *makai* of the highway near Maiha Street. The condominium units here are low-rise, with prices mostly in the moderate range, and are clustered tightly around the bay. A number are located right on the beach, others a short walk away. The quality of the units vary considerably, but generally a better location on the bay and better facilities demand a higher price. The complexes are small, most under 50 units, and all but one has a pool.

At the nearby **Napili Plaza** shopping center you'll find a full-size grocery store, restaurants and shops. It includes Boss Frog's Dive and Surf Shop, Mama's Ribs & Rotisserie, Maui Tacos, Subway and Napili Market (a full-size grocery store). There is Heaven Spa & Gifts, Napili Art Cetera Gallery, a beauty salon, dry cleaners and other services. The Maui Family Support Services has an arts-and-crafts fair held here every Wednesday and Saturday from 9 a.m. to 4 p.m. along with a beauty salon, dry cleaners and other services.

KAPALUA

Kapalua Bay is a small cove of pristine white sand nestled at the edge of a coconut palm grove. This area of Maui tends to be slightly wetter than in neighboring Lahaina, and the winds can and often do pick up in the afternoon. The story of **Kapalua** begins in ancient times, for it is said that Mauna Kahalawai, the immense volcano that formed the West Maui Mountains, is the juncture between Heaven and Earth. Hawaiians settled in this region in abundance, they built their *lo'i*, or flooded fields, for growing their staple crop, taro. They harvested fish, *'ama'ama*, *moi*, *akule* and *opelo*, from the clear waters, never taking more than they needed, and always giving thanks. It was an area rich in blessing, much of it sacred. There was a temple of medicine and one for astronomy. The highest chiefs and their families gathered for sports and games in this place, which they deemed their special retreat and playground. They built *holua* sleds for sliding down the grassy slopes. They rolled lava balls in their game of *ulu maika*, lawn bowling. They wrestled, competed in spear hurling, swam and surfed the waves at Honolua on giant *koa* boards.

> Kapalua is home to a number of outstanding annual events. The Kapalua Tennis Jr. Vet/Sr. Championship is held each May. In June both the Maui Chamber Music Festival and the Earth Maui Nature Summit are held at the Kapalua Resort. Presented by Kapalua Nature Society, the event is designed to foster an appreciation of Maui's natural environment. (In 1996 the Kapalua Resort property became the first Audubon Heritage Sanctuary in the world.) AT&T's "Golf in the Environment" tournament is just one of the summit's nature-oriented events. The Kapalua Wine and Food Symposium is offered in July, the Kapalua Open Tennis Tournament in September, and the Kapalua Betsy Nagelson Tennis Invitational is held the end of November and/or the first part of December. The nationally televised Kapalua International is held in November when top PGA golfers test their skills on Kapalua's Plantation Course. In 1999, Kapalua became home to the PGA Tours Mercedes Championships. The Ritz-Carlton also sponsors some wonderful events. Every Easter weekend they hold the Celebration of the Arts; throughout the year they host an Artists-in-Residence program, and every December there's a tree-lighting ceremony.

Ruins of ancient temples, fishing shrines and agricultural terraces can still be seen along the streams and shores, and people who sometimes find huge lava balls marvel at the prowess of the ancient bowlers. In earlier times, the Hawaiian lands were divided into *ahupua'a*. These pie-shaped land sections traverse forest to sea. They give each person access to various elevations for different crops, and an outlet to the ocean for fishing. There were seven beautiful *ahupua'a* called Honolua, Honokahua, Honokawai, Honokohau, Kahana, Mahinahina and Mailepai. They were joined to form Honolua Ranch, and parts later became Kapalua Resort.

The most important historic site at Kapalua is the **Honokahua Burial Grounds**, which were unearthed when digging began for The Ritz-Carlton, Kapalua. As the significance of the discovery became apparent, the entire hotel was redesigned and moved inland. The mound, which contains over 900 ancient Hawaiian burials dating between 610 and 1800, has been recognized as a sacred site. The mound is now carpeted in lush grass and bordered by native *naupaka* bushes. Also at this site is a portion of the 16th-century *Alaloa*, or King's Trail, a footpath that once encircled the island.

The modern-day history of Kapalua dates back to 1836 when the Baldwin family of New England settled on the island of Maui as missionaries. The Baldwin family home is now a historical landmark in

Lahaina. After 17 years of service, Doctor Baldwin was given 2,675 acres, the lands of Mahinahina and Kahana *ahupua'a*, to use for farming and grazing. By 1902 the area known as Honolua ranch had grown to 24,500 acres as a result of marriages, purchases and royal grants. The ranch crops included taro, mango, aloe and coffee beans. Fishing, along with cattle raising, also took place here. Kapalua became a bustling enclave on the island, with a working ranch that supplied pork and beef to the port of Lahaina. David Fleming arrived from Scotland and became the ranch manager. He experimented with a new fruit, *hala-kahiki*, or pineapple, and planted four acres. The ideal environment produced a very sweet pineapple. It was determined that the coffee operation should be moved upland to make room for a pineapple cannery, homes and bungalows for workers.

The area grew to include a railroad, store, churches, a golf course, tennis courts and a new house for Fleming. Honolua Ranch became Baldwin Packers, the largest producer of private-label pineapple and pineapple juice in the nation. In the years that followed, Kapalua's acres of grassy slopes were transformed into geometric patterns of silver-blue pineapple fields and the first crop of this fruit was harvested in 1914. By 1946 the cattle operation had ceased. In the next two decades, Baldwin Packers merged with Maui Pineapple and in 1969 became Maui Land & Pineapple Company, Inc.

In the 1970s a new master plan for Kapalua began to take place when Colin Cameron (a fifth-generation descendent of the Baldwin family) chose 750 acres of his family's pineapple plantation for the development of this upscale resort. The result was the Kapalua Bay Hotel and Ocean Villas (which opened in 1979) and the surrounding resort area that now includes vacation rental villas and homes, a residential community, golf courses and The Ritz-Carlton, Kapalua resort. Today the Kapalua area encompasses 1,500 acres surrounded by 23,000 acres of pineapple plantation and open fields.

Perhaps the most unusual program that Maui Land & Pineapple Company, Inc. has undertaken is to develop a home for Koko, the gorilla. Dr. Francine "Penny" Patterson has been working with Koko for over 20 years, teaching her communication through sign language. Future plans call for Koko to relocate to 70 acres in West Maui. The compound will be called the Allan G. Sanford Gorilla Preserve in memory of the son of Mary Cameron Sanford, chair of Maui Land & Pineapple. Koko will be joined by two male companions, Michael and Ndume. Visitors will not be permitted at the compound, but there are plans for a visitor center that will have remote viewing via video cameras. For more information call the Gorilla Foundation (800-63-GO-APE).

The road beyond Kapalua is paved and in excellent condition and offers some magnificent shoreline views. It is not as narrow and windy as the Hana Highway, but best negotiated in the daylight as it does twist and turn. **Slaughterhouse (Mokuleʻia) Beach** is only a couple of miles beyond Kapalua and you may find it interesting to watch the body surfers challenge the winter waves.

Just beyond is **Honolua Bay**, where winter swells make excellent board surfing conditions. A good viewing point is along the roadside on the cliffs beyond the bay.

Continuing on, you may notice small piles of rocks like granite snowmen. This is graffiti, Maui style. They began appearing several years ago and these mini-monuments have been sprouting up ever since. There are some wonderful hiking areas here as well. One terrain resembles a moonscape, while another is a windswept peninsula with a symbolic rock circle formation.

As you travel from Kapalua around the top of the island to Kahului there is plenty to see. Some of the cliffs have incredible scenic viewpoints. You will also pass the village of **Kahakuloa**. Some of the residents living here are descendants from the original settlement some 1,500 years ago. It was not many years ago that electricity finally arrived, but much is still done in the way of old Hawaiʻi. Tours of the town are available. (See "Land Tours" in Chapter 6.) Travel time from Napili to Wailuku in this alternate direction is about 1.5 hours. The road beyond is a slow and scenic drive and many parts of it are windy with room enough for only one car. However, don't venture on if you are in a hurry. On occasion, parts of the road have been washed away, closing it. Some rental car companies may restrict your travel on this route.

Kapalua Shops (located adjacent to the Kapalua Bay Hotel & Ocean Villas) offers a showcase of treasures. Here you will find The Kapalua Logo Shop (808-669-4172), where everything from men's and women's resort wear to glassware displays the Kapalua butterfly logo. Kapalua Kids (808-669-0033) features fashions for infants through boys and girls size 7.

There is a lot to enjoy at the **Kapalua Shops** (808-669-3754). A Hawaiian quilt-making class (808-665-1111) is offered Monday 9:30 a.m. to 12:30 p.m. Registration is the Sunday before at noon. The $50 per person fee includes a $30 quilting kit. Ukulele, slack key and steel guitar are performed Tuesday 10:30 to 11:30 a.m. Lei making with Auntie Nani is held Wednesday 1 to 2 p.m. A $2 charge per person for materials. Learn not only the basics of lei making with locally grown flowers, but the history and background of this Hawaiian art. Thursday 10 to 11 a.m. you can enjoy a free traditional ancient Hawaiian hula performance. On Friday, learn beginning hula with Kealani from 10:30

to 11:30 a.m. A West Maui Hike is offered daily 8 a.m. to noon; contact the resort activity desk at 808-669-8088 for reservations. Must be 10 years or older. The Maui Pineapple Plantation Tour (reservations 808-669-8088) is offered Monday through Friday 9:30 a.m. to noon and 12:30 p.m. to 3 p.m. Tours are approximately 2½ hours with breathtaking views of the West Maui Mountains and a visit to the fields of the only pineapple canning operation in the United States. Must be 10 years or older. Cost is $29. And keep in mind the Art School at Kapalua for your kid's summer options. All activities are open to non-resort guests.

Ma'alaea-Kihei-Wailea-Makena Area

MA'ALAEA

Ma'alaea, to many, is just a sign post en route to Ka'anapali, or a harbor for the departure of a tour boat. (Some even think that Buzz's Wharf, with its more visible and prominent sign, is the real name of the town!) However, Ma'alaea (which means "area of red dirt") is the most affordable and centrally located area of the island.

Ten minutes from Kahului, 25 minutes from Lahaina and 15 minutes from Wailea—it's easy to see all of the island while headquartered here. You can hop into the car for a beach trip in either direction. Even better is the mere six-mile jaunt to Kahului/Wailuku for some of Maui's best and most affordable eateries. This is a quiet and relaxing vacation retreat as well as a popular residential area. Seven of the ten condominium complexes are located on a sea wall on or near the harbor of Ma'alaea, while the other three are on one end of the three-mile-long Ma'alaea Bay beach.

The ocean and beach conditions are best just past the last condo, the Makani A Kai. There is less turbidity, providing fair snorkeling at times, good swimming and even two small swimming areas protected by a reef. (These are found on either side of the small rock jetty with the old pipe.) This length of beach is owned by the government and is undeveloped, providing an excellent opportunity for beach walkers who can saunter all the way down to Kihei. The condominium complexes are small and low-rise with moderate prices and no resort activities. The vistas from many of the lanais are magnificent, with a view of the harbor activity and the entire eastern coastline from Kihei to Makena, including majestic Haleakala, as well as Molokini, Kaho'olawe and Lana'i. The view is especially pleasing at night and absolutely stunning during a full moon when its light shimmers across the bay and through the palm trees with the lights of Upcountry, Kihei and

Wailea as a backdrop. No other part of the island offers such a tranquil and unique setting. Another plus are the almost constant tradewinds that provide non air-conditioned cooling as opposed to the sometimes scorching stillness of the Lahaina area.

The Ma'alaea Harbor area is a scenic port from which a number of boats depart for snorkeling, fishing and whale watching. Buzz's Wharf restaurant is one of the oldest and still a prominent landmark; **Harbor Shops at Ma'alaea** has been an exciting addition to the area. In the shopping center you'll find Kaua'i Island Soap Factory has opened their first outer-island store and makes products on location. Interesting to watch! Shaper's is a surf

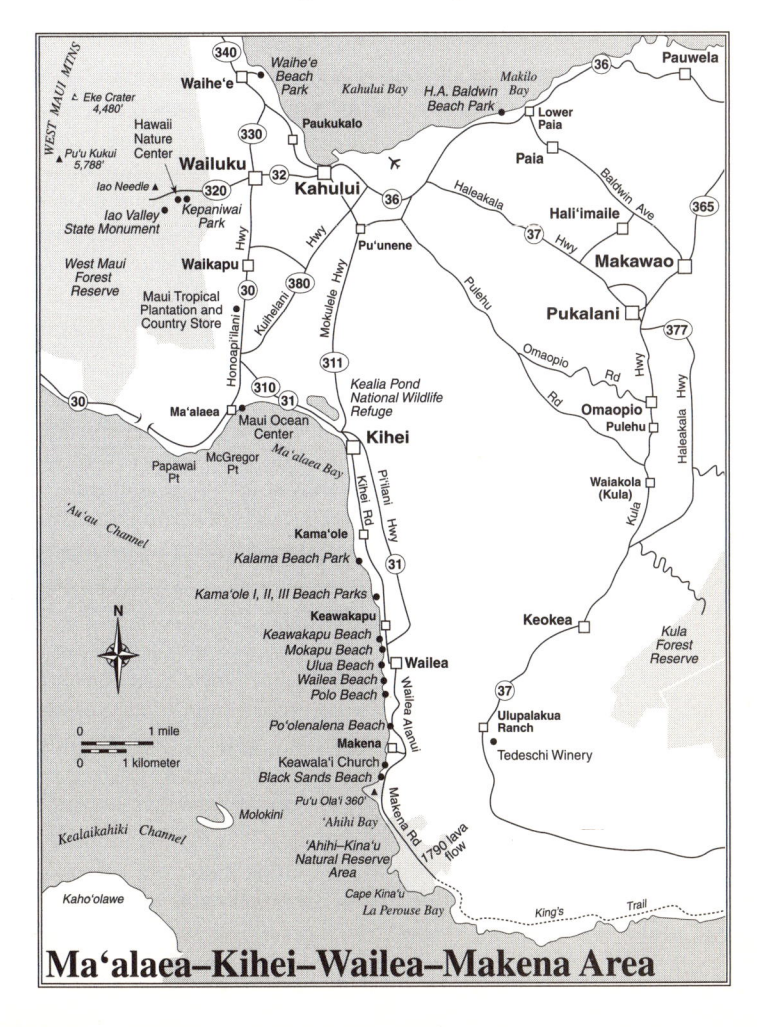

Ma'alaea–Kihei–Wailea–Makena Area

> Summer in Ma'alaea is a time for surfing. Summer swells coming into the bay reportedly create the fastest right-breaking ridable waves in the world and are sometimes referred to as "the freight train." The local kids are out riding from dawn to dusk. Winter brings calmer seas with fair snorkeling over the offshore reef. The calm conditions, undisturbed by parasailing and jet-skiing, also entice the humpback whales into the shallow waters close to shore.

shop with a surfing museum inside and the Pacific Whale Foundation has an exhibit.

In 1998 Coral World International opened their **Maui Ocean Center** as the first and most compelling feature of the Ma'alaea Harbor Village. The aquarium is the only one of its kind in Hawai'i. More information on the center is in Chapter 6 under "Museums and Gardens." Allow a minimum of two hours to visit the Maui Ocean Center, which offers tours, films and classes on their exhibits: an aquarium; reef, turtle and ray pools plus an outdoor touch pool; a shark tank and Whale Center. There is a great gift shop for young and old alike. Oceanview restaurant plus kiosk for fast food and snacks. Open 9 a.m. to 5 p.m. Admission $19 adults, $13 children. 808-270-7000.

KIHEI

This section of East Maui has a much different feel than West Maui or Lahaina. There are no large resorts with exotically landscaped grounds, very few units on prime beachfront and more competition among the complexes, making this area a good value for your vacation dollar. (And a good location for extended stays.) Kihei always seemed to operate at a quieter and more leisurely pace than Ka'anapali and Lahaina, but the last couple of years has seen a significant upsurge of development, not of condos but of shopping complexes.

There is no real distinct dividing line, but I have always sensed that North Kihei and South Kihei are two unique areas. **North Kihei** is 15 minutes from the Kahului Airport and located at the entrance to South Kihei; the condominiums in North Kihei stretch along a gentle sloping white-sand beach. The pace is quieter here than in South Kihei and I feel that the beaches are better.

Traveling south from Ma'alaea you'll pass large wetlands and **Kealia Pond National Wildlife Refuge** (note warnings to watch for sea turtles that sometimes make their way onshore here to nest and lay their eggs). Among the endangered species currently making their home in Kealia Pond are the Hawaiian coot and Hawaiian stilt. Kids and adults alike will enjoy a self-guided tour of the refuge's coastal wetlands and sand dunes. You'll see turtles (and whales) from the elevated vantage point, with the aid of interpretive signs along the elevated boardwalk (approximately .75 mile) on the tour trail. The family can learn about the cultural history of the area, bird identification, biology, ecology and watershed. 808-875-1582.

South Kihei began its growth after that of West Maui and the result is a sprawling six-mile stretch of coastline littered with more than 50 properties, nearly all condominiums, with some 2,400 units in rental programs. Few complexes are actually on a good beach. However, many are across Kihei Road from one of the Kama'ole Beach Parks. A variety of beautiful beaches are just a few minutes' drive away.

The only historical landmark in North Kihei is a **totem pole** near the Maui Lu Resort that commemorates the site where Captain Vancouver landed.

The **Maui Research & Technology Park** is located up from the highway on Lipoa Street. Although generally not open to the public, it is worth a mention since their high-performance computing center is one of less than two dozen in the entire nation. It is also one of the largest configurations of IBM super-computing technology in the U.S.

The small **Kealia Shopping Center** is located between the Kihei Sands and Nani Kai Hale. Another small shopping area is found at the Sugar Beach Condominiums. Several snack shops can be found along Kihei Road in this area. Down in South Kihei you'll have plenty of shopping centers to choose from.

A shopping center, Maui Nui Park in North Kihei, has been proposed for the triangle of land where you can turn to go to the Pi'ilani Highway down to Kihei Road or up to Lahaina. Check the *Maui Update* newsletter for developments.

Every corner of Kihei is sprouting a shopping mall. The complexes all seem to have quick markets, video stores and at least one T-shirt shop. Traveling down Kihei Road, the first center is **Azeka Place Makai** (808-874-8400), aka Azeka Place I, where Bill Azeka opened his first store in 1950. The Azeka Snack Shop continues to offer great deals on island-style plate lunches. The Royal Thai Cuisine and Home Maid Bakery and Deli are other dining options. On my last visit virtually all of the tourist shops were empty. Unknown is what renovations or newcomers may fill the shops.

Located across the street is **Azeka Place Mauka** (also called Azeka Place II) with several jewelry and clothing stores, a baby accessory shop, a bank, Panda Express, a Mexican restaurant cyber café (Restaurante Pasatiempo), the Coffee Store, a noodle restaurant and Peggy Sue's. Pi'ikea slices through and travels up to the Pi'ilani Highway and the Pi'ilani Village Shopping Center with a huge Safeway. Be careful crossing! The cars whiz down. Across the street is another portion of the mall that has a sign that reads "Longs Drugs Kihei Center." Here you'll find eateries that include Sushi Paradise and Antonio's. Opposite this mall is McDonald's.

If you're traveling toward Wailea, on your right will be Star Market, on your left a Chevron station and behind this is Paradise Plaza. Behind the service station is Shaka Pizza. They have fabulous New York subway-style pizza, so be sure to give them a try.

The **Lipoa Shopping Center** is a block down Lipoa Street and offers several eateries.

Just past the Kapulanikai condominiums, the **Kukui Mall** is an attractive one. This large complex is done in Spanish-style architecture with a wide assortment of shops. The kids might want to spend some time on a rainy afternoon at the Fun Factory. They have an assortment of video and arcade games. A number of gift and sundry shops round out this mall.

Across the street from the Kukui Mall is the **Aloha Market**. Looks like lots of jewelry and T-shirts but I've honestly never stopped in.

A bit farther is the **Kihei Town Center**, which offers a selection of shops including sporting goods, novelty items, clothing and the Foodland grocery.

On the same side of the street look for the development of **Kihei Kalama Village**, a cluster of shops, restaurants and small eateries. Its original swap meet–type venue of open-air stalls was transformed and renovated to a bit more formal atmosphere with a large open steel pavilion to shelter the stalls and shops amid landscaped gardens and monkey pod trees. Don't miss Frederick's Studio for some low-maintenance aquarium items. These blown-glass fish, crab and other aquatic critters are made on site and are fun gifts. A branch of Tuna Luna has great affordable gift items. Hungry? You'll find great affordable dining at Pita Paradise—a favorite of mine.

The next few shopping areas almost run together. The **Dolphin Plaza** at 2395 South Kihei Road is across from Kama'ole I Beach.

Between the Dolphin Plaza and Rainbow Mall is the tiny **Kama'ole Beach Center** at 2411 South Kihei Road Here you'll find Hawaiian Moons Natural Foods, which features health foods, vitamins and organically grown produce and some cooked hot dishes.

The **Rainbow Mall** is a small center also on the *mauka* (towards the mountain) side of South Kihei Road. They offer jewelry and souvenir stores, and a stand that serves shave ice and espresso. Haleakala

Trading Co. offers arts and crafts made by local Maui artists—everything from paintings to perfumes.

Kamaʻole Shopping Center is one of the larger malls and offers several restaurant selections. There is also a Maui Dive Shop, Whalers General Store and several clothing shops.

The last shopping center in Kihei, across from Kamaʻole III Beach, is the **Kai Nani Shopping Center**.

Now that I've covered Kihei Road, you can venture up to the **Piʻilani Shopping Village**. To reach it from Kihei Road, turn *mauka* (toward the mountain) between the Longs Center and the Azeka Place II shopping center on Piʻikea Road. You'll find the largest Safeway in the islands and it is open 24 hours a day. You'll also find the second Maui location for Hilo Hattie's, as well as Jamba Juice, Waldenbooks and Starbucks. Assorted gift and clothing stores.

WAILEA

Wailea, developed by Alexander and Baldwin, is a well-planned and beautifully manicured resort on 1,500 acres just south of Kihei. There are outstanding luxury resorts and condominiums, as well as championship golf courses and a large tennis center.

The spacious and uncluttered layout of Wailea is impressive, as is its series of lovely beaches. Spend some time sitting on a beach under the palm tree. There is a paved shoreline trail that travels between the Fairmont Kea Lani up to the Grand Wailea Resort, making it a wonderful option for a stroll, day or night.

The Wailea beaches are actually well-planned and nicely maintained public parks with excellent access, off-street parking and most have restrooms and rinse-off showers. Ulua Beach is a personal favorite. Be sure you spend some time strolling through the imaginative grounds of the **Grand Wailea Resort Hotel**. The sea remains the theme throughout the resort. At the entry look closely for the Hawaiian sea spirits that are hidden amid this cascading waterfall. Each of the many Hawaiian sculptures has a legend or history—King Kamehameha stands out near the entry and was created by Herb Kane, a noted specialist on Polynesian culture and history. He also created many of the mermaids, dancers and fisherman found by the resort's lagoons and streams. Inside the resort you'll find Hena, the mother of the demigod Maui. In the open-air walkway of the Haleakala Wing there are 18 bronzes around the grounds that were sculpted by world-famous artist Fernard Leger. Jan Fisher sculpted 10 life-size pieces for the resort including the maidens bathing and the two trios of hula dancers at the entry of the atrium. Be sure to take note of the beautiful relief painting on the walls of the Grand Dining Room. The murals were painted by Doug Riseborough and depict his version of the legend of the demigod Maui. In the center of the dining room is a sculpture done by Shige Yamada entitled "Maui Captures the Sun." Just outside the dining room is a small stage with a fabulous Hawaiian mosaic.

The resort offers a complimentary art tour twice weekly led by art curator Michael Gilbert. The center courtyard is called the Botero Gallery. These sculptures seem to be getting the most discussion—both good and bad! Fernando Botero is a contemporary artist from Colombia and his work is "oversized." The huge Hawaiian woman reclining on her stomach (smoking a cigarette in the buff) weighs 3,000 pounds and is appraised at $4 million. If you're on the upper levels, be sure to look down to see her from another interesting perspective.

The Shops at Wailea is a 150,000-square-foot shopping center with many known names, from Louis Vitiation, to Tiffany and Tommy Bahamas, Endangered Species, Gap, Banana Republic and Carter. Among the popular local tenants are Serendipity, Sacco Designs, Lahaina Galleries, Reyn's, Crazy Shirts and Honoloa Surf Company. The center features not one but two waterfalls, numerous fountains and escalators.

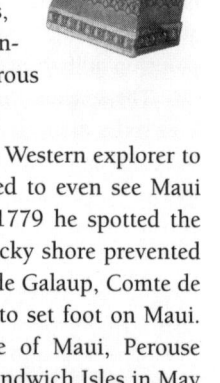

Captain James Cook may have been the first Western explorer to visit and map the Hawaiian islands, but he failed to even see Maui during his first voyage. On his second trip in 1779 he spotted the northeast coastline of Maui, but a rugged and rocky shore prevented him from landing. It was Admiral Jean-Francois de Galaup, Comte de La Perouse, who was the first Western explorer to set foot on Maui. Seven years after Cook had anchored offshore of Maui, Perouse departed from Easter Island and arrived in the Sandwich Isles in May 1786. His two frigates, the *Astrolabe* and the *Boussole*, sailed around the Hana coast searching for a location to land. Discovering Maui's south shore, he decided to land at Keoneʻoʻio to conduct trading with the Hawaiians. He was greeted by local Hawaiians who were friendly and eager to trade. They exchanged gifts and La Perouse visited a total of four villages. This three-hour visit resulted in the Keoneʻoʻio Bay being called La Perouse Bay.

Hiking beyond La Perouse affords some great ocean vistas. You'll see trails made by local residents in their four-wheel-drive vehicles and fishermen's trails leading to volcanic promontories overlooking the ocean. You may even spot the fishing pole holders that have been securely attached to the lava boulders. The **Hoapili Trail** begins just past La Perouse Bay and is referred to as the King's Highway. Another interesting hike is at the **Puʻu Olaʻi cinder cone**, the red-earth hillock that juts out to the sea just beyond the cover fronting the Maui Prince Hotel. It is one of Haleakala's craters (under which is a large cave) and is said to be the sacred dwelling place of Mano, the ancestral shark deity. See "Hiking" in Chapter 6 for more information. Here are the last really gorgeous and undeveloped recreational beaches on Maui.

The paved road (Makena Alanui) runs from Wailea past the Makena Surf and Maui Prince Hotel, exiting onto the Old Makena Road near the entrances to Oneuli (Black Sand) Beach and Oneloa (Big Makena)–Pu'u Ola'i (Little Makena) beaches. Past 'Ahihi-Kina'u Natural Reserve on Old Makena Road you will traverse the last major lava flow on Maui, which still looks pretty fresh after some 250 years, and the road continues to La Perouse Bay (see Chapter 5 for more beach information).

The **Keawala'i Church**, founded in 1832, was once the cultural and spiritual center of the community. The structure, completed in 1854, is three feet thick and made of melted coral gathered from the sea. It is surrounded by ti leaf that was planted because of the Hawaiian belief that it provides protection and healing. This charming historical church sits quietly along the ocean in Makena and is home to an active Protestant congregation. Services are in both English and Hawaiian.

Kahului–Wailuku Area

The twin towns of Wailuku and Kahului are located on the northern, windward side of the island. Wailuku is the county seat of Maui while Kahului houses not only the largest residential population on the island, but also the main airport terminal and deep-water harbor.

Kahului has a very colorful history beginning in the 1790s with the arrival of King Kamehameha I from the Big Island of Hawai'i. The meaning of Kahului is "winning" and may have had its origins in the battle that ensued between Kamehameha and the Maui chieftain. The shoreline of Kahului Bay began its development in 1863 with the construction of a warehouse by Thomas Hogan. By 1879, a landing at the bay was necessary to keep up with the growing sugar cane industry. Two years later, in 1881, the Kahului Railroad Company began. The city of Kahului grew rapidly until 1900, when it was purposely burned down to destroy the spreading of a bubonic plague outbreak. The reconstruction of Kahului created a full-scale commercial harbor, which was bombed along with Pearl Harbor on December 7, 1941. After World War II, a boom began with the development of reasonably priced homes to house the increasing number of people moving to the island. The expansion has continued ever since.

Wailuku has been the center of government since 1930. It is now, slowly, experiencing a rebirth. It is often overlooked by visitors (who miss out on some wonderful local restaurants and interesting shopping).

Ka'ahumanu Church, Maui's oldest remaining church, was built in 1837 at High and Main streets in Wailuku.

Hale Hoikeike houses the **Bailey House Museum**, circa 1834. To reach it, follow the signs to Iao Valley and you will see the historical landmark sign on the left side of the road. Here you will find the Bailey Gallery (once a dining room for the female seminary that was located at this site) with the paintings of Edward Bailey done during the 19th century. His work depicts many aspects of Hawaiian life during earlier days. Also on display are early Hawaiian artifacts and memorabilia from the missionary days. The staff is extremely knowledgeable and friendly. They also have an array of Hawaiian history, arts, crafts and photographic books for sale. Originally, the Royal Historical Society was established in 1841, but it was not until 1956 that it was reactivated as the Maui Historical Society. The museum was dedicated on July 6, 1957. Of special interest are the impressive 20-inch-thick walls that are made of plaster using a special missionary recipe that included goat hair as one ingredient (talk about recycling!). The thick walls provided the inhabitants with a natural means of air conditioning. Open Monday to Saturday 10 a.m. to 4 p.m. Admission $5 adults, $4 seniors 60 and over, $1 kids 7 to 12, free six and under. 808-244-3326.

The **Maui Jinsha Mission** is located at 472 Lipo Street in Wailuku. One of the few remaining old Shinto shrines in the state of Hawai'i, this mission was placed on the National Register of Historic Places in 1978.

The **Halekii** and **Pihana State Monuments** are among Maui's most interesting early Hawaiian historical sites. Both are of considerable size and situated atop a sand dune. These temples were very important structures for the island's early *ali'i*. Their exact age is unknown, although one source reported that they were used from 1765 to 1895. The Halekii monument is in better condition as a result of some reconstruction done on it in 1958. Follow Waiehu Beach Road across a bridge, then turn left onto Kuhio Place and again on Hea Place. Look for and follow the Hawai'i Visitors Bureau markers. Some say the Pihana *heiau* was built by the *menehunes* (Hawai'i's lit-

---

The **Hawai'i Nature Center** at Iao Valley comprises a towering glass solarium and offers unique hands-on exhibits and experiences focusing on Hawai'i's natural history. See "Museums/Gardens" in Chapter 6 for more information. Open 10 a.m. to 4 p.m. Adults $6, $4 children 4 to 11, free under 4. 808-244-6500; fax 808-244-6525

Kahului–Wailuku Area

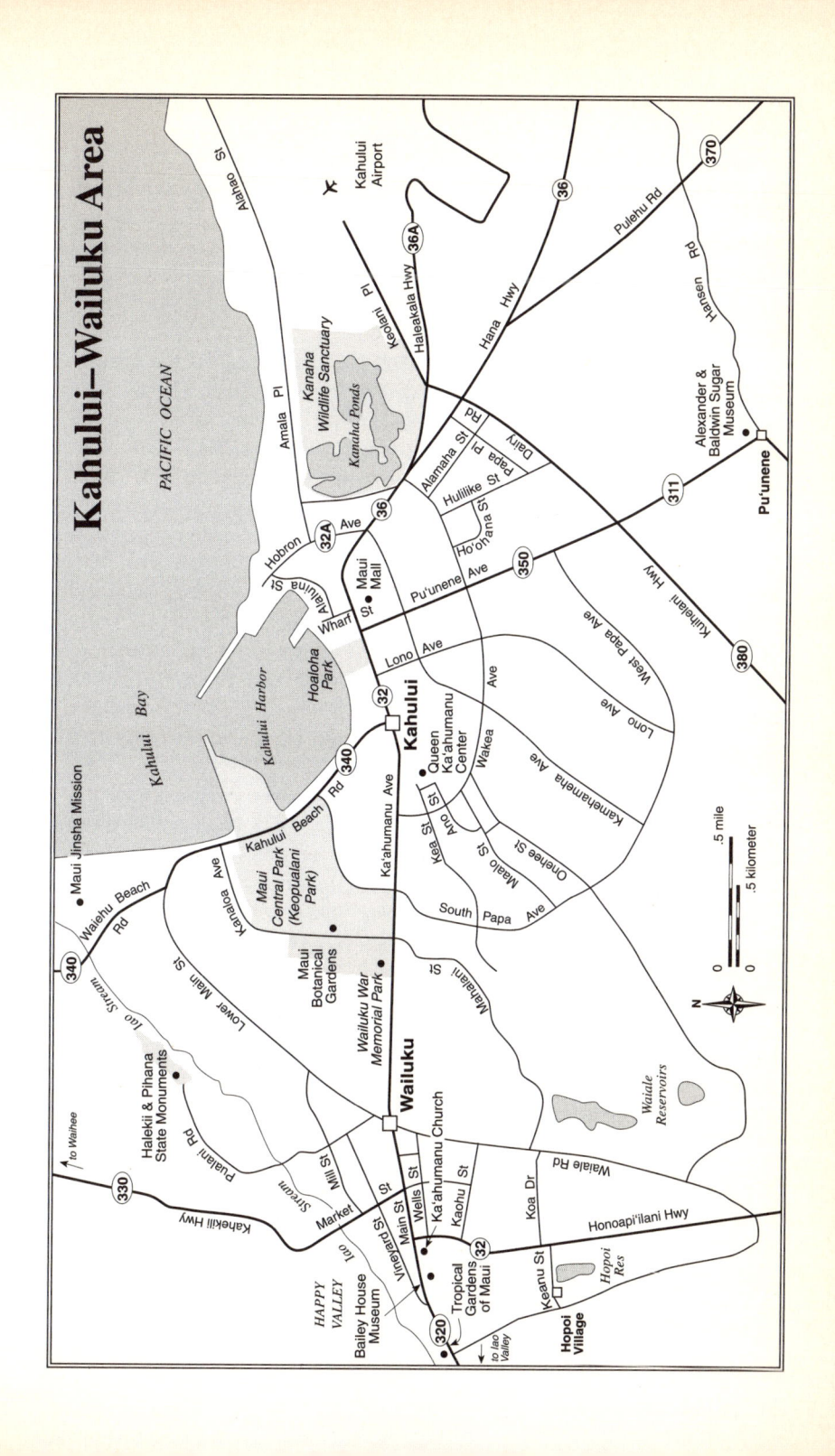

tle people), others believe the construction was done under the guidance of the Maui chieftain, Kahekili.

The **Iao Valley** is a short drive beyond Hale Hoikeike. Within the valley is an awesome volcanic ridge that rises 2,250 feet and is known as the Iao Needle. A little known fact is that this interesting natural phenomena is not a monolithic formation but rather the end of a large, thin ridge. (A helicopter view will give you an entirely different perspective.) Parking facilities are available and there are a number of hiking trails.

The **Tropical Gardens of Maui** is a botanical garden that features the largest selection of exotic orchids in the Hawaiian islands. For a small fee you can stroll the grounds where they grow. Or just stop and visit their gift shop filled with tropical flowers and Maui-made products. Plants can be shipped home. Snack bar and picnic tables available. Open Monday through Saturday. Admission $3. 808-244-3085.

The **Heritage Garden—Kepaniwai Park** is an exhibit of pavilions and gardens that pays tribute to the culture of the Hawaiians, Portuguese, Filipinos, Koreans, Japanese and Chinese. Picnic tables and barbecues are available for public use. They are located on Iao Valley Road. Open daily. Also a popular site for weddings and other functions, it is available for rent from the Maui Parks Department. 808-270-7230 or 808-270-7389. A free public swimming pool for children is open weekends and holidays from 9 to 11:45 a.m. and again from 1 p.m. until 4:30 p.m.

Just outside Wailuku on Highway 30 between Wailuku and Ma'alaea, is Waikapu, home of the **Maui Tropical Plantation and Country Store**. This visitor attraction has become one of the top ten most heavily visited in the state of Hawai'i. The 50 acres, which opened in 1984, have been planted with sugar cane, bananas, guava and other island produce. A 10-acre visitor center includes exhibits, the Country Store (a marketplace), nursery and restaurant. There is no admission for entry into the store or the restaurant, but there is a charge ($9.50 adults, $3.50 children 3 to 12) for the narrated tram ride around the fields. The tram ride departs between 10 a.m. and 3:15 p.m. (last tram 2:30 on Friday). Frequency of the tram varies with the days of the week. The trip includes several stops for samples of fresh fruit. Open daily 9 a.m. to 5 p.m. 808-244-7643; www.mauitropicalplantation.com.

In addition to baseball and mini-soccer fields, the $11 million, 110-acre **Maui Central Park** (Keopualani Park) offers four playground areas, walking and jogging paths and a skateboard park. There are 50 picnic tables scattered throughout. Go up Ka'ahumanu to Kanaloa Street and turn by the Wailuku War Memorial Park, now home of the Hula Bowl that is held there in January. Adjoining is the **Maui Botanical Gardens**.

A popular Saturday morning stop for local residents and visitors alike is the **Maui Swap Meet**, held at grounds around the Christ the King Church, next door to the post office off Puʻunene Highway 35. You'll find us referring to this event for various reasons throughout this guide. For a 50¢ admission (children free) you will find an assortment of vendors selling local fruits and vegetables, new and used clothing, household items and many of the same souvenir-type items found at higher prices in resort gift shops. I recently discovered one fellow selling "designer" sunglasses and handbags at one third the price of retail stores. He professed they were the real thing, not knock-offs, but I'm not too sure about that. The swap meet is also a great place to pick up tropical flowers, and for only a few dollars you can lavishly decorate your condo during your stay. Protea are seasonally available here for a fraction of the cost elsewhere (and they are *not* knock-offs). This is also the only place to get true spoonmeat coconuts. These are fairly immature coconuts with deliciously mild and soft meat and filled with sweet coconut milk. I usually stock up on a week's supply at a time. These coconuts are the ones that are trimmed off the trees while still green and far different from the hard brown ones in the supermarkets. One booth I discovered had coconuts that could be inscribed with a message and mailed home as a postcard. Plain were around $10 including postage, painted were $15. Another must-purchase are goodies from Four Sisters Bakery (if they aren't here, check them out at their bakery location in Wailuku). Swap meet hours are 8 a.m. to noon. This is an outstanding family outing to central Maui. Combine it with breakfast or lunch at one of the local restaurants nearby. 808-877-3100

The **Kanaha Wildlife Sanctuary** is off Route 32, near the Kahului Airport, and was once a royal fish pond. Now a lookout is located here for those interested in viewing the stilt and other birds that inhabit the area.

The **Alexander and Baldwin Sugar Museum** is located at 3957 Hansen Road in Puʻunene. Puʻunene is on Highway 35 between Kahului and Kihei. The tall stacks of the working mill are easily spotted. The museum is housed in a 1902 plantation home that was once occupied by the sugar mill's superintendent. You'll find an informative assortment of memorabilia as well as an actual working scale model of a sugar mill. Hours are Monday through Saturday 9:30 a.m. to 4:30 p.m. Open Sunday only in February, March, July and August. Admission $5 adult, $2 children under 18, free children under 6. 808-871-8058.

A **historic tunnel of trees** once lined the Puʻunene Road between the mill and Kahului. The trees were taken down to make room for state and county road improvements. The earpods and monkeypods were more than 65 years old, but had suffered from time and were frankly rather pitiful. Thirty-five new monkeypods trees have been planted on both sides of the road to replace them.

Market Street in Old Wailuku Town is alive with the atmosphere of Old Hawaiʻi. The area, rich in history, was built on the site of ancient *heiaus* and has witnessed decisive Hawaiian battles. Later, the area hosted the likes of Mark Twain and Robert Redford. Now Wailuku emerges into a new century with a tip of the hat to the last. This rebirth is evident in Wailuku with the Main Street Promenade. The turn-of-the-20th-century architecture, old-style walkways, faux gaslight fixtures and a linear courtyard are all part of the ambitious revitalization plan. An open-air food court was planned as a "draw" for both residents and visitors to eat, stroll and be merry. Iron-wrought benches and historic pictures of territorial Wailuku accent the one-acre, three-story building complex of office, retail shops, additional parking and restaurants that comprise the 2000 block of Main Street.

Looking for farm-fresh produce at bargain prices? Check out the **farmer's market** next to the Iao Theater. Open 7 a.m. to 7 p.m.

You'll find a nice little café with internet connection on the corner of Market. If you're interested in all that glitters be sure to stop by **Precision Goldsmiths** at 16 North Market Street; 808-986-8282. The three proprietors of this little gem of a store produce world-class jewelry using high-tech equipment along with old-world craftsmanship. Whether you want a special piece reminiscent of your Hawaiʻi visit, a unique or traditional wedding set, or a design of your own, these award-winning designers/jewelers have the artistic talent and personal desire to meet your jewelry wishes. Darren, Brian and Gary invite you to stop in and visit their showroom Monday through Friday 9 a.m. to 5 p.m. Discover the ever present aloha spirit at this jewelry store. You can also call to arrange after-hour appointments. www.precisiongoldsmith.com.

Set against the lush backdrop of the Iao Valley and the West Maui Mountains, this area offers a quaint alternative to the hustle-bustle vacation centers of Lahaina and Kihei. Surrounding this area is a multitude of wonderful and inexpensive ethnic restaurants. So don't limit your excursion to the few shops on the corner of Market and Main streets.

A short drive down Market Street is **Takamiya's Market**. They have a large selection of ready-cooked foods. Another grocery store,

Ooka Supermarket on Main Street, has some of the island's best grocery values. They also have some interesting local foods.

There are three large shopping centers in Kahului, all on Ka'ahumanu Avenue. The **Maui Mall** is only a two-minute drive from the airport. Across the street from Safeway and the Ross Dress for Less store, this is where you'll find Star Market and a Longs Drugs that is great for picking up sundry and souvenir items. There are also a variety of small shops and restaurants and a Maui institution: *tasaka guri guri*, a kind of local creamy sherbet you can order with or without beans at the bottom of the cone. The **Paper Airplane Museum** (808-877-8916) features the unique juice-can creations of the Tin Can Man along with aviation model exhibits and pictures depicting the history of aviation in the Hawaiian islands.

The older, local-style **Kahului Shopping Center** is lined with monkeypod trees and filled with local residents playing cards. Check out Ah Fook's grocery for their bentos. The largest shopping center is **Queen Ka'ahumanu Center**, with a second level that includes a food court. Three major department stores Sears, Macy's and Liberty House anchor this mall with the island's largest selection of clothing and gift shops in between. Here is where you'll find the Disney Store, Waldenbooks, Gap, Kids' Foot Locker and a large food court. A great place to spend a rainy day on Maui so shop, eat and see a movie.

If you don't have accommodations with a kitchen or mini-refrigerator, you might want to pick up a styrofoam-type ice chest at one of these centers. Stock it with juices, lunch meats and whatnot to enjoy in your hotel room and for use on beach trips or drives to Hana and Haleakala. (Check with your hotel regarding small in-room refrigerators.)

There is a **Big Kmart** at the intersection of Dairy Road and the Hana Highway and next door is **Costco**, a wholesale warehouse. Membership is required, but it is good at any of their Hawai'i or mainland stores. Costco has some great deals; be sure to check out their Hawaiiana CD music and books—not a complete selection, but good prices on those items that they do stock. Big Kmart has convenient hours (7 a.m. to 10 p.m.) and some very good values on everyday items such as sandals. The downside is that the combination of Costco and Big Kmart has really increased the traffic on Dairy Road. **Walmart** and **Home Depot** are also located here.

Adding to the congestion is the **Maui Marketplace**, which includes a number of large, mainland-style outlets. This is where you'll also find Borders Books, Music & Café and Starbucks.

Triangle Square (isn't that an oxymoron?) is located nearby at the intersection of the Hana and Haleakala Highways. Hi-Tech Surf Sports, Maui Sails and Nevada Bob's are here.

Upcountry

The western slopes of Haleakala are generally known as Upcountry and consist of several communities including Makawao and Pukalani. The higher altitude, cooler temperatures and increased rainfall make it an ideal location for produce farming. A few fireplace chimneys can be spotted in this region where the nights can get rather chilly. Upcountry, where the air is cool and clear, is an awesome location to spend at least part of your vacation holiday; if you love hiking and the outdoors the opportunities are in your backyard. My suggestion is if you have a two-week vacation spend three or four of them in Upcountry.

Haleakala means "house of the sun" and is claimed to be the largest dormant volcano in the world. While it rises 10,023 feet above sea level, the greater portion of this magnificent mountain lies below the ocean. If measured from the sea floor, Haleakala would rise to a height of nearly 30,000 feet. The volcano is truly awesome and it is easy to see why the old Hawaiians considered it sacred and the center of the earth's spiritual power.

Haleakala National Park was created in 1916, but the first ranger did not arrive until 1935. In July 1945 the park, concerned about the vandalism of endangered plants, began checking visitors' cars. The park encompasses two districts, the Summit District and the Kipahulu District. The Kipahulu District, on the South Shore near Hana, will be discussed later. The charge for entry to the Summit District is $10 per car, U.S. residents 62 and older enter free. Free admission if you have a current card for the National Park System ($50 for a yearly pass to all parks). The most direct route is to follow Highway 37 from Kahului, left onto Highway 377 above Pukalani, and then left again onto Highway 378 for the last 10 miles. While only about 40 miles from Kahului, the last part of the trip is very slow. There are numerous switchbacks and bicycle tours doing the 38-mile downhill coast. Two hours should be allowed to reach the summit.

Sunrise at the summit is a popular and memorable experience, but plan your arrival accordingly. Many visitors have missed this spectacular event by only minutes. The *Maui News*, the local daily, prints sunrise and sunset times. The park offers a recording of general weather information and viewing conditions that can be accessed by calling 808-577-5111. Be sure you have packed a sweater as the summit temperature can be 30 degrees cooler than the coast and snow is a winter possibility. Early to mid-morning from May to October generally offers the clearest viewing. However, fog (or vog) can cause very limited visibility and a call may save you a trip.

Upcountry

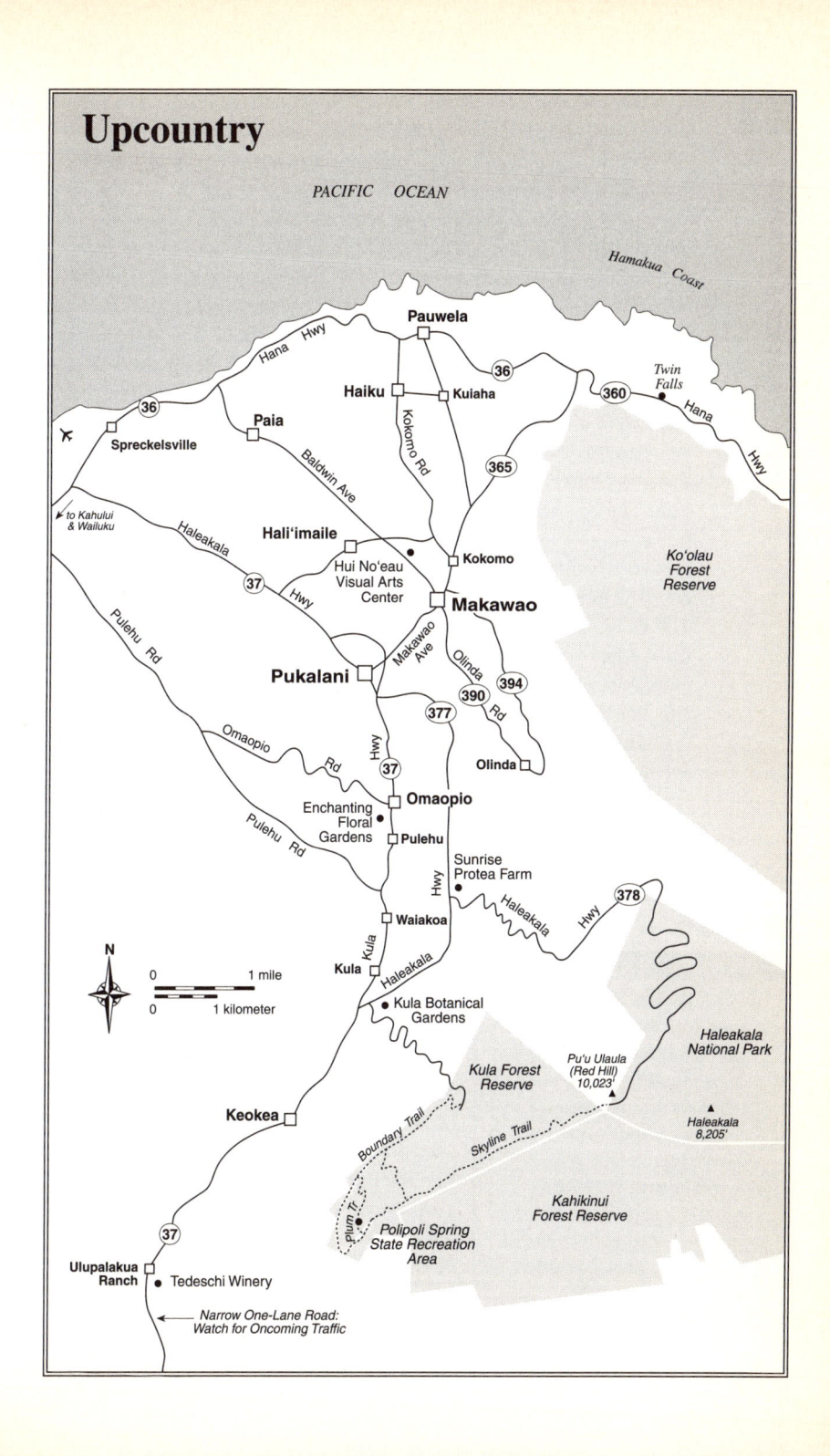

The first stop for visitors is **Park Headquarters** (808-572-4400). Hiking and camping information and permits are available here (see "Hiking" in Chapter 6 for information on trails). You can also see an example of the rare **silversword** that takes up between 20 to 50 years to mature, then blooms in a profusion of small purplish blossoms in July or August. It then withers and dies in the fall. Some years many silverswords may flower, in other years there may be none. The Hawaiian word for silversword is *'ahinahina*. (Hina is the goddess of the moon.) Once, the silverswords grew in abundance and were even used on floats for parades in the early part of the 1900s. By the 1930s, however, wild cattle, goats and sheep found them so appealing that there were only a few thousand silversword plants remaining.

Exhibits on Haleakala history and geology are in the **Haleakala Visitors Center**, located at an elevation of 9,745 feet. It is open daily from sunrise to 3 p.m., hours may vary. A short distance by road will bring you to the **Summit Building** located on the volcano rim. This glassed-in vantage point (the Pu'u Ulaula outlook) is the best for sunrise. The rangers give morning talks here at 9:30, 10:30 and 11:30 a.m. The view, on a good day, is nothing short of awesome. The inside of the volcano is 7 miles long, 2 miles wide and 3,000 feet deep. A closer look is available by foot or horseback (see "Horseback Riding" in Chapter 6).

The park service maintains 30 miles of well-marked trails that access three cabins and two campgrounds. The three cabins are Holua, Kapalaoa and Paliku, all located within the Haleakala Wilderness Area. These cabins are for "real" hikers as they are accessible only by trail. (The closest cabins are 4 to 10 miles away from the trailheads.) These cabins are available through a lottery system. See "Camping: Haleakala National Park" in Chapter 6 for detailed information.

Haleakala Observatories can be seen beyond the visitor center, but the buildings are not open to the public. They house a solar and lunar observatory operated by the University of Hawaii, television relay stations and a Department of Defense satellite station. Eight telescopes (located on the top of Haleakala) perform work for the Department of Defense in space surveillance and optical research and development. www.ulua.mhpcc.af.mil/~det3.

If time allows, there is more of Upcountry to be seen. The **Kula** area offers rich volcanic soil and commercial farmers harvest a variety of fruits and vegetables.

HIKING HALEAKALA

A 2.5-hour hike down **Sliding Sands Trail** into the Haleakala Volcano is offered by the park service regularly. Check bulletin boards for schedules. They depart from the Haleakala Visitors Center. A hike featuring native Hawaiian birds and plants is scheduled regularly. Keep your eye out for the many nene (geese) that inhabit the volcano. Check with the ranger headquarters (808-572-4400) to verify trips, dates and times.

Haleakala National Park

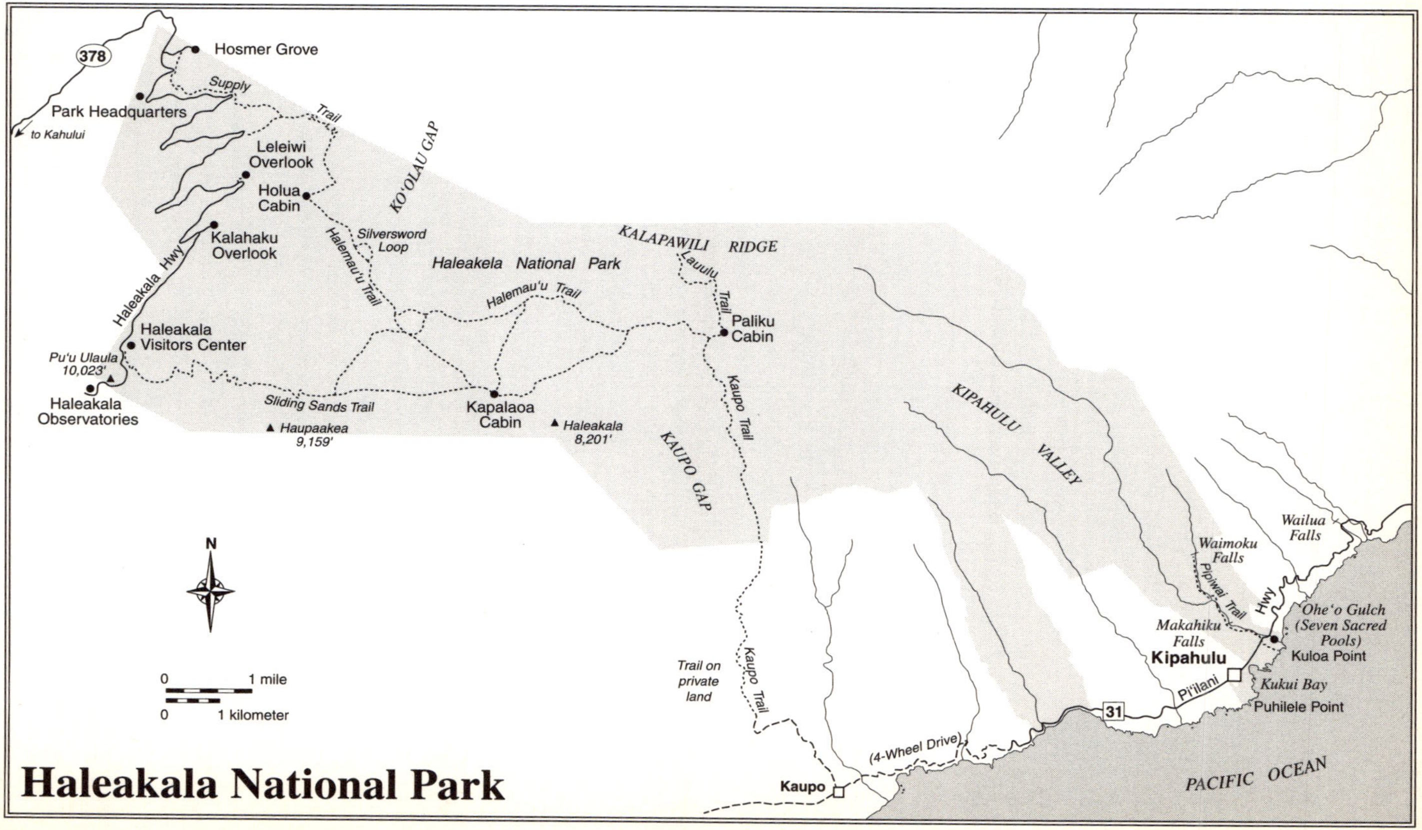

Grapes, apples, pineapples, lettuce, artichokes, tomatoes and, of course, Maui onions are only a few examples. The town can be reached by retracing Highway 378 to the Upper Kula Road, where you turn left. The protea, a floral immigrant from South Africa, has created a profitable business as well.

The **Kula Botanical Gardens** charges $5 adults, $1 children 6 to 12 years to tour their six-acre facility with over 2,000 plants. Open 9 a.m. to 4 p.m. 808-878-1715.

The **Enchanting Floral Gardens**, on Highway 37 in Kula, charges $5 adults, $1 children for a self-guided botanical tour. Open 9 a.m. to 5 p.m. 808-878-2531.

The **Sunrise Protea Farm** in Kula has a small but diverse variety of protea growing adjacent to their market and flower stand for shipment home. Dried assortments begin at about $25. Picnic tables available. 808-876-0200.

Be sure and stop in Keokea at **Grandma's Coffee House**. This wonderfully cozy restaurant is the place for some freshly made, Maui-grown coffee, hot-out-of-the-oven cinnamon rolls or a light lunch. See Chapter 4 for more information.

Polipoli Springs State Recreation Area is a state park high on the slopes of Haleakala above Kula at an elevation of 6,200 feet. Continue on Highway 377 past Kula and turn left on Waipoli Road; if you end up on Highway 37, you've gone too far. The sign indicating Poli Poli may be difficult to spot, so you could also look for the sign indicating someone's home that reads "Walker" (assuming it's still there). It's another 10 miles to the park. Fortunately, the road has been paved, making accessibility easy. The 10-acre park offers miles of trails, a picnic area, restrooms, running water, a small redwood forest and great views. This is an excellent trail for the non-athlete or family. Keep your eye out for earth that appears disturbed. This is an indication of one of the wild boars at work. While not likely, I still advise you to keep your ears alert—you don't want to encounter one. On one occasion while hiking with my family we heard them rumbling in the brush near the trail.

Approximately nine miles past the Kula Botanical Gardens on Highway 37 is the **Ulupalakua Ranch**. The **Tedeschi Winery** (808-878-6058), part of the 30,000-acre ranch, made its debut in 1974. The king's cottage houses the Tasting Room, which provides samples of their pineapple champagne and red table wines at a mango-wood bar (handcrafted from one of the many trees at the surrounding ranch). Their latest label is a raspberry dessert wine. Free daily guided tours are offered between 10 a.m. and 5 p.m. The tour begins at the Tasting Room, then continues on to view the presses used to separate the juice from the grapes, the large fermenting tanks, and finally the corking and the labeling rooms. It is an interesting behind-the-scenes tour.

If you continue on past the ranch on Highway 37, it's another very long 35 miles to Hana with nothing but beautiful scenery. Don't let the distance fool you. It is a good three-hour trip (each way), at least, over some fairly rough sections of road that are not approved for standard rental cars. During recent years this road has been closed often to through traffic due to severe washouts. Check with the county to see if it is currently passable. I'd recommend doing just the first part of the road, driving as far as Kaupo. (See "Hana Highway" section below for more information.)

If you are not continuing on, I suggest you turn around and head back to **Pukalani** and **Makawao**. You can take the route down via Makawao, the colorful "cowboy" town, and then on to Paia or Hali'imaile. Both have several good restaurants.

The **Hui No'eau Visual Arts Center** may at first seem a little out of place, located at 2841 Baldwin Avenue, down the road from Makawao. However, there could not be a more beautiful and tranquil setting than at this estate called Kaluanui, built in 1917 by famous Honolulu architect C.W. Dickey for Harry and Ethel Baldwin. The house was occupied until the mid-1950s, and in 1976 Colin Cameron (grandson of Ethel Baldwin) granted Hui No'eau the use of Kaluanui as a visual arts center. A gift shop is open year round and the first part of December they have a special Christmas boutique. Near the entrance to the nine-acre estate are the remains of one of Maui's earliest sugar mills. It utilized mule power and was the first Hawaiian sugar mill to use a centrifuge to separate sugar crystals. What were once stables and tack rooms are now ceramic studios. Open daily 9 a.m. to 1 p.m. 808-572-6560.

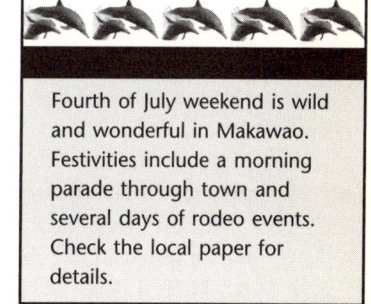

> Fourth of July weekend is wild and wonderful in Makawao. Festivities include a morning parade through town and several days of rodeo events. Check the local paper for details.

Maui Fresh Fruit Store and Farmer's Market is located in Hali'imaile, sandwiched between the Hali'imaile General Store and the plantation office. This is *the* place to pick up pineapples ready to take back to the mainland. They have history on the 100-year Maui Pineapple Company's plantation with photos and memorabilia. Local Maui growers offer their fresh fruits and vegetables here. Open Monday through Saturday 10 a.m. to 6 p.m. 808-573-5129; e-mail: mauipineapplestore@maui.net.

The town of Makawao offers a Western flavor with a scattering of shops down its main street. There are several good restaurants and grocery stores if you are feeling hungry. I recommend the **Komoda Store** for its popular bakery, but get there early if you want any of their famous cream puffs. **Olas's** and **Gallery Maui** on Makawao Avenue offer an intriguing selection of gifts (like obi sash wall hangings and stained-glass screens), and just up the street is the Maui School of Therapeutic Massage (808-572-2277), where you can treat yourself to a relaxing massage for just $25.

The Courtyard at 3620 Baldwin Avenue houses **Viewpoints Gallery** (808-572-5979), a fine cooperative gallery featuring local artists, and a cluster of interesting gift shops including **Hot Island Glass**. This glass-blowing studio and gallery is a Makawao must-see.

Nearby **Pukalani Terrace Center** has a grocery store and a few small shops. There is a Pizza Hut for take-out only, KFC, Subway as well as Royal King's Garden for Asian food or local style at Maui Mixed Plate.

Hana Highway

If you're traveling to Hana, plan on spending at least one night. Traveling with a family and making all the stops to see all the sights will be much more pleasant (and less exhausting) if it can be done leisurely. The road is very windy so another option for some is to fly from Kahului into Hana and save several hours on the twisting road. Check with your family physician if your children have trouble with motion sickness. My son had never had a problem with it until we were on the road to Hana. There are plenty of bed and breakfasts along the way if you'd like to linger longer along the Hana Highway.

The **Maui Crafts Guild** is owned and operated by a group of local artisans. *Koa* furniture, pottery, weaving, wall sculptures, wood serving pieces, prints and basketry are featured—very lovely, but expensive, hand-crafted items.

If you've heard any discussion at all about Maui, it has probably included a mention of the Hana Highway. The twisted, narrow route follows the windward shore down to Hana on the southern coast of the island. Hana is about as far away as you can get from tourism. More native Hawaiians live in this area than in any other part of Maui. A substantial reason for the isolation of Hana is the Hana Highway. Hana attracts the average traveler who yearns to get a taste of real Hawai'i as well as the celebrity attempting to find a little seclusion. Leaving Wailuku along Highway 36 you will continue to mile-marker 16; at this point Highway 365, also known as Kaupakulua Road, intersects. This is where the mile-markers return to zero, and this may be considered the official start of the Hana Highway.

There are a couple of good resources you might consider taking along on your drive. If you'd like a self-guided yet narrated tour, for less than $20 you can purchase a cassette tape "Best of Maui" that will guide you to the stops along the way. The tape allows you to drive at your own pace while listening to information on the legends and history of the islands. However, I listened to it but didn't find any information on the tape that wasn't included in this guidebook.

As I discuss later, it is a lengthy drive and will require a full day. (Insider's secret: Hana can best be enjoyed before and after the throngs of daily visitors who make this drive, so try to stay in Hana for a few days.) If you can't plan an extended stay in Hana, you might consider at least an overnight stop at one of the many accommodations to break up the long drive to this isolated east coast of Maui. The best travel days are Saturday and Sunday, since road crews are generally not at work and you won't encounter the many delivery trucks that keep Hana supplied with all its goods.

Here is a different Maui from the sunny, dry resort areas on the leeward coast. The windward coast here is turbulent with magnificent coastal views, rain forests and mountain waterfalls that create wonderful pools for swimming. However, *do not* drink the water from these streams and falls. The water has a high bacteria count from the pigs that live in the forests above. The beaches along the Hana Highway are unsafe for swimming.

The trip to Hana by car from Kahului will take at least three hours, one way, which allows for plenty of time to make some stops, enjoy these waterfalls up close and experience this unique coastline. Add another 45 to 60 minutes for travel from Lahaina/Kapalua areas.

Anyone who endures the three-hour (at least) drive to Hana deserves to sport the "I survived the Road to Hana" T-shirts that are sold locally. While it may be true that it is easy to fall in love with Hana, getting there is quite a different story. Even with greatly improved road conditions as a result of repaving, the drive to Hana is not for everyone. It is not for people who are prone to motion sickness, those who don't like a lot of scenery, those who are in a hurry to get somewhere, or those who don't love long drives. However, it is a trip filled with waterfalls and lush tropical jungles (which flourish in the 340-inch average annual rainfall).

Maps are deceiving. It appears you could make the 53-mile journey in much less than three hours, but there are 617 (usually hairpin) curves and 56 miniature bridges along this narrow road. And believe it or not, each of these bridges has its own Hawaiian name. You'll note in places that the road is so narrow there isn't even room to paint a center line! With drivers visually exploring the many scenic wonders, you may find cars traveling in the middle of the road, thus making each turn a potentially exciting experience.

The Hana Highway was originally built in 1927 with pick and shovel (which accounts for its narrowness) to provide a link between Hana and Kahului. In days gone by when heavy rains caused washouts, it is said that people would literally climb the mud barricades and swap cars, then resume their journey. Today there can be delays on the road of up to two hours if the road is being worked on or a landslide has occurred. Despite all this, hundreds of people traverse this road daily, and it is the supply route for all deliveries to Hana and the small settlements along the way.

Now, if I haven't dissuaded you, and you still want to see spectacular undeveloped scenery, plan to spend the whole day (or even better, stop overnight) in Hana. If you are driving, be sure to leave as early in the morning as possible. You don't want to be making a return trip on this road in the dark. Be sure to get gas (the last stations before Hana are in Kahului or Paia) and be sure you pack your own food and drink. With the exception of an occasional fruit stand, there is no place to eat and only limited stops for drinking water

Picnics in Paia is a popular stop for a picnic lunch—their newsprint menu even offers a Hana map with points of interest. For something a little more unusual try packing along some local-style foods or a bento. Takamiya's Market on Lower Market Street has an unbelievable assortment of cooked, pre-packaged food made fresh daily.

Whether you are planning a day or an extended visit in Hana, packing some rain gear and a warm sweater or sweatshirt is a precaution against the sometimes cooler weather and rain showers. Don't forget your camera, but remember not to leave it in your car unattended. I strongly recommend you take along some mosquito repellent.

If you drive, select a car with an automatic transmission (or else be prepared for constant shifting). Another choice is to try one of the affordable van tours (or splurge with a company such as Temptation Tours) that go to Hana and leave the driving to them. Be aware that drivers will be so busy watching the road, they won't have much opportunity to enjoy the spectacular scenery. If you don't wish to retrace your route along the windward shore's Hana Highway, check to see whether the tours are operating their vans around the other, leeward side of the island. This route follows the Pi'ilani Highway and travel will depend on the road conditions. And you thought the Hana Highway was rugged? This route can be traveled in your personal vehicle, but rental car disclaimers warn against or prohibit travel along

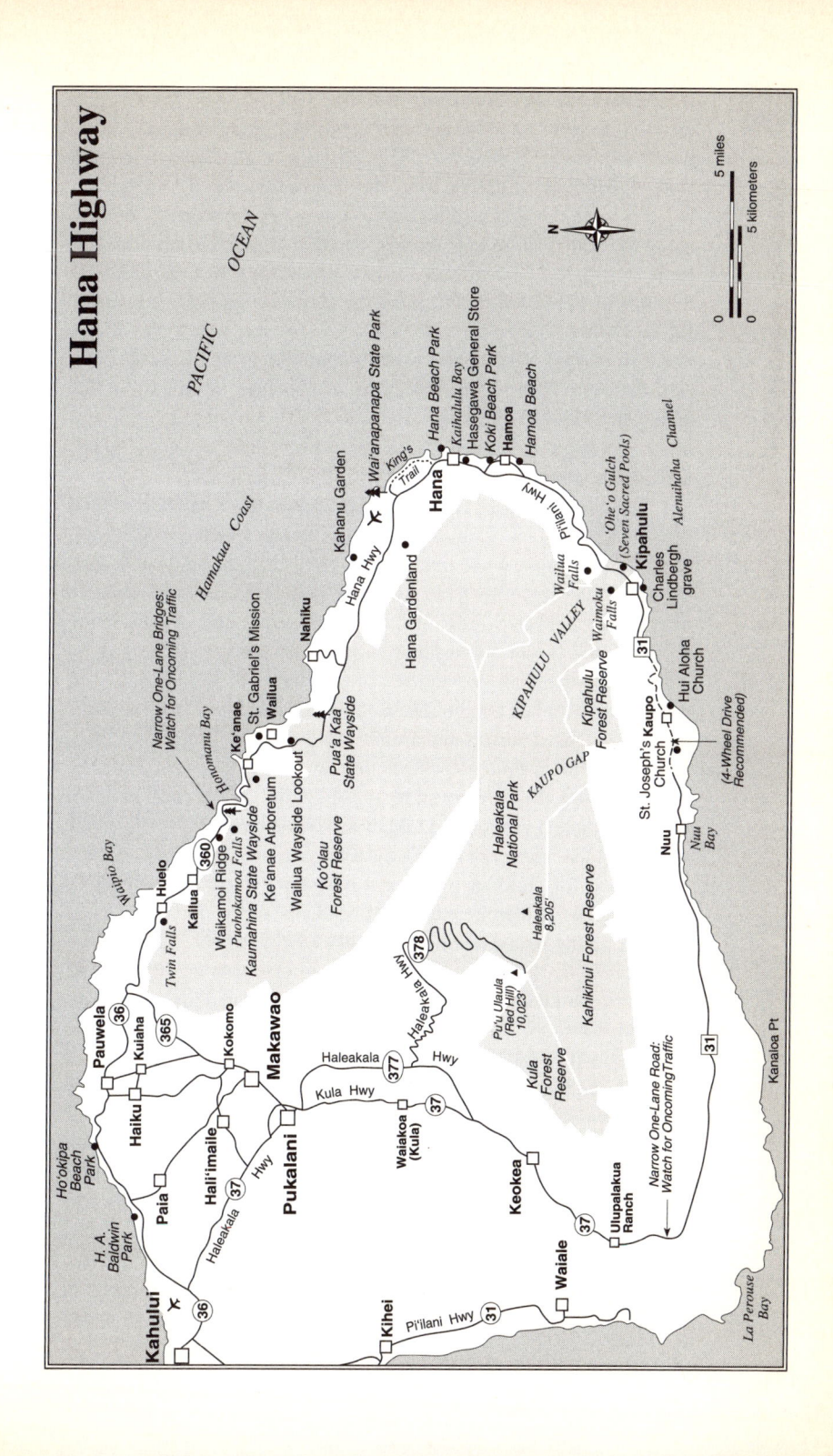

Hana Highway

it. The exception is some companies that rent four-wheel-drive vehicles. Check with the rental companies for their guidelines and restrictions. The scenery along the Pi'ilani Highway, on this dry leeward side, is strikingly different from the windward coastal rain forests. Good tour guides will also be able to point out the sights of interest along the way that are easy to miss. Another alternative is to drive to Hana and then fly out of Hana's small airport back to Kahului.

A little beyond Wailuku, along the highway that leads to Hana, is the small town of **Paia**. Paia means "noisy," but the origin of this name is unclear. This quaint town is reminiscent of the early sugar cane era when Henry Baldwin located his first sugar plantation in this area. The wooden buildings are now filled with antiques, art and other gift shops to attract the passing tourist. The advent of windsurfing has caused a rebirth in this small charming town.

Just two miles past Paia is one the island's most popular seafood restaurants on Maui, Mama's Fish House. If the winds are right, you will be able to spot what appear to be colorful giant butterflies darting along the ocean offshore. This is **Ho'okipa**, thought by some to offer the world's best windsurfing. There won't be much activity in the morning, but if you are heading past here in mid- to late afternoon when the winds pick up, you are sure to see numerous windsurfers daring both wind and wave. These waves are enough to challenge the most experienced surfers and are not for the novice except as a spectator sport. You'll note that on the left are the windsurfers while the waves on the right are enjoyed by surfers. A number of covered pavilions offer shaded viewing, and the beach, while not recommended for swimming, has some tidepools (of varying size depending on the tidal conditions) for children to enjoy a refreshing splash. This beach is also a popular fishing area for local residents and you may see some folks along the banks casting their lines.

At mile-marker 11 and mile-marker 14 are turnoffs to Haiku and Makawao. **Haiku** is a couple of miles inland and noted for its two canneries that have been converted into local, Hawaiian-style mini-malls. The first is the **Haiku Cannery**, and if you're hankering for some of Maui's finest local grinds or a box lunch for the road, then definitely make a stop at Hana Hou Café located here. Farther up, the **Pauwela Cannery** is home to Pauwela Café, where you'll find find excellent homemade breakfasts and lunches. Just past mile-marker 15 is **Maui Grown Market** and a chance to pick up some picnic food fare and beverages. The Hawaiian translation for Haiku is "abrupt break"; it is not unusual to experience some overcast, rainy weather here. Highway 36 ends just past mile-marker 16. At this point on Highway 365 there is an intersection with Kaupakulua Road. The Hana Highway continues from here, but it is now Highway 360 and the mile-markers begin again at zero. So begins the Hana Highway.

Just past mile-marker 2 you will reach the Hoolawa Bridge. You will probably spot a number of cars on the roadside as well as a fruit stand, the first of many you'll find along the road to Hana. The trek is up the one-mile trail to the waterfall. This area, known as **Twin Falls**, offers a pleasant spot for swimming. The first pool has two waterfalls, but by hiking a little farther, two more pools of crystal-clear water created by waterfalls can be easily reached. This is a fairly easy hike, so a good one for the entire family. Remember, don't drink the stream water here or from any other freshwater stream or pool. Mosquitoes can be prolific so pack bug spray.

There are no safe beaches along this route for swimming, so for a cool dip, take advantage of one of the freshwater swimming holes. Be adventurous and stop along one of the bridges. Most have trails running up to the waterfalls, but please respect posted, private lands.

A bit past mile-maker 3 is **Huelo**. A short drive at the turnoff will take you down to a historic coral block church built in 1853.

Past mile-marker 9 (about .4 mile) is the **Waikamoi Ridge Nature Trail**. And near mile-marker 10 is the **Waikamo Bridge**. A trail to the right of the bridge goes up from the first to a beautiful, higher second pool. Also near mile-marker 10 is **Garden of Eden**. They have a picnic area, restrooms, viewpoints and a nature area. There are parrots that you can get a photo shoot with and they have done an excellent job of labeling the local floral. Open 8 a.m. to 3 p.m. Admission $7.50 per car.

Puohokamoa Falls is located near mile-marker 11. There is a pull-off area with parking only for a couple of cars. This small picnic area offers one covered table (in the event of one of the frequent windward coast rain showers). A short tunnel trail through lush foliage leads to a spectacular swimming hole beneath the waterfall.

Kaumahina State Wayside is located just past mile-marker 12. Here you'll find a lovely park. This area overlooks the spectacular Honomanu Gulch, the rugged Maui coastline and in the distance the Ke'anae Peninsula. This is a good opportunity to make use of the restroom facilities.

There is a dirt turnoff a half mile past mile-marker 13. It travels down to **Honomanu Bay**. This a pristine and peaceful black-lava bay. There is another entrance to the same bay by mile-marker 14 down a rougher piece of road.

Just past Camp Ke'anae is the **Ke'anae Arboretum**. This free six-acre botanical garden is managed by the Department of Land and Natural Resources and is home to myriad tropical plants. A number

> Just past the Ke'anae Arboretum is a dead-end that turns off *makai* (to the sea). Follow it down to the ocean and enjoy some spectacular pinnacle lava formations along this peninsula. With the azure Pacific pounding onto the volcanic coastline, it is truly spectacular. The small island offshore is **Mokumana Island**, a sanctuary for seabirds. This is a great stop to let the kids run around and stretch their legs. At Keanae Landing you'll find a little stand that serves up freshly made banana bread and delicious fruit smoothies (two fellows we spoke with had driven over from Kahului just to buy banana bread). Located here is the small **Ke'anae Congregational Church**. The church was built in 1860 of lava and coral and invites visitors to come in and sign their guestbook.

of the plants have been labeled for your assistance in identification. Traveling farther up the trail you can view taro patches and hike into the rainforest.

The **Ke'anae Peninsula** was formed by a massive outpouring centuries ago from the volcano Haleakala. The lava poured out of the volcano, flowed down the Ko'olau Gap and stopped in this valley. Today it is an agricultural area with taro, the principal crop. The taro root is cooked and mashed and the result is a bland, pinkish brown paste called poi. Poi was a staple in the diets of early Hawaiians and is still a popular local food product that can be sampled at luaus or purchased at local groceries. Alone, the taste has been described as resembling wallpaper paste (if you've ever tried wallpaper paste) but it is meant to be eaten with other foods, such as *kalua* pig. It is a taste that sometimes needs time to acquire. I understand island grandmothers send fresh poi to the mainland for their young grandbabies. Poi is extremely healthy, full of minerals and well tolerated by young stomachs.

At mile-marker 18 turn *makai* (left) and you'll reach the main attraction in Wailua, **Our Lady of Fatima Shrine**, also known as the **Miracle Church**. This historical landmark has a fascinating history. In the mid-1800s the community lacked building materials for their church. The common practice was for men to dive into the ocean and bring up pieces of coral. Obviously, this was very laborious and time consuming. Quite suddenly a huge storm hit and, by some miracle, deposited a load of coral onto the beach. The story continues that following the construction of the church, another storm hit and returned the remaining coral back to the sea. Now painted, the coral church walls are still standing today. It is set back from the road.

Another church on the road is the 100-year old **St. Gabriel's Mission**. Upcoming around a bend in the road near mile-marker 19 is the **Wailua Wayside Lookout.** Look carefully for the turnoff on the right. Park and follow the tunnel made by the *hau* plants up the steps to the lookout. The short trek up is worth the excellent view. Back up to the highway and head a few hundred yards to the next lookout. Here you can take a few photos of the incredible Keʻanae Peninsula. There are no signs, but it is easy to spot this gravel area on the left of the roadside.

The slice of this green wonderland seen from the winding Hana Highway is just a small piece of the rugged wilderness above. The **waterfalls** are spectacular along the road, but consider what they are like from the air! I had no idea of the vastness of this tropical forest until I experienced a bird's-eye view. Almost every waterfall and pool is preceded by another waterfall and pool above it, and above it there are yet others.

A half mile past marker 22 is **Puaʻa Kaa State Wayside.** This picture-perfect state park offers two waterfalls that are only a short walk from the roadside. This is a favorite stop for a picnic lunch. The waterfalls and pools combine with this lush tropical locale to make you feel sure a *menehune* must be lurking nearby. Restrooms and drinking water are available here, too. Keep your eye out for mongoose. They have been "trained" by some of the van tour guides to make an appearance for a handout at some of these wayside stations. The best place to get a look at them is usually near the garbage cans. If you don't spot a mongoose, you'll probably meet one of many stray cats. They seem to subsist on the garbage that visitors leave here.

With a little effort a sharp observer can spot the open ditches and dams along the roadside. These are the **Spreckles Ditches** built over 100 years ago to supply water for the young sugar cane industry. These ditches continue to provide the island with an important part of its supply of water.

At mile-marker 25 just past the bridge on the left is a road to Nahiki. This was once a rubber plantation that operated from 1905 to 1916. No real signs left. Between mile-markers 26 and 27 is **Nahiki Tropicals** with plenty of plants available to ship home to family, friends or yourself. If you're hungry there is a little village on your left. **Nahiki Gallery and Gifts** offers some shopping options and the outdoor deli has fish kabobs, *kalua* pork sandwiches, corn on the cob and even baked breadfruit. A fruit stand, too.

Just before mile-marker 31, the road begins to straighten out. Look for the flagpoles to **Hana Gardenland,** which has gardens and trails to explore.

The National Tropical Botanical Garden operates the 126-acre **Kahanu Garden,** reached by turning *makai* (toward the sea) on Ulaino Road, just past mile-marker 31. It is 1.5 miles to the entrance of the garden. The garden is located at Kalahu Point, which is also the location of Hawai'i's largest *heiau*, the six-centuries-old **Pi'ilanihale Heiau**; it was constructed by the sons of Maui chief Pi'ilani in his honor. Restoration of the *heiau* is ongoing and two gardens have been added. Self-guided tours Monday through Friday 10 a.m. to 2 p.m. (closed some holidays). Adults $10, children 12 and under free. 808-248-8912; e-mail: kahanu@ntbg.org.

Wai'anapanapa State Park is four miles before Hana at milemarker 32. It covers an area of 120 acres. Translated, Wai'anapanapa means "glistening water." This area offers a number of historical sites, ancient *heiaus* and early cemeteries. You can spot one of the many lava rock walls used by the early Hawaiians for property boundaries, animal enclosures and also as home foundations. Wai'anapanapa is noted for its unusual black-sand beach made of small, smooth volcanic pebbles. From the rocky cliff protrudes a natural lava arch on the side of Pailoa Bay. This can be reached by following the short path down from the parking lot at the end of the road. The ocean here is not safe for swimming, but there is plenty to explore.

Splash on some mosquito repellent, tennis shoes are a good idea, and follow the well-marked trails to the **Wai'anapanapa Caves**. The trail is lined with thick vines, a signal left by the early Hawaiians that this area was *kapu* (off limits). The huge lava tubes have created pools of cold, clear water. An ancient cave legend tells of a beautiful Hawaiian princess named Popoalaea who fled from Kakae, her cruel husband. She hid in the caves, but was discovered and killed. At certain times of the year the waters turn red. Some say it is a reminder of the beautiful slain princess, while others explain that it is the infestation of thousands of tiny red shrimp.

> If you plan on arriving in Hana after 5 p.m., make sure you have either dinner plans at the Hotel Hana Maui or some food for your evening meal. The Hana Ranch Restaurant is open only a couple of nights a week for full dinners. All other local restaurants close by 5 p.m., as does the Hasegawa General Store.

In ancient times there was a trail that circumnavigated the entire island along a coastal route. Known as the King's Highway, it once traversed 138 miles. Maui is the only island to have had a trail that connected the entire island. Remnants of the King's Highway can be found from here to La Perouse Bay. Examining the King's Highway you can almost imagine the Hawaiians of years gone by traveling over these smooth stones. The stones were placed on top of the sharp lava rock for obvious reasons. The effort it took to place this many stones must have been tremendous. You can follow this trail east toward Hana, passing a blowhole as well as *heiau* ruins and ending near Hana town at Kainalimu Bay. The trail also goes north toward the Hana Airport for a short distance.

Camping is allowed at Wai'anapanapa in their rustic cabins available for rent, $5 per family per night per campsite, with maximum 10 people. (See Chapter 3 for more information.)

Now, back in the car for a drive into downtown **Hana**, but don't blink, or you might miss it. Hana offers a quiet retreat and an atmosphere of peace (seemingly undisturbed by the constant flow of tourist cars and vans) that has lured many a prominent personality to these quiet shores. Restaurant choices are extremely limited. The diversity between eating at Tutu's at Hana Bay and the fine dining of the Hotel Hana Maui is quite striking. Shopping is restricted to the Hasegawa General Store, the Hana Ranch Store or a few shops at the Hana Hotel.

Hana Cultural Center opened in 1983. It contains a collection of relics of Hana's past in the old courthouse building and a small museum. Located on Uakea Road Street near Hana Bay, watch for signs. Open Monday through Friday 10 a.m. to 4 p.m., and half days on Saturday and Sunday. Admission $2. 808-248-8622.

Hana Bay has been the site of many historical events. It was a retreat for Hawaiian royalty as well as an important military point from which Maui warriors attacked the island of Hawai'i, and then were, in turn, attacked. This is also the birthplace of Ka'ahumanu (1768), Kamehameha's favorite wife. (See Chapter 5 for more information.)

The climate on this end of Maui is cooler and wetter, creating an ideal environment for agricultural development. The Ka'eleku Sugar Company established itself in Hana in 1860. Cattle raising, also a prominent industry during the 20th century, continues today. You can still view the *paniolos* (Hawaiian cowboys) at work at nearby **Hana Ranch**. There are 3,200 head of cattle that graze on 3,300 acres of land. Every three days the cattle are moved to fresh pastures. My family was thrilled when a *paniolo* flagged us to stop on the road outside Hana while a herd of cattle surrounded our car en route to greener pastures.

Hana has little to offer in the way of shopping. However, the **Hasegawa General Store** offers a little bit of everything. It has operated since 1910, meeting the needs of visitors and local residents alike. Several years ago the original structure was burned down, but they reopened in the old Hana Theatre location. This store has even been immortalized in song. You might just run into one of the celebrities who come to the area for vacation. Hours are Monday through Saturday 8 a.m. to 5 p.m., Sunday 9 a.m. to 5 p.m.

On **Lyon's Hill** stands a 30-foot-tall lava-rock cross in memory of Paul Fagan, a founding father of modern-day Hana. It was built by two Japanese brothers from Kahului in 1960. Although the access road is chained, the front desk of the Hotel Hana-Maui will provide a key. The short trip to the top will reward the visitor with a spectacular panoramic view of Hana Bay and the open pasture land of the Hana Ranch. About a quarter of a mile up toward the cross you'll find the beginning of a jogging/walking trail that follows the track of the old narrow-gauge railroad once used on the plantation. The path runs for about 2.5 miles.

Kaihalulu Beach (Red Sand Beach) is located in a small cove on the other side of Kauiki Hill from Hana Bay and is accessible by a narrow, crumbly trail more suited to mountain goats than people. The trail descends into a lovely cove bordered by high cliffs and is almost entirely enclosed by a natural lava barrier seaward. Far too many accidents have happened on this dangerous access so we can't recommend it. (See Chapter 5 for more details.)

Hamoa Beach is a gorgeous beach that has been very attractively landscaped and developed by the Hotel Hana-Maui in a manner that adds to the surrounding lushness. The long sandy beach is in a very tropical setting and surrounded by a low sea cliff. As you leave Hana toward the Pools of 'Ohe'o, look for the sign 1.5 miles past the Hasegawa store that says "Koki Park–Hamoa Beach–Hamoa Village." Follow the road, you can't miss it.

You'll quickly pass fields of grazing world-famous Maui beef cattle and re-enter the tropical jungle once more. Numerous waterfalls cascade along the roadside and after ten curvy, bumpy miles on a very narrow two-lane road (a 45- to 60-minute drive) you arrive at one of the reasons for this trip, the **Kipahulu Valley** and **Haleakala National Park**. The Kipahulu Ranger Station offers cultural demonstrations, talks and guided walks. Parking fee, $10 per vehicle. 808-248-7375.

Looking for the Seven Sacred Pools? They don't exist! The National Park Service notes that the term "Seven Sacred Pools" has been misused in this area for more than 50 years. The name was first promoted in 1946 by the social director of a newly developed hotel in Hana to attract visitors to the area. Along the stream there are actually more than 24 large and small pools along the one-mile length of the gulch, so even the term "Seven Pools" is misleading and inaccurate. The term *'Ohe'o* refers to the name of the area where the Pipiwai Stream enters the ocean. When the Kipahulu District was acquired by Haleakala National Park in 1969, park rangers interviewed native Hawaiians born and raised in the area to document its history. Without exception all local residents claimed that none of the pools was ever considered sacred. In 1996 the Haleakala National Park finally settled on a name. So now when you head to Kipahulu you can visit the **Pools of 'Ohe'o.**

Beneath the narrow bridge water cascades over the blue-gray lava to create the lovely lower pools. These are just a few of the more than 20 pools that have been formed as the water of this stream rushes to the ocean. When not in flood stage, the pools are safe for swimming so pack your suit (*caution:* no diving allowed). Swimming off the black-sand beach is very dangerous and many drownings and near-drownings have occurred here. The best time to enjoy the park may be in late afternoon when the day visitors have returned to their cars for the drive home. (This is another good reason to make Hana an overnight trip.) The bluff above the beach offers a magnificent view of the ocean and cliffs, so have your camera ready.

This area is of historical significance and signs warn visitors not to remove any rocks. A pleasant hike will take you to the upper falls. The falls at **Makahiku** are 184 feet high and there is a fairly easy half-mile hike that passes through a forest. **Waimoku Falls** is another mile and a half. Three to four hours should be allowed for this hike that traverses the stream and winds through a bamboo forest. Heavy rains

HANA'S HOURS

The **Hana Ranch Store** is open daily and the **Hana Resort** has a gift shop and boutique. The oldest building in town, built in 1830, currently houses the laundry facility for the Hana Hotel.

St. Mary's Church (808-248-8030) Saturday Mass 5 p.m., Sunday 9 a.m.

Wananalua Protestant Church (808-248-8040) Established in 1838. Church services 10 a.m. Sunday

Hana Ranch Store (808-248-8261) 7 a.m. to 7 p.m. daily

Hasegawa General Store (808-248-8231) Monday through Saturday 8 a.m. to 5:30 p.m., Sunday 9 a.m. to 4:30 p.m.

Hana Community Health Center (808-248-8294) Emergencies 24 hours. Monday through Thursday 8 a.m. to 10 p.m., Friday 8 a.m. to 8 p.m., Saturday 8 a.m. to 5 p.m. Closed Sunday

Bank of Hawaii (808-248-8015) Monday through Thursday 3 to 4:30 p.m., Friday 3 to 6 p.m. (Hana must have been the place where they coined the term "Banker's Hours")

Library (808-248-7714) Monday 8 a.m. to 8 p.m., Tuesday through Friday 8 a.m. to 5 p.m. Closed Saturday and Sunday

Post Office (808-248-8258) Monday through Friday, 8 a.m. to 4:30 p.m.

Hana Theater (808-248-7568)

in the mountains far above can result in flash floods. Avoid swimming in these upper streams or crossing the stream in high water. Check with the park rangers who keep advised as to possible flooding conditions. Also check with the park service (808-248-7375) to see when the free ranger-guided hikes are available. Cultural demonstrations are given daily, check the bulletin boards for schedules.

Camping at Kipahulu is available at no charge. Be advised there is no drinking water. Bottled water may be available for a minimal cost at the ranger station, but I suggest you arrive with your own supply.

One interesting fact about Kipahulu is that many of the marine animals here have evolved from saltwater origins. Others continue to make the transition between the ocean's salty environment and the fresh water of the Palikea stream. One of the most unusual is the rare *oopu* that breeds in the upper stream, migrates to the ocean during its youth and then returns to the stream to mature. After a glimpse of the many waterfalls, this appears to be a most remarkable feat. The ingenious *oopu* actually climbs the falls by using its lower front fins as a suction cup to hold onto the steep rock walls. Using its tail to propel itself, the *oopu* then travels slowly upstream.

The upper Kipahulu Valley is a place visitors will never see. Under the jurisdiction of the park service, it is one of the last fragments of the native rain forests. The native plants in the islands have been destroyed by the more aggressive plants brought by the early Hawaiians and visitors in the centuries that followed. Some rare species, such as the green silversword, grow only in this restricted area.

Two miles farther on is the **Charles Lindbergh grave**, located in the small cemetery. Just past mile-marker 41 you'll see a sign for the Pala Pala Hoomanu Congregational Church. Turn *mauka* (toward the ocean) on this road called Ho'oma, and a sign indicating the 1850 **Kipahulu Hawaiian Church**. Lindbergh chose this site only a year prior to his death in 1974, after living in the area for a number of years. However, he never envisioned the huge numbers of visitors that would come to Hana to enjoy the scenery and visit his gravesite. A little-known fact are the graves near Sam Pryor and Pryor's wife, Mary, that bears only a single name and a hand-scribbled date on the worn cement marker. I was told these are the graves of six pet monkeys. Sam Pryor, the president of Pan American Airways, was instrumental in encouraging Lindbergh to relocate to Hana following the death of Lindbergh's young child. Pryor apparently had an affection for those primates, and so buried his pets in this churchyard. Please respect the sanctity of this area.

It is possible to travel the back road from Hana through Upcountry and back to Kahului. Sometimes the trip is more arduous than others depending on the road conditions. The trip from Hana to

Ulupalakua is a very slow 37 miles. This is Maui's desert region and it is a vivid contrast to the lush windward environs. You will be following Highway 31 (Pi'ilani Highway) from Hana along the southern coast until you gradually move inland and begin the ascent up the slopes of Upcountry, joining Highway 37 or the Kula Highway.

While some consider this road an adventure, others term the drive fool-hardy. They are both correct. Keep in mind that rental car companies have restrictions on travel along this route. Namely, if you get stuck or break down, it is your problem. These restrictions may not apply if you rent a four-wheel-drive vehicle, but check with the specific rental car company to be sure. It is very important to determine the current condition of the road and the current and future weather. Many of the ground tour vans now continue around this part of the island.

While very parched, this route presents a hazard that can take visitors unaware. Flash floods in the mountains above, most likely during November to March, can send walls of water down the mountain, quickly washing out a bridge or overflowing the road. The road is sometimes closed for months due to serious washouts. Check with the county to see the current status of this route. Another good source of road information are the local folks in Hana. Although their viewpoints might differ, they generally seem to be well informed about the road conditions. I checked with no fewer than ten people before ascertaining that I might make it through. Recent rains can cause parts of this "road" (term used loosely) to become huge, oozing, muddy bogs. Currently the road is eroded for about two or three miles. Travel is reduced to about five miles an hour, or less, over these portions. Another two or three miles are slightly better. The Drive Slowly signs that are posted are quite sincere (but hardly necessary).

The first section of the road past the O'heo area seems easily navigable. However, fairly quickly you may wonder if you made an incorrect turn and ended up on a hiking trail. This section of the unimproved road lasts 4.5 very long miles. You'll be challenged by steeply dropping cliffs to your left and the rocky walls on your right, chiseled just enough to let only a single car go by. However, if you have second thoughts at this point, you may be out of luck—there isn't room to turn around. The most harrowing portions, besides the huge muddy ruts, are the blind corners. Luckily the road had been graded when I made my last trip in late 2002 around the bottom of the island and it was fairly level and a smoother ride than on other occasions. If you have an open-top jeep be sure you fight for the front seat or you'll be eating a lot of dust.

There are several landmarks along this road, one of them the **Hui Aloha Church** built in 1859. There are small pullouts along the roadside that are worth a stop for a photo or two.

The next landmark of civilization is the **Kaupo Store**. It has been operating since 1925. If they are open, you can head to the back of the store and choose from one of several refrigerators for a cool soda or the freezer for an ice cream. The walls are lined with an assortment of antiques, none of which are for sale. There are old bottles, an impressive collection of old cameras, radios and antique drug store items.

The scenic attractions are pretty limited for the next few miles. There is scenic **St. Joseph's Church**, built in 1862. Take note of the many lava rock walls along the roadside. This area supported a large native Hawaiian population and these walls served as boundaries as well as retaining walls for livestock, primarily pigs. The walls are centuries old and unfortunately have suffered from visitor vandalism and destruction by the range cattle. Cattle are now the principal area residents. However, more people are gradually moving into this area.

You'll note the remnants of an old church on a bluff (*makai*) overlooking the ocean. This is the headquarters of **Ka'ohana O Kahikinui**. This self-help organization is attempting to put the Hawaiians back on Hawaiian land.

As you enter Upcountry and civilization once more, look for the Tedeschi Winery at the Ulupalakua Ranch. On the way back down (before 4 p.m.) you might stop at the Kula Botanical Gardens, which feature a look at the unusual protea flowers. (See the "Upcountry" section earlier in the chapter for more information.)

CHAPTER 3

Where to Stay

Maui has more than 18,000 hotel rooms and condominium units in vacation rental programs, with the bulk of the accommodations located in two areas, West Maui and the south shore of East Maui. This chapter contains a list of essentially all of the condominiums that are in rental programs, as well as the island's hotels and bed-and-breakfast homes.

If you are physically impaired, see "Travel Tips for the Physically Impaired" in Chapter 1. While many accommodations do have facilities to accommodate the physically impaired, you may encounter difficulty with some of the tourist attractions. Access to many of them is limited.

If you are traveling with children, refer to Chapter 1 for information on children's programs at a host of resorts.

THINGS TO KNOW ABOUT USING THIS CHAPTER

As with the other chapters, we've divided Maui into six geographic regions: Lahaina, Kaʻanapali–Kapalua Area, Maʻalaea–Kihei–Wailea–Makena Area, Kahului–Wailuku Area, Upcountry and Hana Highway. Accommodations are listed alphabetically within these regions. For each of the properties you will find the local address or P.O. Box as well as local, fax and toll-free numbers. I have also included e-mail addresses and websites. You can usually e-mail via website as well. For ease in locating information, the properties are also indexed alphabetically in the Lodging Index at the end of the book.

Condos are abundant, and the prices and facilities they offer can be quite varied. Other options include hotels, private cottages and B&Bs; B&Bs are marked with a dresser. I have tried to indicate personal preferences by the use of a ★. I felt these were the best buys or special in some way. However, it is impossible for us to stay in or view all the units within a complex, and since condominiums are privately owned, each unit can vary in its furnishings and its condition. Please see the "Best Bets" section for more highlights.

In many cases there are a variety of rental agents handling units in addition to the on-site management; an assortment of these have been listed. When you determine which condo interests you, call all of the agents. Be aware that while one agent may have no vacancy, another will have several. The prices can also vary (sometimes greatly) from one to another. The quality of the furnishings and the care of the unit may also vary. The prices I have listed are generally the lowest available (although some agents may offer lower rates by reducing certain services such as daily maid service). Unfortunately, I've had at least one occasion where the cheaper rate resulted in a condo that needed not only a good cleaning, but complete renovation. However, a reputable rental agent will not let a unit fall into disrepair. I can recommend **Maui and All Island Condominiums**; be sure to ask about their seasonal specials. **Kihei Maui Vacations** is also very good with their broad range of properties in South Maui. **Whalers Realty** in West Maui offers moderate to expensive properties at rates lower than the posted rack rates. At the end of this chapter is an alphabetical listing of rental agents. Due to space, not all rental agents have been included in the individual property listings.

Prices are listed to aid your selection and, while these were the most current available at press time, they are subject to change without notice. As island vacationers ourselves, I found it important to include this feature rather than just giving you broad categories such as budget or expensive. After all, one person's "expensive" may be "budget" to someone else! The prices are listed with a slash dividing them. The first price listed is the high-season rate, the second price is the low-season rate. A few offer a flat yearly rate so there will only be a single price.

For the sake of space, I have made use of several abbreviations. The size of the condominiums are identified as studio (S BR), one bedroom (1BR), two bedroom (2BR) and three bedroom (3BR). The numbers in parentheses following this refer to the number of people that can occupy the unit for the price listed, e.g., 2BR (4). The description will tell you how much it will cost for additional persons over two, e.g., extra person $10/night. Some facilities consider an infant as an extra person, others will allow children free up to a specified age. The abbreviations *o.f.*, *g.v.*, *o.v.* and *m.v.* refer to oceanfront, gardenview, oceanview and mountainview units.

WHERE TO STAY?

The *Lahaina* and *Ka'anapali* areas offer the visitor the hub of the island's activities, but accommodations are a little more costly. The beaches are especially good at Ka'anapali. The Ka'anapali Beach Resort boasts the most convention space of any of the neighboring islands, with the Maui Marriott, Westin Maui and the Hyatt Regency also being popular locations. All the hotels are located beachfront, although some of the condos are situated above the beach in the golf course area. All are priced in the luxury range. The wide avenues and the spaciousness of the resort's lush green and manicured grounds are most impressive. No on-street parking and careful planning have successfully given this resort a feeling of spaciousness. Nestled between a pristine white-sand beach and scenic golf courses with a mountain range beyond, this may be the ideal spot for your vacation.

The values and choice of condos are more extensive a little beyond Ka'anapali in *Honokowai*, *Kahana* (Lower Honoapi'ilani Highway area), and further on at *Napili*. However, perhaps because of the shape of the sloping ridges of the West Maui Mountain, there can be slightly cooler temperatures here and oftentimes more rain. Some of the condominiums in this area, while very adequate, may be a little overdue for redecorating. While many complexes are on nice beaches, many are also on rocky shores. Many people return year after year to this quiet area, away from the bustle of Lahaina and Ka'anapali and where condo prices are in the moderate range.

Kapalua offers high-class and high-price condominium and hotel accommodations. *Ma'alaea* and *Kihei* are a half-hour drive from Lahaina and offer some attractive condo units at excellent prices and, although few are located on a beach, there are plenty of easily accessible public beach parks. Many Maui vacationers feel that Kihei offers better weather in the winter months, which may be true with annual rainfall only about 3 inches on Maui's southern shore. There are plenty of restaurants here and an even broader selection can be found by driving the short distance to Wailuku to sample some local fare.

The *Wailea* and *Makena* areas are just beyond Kihei and are beautifully developed resorts. The beaches are excellent for a variety of water activities; however, it is significantly more expensive than neighboring Kihei. The introductory section to each area offers additional information.

The twin towns of *Wailuku* and *Kahului* are located on the northern, windward side of the island. There are three motel-type accommodations around Kahului Harbor and while the rates are economical and the location is somewhat central to all parts of the island, I cannot recommend staying in this area for other than a quick stopover that might require easy airport access. This side of the island is generally more windy, overcast and cooler, with few good beaches. Except for the avid windsurfer, I feel there is little reason to headquarter your stay in this area. However, there are many good reasons to linger and explore.

Accommodations in *Upcountry* include two small lodges in Kula, a few cabins available from the park service for overnight use while hiking in the Haleakala Wilderness Area (Haleakala is actually not a crater, rather an erosional valley), and a number of interesting bed-and-breakfast establishments and cottages.

Along the *Hana Highway*, you'll find plenty of B&Bs as well as a lovely resort, a few condos and some homes for rent.

HOW TO SAVE MONEY

Maui has two price seasons: high or "in" season and low or "off" season. Low season is generally considered to be April 15 to about December 15, and the rates are discounted at some places as much as 30 percent. Different resorts and condominiums may vary these dates by as much as two weeks and a few resorts are going to a flat, year-round rate. Ironically, some of the best weather is during the fall when temperatures are cooler than summer and there is less rain than the winter and spring months. (See "Weather" in Chapter 1 for year-round temperatures). For longer than one week, a condo unit with a kitchen can result in significant savings on your food bill. While this will give you more space than a hotel room at a lower price, you may give up some resort amenities (shops, restaurants, maid service, etc.). There are several large grocery stores around the island with fairly competitive prices, although most things at the store will run slightly higher than on the mainland. (See "Grocery Shopping" in Chapter 1.)

LONG-TERM STAYS

Almost all condo complexes and rental agents offer the long-term visitor moderate to substantial discounts for stays of one month or more. Private homes can also be booked through the rental agents listed at the end of the chapter.

A Reminder: The accommodations are listed alphabetically within six regions. You will also find a Lodging Index at the back of this book to provide further assistance.

Money can be saved by using the following tips when choosing a place to settle. First, it is less expensive to stay during the off or low season. Second, there are some areas that are much less expensive. Although Kahului has some motel units, I can't recommend this area as a place to headquarter your stay. The weather is wetter in winter, hotter in summer, generally windier than the other side of the island, and there are few good beaches. Two renovated old hotels in Wailuku now offer serviceable, basic and affordable accommodations for the budget minded. They should especially appeal to the windsurfing community with nearby Ho'okipa Beach. There are a couple of hostel type accommodations in this area. There are some good deals in the Ma'alaea and Kihei areas, and the northern area above Lahaina has some older complexes that are reasonably good values.

Third, there are some pleasant condo units either across the road from the beach or on a rocky, less attractive beach. This can represent a tremendous savings, and there are always good beaches a short walk or drive away. Fourth, hotel rooms or condos with garden or mountain views are less costly than an oceanview or oceanfront room. In fact, my traveling buddies and I find the mountainview rooms, especially in Ka'anapali, to be superior. The mountains are simply gorgeous and I'd rather be on the beach than look at it! Most condominiums offer maid service only upon check-out. A few might offer it twice a week or weekly. Additional maid service may be available for an extra charge. A few condos still do not provide in-room phones or color televisions, and fewer still have no pool.

A few words of caution: Condominium units within one complex can differ greatly and, if a phone is important to you, ask. Some may also add up to $1 per in-room local call, others have no extra charge for local calls. Some units have washers and dryers in the rooms, while others do not. Many have coin-operated laundry facilities on the premises. Generally all units have microwaves in their kitchens. All condos have TVs and swimming pools unless otherwise specified.

Travel agents will be able to book your stay in all Maui hotels and in most condominiums. If you prefer to make your own reservation, I have listed the various contacts for each condominium so that if you're willing to do the legwork, you could save a few dollars. Rates vary between rental agents, so check all those listed for a particular condominium. I have indicated toll-free (prefixes: 800, 866, 877 or 888) numbers when available. Some may not be accessible from Canada, so for those, check the rental agent list at the end of this chapter. Look for an 808 area code preceding the non-toll free numbers. (It gets confusing with all those 8s.) You might also check the classified ads in your local newspaper for owners offering their units, which may be a better bargain. I've provided e-mail addresses where possible. Although prices can jump, most go up only 5 to 10 percent per year. Prices listed do not include the occupancy tax, which is currently 7.16 percent hotel tax plus 4 percent sales tax. Ouch!

GENERAL POLICIES Condominium complexes require a deposit, usually equivalent to one- or two-nights stay, to secure your reservation and insure your room rate from price increases. Some charge higher deposits during winter or over Christmas holidays. Generally a 30-day notice of cancellation is needed to receive a full refund. Most require payment in full either 30 days prior to arrival or upon arrival, and many do not accept credit cards. The usual minimum condo stay is three nights, with some requiring one week in winter. Christmas holidays may have steeper restrictions with minimum stays as long as two weeks, payments 90 days in advance, and heavy cancellation penalties. It is not uncommon to book as much as two years in advance for the Christmas season.

Monthly and oftentimes weekly discounts are available. Room rates quoted are generally for two people. Additional persons run $8 to $15 per night per person with the exception of the high-class resorts and hotels, where it may run as much as $25 to $35 extra. Many complexes can arrange for crib rentals. (See "Traveling with Children" in Chapter 1.) I have tried to give the lowest rates generally available, which might not be through the hotel or condo office, so check with the offices as well as the rental agents. When contacting condominium complexes by mail, be sure to address your correspondence to the attention of the manager. The managers of several complexes do not handle any reservations so I have indicated to whom you should address reservation requests at these properties. If two addresses are given, use the P.O. Box rather than street address.

Lodging Best Bets

Get-Away-from-It-All Destinations There are several excellent options if you want to slow down and feel the true aloha of Hawai'i. • Hop on a plane or take Expedition and head off to Lana'i and spend a few days at the Lodge at Koele or Manele Bay Resort. You won't find a more lavish and lovely setting. • Fly or drive to Hana and experience the quiet and tranquil beauty of the Hotel Hana-Maui. Stay in an oceanfront sea cottage or one with a lanai jacuzzi and just feel the tension ooze out of every muscle as you watch the sunrise. • Stay at the Silver Cloud Upcountry Guest Ranch. You'd never imagine you were just minutes away from the buzz of resorts. Located in Ulupalakua this is a tranquil retreat that I just can't say enough about. And the breakfasts are killer.

Most Intimate Accommodations The Victorian-style Lahaina Inn is a step back into time. No ocean view here or televisions, but wonderfully romantic. A great couple destination. • Plantation Inn is equally charming with a tropical feel and the added amenities of air conditioning, a pool and TV. This one would be a great location with or without children.

Condos If You Can Splurge Makena Surf is a terrific, luxury property with elegant, ideally located and beautifully appointed units. You can really get away from it here. • The Ka'anapali Alii has long been a favorite of mine.

Discount Accommodations Check the internet for specials. One website www.hotwire.com offers great deals on "mystery" accommodations. Also check out www.accomline.com. There is a membership fee for the latter or book with them and they charge you a dollar or two a night more for your booking and waive the membership fee.

LAHAINA Puamana—A nice residential type area of two-plex and four-plex units, some oceanfront. Plenty of room for kids to run around. **Lahaina Shores**—A moderately priced colonial-style high-rise right on the beach and within walking distance of Lahaina shops. Fronting reef makes for calm waters for kids who enjoy the ocean. **Lahaina Inn**—A great couple getaway, not oriented to children. **Plantation Inn**—Tastefully done with all the elegance of bygone days and in the middle of town.

KA'ANAPALI Hyatt Regency Maui Resort and Spa—An elegant and exotic setting with a wonderful selection of great restaurants. **Maui Marriott Resort & Ocean Club**—A hotel/timeshare. **Westin Maui**—A gorgeous resort and a pool lover's paradise. **Ka'anapali Alii**—One of only three condominiums that are oceanfront. Luxurious, expensive and spacious. (My choice to purchase a unit with future lottery winnings!) **Royal Lahaina Resort**—A beautiful property on sandy Ka'anapali Beach. **The Whaler**—Condominiums at the heart of Honoka'o'o Beach adjacent to the Whalers Village Shopping Center.

HONOKOWAI Ka'anapali Shores—A high-rise surrounded by lovely grounds on the best beach in the area. **Papakea**—A low-rise complex with attractive grounds and pool. **Embassy Vacation Resort**—A mix

---

The complimentary services of *Concierge Connection* can provide you with accommodations as well as package discounts, coupons and percentage-off cards for restaurants and activities. They even offer resort-guest prices for golf courses or the Grand Wailea Spa. They offer free advice, information and recommendations on all other aspects of your Maui vacation—with discounts on those, too. Call Sandy 888-875-9366, 808-875-9366 on Maui, or e-mail: connect@maui.net.

TREEHOUSES

Nestled in the Nahiku rainforest, along the Hana Highway, you'll find **Nahiku Tree House** the perfect place to get away from it all. A lofted sleeping area with linens provided, full bathroom, a large lofty deck and time to catch up on that book you've been meaning to read. Nahiku is just past mile-marker 25 on the Hana Highway. A four-wheel-drive vehicle is recommended or you can walk the last 100 or so yards to the treehouse. A little too primitive for my tastes, but it is a Boy Scout's dream come true. 773-472-4080; www.nahiku.com. **Tree Houses of Hana** operate more treehouses. 808-248-7241; www.maui.net/~hanalani; e-mail: hanalani@maui.net.

between a condo and a hotel with breakfast included. Spacious rooms and a good sandy beach.

KAHANA Sands of Kahana—Spacious units on a nice white-sand beach. **Kahana Sunset**—Low-rise condos surrounding a secluded cove and beach.

NAPILI Napili Sunset—Centered right on the edge of Napili Bay, rooms are well kept. **Napili Kai Beach Resort**—A quiet facility on the edge of Napili Bay. Large grounds and a restaurant on site. Resort activities are offered. **Honokeana Cove**—Great value and private location.

KAPALUA The **Kapalua Bay Hotel and Ocean Villas** and **The Ritz-Carlton, Kapalua** are both outstanding properties offering quiet elegance, top service and great food with all the amenities. The area's villas and luxury homes offer spacious living and complete kitchen facilities. Rentals are located in five different areas, and there are a number of rental agents. Any of the units would be excellent; however, they are not all located within easy walking distance of the beach. A shuttle service is available for all resort guests.

MA'ALAEA Kana'i a Nalu—Attractive complex with all two-bedroom units on a sandy beachfront, affordably priced. **Lauloa**—Well-designed units oceanfront on the sea wall. **Makani A Kai**—Located on a sandy beachfront, two-bedroom units are townhouse style.

NORTH KIHEI Kealia and Ma'alaea Surf.

SOUTH KIHEI Maui Hill—Situated on a hillside across the road from the ocean, some units have excellent ocean views. The three-bedroom units here are roomy and a good value for large families. **Haleakala Shores**—Across from Kama'ole III Beach Park. **Mana Kai Maui**—One of Kihei's larger resorts, the units are fair but an extra plus is that they are located on good beaches.

WAILEA It's hard to go wrong in wonderful Wailea. Affordable accommodations are not what the visitor will find here, but there are a variety of excellent condominiums and hotels from which to choose. Each is different, each is lovely and in fact there is not one property that I would not recommend. Many have wonderful kids programs. **Wailea Marriott, an Outrigger Resort**—A lovely resort featuring a tropical flavor with spacious grounds, excellent restaurants and two great beaches. They are continuing to develop a wonderful Hawaiiana program. **Renaissance Wailea Beach Resort**—This complex is smaller and more intimate as resorts go; it has lush, tropical grounds, and it is fronted by one of the island's finest beaches. The **Grand Wailea Resort Hotel & Spa**—This is an enormous resort, but also enormous fun. The pools are incredible, but if you prefer the ocean, there is the excellent Wailea Beach. There is something for everyone in the family. **Four Seasons Resort**—This resort is purely and simply elegant. From it's white porte-cochere you enter a tranquil and serene environ. Simply sit by the pool or enjoy a day on the beach. No need to go further. The **Fairmont Kea Lani Hotel**—This is an all-suites resort, a blend of the best of resorts and the comforts of a condominium, all on Polo Beach. **The Palms at Wailea**—Very spacious units can comfortably accommodate a family. Tastefully appointed, the gardenview units are very affordable and only a short walk to the beach. **Polo Beach**—Luxury condominium units with easy access to two small but good beaches.

MAKENA The **Maui Prince Hotel** and **Makena Surf**—Both are first-class, luxury accommodations on beautiful beaches.

Lahaina

Best Western Pioneer Inn
658 Wharf Street, P.O. Box 243, Lahaina, HI 96764. 800-457-5457; fax 808-667-5708; 808-661-3636; www.pioneerinnmaui.com; e-mail: pioneer@maui.net.

With its colorful history, Pioneer Inn remains a nostalgic Lahaina landmark, the oldest accommodation on the island. Best Western International took over property management of this nostalgic landmark in 1998 and began room renovation to include queen beds, tiled modern bathrooms and air conditioning as well as ceiling fans, TV, radio and direct-dial telephones. A courtyard swimming pool.

Garden Gate Bed and Breakfast
67 Kaniau Road, Lahaina, HI 96761. 800-939-3217; 808-661-8800; fax 808-661-0209; www.gardengatebb.com; e-mail: jaime@gardengatebb.com.

Hosts Jaime and Bill Mosley offer rooms with private bath, phones, refrigerators, TVs, VCRs, air conditioning, ceiling fans and ocean or garden views. Continental breakfast daily except Sunday. Garden Gate is centrally located near Historic Old Lahaina Town. Three-night minimum (but they can be flexible on this).

Rates: $79-$99 per person double occupancy, $115-$130 deluxe suite, $275 per night for 2-bedroom, two-bath condo; extra person $15/night

House of Fountains

1579 Lokia Street, Lahaina, HI 96761. 800-789-6865; 808-667-2121; e-mail: private@maui.net; www.alohahouse.com.

This B&B is located three blocks from the beach. Accommodations are in a 7,000-square-foot home. Air-conditioned rooms furnished with queen bed and private bath. There's *koa* wood furniture and the rooms have a Hawaiiana style. German breakfast. Your host is Daniela Clement. House of Fountains received the Kahili award from the Hawaii Visitors Bureau for the most Hawaiian accommodation in 2002.

Rates: $95-$145

★ Lahaina Inn

127 Lahainaluna Road, Lahaina, HI 96761. 800-669-3444; 808-661-0577; fax 808-667-9480; e-mail: inntown@lahainainn.com; www.lahainainn.com.

Built in 1938 by Tomezo Masuda for his general store, Maui Trading Company, this property was a popular place for World War II Army men to "hang loose." Dickie, the Masudas' black German shepherd, became legendary for his mail run. He would make the trip to the Lahaina post office to fetch the store's mail. In 1949, the Tabata family purchased the business, but by the early 1960s the business failed and the building was placed at public auction. George Izaki bought the property and made the street-level store into four business spaces and transformed the second floor into a hotel. A fire destroyed the business in the mid-1960s. The interior was reconstructed and the Lahainaluna Hotel was developed in the second-story level. There were 19 rooms and three baths. The hotel gradually deteriorated. When I toured the property for the first edition of this guidebook in the early 1980s, the Lahainaluna was renting for $20 a night, and that was a lot for what you got.

In 1986 Rick Ralston, who also owned Crazy Shirts, undertook renovations and the transformation was dramatic. Gone are the cheap "rustic" units. Lahaina Inn is now an elegant 12 room bed-and-breakfast hotel in the heart of Lahaina Town. It provides an atmosphere of comfortable luxury with all the charm and romance of an intimate inn at the turn of the 20th century. The rich warm furnishings of your standard double room or parlor suite set the stage for you to realize your dreams. Each room is individually decorated with authentic period furnishings, hand-quilted bed covers, antique lamps and oriental carpets. Relax in air-conditioned comfort or sit back in rocking chairs on your own balcony lanai. A continental breakfast is provided every morning from an antique sideboard and stocked with Kona coffee, tea, fruit juice, muffins and croissants. In-room phones offer free local calls. Considering you are in the center of town, the rooms are surprisingly quiet. If you can do without the ocean view, I can't imagine a more romantic, charming and intimate way to spend your Maui vacation. Adjacent is David Paul's Lahaina Grill. Parking $5 per day. Honeymoon packages. Children over age 15 are welcome.

Rates: m.v. $119/$109; o.v. $139/$119; Makai Room o.v. $169/$159; Mauka Room o.v. and m.v. $169/$159; Lahainaluna Room $169/$159

Lahaina Roads

1403 Front Street, Lahaina, HI 96761. 808-661-3166. Agents: Melinda Mower 800-572-5642, 808-662-0812; Sherry Barbier 800-847-0761, 808-667-4663.

These 42 700-square-foot, one-bedroom/one-bath oceanfront condominiums are decorated with tropical decor. They are equipped with full kitchen, telephone, bedroom air conditioning and ceiling fans. The large lanai overlooks the ocean and offers an incredible view of the warm Pacific. Covered parking and elevator to upper levels.

Rates: $129-$149.

Sherry Barbier rates: from $149

★ Lahaina Shores Beach Resort

475 Front Street, Lahaina, HI 96761. 808-661-4835 (hotel only, no reservations). Agents: Classic Resorts 800-628-6699; Whalers Realty 800-676-4112; Chase 'n Rainbows 800-367-6092.

This seven-story plantation-style building offers 200 oceanfront units with air conditioning, lanais, full kitchens, daily maid service and laundry facilities on each floor. The beach here is fair and the water calm due to offshore reefs, but shallow with coral. With a family staying at Lahaina Shores you have the opportunity to enjoy the beach directly in front; there's also a pool and patio. Lahaina Town is only a short walk away, plus this complex neighbors the 505 Front Street Shopping Center, which offers several restaurants and a small grocery/convenience store.

Classic Resorts rates: S BR (2, max 3) m.v.-o.f. $180-$215; 1BR (2, max 4) m.v. $250, o.f. $280; penthouse (2, max 5) m.v. $290-$315

Hotel rates: S BR m.v. $170/$150, o.f. $205/$185; 1BR m.v. $240/$200, o.f. $270/$225; penthouse $235-$305

Maui Islander Hotel

660 Wainee Street, Lahaina, HI 96761. 808-667-9766. Maui Islander 800-367-5226. Managed by Outrigger Resorts: 800-OUTRIGGER.

The 374-unit property includes 11 two-story buildings set on nearly 10 acres, featuring hotel rooms, studios, deluxe studios, and one- and two-bedroom suites. All include full kitchens, except for the hotel rooms, which have mini-refrigerators. Located in the heart of Lahaina Town, less than a 5-minute walk to the sea wall, yet far enough away to be peaceful. The back of the building borders the Honoapi'ilani Highway, so front units may be a bit quieter. Daily maid service, air conditioning, laundry facilities, tennis courts, pool.

Rates: Hotel room $140, 1BR $199, 2BR $279, family suite $179

★ Old Lahaina House Bed & Breakfast

P.O. Box 10355, Lahaina, HI 96761. 800-847-0761; 808-667-4663; fax 808-667-5615; e-mail: info@oldlahaina.com; www.oldlahaina.com.

Host Sherry Barbier offers four rooms in her home in the historic Lahaina area. All rooms have air conditioning, private bath and have access to refrigerator and microwave. Breakfast is included except on Sunday. Swimming pool. They are across the street from a neighborhood beach and four blocks from Lahaina Harbor. Sherry also offers a number of other condo and home rentals around West Maui.

Rates: Exclusive Suite with queen bed, full kitchen and washer/dryer $150-$205, Deluxe with king bed $114-$125, Standard with queen bed and microwave $89-$99, Budget with twin beds $69-$89

The Plantation Inn

174 Lahainaluna Road, Lahaina, HI 96761. 800-433-6815; 808-667-9225; fax 808-667-9293; e-mail: info@theplantationinn.com; www.theplantationinn.com.

This child-friendly 18-room B&B has all the charm of a historic inn, while incorporating all the benefits of modernization. You'd never know you were just footsteps away from the bustle of Front Street Lahaina. Filled with antiques, beautiful Victorian decor, hardwood floors and stained glass, they also offer air conditioning, refrigerators and VCRs. Some units on the ground floor have lovely patios that extend out to the pool area. The second-floor units have balconies. Some units even have kitchens and jacuzzi tubs. Located just blocks from the ocean in the heart of Lahaina, it has a 12-foot deep tiled pool and a spa. (A nice touch that the spa is open 24 hours.) An added bonus is Gerard's restaurant, featuring fine French cuisine for your evening dining pleasure, and all guests of The Plantation Inn receive a $50 dining credit. For breakfast, fresh fruit, outstanding French toast and other specialties along with piping hot coffee are served in their lovely poolside pavilion or around the pool. Added value packages (based on two persons) include a Romance Package, Gourmet Package, Lahaina Whale Encounter, or Best of Maui.

Rates: Standard $157, superior $177, deluxe $197, suites $220-$240

★ Puamana

P.O. Box 11108, Lahaina, HI 96761. 800-628-6731; 808-667-2551. Agents: Maui & All Island 800-663-6962; Maui Beachfront Rentals 888-661-7200.

A series of duplexes and fourplexes in a garden setting with 228 units. This large oceanside complex resembles a residential community much more than a vacation resort. The variation in price reflects location in the complex, oceanfront to gardenview. There's a beach suitable for swimming.

Maui Beachfront Rentals rates: 1BR 2BTH g.v. $131/$114, 3BR 2BTH o.f. $293-$368/$286-$315

Puunoa Beach Estates

45 Kai Pali Place, Lahaina, HI 96761. Agents: Classic Resorts 800-628-6699; Whalers Realty Management 800-676-4112.

Amenities include full-size swimming pool, jacuzzi, his and hers sauna, and paddle tennis courts. Units include laundry rooms, lanais, master bath with jacuzzi, full bar and daily maid service. These luxury units are located on Pu'unoa Beach in a residential area just north of Lahaina. Beautiful and spacious air-conditioned units, convenient to restaurants and shops. The beachfront has a coral reef that makes for calm conditions for children, but swimming or snorkeling are poor due to the shallowness and coral.

Whalers rates: 3BR 4BTH o.f. $800/$700

Classic Resorts rates: $650-$800

★ Wai Ola

P.O. Box 12580, Lahaina, HI 96761. 808 662-0812; e-mail: waiola@maui-vacations.com; www.waiola.com. P.O. Box 11108, Lahaina, HI 96761. 800-628-6731; 808-667-2551. Agents: Maui & All Island 800-663-6962; Maui Beachfront Rentals 888-661-7200.

This elegant 5,000-square-foot vacation rental home is conveniently located between Lahaina Town and Ka'anapali. Close to Maui's world-famous beaches, golf courses, shopping and fine restaurants. It offers 4 bedrooms and a private cottage. This beautifully maintained property enjoys panoramic ocean views and spectacular sunsets.

Rates: $135-$150; cottage $175

Ka'anapali–Kapalua Area

Note: A number of the resort hotels charge guests a daily parking fee.

KA'ANAPALI

★ Hyatt Regency Maui Resort and Spa
200 Nohea Kai Drive, Lahaina, HI 96761. 800-223-1234; 808-661-1234.

This magnificent complex is located on 40 beachfront acres and offers 806 rooms and suites. The beach is beautiful, but has a steep drop-off. The adjoining Hanokao'o Beach Park offers a gentler slope into deeper water. The two-acre pool area is an impressive feature resembling a contemporary adventure that Robinson Crusoe could only have dreamed of. The pool is divided by a large cavern that can be reached on either side by swimming beneath a waterfall. The more adventurous can try out their waterslide. One side of the pool is spanned by a large swinging rope bridge. The kids just love walking back and forth with the swaying motion. And the Hyatt has a children's fantasy pool. It's a 3,000-square-foot sandy play pool with fountains, mist, a 24-foot slide and ocean features that resemble a tide pool. Penguins, jewel-toned *koi*, parrots, swans, cranes and flamingos around the grounds require full-time game keepers. The tropical birds are so at home here that some are reproducing, a rarity for some of these species in captivity. The lobby is a blend of beautiful pieces of oriental art and paths that lead to the grounds. Non-guests should definitely visit the Hyatt for a self-guided tour of the grounds, the art, the elegant shops, the fine restaurants or their luau show. There are children's daycamps and evening programs. The Regency Club at the Hyatt consists of two floors that feature special services, including continental breakfast, evening cocktails and appetizers. No charge for children 18 and under sharing with parents.

Rates: Terrace $345; Golf/Mountain $385, partial o.v. $445, o.v. $565; Regency partial o.v. $585, o.f. $650, ocean suite $850; other suites $1,250-$3,000. Additional persons 19 and older $35 per night, $50 per night in Regency Club

---

The off-Broadway show *Tony n' Tina's Wedding* debuted at the Hyatt Regency Maui Resort and Spa in late 2002. You'll be a part of the wedding and the reception as these two New York Italian families join in marriage. And it has a splash of local aloha. Self-parking is free to everyone, valet parking is $10 per visit but completely validated if you eat at the restaurants.

★ **Ka'anapali Alii**
50 Nohea Kai Drive, Lahaina, HI 96761. 800-367-6090. Agents: Classic Resorts 800-628-6699; Whalers Realty 800-676-4112; Maui Beachfront Rentals 888-661-7200.

All 264 units are very spacious and beautifully furnished, with air conditioning, microwaves, washer/dryer and daily maid service. Other amenities include security entrances and covered parking. The 1-bedroom units have a den, which actually makes them equivalent to a 2-bedroom. Three lighted tennis courts, pool (also a children's pool) and exercise room. No restaurants on the property, but shops and restaurants are within easy walking distance. A very elegant, high-class and quiet property with a very cordial staff and concierge department. Okay, you want to know a secret? This is one of my favorites!

Classic Resort rates: 1BR g.v. $350, m.v. $375, partial o.v. $400, o.v. $425, premier $500, o.f. $525; 2BR g.v. $275, m.v. $500, partial o.v. $530, o.v. $580, premier $635, o.f. $665, o.f. premier $750, suite $900

Ka'anapali Beach Hotel
2525 Ka'anapali Parkway, Lahaina, HI 96761. 800-262-8450; 808-661-0011; fax 808-667-5616 (guests), fax 808-667-5978 (administration); e-mail: info@kbhmaui.com; www.kbhmaui.com.

Located on Ka'anapali Beach near Black Rock and Whalers Village Shops, this 430-room hotel has been welcoming guests since 1964. A great location, but not a "posh" resort, this special place is Maui's most Hawaiian hotel where the staff is regularly instructed in Hawaiian culture. The hotel has earned its reputation as Maui's most Hawaiian hotel. There are four wings to this property that embrace a tropical courtyard featuring gardens, walkways, a whale-shaped swimming pool and an outdoor bar and grill. Each room is decorated with airy, island decor and offers a private balcony or lanai, air conditioning, mini-refrigerator, color cable TV, in-room safes and coffee maker. Nonsmoking rooms are available. Five rooms are equipped for the disabled traveler. The hotel offers two restaurants plus a poolside grill and bar. This is the best value on Ka'anapali Beach. A variety of Hawaiian activities are scheduled daily. Among them are leaf printing, ti leaf skirt making, hula classes, lei making and *lauhala* weaving. Throughout the week there are craft fairs and special employee entertainment each morning at the complimentary 'Ohana Welcome Breakfast. Each night at sunset there's a free hula show in the Tiki Terrace Courtyard. Coin-operated laundry facilities on the property. "Aloha Passport for Kids" is an amenity program, free for all children 12 and younger; see "Childcare Programs" in Chapter 1 for details. All guests receive a complimentary 10-minute phone card and, upon departure, a very special farewell ceremony and souvenir *kukui* lei. Cribs available at no charge. Rollaway bed $15 per night. Children under 18 free when sharing room with parents using existing bedding. Children 5 years and younger eat free at the hotel restaurants when accompanied by a paying adult. Special package rates include "Awake to Paradise" with complimentary daily breakfast, or "Room and Wheels," which includes a compact rental car for and additional $10. "Fifty Plus" offers special rates for seniors with ID card required at check-in, while the "Ka'anapali Whale Encounter" and "Best of the Beach" packages incorporate some wonderful options on Maui activities. Children 17 and under staying in parent/guardian room and using existing beds are free. Higher rates for holiday period.

Rates: Aloha Value Special $169 (no breakfast), g.v. $195, partial o.v. $220, o.v. $265, o.f. $290; extra person $25/night

Ka'anapali Plantation

150 Pu'ukolii Road (P.O. Box 845), Lahaina, HI 96761. Agent: Chase 'n Rainbows 800-367-6902.

Sixty-two one-, two- and three-bedroom units in a garden setting overlooking golf course and ocean.

Rates: 2BR $175/$155, 3BR $215/$155

★ Ka'anapali Royal

2560 Keka'a Drive, Lahaina, HI 96761. 808-661-8687. Agents: Whalers Realty 800-676-4112; Maui Beachfront Rentals 888-661-7200; Chase 'n Rainbows 800-367-6092; RSVP 800-663-1118.

Situated on the 16th fairway of the Ka'anapali golf course overlooking the Ka'anapali Resort and Pacific Ocean, these very spacious condos (1,600 to 2,000 square feet) offer air conditioning, lanais, daily maid service and washer/dryers. Note that while all units have two bedrooms, they may be rented as a one bedroom based on space availability. Units are rented out by individual owners or rental agents. No on-property rental agent.

Maui Beachfront rates: 2BR o.v. $234/$208, g.v. $208/$192

Maui Eldorado

Located on Ka'anapali North Golf Course. 2661 Keka'a Drive, Lahaina, HI 96761. 800-367-2967 U.S., 800-663-1118 Canada; 808-661-0021.
Managed by and reservations through Outrigger Resorts: 800-OUTRIGGER.

There are 204 air-conditioned units with private lanais and free HBO on cable TV. Daily maid service. Three pools. Free shuttle to private cabana for Maui Eldorado guests on nearby Ka'anapali beachfront.

Rates: S BR (1-2) g.v. $195, partial o.v. $220; 1BR (1-4) g.v. $255, partial o.v. $285; 2BR (1-6) g.v. $370, partial o.v. $395

Maui Ka'anapali Villas

2805 Honoapi'ilani Highway, Lahaina, HI 96761. 808-667-7791. Agents: Aston 800-922-7866; Chase 'n Rainbows 800-367-0092.

Located on fabulous, sandy Ka'anapali Beach, these units (except the hotel rooms) are all air-conditioned and have kitchen facilities. The upper floors of the tower unit have wonderful mountain or ocean views. All are privately owned and some units need updating. Three swimming pools, beach concessions, store nearby. Walking distance to Whalers Village shops and restaurants and adjacent to the Royal Ka'anapali Golf Course. Inquire about their Island Hopper Rates, which offer sizeable discounts.

Aston rates: Hotel room (2) $210/$160, studio w/kitchen (2) $230-$295/$195-$250, 1BR (4) g.v. $290/$250, o.v. $340/$330, oceanside $355/$315, 2BR 2BTH $500

★ *Maui Marriott Resort & Ocean Club*
100 Nohea Kai Drive, Lahaina, HI 96761. 800-228-9290; 808-667-1200; fax 808-667-8300.

After millions of dollars in major renovation the hotel resort is now a timeshare. You'll find a 3.5-acre "superpool" with waterslides, whirlpool spas, swim-through grottos and a children's beach. On-property restaurants include Va Bene Italian Beachside Grill and Nalu Sunset Bar & Sushi. I recommend you call about prices. Since they are now selling timeshare units they have some great packages to introduce guests to their property. You can get additional discounts by attending their sales meeting and hearing more about buying time-share options.

Rates: g.v. $329, pool o.v. $384, o.v. $444, o.v. deluxe king suite $649

★ *Royal Lahaina Resort*
2780 Keka'a Drive, Lahaina, HI 96761. 800-44-ROYAL; 808-661-3611. Managed by: Hawaiian Hotels & Resorts 800-22-ALOHA; www.hawaiianhotels.com.

The 592 units are located on beautiful Ka'anapali Beach just north of Black Rock. Located on 27 tropical acres, all cottage suites have kitchens and are situated around the lush, spacious grounds. Coffee and teamakers are in-room amenities and their five beachside Ehu Kai suites are decorated with a Hawaiian style. The suites' bedrooms include a king-size bed with Hawaiian quilt spread and a sitting area; the adjoining living room features an entertainment center with color television, dining area and daybed. The suites' parlors feature queen-size sofa beds. A pair of full bathrooms and a complete kitchen round out these lovely suites, which can accommodate 5 guests. As part of the Royal Lahaina's complimentary *"Na Mea Hawai'i"* ("Things Hawaiian") program, guests have the opportunity to gain insight into Hawai'i's culture. Regularly scheduled activities and demonstrations include flower lei making, *lauhala* and coconut weaving, *tapa* crafts, Polynesian wood carving and Hawaiian quilting.

A mini-shopping mall is conveniently located on the property. Nearby is the Royal Lahaina Tennis Ranch. The resort has 11 courts and a 3,500-seat tennis stadium. The Royal Lahaina also offers three swimming pools. Restaurants on the property are the Royal Ocean Terrace, Basil Tomatoes and Beachcomber's. Made in the Shade is a poolside restaurant and the Royal Scoop is an ice cream and sandwich shop. Nightly luaus are offered in the luau gardens. Children under 17 sharing parents' room in existing beds are free. Additional amenities include beach cabanas for half- or full-day rental and beach rental equipment; there are also complimentary windsurfing lessons. HH&R offers a complimentary newsletter that features special discounts at all their properties, plus coupons on goodies during your stay. It is well worth a phone call to receive these bonus offers. To subscribe to Essence of Paradise call 800-222-5632 or write them at 2404 Townsgate Road, Westlake Village, CA 91361. Check the website for substantial discounts and internet specials.

Rates: Main Tower g.v. $270, o.v. $230, o.f. $440, g.v. cottage $220, o.v. cottage $230

★ Sheraton Maui

2605 Ka'anapali Parkway, Lahaina, HI 96761. 808-661-0031; 888-488-3535; www.sheraton.com/hawaii.

One of the first resorts to be built along Ka'anapali, the property opened in 1963. The 510-room resort stretches over 23 beachfront acres. The rooms include 16 luxury suites, 20 family suites, 10 junior suites, 15 handicapped accessible rooms and 10 rooms designated for hearing impaired. The buildings, each no taller than six stories, seem to emerge naturally from the surroundings. Each is named as a *hale* ("house"). The main structure of the original property remains, but the *makai* wing (nearer the ocean) is now Hale Nalu (House of the Surf), while the *mauka* portion is Hale Anuenue (House of the Rainbow). The Hale Moana (House of the Ocean) is on the point at black rock. The Hale Lahaina and Hale Ohana are in the middle of the property.

Standard guest rooms feature air conditioning, lanai, small refrigerator, iron and ironing board, coffee maker, TV and guest safe. The Sheraton can provide a room that fits the size of your *ohana* (family). They feature 20 family suites designed with three beds (two double beds and one pull-down double bed). Family suites also feature two connecting lanais with lounge chairs and tables. A nifty room divider can create two rooms for additional privacy. The bathroom is even family-sized, with two showers, one tub and a showerhead that is adjustable for those smaller family members. Children 17 and under staying in the same room and using existing bedding are free. Cribs are available at no charge and babysitting services are available in addition to their children's program held within walking distance held at their sister property, the Westin Maui. Daily culturally enhanced programs welcome children ages 5 to 12 years. A nominal fee applies and night programs are also available. Another family plus is the "Kids Eat Free" program where children 12 and under enjoy complimentary meals, one child per paying adult.

The lighting of the torches off Black Rock and Hawaiian music still welcome the sunset. Bridges, lagoons and lava rock landscape the extended grounds and there are two restaurants, Teppan Yaki Dan and the open-air Keka'a Terrace. Other options include the Lagoon and Sundowner Bars, Reef's Edge Lounge and the Honu Snack Shop. A 142-yard freshwater swimming pool and kiddie pool are available for resort guests. Poolside bars offer cool, refreshing cocktails and hot barbecue snacks throughout the day. There is a daily resort fee that includes self-parking (additional $5 for valet parking). The room fee includes free local calls, free credit card and long distance access fees, free in-room safe, daily newspaper, daily coffee (in-room), flower lei greeting and complimentary use of their fitness center.

Rates: g.v. $350, m.v. $420, partial o.v. $445, o.v. $510, o.f. $570, deluxe o.v. $580, deluxe o.f. $610; Ohana Family Suites $750; other suites from $825; extra person $50/night; maximum four persons per room

★ **Westin Maui**
2365 Ka'anapali Parkway, Lahaina, HI 96761. 808-667-2525; 800-228-3000; www.westinmaui.com.

This is a gorgeous resort offering 761 deluxe rooms, including 28 suites. The Westin Maui has an ocean tower of 11 stories with 556 guest rooms and a beach tower with 206 guest rooms and suites. They offer nonsmoking floors. The rooms have been designed in comfortable hues of muted peach and beige. Complimentary shuttle service is offered to the Royal Lahaina Tennis Ranch, the largest tennis facility on Ka'anapali with 11 tennis courts and 6 courts lit for night play. Conference and banquet facilities are available as well as an array of gift, art and fashion shops. Eight restaurants and lounges overlook the ocean, waterfalls and pools. The hotel exercise room includes weight rooms, sauna and whirlpools. Take a self-guided tour of the grounds and enjoy Westin's family of birds and their tropical surroundings. This resort's $2.5 million art collection could put a museum to shame. Parents may enjoy a brief respite while the kids enjoy the resort's Keiki Kamp Ka'anapali for youth ages 5 to 12 years. (See "Childcare Programs" in Chapter 1 for details.) On-property restaurants include tropica (no capital!) and 'OnO Surf Bar & Grill. No extra charge for children 18 or under sharing the same room as parents. A 25 percent discount is available for additional rooms occupied. Early departure fee will be assessed. A resort fee of $10 per day plus tax will be posted to all accounts for amenities and services (this includes parking).

Rates: Terrace $350, g.v. $380, golf or m.v. $420, partial o.v. $450, o.v. $520, deluxe o.v. $590, o.f. $630, suites $850-$3,500; extra person $45

★ *The Whaler*
2481 Ka'anapali Parkway, Lahaina, HI 96761. 808-661-4861. Managed by Aston Resorts 800-922-7866. Agents: Whalers Realty 800-676-4112; RSVP 800-663-1118; Maui Beachfront Rentals 888-661-7200; Maui & All Island 800-663-6962.

Choice location on an excellent beachfront in the heart of Ka'anapali next to the Whalers Village shopping center. A large pool area is beachfront and they provide a children's program during the summer. Underground parking.

Rates: S BR 1 bath (2) g.v. $235/$205, o.v. $255/$230; 1BR 1 bath (4) g.v. $330/$275, o.v. $360/$330; 1BR 2 bath g.v. (4) $345/$285, o.v. $380/$315, o.f. $485/$415; 2BR 2 bath g.v. (6) $535/$435, o.v. $600/$470, o.f. $700/$570

HONOKOWAI

As you leave the Ka'anapali Resort you will pass the site of the old Ka'anapali Airport and the new Ka'anapali Ocean Resort. Ahead, four large condo complexes signal the beginning of Honokowai, which stretches north along Lower Honoapi'ilani Highway.

★ *Embassy Vacation Resort—Ka'anapali Beach*
104 Ka'anapali Shores Place, Lahaina, HI 96761. 800-669-3155; 808-661-2000.

On 7.5 acres, this pink pyramid structure with a three-story blue waterfall cascading down the side can't be missed. This accommodation blends the best of condo and resort living together. The pool (heated in the winter) area is large and tropical with plenty of room for lounge chairs. The lobby is open air and their glass-enclosed elevators will whisk you up with a view. On the lower roof, mezzanine level, families can enjoy the miniature golf course. Each one-bedroom suite is a spacious 820 square feet, two-bedroom suites are 1,100 square feet. Each features lanai with ocean or scenic views. Master bedrooms are equipped with a remote-control 20-inch television and a large adjoining master bath with soaking tub. The living room contains a massive 35-inch television, stereo receiver, VCR player and cassette player. Living rooms have a sofa that pulls out into a double bed. A dining area with a small kitchenette is equipped with a microwave, small refrigerator and sink. Ironing equipment available upon request. Their two Presidential Suites are 2,100 square feet and offer two bedrooms, two full baths and a large kitchen. One features an oriental theme, the other is decorated with a contemporary California flare. On-site restaurants include North Beach Grille and a shop for sandwiches and sundries. Their children's program, Beach Buddies, is dedicated to perpetuating and preserving the heritage of the islands. "As a *Keiki O Ka Aina Ika Pono* (child of the land), let us share with you a 'Hawaiian Experience' rich in culture and tradition." (See "Childcare Programs" in Chapter 1.) Their health facility has state-of-the-art exercise equipment. They also offer salon and spa services. The resort has a gazebo for wedding ceremonies as well as a 13,000-square-foot meeting facility. Package plans also available.

Rates: 1BR scenic view (1-4) $349, o.v. $389, deluxe o.v. $395, o.f. $459; 2BR suite (1-6) $629; Presidential Suite $1,500

Hale Kai

3691 Lower Honoapi'ilani Highway, Lahaina, HI 96761. 800-446-7307; 808-669-6333; fax 808-669-7474; e-mail: halekai@halekai.com; www.halekai.com. Agent: Chase 'n Rainbows 800-367-6092.

Forty units in a two-story building. The units have lanais, kitchens and a pool as well as VCRs and CDs. A simple and quiet property. Laundry room next to office.

Rates: 1BR (2) $120/$105, 2BR (4) $150-$155/$135-$140, 3BR (6) $200; extra person $15/night

Hale Mahina Beach Resort

3875 Lower Honoapi'ilani Highway, Lahaina, HI 96761. 800-367-8047 ext. 441; 808-669-8441; e-mail: halemahinabeachresort@msn.com. Agents: Chase 'n Rainbows 800-367-0092; Maui Lodging 800-487-6002.

Hale Mahina means "House of the Pale Moon" and offers 52 units in two four-story buildings and one two-story building. All feature lanais, ceiling fans, microwaves, washer/dryer, barbecue area, jacuzzi.

Chase 'n Rainbows rates: 1BR $160/$140, 2BR $195/$175

Hale Maui Apartment Hotel

P.O. Box 516, Lahaina, HI 96761. 808-669-6312; www.maui.net/~halemaui.

All one-bedroom units sleep 5. Lanais, limited maid service, coin-operated washer/dryer, barbecue. Weekly and monthly discounts. Three-night minimum.

Rates: 1BR (2, max 5) $85-$95; extra person $15/night

★ Hale Ono Loa

3823 Lower Honoapi'ilani Highway, Lahaina, HI 96761. 808-669-6362. Agents: Maui Accommodations 800-252-MAUI; Maui Lodging 800-487-6002; Chase 'n Rainbows 800-367-6092.

Sixty-seven oceanfront and oceanview units. Beachfront is rocky. The units I toured were roomy and nicely furnished with spacious lanais. The grounds and pool area were pleasant and well groomed. A good choice for a quiet retreat. Grocery store nearby. Some rental agents may offer two-bedroom units.

Maui Lodging rates: 1BR 1BTH $85-$110 (4), 2BR $135-$165

Hoyochi Nikko

3901 Lower Honoapi'ilani Highway, Lahaina, HI 96761. 800-487-6002; 808-669-8343; e-mail: hoyochi@aol.com. Agent: Maui Lodging 800-487-6002.

All 18 units are one bedroom (some with lofts), oceanview on a rocky beachfront with sandbar. Air conditioning. The two-story building bears an oriental motif. Underground parking, "Long Boy" twin beds, some with queens, stacking washer/dryer in units. Barbecue.

Maui Lodging rates: $100-$165

★ Aston Ka'anapali Shores

100 Ka'anapali Shores Place, Lahaina, HI 96761. 808-667-2211. Agents: Managed by Aston 800-922-7866; Maui & All Island 800-663-6962; Chase 'n Rainbows 800-367-6092; Whalers Realty 800-676-4112.

All 463 units offer telephones, free tennis, daily maid service and air conditioning. Nicely landscaped grounds and a wide beach with an area of coral reef cleared for swimming and snorkeling. This is the only resort on north Ka'anapali Beach that offers a good swimming area. Putting green, jacuzzi and the Beach Club restaurant located in the pool area. The resort features a year-round program for children ages 3 to 10 years; check "Childcare Programs" in Chapter 1. Activities are all held on property grounds and include hula and crafts. Program for resort guests only. Inquire about Aston's Island Hopper Rates, which offer sizable discounts.

Aston rates: Hotel Room w/refrigerator $200/$175; S BR (1-2) g.v., partial o.v. $300/$225; 1BR (1-4) standard $350/$255, g.v. $385/$285, o.v. $465/$325; 2BR (1-6) g.v. $550/$395, o.v. $630/$455, o.f. $730/$535; Suites $900-$1,000/$675-$775

Kaleialoha

3785 Lower Honoapi'ilani Highway, Lahaina, HI 96761. Kaleialoha agent: 800-222-8688; 808-669-8197; www.maui.net/dwhipple/kaleialoha.com. Other agents: Maui Beachfront Rentals 888-661-7200.

Sixty-seven units in a four-story building.

Rates: 1BR (2, max 4) superior $125, deluxe $115, mountain view $95; extra persons 2 years and older $10/night

Kulakane

3741 Lower Honoapi'ilani Highway (P.O. Box 5236), Lahaina, HI 96761. 800-367-6088; 808-669-6119; fax 808-669-9694; www.kulakane.com; e-mail: kulakane@maui.net.

Forty-two oceanfront units with fully equipped kitchen, laundry facilities. Lanais overlook ocean but no sandy beach.

Rates: 1BR $127, 2BR $175

Kuleana

3959 Lower Honoapi'ilani Highway, Lahaina, HI 96761. 800-367-5633; 808-669-8080. Agents: Maui Lodging 800-487-6002; Chase 'n Rainbows 800-367-6092.

All 118 one-bedroom units have queen-size sofa bed in living room. Large pool with plenty of lounge chair room and tennis court. A short walk to sandy beaches.

Rates: 1BR o.v. $90-$105, o.f. $125; 2BR o.f. $185-$205

Lokelani

3833 Lower Honoapi'ilani Highway, Lahaina, HI 96761. 800-367-2976; 808-669-8110; fax: 808-669-1619; e-mail lokelanihi@aol.com; www.maui.net/~lokcondo. Agent: Chase 'n Rainbows 800-367-6092.

Three 3-story, 12-unit buildings with beachfront or oceanview units. The one-bedroom units are on beach level with lanai, two-bedroom units are townhouses with bedrooms upstairs and lanais on both levels. Washer/dryers.

Rates: 1BR (2) $125, 2BR townhouses (1-6) $170-$190; add $10 per night December 1 to May 1

★ Mahana

110 Ka'anapali Shores Place, Lahaina, HI 96761. 808-661-8751. Agents: Managed by Aston Resorts and Hotels 800-922-7866; Maui & All Island 800-663-6962; Whalers Realty 800-676-4112; Chase 'n Rainbows 800-367-0092; Maui Lodging 800-487-6002.

Mahana means "twins" as in two towers. All units oceanfront. Two 12-story towers with two tennis courts, heated pool, central air conditioning, saunas, elevators, small pool area. Located on narrow beachfront with offshore coral reef precluding swimming and snorkeling. A better swimming area is 100 yards up the beach. I haven't stayed here, but over the years have heard from many readers that they wouldn't stay anywhere else. Higher rates from Aston may include added amenities, such as daily maid service. Inquire about Aston's Island Hopper Rates, which are significantly discounted from the following.

Aston rates: S BR 1 bath (1-2) o.f. $295/$225, 1BR 1 bath (1-4) o.f. $385/$290, 2BR 2 bath (1-6) o.f. $625/$450

Chase 'n Rainbows rates: S BR $120/$110, 1BR $140/$120

Mahina Surf

4057 Lower Honoapi'ilani Highway, Lahaina, HI 96761. 800-367-6086; 808-669-6068; fax 808-669-4534; www.mahina.surf.com. Agent: Maui Beachfront Rentals 888-661-7200.

Fifty-six one-bedroom and one-bedroom-with-loft units. Dishwashers. Located on rocky shore, the nearest sandy beach is a short drive to Kahana. A large lawn around the pool offers plenty of lounging room.

Maui Beachfront Rentals rates: 1BR o.v. $125-$160/$110-$145, 2BR o.v. $155-$190/$140-$175

Makani Sands
3765 Lower Honoapi'ilani Highway, Lahaina, HI 96761. 800-227-8223; 808-669-8223; fax 808-665-0756. Agents: Maui Lodging 800-487-6002; Chase 'n Rainbows 800-367-6092;

Thirty units in a three-story building. Dishwashers, washer/dryers, elevator. Oceanfront with small sandy beach. Some units with air conditioning. Onsite property managers.

Rates: 1BR (2) $125, 2BR (4) $170, 3BR (6) $205-$295

Maui Kai
106 Ka'anapali Shores Place, Lahaina, HI 96761. 800-367-5635; 808-667-3500; e-mail: mauikai@worldnet.att.net. Agents: Maui Beachfront Rentals 888-661-7200; Chase 'n Rainbows 800-367-6092.

A single ten-story building with 79 units. Offering central air conditioning, private lanais, fully equipped kitchens and amenities including a swimming pool, jacuzzi, laundry facilities, plus free parking. Some studio units may be available. Weekly/monthly discounts.

Hotel rates: S BR $155/$145, 1BR $188-$199/$180-$190, 2BR $294/$280

Maui Beachfront Rentals rates: 1BR 1BTH o.f. $148/$131

Maui Sands
3559 Lower Honoapi'ilani Highway, Lahaina, HI 96761. Agents: Maui Resort Management 800-367-5037; Whalers Realty 800-676-4112.

All 76 units have air conditioning and kitchens. Limited maid service. Microwaves, coin-op laundry facility, and rollaways and cribs available $9 night. A very friendly atmosphere where old friends have been gathering each year since it was built in the mid-1960s. They feature a large pool area with barbecues. Large boulders line the beach. A good family facility.

Rates: 1BR (2, max 3) g.v. $105/$95, garden w/o.v. $125/$115; 2BR g.v. 150-$160/$130-$145, o.f. $180/$160

Noelani
4095 Lower Honoapi'ilani Highway, Lahaina, HI 96761. 800-367-6030; 808-669-8374; fax 808-669-7904; e-mail: noelani@maui.net; www.noelani-condo-resort.com.

Fifty oceanfront units in one 4-story building and two 2-story structures. Kitchens with dishwashers and washer/dryers in 1-, 2- and 3-bedroom units. Three-bedroom units feature a sunken living room as do the two-bedroom units on the third floor. Complex has two pools and maid service mid-week. Located on a rocky shore, nearest sandy beach is short drive to Kahana. Under 18 free.

Rates: S BR 1 bath (1-2, max 2) $122/$107, Studio deluxe (1-2, max 3) $135/$119; 1BR 1 bath (1-2, max 4) $165/$147; 2BR 2 bath (1-2) $217; 3BR 3 bath (1-6, max 8) $267; extra person $10/night

Nohonani

3723 Lower Honoapi'ilani Highway, Lahaina, HI 96761. 800-822-7368; 808-669-8208; fax 808-822-RENT; e-mail: alohablu@maui.net.

Two 4-story buildings contain 22 oceanfront two-bedroom units and 5 one-bedroom units. Complex has large pool, telephones and is one block to grocery store. On-property management. Weekly and monthly discounts. Three-night minimum. No credit cards from on-site reservations.

Rates: 1BR (1-2) $122/$117, 2BR (1-4) $160/$140; extra person $15/night

Paki Maui

3615 Lower Honoapi'ilani Highway, Lahaina, HI 96761. 808-669-8235. Agents: Aston Hotels & Resorts 800-922-7866; Maui & All Island 800-663-6962; Chase 'n Rainbows 800-367-6092.

This complex surrounds a garden and waterfall. No air conditioning.

Rates: 1BR (1-4) $210-$265/$165-$210, 2BRS (1-6) $310-$345/$240-$270

★ Papakea

3543 Lower Honoapi'ilani Highway, Lahaina, HI 96761. Agents: Maui Resort Management 800-367-5037, 808-669-4848; Aston Hotels & Resorts 800-922-7866; Maui Beachfront Rentals 800-676-4112; Maui & All Island 800-663-6962; Whalers Realty 800-676-4112; RSVP 800-663-1118; Chase 'n Rainbows 800-367-0092.

There are five 4-story buildings with 364 units. Two pools, two jacuzzis, two saunas, tennis courts, putting green, washer/dryers and barbecue area. The shallow water is great for children due to a protective reef located 10-30 yards offshore, but poor for swimming or snorkeling. A better beach is down in front of the Ka'anapali Shores. One of the nicer grounds for a condominium complex, Papakea features lush landscaping and pool areas. A comfortable and quiet property that I recommend especially for families. Nonsmoking units available.

Maui Resort Management rates: S BR (2) g.v. $125-$135/$115; 1BR (4) $135-$160/$125-$160, 1BR 2BTH (4) $150-$180/$165; 2BR (6) $160-$200/$155-$175

Pikake

3701 Lower Honoapi'ilani Highway, Lahaina, HI 96761. 800-446-3054; 808-669-6086. Agent: Maui Lodging 800-487-6002.

A low-rise, two-story, Polynesian-style building with only 12 apartments completed in 1966. Private lanais open to the lawn or balconies. The beach is protected by a sea wall. Central laundry area. Ceiling fans, no air conditioning. All units are oceanfront.

Rates: 1BR (2, max 4) $130/$115, 2BR (4, max 6) $170/$150; extra person $10/night

Polynesian Shores

3975 Lower Honoapi'ilani Highway, Lahaina, HI 96761. 800-433-6284, 800-488-2179 (from Canada); 808-669-6065; e-mail: polyshor@maui.net. Agent: Chase 'n Rainbows 800-367-6092.

Fifty-two units on a rocky shore but nice grounds with deck overlooking the ocean. Heated swimming pool.

Rates: 1BR 1 bath (2) $145/$135, 2BR 2 bath (2) $185/$175, 2BR 2 Bath End (4) $215/$200; 3BR 3 bath (4) $245/$225

KAHANA

Hololani

4401 Lower Honoapi'ilani Highway, Lahaina, HI 96761. 800-367-5032; 808-669-8021; fax 808-669-7682. Agents: Chase 'n Rainbows 800-367-0092, Maui Beachfront Rentals 888-661-7200.

Twenty-seven oceanfront units on sandy, reef protected beach. Covered parking. Children under five free. No credit cards.

Maui Beachfront Rentals rates: 2BR 2 BTH (6) o.f. $182/$158

Kahana Beach Resort

4221 Lower Honoapi'ilani Highway, Lahaina, HI 96761. 808-669-8611; 888-941-3004.

Most of the rooms are studios with only a single one-bedroom unit on each floor. The property is on the ocean, but the shoreline is rocky. A small onsite pool, but guests have use of the adjacent Sands of Kahana pool and facilities. Rates higher during Christmas holidays.

Rates: S BR $175, 1BR $300

Kahana Outrigger

4521 Lower Honoapi'ilani Highway, Lahaina, HI 96761. 800-987-8494; 808-669-6550. Agents: Maui & All Island 800-663-6962; Chase 'n Rainbows 800-367-0092; Maui Beachfront Rentals 888-661-7200.

Sixteen spacious three-bedroom oceanview condo suites in a low-rise complex on a narrow sandy beachfront. Units have microwaves, washer/dryers and are appointed with Italian tile. These are rented as vacation "homes" with no on-property service provided.

Maui Beachfront Rentals rates: 3BR 2BTH o.f. $338/$312, 3BR 3BTH o.v. $281/$250, 3BR 2BTH o.v. $260/$229

★ Kahana Reef

4471 Lower Honoapi'ilani Highway, Lahaina, HI 96761. 800-253-3773; 808-669-6491; fax 808-669-2192. Managed by Aston Hotels & Resorts 800-922-7866. Agents: Maui Condo & Home 800-822-4409; Maui & All

Island 800-663-6962; Chase 'n Rainbows 800-367-6092; Maui Beachfront Rentals 888-661-7200; Whalers Realty 800-676-4112.

Eighty-eight well-kept units. Limited number of oceanfront studios available. Laundry facilities on premises. A good value. Amenities such as maid service may influence price differential.

Maui Condo & Home rates: 1BR $160/$130

★ Kahana Sunset

P.O. Box 10219, Lahaina, HI 96761. 800-669-1488; 808-669-8011; fax 808-669-9170. Agents: Village Resorts 800-367-7052, fax 808-661-8315; RSVP 800-663-1118.

Ninety units in 6 two- and three-story buildings on a beautiful and secluded white-sand beach. Units have very large lanais, telephones and washer/dryers. Each unit has its own lanai, but they adjoin one another, adding to the friendly atmosphere of this complex. One of the very few resorts with a heated pool, heated children's pool and barbecue. You can drive up right to your door on most of the two-bedroom units, making unloading easy (and with a family heavy into suitcases that can be a real back saver). These are not luxurious units, but it is a location that is difficult to beat.

Rates: 1BR g.v. $205-$220/$130-$165, ocean/garden view $240/$180; 2BR ocean/garden view $230/$195, o.v. $250-$275/$210-$245, o.f. $350-$370/$280-$325

Kahana Villa

4242 Lower Honoapi'ilani Highway, Lahaina, HI 96761. 808-669-5613. Agents: Chase 'n Rainbows 800-367-6092; Maui Beachfront Rentals 888-661-7200.

Across the road from the beach. Units have microwaves, washer/dryers, telephones. Daily maid service. Property also has sauna, tennis courts, convenience store and Erik's Seafood Grotto restaurant. Some studios also available through agents.

Maui Beachfront Rentals rates: 1BR 1 bath (1-4) g.v. $125-$135/$114-$125, o.v. $146-$185/$135-$164; 2BR 2 bath (1-6) g.v. $140/$130, o.v. $178/$158

★ Kahana Village

4531 Lower Honoapi'ilani Highway, Lahaina, HI 96761. 800-824-3065; 808-669-5111; www.kahanavillage.com. Other agents: Maui & All Island 800-663-6962; RSVP 800-663-1118; Chase 'n Rainbows 800-367-6092.

Attractive townhouse units. Second-level units are 1,200 square feet, ground-level three-bedroom units have 1,700 square feet with a wet bar, sunken tub in master bath, Jenn-aire ranges, microwaves, lanais and washer/dryers. They offer a heated pool and attractively landscaped grounds. Nice but narrow beach offering good swimming.

Rates: 2BR o.v. $240/$205, o.f. $280/$240; 3BR o.v. $330/$280, o.f. $395/$335

Royal Kahana

4365 Lower Honoapi'ilani Highway, Lahaina, HI 96761. 800-447-7783; 808-669-5911; fax 808-669-5950. Management and reservations: Outrigger Resorts 800-OUTRIGGER. Other agent: Chase 'n Rainbows 800-367-6092.

Built in 1975 with 236 oceanview units on Kahana Beach, this 12-story high-rise complex is near grocery stores, restaurants and shops. Underground parking and air conditioning. Daily maid service. A nice pool area with sauna. Tennis courts. All suites include full kitchens and washer/dryer in unit. Free parking. Extra person charge $15 per night includes rollaways. Cribs available. Two-night minimum stay.

Rates: Studio (1-3) g.v./o.v. $210, o.v. $230; 1BR 1 bath (1-2) g.v $265, o.v. $285, o.f. $345; 2BR 2 bath (1-6) g.v. $320 /o.v.$350, o.f. $460

★ Sands of Kahana

4299 Lower Honoapi'ilani Highway, Lahaina, HI 96761. Managed by Sullivan Properties: 888-669-0400; e-mail: info@sands-of-kahana.com; www.sands-of-kahana.com. Agent: Chase 'n Rainbows 800-367-6092.

Ninety-six units on Kahana Beach. I stayed here some years back and enjoyed the spacious rooms and nicely appointed amenities. I was surprised to discover it is among many in Kahana that are going timeshare. While they do still rent to the public for now, you'd have to avoid the constant sales pitches and gathering of folks for sales talks. Pool, children's pool, jacuzzi and three tennis courts. Three rates indicate holiday season, on season and off season.

Rates: 1BR value view $190/$150/$130, o.v. $225/$185/$165, o.f. $265/$225/$205; 2BR value view $255/$205/$180, o.v. $295/$245/$220, o.f. $335/$285/$260; 3BR o.v. $365/$305/$275, o.f. $410/$350/$320; Penthouse $300-$435

Valley Isle Resort

4327 Lower Honoapi'ilani Highway, Lahaina, HI 96761. 808-669-5511 (for brochure only, no reservations) Agents: Maui Lodging 800-487-6002; Chase 'n Rainbows 800-367-0092; Maui & All Island 800-663-6962.

Partial air conditioning. Located on Kahana Beach. Chase 'n Rainbow has most of the private condo rentals at this property.

Rates: $100 range for studios, $110-$120 for one bedrooms and 2 bedrooms in the $150 range depending on view and location

NAPILI

Hale Napili

65 Hui Road, Napili, HI 96761. 800-245-2266; 808-669-6184; fax 808-665-0066.

Eighteen oceanfront units on Napili Bay. Daily maid service except Sunday. Ceiling fans, microwaves, lanais and laundry facilities on property. No pool. Three-night minimum. Children 12 and under free.

Rates: Studio (2) g.v. $110/$100, o.f. $150/$140; 1BR (2) o.f. $175/$160; extra person $15/night

★ **Honokeana Cove**
5255 Lower Honoapi'ilani Highway, Lahaina, HI 96761. 800-237-4948; 808-669-6441; e-mail: honokeana-cove.com; www.honokeana-cove.com. On-site agent: 800-237-4948.

Thirty-eight oceanview units on Honokeana Cove near Napili Bay. Attractive grounds—and friendly sea turtles. Probably one of the best values in West Maui and that is evidenced by the many returning guests. In calm weather you'll find lots of folks snorkeling in the cove. While each condo is privately owned and furnished with the owner's individual tastes, you'll find all units equipped with cable television, VCR, microwaves, blenders, etc. Private lanai with ocean views. Weekly and monthly discounts.

Rates: 1BR 1 bath (2) $127, 1BR 2 bath (2) $135, 2BR 1 bath $146; 2BR 2 bath (4, max 4) $175; 3BR 2 bath (4, max 6) $207; townhouse (4) $204; extra person $10-$15/night

Mauian
5441 Honoapi'ilani Highway, Lahaina, HI 96761. 800-367-5034; 808-669-6205; fax 808-669-0129; e-mail: info@mauian.com; www.mauian.com.

Forty-four studio apartments on Napili Bay. The Mauian hotel on Napili Beach is a small, charming hideaway nestled along the gentle waters of Napili Bay. The two-acre beachfront property features 44 studios with fully equipped kitchens and private lanais. They cannot guarantee any specific room number, but they will make every attempt to accommodate those guests requesting a particular building location. Check website for special discounts. Rooms have one queen and two twin day beds. The Mauian has been offering Hawaiian hospitality since 1959 and is owned and operated by a long-time Hawaiian family. The Mauian offers guests a relaxed island-style haven with no unwanted disturbances—the units do not have telephones or television. A courtesy phone is available in the lobby. Barbecue area. Many guests have returned to vacation at this quiet corner of Napili for years.

Rates: S BR g.v. $165/$145, o.v. $185/$165, o.f. $195/$180

Napili Bay Resort
33 Hui Drive, Lahaina, HI 96761. 808-669-6044. Agents: Maui Beachfront Rentals 888-661-7200; Chase 'n Rainbows 800-367-6092.

This older complex on Napili Bay is neat, clean and affordably priced. Studio apartments offer one queen and two single beds, lanais, kitchens, daily maid service. Coin-op laundromat with public phones. Many of the individually owned studios are rented directly from the owners.

Maui Beachfront Rentals rates: o.f. $109, o.v. and partial o.v. $95

Napili Gardens

5432 Honoapi'ilani Highway, Lahaina, HI 96761. Contact Liz Anderson, e-mail: liz@mauigateway.com; 808-870-2043.

Lovely custom townhouses that offer double car garages, private rear yards, gourmet kitchens, lanais, plus washer/dryer. Located a short walk to the beach.

Rates: 3BR 2.5 baths $250/$200

★ Napili Kai Beach Resort

5900 Honoapi'ilani Highway, Lahaina, HI 96761. 800-367-5030; 808-669-6271; fax 808-669-0086; e-mail: stay@napilikai.com; www.napilikai.com.

Units feature lanais, kitchenettes and telephones. Complimentary tennis equipment, beach equipment, putters and snorkel gear. Daily coffee and tea party in Beach Club. Sea House restaurant located on grounds. Four pools and Hawai'i's largest jacuzzi. The key here is location, location, location. The grounds are extensive and the area very quiet. A relaxed and friendly atmosphere, a great beach and a variety of activities may tempt you to spend most of your time enjoying this very personable and complete resort. A popular location for family reunions. A kids' program is offered during the summer months for youth between the ages of six and twelve. See "Childcare Programs" in Chapter 1. Two-night deposit, 14-day refund notice. Christmas rates slightly higher. Group rates available and packages, too.

Rates: Hotel room (2) g.v. $190, o.v. $225; S BR g.v. $220, o.v. $250, beachfront $290, o.f. $305; 2BR Suite g.v. $410, o.v. $475-525, o.f. $675; 3BR Suite g.v. $535, o.v. $700; Hideaway Suite g.v. $550

Napili Point

5295 Lower Honoapi'ilani Highway, Lahaina, HI 96761. Napili Point Resort Rental 808-669-9222; 800-669-6252; e-mail: napiliptresort@cs.com; www.napili.com.

Located on rocky beach, but next door to beautiful Napili Bay. Units have washer/dryer, full kitchens with dishwashers and daily maid service. King- or queen-size beds in one-bedroom units. No air conditioning, most units have ceiling fans. Cribs available. Two pools. In some suites the second bedroom is loft-style.

Napili Point rates: 1BR o.v. $229/$199, o.f. $249/$219, Point o.f. $269/$239; 2BR o.v. $329/$259, o.f. $359/$289, Point o.f. $399/$319

Napili Shores

5315 Lower Honoapi'ilani Highway, Lahaina, HI 96761. 808-669-8061; fax 808-669-5047. Management and reservations: Outrigger Resorts Hawaii 800-OUTRIGGER; Maui Beachfront Rentals 888-661-7200; RSVP 800-663-1118.

On fabulous Napili Bay, 152 units with lanais, one-bedroom units have dishwashers. Laundry facilities on premises as well as two pools, adult hot tub, croquet and barbecue area. Restaurants, cocktail lounge and grocery store on property. Studios have one queen and one twin bed. Cribs and rollaways available.

Outrigger Resorts rates: S BR g.v. $182, o.v. $210, o.f. 238; 1BR g.v. $215, o.v. $244

Maui Beachfront Rentals rates: S BR (2, max 3) $140/$99, 1BR (2, max 4) $140/$120 (limited number of units)

★ Napili Sunset
46 Hui Road, Lahaina, HI 96761. 800-447-9229 U.S.; 800-223-4611 Canada; 808-669-8083; fax 808-669-2730; e-mail: info@napilisunset.com; www.napilisunset.com.

Forty-one units located on Napili Bay. Daily maid service. Ceiling fans, no air conditioning. These units have great ocean views and are well maintained. A very friendly atmosphere. The studio units are nicely kept, but I'd recommend the oceanfront one bedrooms. You can't get any closer to the beach than here. Three-night minimum.

Rates: S BR g.v. $120/$105 (2), 1BR 1 bath (2, max 5) beachfront $225/$205, 2BR (4) 2 bath o.f. $315/$265; extra person (over 2 years old) $12/night

Napili Surf
50 Napili Place, Lahaina, HI 96761. 800-541-0638; 808-669-8002; fax 808-669-8004; www.napilisurf.com.

These 53 units are on Napili Bay. Two pools, barbecue, shuffleboard, lanais, daily maid service and laundry facilities. Five-night minimum. No credit cards. Inquire about specials and monthly discounts.

Rates: S BR (2, max 3) g.v. $130, o.v. $175, o.f. $190; 1BR (2, max 5) partial o.v. $205, o.v. $225, o.f. $280; extra person $15/night

Napili Village Suites
5425 Honoapi'ilani Highway, Lahaina, HI 96761. 800-336-2185; 808-669-6228; fax 808-669-6229. Agent: Maui Beachfront Rentals 888-661-7200.

All vacation apartments are 500 square feet and feature king- or queen-size beds. Daily maid service. Laundry facilities on premises. Located a short walk from Napili Bay. Children 5 and under are free.

Rates: (2) g.v. $99/$89, o.v. $109/$99, g.v. deluxe $119/$109

One Napili Way
5355 Lower Honoapi'ilani Highway Road #101, Napili, HI 96761. 808-669-2007; 800-841-MAUI; e-mail: onenapi@aloha.net; www.onenapiliway.com.

There are 14 condos available as one-, two- or three-bedroom units. Master baths feature jacuzzi tub, all units have washer/dryer. Four-night minimum.

Rates: 1BR (1-4) $250, 2BR (1-6) $310, 3BR (1-8) $340

KAPALUA

Kapalua, "arms embracing the sea," is the most northwestern development on Maui. Kapalua Bay has garnered top accolades from Dr. Beach and his "Best Beaches in the World" awards. It is a prefect crescent lined with palm trees. Many of the condominiums are nestled around the golf courses and you need to take a shuttle down to the beach, drive (limited parking) or walk. The Kapalua Bay Hotel and Ocean Villas is just steps away from the bay. The Ritz-Carlton, Kapalua is situated above D.T. Fleming Beach, which is not as protected and safe as Kapalua Bay. Either resort offers outstanding amenities and every aspect of your stay will leave you feeling relaxed and pampered. More than 400 condominium units are located in the Ridge, Golf and Bay Villas at Kapalua Villas. Spacious luxury homes and estates are also available as vacation rentals. The logo for Kapalua is the butterfly, and with a close look you can see that the body of the butterfly is a pineapple.

★ Kapalua Bay Hotel and Ocean Villas

1 Bay Drive, Kapalua, HI 96761. 800-367-8000; 808-669-5656; fax 808-669-4694; www.kapaluabayhotel.com.

The hotel offers 191 luxury hotel rooms and suites in an open-air terraced low-rise. Spacious rooms have service bars, mini-refrigerators, video cassette players and his-and-her vanities. Air conditioning and private lanais in all units. Their stunning lobby features floor-to-ceiling glass windows with that breathtaking view of Moloka'i and Lana'i showcased. The views continue in their fitness center located above the lobby. There's a plethora of exciting Hawaiian cultural activities held at the adjoining Kapalua Shops. The Bay Club and the Gardenia Court are the hotel's outstanding restaurants. The Lehua Lounge serves afternoon tea in the open-air lobby; a variety of appetizers and desserts with accompanying piano music are available in the evening. The Plumeria Terrace offers daytime meals poolside. (The pool is butterfly-shaped and located near the ocean.) The resort's three championship golf courses and two tennis facilities (20 plexipave courts, 9 lighted) are all available for guest use. A beauty salon and exercise room are on property and a children's program (see "Childcare Programs" in Chapter 1 for details) is available. Lovely grounds, excellent beach and breathtaking bay. The expanse of lawn gives way to lush tropical foliage, waterfalls, pools and gardens. This is elegance on a more sophisticated scale than the glitter and glitz of the Ka'anapali resorts. Two children 17 or younger free if sharing room with parent. Cribs available at no charge. Three-night deposit high season, one-night deposit low season; 14-day refund notice. Modified American Plan is available at $65 per person. Room & Car, Golf, Family and other packages offer value with extra amenities.

Rates: g.v. $360, partial o.v. $410, o.v. $480, o.f. $540, deluxe o.f. $610; 1 and 2BR suites available

★ Kapalua Villas

Kapalua Villas: 500 Office Road, Kapalua, HI 96761. 800-545-0018 U.S. & Canada; 808-669-8088; fax 808-669-5234; www.kapaluavillas.com. Other agents: Kapalua Hotel (Villa Suites) 800-367-8000.

There are over 270 vacation rental units in the Ridge, Golf and Bay Villas and each is spacious and beautifully appointed. Individually decorated and private, they feel much more like a home than a condominium and make wonderful units for a large family or couples traveling together. Rates from the Kapalua Villas include a 24-hour reception center, maid service, concierge, activity desk and complimentary tennis. (These amenities do not apply if you rent through other agencies.) Their units offer kitchens, washer/dryers and ceiling fans with 2 TVs, 2 telephones and a VCR. Recreational facilities include several pools, outdoor barbecues and tropical garden areas. The resort includes The Bay Course and The Village Course, two 18-hole championship golf courses designed by Arnold Palmer, as well as the Plantation Course, designed by Coore & Crenshaw. Two tennis facilities offer 20 courts (9 lighted) and there is a shopping area with myriad boutiques. There are also several excellent restaurants in the area from which to choose. The Kapalua Villas also offer luxury homes within the private gated community of Pineapple Hill at Kapalua. With nearly 4,000 square feet of living space, these magnificently furnished homes offer deluxe kitchens, whirlpool and steam baths, private outdoor pools and/or whirlpool spas and daily maid service. A 5-bedroom, 7,700-square-foot, multimillion-dollar estate is also available at The Plantation Estates. Prices are reflected by location and view and vary with each agent. A little calling may be worth your while. I'd suggest starting with Kapalua Villas.

Rates: 1BR (max 4) fairway v. $239/$199, o.v. $269/$239, o.f. $299/$279; 2BR (4, max 6) fairway v. $355/$299, o.v. $430/$379, o.f. $505/$469. Luxury homes: 3BR (max 6) and 4BR (max 8) $1695/$1650; 5BR estate $4,000-$7,500

★ The Ritz-Carlton, Kapalua

1 Ritz Carlton Drive, Kapalua, HI 96761. 808-669-6200; fax 808-669-1566; www.ritzcarlton.com.

The 550-room oceanfront resort at D. T. Fleming Beach has a Hawaiian motif with a plantation feel that features native stonework throughout the hotel. Accommodations include 377 kings, 171 doubles, 65 Club Rooms and 58 suites. Amenities include twice-daily made service, in-room terry robes, complimentary in-room safe, multilingual staff, babysitting and children's programs, and full-service beauty salon. The Ritz-Kids program is a half- or full-day program that explores the wonders of Maui; see "Childcare Programs" in Chapter 1. While the kids are at play, spoil yourself with one of the many spa services at the fitness center; oceanside or in-room massage is available. Ten tennis courts plus a 10,000-square-foot, three-level swimming pool are among the amenities. Dining options include The Terrace restaurant, the poolside Banyan Tree, the Beach House, the Lobby Lounge, and the Pool Bar. See Chapter 4 for more information. Plenty of annual events are held at Kapalua; see "Calendar of Annual Events" in Chapter 1.

The Ritz-Carlton is certainly a jewel for West Maui. I enjoyed a couple of days and checked out the Club Floor. These special floors, available at many of the finer properties on Maui, have added security. A special key was required in the elevator to reach your floor. A special "Club" lounge area offered snacks almost continually. The continental breakfast was more than one would expect, with some wonderful cereals, pastries, freshly squeezed juices and fresh fruits. The midday snack included light sandwiches and fresh vegetables or fruits. The early-evening hours provided appetizers and wine or drinks. After dinner were chocolates and cordials. There were also cold drinks and hot coffee available all day. The lounge/dining room was elegant yet homey, and the balconies provided entertaining views of golfers playing the course. The kids really enjoyed running down for a snack whenever they felt like it. In fact, they seldom were hungry at mealtimes and probably could have survived for weeks on the goodies served on the Club Floor. This is the way to be pampered in paradise! The guest rooms were spacious and beautifully appointed. Inquire about special packages and promotions.

Rates: g.v. $375, o.v. $445, deluxe o.v. $535; The Ritz-Carlton Club $635; 1BR Suites g.v. $635, o.v. $675; Club Suite $975; 1BR and 2BR Suites $1,035-$4,035

Ma'alaea–Kihei–Wailea–Makena Area

MA'ALAEA

Hono Kai
280 Hauoli Street, Wailuku, HI 96793. 808-244-7012. Agent: Ma'alaea Bay Rentals 800-367-6084.

Forty-six units located on the beach. Choice of gardenview, oceanview or oceanfront. Laundry facilities, barbecue, pool. This complex is on the beach and gains the attention of the budget-conscious traveler, but don't expect any frills. Five-night minimum stay.

Rates: 1BR g.v. $120/$90, o.f. $165/$125; 2BR g.v. $160/$120, o.f. $180/$145; 3BR $200/$150

Island Sands

150 Hauoli Street, Wailuku, HI 96793. Island Sands Resort Rentals 800-826-7816; 808-244-0848; fax 808-244-5639. Agents: Ma'alaea Bay Rentals 800-367-6084; Condominium Rentals Hawaii 800-367-5242, 808-879-2778.

Eighty-four units in a 6-story building. One of Ma'alaea's larger complexes located along the sea wall. Offers a Maui-shaped pool, a grassy lawn area, barbecue. Many of these units also have a lanai off the master bedroom; however, the lanais have a concrete piece in the middle of each railing that somewhat limits the view while sitting or lying in bed. Washer/dryers and air conditioning. Elevators. Weekly and monthly discounts. Four-night minimum. Children under three free; $200 deposit with 15-day refund notice.

Ma'alaea Bay Rentals rates: 1BR o.f. $135/$115, 2BR ranging up to $185; extra person $7.50/night

★ Kana'i a Nalu

250 Hauoli Street, Wailuku, HI 96793. Agent: Ma'alaea Bay Rentals 800-367-6084.

Eighty units with washer/dryers in four buildings with elevators. No maid service. This is the first of three condominiums along a sandy beachfront. Its name means "parting of the sea, surf, or wave." The complex is V-shaped with a pool area in the middle. Nicely landscaped grounds, a decent beach and only a short walk along the beach to the best swimming and playing area along this section of coastline. While over the last couple of years the high-season prices have jumped a bit, the low-season rates have consistently remained an excellent value. Overall one of the best values in the Ma'alaea area. Have you wondered where the author of this guide stays? If I am not moving around the island, sampling different properties, you'll find me catching my breath here, and enjoying the sunny shores and gentle breezes of Ma'alaea. Five-night minimum, ten nights over Christmas. Weekly/monthly discounts.

Rates: 2BR (4) o.v. $185/$130, o.f. $225/$165

★ Lauloa

100 Hauoli Street, Wailuku, HI 96793. 808-242-6575. Agent: Ma'alaea Bay Rentals 800-367-6084.

Forty-seven 2-bedroom, 2-bath units of 1,100 square feet. One of the Lauloa's best features is their floor plan. The living room and master bedroom are on the front of the building with a long connecting lanai and sliding glass patio doors that offer unobstructed ocean views.

A sliding shoji screen separates the living room from the bedroom. Each morning from the bed you have but to open your eyes to see the palm trees swaying in front of the panoramic ocean view. The second bedroom is in the back of the unit. These two-bedroom units are spacious and are in fair to good condition (depending on the owner). Each has a washer/dryer in the unit. The pool area and grounds are along the sea wall. There are often local fishermen throwing nets and lines into the ocean. Five-night minimum. Maid service extra charge. Monthly discounts.

Ma'alaea Bay Rentals rates: 2BR 2 bath (4) o.f. reef $160/$125

Ma'alaea Banyans

190 Hauoli Street, Wailuku, HI 96793. 808-242-5668. Agent: Ma'alaea Bay Rentals 800-367-6084.

Seventy-six oceanview units with lanai and washer/dryer. Weekly and monthly discounts. Oceanfront on rocky shore, short walk to beach. Pool area, jacuzzi, barbecues.

Ma'alaea Bay Rentals rates: 1BR (2) o.f. reef $115/$110; extra person $10/night

Ma'alaea Kai

70 Hauoli Street, Wailuku, HI 96793. 808-244-7012. Agent: Ma'alaea Bay Rentals 800-367-6084.

Seventy oceanfront units. Laundry facilities, putting green, barbecue and elevators. Located on the harbor wall, the rooms are standard and quite satisfactory. Most have washer and dryer in the room. Pool area and large pleasant grounds in front along the harbor wall. A few blocks' walk down to a sandy beach. Weekly and monthly discounts.

Rates: 1BR (2) o.f. reef $95/$80, 2BR (4) o.f. reef $130/$90

Ma'alaea Yacht Marina

30 Hauoli Street, Wailuku, HI 96793. 808-244-7012. Agent: Ma'alaea Bay Rentals 800-367-6084.

All units are oceanfront, a beach is nearby. The units I viewed were pleasant with a wonderful view of the boats from most units and the added plus of having security elevators and stairways. Many of the units have no air conditioning; laundry facilities are located in a laundry room on each floor. A postage stamp–size grassy area in front and a small but adequate pool.

Ma'alaea Bay Rentals rates: 1BR (2) o.f. reef $115/$100, 2BR (4) o.f. reef low season only $120

★ Makani a Kai

300 Hauoli Street, Wailuku, HI 96793. Agent: Ma'alaea Bay Rentals 800-367-6084.

These deluxe oceanfront and oceanview units are on the beach. Laundry room on property, pool, barbecue. This is the last property along the beach in Ma'alaea. Beyond this is a long stretch of sandy beach along undeveloped state land and about a four-mile jaunt down to North Kihei—great for you beach walkers. The two-bedroom units are townhouse style. This is a very pleasant place to headquarter your Maui vacations. Five-night minimum, ten days over Christmas.

Rates: 1BR $125-$175/$110-$135; 2BR $185-$225/$125-$160

Milowai

50 Hauoli Street, Wailuku, HI 96793. Agents: Milowai Rentals 808-242-1580, fax 808-242-1634; Kihei Maui Vacations 800-541-6284; Ma'alaea Bay Rentals 800-367-6084.

One of the larger complexes in Ma'alaea with a restaurant on location, The Waterfront. They offer a large pool area and a barbecue along the sea wall. The corner units are a very roomy 1,200 square feet with windows off the master bedrooms. Depending on condo location in the building, the views are of the Ma'alaea Harbor or the open ocean. The one-bedroom units have a lanai off the living room and a bedroom in the back. Washer/dryer. Weekly/monthly discounts.

Ma'alaea Bay Rentals rates: 1BR (2) o.f. reef $115/$100, 2BR (4) o.f. reef $165/$120

KIHEI

Along with Ma'alaea, Kihei is a favorite place to stay because of the good units, central but quiet location, nice beach, cooling breezes and certainly some of the island's best vacation buys.

Hale Alana

Located in Maui Meadows. P.O. Box 160, Kihei, HI 96753. 800-871-5032; 808-875-4840; fax 808-879-6851; e-mail: maui@alohajourneys.com; www.alohajourneys.com.

Your hosts are Karen and Ken Stover. There are two master bedrooms and a third bedroom with two double beds. Great ocean vistas from the private deck and beautifully appointed all around. Two cottages are also available. One-week minimum from December 15 to April 15.

Rates: house (4) $264/$220, $30 each additional guest; cottages (2, max 4) $100/$80, $20/$15 each additional guest

Hale Hui Kai

2994 South Kihei Road, Kihei, HI 96753. 808-879-1219; fax 808-879-0600; 800-809-MAUI; www.beachbreeze.com.

Oceanfront on Keawakapu Beach. Five-night minimum or cleaning fee charged. No credit cards.

Rates: 2BR 2BTH (2) o.f. $260-300/$200-$260, side o.v. $180-$250/$165-$250, g.v. $180-$220/$140-$190; extra person $15-$20/night

Hale Kai O' Kihei

1310 Uluniu Road (P.O. Box 809), Kihei, HI 96753. 808-879-2757; 800-457-7014; fax 808-875-8242. Agent: Condo Rentals Hawaii 800-367-5242.

Fifty-nine oceanfront units with lanais in three-story building. Sandy beachfront. Shuffleboard, putting green, barbecues, laundry, recreation area.

Condo Rentals Hawaii rates: 1BR (2) $112-$139, 2BR (4) $135-$168

Hale Kamaole

2737 South Kihei Road, Kihei, HI 96753. 800-367-2970; 808-879-2698. Agents: Maui & All Island 800-663-6962; Condo Rentals Hawaii 800-367-5242; Maui Condo & Home 800-822-4409; Maui Condominiums 800-663-6962 U.S. & Canada.

There are 188 units in 5 buildings (2- and 3-story, no elevator) across the road from Kama'ole III Beach. Laundry building, barbecues, 2 pools, tennis courts. Some units have washer and dryers. Cleaning fee charged for less than 6 nights.

Condo Rentals Hawaii rates: 1BR $115-$145, 2BR 2BTH $141-$194

Hale Pau Hana

2480 South Kihei Road, Kihei, HI 96753. 808-879-2715; 800-367-6036; fax 808-875-0238; www.hphrewsort.com. Agents: RSVP 800-663-1118; Condominium Rentals Hawaii 800-367-5242; Kihei Maui Vacations 800-541-6284.

Seventy-eight oceanview units in four buildings. Laundry area, elevator, laundry facilities. Located on Kama'ole II Beach. Credit cards accepted but with surcharge.

Rates: The Tower $235-$276/$170-$230; The Two Story $225-$235/$160-$165

★ Haleakala Shores

2619 South Kihei Road, Kihei, HI 96753. 800-869-1097; 808-879-1218. Agents: Kihei Maui Vacations 800-541-6284; Bello Realty 800-541-3060.

Seventy-six 2-bedroom units in two four story buildings. Located across the road from Kama'ole III Beach. Washer/dryer. Covered parking. A good value. Rentals through on-site manager are check only, no credit cards.

Bello Realty rates: 2BR 2 BTH (1-4) $120/$90

Kamaole Beach Royale

2385 South Kihei Road, Kihei, HI 96753. 800-421-3661; 808-879-3131; fax 808-879-9163; e-mail: davi@aloha.net. Agent: Kumulani 800-367-2954.

Sixty-four units with washer/dryers and single or double lanais in a single seven-story building across from Kama'ole I Beach. Recreation area, elevator, roof garden. No credit cards through on-site rental agent and a minimum stay of five nights required.

Rates: 1BR 1 bath (2) $105-$115/$80-$90; 2BR 2 bath (2) $130-$145/ $105-$120; 3BR 2 bath (2) $160-$170/$135-$145; extra person $10/night

Kamaole Nalu

2450 South Kihei Road, Kihei, HI 96753 808-879-1006; fax 808-879-8693; 800-767-1497; e-mail: info@kamaolenalu.com; www.kamaole nalu.com. Agent: Maui & All Island 800-663-6962.

Thirty-six two-bedroom, two-bath units with large lanai, dishwasher and washer/dryer in a 6-story building. Located between Kama'ole I and II Beach Parks with all units offering ocean views. Weekly maid service during high season. Three-day minimum.

Rates: 2BR 2 bath (2) value view o.f. $195, deluxe o.v. $175, o.v. $155, g.v. $135; high season runs approximately $20/night extra; extra person $12-$15/night

Kamaole Sands

2695 South Kihei Road, Kihei, HI 96753. 808-874-8700; fax 808-879-0666. Managed by Castle Resorts Reservations 800-367-5004 U.S. & Canada. Agents: Kumulani 800-367-2954; Maui Condo & Home 800-822-4409; Bello Realty 800-541-3060; Kihei Maui Vacations 800-541-6284; Maui Condo & Home 800-822-4409; Maui Condominiums 800-663-6962 U.S. & Canada; Kihei Maui Vacations 800-541-6284; Maui & All Island 800-663-6962.

Ten 4-story buildings totaling 315 units. Includes daily maid service, 4 tennis courts, wading pool, babysitting services, 2 jacuzzis and barbecues. Located on 15 acres across the road from Kama'ole III Beach.

Castle Resorts rates: 1BR (1-4) Standard, Superior, Partial o.v. $195-$220/$170-$220; 2BR (1-6) Standard, Garden View, Partial o.v. $285-$335/$260-$310; 3BR (1-7) Partial o.v. $375/$415

Kathy Scheper's Maui Accommodations

800-645-3753; 808-879-8744; fax 808-879-9100; e-mail: vacation@maui 411.com; www.maui411.com.

Kathy offers a beach cottage and studio located on her property in Kihei at very reasonable rates. The cottage sleeps four. The studio is suited for one or two on a budget. It includes a small refrigerator, microwave oven, TV and a half bath. A tropical garden patio has a private outdoor shower. The beach is a short walk away. She also rents units at the Kai Nani Beach Condo.

Rates: Beach Cottage $125/$85, Studio $59/$39, Condo at Kai Nani $95/$75

Kauhale Makai (Village by the Sea)

930-938 South Kihei Road, Kihei, HI 96753. 808-879-8888. Agents: Maui & All Island 800-663-6962; Maui Condo & Home 800-822-4409; Kumulani 800-367-2954; RSVP 800-663-1118; Maui Condominiums 800-663-6962 U.S. & Canada; Kihei Maui Vacations 800-541-6284.

Two 6-floor buildings offer 169 air-conditioned units with phones. Complex features putting green, gas barbecues, plus kids' pool, sauna and laundry center. The beach here is usually strewn with coral rubble and seaweed, but area condos have taken to "vacuuming" it daily.

Maui Condo & Home rates: S BR (2) $110/85, 1BR (2) $120/$95, 2BR (4) $190/$150

★ Kealia

191 North Kihei Road, Kihei, HI 96753. 800-367-5222; 808-879-9159. Agent: Maui Condo & Home 800-822-4409.

Fifty-one air-conditioned units with lanais, washer/dryers and dishwashers. Maid service upon request. The one-bedroom units are a little on the small side, but overall a good value. Well-maintained and quiet resort with a wonderful sandy beach. Shops nearby.

Maui Condo rates: S BR $120/$90; 1BR partial o.v. $140/$110, 1BR o.f. $175/$135; 2BR o.f. $210/$175

Kihei Akahi

2531 South Kihei Road, Kihei, HI 96753. 808-879-1881. Agents: Maui Condominiums 800-663-6962 U.S. & Canada; Condo Rentals Hawaii 800-367-5242; Maui Condo & Home 800-822-4409; Kihei Maui Vacations 800-541-6284; All Island 800-663-6962; RSVP 800-663-1118.

Across from Kamaʻole II Beach Park, 240 units with washers and dryers. 2 pools, tennis court, barbecues. Prices higher for units with air conditioning.

Condo Rentals Hawaii rates: S BR $90-$119; 1BR $109-$139, 1BR a.c. $115-$145; 2BR $141-$188, 2BR a.c. $141-$194

Kihei Alii Kai

2387 South Kihei Road, Kihei, HI 96753. 808-879-6770; 800-888-MAUI. Agents: Leisure Properties (P.O. Box 985, Kihei, HI 96753) 800-888-MAUI; Maui & All Island 800-663-6962; RSVP 800-663-1118; Bello Realty 800-541-3060; Kihei Maui Vacations 800-541-6284.

Four buildings with 127 units, all with washer/dryers. No maid service. Complex features pool, jacuzzi, sauna, two tennis courts, barbecue. Across the road and up the street from beach. Nearby restaurants and shops. Other rental agents offer 2-bedroom units as well.

Bello Realty rates: 1 BD 1BTH w/loft $115/$95

Kihei Bay Surf

715 South Kihei Road (Manager Apt. 110), Kihei, HI 96753. 808-879-7650. Agents: Kihei Maui Vacations 800-541-6284; Maui Vacation Properties 800-782-6105; Maui & All Island 800-663-6962; RSVP 800-663-1118.

Kihei Bay Surf offers 118 studio units in 7 two-story buildings. Pool-area jacuzzi, barbecue, laundry area, tennis. Across the road from Kamaʻole I Beach.

RSVP rates: from $64

Kihei Bay Vista
679 South Kihei Road, Kihei, HI 96753. 808-879-8866. Agents: Kihei Maui Vacations 800-541-6284; Bello Realty 800-541-3060.

Complex offers pool, spa, jacuzzi, putting green, air conditioning, washer/dryer, lanais and full kitchens. A short walk across the road to Kama'ole I Beach. Overlooking Kalepolepo Beach.

Kihei Maui Vacations rates: 1BR units $129/$119

★ Kihei Beach Resort Vacation Condominiums
36 South Kihei Road, Kihei, HI 96753. 800-367-6034; 808-879-2744; fax 808-875-0306; www.kbr.com. Agents: Kihei Maui Vacations 800-541-6284; Maui Condo & Home 800-822-4409; Maui & All Island 800-663-6962.

Beachfront units all with great ocean views, microwaves, phones. Kihei Beach Resort offers central air conditioning, recreation area, elevator, limited maid service. Conveniently located in North Kihei. The lobby has a pleasant guest lounge with coffee served each morning. Laundry facilities available (coin-op); however, some units have their own washer/dryer. Sparkling bathrooms with attractive taupe-hued tile. The units are cozy and well-maintained. Great whale watching and the beach is truly just footsteps away.

Maui Condo & Home rates: 1BR 1BTH o.f. $185/$135, 2BR 2BTH o.f. $260/$205

Kihei Garden Estates
1299 Uluniu Street, Kihei, HI 96753. 808-879-5785; 800-827-2786. Agents: Kihei Maui Vacations 800-541-6284, Maui Condominiums 800-663-6962 U.S. & Canada.

Eighty-four units in eight two-story buildings. Jacuzzi, barbecues. Across the road and a short walk to beaches. Weekly and monthly discounts. Four-day minimum or cleaning fee charged. No credit cards.

Kihei Maui Vacations rates: 1BR (2, max 4) $109-$144/$94-$124

Kihei Holiday
483 South Kihei Road, Kihei, HI 96753. 808-879-9228. Agents: Kihei Maui Vacations 800-541-6284; RSVP 800-663-1118.

Units are across the street from the beach and have lanais with garden views. Pool area, jacuzzi and barbecues.

RSVP rates: from $84

Kihei Kai
61 North Kihei Road, Kihei, HI 96753. 800-207-3565; 808-879-2357.

Twenty-four units in a two-story beachfront building. Recreation area, laundry room, units have air conditioning or ceiling fans. barbecue. On seven-mile stretch of sandy beach, near windsurfing.

Rates: 1BR (2, max 4) g.v. and o.v. $105/$95, beachfront $125/$115

Kihei Kai Nani

2495 South Kihei Road, Kihei, HI 96753. 808-879-1430; 800-473-1493; e-mail: kkndiaz@maui.net. Agents: Maui Condominiums 800-663-6962 U.S. & Canada; Bello Realty 800-541-3060; Maui & All Island 800-663-6962.

This complex is one of the older ones along Kihei Road, composed of 180 one-bedroom units with lanai or balcony in a two- and three-story structure. Laundry room and recreation center. Across from Kama'ole II Beach. No credit cards through front-desk reservations.

Bello Realty rates: $95/$75

Kihei Resort

777 South Kihei Road, Kihei, HI 96753. Agents: Kihei Maui Vacations 800-541-6284; RSVP 800-663-1118.

Sixty-four units in a two-story building located across the street from the ocean; barbecues, pool-area jacuzzi. Two-bedroom units may be available from some rental agents. No credit cards. Weekly discounts.

RSVP rates: 1BR (2) from $74

Kihei Maui Vacations rates (for 4-6 day stay): 1BR $94/$75, 2BR $124/$94

Kihei Sands

115 North Kihei Road, Kihei, HI 96753. 808-879-2624; 800-882-6284; e-mail: kiheisands@msn.com; www.kiheisands.com.

Thirty air-conditioned oceanfront units, kitchens include microwaves. Shops and restaurant nearby. Coin laundry area. Four-night minimum summer, seven nights winter.

Rates: 1BR (2) g.v. $110/$90, o.v. $125/$105, o.f. $145/$125; 2BR (4) g.v. $150/$120, o.f. $170/$140; 3BR g.v. $155/$125; extra person $6/night.

Kihei Surfside

2936 South Kihei Road, Kihei, HI 96753. 808-879-1488; 800-367-5240. Agents: Maui Condo & Home 800-822-4409; Condo Rentals Hawaii 800-367-5242; Maui & All Island 800-663-6962.

Eighty-three units on rocky shore with tidepools. Only a short walk to Keawakapu Beach. Large grassy area and good view. Coin-op laundry on premises.

Condo Rentals Hawaii: 1BR $127-$168, 1BR deluxe $137-$183

Koa Lagoon

800 South Kihei Road, Kihei, HI 96753. 800-367-8030; e-mail: barron@mauigateway.com. Managed by Bello Realty 800-541-3060.

These 42 oceanview units are in one six-story building. Washer/dryers, pool-area pavilion and barbecues. Located on a small sandy beach that is often plagued by seaweed that washes ashore from the offshore coral reef. This stretch of Kihei is very popular with windsurfers. Five-night minimum; cleaning fee for less than 5 days.

Rates: 1BR 1 bath (2, max 4) $160/$130, 2BR 2 bath (4, max 6) $130/$100

Koa Resort
811 South Kihei Road, Kihei, HI 96753. 808-879-1161. Agents: Kihei Maui Vacations 800-541-6284; Bello Realty 800-541-3060.

There are 54 units on spacious 5.5-acre grounds in 2 five-story buildings. Located across the road from the beach. Two tennis courts, spa, jacuzzi, putting green. Units have washer/dryers.

Bello Realty rates: 1BR 1 bath $105/85; 2BR 1 bath $120/$100, 2BR 2 bath $130/$119; 3BR 2 bath $155/$135, 3BR 3 bath $180/$160

Leilani Kai
1226 Uluniu Street (P.O. Box 296), Kihei, HI 96753. 808-879-2606; fax 808-879-0241; e-mail: lkresort@msn.com; www.lkresort.com.

Eight garden apartments with lanais. Monthly discounts. Three-night minimum or cleaning fee added.

Rates: Studio (2) $73, 1BR (2 $84), 1BR deluxe (4)$95, 2BR (4)$100

Leinaala
998 South Kihei Road, Kihei, HI 96753. 808-879-2235; 800-334-3305 U.S. & Canada; fax 808-879-8366. Agent: Maui Condo & Home 800-822-4409.

Twenty-four one- and two-bedroom units in a four-story building. Tennis courts at adjoining park. Pool, cable TV. Oceanview. The property is fronted by a large park that stretches out to the ocean. Popular area for windsurfing, but lots of better sandy swimming beach parks a short drive away.

Maui Condo & Home rates: 1BR (2) $135/$100, 2BR (4) $180/$135

★ Luana Kai
940 South Kihei Road, Kihei, HI 96753. 808-879-1268; 800-669-1127; fax 808-879-1455, www.luanakai.com. Agents: Maui & All Island 800-663-6962; Kihei Maui Vacations 800-541-6284; Kumulani 800-367-2954.

Located adjacent to a large oceanfront park with public tennis courts, 113 units with washer/dryers on 8 acres. The grounds are nicely landscaped and include a putting green, barbecue area, pool area, sauna and jacuzzi. The beach, however, is almost always covered with coral rubble and seaweed.

Rates: 1BR (2) partial o.v. $119-$139/89-$109, o.v. $129-$149/$99-$119; 2BR (6) partial o.v. $139-$159/$109-$129, o.v. $149-$169/$119-$139; 3BR partial o.v. deluxe $269/$239

★ Ma'alaea Surf
12 South Kihei Road, Kihei, HI 96753. 800-423-7953; 808-879-1267; fax 808-874-2884; e-mail: msurf@maui.net; www.maalaeasurfresort.com. Agent: Maui Condo & Home 800-822-4409.

Sixty units in 8 two-story oceanfront buildings. These townhouse units have air conditioning and microwaves. Daily maid service, except Sundays and holidays. Two pools, two tennis courts, shuffleboard. Laundry facilities in each building. Very attractive and quiet low-rise complex on a great beach. In this price range, these spacious and attractive units, along with five acres of beautiful grounds, are hard to beat.

Rates: 1BR 1 bath (2, max 4) o.v. $205, o.f. $230; 2BR 2 bath (4, max 6) ground floor or townhouse o.v. $277-$307, o.f. $307-$350

Maui Condo & Home rates: 1BR $210/$160, 2BR $300/$225

★ Mana Kai

2960 South Kihei Road, Kihei, HI 96753. 808-879-1561; 800-525-2025; fax 808-874-5042. Agents: Condo Rentals Hawaii 800-367-5242; Kumulani 800-367-2954; Maui & All Islands 800-663-6962.

Eight-story building with 132 rooms. The studio units have a room with an adjoining bath. The one-bedroom units have a kitchen and the two-bedroom units are actually the hotel unit and a one bedroom combined, each having separate entry doors. The Mana Kai offers hotel-like services, no minimum stay and daily maid service. This complex has laundry facilities on each floor, an oceanfront pool and a restaurant off the lobby. The Mana Kai is nestled at the end of Keawakapu Beach, and offers a majestic view of the blue Pacific, the 10,000-foot-high Haleakala and Upcountry Maui. It is the only major facility in Kihei on a prime beachfront location. Keawakapu Beach is not only very nice, but generally very underused.

Condo Rentals Hawaii rates: Hotel room (2) $ 95-$135; 1BR 1BTH (2) o.v. $175-$225, 1BR deluxe $191-$245; 2BR o.v. $217-$300

Aston Maui Banyan

2575 South Kihei Road. Managed by Aston Resorts: 800-922-7866. Agents: Maui & All Island 800-663-6962; Kihei Maui Vacations 800-541-6284; Bello Realty 800-541-3060; Kumulani 800-367-2954; Maui Condo & Home 800-822-4409; Maui Condominiums 800-663-6962 U.S. & Canada.

Overlooking Kama'ole II Beach, these suites feature kitchens, washer/dryer, lanai, air conditioning, cable TV and telephone. Facilities include tennis court, pool and jacuzzi. Putting green and barbecue area. Hotel rooms have no kitchens. Aston rates include daily maid service.

Aston rates: Hotel Room (1-2) standard $190/$145; 1BR (max 4) $250-270/$185-$200; 2BR (max 6) $325-$365/$245-$275

Maui Coast Hotel

2259 South Kihei Road, Kihei, HI 96753. 808-874-MAUI; fax 808-875-4731; 800-426-0670; www.mauicoasthotel.com.

Owned and operated by West Coast Hotels, they offer 265 rooms—114 of them suites. The hotel offers a pool area plus children's wading pool, two outdoor whirlpools, Spices Restaurant in front, two night-lit tennis courts and complimentary laundry facilities. This is a great concept, a hotel with condominium conveniences, such as a small in-room refrigerator. Coffee makers with complimentary coffee, free cribs, jetted tubs in suites and room service. However, I found the standard room was too crowded with one king bed and the two kids on a sofa bed. Compared to the Wailea Resorts, this is a no-frills hotel option. Nicely appointed property located across the road from the Kama'ole Beach Parks.

Rates: Standard Hotel room $165, partial o.v. $175; alcove suite $195, partial o.v. $205; 1BR suite $235; 2BR suite $350; extra person/rollaway $20/night

★ Maui Hill
2881 South Kihei Road, Kihei, HI 96753. 808-879-6321. Agents: Aston Hotels 800-922-7866; RSVP 800-663-1118.

Twelve buildings with a Spanish flair clustered on a hillside above the Keawakapu Beach area; 140 attractively furnished units with washer/dryers, air conditioning, microwaves, dishwashers and large lanais. Daily maid service. There is a moderate walk down and across the road to the beach. Upper units have better ocean views. The 3-bedroom units are very spacious. Large pool and tennis courts.

Aston rates: 1BR (1-4) o.v. $280/$215, 2BR (1-6) o.v. $280, 3BR o.v. $385

Maui Kamaole
2777 South Kihei Road, Kihei, HI 96743. 808-879-7668. Agents: Kihei Maui Vacations 800-541-6284; Condo Rentals Hawaii 800-367-5242; Maui & All Island 800-663-6962; Maui Condominiums 800-663-6962 U.S. & Canada.

Located on a bluff overlooking the ocean; across the street and a short walk down to Kama'ole III Beach Park or Keawakapu Beach. 1BR units are 1,000 to 1,300 square feet and 2BR units are 1,300 to 1,600 square feet This four-phase development is located on 23 oceanview acres. All are low-rise fourplex buildings grouped into 13 clusters, each named after Hawaiian flora. Weekly discounts available.

Condo Rentals Hawaii rates: 1BR 2BTH g.v. $132-$180, 1BR 2BTH o.v. $143-$200; 2BR 2BTH g.v. $148-$225, o.v. $178-$260

Maui Lu Resort
575 South Kihei Road, Kihei, HI 96753. 808-879-5881. Managed by Aston 800-922-7866.

One of the first resorts in the Kihei area and unusual with its spacious grounds: 180 units on 26 acres. Pool is shaped like the island of Maui. Many of the hotel rooms are set back from South Kihei Road and the oceanfront units are not on a sandy beachfront. Ask about the Aston Island Hopper rates if you're planning on visiting multiple islands.

Aston rates: Hotel Room with refrigerator (1-2) g.v. $108, superior g.v. $125, deluxe o.v. $155, o.f. $180

Maui Oceanfront Inn
2980 South Kihei Road, Kihei, HI 96753. 800-263-3387; www.mauiocean frontinn.com.

Located on Keaweakapu Beach. An 88-room boutique-style oceanfront inn, they feature classic Hawaiian art and furnishings in each room which augments the natural elegance and beauty of Hawaii. Mountain view and garden view guest rooms feature queen bed, entertainment center, built-in refrigerator, coffee maker and air conditioning. Front building has oceanfront units. Two rooms, connected by a door, can create a suite. Very cute and this beach is one of my favorites. A good value for an oceanfront location.

Rates: g.v. $208/$188, m.v. $198/$166

Maui Parkshore
2653 South Kihei Road, Kihei, HI 96753. 808-879-1600. Agents: Maui & All Island 800-663-6962; Maui Condo & Home 800-822-4409.

Sixty-four two-bedroom, two-bath oceanview condos with washer/dryers and lanais in a 4-story building (elevator) across from Kama'ole III Beach. Pool-area sauna.

Maui Condo & Home rates: 2BR 2 bath (4) $160/$125

Maui Sunset
1032 South Kihei, Road, Kihei, HI 96753. 808-879-0674; 800-843-5880. Agents: Kihei Maui Vacations 800-541-6284; RSVP 800-663-1118; Maui & All Island 800-663-6962; Kumulani 800-367-2954; Maui Condo & Home 800-822-4409.

Two multistory buildings with 225 air-conditioned units. Tennis courts, pitch-and-putt golf green and sauna. Large pool, exercise facility, barbecues. Located on beach park with tennis courts. They resolve their longtime problem of seaweed and coral rubble on the beach with a daily beach "sweeping."

Maui Condo & Home rates: 1BR $130/$100, 2BR $180/$145

Maui Vista
2191 South Kihei Road, Kihei, HI 96753. 808-879-7966; 800-367-8047 ext. 330. Agents: Maui & All Island 800-663-6962; Kihei Maui Vacations 800-541-6284; Marc Resorts 800-535-0085; Maui Condo & Home 800-822-4409; Bello Realty 800-541-3060; Maui Condominiums 800-663-6962 U.S. & Canada.

Three 4-story buildings, across from the beach, 280 units. Some have air conditioning, some have washer/dryers. All have kitchens with dishwashers. The two-bedroom units are fourth-floor townhouses. Some oceanview units. Six tennis courts, three pools, barbecues. A great value if you don't mind a short walk to the beach, but I had problem with sound from a neighboring unit.

Kihei Maui Vacations rates: 1BR $129-$159/$129-$149; 2BR units available through some rental agents

Menehune Shores
760 Kihei Road, Kihei, HI 96753. 808-879-0076. Agent: Menehune Reservations (no credit cards), P.O. Box 1327, Kihei, HI 96753, 800-558-9117 U.S. & Canada; 808-879-3428; fax 808-879-5218. Other agents: RSVP 800-663-1118; Kihei Maui Vacations 800-541-6284.

Six-story building, 115 units with dishwashers, washer/dryers and lanais. A recreation room with roof garden and a whale-watching platform, and shuffleboard. The ocean area in front of this condo property is the last remnant of one of Maui's early fish ponds. These ponds, where fish were raised and harvested, were created by the early Hawaiians all around the islands.

Rates: 1BR 1 bath (2) $134/$94; 2BR 2 bath (2) $154/$129; 3BR 2 bath (6) $179/$149

My Waii Beach Cottage
2128A Ili'ili Road, Kihei. Agent: Linda R. Owen, 3538 207th SE, Issaquah, WA 98029. 800-882-9007; e-mail: info@mywaii.com; www.mywaii.com.

Linda offers a deluxe one-bedroom, two-bath oceanfront cottage. It is located 500 yards from Kama'ole Beach I and the front lawn area also adjoins a small beach. The cottage has a TV, VCR, stereo with CD, full kitchen, microwave, 3 telephones, ceiling fans. There is a dual king in the bedroom and a queen-size Murphy bed in the living room. Minimum stay of 5 nights or you'll be charged a cleaning fee.

Rates: $190; extra person (max 4) $10 each

★ Nani Kai Hale
73 North Kihei Road, Kihei, HI 96753. 808-879-9120; 800-367-6032. Agents: Maui & All Island 800-663-6962; Maui Condo & Home 800-822-4409; Maui Condominiums 800-663-6962 U.S. & Canada.

A six-story building holds 46 units. Under-building parking, laundry on each floor, elevator. Patio and barbecues by beach. Lanais have ocean and mountain views.

Maui Condo & Home rates: 1BR 2BTH (2) o.v. $155/$110, 2BR 2BTH o.v. $200/$160

Nona Lani
455 South Kihei Road (P.O. Box 655), Kihei, HI 96753. 800-733-2688; 808-879-2497; fax 808-891-0273; www.nonalanicottages.com.

Eight individual cottages with kitchens, TV, queen bed plus a rollaway and day bed, full bath with tub and shower, and lanais. Rooms have queen bed and bathroom, TV, ceiling fan and air conditioning. Large grounds, public phone, two barbecues and laundry facilities. Located across the road from sandy beach. No credit cards. Weekly discounts.

Rates: Rooms $85/$75, cottages $99/$90

Punahoa

2142 Ili'ili Road, Kihei, HI 96753. 800-564-2720; 808-879-2720.

Fifteen oceanview units with large lanais, telephones. No pool. Elevator, laundry facilities, beaches nearby. Some have air conditioning. No credit cards. Three seasons: May 1 to October 31 (low season); November 1 to December 14 and April 1 to April 30 (mid season); and December 15 to March 31 (high season).

Rates: S BR (2) $130/$109/$94, 1BR (2, max 4) $185/$150/$130; 2BR (2, max 6) $220/$190/$160; 1BR penthouse $198/$160/$145

Royal Mauian

2430 South Kihei Road, Kihei, HI 96753. 808-879-1263; 800-367-8009; fax 808-367-8009. Agents: Maui Condo & Home 800-822-4409; Kihei Maui Vacations 800-541-6284.

Complex has shuffleboard, carpeted roof garden and is next to the pleasant Kama'ole II Beach Park; 107 units with lanai and washer/dryer in a six-story building.

Maui Condo & Home rates: 1BR 1 bath or 2 bath o.f. (2) $18-$135; 2BR o.f. $235/$180; some 3BR may be available through some rental agents

Shores of Maui

2075 South Kihei Road (P.O. Box 985), Kihei, HI 96753. 808-879-9140; 800-367-8002. Agent: Leisure Properties 800-367-8002.

This 50-unit two-level complex in garden setting offers barbecues, tennis courts and spa. Located across the street from a rocky shoreline and north of Kama'ole I Beach Park. Three-night minimum stay, one-week minimum over Christmas holidays. One of Kihei's good values.

Rates: 1BR $100/$75, 2BR $130/$105

Sugar Beach Resort

145 North Kihei Road, Kihei HI 96753. 808-879-7765. Agents: Maui & All Island 800-663-6962; RSVP 800-663-1118; Maui Condo & Home 800-822-4409; Condo Rental HI 800-367-5242.

Several six-story buildings with elevators, 215 units. Air conditioning. Jacuzzi, putting green, gas barbecue grills. Sandwich shop and quick shop market on location. A nice pool area and located on an excellent swimming beach. Popular with families, so expect lots of kids.

Condo Rental HI rates: 1BR g.v. $116-$162, o.v. $128-$172, o.f. $139-$183; 2BR o.v. $218-$325

Maui Condo & Home rates: 1BR o.v. $170/$125, o.f. $195/$145; 2BR o.v. $300/$220

Sunseeker Resort
551 South Kihei Road (P.O. Box 276), Kihei, HI 96753. 800-532-MAUI; 808-879-1261; fax 808-879-1261.

Units include studios with kitchenettes, and one bedrooms with kitchens. Monthly discounts available. No room phones, no pool. Across the street from beach. Popular area for windsurfing.
Rates: $60-$75

Wailana Inn
14 Wailana Place, Kihei, HI 96753. 800-399-3885; 808-874-3131; www.wailanabeach.com.

Eleven small and large studios. Across the road from the beach. Rooftop sun deck and hot tub. Full and king beds with kitchen or kitchenettes. Laundry room on the property.
Rates: $75-$140

Wailana Kai
34 Wailana Place, Kihei, HI 96753. 866-891-1626; 808-891-1626; www.wailanakai.com.

One-bedroom units have sofa sleepers in living area. Private phone lines, pool, laundry facilities.
Rates: 1BR 1BTH $90, 2BR 2BTH $110

WAILEA

Diamond Resort
555 Kaukahi Street, Wailea, HI 96753. 808-874-0500.

The 72-suite resort comprises 18 two-story buildings on 15 acres. Each suite is 947 square feet and includes a master bedroom, dining area, kitchenette, sitting area, lanai and bath. Suites have ocean views, golf course views, or views of Haleakala. Two of their suites have been designed for physically challenged guests and four suites are non-smoking. The spa facility, which includes a men's and women's *daiyokujo* (traditional Japanese bath), a waterfall to gently massage your neck and shoulders as well as a soothing Finlandia sauna, is one of the resort's highlights. The grounds are lovely with quiet waterfalls and bridges along the paths. A lovely and tranquil setting. Their Restaurant Taiko and Le Gunji are both fine dining restaurants. Capische? is open evenings for casual dining or cocktails and live entertainment. Includes complimentary use of the spa.
Rates: g.v. $240, partial o.v. $270, deluxe o.v. $340

★ Fairmont Kea Lani Hotel, Suites & Villas
4100 Wailea Alanui, Wailea, HI 96753. 808-875-4100; 800-882-4100; www.kealani.com.

There are 413 suites plus 37 one-, two- and three-bedroom oceanfront villas. Designed after Las Hadas in Manzanillo, the name means

"White Heavens." Its Mediterranean style seems like a sultan's enormous villa dramatically set on 22 acres. You enter a drive lined with Norfolk pines and beyond the portecochere there is a large open lobby area with a fountain covered by nine domes. Decorations are in Hawaiian florals with mosaic tile ceilings and floors.

The spacious (840 square feet) one-bedroom suites each have a private balcony. (There are 45 pairs of connecting suites for those traveling with larger families.) Each is decorated in hues of cream and white and has a sunken marble tub, an enormous walk-in shower, king or two double beds, and two closets. A cotton kimono is provided for guests. The living room features a state-of-the-art compact and laser disc system, TV and VCR. Fresh-ground coffee and coffee maker are provided daily in the suite and a mini-kitchen offers a microwave, a small sink and mini-bar. An iron and ironing board are also available. In addition to the suites, there are also 37 townhouse-style villas that overlook Polo Beach—a little expensive, but it would be easy to feel at home here. Each has a private lanai, huge walk-in closets, full-size kitchen, washer and dryer, a generous living room and eating area. If you don't want to make that walk to the beach, you can just meander out onto the lanai and take a dip in your private swimming pool. That's right. Each villa has its own pool!

The exercise room is complimentary for guests. Massage, body treatments, facials and fitness programs are available in their luxury spa facility. (See "Spas/Fitness Centers/Health Retreats" in Chapter 6 for more information.) Restaurants include Caffe Ciao, Nick's Fishmarket Maui, and Polo Beach Grille and Bar. Complimentary daily golf clinics; for those who prefer to be beach bound they offer beach rental equipment, everything from a single kayak to a pool float. Beach butlers are on hand to ensure you have a great day at the beach. For a fee the resort offers "Keiki Lani" for youths 5 to 11 years of age; see "Childcare Programs" in Chapter 1 for details. Sean the clown/juggler also stops by several times each week. Honeymoon, wedding, family and golf packages are available.

Rates: 1BR suite scenic view (4) $265, o.v. (4) $350, deluxe o.v. (4) $450; 1BR villa (1-4 persons) o.v. $795, o.f. $895; 2BR villa (1-6 persons) o.v. $895, o.f. $995; 3BR villa (1-8 persons) o.v. $1,095, o.f. $1,195

★ *Four Seasons Resort Wailea*
3900 Wailea Alanui, Wailea, HI 96753. 808-874-8000; 800-334-MAUI; fax 808-874-2222; www.fourseasons.com.

This gorgeous property offers 380 oversized guest rooms (600 square feet) on eight floors encompassing 15 beachfront acres on Wailea Beach; the suite offers a large living room, one bedroom, full kitchen and a 439-square-foot lanai. This full-service resort features two pools (one large and one smaller lava pool) and a jacuzzi on each end of the main pool, one of which is set aside for children only. The layout of the grand pool provides shelter from the afternoon breezes. In addition there are two tennis courts, a croquet lawn, health spa, beauty salon, three restaurants and two lounges. The public areas are spacious, open and ocean oriented. (If I had a category for "Best Bathrooms" these would be the winners. They are elegantly decorated and each stall is like a mini-suite.) A very different mood from other Maui resorts, the blue-tiled roof and cream-colored building create a very classic atmosphere. Even the grounds, although a profusion of colors with many varied Hawaiian flora, vaguely resemble a Mediterranean villa. Throughout the resort's gardens and courtyards are an array of attractive formal and natural pools, ponds, waterfalls and fountains.

Their guest policy features real aloha spirit, with no charge for use of the tennis courts or health spa and complimentary snorkel gear, smash or volleyball equipment. For the younger guests, strollers, car seats, high chairs, cribs and even complimentary baby baths and bottle warmers are available. Their year-round, complimentary "Kids for All Seasons " program is geared for children ages five through twelve; see "Childcare Programs" in Chapter 1. Guest services, which distinguish the Four Seasons from other properties, include their early-arrival/late-departure program. Guests have their luggage checked and are escorted to The Health Centre, where a private locker is supplied for personal items. The resort makes available for these guests an array of casual clothing from work-out gear and jogging suits to swimwear.

The Four Seasons Resort is peaceful and elegant. No glitz here, just what you come to Paradise for. A "children's only" hot tub allows the second adult hot tub to be a quiet respite. There are plenty of complimentary cabanas around the pool area and on the beach. Pool and beach staff are on their toes providing prompt attention to guests in setting up their lounge chairs with towels and providing chilled towels or spritzers to cool the face. Ferraro's, the poolside restaurant and bar, makes it easy to spend the entire day without leaving your lounge chair. The snorkeling is best out to the left near the rocky shoreline, but go early in the day. Like clockwork, around noon the wind picks up and the water clarity rapidly deteriorates. Another plus for the Wailea area is the walkway that spans the shoreline between resorts. It is a pleasant walk over to the neighboring southern resort, the Fairmont Kea Lani; the Grand Wailea to the north is definitely worth a stroll (go during the day and again at night for a very different experience).

Numerous special package offers include a room and car, golf, romance and family packages. Restaurants include Pacific Grill and Spago. Amenities for guests on the Club Floor include a private lounge, 24-hour concierge, complimentary breakfast, afternoon tea, evening cocktails and after-dinner liqueurs. Under age 18 free when sharing same room with parents, except on Club Floor add $60/night per child ages 5 to 17. Ask about special seasonal discounts, family rates (for a second room for children under 18) and packages. Prices are regular season and value season.

Rates: mountain side $335 all year, g.v. $425/$410, partial o.v. $505/$490, o.v. $590/$570, o.v. prime $665/$645. Club Floor: o.v. $730. Executive Suites $610-$1,105. Additional 1BR and 2BR suites $755-$6,700.

★ Grand Wailea Resort Hotel & Spa

3850 Wailea Alanui, Wailea, HI 96753. 808-875-1234; 800-888-6100; fax 808-874-2442; e-mail: info@grandwailea.com; www.grandwailea.com.

This beautifully appointed 780-room resort is a must-see, even if you aren't lucky enough to stay. In fact, make at least two trips—a second at night to enjoy dinner and tour the grounds when they are alight like a twinkling fairyland. Over $20 million was spent on the waterfalls, streams, rapids, slides, reflecting pools, swimming pools, river pool, scuba pool, saltwater lagoon and spa features. Strikingly beautiful, the formal reflecting pool leads you to the sweeping Wailea Beach. Beyond this pool is the hibiscus pool made of Mexican glass tile with gold leaf and lined with wide Mediterranean-style cabanas. The "activity pool" is a 770,000-gallon, 27,500-square-foot pool with nine large, free-form pools at various levels beginning at a height of 40 feet and dropping to sea level. Painted tiles depicting turtles and tropical fish in varying shades of green and blue line the bottom and sides, while huge rocks line the pools. At one end of the pool is an incredible waterslide, a 225-foot twisting ride that drops three stories. The "jungle pool," another part of the Wailea Canyon Activity Pool, offers a rope swing.

The pools are connected by a 2,000-foot river that carries swimmers at varying current speeds, ranging from whitewater rapids to a lazy cruise. Along the way are hidden grottos, three jacuzzis and saunas, seven slides, numerous waterfalls and bumpy whitewater rapids that have been created using special aquatic devices. At the bottom of the river is a one-of-a-kind water elevator that lifts the swimmers back up to the top again. Below the rocky waterfall is the scuba pool that gets prospective divers in the mood with an underwater mural featuring a coral reef, and sea life made of tiles. It takes 50,000 gallons of water a minute to sustain this aquatic system. Streams and pools also meander through elaborate gardens in Hawaiian and Japanese themes throughout the resort. Spa Grande is Hawai'i's largest spa that spans 50,000 square feet in the atrium wing of the resort; See "Spas/Fitness Centers/Health Retreats" in Chapter 6. Six restaurants give guests plenty of choices: Kincha, Grand Dining Room Maui, Café Kula, Humuhumunukunukua'pua'a, Bistro Molokini, and the Volcano Bar. There is also a swim-up bar!

I am fascinated by the blend of enormity and grandeur with Hawaiian themes, tempered with outstanding craftsmanship. It seems to work. There is actually a great deal of fine detail (notice the twisted *ohia* wood rails that line the pathways) and I especially like the attention paid to the Hawaiiana aspects. The resort is visually very stimulating and each time you stroll around the resort you're sure to see something new. The chapel, set in the middle of the grounds, is a popular spot for weddings. The woodwork and stained-glass windows are absolutely beautiful, and take note of the chandeliers above made of exquisite Maurano glass. The 28,000-square-foot ballroom is a meeting planner's dream, with concealed projection screens, specialized audio equipment—the works! The ballroom also has three huge, beautiful and unique artworks in gold and silver leaf that depict the story of Pele, the fire goddess, and her two sisters. Don't neglect a look up at the 29,000-pound, Venetian-glass chandelier imported from Italy.

Now the rooms! There are 780 rooms, each 650 square feet, and 52 suites. The presidential suite (5,500 square feet) is a mere $10,000 per night and features what is lovingly referred to as the Imelda Marcos shoe closet, a private sauna, a room-sized shower with ocean view in one bathroom and a *koa* tub. Lots of marble was used throughout all the rooms and is accented by subtle beige wallpaper. This may be the one resort that your kids will *insist* you come back to again and again. After you visit the kids' camp you will, at least momentarily, wish you could pass for a 10 or 11 year old. See "Childcare Programs" in Chapter 1 for more information. All-in-all, if you're seeking an action-packed resort vacation, you'll find it all here. Not everyone wants the activity of a resort, but this one certainly has something for everyone.

Rates: Terrace $450, g.v. $550, Premium g,v. King $610, o.v. $650, Deluxe o.v. $700, Premium o.v. King $760; Suites $1,575-2000. Napua Tower rooms: Napua Club $800, 1BR and 2BR Napua suites $2,200-$10,000

★ **The Palms at Wailea**
3200 Wailea Alanui Drive, Wailea, HI 96753. 808-879-5800. Agents: Outrigger Hotels Hawaii 800-OUTRIGGER; Maui Condo & Home 800-822-4409; Kihei Maui Vacations 800-541-6284; Bello Realty 800-541-3060.

One- and two-bedroom condominiums on a bluff overlooking the Wailea area with views of the islands of Kaho'olawe and Lana'i.

Two-story buildings with a total of 77 luxury units. Amenities include partial air conditioning (in bedrooms, not living rooms), VCR, in-room laundry, pool and spa. Each unit is privately owned, but all are kept up to a high standard. As part of the Wailea Resort Community, this property offers access to the two Wailea golf courses and tennis complex. Daily maid service with some rental agents. These condos are a great value and you're in beautiful Wailea. Even the one-bedroom units are incredibly spacious. Only a short walk to the beach. The upper units have lovely ocean vistas, the lower ones provide nice garden patio views. The kitchens are enormous and obviously designed to be adequate for long-term tenants. For value and location, The Palms at Wailea get our star of approval. Outrigger rates include daily maid service.

Outrigger rates: 1BR g.v. villa (1-4) $235, o.v. villa $265; 2BR g.v. villa (1-6) $270, g.v. villa deluxe $285, o.v. villa $300

★ **Polo Beach Club**
20 Makena Road, Wailea, HI 96753. 808-879-8847. On-site agent: Destination Resorts 800-367-5246.

Seventy-one apartments in an 8-story building located on Polo Beach. The units are luxurious and spacious. Underground parking, pool area and jacuzzi. Located next to the Fairmont Kea Lani Resort. Three-night minimum; 14-night minimum during Christmas holidays.

Destination Resorts rates: *High Season:* no 1BR available; 2BR $400-$515. *Low Season:* 1BR o.v. $350, o.f. $375, prime not available; 2BR o.v. $400, o.f. $45, prime o.f. $515; extra person (over 4) $20

★ **Renaissance Wailea Beach Resort**
3550 Wailea Alanui, Wailea, HI 96753. 800-992-4532; 808-879-4900; fax 808-874-5370.

This luxury resort covers 15.5 acres above beautiful Mokapu Beach with 345 units, including 12 suites. Each guest room is 500 square feet and offers a refrigerator, individual air conditioner and private lanai. The rooms are decorated in soothing rose, ash and blue tones. An assortment of daily guest activities are available as well as a year-round children's program called Camp Wailea; see "Childcare Programs" in Chapter 1 for details. Guest services include complimentary in-room coffee, daily paper, complimentary video library, traditional Hawaiian craft classes and demonstrations, massage therapy and fitness center. Wailea offers complimentary shuttle service to shopping, golf and tennis within the Wailea Resort area. Fat City, a "multi-colored cat of undetermined lineage," has become the unofficial resort resident. In fact, she has endeared herself to so many guests that she receives mail on a regular basis. Mokapu Beach Wing is a separate beachfront building with 26 units that feature open-beamed ceilings and rich *koa* wood furnishings, plus a small swimming pool. The resort's restaurants are the Maui Onion, Palm Court and Hana Gion. The Sunset Terrace has an excellent vantage point for a beautiful sunset. The beach offers excellent swimming. The best snorkeling is just a very short walk over to the adjoining Ulua Beach. The grounds are a beautiful tropical jungle with a very attractive pool area. Also inquire about their "roomful of packages," which includes romance options (chocolate-dipped strawberries included) or room and car as well as room and breakfast. They have some outstanding rates that definitely make this property a best bet for a fine Wailea resort. They also offer discounted rates at the Wailea golf courses if you are a guest. Check with reservations for seasonal specials.

Rates: Deluxe Terrace $360, Deluxe Garden $420, Deluxe o.v. $480, Oceanfront Mokapu $650, Beach Suites $1,050-$4,000.

★ Wailea Marriott, an Outrigger Resort

3700 Wailea Alanui, Wailea, HI 96753. 808-879-1922; fax 808-874-8331; 888-859-8262. Reservations: Outrigger Resorts 800-OUTRIGGER.

The resort underwent $25 million in major improvements during 2000. When you arrive at the porte-cochere, the banyan trees are the focal point and a waterfall is the centerpiece. You'll find the lovely ocean view and the beautiful *koa* rockers tempt guests to sit, relax and enjoy. (Pretend you're on the deck of a luxurious cruise ship of the 1930s or '40s.) The lobby design is unpretentious, old Hawaiian and classic. The artwork is subtle with intricate chests from Japan, huge stone mochi bowls, New Guinea roof finials, and Big Island calabashes. The popular Hula Moons Restaurant is off the main lobby. Just beyond the main lobby, the stairway descends down and winds past a lily pond (a popular wedding site) to the central pool area. On the lower level you'll find the Kumu Bar & Grill. The guest rooms have a silversword theme with seafoam green accents in the fabrics, wallcovering and carpeting that matches the aloha wear worn by the staff. Amenities in the rooms include a refrigerator, dataports, coffee maker with complimentary coffee and an in-room safe. Located on 22 acres they have a half-mile of oceanfront property and access to two great beaches, Ulua and Wailea. There is a seven-story tower and six low-rise buildings. The wonderful layout of this resort allows 80 percent of all guest rooms to have an ocean view and the grounds are spacious and sprawling. No "packing them in" feel here! The resort's third pool is adjacent to the luau pool. This miniature water park, called "Wailele," which means jumping waters, will delight the *keikis* with two water slides, climbing areas, lots of water spray and interactive possibilities. The main pool area is still spacious with lots of decking for a day in the sun with a good book. The resort offers the excellent *Hoolokahi* program, a series of Hawaiian classes available to guests and non-guests for a nominal fee, as well as a kids' program. This is also home to one of the Maui's best luaus. A number of exciting annual events are sponsored by the resort. Golf, tennis and honeymoon package plans also available. They have complimentary parking and no resort fees. Children age 17 and under are free when staying with parents and occupying existing beds. Single/double occupancy are one rate all year.

Rates: g.v. $325, m.v. $375, o.v. $425, o.f. $475, deluxe o.f. $525, Suites $650-$3,000

Wailea Villas

3750 Wailea Alanui, Wailea, HI 96753. 808-879-1595; 800-367-5246.
Agents: Destination Resorts Wailea 808-879-1595, 800-367-5246; Maui Condo & Home (Grand Champion & Ekolu) 800-822-4409; Kumulani 800-367-2954 (only Ekahi Condos); Maui Vacation Properties 800-782-6105; Maui & All Island 800-663-6962; Bello Realty 800-541-3060.

Some agents may have a few units for slightly better prices than those quoted below. The price range reflects location in the complex. Children under 16 free in parents' room. Destination also provides added amenities such as daily housekeeping service and concierge service and they feature package specials. I haven't stayed in any of these properties so couldn't really judge them by anything other than a walk-around. The less-expensive properties on the hill are a better value, but if you're a beach lover, you might prefer the luxury of having it footsteps away. I've heard some positive feedback in general, but did have one complaint that the property wasn't very kid-friendly.

Ekolu Village—Located near the tennis center and the Wailea golf course.

Destination Resorts rates, three-night minimum stay: 1BR (2) g.v. $190/$170, o.v. $235/$214; 2BR (4) g.v. $230/$204, o.v. $275/$250

Ekahi Village—On the hillside above the south end of Keawakapu Beach; some units are right above the beach.

Destination Resorts rates, three-night minimum stay, seventh night free available low season in some categories: 1BR (2) g.v. upper village studio $180/$160, g.v. lower village $195/$170, o.f. upper village $205/$180, o.v. lower village $225/$200; 2BR: g.v. upper village $330/$280, g.v. lower village $370/$330, o.v. upper village $360/$320, o.v. lower village $410/$350; 1BR (2) $210-$260/$190-$230; 2BR (4) $295-$370/$250-$330

Elua Village—Located on Ulua Beach, one of the best in the area. I would recommend these units, expensive though they are! Five-night minimum stay. Fourteen-day minimum during Christmas holidays. No off-season discounts. An additional $60 check-in fee per reservation charged by Elua Village Owners Association.

Rates: 1BR g.v. $295, o.v. $355, o.f. $465, prime o.f. $510; 2BR g.v. $395, o.v. $445, o.f. $590, prime o.f. $635; 3BR g.v. $585, o.v. $625, o.f. $725, prime o.f. $825

Grand Champion Villas—*155 Wailea Iki Place, Wailea, HI 96753. Agents: Maui Condo & Home 800-822-4409; Destination Resorts 800-367-5246; Bello Realty 800-541-3060; Kihei Maui Vacations 800-541-6284.*

Twelve lush acres comprising 188 luxury condominium units with garden view, golf view or oceanview units. The fourth and newest of the Wailea Villas, this is a sportsman's dream, located between Wailea's Blue Golf Course and the "Wimbledon West" Tennis Center. Bookings through Destination Resorts include daily maid service and concierge service. Golf, tennis and/or car packages available.

Destination Resorts rates include 4th night free plan, three-night minimum stay, 14 days during Christmas holidays: 1BR (2) g.v. $200/$180, partial o.v. $250/$230, o.v. $260/$240; 2BR g.v. $265/$250, partial o.v. $285/$260, o.v. $300/$280; 3BR o.v. $385/$365, partial o.v. $365/$345

MAKENA

Just south of Wailea is Makena, which will probably be one of the last resort areas to be developed on Maui. This is an upscale and peaceful location, great for family vacationers who don't care to be at a resort area that is filled with people.

★ *Makena Surf*
96 Makena Alanui Road, Makena, HI 96753; www.makenasurf.com. Agents: Destination Resorts 800-367-5246; Maui Condo & Home 800-822-4409.

Jim Osgood privately rents his two-bedroom unit (e-mail: jim@makenasurf.com; 425-391-8900). Located 2 miles past Wailea. All units are oceanfront and more or less surround Paipu (Chang's) Beach. These very spacious and attractive condos feature central air conditioning, fully equipped kitchens, washers and dryers, wet bar, whirlpool spa in the master bath, telephones and daily maid service. Two pools and four tennis courts are set in landscaped grounds. Three historic sites found on location have been preserved. I stayed here for the first time a few years back. It was even better than I had imagined. When it was first built it seemed that the Makena Surf was very out of the way and removed from the rest of the Wailea area. That isn't the case anymore, but this property is still very private. The units are well maintained and luxuriously appointed. Looking out from the oceanfront units it is hard to imagine that this isn't your own private island. Pull up a lounge chair, open that bottle of wine and watch the whales frolic as the sun sets gloriously in the Pacific beyond them. It doesn't get any better than this! Destination Resorts handles most of the rental units. Five-night minimum stay. An additional $50 (plus tax) is charged for check-in fee per reservation and is charged by the

Makena Surf Owners Association. Seventh night is free in some categories during certain seasons with Destination Resorts.

Destination Resort rates: *High Season*: 1BR (2) o.f. $490; 2BR (4) o.f. $490-$560, prime o.f./beachfront $610-$675; 3BR (6) o.f. $725, prime o.f. $775; 4BR o.f. $1,200. *Low Season*: 1BR o.f $417-$475; 2BR o.f. $490-$520, prime o.f. $610, prime beachfront $675; 3BR o.f. $725, prime o.f. $775; 4BR o.f. $1,200. Extra person $20

★ Maui Prince Hotel
5400 Makena Alanui, Makena, HI 96753. 808-874-1111; 800-321-6284.

In sharp contrast to the ostentatious atmosphere of some of the Ka'anapali resorts, the Maui Prince radiates understated elegance. Its simplicity of color and design, with an oriental theme, provides a tranquil setting and allows the beauty of Maui to be reflected. The central courtyard is the focal point of the resort, with a lovely traditional water garden complete with a cool cascading waterfall and ponds filled with gleaming *koi*. The 310 rooms are tastefully appointed. The units have two telephones and a small refrigerator. Terry robes are available for use during the guest's stay. A 24-hour full room-service menu adds to the conveniences. They offer the Prince Keiki Club program; see "Childcare Programs" in Chapter 1 for details. There is plenty of room for lounging around two circular swimming pools or in a few steps you can be on Maluaka (Nau Paka) Beach with its luxuriously deep, fine white sand and good snorkeling, swimming and wave playing. The resort comprises 1,800 acres including two championship golf courses. Restaurants include Prince Court, Cafe Kiowai and Hakone. Package plans include Single Golfer Package, Room & Meal Package, Sporting Clays Package, Tennis for Life Package, Sunset Romance Package, Unlimited Golf Package and more.

Rates: Partial o.v. $230, o.v. $290, o.v. prime $330, o.f. $380; Suites $420-$820; no charge for third person using existing beds

Kahului-Wailuku Area

Banana Bungalow Maui—Hotel & International Hostel
310 North Market Street, Wailuku, HI 96793. 808-244-5090; 800-8-HOSTEL; e-mail: info@mauihostel.com; www.mauihostel.com.

Jim Heine reminds readers that his hostel is not a "youth" hostel, but accepts guests of all ages and can accommodate families of various ages and sizes; this is the only owner-operated hostel on Maui. His private rooms accommodate up to two people in beds, with a third on the floor with a futon mattress he provides. Young children sharing existing beds are free. Families of four to six can be accommodated in a dorm-style room where everyone can have their own bed. This historic plantation-style hostel has an indoor kitchen. The backyard boasts a tropical garden with hammocks and picnic tables. Jim also provides a free island tour: "Local tour companies charge as much as $125 for some of the tours we do for free and we visit all the secret places they do not!" Tours are aboard a 15-passenger van and guests can relax in the large jacuzzi when they return. He offers free internet access, free airport drop-off, free morning beach shuttle, free windsurf gear storage and discounts on windsurf equipment and car rentals. This international hotel and hostel, with clean and comfortable accommodations and a social atmosphere, attracts budget travelers, windsurfers and international backpackers. Rooms are equipped with closet, chair, mirror and nightstand. Bathrooms are shared. Passport or plane ticket off-island required for check-in. Check out is 10 a.m. and the office is closed 11 p.m. to 8 a.m. Laundry facilities on property. There are co-ed and women-only dorm rooms; private rooms have two twin beds or one queen bed.

Rates: Dorm rooms $17.50; private rooms $32 single, $45 double, $55 triple

Maui Beach Hotel
170 Ka'ahumanu Avenue, Kahului, HI 96732. 808-877-0051.

This two-story, 152-room hotel is located oceanfront on Kahului Bay. All rooms have air conditioning and TV; some have balconies. Complimentary airport shuttle. Restaurant on property.

Rates: from $98

Maui Palms
170 Ka'ahumanu Avenue, Kahului, HI 96732. 808-877-0051. Agent: Castle Resorts www.castleresorts.com.

This property is a 103-unit low-rise hotel with Polynesian decor. Built in 1953, the larger Maui Palms was constructed in 1968. In 1979 the Maui Beach purchased the Palms. I wouldn't recommend this property as a vacation stay, but it is convenient if you need a place for a night before an early morning flight from the Kahului Airport. Free airport pickup.

Rates: from $100

★ Old Wailuku Inn at Ulupono
2199 Kaho'okele Street, Wailuku, HI 96793. 808-244-5897; 800-305-4899; fax 808-242-9600; www.mauiinn.com.

Your hosts are Janice and Tom Fairbanks. Built in 1924 by a wealthy island banker as a wedding gift for his daughter-in-law, this historic Wailuku home has been lovingly restored. They were awarded the Kahili "Keep it Hawai'i" Award for Accommodations (from the Hawai'i Visitors & Convention Bureau) for, "saluting the former 1920 plantation home for blending a nostalgic ambiance while at the same time providing all comforts and conveniences for the modern day traveler." In 2000 *Travel & Leisure* named the inn number five of the top ten B&Bs in the U.S. The rooms and overall theme of the inn are a tribute to Hawai'i's famed poet of the 1920s and '30s, Don Blanding. All rooms have high ceilings, wide crown molding, hardwood floors and all the comforts provided by cable television, VCR, ceiling fans, private baths and heirloom Hawaiian quilts. Full gourmet breakfast and daily maid service are included. Ten rooms. Two-night minimum.

Rates: $120-$180 per night; extra person $20/night

Upcountry

Banyan Tree Vacation Rentals
808-572-9021; fax 808-573-5072; e-mail: banyan@hawaii-mauirentals.com; www.hawaii-mauirentals.com.

Located on two acres in upcountry Maui, known in past decades as "Sunnyside" for it's temperate climate. The three-bedroom three-bath home, hidden beneath exotic banyan and monkeypod trees, had a previous life as the home of a plantation manager. Adjacent to the home are private cottages with full or half kitchens. The main house has a restaurant kitchen. Your host is Suzy Papanikolas. Weekly and monthly rates are available.

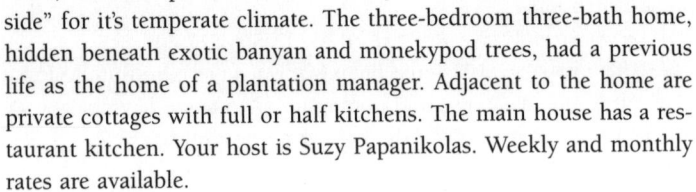

Rates: Plantation home $300/night, Cottage apartments $85-$110

Haiku Getaway, B&B Vacation Rentals
1765 Haiku Road, Haiku, HI 96708. Tel/fax 808-575-9362; 800-680-4946; e-mail: info@vacationrentalmaui.com; www.vacationrentalmaui.com.

Conveniently located just 20 minutes from the airport on your way to Hana, minutes from Ho'okipa Beach Park, Maui's most beloved windsurfing spot, and within walking distance of the Pauwela Cannery. The property is very tropical and private. The two-bedroom cottage has a master bedroom with twins or king option, plus a queen-size guest bedroom. With a private washer/dryer and fenced yard it is a great value for a traveling family. The Gardenia Suite features a queen-size bed and full kitchen. The Tangerine Room has a queen bed and mini-kitchen. All units have access to the gas barbecue on the property and their own private phones, TV, VCR, CD player and ceiling fans. Children 3 and under no charge. A cleaning fee may apply for stays under 2 weeks.

Rates: Cottage $100, Gardenia Suite $90, Tangerine Room $70; extra person $10/night

Hale Huelo Bed & Breakfast
P.O. Box 1237, Haiku, HI 96708. 808-572-8669; fax 808-573-8403; e-mail: halehuelo@maui.net.

Doug Barrett is your host. Rooms have modern bathrooms and small, convenient mini-kitchens. The ocean view is spectacular from all the suites. The atmosphere is country Hawaiian with a touch of Japanese. Other amenities include a swimming pool, secluded hot tub and a bathroom shower that can be entered from inside or straight from the outdoor patio (no need to shower off just to get to the shower).

Rates: $110 off-season (5/1 through 10/31), $125 high season (11/1 through 3/31)

Haleakala National Park
Lottery: Haleakala National Park, Attention Cabins, P.O. Box 369, Makawao, HI 96768-0369; 808-572-4400.

Wilderness cabins at Holua, Paliku and Kapalaoa require a permit. Built by the Civilian Conservation Corps in the 1930s, each cabin has a wood-burning stove, cooking utensils and dishes, 12 padded bunks, pit toilets and limited water and firewood. There is no electricity. Water must be treated. In times of drought, all cookware will be removed and you will need to carry all your water in with you. Each cabin is allocated to one party as a unit, up to 12 people per night. You must enter the reservation lottery by writing to the address above at least 90 days before you get to Maui. Tell them the dates you want (the more flexible you are, the better your chances), which cabin, and how many people. Or call 808-572-4400 between the hours of 1 and 3 p.m.

Rates: $40 (1-6 people); $80 (7-12 people)

Kula Cottage
40 Puakea Place, Kula, HI 96790. 808-871-6230 ext. 17; 808-878-2043; fax 808-871-9187; www.gilbertadvertising.com/kulacottage; e-mail: cecilia@gilbertadvertising.com.

Three thousand feet up on the slopes of Haleakala, in a lush half-acre mountain setting, is this one-bedroom hideaway. The cottage is equipped with a wood-burning fireplace, a full kitchen, laundry, private driveway, gas barbecue and a queen-size bed. Two-night minimum stay.

Rates: $95

Kula Lodge
RR 1, Box 475, Kula, HI 96790. 808-878-1535; 800-233-1535; fax 808-878-2518; e-mail: info@kulodge.com; www.kulalodge.com.

Five and a half miles past Pukalani is the Kula Lodge. Five rustic chalet-like cabins located at the 3,200-foot elevation. There's a restaurant on the property. Chalets 1 each have queen bed, fireplace, lanai, and stairs to loft with 2 twin beds, while Chalets 3 each have queen bed, and ladder to loft with two futon. The single-story Chalet 5 has a queen bed and studio couch

Rates: Chalet 1 and 2 $165, Chalet 3 and 4 $135, Chalet 5 $110; extra charge $30 for more than two guests

★ Kula Lynn Farm

P.O. Box 847, Kula, HI 96789. 808-878-6176; 800-874-2666 ext. 211; e-mail: captcoon@gte.net.

Your hosts are a part of the Coon family (Trilogy Excursions). The lower-level apartment is 1600 square feet with a full kitchen and patio deck. The home is located in beautiful Upcountry on the slopes of Haleakala, in lower Kula.

Rates: $95; extra person $15/night

Maluhia Hale

Located at Twin Falls, about 18 miles from the airport. P.O. Box 687 Haiku, HI 96708. 808-572-2959; e-mail diane@peaceful-home.com.

Diane rents a private cottage with a full ocean view and king-size bed. The furnishings are antiques that reflect an open and spacious feeling. There is a kitchenette stocked with coffee, tea and a light breakfast of muffins and fruit is provided. There is a glass sitting room with a twin bed and a screen porch for relaxing on. No credit cards, no smoking. Two-night minimum.

Rates: $125 double, $150 triple

Maui Dream Cottages

265 West Kuiaha Road, Haiku, HI 96708. 808-575-9079; fax 808-575-9477; www.planet-hawaii.com/haiku; e-mail: gblue@aloha.net.

Gregg Blue offers two dream cottages. Both are equipped with washer/dryer, phone, TV/VCR and sleep 2 to 5 people. There are ocean views from inside both houses.

Rates: $490 per week for two; each additional adult $10/night

Polipoli Springs State Recreation Area

Division of Parks, P.O. Box 537, Makawao, HI 96768.

A single cabin, which sleeps 10, has bunk beds, water, a cold shower and kitchenware. Sheets and towels can be picked up along with the key.

Rates: $45 (1 to 4 persons), extra person $5/night

★ Silver Cloud Upcountry Guest Ranch

1373 Thompson Road Kula, HI 96790. 808-878-6101; fax 808-878-2132; U.S. & Canada 800-532-1111; www.silvercloudranch.com; e-mail: slvrcld@maui.net.

The Silver Cloud ranch was originally part of the Thompson Ranch, which had its beginnings on Maui in 1902. The nine-acre ranch is located at the 2,800-foot elevation on the slopes of Haleakala. Owners Mike Gerry and Ana Lee Apple offer 12 rooms, suites and cottages, each with private bathrooms and most with private lanais and entrances. The King Kamehameha and Queen Emma rooms are located in the main house with a private lanai (the view of the lush Upcountry and the slopes down to the ocean are phenomenal). The Lana'i Cottage offers total privacy with a complete kitchen, clawfoot bathtub and wood-burning stove. The cottage is surrounded by a lovely flower garden and lanai. The Mauka Hale has studios with kitchenettes and lanais. The Bunkhouse's Haleakala Suite is a larger facility with a bedroom, separate living area, fireplace and complete kitchen. The Makawao and Ulupalakua Studios also have gas fireplaces. All room rates include a fabulous full breakfast and use of the main house and kitchen; $15 surcharge added for one-night stay. Not only is this the ideal place to slow down and get away from the rat race, but a fabulous retreat for a wedding or family reunion.

Rates: Aloha Room g.v. $110, Bamboo Room g.v. $122, Haleakala Suite $188, Lana'i Cottage $195; a number of studios, rooms and suites $136; extra person $15/night

Hana Highway

Aloha Cottages
P.O. Box 205, Hana, HI 96713. 808-248-8420.

These simple but comfortable furnished 2- to 3-bedroom cottages are located in a residential area, just a short walk to Hana Bay. No in-room phones, but messages will be taken. There are pay phones nearby. Television optional. Daily maid service. No credit cards.

Rates: $60-$90; extra person $10-$20/night

Haiku Lani
808-575-9037; 808-575-9065; e-mail: drcod@maui.net.

This is a 750-square-foot, 2-bedroom, 1-bath cottage located on a rural half-acre in Haiku. One room has a king bed, the other a double. It's near popular windsurfing beaches. One-week minimum or pay a cleaning fee.

Rates: $550/week

Halfway to Hana House
P.O. Box 675, Haiku, HI 96708. 808-572-1176; fax 808-572-3609; e-mail: gailp@maui.net; www.halfwaytohana.com.

Located 20 minutes from Paia town along the scenic Hana Highway. The romantic guest studio has a spectacular ocean view, hammock for two in the palms, private entrance and bath, mini-kitchen and covered patio. Three-night minimum preferred. Breakfast is an additional $8 per person or $15 for two.

Rates: $85

Hamoa Bay Bungalow and Hamoa Bay House

P.O. Box 773, Hana, HI 96713. Contact Robin Gaffney at 808-248-7884; fax 808-248-7047; e-mail: hamoabay@maui.net; www.hamoabay.com.

The 600-square-foot studio cottage "bungalow" has a fully equipped kitchen, a king-size bamboo bed, a jacuzzi bath for two, a CD/tape player, a VCR and videos, a microwave and laundry facilities. The Balinese-inspired Hamoa Bay House offers mountain, jungle and sea views. You'll find king- and queen-size beds, a barbecue area, laundry facilities and an outdoor lava-rock shower. No smoking indoors. Three-night minimum.

Rates: Bungalow $195; house $250 for 2 people, $350 for 4 people

Hana Kai-Maui

P.O. Box 38, Hana, HI 96713. Located at 1533 Uakea Road in Hana. 800-346-2772; 808-248-8426, 808-248-7506; fax 808-248-7482; e-mail: hanakai@maui.net; www.hanakai.com.

These 18 studio and one-bedroom condominiums are nestled on Hana Bay. All units have fully equipped kitchens and private lanais. There is daily maid service. Amenities include a spring-fed pool and barbecue area.

Rates: Studio (2) $125-$145, 1BR (4) $145-$195

Heavenly Hana Inn

P.O. Box 790, Hana, HI 96713. Tel/fax 808-248-8442; e-mail: hanainn@maui.net; www.heavenlyhanainn.com.

This tranquil inn features two one-room suites and one two-room suite; each has a Japanese-style bath, a lanai and a private entrance, and a small sitting room with cable TV. The spacious bathrooms include a soaking tub. There are no in-room telephones. If you'd like to breakfast here, arrangements must be made a week before arrival; cost is $15 per person. No smoking. Two-night minimum.

Rates: 1-room suite $185-$200, 2-room suite $250

Hana Gardenland

808-248-8610; www.hanapalmsretreat.com.

Both the Garden House and the Palms House are located within the private five-acre Hana Gardenland. The Garden House has two separate and complete residences. They share an outdoor covered hot tub. The Garden Upper Residence has three bedrooms: a sun room with queen bed, a bedroom with two twin beds (or one king), and a bedroom with queen bed, bathroom, full kitchen, large living and dining area. Two-night minimum. The Garden Lower Residence has two bedrooms: a bedroom with two twin beds (or one king) and a bedroom with queen bed, bathroom, full kitchen, living and dining area. Two-night minimum. The Palms House has two bedrooms: Upper large master bedroom queen bed upstairs with half bath, downstairs bedroom queen bed, full kitchen, living room, sun porch dining area, bathroom, outdoor covered shower/bath on porch, outdoors covered hot tub. One-week minimum. Hana Gardenland is 3.5 miles before you reach the town of Hana (driving from Kahului). Look for mile-marker 31 and turn right on Kalo Road. You will see the Garden Café sign on the corner.

Rates: Garden Upper $175, Garden Lower $125, Palms House $225/night

★ **Hotel Hana-Maui at Hana Ranch**
P.O. Box 8, Hana, HI 96713. 800-321-HANA; 808-248-8211; fax 808-248-7202; www.hotelhanamaui.com.

This "island on an island" is Maui's most secluded resort. The 93-room hotel resembles a small neighborhood with single-story units scattered about the grounds. The simple yet elegant rooms have wet bars, hardwood floors and tiled bathrooms with deep tubs and "walk-in" showers. Wicker and bamboo are also prominent. The resort prides itself on the fact that it has no televisions or in-room air conditioning. The 47 fabulous sea ranch cottages resemble early plantation-style houses; some of these oceanview and oceanfront cottages also have private hot tubs. What a way to get away! Built in 1928, the resort's Plantation Guest House can be used as a guest home; it offers two bedrooms, two baths, a large living room with fireplace, dining room, library, bar and complete kitchen. This 4,000-square-foot building, set on four lush acres, was once the home of August Unna, Hana's first plantation owner.

Resort guest services include a free shuttle to and from Hana Airport, daily maid service, tennis courts, two heated pools and an outdoor jacuzzi, a fitness and wellness center, three-hole par-3 practice course with complimentary clubs and balls, and Hawaiian arts and crafts. They provide a Hawaiian buffet with entertainment on Friday evenings in the dining room. Many of the performers are hotel employees or their family members, which affords a more authentic and very charming show. They also offer Hawaiian music in the bar Thursday through Sunday. Dining options include the upscale Main Dining Room and the informal Hana Ranch Restaurant; the bar serves *pupus* and lighter fare. They also provide pool service and in-room service.

A variety of activities are available during the day and evening. A free shuttle goes to beautiful Hamoa Beach with private facilities and complimentary beach and snorkeling equipment for hotel guests.

> In the early 1940s, the end of Hana's sugar industry was close at hand; its 5,000 residents had dwindled down to only 500. Industrialist Paul Fagan consolidated five sugar plantations into a cattle ranch and built a small hotel in 1946, rejuvenating Hana. Originally known as the Kauiki Inn, Fagan's ten-room hotel was expanded over the years and eventually renamed the Hotel Hana-Maui. This Hana landmark, along with the ranch and flower nursery, now employs approximately a third of the town's 1,000 residents.

There are many hiking trails and lots to see horseback riding. Guests can book tours to 'Ohe'o Gulch or the nearby underground caverns, or arrange for guided horseback excursions (fee). Children's activities and overnight sitters are also available. The Paniolo Lounge is a bar with a large fireplace and an open deck with a quiet adjoining lounge. Enjoy some quiet reading in the library, which contains rare volumes of early Hawaiiana as well as popular novels. There is also a small boutique in addition to a beauty salon. The Club Room has free internet access and a television; evening lectures are sometimes given here. The two swimming pools are equally beautiful with different settings, and I made time to lay in the hammock under the palm tree and listen to the ocean. A more tranquil setting is difficult to imagine. Prices are based on single or double occupancy.

Rates: *Bay Cottages*: garden jr. suite $295, deluxe jr. suite $325, o.v. hotel room $325, o.v. jr. suite $365; *Sea Ranch Cottages*: o.v. cottage $395, deluxe o.v. cottage $445, o.v. cottage with spa $495, o.f. cottage $495, o.f. cottage with spa $545, o.f. suite with spa $725; *Plantation Guest House*: $1,500; extra person $50/night

Huelo Point Lookout
P.O. Box 790117, Paia, HI 96779-0117. 800-871-8645; 808-573-0914; e-mail: dreamers@maui.net; www.mauivacationcottages.com

Innkeepers Jeff and Sharyn Stone offer five unique lodging options on their two-acre garden estate. Sweeping ocean and mountain views, hot tubs, a 44-foot rock-walled swimming pool and an organic herb-and-vegetable garden provide a laidback North Shore vacation for the whole family. The Haleakala Cottage has a full kitchen with a dishwasher, king bed, tropical flowers and mountain views. Situated on an acre of lush greenery, the Star Cottage has plenty of windows, ocean and mountain views, a king bed and a private hot tub. Perfect for honeymooners, the two-story Rainbow Cottage will spoil you with fantastic views, private lanais and hot tub. An elegant spiral staircase leads to the skylit master bedroom with a king bed. The 800-square-foot Sunrise Suite's glass-walled living room provides panoramic views, the bedroom suite has a king bed, and the bathroom comes with a view and tub for two. And the large two-story Lookout House, which accommodates up to eight people, has panoramic views, a private lanai with hot tub, wraparound porches, a kitchen, a dining room, and plenty of room for the kids. A massage, yoga classes or even gourmet meals can be arranged. Children must be "swim safe" as neither the pool or hot tub are enclosed. It's a 30- to 40-minute drive from Kahului airport along the road to Hana. No credit cards. Lookout House has a one-week minimum.

Rates: Haleakala Cottage $185-$195, Star Cottage $225-$255, Rainbow Cottage $285-$355, Sunrise Suite $325-$360, Lookout House $2,650-$2,850/week; extra person $30/night

Inn at Mama's Fish House

799 Poho Place, Paia, HI 96779. 800-860-HULA; 808-579-9764; www.mamasfishhouse.com; e-mail: info@mamasfishhouse.com.

Fully equipped oceanfront apartments with private lanais. Laundry facilities and gas grills available. Three-night minimum required.

Rates: S BR $75, 3BR 2 BTH $195, 1BR suites $75, 2BR suites up to $350

Pilialoha Bed & Breakfast Cottage

2512 Kaupakalua Road, Haiku, HI 96708-6024. 808-572-1440; fax 808-572-4612; e-mail: cottage@pilialoha.com; www.pilialoha.com.

Your hosts are Bill and Machikio Keyde. Pilialoha, which means "friendship" in Hawaiian, is a split-level guest cottage on a private two-acre Haiku property. The cottage's master bedroom has a queen bed; an adjoining room has a twin bed. There's an open-air deck and full kitchen, which is stocked with an assortment of teas and coffees. Maximum capacity is three people (a child or baby is counted as one person). Three-night minimum.

Rates: $110/night for one, $130 for two, $150 for three

Wai'anapanapa State Park

54 South High Street, first floor, Wailuku, HI 96793. 808-243-5354.

The State Park Department offers 12 cabins that sleep up to six people. The units have electric lights, hot water, showers and toilet facilities (bring your own soap). There is a living room with two single beds and one bedroom with two bunks. Completely furnished with bedding, bath towels, dish cloth, and cooking and eating utensils. There's an electric range (no oven) and refrigerator. Mosquito repellent is strongly recommended, even for a short walk through the pool area. A five-day maximum stay is the rule and guests are required to clean their units before departure, leaving soiled linens. A 50 percent deposit is required for reservations and they are booked way ahead (six months to one year). Children are considered those ages 11 and under. No pets are allowed.

Rates: $45 for 1-4 persons; extra person $5/night

YMCA Camp Ke'anae
In Ke'anae. 808-248-8355. Reservations and information available through the Maui YMCA office at 250 Kanaloa Avenue, Kahului, HI 96732; 808-242-9007; onsite phone 808-248-8355.

Located a half mile past mile-marker 16, the YMCA's Camp Ke'anae offers overnight dorm-style accommodations for men and women (housed separately). Arrival is requested between 4 p.m. and 6 p.m. Bring your own food and sleeping bag.

Rates: $10

Rental Agents

BED & BREAKFAST AGENCIES

An alternative to condominiums and hotels are the bed-and-breakfast organizations. They offer homes around the island at some very reasonable rates.

Affordable Accommodations Maui
2825 Kauhale Street, Kihei, HI 96753. 808-879-7865; fax 808-874-0831; e-mail: info@affordablemaui.com; www.affordablemaui.com.

Linda Little runs this agency, which offers bed and breakfasts, studios, cottages, condominiums and homes. Prices range from a $50/night budget accommodation to $5,000/night luxury home. Their objective is to find just the right place for you at your preferred price range. They can also arrange for outer island accommodations and rental cars.

Bed & Breakfast Hawai'i
P.O. Box 449, Kapa'a, HI 96746. 800-733-1632; 808-822-7771; fax 808-822-2723; e-mail: reservations@bandb-hawaii.com; www.bandb-hawaii.com.

This agency is among the best known. To become a member and receive their directory (which includes the other islands) contact them.

CONDOMINIUM AND HOME RENTAL AGENCIES

AA Oceanfront Condo Rentals
800-488-6004; 808-879-7288; fax 808-879-7500; e-mail: info@aaoceanfront.com; www.makena.com.

Rents properties from North Kihei to Makena in all price categories. There is a cleaning fee for less than 5 nights. They also rent cars.

Aston Hotels & Resorts
2255 Kalakaua Avenue #500, Honolulu, HI 96815. 808-931-1400; 800-321-2558 U.S., 800-445-6633 Canada; www.aston-hotels.com.

Bello Realty-Maui Beach Homes
P.O. Box 1776, Kihei, HI 96753. 808-879-2598; 800-541-3060 U.S. & Canada; e-mail: pam@bellomaui.com; www.bellomaui.com.

Specializing in the Kihei area, Bello rents condos and homes by the day, week or month. Their rates look pretty competitive.

Castle Group
745 Fort Street, Honolulu, HI 96813. 800-367-5004; fax 800-477-2329; www.castle-group.com.

Chase 'n Rainbows
P.O. Box 11478, Lahaina, HI. 800-367-6092 U.S. & Canada; 808-667-7088; fax 808-661-8423; e-mail: info@chasenrainbows.com; www.chasenrainbows.com

Also does car rentals.

Classic Resorts
50 Nohea Kai Drive, Lahaina, HI 96761. 800-642-6284; 808-661-3339; fax 808-667-1145; e-mail: info@classicresorts.com; www.classicresorts.com.

Condominium Rentals Hawaii
362 Huku Li'i Place #204, Kihei, HI 96753. 800-367-5242 U.S.; 800-663-2101 Canada; 808-879-2778; e-mail: res@crhmaui.com; www.crhmaui.com.

★ **Destination Resorts**
800-367-5246; 808-879-1595; fax 808-874-3554; e-mail: info@drhmaui.net; www.destinationresortshi.com.

Elite Properties Unlimited
505 Front Street #228, Lahaina, HI 96761. 800-448-9222 U.S. & Canada; 808-665-0561; fax 808-669-2417; e-mail: homes@eliteprop.com; www.eliteprop.com.

Rents family homes and luxury estates (3 to 7 bedrooms) on all four major islands. Weekly and monthly rentals. One-week minimum. Maid service, chefs and concierge services available.

Hana Alii Holidays
P.O. Box 536, Hana, HI. 800-548-0478; 808-248-7742; e-mail: info@hanaalii.com; www.hanaalii.com.

They handle rental homes in Hana with more than a dozen ranging from $75-$300/night.

★ **Hana Alii Holidays Vacation Rentals**
P.O. Box 536, Hana, HI. 800-548-0478; 808-248-7742; e-mail: info@hanaalii.com; www.hanaalii.com.

They have a number of oceanview and oceanfront homes or cottages. Cottages for two start from $100/night; three-bedroom units are in the $250 range.

Hana Plantation Houses
P.O. Box 249, Hana, HI 96713. 800-228-HANA; 808-248-7868; www.hana-maui.com.

Blair and Tom have a variety of excellent properties, from plantation-style homes to quaint cottages. Full payment is required in advance. Rates are $100/night and up.

Hawaiian Hotels & Resorts
800-222-5642 U.S. & Canada; 805-497-7934; e-mail: hhr@hawaii hotels.com; www.hawaiihotels.com.

Hawaiian Island Vacation
800-231-6958; 808-871-4981; fax 808-871-4624; e-mail: info@hawaiian island.com; www.hawaiianisland.com.

Condo and car vacation packages; interisland air travel.

Kathy Scheper's Maui Accommodations
1587 North Alaniu Place, Kihei, HI 96753. 800-645-3753; 808-879-8744; fax 808-879-9100; e-mail: vacation@maui411.com; www.maui411.com.

Condo in Kihei and penthouse at Hale Mahina.

★ Kihei Maui Vacations
800-542-6284 U.S.; 800-423-8733 ext. 4000 Canada; 808-879-7581.

In addition to condos they offer homes and cottages in the Kihei, Wailea and Makena areas. No credit cards.

Kumulani Vacations & Realty
P.O. Box 1190, Kihei, HI 96753. 800-367-2954 U.S. & Canada; 808-879-9272; e-mail: info@kumulani.com; www.kumulani.com.

Can assist with almost any island property and interisland connections.

Ma'alaea Bay Rentals
280 Hauoli Street, Ma'alaea Village, HI 96793. 800-367-6084; 808-244-7012; fax 808-242-7476; e-mail: reservations@maalaeabay.com; www.maalaeabay.com.

Marc Resorts
2155 Kalakaua Avenue, 7th floor, Honolulu, HI 96815. 800-535-0085; 808-992-9700; fax 800-663-5085; e-mail: aloha@marcresorts.com; www.marcresorts.com.

★ Maui and All Island Condominiums and Cars
P.O. Box 1089, Aldergrove, BC, Canada V4W 2V1. U.S. Mailing address: P.O. Box 947, Lynden, WA 98264. 800-663-6962 U.S. & Canada; 604-856-4190; fax 604-856-4187.

Approximately 25,000 condos and homes rented weekly, biweekly and monthly.

Maui Beachfront Rentals
256 Papalaua Street, Lahaina, HI 96761. 888-661-7200; 808-661-3500; e-mail: beachfrt@maui.net; www.mauibeachfront.com.

Maui Condo and Home Realty
P.O. Box 1840, Kihei, HI 96753. 800-822-4409; 808-879-0028; fax 808-875-1769; www.mauicondo.com.

Homes and condos in the Kihei–Wailea area.

Maui Lodging
800-487-6002; 808-669-0089; fax 808-669-3937; e-mail: info@mauilodging.com; www.mauilodging.com.

Maui Resort Management
3600 Lower Honoapi'ilani Highway, Lahaina, HI 96761. 800-367-5037; 808-669-1902; e-mail: getaway@maui.net; www.mauigetaway.com.

Maui Vacation Properties
P.O. Box 1359, Haiku, HI 96708. 800-782-6105; 808-575-9228; fax 808-575-2826; e-mail: info@mauivacationproperties.com; www.mauivacationproperties.com.

Islandwide rental condos, homes and cottages.

Maui Vacations
Melinda Mower. 494 Wainee Street, Lahaina, HI 96761. 800-572-5642; 808-662-0812; fax 808-661-8045; e-mail: info@maui-vacations.com; www.maui-vacations.com.

Offering mountain view, ocean view and beachfront vacation rental condos, homes and cottages in Lahaina Town and throughout beautiful West Maui.

Maui Windsurfari
808-871-7766; 800-736-6284; e-mail: info@windsurfari.com; www.windsurfari.com.

Vacation rental agency offering private homes, cottages and condos from $50 up. Many of their vacation rentals are unusual with close proximity to windsurfing locations. Packages include accommodations, rental car, windsurfing equipment and excursions.

My Vacation Properties by Windsurfing West, Ltd.
P.O. Box 1359, Haiku, HI 96708. 800-782-6105; 808-575-9228; fax 808-575-2826; e-mail: windsurf@maui.net; www.maui.cc.

Their list of condo rentals covers the North Shore, South Shore and Upcountry. Along with condos they have quality villas, rental homes and quaint cottages. Rates range from $60 to $1,000 per night. Even if you're not a windsurfer, you might want to check into their "Accommodations Only" packages. They can also arrange equipment rentals and lessons.

My Waii Beach Cottage
3537 207th SE, Issaquah, WA 98029. 800-882-9007; e-mail: info@mywaii.com; www.mywaii.com.

Great oceanfront cottage located at 2128A Ili'ili Road, Kihei.

Outrigger Hotels Hawaii
2335 Kalakaua Avenue, Honolulu, HI 96715-2941. 800-OUTRIGGER; 303-369-7777; www.outrigger.com; e-mail: reservations@outrigger.com.

Premier Destinations
3478 Buskirk Avenue, Suite 275, Pleasant Hill, CA 94523. 800-367-7052; e-mail: stay@premier-resorts.com; www.premier-resorts.com.

RSVP
1575 West Georgia Street, 3rd floor, Vancouver, BC, Canada V6G 2V3. 800-663-1118 U.S. & Canada; e-mail: karen@rsvphawaii.com; www.rsvphawaii.com.

Ask about specials they may have for free rental cars, senior rates, military discounts, etc.

Upcountry Maui Rentals
808-280-0404; e-mail tanmayomaui@yahoo.com.

Semi-furnished rooms at $345-$495 per month includes utilities and use of hot tub. They also have a cottage available for vacation or long-term rental.

★ Whalers Realty Management Co.
Kaʻanapali Professional Center, Suite C, 2530 Kekaʻa Drive, Lahaina, HI 96761. 800-676-4112; 808-661-3484; fax 808-661-8338; e-mail: vacation@whalersrealty.com; www.whalersrealty.com

They offer high-quality condos at reasonable prices.

CHAPTER 4

Where to Dine

Whether it is a teriburger at a local café or a romantic evening spent dining next to a swan lagoon, Maui offers something for everyone. I'm confident that you will enjoy exploring Maui's diverse dining options as much as I have.

The dramatic growth in restaurants has finally overwhelmed me! In an effort to avoid this book becoming a two-volume set, I have decided to delete those restaurants that I find less interesting, those so far off-the-beaten path that you would not likely venture to or perhaps simply not so good. In the case of new restaurants, I have tried to include them so you can evaluate the newest dining opportunities on the island and I will continue to keep you posted in the quarterly newsletter, *The Maui Update*. There are wonderful dining options around the island, but be sure to take special note of the dining opportunities in Kahului and Wailuku. You'll get the most for your dining dollar. And, of course, even with the help of many, many friends, we can't eat at every restaurant before the revision of each guidebook (although we really try!). So I'd love to hear from you. It is quite a job to keep up on the restaurants that come and go! Some will become a permanent part of the Maui dining scene, others will quickly disappear.

The restaurants are divided into the same geographical sections of the island as the "Where to Stay" chapter. The restaurant descriptions/listings are separated by price range, and listed alphabetically within those price ranges. This should simplify looking for that perfect place for breakfast, lunch or dinner based on the location where you find yourself. They are also indexed alphabetically as well as by food type. The price ranges are: "*inexpensive,*" mostly under $15, "*moderate,*" most entrees $15 to $25, and "*expensive,*" $25 and above. As a means of comparison, I have taken an average meal (usually dinner), excluding tax, alcoholic beverages and desserts, for one person at that restaurant. The prices listed were accurate at the time of publication, but I cannot be responsible for any price increases. For quick reference, the type of food served at the restaurant described is indicated next to the restaurant name. Sample menu offerings are also included as a helpful guide. *Tip:* Check the local free papers for restaurant ads. You might find some seasonal specials or early-bird dinner offerings. In addition, favorite restaurants are generally either a real bargain for the price, serve a very high quality meal, or just have something special to recommend them, and are indicated by a ★.

My recommendations for best family-dining restaurants are indicated with a girl with a hat. While many restaurants offer *keiki* menus, we feel these recommended restaurants have great food, good value (although some are fine-dining establishments and will not be inexpensive) and wonderful atmosphere/ambience. If there's no *keiki* menu, most restaurants are happy to down-size standard portions and reduce the cost.

Many smaller restaurants post dinner hours as *n* p.m. to closing. While most close around 9 p.m., many will adjust the time to close their doors based on business each evening. Special events, holidays, weekends and particularly busy vacation seasons warrant later hours.

There are numerous fast food/chain restaurants, but I have only included the larger, more "restaurant-like" ones in key locations. I have also tried to include all the locally owned places—the inexpensive little "finds" you won't see back home. Among those not listed are Subway, McDonald's, Pizza Hut, Taco Bell, Little Caesar's (inside Big Kmart), Wendy's, Arby's, Carl's Jr., KFC and Dairy Queen. They all serve the same food you'd expect, but most have slightly higher prices than the mainland. Keep an eye out for special offers and promos, which tend to be the same price as the mainland. The Burger King in Lahaina has a very good location on Front Street with patio seating across from the Banyan Tree and a view of the ocean beyond it. McDonald's has the usual fare, but with some unusual items added in: for breakfast you can have Portuguese sausage with rice and chase it down with a chilled guava juice; then for lunch, try a big bowl of saimin.

There are several food courts around the island. In Lahaina, the Pineapple Food Court at the Lahaina Cannery Mall is an excellent stop for the traveling family; with so many selections, everyone will find exactly what they want and it won't pinch the pocketbook. You'll also find food courts at Whalers Village in Ka'anapali, and Queen Ka'ahumanu Center and Maui Marketplace in Kahului–Wailuku. Although not a food court, there are several small food outlets in Maui Mall.

Ethnic Foods

The cultural diversity of the Hawaiian islands benefits visitors and residents alike. As immigrants arrived, they brought with them many varied foods from their native lands; some may be familiar while others are new and interesting. little background on some ethnic foods may tempt you to try a few new foods as a part of your dining adventure on Maui.

CHINESE FOODS

Bean threads: thin, clear noodles made from mung beans
Char siu: roasted pork with spices
Chow mein: thin noodles prepared with veggies and meat in various combinations, also cake-noodles style
Crack seed: preserved fruits and seeds, some are sweet, others are sour
Egg/Spring/Summer roll: deep-fried or fresh pastry roll with various veggie, meat or shrimp fillings
Kung pao chicken: deep-fried or sauteed spicy chicken pieces
Long rice: clear noodles cooked with chicken and vegetables
Mongolian beef: thinly sliced charbroiled beefsteak
Peking duck: charbroiled duck with *char siu* flavoring
Pot stickers: semisoft pan-fried filled dumplings
Sweet-and-sour sauce: sugar-and-vinegar-based sauce with tomato sauce, salt and garlic flavorings
Szechuan sauce: hot chili–flavored sauce used extensively in beef, chicken, pork, seafood dishes
Won ton: crispy deep-fried dumpling with meat or veggie fillings; also soft style cooked in soups or noodle dishes

FILIPINO FOODS

Adobo: chicken or pork cooked with vinegar and spices
Cascaron: a donut made with rice flour and rolled in sugar
Chicken papaya: chicken soup with green papaya and seasonings
Dinadaraan: blend of prepared pork blood and meats
Halo halo: a tropical fruit sundae that is a blend of milk, sugar, fruits and ice
Lumpia: fried pastry filled with vegetables and meats
Pancit: noodles with vegetables or meat
Pinacbet: stir-fry of bitter melon, okra, pork and various seasonings
Pork and peas: traditional entree of pork, peas, flavorings in a tomato paste base
Sari sari: soup entree of pork, veggies and flavorings

HAWAIIAN FOODS

Haupia: a sweet custard made of coconut milk

Kalua pig: roast pig cooked in an underground *imu* oven, very flavorful

Kulolo: a steamed pudding using coconut milk and grated taro root

Laulau: pieces of pork or chicken, flavored with butterfish, topped with luau (taro) leaves, wrapped in ti leaves, then steamed

Lomi lomi salmon: diced and salted salmon with tomatoes and green onions

Long rice: clear noodles cooked with squid or chicken broth

Opihi: saltwater limpets eaten raw and considered a delicacy

Poi: pureed taro corms, best eaten fresh

Poke: raw fish that has been spiced. A variety of fish are used and are often mixed with seaweed; for example, ahi *poke* is raw tuna while *tako poke* is marinated octopus

JAPANESE FOODS

Chicken katsu: deep-fried, breaded chicken pieces served with *katsu* sauce

Donburi: chicken, pork or fish entree with veggies and special soy sauce served over steaming rice and topped with egg

Kamaboko: fish cake of white fish and starch steamed together

Miso soup: soup of fermented soy beans

Okazuya: this is a style of serving where you select dishes from a buffet line; the food represents a variety of ethnic cuisines

Sashimi: very fresh firm raw fish, usually yellowfin tuna (*ahi*), sliced thin and dipped in wasabi-*shoyu* sauce;

Shabu shabu: thinly sliced beef with veggies, noodles and *ponzu* sauce

Soba/saimin: thin noodles served with/without broth; cold soba served as salad with vegetables

Sukiyaki: thinly sliced beef with veggies, noodles and tofu in a broth

Sushi: white rice rolls or cakes with various seafood, seaweed and veggie fillings

Tempura: deep-fried shrimp, fish, seafood and veggies dipped in a light flour batter

Teriyaki: flavorful, savory soy sauce and ginger marinade for beef, chicken, pork and seafood

Tonkatsu: pork cutlet grilled golden brown, served with *tonkatsu* sauce

Udon: noodles served with soup broth, green onions, fish cake slices, optional meat

Wasabi: very spicy green horseradish root used to dip sushi into

KOREAN FOODS

Kalbi ribs: flavored similarly to teriyaki, but with chili pepper, sesame oil and green onions

Kim chee: spicy pickled cabbage flavored with ginger and garlic
Mandoo: fried dumplings with meat and vegetable fillings
Mandoo kook, Bi bim kook, yook kae jang: soups served with *mandoo* dumplings, noodles, vegetables, variety of meats
Meat or fish jun: fried or broiled beef or fish with teriyaki-type sauce
Spicy barbecue beef, chicken or pork: broiled soy sauce–flavored beef, chicken or pork laced with spicy hot chili

LOCAL FAVORITES

Bento: a box lunch might include tempura shrimp, veggies, scoop of noodles, sushi roll or rice
Loco moco: a combination of hamburger patty atop a bowl of rice with fried egg and gravy
Plate lunches: a traditional favorite might include teriyaki beef or chicken, hamburger with gravy, roast pork, fried fish or any of several other entrees, always served with rice and often a scoop of macaroni salad
Saimin: noodles served in broth with fish cake, veggies
Shave ice: ground ice—mainlanders know it as snowcones, except the ice is more finely shaved—topped with flavored syrups such as strawberry, pineapple, guava, vanilla, mango, root beer, *lilikoi*.

PUERTO RICAN FOODS

Pasteles: an exterior of grated green banana that is filled with pork and vegetables

THAI/VIETNAMESE FOOD

Fried noodles/fried rice: crispy/soft fried noodles with meat entree and soft rice with meat and vegetables
Green curry: choice of meat entree with peas, string beans, coconut milk and sweet basil
Mein noodles: egg noodle soup with shrimp, seafood or other entree
Musaman curry: curry with onion, peanuts, carrots and potatoes in coconut milk
Pad Thai: Thai-style pan-fried noodles with choice of meat entree or veggies garnished with sprouts
Pho noodle soup: noodle soup with beefsteak, meatball, chicken or combination with veggies
Red curry: choice of meat entree with bamboo shoots in coconut milk and sweet basil
Rice noodle soup: rice stick noodles with shrimp, pork, fish cake, squid or other seafood
Satay sticks: broiled chicken, pork or beef on skewer sticks, served as a side dish

Vermicelli cold noodles: thin, clear noodles combined with meat or seafood entree and veggies

Yellow curry: chicken with coconut milk and potatoes

A FEW WORDS ABOUT FISH

Whether cooking fish at your condominium or eating out, the names of the island fish can be confusing. While local shore fishermen catch shallow-water fish such as goatfish or *papio* for their dinner table, commercial fishermen angle for two types. Steakfish are caught by trolling in deep waters and include ahi, *ono* and mahi-mahi. The more delicate bottom fish include *opakapaka* and *onaga*, which are caught with lines dropped as deep as 1,500 feet to shelves off the island coastlines. Here is some background on what you might find on your dinner plate.

Ahi: yellowfin (Allison tuna) is caught in deep waters off Kaua'i and weighs 60 to 280 pounds; pinkish red meat is firm yet flaky and popular for sashimi.

Aku: a bluefin tuna that has a stronger taste than ahi.

Albacore: a smaller version of the ahi, averages 40 to 50 pounds and is lighter in both texture and color; also called *koshibi*.

A'u: the broadbill swordfish, or marlin; a dense and sometimes dry fish.

Ehu: orange snapper.

Hapu: Hawaiian sea bass.

Kamakamaka: Island catfish, very tasty but a little difficult to find.

Lehi: a silver-mouth member of the snapper family, with a stronger flavor than *onaga* or *opakapaka* and a texture resembling mahimahi.

Mahimahi: called the dolphin fish, but has no relation to Flipper or his friends; caught while trolling and weighs between 10 to 65 pounds; excellent white meat that is moist and light and very good sauteed; a seasonal fish that commands a high price when fresh. **Beware**: while excellent fresh, mahimahi is often served in restaurants having arrived from the Philippines frozen, making it far less pleasing. A clue as to whether it's fresh or frozen may be the price tag. If it runs less than $10 to $15 it is probably the frozen variety. Fresh mahimahi will run more.

Mu'u: I tried this mild white fish at the Makawao Steak House years ago and was told there is no common name for this fish. I've never seen it served elsewhere in restaurants.

Onaga: caught in holes that are 1,000 feet or deeper, this red snapper has an attractive hot-pink exterior with tender, juicy white meat inside.

Ono: also known as *wahoo*; a member of the barracuda family, its white meat is firm and more steaklike. *Ono* means "delicious" in Hawaiian.
'Opae: shrimp
Opakapaka: pink snapper; meat is very light and flaky with a delicate flavor.
Papio: a baby *ulua* caught in shallow waters.
Uku: grey snapper, light, firm and white meat with a texture that varies with size.
Ulua: also known as pompano, this fish is firm and flaky with steak-like, textured white meat.

Dining Best Bets

Top Restaurants   My criteria for a top restaurant are excellence of food preparation and presentation, a pleasing atmosphere, and service that anticipates or responds promptly to one's needs. While the following exemplify these criteria, they are also all "deep pocket" restaurants, so expect to spend $100 or more for your meal, wine and gratuity for two. Generally, anything you have will be excellent. Remember, even the best restaurants may have an "off" night, but these are seldom. Also, chefs and management do change, rendering what you may have found to be excellent on one occasion to be quite different the next. However, the following have proven to be consistent through the years. Enjoy your meal, enjoy being a little bit spoiled, and remember that muumuus are great for covering up all those calories.
Lahaina: Chez Paul; David Paul's Lahaina Grill; Gerard's. *Ka'anapali–Kapalua Area*: Spats Trattoria; Swan Court. *Ma'alaea–Kihei–Wailea–Makena Area*: Hakone; Prince Court; Spago.

Top Restaurants in a More Casual Atmosphere   While some of these restaurants are slightly less expensive, it is still easy to spend $70 or more for dinner for two. They serve a superior meal in a less formal atmosphere. *Lahaina*: Canoes; Longhi's. *Ka'anapali–Kapalua Area*: Gardenia Court; Hula Grill; 'OnO Surf Bar & Grill; Plantation House; Roy's Kahana Bar & Grill; Roy's Nicolina; Westin's tropica; Va Bene. *Ma'alaea–Kihei–Wailea–Makena Area*: Five Palms Beach Grill; Le Gunji; Nick's Fishmarket; Sarento's, Sea Watch Restaurant; Restaurant Taiko, Waterfront Restaurant. *Upcountry*: Hali'imaile General Store. *Hana Highway*: Mama's Fish House.

Best Restaurants with a View   Café O'Lei, Lahaina; Castaway Café, Ka'anapali; Ferraro's, Four Seasons, Wailea; Five Palms Beach Grill, Kihei; Kapalua Island Grill; Kula Lodge, Kula; Plantation House, Kapalua; Sarento's, Wailea; Sea Watch Restaurant, Wailea

"Local" Restaurants For years I have delighted in exploring the many small, family-owned "local" restaurants in Kahului, and especially in Wailuku. The food in these establishments is not only plentiful and well prepared, but also very inexpensive. The service is often better and friendlier than at many of the resort establishments. *Ka'anapali–Kapalua Area*: Honokowai Okazuya & Deli. *Kahului–Wailuku Area*: A Saigon Café; Fiesta Time; Mama Ding's; Nazo's; Saeng's Thai Cuisine; Sam Sato's; Siam Thai; Tasty Crust; Tokyo Tei. *Hana Highway*: Hana Hou.

Most Romantic Check out the Dinner Under the Stars offered by the Sheraton on Ka'anapali Beach. They have three menus from which to choose: Moonlit ($115), Cupid ($130) or Stargazed ($150), or arrange your own customized selection of dining items. and can be tailored to specific wishes. Several romantic and spectacular locations on the property—by a waterfall, at the beach, on the ocean lawn, etc. You and yours have your private server who sees to your every wish. A romantic experience not to be forgotten.

Best Ambiance Gerard's in Lahaina, Plantation House in Kapalua, Swan Court at Hyatt Regency Maui. *Oceanside dining:* Hula Grill in Ka'anapali, Sea Watch Restaurant in Wailea, Five Palms Beach Grill in Kihei, Mama's Fish House in Paia, General Store in Hali'imaile.

Sushi Bar Sansei Restaurant in Kihei and Kapalua.

French Gerard's in Lahaina, Chez Paul in Olowalu.

Seafood Mama's Fish House in Paia, Gerard's in Lahaina (although not a seafood restaurant, their fresh fish is outstanding), Waterfront Restaurant in Ma'alaea and Nick's Fishmarket at Fairmont Kea Lani in Wailea.

Seafood Buffet All of the top restaurants have wonderful seafood, but an all-you-can-eat buffet is a seafood lover's dream come true. Kapalua Bay Resort's Gardenia Court Restaurant, The Ritz-Carlton's Terrace Restaurant, Prince Court, Hula Moons Restaurant in Wailea, 'OnO at the Westin.

Daily breakfast buffets Swan Court (Hyatt Regency Maui), Va Bene at the Maui Marriott, Gardenia Court at the Kapalua Bay Hotel, 'OnO Surf Bar & Grill at the Westin, Wailea Marriott's Hula Moons Restaurant, the Fairmont Kea Lani's restaurant, and Palm Court at the Renaissance. The least expensive and most casual is at the Ka'anapali Beach Hotel's Tiki Terrace.

Sunday Brunches There are no "best" Sunday brunches—they're all wonderful. (And you may not have to eat for the next two days.) Sunday brunches run $30-$40, with some serving champagne; all include a larger area of entree items than their daily breakfast buffet. Swan Court (Hyatt Regency Maui), The Gardenia Court Restaurant (Kapalua Bay Hotel), Tiki Terrace (Ka'anapali Beach

Hotel), the Westin's tropica, Hula Moons Restaurant (Wailea Marriott, an Outrigger Resort), the Fairmont Kea Lani Restaurant, Prince Court (Maui Prince Hotel).
Salad Bars   Canoes in Lahaina.
Pizza   BJ's Chicago Pizzeria in Lahaina.
Hamburger with a View   Cheeseburger in Paradise or Kimo's in Lahaina.
Sandwiches   The Peking Duck sandwich at Longhi's, Mr. Sub in Lahaina, Sub Paradise in Kahului, the *kalua* turkey sandwich at Pauwela Café in Haiku, the Vietnamese sandwiches at Ba-Le in Lahaina Cannery Mall and Kahului's Maui Marketplace.
Appetizers   The lettuce wraps at Café O'Lei or Ma'alaea Grill; the Asian coconut milk soup at Spago; the crab cake at Erik's Seafood and Sushi; the rock shrimp cake at Sansei; the carpaccio or *frutta di mare* (a lavish array of seafood appetizers) at Sarento's; the fresh foie gras with scallops at Restaurant Taiko; or the chef's sample trio at Café Sauvage in Lahaina.
Dessert   "Brownie to Da Max" sundae at Plantation House. BJ's Chicago Pizzeria's own invention, the "pizookie," is a winner. And who couldn't love Kimo's hula pie?
Hawaiian   Tiki Terrace at the Ka'anapali Beach Hotel, Hana Hou in Haiku, Cary & Eddie's Hideaway in Kahului.
Family Dining Experience, Cost Is No Object   Hard Rock Cafe, Cheeseburger in Paradise, Bubba Gump Shrimp Company.
Good and Cheap   Early-bird dinners at Ka'anapali Beach Hotel's Ka'anapali Mixed Plate (4-6 p.m.), Kobe Japanese Steak House (5:30 or 6 p.m. seating), Canoes in Lahaina (5-6 p.m.), Coconut Grove in Lahaina (5:30-7 p.m.) and Café Sauvage in Lahaina (5-6:30 p.m.). If you're a "late bird" then check out Sansei Sushi for their after-hours half-price appetizers starting at 10 p.m.
Dinner Value   Honokowai Okazuya & Deli in Honokowai.
Shave Ice   Ashley's Internet Cafe at Kahana Gateway, W & F Washerette Snack Bar in Kahului and the Snack Shop at Suda's Store (it sells shave ice only between 1 and 5 p.m., after Suda's main store closes).
Bakeries   The Bakery in Lahaina (wonderful French pastries), central Maui's Home Maid Bakery (fantastic bread pudding), The Four Sisters Bakery in Wailuku, The Maui Bake Shop in Kahului

> **EARLY-BIRD DINNERS**
> Hours vary, but early-bird dinners are a small window usually beginning around 5-5:30 p.m. and ending by 6 p.m. Meals are often the same ones you would pay more for an hour later, but selections are limited. This used to be a huge marketing trend but very few are offered Be sure to check in some of the brochures and the seasonal dinner specials.

> ## FOOD FESTIVALS
>
> Grand Chefs at Kea Lani teams prominent chefs from the mainland and Hawai'i for a variety of events; the Lana'i Visiting Artists program at the Lodge at Koele frequently features guest chefs. April's "Ulupalakua Thing" is an agricultural fair with food samplings. The Kapalua Wine Symposium and Seafood Festival in July is a chance to taste seafood from the island's best chefs. September's Taste of Lahaina offers both a dinner and food festival at which you can sample food from a variety of Maui restaurants. For details on these and other upcoming culinary events call Interactive Events 800-961-9196 or e-mail: events@maui.net. (They can also help you create your own culinary event, whether it's meeting a favorite chef, adding to a cookbook collection, touring an agricultural farm or food manufacturing company, or attending a cooking class.)

(fine pastries and cakes). Komoda Store and Bakery in Makawao (808-572-7261) is famous for its cream puffs. Arrive past noon and you'll likely not get any!

Vegetarian Hokus Pokus restaurant in Paia probably has the largest strictly-vegetarian menu. Simple Pleasures Café in Wailuku has a daily selection of excellent vegetarian and vegan dishes. Down to Earth is a "health food" store located in Kahului and Makawao; in addition to their grocery items they offer hot vegetarian dishes and a salad bar priced by the pound.

Luau The luau at Wailea Marriott, An Outrigger Resort; the Old Lahaina Luau.

Night Spots Hapa*s in Kihei, Casanova's in Makawao. Check in the entertainment section of the *Maui News* for happening events.

Lahaina

Inexpensive-priced Dining

A & J Kitchen Deli & Bakery (Local)
Lahaina Center, 900 Front Street; 808-667-0623.

Hours: Sunday 9:30 a.m.-4 p.m. Monday-Thursday 9:30 a.m.-8 p.m., Friday-Saturday until 9 p.m. *Sampling:* Big breakfasts are just the ticket for the hearty eater, with 3 eggs, rice, Spam or another breakfast meat for $6.49. Breakfast sandwich, pancakes and eggs ($6.59-$6.99). Kids' menus, too. Try local plates with two scoops rice, *kim chee* or macaroni salad and entrees like chicken *katsu*, *mochiko* chicken or chili and rice ($5.50-$7.99). Korean plates include *kalbi* ribs, meat *jun*, and even *mandoo* soup. Chef's favorites include egg foo yong, oyster-sauce chicken and *char-siu* fried rice ($6-$7). Also deli sandwiches and burgers. Taking the gang to the beach? Try their "Lunch Pak" or "Pack & Go" with an assortment of barbecue beef, chicken and ribs. *Comments:* Their $5 lunch menu is Monday through Friday 11 a.m.-4 p.m. and they deliver. Plus 4 hours free validated parking at Lahaina Center.

Aloha Mixed Plate *(Local/Hawaiian)*
1285 Front Street, across from the Lahaina Cannery; 808-661-3322.

    Hours: Breakfast 7:30-10 a.m. Lunch/dinner 10 a.m.-10 p.m. Happy Hour 3-6 p.m. and 10 p.m.-midnight. *Sampling:* Plate lunches, saimin, "grilled stuff," burgers and sandwiches ($4.50-$7.95). Hawaiian plate lunches include *kalua* pig, *laulau*, and even *lomi lomi* salmon and *haupia* ($7.95-$12.95). *Comments:* Pleasant outdoor patio dining, oceanfront, too.

The Bakery *(French/American Pastries)*
911 Limahana (turn off Honoapi'ilani Highway by Pizza Hut); 808-667-9062.

    Hours: Monday-Friday 5:30 a.m.-3 p.m. Saturday 5:30 a.m.-2 p.m. Sunday 5:30 a.m.-noon. *Sampling:* Chocolate almond and whole-wheat cream cheese croissants, cinnamon rolls topped with pecans or honey or filled with raisins, and coconut macaroons. A daily selection of stuffed croissants usually sells out quickly. Also don't forget the great fresh breads and fruit tortes ($1.50-$5). *Comments:* Basically a to-go eatery. Arrive early in the day for better selection. Everything is delicious and it's well worth the stop if you are a pastry lover.

Bamboo Bar & Grill *(Vietnamese/Thai/Sushi)*
505 Front Street; 808-667-4051.

    Hours: 10 a.m.-1 a.m. *Sampling:* The menu highlights Vietnamese and Thai cuisine with lemongrass chicken or shrimp, green bean beef, Thai coconut shrimp, and fish clay pot. Deep fried whole fish, too ($7.95-$15.95). *Comments:* This little café features a full menu of Asian cuisine and has a sushi outlet in the back. "Take Sushi" is open Wednesday-Saturday for lunch (11 a.m.-2 p.m.) and dinner (5-11:30 p.m.).

★ **BJ's Chicago Pizzeria** *(Italian)*
730 Front Street; 808-661-0700.

    Hours: 11 a.m.-11 p.m. *Sampling:* Start with BJ's bruschetta, toasted ravioli or their own invention, the pizza-dilla: quesadilla-like triangles of pizza dough with a creamy topping of artichoke, spinach and cheese ($5.95-$9.95). Then order a basic cheese and tomato ($8.95/$12.95/$14.95 for S/M/L) and add your own toppings or try one of their innovative specialties like "BBQ Chicken or Shrimp Thermidor" ($15.65/$20.95/$23.55). Calzones for one

($5.95) or two ($9.95), too. BJ's specialty salads include chopped Italian, sesame chicken or chopped barbecue chicken ($4.95-$9.70). Lots of pasta dishes ($8.50-$13.95), as well as homemade sandwiches on BJ's freshly baked rolls including meatball, Italian sub, and three varieties of chicken: barbecue, Caesar or Italian ($6.95-$7.45). *Comments:* This Front Street landmark is filled with woodwork, murals and historic photographs. Same menu all day (lunch specials until 4 p.m.). The deep-dish Chicago-style pizza has a crust that is thick while surprisingly light, and the toppings are fresh and innovative. Wash it down with a festive Tropitini, a spirited ice cream cooler, or BJ's original-recipe mai tai made with Grand Marnier. But leave room for dessert. You won't be able to resist the Pizookie n' Cream: a chocolate chip or white chocolate and macadamia cookie baked fresh in a mini-pizza pan and served warm with vanilla ice cream.

Blue Lagoon Tropical Bar and Grill *(American)*
Wharf Cinema Center (lower level), 658 Front Street; 808-661-8141.
   Hours: Breakfast 9 a.m.-noon; continuous menu 10 a.m.-9:30 p.m. Happy Hour 3-6 p.m. and 9-11 p.m. Tropical bar open until 2 a.m. *Sampling:* Breakfast offers *loco moco*, shangri-la scramble (their signature breakfast dish), or try pancakes or sweet French toast ($4.95-$8.95). Burgers and sandwiches include french fries or pasta salad and range from French dips to BLT or burgers ($5.95-$9.95). House specialties include *kalua* pork and cabbage or their beer-battered fish and chips. Pizzas, soups pastas and salads round out the choices ($5.96-$14.95). *Comments:* Eat in the courtyard of the shopping center (surrounded by waterfalls and *koi* ponds).

Captain Dave's Fish & Chips/Pipeline Pizza *(Fish & Chips/Pizza)*
Lahaina Marketplace, 129 Lahainaluna Road off Front Street; 808-667-6700.
   Hours: Sunday-Thursday 8 a.m.-9:30 p.m. Friday-Saturday 8 a.m.-10 p.m. *Sampling: Ono* and chips, prawns and chips, clams and chips, calamari and chips, grilled *ono* or chicken strips; half orders also available. ($6.69-$8.80). Salads ($3.95-$6.95). Pizzas ($5.95-$7.95). *Comments:* All main-menu fish items can be ordered fried (in 100 percent canola oil) or broiled and come with french fries, Maui coleslaw (with pineapple) and homemade tartar or cocktail sauce. They also deliver.

★ **Cheeseburger in Paradise** *(American)*
811 Front Street; 808-661-4855. Sister location called Cheeseburger, Mai Tais & Rock 'N Roll at Shops at Wailea, 3750 Wailea Alanui; 808-661-4855.
   Hours: Breakfast 8-11 a.m., lunch/dinner 11 a.m.-11 p.m. *Sampling:* A 100 percent natural Meyer Angus beef cheeseburger, or cheeseburger squared (double everything). The spicy island chicken sandwich is covered with Cajun spices, the Polynesian chicken salad sandwich has chunks of fresh grilled chicken blended with mango

chutney, peppers, pineapple and other goodies. Gobble up a Portuguese turkey burger, garden burger or tofu burger. Calamari sandwich, tuna salad and other seafood sandwiches and a half-dozen salad selections. A basic cheeseburger is $7.50. Other sandwich selections $5.95-$9.95. Add seasoned fries for $3.75, *ono* onion rings for $4.75, chili cheese fries for $6. Finish off your cheeseburger your way with Ortega chilies, grilled Maui pineapple, bacon, guacamole or mushrooms $1-$2. *Comments:* A casual and fun atmosphere with open-air dining and wonderful views of the Lahaina Harbor and Front Street from the upstairs loft. You can't go wrong with a cheeseburger and fries, and the other stuff is good, too. Live music nightly. Make sure you try some of their tropical drinks like Trouble in Paradise (or if you want to stay *out* of trouble, try the thick and chunky non-alcoholic Oreo cookie smoothie). It can be crowded at meal times, but the lines move along pretty quickly.

Cool Cat Café *(Diner)*
Wharf Cinema Center, 658 Front Street; 808-667-0908.
   Hours: Sunday-Tuesday 11 a.m.-midnight. Friday-Saturday 11 a.m.-2 a.m. Continuous menu for lunch and dinner. Take-out available. *Sampling:* Appetizers ($4.89-$9.89) include hula sticks (pineapple with sweet Maui onion marinated and charbroiled), onion rings, chili fries or ahi sticks. Burgers (all 1/3 lb. beef patty) include the Bogey Burger topped with bacon and cheese, the Marilyn Burger (because "some like it hot") with melted jack cheese and green ortega chile peppers, and The Duke, where you get your burger topped with bacon, cheese, onion rings and their special barbecue sauce. Other sandwiches include the Elvis melt (tuna), Betty Boop (BLT) or Chubby Chicken ($3.59-$9.89). Dinner selections are served with potato or rice and salad and include rib-eye steak, sweet baby back ribs or fresh catch of the day ($12.89-$16.89). Kids' menu, too ($3.59-$4.99). *Comments:* Take a trip down memory lane with their black-and-white floor, mirrored walls and 1955 Seeburg 100 jukebox. Chrome chairs, Formica tables and a counter with barstools where you can sip on some real ice cream shakes and malts. A full bar with seating inside and outside. Live music.

Denny's *(American)*
Lahaina Square Shopping Center, 840 Wainee Street; 808-667-7898. Also at Kama'ole Shopping Center, 2463 South Kihei Road; 808-879-0604.
   Hours: Open 24 hours a day. *Sampling:* Traditional Denny's burgers, sandwiches and dinners plus island favorites like saimin, mahi sandwich, teri burger, local-style plate lunches, fresh catch, and Spam and eggs (would that make it a "Spam slam"?). Prices from $5 (pancakes)

to $15 (steak and shrimp). Breakfast served anytime. Senior specials and kids' meals available. *Comments:* Wine and beer.

Gaby's Pizzeria & Deli *(Italian)*
505 Front Street; 808-661-8112.

Hours: 11 a.m.-midnight. Happy Hour 4-6 p.m. *Sampling:* Try one of their "original pizza rolls" ($8.95-$10.95) or house-special pizzas, Neapolitan or Sicilian ($22-$24). Half pizzas available as well, or by the slice. Their deli features assorted meats and Italian specialty items, or try their hot and cold sandwiches ($5.95-$8.95) as well as pasta dishes ($9.95-$12.95).

House of Saimin *(Local)*
Old Lahaina Center; 808-667-7572.

Hours: Monday 5-10 p.m. Tuesday-Thursday 5 p.m.-2 a.m. Friday and Saturday until 3 a.m. Closed Sunday. *Sampling:* Saimin, soups, sandwiches, burgers, stews ($3.50-$5.50). *Comments:* One big central counter and late-night hours—in the tradition of Kauaʻi's Hamura Saimin—though not quite as funky, or as much fun! I've found better saimin elsewhere.

Kahuna Kabob *(Healthy/Local)*
Lahaina Marketplace; 808-661-9999.

Hours: 9 a.m.-9:30 p.m. *Sampling:* From the grill choose shrimp, chicken, steak or fish kabob ($6.50-$9.50). Looking for a lil' somethin' else? Then try their chili rice plate with cheese, steamed veggies, garlic bread or potato salad ($1-$4.20). A basic burger, Boca burger or kahuna burger ($6.95). *Comments:* Dining around the courtyard at shaded tables. Reasonably priced and a cool respite from your day in Lahaina Town.

Kamaaina Kitchen *(Local/Korean)*
Wharf Cinema Center, 658 Front Street; 808-661-4888 or 808-662-3421.

Hours: Monday-Saturday 7 a.m.-9 p.m. Sunday 7 a.m.-2 p.m. *Sampling:* Basic breakfasts include one, two or three eggs, omelets, pancakes and waffles ($4.99-$9.95). Lunches range from plate lunches with *kalbi* ribs or *shoyu* chicken to sandwiches such as a classic club or a burger ($7.99-$12.99). Italian pasta dishes, too ($12.95-$22.95). *Comments:* This is actually two restaurants in one. One side opens for breakfast and the other for lunch and dinner. Family owned and operated.

Lahaina Cannery Mall *(Food Court)*
1221 Honoapiʻilani Highway, Lahaina; 808-667-0952; *www.lahainacannerymall.com.*

A great place for family dining where there is something for everyone. In addition to national chain restaurants, you'll find *Edo*

Japan (teppanyaki, sushi, rice bowls), *L&L Drive-Inn* (local-style plate lunches), *Athens Greek Restaurant* (gyros, shish kebabs), *Chopsticks Express* (Chinese plate lunches), *South Philly Steak & Fries* (cheese steaks) and *Compadres* (see individual listing). *Greenleaf's Grille* has "upscale fast food for today's healthy lifestyle." Try ★ *Ba-Le Sandwiches* for one of their *pho* soups or their awesome sandwiches served on their freshly baked French bread.

Lemongrass *(Vietnamese)*
930 Wainee Street, Lahaina; 808-661-4466.

Hours: 10:30 a.m.-9 p.m. *Sampling:* The menu is the same for lunch or dinner, which makes dinner a great deal. Soups and appetizers (from $4.95), as well as rice plates and entree dishes ($6.95-$12.95). *Comments:* If you aren't familiar with Vietnamese cuisine, give them a try.

Maui Swiss Café *(Eclectic/Internet Café)*
640 Front Street; 808-661-6776; www.swisscafe.net.

Hours: 9 a.m.-6 p.m. *Sampling:* Hot and cold sandwiches include turkey broccoli melt, roast beef, ham or turkey and a number of vegetarian sandwiches and salads as well. Pizza, too. Prices are affordable at $5.95-$7.95. *Comments:* Sip a coffee drink, a smoothie or a milkshake while checking your e-mail. At 15¢ per minute/$2 minimum and with a speedy DSL connection, you don't waste anytime or money logging on. Or you can get a rate of $10 minute with a $20 prepaid card. Located off Front Street between the Wharf Cinema Center and Burger King.

Maui Tacos *(Healthy/Mexican)*
Lahaina Square Shopping Center, 840 Wainee Street; 808-661-8883. Other locations at Napili Plaza, 808-665-0222; Kama'ole Beach Center, 808-879-5005.

Hours: 9 a.m.-9 p.m. *Sampling:* Potato enchiladas, hard or soft tacos, quesadillas, chimichangas, nachos, and over a dozen varieties of special hand-held burritos in fish, steak, chicken, beef or vegetarian combinations with black beans ($1.99-$6.95). *Comments:* Guacamole and salsa made fresh everyday. No lard, no MSG—they use only vegetable oil, fresh beans and lean meats. The complimentary salsa bar offers several choices with jalapenos, onions, cilantro, hot sauce and more. I found better Mexican food elsewhere but lots of folks seem to like this chain.

Mr. Sub *(Sandwiches)*
129 Lahainaluna Road; 808-667-5683.

Hours: Monday-Friday 7 a.m.-5 p.m. Saturday until 4 p.m. Closed Sunday. *Sampling:* Sandwiches with one or two items like turkey, tuna, egg salad, roast beef, and Danish ham ($4.50-$6.25). Specialty sandwiches ($5.95-$8.50) or wraps ($4.95-$5.95). Caesar, chef's, Chinese chicken, garden and fruit salads, or chicken or tuna in half a papaya ($3.50-$7.25). Great choice of breads, too. *Comments:* This place offers some of the best subs on the island and also features "wraps"—chicken Caesar, Salsa or Ranch rolled up burrito-style in a tasty spinach or jalapeno cheese tortilla. Pick up some for a picnic lunch. Free delivery in Lahaina Town Monday-Saturday 11 a.m.-2 p.m.

Moose McGillycuddy's *(American)*
844 Front Street, upper level of Mariner's Alley, a small shopping alley at the north end of town; 808-667-7758.

Hours: Breakfast 7:30 a.m.-11 a.m. Lunch 11 a.m.-4 p.m. Dinner 4-10 p.m. *Sampling:* Early birds can take advantage of the special for $1.99 (served 7:30-8:30 a.m.) Late risers can dine on "chicken feed"—3 eggs, meat and potatoes, *loco moco*, moose cakes, breakfast quesadilla or French toast ($3.95-$6.95). For lunch sample a gourmet burger served with fries and your choice of toppings ($5.95-$9.45). Sandwiches such as fresh fish, calamari steak or French dip and entrees such as chicken fajitas, lasagna, fish tacos or spaghetti ($5.95-$9.95). Dinner entrees include mahi macadamia, Moose's prime rib, chicken fried steak, fresh ahi, or Mexican and Italian entrees ($9.95-$15.95). There's chocolate "moose" for dessert (what else?) and an extensive selection of fun, tropical drinks. *Comments:* A great stop for breakfast in Lahaina. Get a table with a balcony view. This place gets hopping at night with lots of young adults and live music. A good food value. And check for early-bird or nightly specials. Late-night entertainment.

★ **No Ka Oi Deli** *(Sandwiches & Salads/Local)*
Anchor Square, 222 Papalaua Street (facing Wainee Street); 808-667-2244.

Hours: 10 a.m.-2 p.m. *Sampling:* A good variety of subs (French dip, teri chicken or beef, pastrami, and seafood, tuna, egg or chicken salad) and salads (chef, Caesar, and Chinese chicken) plus daily plate-lunch specials ($4.25-$5.95). Side specialties, too, like spinach rolls. Fountain drinks, smoothies and shave ice. Homemade cookies or order a picnic to go. *Comments:* "Home of the Famous HOP WO Bread": The Hop Wo Store was a landmark on Front Street from 1917 to its closure in 1985 and now a younger generation of this family has begun what they hope will be a new Lahaina landmark. "Ono" baking weekends offer *manapua* and small pies on Saturdays, Hop Wo bread and biscuits on Sundays or cinnamon rolls and twist donuts. Check out "'Da Wall of Yummies" for crack seed and mochi crunch.

Pancho and Lefty's *(Mexican)*
Wharf Cinema Center, 658 Front Street; 808-661-4666.

Hours: Breakfast Thursday-Sunday 9 a.m.-noon. Lunch daily 11 a.m.-10 p.m. *Sampling:* Mexican- or American-style breakfasts. Lunch/dinner menu includes Mexican burgers, burritos, chimichanga, chile relleno, or seafood salad ($8.95-$14.95). If you have room for dessert try the deep-fried ice cream. Full bar service.

Penne Pasta Café *(Italian)*
180 Dickenson Street; 808-661-6633.

Hours: Monday-Thursday 11 a.m.-9:30 p.m. Friday 11 a.m.-10 p.m. Saturday 5-10 p.m. Sunday 5-9 p.m. *Sampling:* This is Mark Ellman's café, you'll know him for his Maui Tacos chain. Pizzas and flatbreads ($1.99-$7.95). Sandwiches such as mozzarella, tomato, basil and greens, or roast chicken salad ($5.95-$7.95). Sample a gamut of pastas from classic fettuccine alfredo to bolognese fettuccine to penne puttanesca and even whole wheat spaghetti with roasted eggplant and tomatoes ($6.50-$9.95). Add garlic ahi ($3.95) or chicken breast ($2.95) to any dish. *Comments:* They deliver Monday-Friday 11 a.m.-2 p.m.

Royal Seafood Chinese Restaurant *(Asian)*
Old Lahaina Center, Papalaua and Wainee streets; 808-661-9955.

Hours: 10 a.m.-9:30 p.m. All-you-can-eat lunch buffet served until 2:30 p.m. *Sampling:* Seafood selections number almost three dozen, plus noodle dishes, soups, egg dishes, and vegetarian selections ($6.95-$16.95).

Sunrise Café *(Sandwiches/Light Meals)*
693A Front Street; 808-661-8558.

Hours: 6 a.m.-6 p.m. *Sampling:* Great patio dining just off the waterfront featuring quiche, pancakes, waffles and bagels ($2.50-$7.95). Lunch and dinner offer gourmet sandwiches and plate lunches such as mango barbecued beef or chicken, roast pork or tofu dishes ($5.95-$7.95). Homemade soups and plenty of salad options. *Comments:* This is a very small, quaint eatery with some nice outside tables or food available to go. It's all homemade and good, but the Hawaiian specialties stand out: *kalua* pork salad with Maui onions, pineapple, steamed cabbage and papaya; stuffed pasta shells with macadamia nut pesto; and mango barbecue chicken breast or *kalua* pork as a plate lunch or a sandwich.

Sushiya *(Local)*
117 Prison Street; 808-661-5679.

Hours: Monday-Friday 6 a.m.-4 p.m. *Sampling:* Local-style plate lunches is their specialty. Some interesting selections, like Spam, sweet potato, shrimp or eggplant tempura for 75¢. *Comments:* I'd hoped this would be a great option for inexpensive local dining on the west side. They must have a good clientele, they've been in business since 1965 but I found it rather disappointing. Still, you can fill up on just a couple of bucks. Take out available.

Take Home Maui *(American)*
121 Dickenson; 808-667-7056.

Hours: 6:30 a.m.-5:30 p.m. *Sampling:* You might pass by this place, but don't! Stop by for a yummy smoothie ($3.25) or sit on the porch and enjoy some quiche, empanadas, veggie lasagna, or sandwich ($2.50-$5). Bagels and breakfast pastries every morning ($2-$6). Ice cream and sodas in the freezer. *Comments:* Papayas, pineapples, onions and Hawaiian coffee are among the items to be shipped or taken home. They offer free airport or hotel delivery. The staff is helpful and friendly—lots of aloha here. Good, too!

Thai Chef *(Thai)*
Old Lahaina Shopping Center; 808-667-2814.

Hours: Lunch Monday-Friday 11 a.m.-2 p.m. Dinner nightly from 5-9 p.m. *Sampling:* Thai crisp noodles, Thai toast, green papaya salad, long rice chicken soup, and chicken, beef, pork or shrimp served with Thai oyster sauce, Thai basil sauce, Thai ginger and more. Sample crab with yellow curry or sautéed mussels with chili sauce ($6.95-$13.95). Combination dinners ($35.95-$61.95). *Comments:* A very lengthy menu ranging from noodle dishes to salads, seafoods, vegetarian fare, and curry dishes. Chef's suggestions offer combinations for 2, 3 or 4 people. Entrees available in mild, medium or hot (!)—second location at the Rainbow Mall in Kihei.

Whale's Tale *(American)*
Next door to Wharf Cinema Center, upstairs of the ABC store, 672 Front Street; 808-667-4044.

Hours: 11 a.m.-10 p.m. Happy hour 2:30-5 p.m. *Sampling:* Same menu all day. Their getting-started stuff includes cheesy fries, spicy chicken wings or shrimp cocktail. Lots of burgers and grilled fish tacos, or quesadillas and fish or chicken sandwiches ($6.95-$10.95). *Comments:* Inexpensive, bar-style fare. Live music nightly.

Yama *(Sushi)*
Lahaina Square Shopping Center, 840 Wainee Street; 808-662-0228.

Hours: Tuesday 2-9:30 p.m. Wednesday-Monday noon-9:30 p.m. *Sampling:* Only serves sushi. Wine and beer.

Zushi *(Japanese)*
Lahaina Square Shopping Center, 840 Wainee Street; 808-667-5142.

Hours: Lunch 11 a.m.-2 p.m. Dinner 5-8:30 p.m. Closed Sunday. *Comments:* Fried chicken teriyaki, tempura, *shoyu* chicken and udon are lunch entrees ($4.95-$9.95). Dinners include cooked fish, combination dinners and slightly higher prices and larger portions of the lunch items ($6.95-$12.95).

Moderate-priced Dining

Bubba Gump Shrimp Company Restaurant & Market *(Seafood)*
889 Front Street; 808-661-3111.

Hours: 11 a.m.-10:30 p.m. *Sampling:* Start with Peel 'n Eat shrimp or Bubba's Far Out Dip (classic spinach with a twist). Entrees include Lt. Dan's Drunken Shrimp, Southern Charmed fried shrimp, Louisiana home-style etouffee (shrimp in a classic Cajun gravy), Dumb Luck Coconut Shrimp. Plenty of other seafood selections like Mama Blue's Crab Pot, Bourbon Street Mahimahi, or Captain's Fish & Chips. Jenny's Peace 'n Love Veggie Plate or a bone-in rib-eye steak are non-oceanic selections ($13.59-$17.99). Sandwiches include fishwich, barbecue pork, chicken or burgers ($7.99-$8.79). For dessert try a Gumpberry Cobbler, Jenny's Strawberry Dream, Alabama Mud Pie or sip on Forrest's Dr. Pepper Float ($3.79-$5.99). *Comments:* Inspired by the award-winning movie *Forrest Gump*, this is a part of the chain that began in Monterey and San Francisco. "Gumpisms" prevail—from the "Run Forrest Run" sign that signals for service to the "box of chocolates" (that "life is like") on the dessert menu. Like newspaper is to fish and chips, the funky boathouse decor and tin bucket table service is to Bubba Gump's. The friendly service and fun food presentations are more than enough to keep you interested, so it's impressive that they offer cut-above extras: tartar sauce with lime and orange rind, cocktail sauce with tequila, homemade cole slaw, and "real" Key lime pie. The all-day menu makes it cheap for dinner, a bit expensive for lunch. Portions can be hit and miss: some are huge, others on the small side, but overall good food and good value. Usually a big crowd, so they've got the appeal.

★ **Café O'Lei** *(Pacific Rim)*
839 Front Street; 808-661-9491.

Hours: Lunch 10:30 a.m.-4:30 p.m. Dinner 5-9 p.m. *Sampling:* Appetizers and salads include my old favorite, Manoa lettuce wraps (chicken, water chestnuts, shiitake mushrooms and ginger), and a new favorite, ahi-stuffed fried calamari. Or enjoy coconut ceviche with lobster and fresh-island fish, feta potato cakes or *kalua* pork quesadilla. Their quinoa salad over baby greens, taro salad, or Caesar ($6.95-$9.95). Continuing with dinner entrees you can select from macadamia nut roast duckling, prime rib, grilled marinated jumbo shrimp or tempura mahi and chips as well as burgers, a crab club or an ahi sandwich ($8.95-$18.95). For dessert sample their pineapple upside-down cake (a specialty), *lilikoi* cheesecake, Kona coffee creme brulee or chocolate mousse cake ($5.95-$6.95). *Comments:* Owned and operated by chefs Dana and Michael Pastula, this was their first West Maui restaurant. Great prices and a fabulous oceanfront location and outstanding quality food, too. Sunset music Tuesday-Saturday. An excellent choice for family dining.

Café Sauvage *(Island Fusion)*
844 Front Street; 808-661-7600.

Hours: 5:30-9:30 p.m. *Sampling:* Starters include ahi *poke*, escargot, seared peppered ahi or calamari ($6-$9), or sample an appetizer pizza ($7-$7.50). Entrees range from crispy chicken roulade, seafood pasta, plum-glazed lamb ($13.95-$24.95).

★ Canoes *(American/Pacific Rim)*
1450 Front Street; 808-661-0937.

Hours: Dinner 5-9.30 p.m. Lounge/bar open 4-10 p.m. *Sampling:* Start with an appetizer of grilled or coconut shrimp, seared ahi or steamed artichoke ($8.95-$13.95). Dinners include fresh catch, garlic prawns, blackened ahi, pina colada shrimp, baby back ribs, macadamia-and-banana-crusted chicken, herb-crusted prime rib, and a variety of steaks ($17.95-$26.95 including salad bar). *Comments:* This A-frame structure has been enhanced by polished wooden canoes hanging from the high ceiling and custom Hawaiian *ohia* wood railing around the open-air patio. Within just a few weeks of opening, they established themselves by taking Best Seafood in that year's Taste of Lahaina. The 25-foot salad bar has 60 items, which are included with entrees. (Salad bar only for $14.95). Go early (5-6 p.m.) and enjoy a 3-course sunset dinner special for only $19.95 (choice of prime rib, fresh fish, or lemon-scented chicken, salad bar, and homemade dessert). Appetizers are half-price from 4-6 p.m. in the lounge. A spectacular oceanfront view, lovely atmosphere, good quality and large portions for your vacation dollar.

Coconut Grove *(Seafood/Hawaiian)*
1312 Front Street; 808-667-1884.

Hours: Lunch: 10:30 a.m.-1:30 p.m. Dinner 5:30-9 p.m. Early Bird 5:30-7 p.m. *Sampling:* Plate lunches served with rice and macaroni salad offer teri beef or chicken, *kalua* pig, pork cutlet, and mahimahi ($5.95), shrimp (coconut, garlic, pineapple or curry) for $6.95, or *laulau* (Fridays only) for $8.95. Burgers ($4.50-$8.50). Dinner entrees include soup or salad followed by specialty entrees like lobster or prawns Tahitian, crusted mahimahi, seafood medley, and fresh fish as well as baked scallops in papaya, barbecue ribs, teriyaki chicken, and a variety of steaks ($16.50-$29.50). Hot Lava

Chocolate Cake, Mud Pie, and Island Banana Lumpia ($4.95-$5.50) are some of the sweet temptations to finish you meal. *Comments:* This place has been in and out of different ownerships and names. They are now back to the original owners and the original name from 1958. They are across the street from the beach and ocean but you can still see the Pacific and enjoy the gentle breezes. Let me know if you dine here and send me your review.

★ **Compadres** *(Mexican)*
Lahaina Cannery Mall; 808-661-7189.

Hours: 8 a.m.-10 p.m., breakfast until noon. *Sampling:* Breakfast ($5-$10) features chorizo, enchilada, burrito egg dishes, huevos rancheros, and "grande" omelets ($7-$11). Gringo specialties include pineapple or macadamia pancakes, and sweet bread French toast ($5-$6). Their lunch/dinner menu includes Quesadillas Internacionales—Baja (topped with Gulf prawns in spicy barbecue sauce), Texas (loaded with fajita steak or chicken with Jack cheese) and Thai (with chicken, Jack cheese, sprouts, peanuts, shredded carrots, and peanut-chili sauce) ($8-$11). Mexican pizza, tortilla soup, fajita nachos, *chingalinga*, six-layer dip, *sopes* (Mexican bruschetta) and Caesar, Cobb, taco and fajita salads are the distinctive starters ($5-$12), while *arroz con pollo*, *camarones* (shrimp) *rancheros*, tequila chicken, seafood enchilada, fish tacos, prawn burrito, and a variety of rellenos are some of the innovative entrees ($9-$15). Mexican club, chicken and guacamole, and Santa Fe chicken are the south-of-the-border sandwiches ($8-$10). *Comments:* I don't usually recommend chain restaurants, but Compadres earns a star for its innovative menu and all-around good dining fare.

Erik's Seafood & Sushi *(Seafood/Oyster & Sushi Bar)*
Old Lahaina Center, 843 Wainee Street; 808-669-4806.

Hours: 11 a.m.-10 p.m. *Sampling:* Fish and chips as well as grilled or fried (*panko*, traditional or tempura) oysters, calamari, shrimp, scallops and lobster. Pastas with clams, fish or chicken and red or white sauce. Shrimp, fish, lobster, chicken sandwiches and burgers. Salads include Caesar, chef's seafood, fresh vegetable, and spinach with smoked salmon dressing. Prices average $7-$8. Cioppino, bouillabaisse, scampi and lobster dishes ($10-$16). Daily Mexican seafood specials. Indian curry with all the trimmings. Oyster and sushi bar (steamed clams, fresh shucked oysters, and full oyster menu). Soup or salad, starch and bread are included with dinner entrees like barbecued shrimp, bouillabaisse, cioppino, lobster thermidor, scampi Olowalu, Coquille St. Jacques and fresh fish, steaks and combinations ($18-$24.95). *Comments:* After 21 years in Kahana, Erik's moved to this location in January 2003. Take-out or full-service dining. Nautical decor with brass lanterns, ship's wheels, and aquariums. Fresh fish market on display with live crab and lobster tanks. *Keiki* menu and smaller "Cabin Boy" portions of fish and chips, pastas and salads. Their early-bird specials have always been more creative than most and still continue: Island Mahi "Oscar," lobster-stuffed boneless chicken breast and crab-stuffed prawns in addition to NY steak or fresh fish ($12.95-$13.95 from 5-6 p.m.) Erik's was the 2002 Taste of Lahaina winner for their crab cake appetizers.

★ **Hard Rock Cafe** *(American)*
Lahaina Center, 900 Front Street; 808-667-7400.

Hours: 11:30 a.m.-10 p.m. *Sampling:* Salads include Chinese chicken, Caesar or Haystack fried chicken ($6.99-$8.99), burgers ($7.99-$9.19), or specialties such as grilled fajitas, fettuccine with grilled shrimp, fire-roasted vegetable pasta, grilled tenderloin or blackened chicken pasta ($8.99-$21.99). Smokehouse specialties such as barbecue ribs, chicken or pig, come with fries, barbecue beans and coleslaw ($9.19-$15.99). Their "Really Big Sandwiches" include jerk chicken, French dip or veggie options ($8.49-$9.19). Full bar service. *Comments:* A lively atmosphere, if the music isn't too loud for you. Memorabilia on the restaurant walls and in the bathrooms include guitars owned by Eric Clapton, Slash of Guns 'N' Roses, the Grateful Dead, and Pearl Jam, plus Beatles photos and instruments. Homage is also paid to Hawai'i, surfing, and beach rock-and-roll, too. Great prices, good food and a trendy reputation make this a very popular eatery, so there may be a line waiting to get in during peak dining hours.

Hecocks *(American)*
505 Front Street; 808-661-8810.

Hours: Breakfast 8 a.m.-1:30 p.m. Lunch 11:30-2:30 p.m. Dinner 5-9 p.m. Bar open later. *Sampling:* Omelets, egg dishes, pancakes, French toast ($4.50-$8.75). Lunch offers salads and sandwiches such as French dip, teriyaki chicken, BLT or tuna ($3.25-$9.95). Dinner entrees feature scallops, seafood picatta, or Italian dishes such as sausage rigatoni, fettuccini alfredo, baby back ribs or seafood dishes ($19.95-$26.95). *Comments:* This restaurant is a waste of the ocean view. The meals I've had here were mediocre, but a great oceanview location for breakfast.

★ **Kimo's** *(American/Seafood)*
845 Front Street; 808-661-4811.

Hours: Lunch 11 a.m.-3 p.m. Dinner 5-10:30 p.m. Bar until 1 a.m. *Sampling:* Burgers, salads, sandwiches ($6.95-$10.95) plus sashimi, shrimp, veggie plate, and artichoke *pupus* ($4.95-$7.95) are available downstairs daily. Dinner at the bar (limited menu) 5-11 p.m. Dinner entrees include Kimo's Caesar salad, freshly baked carrot muffins and sourdough rolls, and steamed herb rice. Fresh fish of the day (prepared in one of five ways) is $19.95-$23.95. Beef, seafood or island favorites such as Polynesian chicken or Koloa Pork Ribs ($15.95-$24.95). *Keiki* menu. *Comments:* They have a waterfront location and, if you're really lucky, you'll get a table with a view. My experience has been very good service and well-prepared fresh fish. They must be doing something right because they've been doing it since 1977. This is where you'll find the original hula pie—it's still the biggest and the best and heads turn every time one of the whipped-cream skyscrapers comes out of the kitchen. They also have a bar on the lower level and an ocean view that includes a pleasant sunset.

★ **Kobe Japanese Steak House** *(Teppanyaki/Sushi Bar)*
136 Dickenson; 808-667-5555.

Hours: 5:30-9:30 p.m. *Sampling:* Teriyaki chicken, sukiyaki steak, filet mignon, and plenty of combination dinners such as fish and chicken, scallops and steak, lobster and steak or shrimp and scallops ($14.95-$32.95). Dinners include soup, shrimp appetizer, vegetables, rice and tea. *Comments:* A sister of the Palm Springs and Honolulu restaurants, they offer teppan cooking (food is prepared on the grill in front of you) and the show is as good as the meal. Sunset specials served 5:30-6:30 p.m. ($11.95-$15.95). Sushi and sashimi items available individually or in chef-selected tray assortments. The sushi bar is popular with local residents and they're very accommodating to visitors. They'll make up your favorite sushi item if it is not on their menu. *Keiki* menu for children under 10 ($7-$11).

Lahaina Coolers *(American)*
Dickenson Square, 180 Dickenson Street; 808-661-7082.

Hours: 8 a.m.-midnight. *Sampling:* A variety of egg specials and omelets ($6.50-$7.50) or make choices from a number of selections to create your own complete breakfast. For lunch they offer sandwiches, burgers, pasta dishes, and salads ($7-$9) or select a quickie plate lunch of *kalua* pig, fresh fish tacos, or hibachi chicken ($8-$11). Dinners feature an interesting selection of salads along with pizzas and pastas ($11-$14). Entrees include their Coolers Waimea Pork Chop, fresh catch, or seafood, chicken, steak variations ($11-$19). *Comments:* Quiet location off Front Street with patio, porch, or indoor open-air dining. Full bar service.

Lahaina Fish Company *(Seafood/American)*
831 Front Street; 808-661-3472.

Hours: Lunch menu served 11 a.m.-midnight. Dinner 5-10 p.m. *Sampling:* Sandwiches and burgers $7.99-$10.99 for lunch fare. Lots of seafood *pupus* from sashimi to oysters, steamer clams to peel-and-eat shrimp. Fish and shellfish entrees, homemade pasta dishes, steaks, local fare and poultry or try combination plates if you can't decide ($9.99-$21.99). For dinner there are several preparations of fresh fish ($21.99-$23.99). *Comments:* Pleasant setting on (in fact, right over) the ocean. Children's menu $6.99.

Pioneer Inn Bar & Grill *(American)*
Pioneer Inn; 808-661-3636.

Hours: Breakfast 6:30 a.m.-11:30 a.m. Lunch noon-5:30 p.m. Dinner 5:30-10 p.m. *Sampling:* Breakfast includes papaya fresh fruit boat, and entrees served with country potatoes and toast. Eggs Benedict, pancakes, French toast, omelets and frittata ($5-$11). The lunch/dinner menu offers an assortment of sandwiches including club, fresh fish and veggie burger as well as Portuguese bean soup and Caesar salad ($5-$9). Entrees include bread and choice of soup or salad and range from cioppino, South Pacific pork tenderloin or primavera alfredo to bacon seared scallops and chicken parmesan ($12.50-$22.50).

Smokehouse Bar & Grill *(Barbecue)*
1307 Front Street, oceanfront behind The Cannery; 808-667-7005.

Hours: Sunday-Thursday 11 a.m.-9 p.m. Friday and Saturday until 10 p.m. *Sampling:* Lunch sandwiches served 11 a.m.-4 p.m. only and include teriyaki chicken breast, veggie burger along with their *kiawe*-smoked roast sandwiches of pork, turkey, beef or ham ($5.45-$7.95). Their dinner menu offers complete dinners with corn on the cob, baked potato, corn bread, and choice of baked beans, cole slaw, fries or rice. Smokehouse platter, chicken, and beef or pork ribs ($12.95-$22.95). Dinner sandwiches and grilled selections ($10.95-$18.95). *Comments:* Very good ribs and cute, cozy oceanfront location. Dining indoors or on their oceanfront patio. Full bar service.

Expensive-priced Dining

★ **Chez Paul** *(French)*
Five miles south of Lahaina, Olowalu; 808-661-3843.

Hours: Monday-Saturday 6-9 p.m. *Sampling & Comments:* Nestled in "you are now entering-you are now leaving" Olowalu (think of Chez Paul as the hyphen), the restaurant is operated by Chef Patrick Callarec (formerly of The Ritz-Carlton, Kapalua), who offers a menu as delightful and distinct as its location. Sample chilled leak and potato soup, wild mushrooms and brie cheese in a flaky puff pastry with port wine sauce, foie gras, or cappuccino of lobster soup with cognac ($9-$24). Entrees are served with freshly baked baguette, potatoes and two seasonal vegetables. Selections include crispy duck with seasonal fruits and pineapple bigarade, rack of lamb with exotic chutney, lobster or fresh island fish poached in champagne and shallots ($33-$45). Save room for fabulous desserts. One of his classics is pineapple and vanilla cream brulee served in a pineapple shell. This small restaurant—in what could be a tiny village in France—opened in 1968 and has maintained its high popularity with excellent food and service. This place is simply fabulous.

★ **David Paul's Lahaina Grill** *(New American)*
Lahaina Hotel, 127 Lahainaluna Road; 808-667-5117, fax 808-661-5478; www.lahainagrill.com.

Hours: Nightly from 6 p.m. *Sampling:* The menu is described as New American Grill cuisine with a Southwestern flair. The appetizer menu is huge and I would be happy dining only on carpaccio of ahi tuna, *kalua* duck quesadilla and toy box tomato salad ($9-$18) but there is more. The excellent menu is constantly changing, but the popular Tequila Shrimp and Firecracker Rice has become a permanent fixture. Enjoy Kona coffee–roasted rack of lamb, Maui onion–rusted seared ahi, *kalua* duck, lemon-pepper linguine, grilled polenta stacks (with goat cheese, grilled eggplant and portobello mushrooms) as well as sautéed mahimahi. The chef's tasting menu combines signature appetizers, salad and meat or seafood courses, finishing off with dessert ($69; two person minimum). For dessert, try the triple-berry pie, creme brulee, or ask about their sampler dessert selection. *Comments:* David Paul Johnson has won local and national awards for his innovative cuisine and artistic presentations and the new owners are continuing with the traditions. The seating area is attractively furnished with a crisp look to it. Black-and-white floors are contrasted with a beautifully detailed fresco blue/green ceiling and French impressionist art. The bar in the main restaurant is wide and suitable for dining and socializing. You can order appetizers and dinner or enjoy the seafood bar and late-night menu until 11 p.m. every evening.

★ **Gerard's** *(French)*
Plantation Inn lobby, 174 Lahainaluna Road; 808-661-8939; www.gerardsmaui.com.

Hours: 6-9 p.m. *Sampling:* The menu changes seasonally with intriguing appetizers, soup and salad selections that might include seared calamari with lime, ginger and sesame oil, goose rillettes scented with sage, or yellowfin tuna and smoked salmon carpaccio ($10.50 up to $115 for Beluga caviar on ice). Salads include duck foie gras on toasted country French bread with truffles or a spinach salad with grilled scallops ($8.50-$24.50). *Les poissons et fruits de mer* include ragout of Kona lobster with asparagus and oyster risotto, fisherman's ahi stew Basque-style; *les viandes et les volailles* offers caramelized pork tenderloin, rack of lamb, veal sweetbreads, veal Wellington or quails stuffed with Lahaina corn and foie gras. And if you still have room, desserts ($8.50) include their homemade island sorbets, *gateau au chocolat*, or fabulous creme brulee. Also available is the Ulupalakua raspberry dessert wine. Their wine list features a range of moderate to expensive selections from California, France and the Pacific Northwest. *Comments:* Dining at Gerard's is just as wonderful as it was years ago when it was in its old, small, hole-in-the-wall location up the street. The ambiance is equal to the fine cuisine with old-fashioned cane chairs crisply attired in tropical patterned upholstery. And although a Maui sunset ocean view is wonderful to enjoy while dining, sitting beneath a mango tree on the veranda of the Plantation Inn while dining at Gerard's is hard to beat. Simply, this is Maui dining at its best.

I'o (Pacific Rim)
505 Front Street; 808-661-8422.

Hours: 5:30-10 p.m. *Sampling:* Scallops on the half shell, coconut prawns or an Asian *kalua* tostada ($8-$12) whet your appetite for entrees that include crispy ahi, lemongrass coconut fish, a vegetarian green Thai curry risotto with tofu, grilled filet mignon or lamb tenderloin ($18-$27). *Comments:* I'o has the same operations and chef as adjacent Pacific 'O. You can hear the music from the Feast of Mele beachfront while you dine. Chef James McDonald is excellent and his food is outstanding; however, I had a bad experience here with the owners and it has discouraged me from ever going back.

★ **Longhi's** *(Continental)*
Old Lahaina Center, 888 Front Street; 808-667-2288. *Another location at Shops at Wailea, 3750 Wailea Alanui, 808-891-8883; www.longhi maui.com.*

Hours: Breakfast 7:30-11:30 a.m. Lunch 11:45 a.m.-4:45 p.m. Dinner from 5 p.m. *Sampling:* A landmark in Lahaina, they have a second location in the Shops at Wailea, where they have a printed menu (except for the many pizzas and specials). But the long-standing tradition of the oral menu remains here in Lahaina. For breakfast enjoy their signature eggs Benedict served over toasted French baguette and available traditional, Florentine or with crab cakes. French toast Longhi style has a touch of Grand Marnier. Other breakfast favorites, too ($8-$16). Lunch: great appetizers and salads to begin or enjoy seafood selections such as prawns Amaretto or Venice, or Shrimp or Scallops Longhi's ($14-$16.50). Sandwiches range from their fabulous Peking duck to their Italian hoagie with manikin peppers, classic NY Reuben or chicken sauté ($8-$15.50). Lots of pasta and pizzas ($9-$14). Dinner offers some of the same lunch selections that they are famous for, as well as lamb chops, filet mignon with bearnaise, eggplant parmesan, and fresh island fish ($17.50-$30). Vegetables available on the side ($7-$10) and salads ($7-$14). The dessert tray is hard to resist, with ever-changing options like chocolate soufflé with ganache, lychee sorbet, fresh peach and cardamom pie, strawberry-carrot cake, chocolate zuppa, coconut *haupia* cream pie, or espresso torte. *Comments:* After more than 25 years on Maui, Longhi's has become a legend in Lahaina. Part of the legend is a verbal menu, recited to you by a friendly waiter who will probably pull up a vacant chair to "chat" about the evening's selections. Other Longhi's legends include the to-die-for jalapeno, pizza and gorgonzola breads served with your meal; the casual setting with lots of windows open to view the bustling Lahaina streets; the accommodating breakfast hours that allow for both early risers and the laziest of late sleepers to enjoy the fresh-baked goods and tasty egg dishes; and of course, Bob Longhi himself, the "man who loves to eat" and hopes you do, too. Longhi's offers espresso and a good wine selection with valet parking nightly.

Pacific 'O *(Pacific Rim)*
505 Front Street; 808-667-4341.

Hours: 5:30-10 p.m. *Sampling:* Dinners start with shrimp won tons, potstickers, or their award-winning "Yuzu Divers," which are crispy coconut rice rolls with seared diver scallops and a zesty *yuzu* lime sauce ($8-$12). Entrees offer coconut macadamia nut–crusted catch, macaroni and cheese (with Vermont white cheddar and shiitake mushrooms), pink peppered beef, Thai Dye Duck (with a coconut curry sauce) or their "Taste of Lahaina" winning dish: Hapa Hapa tempura with sashimi blocks wrapped in dry seaweed and fried to medium-rare ($22-$29). *Comments:* Executive Chef James McDonald is creative and inventive. *Pupus* are served on a marble slab with sauces painted in colorful designs. A great oceanfront location although the atmosphere is a bit casual for the pricey menu. Poor customer service by one of the two owners deprives the good food of a star. Live jazz Fridays and Saturdays.

★ **Ruth's Chris Steak House** *(Steakhouse)*
Lahaina Center, 900 Front Street; 808-661-8815. Another location at Shops at Wailea, 3750 Wailea Alanui; 808-874-8880.

Hours: 5-9 p.m. *Sampling:* Begin with shrimp remoulade, sizzlin' blue crab cakes or carpaccio tenderloin ($5.95-$16.95), or a salad of fresh asparagus and hearts of palm, Caesar or mixed greens ($5.95-$6.95). They state on the menu, and I've heard from guests as well, that the portions are large and you'd do well to share. Entrees are a la carte and include veal chop with hot and sweet peppers, center-cut pork chops, filet, rib eyes, lamb chops, broiled chicken or catch of the day ($19.95-$36.95). Add potatoes, rice or vegetables ($2.95-$7.95).

Their signature dessert is a New Orleans favorite, bread pudding with whiskey sauce, or sample their caramelized banana cream pie or chocolate sin cake ($5.75-$6.50). *Comments:* An upscale restaurant chain. If you're looking for beef, this is the place. They use only premium cuts and the beef is fresh, never frozen. A good wine list as well. And a little history: it was in 1965 that Ruth Fertel bought a restaurant named "Chris Steak House" and she acquired the right to use that name as long as the restaurant remained in the original location. But after a fire forced her to move, she needed a new name. Adding her name to the logo seemed a simple solution, so Ruth's Chris Steak House came to be.

Ka'anapali–Kapalua Area

Inexpensive-priced Dining

Ashley's Internet Cafe *(Sandwiches/Internet Café)*
Kahana Gateway, 4405 Honoapi'ilani Highway #207; 808-669-0949; www.ashleysmaui.com.

Hours: 10:30 a.m.-9 p.m. Store open until 9:30 p.m. *Sampling:* Deli sandwiches offer turkey, ham, roast beef, tuna, egg salad, or veggie on choice of bread and toppings. Made-on-Maui premium Roselani ice cream, soft-serve Colombo yogurt, or "real" shave ice. Most everything is under $6. *Comments:* Chow fun and crab cole slaw are some of the *ono* daily specials. The chow fun was pretty tasty but I'd have to give a big thumbs up to the *kalua* pig. Get your shave ice with or without ice cream or yogurt. Yum! They also have DVD and VHS movie rentals and fax service along with internet connection (25 cents per minute with a $3 minimum.)

Beach Club *(American)*
Aston Ka'anapali Shores, 100 Ka'anapali Shores Place; 808-667-2211.

Hours: Breakfast 7-11 a.m. Lunch 11:30 a.m.-3 p.m. Café menu (light fare and Happy Hour) served 3-9:30 p.m. Dinner 5:30-9:30 p.m. *Sampling:* Large selection of omelets and other breakfast fare. Lunch primarily hot and cold sandwiches. Dinner features the usual array of chicken, beef and fish.

China Boat *(Cantonese-Szechuan-Mandarin)*
4474 Lower Honoapi'ilani Highway, Kahana; 808-669-5089.

Hours: Monday-Saturday 11:30 a.m.-10 p.m. Sunday 5-9 p.m. *Sampling:* Appetizers feature potstickers, jelly fish, spicy wonton. Entrees include mu shu chicken or pork, big clams with black bean sauce, seafood noodle soup, or sesame beef ($7.95-$16.95). *Comments:* Free delivery in the Ka'anapali and Kapalua areas.

C.J.'s Deli & Diner *(Deli)*
Fairway Shops, Honoapi'ilani Highway in the strip mall near the Ka'anapali Resort's second entrance; 808-667-9680.

Hours: 5:30 a.m.-7:30 p.m. *Sampling:* Breakfasts start with an early-bird special with eggs, breakfast meat and coffee ($4.95 before 7 a.m.). Other good morning offerings include plenty of omelets, pancakes, waffles and French toast ($3.50-$7.95). Lunches include an old-fashioned burger, deli-style sandwiches and some super salads. Side orders range from fettuccine marinara, pineapple fried rice, sautéed mushrooms or garlic bread (95¢-$2.95). And their kids' menu is dynamite. Check out a sharkbite cheeseburger, frankensteinfurter or mega cheese sandwich with fries, grilled chicken breast, mac and cheese with veggies, or lizard toes and squid eyes soup (their menu makes spoofs, but they do have soup). All items include soda, juice or milk ($3.95). Give "The Perfect Panini" a try. These Italian-style grilled sandwiches on focaccia are served with grilled chicken, portobello mushrooms and prosciutto and tomato. Try a plate lunch served with vegetables, and rice or mashed potatoes with chicken parmesan, sautéed mahimahi, grilled pork chops are a few of the selections ($6.95-$10.95). A tasty selection of sweet treats: banana split, island cheesecake, fresh-baked pies or shakes, floats and smoothies. *Comments:* It's no wonder folks line up to sample Christian Jorgansen's tasty breakfast and lunch fare. Pastries, even donuts, are made fresh on the premises. Initial reports are that the wait for food is a bit too long; it's understandable with the immediate popularity of the restaurant but we hope things smooth out for them quickly.

(The) Coffee Store *(Coffee/Pastries)*
Napili Plaza; 808-669-4170. Other locations at 1279 South Kihei Road, 808-875-4244; Queen Ka'ahumanu Center, 275 Ka'ahumanu Avenue, Kahului, 808-871-6860.

Hours: 6:30 a.m.-8 p.m. *Sampling:* Muffins, cinnamon rolls, sticky buns, desserts and assorted pastries. Soup, salad, sandwiches (regular or wrap style), quesadillas ($2.95-$7.75). *Comments:* They also have locations in Kihei and Kahului. Freshly roasted coffee and coffee drinks (with some unusual selections like a banana mocha cooler or an Electric Brown Cow). Juices and flavored Italian sodas or smoothies.

Dollies *(American/Italian)*
Kahana Manor, 4310 Honoapi'ilani Highway; 808-669-0266.

Hours: 11 a.m.-midnight. *Sampling:* Sandwiches include grinders, roast beef, or Cajun chicken or salads ($5.95-$7.95). Pizza selections, or create your own (from $15). Plenty of *pupus* ($3.75-$7.95) or sample one of their fettuccine dishes. *Comments:* Food to go. Good selection of beer, wine and coffee drinks. Popular spot with local residents.

Gazebo *(American)*
Napili Shores Resort, 5315 Lower Honoapi'ilani Highway; 808-669-5621.

Hours: 7:30 a.m.-2 p.m. *Sampling:* Breakfast offers an assortment of omelets (from spinach to shrimp) and egg dishes, but they are most popular for their macadamia nut pancakes; pineapple and banana run a close second ($5.25-$7.95). Lunch selections include burgers and sandwiches (Monte Cristo, shrimp melt, chicken Monterey, patty melt) plus Caesar, shrimp, tuna and Southwestern chicken salads ($5.75-$8.25). *Comments:* It's "paper-plate" casual (even with real plates) and popular with Maui residents for the friendly atmosphere and a wonderful ocean view.

★ **Honokowai Okazuya & Deli** *(Local/Eclectic)*
AAAAA Rent-A-Space Mall, 3600 Lower Honoapi'ilani Highway; 808-665-0512.

Hours: Monday-Saturday 10 a.m.-2:30 p.m., 4:30-9 p.m. Closed Sunday. *Sampling:* Chicken *katsu*, Mongolian beef, *panko* fried mahi, teriyaki steak, veggie frittata, Szechuan eggplant, egg fu yung, Grandma's spicy tofu, pasta primavera, spaghetti with meatballs or sausage. Hot sandwiches (meatball, Italian sausage, turkey or tuna melt, broiled chicken, mahi) plus turkey, ham, club, BLT. Most menu items $5.25-$6.45. *Comments:* Former chefs from Ming Yuen and Buzz's Wharf offer what they call the "Best Take-out in Town"—an eclectic selection of local, Italian, Japanese, deli and vegetarian. Lunch and dinner plates come with rice and a choice of macaroni salad or stir-fried vegetables. Readers have written to rave about it and I agree. A must try! Call ahead and order or you'll be watching all those folks who called ahead picking up their orders while your stomach growls.

Honolua General Store *(American)*
Past Kapalua as you drive through the golf course. Just above The Ritz-Carlton; 808-669-6128.

Hours: 6 a.m.-3 p.m. (Sometimes bentos to-go are available in their warmer oven after 3 p.m.) *Sampling:* Breakfasts include pancakes, eggs and such. Lunches include four local-plate selections daily that might include stew or teri chicken or a smaller portion called a hobo, which is just a main dish and rice. Sandwiches and grilled items include tuna melt, burgers and hot pastrami served with fries. The Spam *musubi*, a local favorite, is usually sold out by noon. And where else can you get a *keiki* corn dog or a peanut butter and jelly? Prices definitely on the low end for Kapalua ($2-$9.) *Comments:* The front portion displays an assortment of Kapalua clothing and some locally made food products as well as gourmet teas and coffees.

Ka'anapali Mixed Plate *(American/Hawaiian)*
Ka'anapali Beach Hotel, 2525 Ka'anapali Parkway; 808-661-0011.
    Hours: Breakfast buffet 6-10:45 a.m. ($10.50 adults/ $7 kids). Lunch buffet 11 a.m.-2 p.m. ($10.95 adults/ $8.95 kids). Early-bird dinner buffet 4-6 p.m. ($10.95 adults/$8.95 kids). Dinner buffet 6-9 p.m. ($13.50 adults/$10 kids). *Sampling:* "All Buffets, All the Time," with dinner offerings that change daily. For example, Friday dinner is Hawaiian style with pork *laulau*, chicken long rice, beef stew and fresh poi. Or visit on Monday for American, Tuesday/Japanese, Wednesday/Italian, Thursday/Chinese or Saturday-Sunday/"Mixed Plate." *Comments:* Pleasant coffee shop decorated with donated mementos that reflect the diverse ethnic and cultural background of the hotel employees. A description of the display items and explanation of the cultural foods is featured in a souvenir booklet given at each table. All buffets include salad bar, beverages and dessert. The best value in Ka'anapali, especially for those with a hearty appetite.

Kahana Terrace Restaurant *(American)*
Sands of Kahana Resort, 4299 Lower Honoapi'ilani Highway; 808-669-5399.
    Hours: Breakfast 7:30 a.m.-2 p.m. Lunch 11 a.m.-5 p.m. *Pupus* 2-9 p.m. Café and dinner menu 5-9 p.m. *Sampling:* Lunches with burgers and specialty sandwiches ($5.95-$8.50). *Pupus* range from potstickers or buffalo wings to pizza and steamers ($7.95-$9.95). Dinners include an all-you-can-eat salad bar ($5.95) with dinner favorites of ginger beef tenderloin with prawns, pasta primavera or NY steak including a trip to the salad bar ($12.94-$25.95). Early-bird specials served in the restaurant 4-6:30 p.m. daily ($11.95-$14.95). *Comments:* Very quiet dining, this restaurant seems to be primarily used by the resort guests. They have a Sunday-afternoon poolside barbecue with all-you-can-eat ribs, teriyaki chicken, hot dogs and fish served 4-8 p.m., $15.95 adults, $6.95 kids 10 and under.

Mama's Ribs -N- Rotisserie *(Barbecue)*
Napili Plaza; 808-665-6262.
    Hours: 11 a.m.-7 p.m. Closed Sunday. *Sampling:* Home-cooked meals for takeout. Rotisserie chicken and barbecue rib dinners are offered along with homemade coleslaw (with fresh apples and raisins), island-style macaroni salad, and barbecue baked ribs simmered with chunks of bacon and onions. Plate-lunch specials (from $5). Full rack of ribs ($18.99) or whole roasted chicken ($10.75) in traditional or

teriyaki citrus marinades along with side dishes such as barbecue baked beans, white rice, cole slaw and tri-pasta salad should feed the masses. They also have "bowl" meals including chili bowl, ban bowl and stew bowl ($2.75-$4).

Nachos Grande *(Mexican)*
Honokowai Marketplace, 3350 Lower Honoapi'ilani Highway; 808-662-0890.
   Hours: 11 a.m.-10 p.m. Bar open until 2 a.m. serving late-night *pupus. Sampling:* Burritos, nachos, enchiladas, tacos and quesadillas served with chicken, beef or vegetarian style ($2.75-$5.99). They feature their own homemade mango salsa. *Comments:* Check out their "wall of flame" with over 100 hot sauces from around the world. And after that, if you need to cool down, sample one of their mango margaritas.

Nalu Sunset Bar & Sushi *(Asian)*
Maui Marriott Resort & Ocean Club, 100 Nohea Kai Drive; 808-667-8292.
   Hours: 5:30-10:30 p.m. *Samplings:* Nalu's features a *pupu* buffet. Appetizers of dim sum, sweet-and-sour rib bites, meatballs, stuffed potato skins, *kalua* pork and cabbage, chicken *katsu* or beef stir fry might be among the selections. Offered Monday-Thursday 5-7 p.m., the buffet is $10 adults, $5 children 10 and under. They also feature sushi creations along with tropical libations. *Comments:* The popular Makai Bar lends itself toward the Pacific (both the view and the menu). It's a full-service bar and has a great sunset vista. Wednesday evenings they offer entertainment.

Ohana Grill and Bar *(American/Deli)*
Embassy Vacation Resort, 104 Ka'anapali Shores Place; 808-661-2000.
   Hours: 11 a.m.-10 p.m. *Sampling:* Shrimp tempura salad, Menehune Caesar, and pizza along with sandwiches such as *kalua* pork, chicken gyro and ahi tuna, burgers and frosty smoothies ($4-$10). They offer a dinner menu with entrees such as lamb chops, prawns and daily catch ($13-$22). *Comments:* Early-bird specials between 5:30 and 6 p.m. with all dinners 25 percent off. Entertainment 6-9 p.m.

★ **Pizza Paradiso** *(Pizza/Italian)*
Two locations: Honokowai Marketplace, 3350 Lower Honoapi'ilani Highway, 808-667-2929; Whalers Village Food Court, 2435 Ka'anapali Parkway, 808-667-0333.
   Hours: 11 a.m.-10 p.m. *Sampling:* Panini ($5.95-$6.75) both hot and cold include mixed grill vegetables, turkey pesto, or Italian meatball. Order a whole pizza pie ($11.95-$25.95) or by the slice. Lots of salads that include pastas or greens ($3.95-$5.95) and an affordable selection of pasta entrees ($6.95-$8.95) available as spaghetti or penne; add chicken, shrimp or clams. Marinara

tomato with herb (available with meatballs or Italian sauce), alfredo or florentine sauces. Their Massimo pesto sauce pasta was a winner of the Taste of Lahaina as was their Mona Lisa, which is creamy gorgonzola with apple and walnuts. The adjoining Hula Scoops offers smoothies, gourmet ice cream, sundaes and desserts, including their tiramisu, which was voted the best in Maui ($2.79-$4.50). Warm up with a variety of hot café drinks or cool down with an espresso shake, a banana mocha cooler or an iced toddy. *Comments:* Pizza Paradiso has received many accolades for their homemade pies made with fresh herbs, mozzarella and secret sauce. Inexpensive gourmet cuisine in a casual setting plus they have "Family Deal" meals that serve up to a family of four with salads from $17.25 for pizza and pastas.

Sports Club Kahana Grill *(Sandwiches)*
Valley Isle Resort, 4327 Lower Honoapi'ilani Highway; 808-669-3538.

Hours: 7 a.m.-11 p.m. Breakfast served until 11 a.m. *Sampling:* Breakfast selections include egg dishes with egg whites only or soy cheese (from $4.95). Salads and sandwiches such as honey-mustard turkey wrap, sesame hummus and vegetable wrap or mango barbecue chicken ($6.95-$8.95). Side orders of green salad, brown rice, potatoes and daily special soups ($1-$3.95). *Comments:* Located in the Maui Muscle Sports Club. Limited seating. Didn't get to try their food but the prices look great.

Moderate-priced Dining

Basil Tomatoes *(Italian)*
Royal Lahaina Resort, 2780 Kekaa Drive; 808-661-3611.

Hours: 5:30-10 p.m. *Sampling:* Classic Italian fare with minestrone soup, fresh clams over linguine, seafood ravioli, rosemary lemon basil chicken, lamb shank osso buco and plenty of pasta dishes ($16.99-$29.99). Desserts range from Italian ices to banana crepes or tiramisu ($3.49-$5.99). *Comments:* Located at the entrance to the Royal Lahaina Resort. Basil Tomatoes' special focaccia bread is served with all entrees. Children's menu. Early-bird specials 5:30-6:30 p.m.

(The) Beach House *(American)*
The Ritz-Carlton, 1 Ritz Carlton Drive, Kapalua; 808-669-6200.

Hours: 11:30 a.m.-4 p.m. Bar service 11:30 a.m.-6 p.m. *Sampling:* Lunch selections range from teriyaki steak and Maui onion sandwich, *kalua* pork sandwich or grilled chicken wrap to a fresh tropical fruit platter with *lilikoi* yogurt ($12-$18). *Comments:* Located adjacent to Fleming Beach, this open-air restaurant utilizes more than 40 fully grown coco palms to offer a natural roof. This is a really spectacular daytime dining location. On a sunny day, you couldn't enjoy a better outdoor dining experience, and if the whales are in town, an added bonus. Parking is available at D.T. Fleming Beach Park.

★ **Castaway Café** *(American with a touch of the islands)*
Maui Ka'anapali Villas Resort, 45 Kai Ala Drive; 808-661-9091.

Hours: Breakfast 7:30 a.m.-2 p.m. Lunch 11 a.m.-2:30 p.m. Light fare 2:30-9 p.m. Dinner 5-9 p.m. *Sampling:* Loco moco, eggs Benedict, omelets or from the griddle (until 11 a.m.) enjoy macadamia nut, banana or pineapple pancakes, or the must-try Kula cinnamon raisin French toast ($4.50-$10.50). Lunches include Paradise chicken salad, burgers and dogs, sandwiches ($6.95-$10.50). Start your evening repast with coconut shrimp or an Asian sampler or perhaps soup or salad ($1.95-$9.95). Entrees are great values. The Hawaiian cordon bleu is enhanced by fresh pineapple, then rolled in coconut and oven baked, served with a lemon butter sauce. The fresh catch is a deal at $21.95 and can be prepared blackened, grilled with lemon butter, or macadamia crusted with tropical fruit salsa ($14.95-$23.95); served with rice or potato and fresh vegetables. Their dessert menu changes, but if you're lucky you can try a piece of their "real" NY cheesecake. *Comments:* They have terrific fish specials daily and our winner for the best French toast. Tuesday is pasta night with two-for-one pasta selections. Great location oceanside (next to the swimming pool at Ka'anapali Villas) and an excellent value. This cozy poolside restaurant is worth finding and with indoor or patio dining you are merely footsteps from the waves. Owner Gary Bush has compiled a remarkable selection of wines and has been recognized by *Wine Spectator Magazine* for the past three years. Full bar service. And the name Castaway? Well, I have to admit that Gary does look just a tiny bit like the Skipper from "Gilligan's Island."

Fish and Games Brewing Company & Rotisserie *(Seafood/Rotisserie & Microbrewery)*
Kahana Gateway, 4405 Honoapi'ilani Highway #207; 808-669-FISH; www.fishandgamerestaurant.com.

Hours: Lunch 11 a.m.-3 p.m. Happy Hour 3-5 p.m. Dinner 5:30-10 p.m. Bar menu available 11 a.m.-1 a.m. *Sampling:* Begin your meal with crispy fried calamari, oysters on the half shell or a cold seafood sampler ($8-$12.95). Entrees include rotisserie chicken, whole roasted pork loin, *kiawe*-smoked prime rib or rack of lamb. Their clam and oyster chowder as well as the Maui onion soup are homemade. Fresh island fish is available cooked in any one of seven different preparations including seven spiced, blackened Cajun or steamed oriental ($15.95-$26.95). The meats are prepared on their rotisserie and the *kiawe* grill. Pizzas and a *keiki* menu also offered. Desserts vary daily. I tried a warm milk chocolate brownie smothered with heated caramel sauce that fared better than the banana espresso bread pudding which seemed to have too many flavors competing. *Comments:* The main dining room has an exhibition kitchen, oyster bar, and retail seafood market. A striking stone hearth rotisserie is surrounded by a marble dining counter and gleaming copper tanks of their glass-enclosed microbrewery. The sports bar side offers state-of-the-art equipment and satellite system. In the back is a separate dining room with elegant wood and brass designs reminiscent of a gentlemen's club.

Giovani's Tomato Pie Ristorante *(Italian)*
Ka'anapali Resort where Ka'anapali Parkway meets Honoapi'ilani Highway by the Ka'anapali Golf Course; 808-661-3160.

Hours: 5:30-9 p.m. *Sampling:* Pick your pasta and combine it with your favorite sauce. Penne with alfredo, linguine with bolognese, and capellini with aioli are only a few of the options ($10.99-$15.79). Stuffed pasta, pizzas or parmigiana dishes with house dinner specials including calamari and seafood pescatore ($13.99-$19.99). Add antipasto or *zuppa* and *saladas* from $3.49. *Comments:* Part of the Jon Applegate chain of restaurants. Kids' meals for 10 and under $6-$10. Downstairs they have Jonny's Burger Joint open 11:30 a.m.-midnight, with the bar open until 2 a.m. There are better pizza and burgers elsewhere in Ka'anapali.

★ **Hula Grill** *(Hawaiian Regional/Seafood)*
Whalers Village, 2435 Ka'anapali Parkway, on the beach; 808-667-6636.

Hours: Dinner 5-9:30 p.m. Barefoot Bar & Café 10 a.m.-9:30 p.m. *Sampling:* The Barefoot Bar serves a continuous lunch/dinner menu featuring appetizers and meal-size salads. Try the *gado gado* salad with peanut sauce ($8.95-$10.95). For dinner try shrimp scampi, wood-grilled ahi steak or banana barbecue ribs ($15-$27). Lots of other delicious fish dishes, chicken and pork. Pizzas available anytime (from $8.95). *Comments:* The Hawaiian Regional cuisine is based on Hawaiian fish and seafood. The casual oceanfront restaurant, reminiscent of a 1930s Dickey-style beach house, is surrounded by tropical gardens and ponds. The interior has a homey atmosphere with a cozy library room for a waiting area. Each room feels like part of a home and a collection of antique hula dolls are on display throughout. The Barefoot Bar is thatched and surrounded by "indoor" sand. There is an exhibition cooking line in front with a large *kiawe*-grill/barbecue, an *imu*-style oven for the pizzas, and a bar-counter to sit and eat and watch it all. Good kids' menu, too. This is the place to see and to be seen. This is a part of the T.S Restaurant chain.

Jameson's Grill & Bar at Kapalua *(Seafood/American)*
200 Kapalua Drive, just across the road from the Kapalua Hotel and a short drive up Kapalua Drive; 808-669-5653.

Hours: Breakfast/lunch 8 a.m.-3 p.m. Café menu 3 p.m.-midnight. Dinner 5-10 p.m. Cocktails 11 a.m.-12:30 a.m. *Sampling:* A few special breakfast selections along with the regular fare. Lunches include burgers, sandwiches, salads and pizza ($4.95-$12.95). A large appetizer selection if you'd just like a meal from that ($4.95-$12.95). Other entrees include pepper-crusted ahi steak served medium rare, rack of lamb, miso-*sake* prawns or Jameson's stuffed shrimp ($17.95-$25.95). *Comments:* The award-winning wine list offers everything from the affordable to the impressive. The location overlooks the 18th hole and affords both ocean and golf course views.

Java Jazz *(Bistro)*
Honokowai Marketplace, 3350 Lower Honoapiʻilani Highway; 808-667-0787; www.javajazz.net.

Hours: Monday-Saturday 6 a.m.-9 p.m. Sunday 6 a.m.-5 p.m. *Sampling:* Breakfast ($5.95-$7.95) features breakfast burrito, omelets, waffles, pancakes and egg dishes. Lunch includes four soups made fresh daily, sandwiches and vegetarian burgers ($5.95-$9.95). Dinners with fresh fish, top-cut steaks ($17.94-$24.95) and homemade desserts. Daily dinner specials. Full bar. *Comments:* They call themselves "House of the Home Hearty Food." Cute little bistro-style café with a bohemian ambiance and a nice espresso bar. Breakfast served all day.

Kekaʻa Terrace *(American)*
Sheraton Maui, 2605 Kaʻanapali Parkway; 808-661-0031.

Hours: Breakfast buffet 6:30-11 a.m. Lunch 11 a.m.-2 p.m. (a la carte). Dinner 5:30-9:30 p.m. (a la carte). Flavors of Hawaii 5:30-9 p.m. *Sampling:* Buffet breakfast runs $19.95. Lunch includes salads such as Polynesian chicken or Kekaʻa Cobb as well as assorted sandwiches such as lemongrass chicken or a Maui wrap with fajita chicken and Maui onion leek spread ($8-$15). Seasonally they offer an evening buffets ($23-$25) and a summer salad bar ($14.95). Begin your dinner with crispy calamari, "Pearl of the Pacific" (their signature dish with cocktail shrimp, smoked scallops and ahi sashimi) or a shrimp and eggplant cake ($8-$14). Continue with fresh catch, baby back ribs, prime rib, bouillabaisse or lobster tail options for dinner ($20-$45). For dinner they offer the "Flavors of Hawaiʻi ($49) a complete dinner with appetizer, soup or salad, intermezzo, entree and dessert, or enjoy a seafood pasta, hibachi salmon, broiled lobster tail, chef's catch prepared one of four ways, bouillabaisse or coconut shrimp ($26-$45). *Comments:* Casual, all-day dining with views of the ocean and the resort's tropical lagoons.

★ **Leilani's on the Beach** *(American/Seafood)*
Whalers Village, 2435 Ka'anapali Parkway, on the beach; 808-661-4495.

Hours: 11 a.m.-11 p.m. *Sampling:* Leilani's on the Beach, located on the lower-level beachside of the restaurant, offers salads, local-style plate lunches and assorted sandwiches including Cajun grilled fish ($8-$12). The dining room opens for dinner with fresh catch, shellfish, grilled steaks, and barbecue ribs all served with rice or potatoes ($15-$23). Save room for Kimo's hula pie. *Comments:* The outdoor lounge and terrace dining room are right on the beach, offering one of the best sunset-viewing spots in Ka'anapali. Leilani's has been here for years and is a good bet for family dining. Specialties are prepared on lava-rock broilers in *koa* wood ovens. Kids' menu. Dinner reservations advised.

North Beach Grille *(Pacific Rim)*
Embassy Vacation Resort, 104 Ka'anapali Shores Place; 808-661-2000.

Hours: 5:30-9:30 p.m. *Sampling:* Chili-glazed calamari, au gratin oysters, fresh island white fish ceviche are among the appetizers ($7.95-$12.50), and for your dinner entree enjoy grilled rare ahi over mashed potatoes, blackened snapper of the day, white clam linguini or roasted vegetable pasta ($14-$33).

'OnO Surf Bar & Grill *(Buffet)*
Westin Maui, 2365 Ka'anapali Parkway, located poolside on the ground floor; 808-667-2525.

Hours: Breakfast 6:30 a.m.-11 a.m. (breakfast buffet 6:30 a.m.-10:30 a.m.). Lunch 11 a.m.-5 p.m. Dinner 5-10 p.m. *Sampling:* Island breakfast buffet is served daily ($19.95 adults, children 4-12 is $1 per year of their age) and is a good value since it includes juices, coffees and fruits. Egg and pancake breakfasts a la carte fetch $14.75-$16.50. Lunches include burgers, or club, Reuben, steak sandwiches, oriental noodle salad, grilled chicken wrap and chicken noodle soup ($7.50-$14). The light eater can have a sandwich or burger for dinner or try out one of their family dinners and entrees. The flat-iron steak is one of the tenderest cuts of beef you'll find. They also have pork chops, sauteed mahi, penne pasta, prawns fettuccine, or savor their three-course prime rib dinner or herbed baked chicken ($16-$25). Their prime rib and seafood buffet is each Saturday 5-9 p.m. For $29.95 ($10 kids 4-12 years) includes iced seafoods and salads, creamy clam and Moloka'i corn chowder; in addition to prime rib hot off the carving station you can enjoy steamed clams and blue mussels in saffron broth, baked mahi, barbecue ribs, *hulihuli* chicken, baked salmon and chef's daily pastas and potatoes. *Comments:* Casual poolside bistro dining. And yes, it is actually spelled 'OnO; some of these restaurants are taxing established grammar.

Outback Steakhouse *(Steakhouse)*
Kahana Gateway, 4405 Honoapi'ilani Highway; 808-665-1822. Another location at Pi'ilani Shopping Center, 281 Pi'ikea Avenue, Kihei (by Safeway), 808-879-8400; www.outback.com.

Hours: 4-10 p.m. *Sampling:* Start with "Aussie-tizers" of Gold Coast coconut shrimp, Aussie cheese fries, Kookaburra wings, grilled shrimp (on the barbie, of course), and their signature Bloomin' Onion ($6.99-$8.99), or go for a Bonzer Salad—Caesar with "chook" (chicken)—or the Queensland with chicken, egg, tomato, bacon and two cheeses ($8.99-$11.99). Entrees include "Down Under Favorites" like Queensland chicken and shrimp, Jackeroo chops, or Alice Springs chicken. "Barrier Reef" favorites include North Atlantic salmon, Toowoomba pasta (seafood fettuccine if you're non-Aussie), or ribs or chicken on the barbie ($14-$24). And it doesn't stop there, mate. There's still the "Chocolate Thunder from Down Under" pecan brownie with ice cream and chocolate sauce. They also have a menu of "Cut Lunches" (chook sandwiches and burgers) ($7.99-$8.49) and a "joey" menu for kids, with most items priced "down under" ($4.99-$6.99). *Comments:* Casual ranch-house atmosphere with hardwood floors, wood-framed booths, and plenty of Aussie artifacts.

Pavillion *(Pacific Rim)*
Hyatt Regency Maui Resort and Spa, 200 Nohea Kai Drive, lower level; 808-661-1234.

Hours: Breakfast 6-11:30 a.m. Grill menu 11:30 a.m.-5 p.m. *Sampling:* The Pavillion "Buffeteria" features casual dining items. Most selections are under $10 and a *keiki* menu includes a fountain drink and french fries. *Comments:* Fairly affordable for resort dining. Very casual indoor or outdoor seating. At night it sometimes serves as the reception area for the theatrical production, Tony 'n Tina's Wedding. And yes, it is Pavillion with two Ls. Guess they started the trend for 'OnO, Capische?, Hapa*s and tropica.

Plumeria Terrace Restaurant and Bar *(International)*
Kapalua Bay Hotel, poolside; 808-669-5656.

Hours: 11 a.m.-4:30 p.m. Cocktails until 5 p.m. *Sampling:* Plumeria crab cakes, buffalo wings and sushi rolls ($8-$14). Sample a *pupu* platter ($16), clam chowder ($7) or a Kula or Caesar salad ($6-$9) and add prawns, ahi or chicken. They have pizza, a chicken sandwich on focaccia bread, plus beef and pawns with Asian noodles ($12-$15). Something sweet? Ice creams and sorbets, plus Kula lime pie, mud pie and cheesecake. *Comments:* The beautiful location of this casual poolside setting features an ocean view from every seat.

Reilley's *(Steaks/Seafood)*
2290 Ka'anapali Parkway, overlooking the golf course; 808-667-7477.

Hours: Lunch 10:30-4 p.m. Dinner 5-9 p.m. *Sampling:* Lunch menu might include a nice selection of Caesar, Cobb and assorted salads along with some sandwiches that are a cut-above the norm. Tempura lobster tail, pan-seared crab cake or yellow velvet soup are among the dinner starters ($5) or house or Caesar salad ($5-$7). Seafood selections offer bouillabaisse, pan-seared Pacific salmon, rack of lamb or maple guava duck breast ($19-$28). Save room for Kona coffee creme brulee, leprechaun pie (mint chocolate chip ice cream in an Oreo cookie crust), or double chocolate mousse tower ($6). *Comments:* Spacious and attractive pub atmosphere. All-you-can-eat prime rib special every Tuesday and Wednesday night. Kona lobster special on Sundays (reservations a must) and dinner jazz each Monday and Tuesday evening to enhance your dining pleasure. Wine and beer and a selection of tropical, "Irish" and coffee drinks.

Royal Ocean Terrace Restaurant *(Buffet)*
Royal Lahaina Resort, 2780 Kekaa Drive; 808-661-3611.

Hours: Breakfast 6-10 a.m. Dinner 5-10 p.m. *Sampling:* Breakfast offers omelets, pancakes and waffles as well as a la carte items ($6-$8.50). The best deal is their "Royal Breakfast" with two eggs, two slices of bacon and toast ($4.99). Their breakfast buffet is one of the best buys on Ka'anapali ($11.50 adults, $6.99 children 6-11, 5 and under free) with fruits, pastries, cereals and yogurt. Hot items include corned beef hash and scrambled eggs along with daily special items such as waffles, banana pancakes or hash browns. Dinner soups, salads and sandwiches ($5.95-$10.95) for the light eater or enjoy teriyaki steak, an aloha luau platter, fish and chips, fresh catch of the day or chicken alfredo ($11.95-$24.95). Theme nights are Prime Rib Sundays and Wednesdays, Spaghetti Mondays, BBQ Mixed Grill on Tuesdays, Porterhouse Steak Thursdays, Fish Sampler Fridays and Herb Chicken Saturdays ($10.95-$21.95). Kids' meals $6.50. Desserts include passion fruit cheesecake or their fabulous Mauna Loa mud pie. *Comments:* This is an attractive, airy restaurant overlooking the pool and ocean. The adjoining Royal Ocean Terrace offers a sunset torch-lighting ceremony at 6:30 followed by Hawaiian musical entertainment. The lounge also offers *pupus* and light meals.

Rusty Harpoon *(American)*
Whalers Village, 2435 Ka'anapali Parkway; 808-661-3123.

Hours: Breakfast 8-11 a.m. Lunch 11 a.m.-5 p.m. Happy Hour 2-6 p.m. Dinner 5 p.m.-midnight. *Sampling:* The only "real" restaurant open at Whalers Village for breakfast. Waffles (no pancakes on their breakfast menu) and assorted egg dishes all start at $7.95. For dinner they feature some unusual specials such as Rusty's Masaman Seafood Curry ($23.95) and a Kobe burger ($14.95). Their honeymoon special is $79.95. Seafood, beef, pasta and chicken entrees ($18.95-$29.95). *Comments:* "Jerome E. Metcalfe's Rusty Harpoon and Tavern on Ka'anapali Beach" added a lot of words to the old restaurant (along with full sports-satellite large-screen TVs) but the diverse menu and great ocean view remain the same.

★ **Sansei Restaurant and Sushi Bar** *(Sushi/Pacific Rim)*
Kapalua Bay Hotel Shops; 808-669-6286. Another location at Kihei Town Center, 1881 South Kihei Road, near Foodland; 808-879-0004

Hours: Saturday-Wednesday 5:30-10 p.m., Thursday-Friday until 1:30 a.m. Karaoke and *pupus* Thursday-Friday 10 p.m.-1 a.m. *Sampling:* No matter what you select, it is going to be great. Start with tea duck egg roll, and you *must* try the *panko*-crusted fresh ahi sashimi. Sansei has repeatedly won awards and received first place for their Asian rock shrimp cake and mango crab salad handroll at Taste of Lahaina. There are plenty of creative rolls such as the Kapalua "Butterfry" roll (fresh snapper, smoked salmon, snow crab and veggies in crispy *panko* butter and served with a tangy *ponzu* sauce; don't you love the play on words?). Or sample their Sansei Special roll with spicy crab, cilantro, fresh cucumber and avocado. Yum! Their fresh Hawaiian ahi carpaccio is soaked with cilantro, peanuts and Thai chili sauce. Another Taste of Lahaina winner is their Japanese calamari salad with a crispy won ton basket filled with Kula greens and topped with fried calamari. Just writing about their food is making me ravenous. I'm a fish lover but for you land lovers they have a fabulous roasted Peking duck breast, tender *shichimi*-seasoned filet of beef and roasted Japanese jerk chicken. Dinner entrees ($10.95-$21.95—lobster higher). But I think it is much more fun to just enjoy the diversity of flavors in the appetizers (Asian tapas) and rolls ($4.95-$10.95). If you really can't decide try their "Omakase" tasting menu made for two featuring the best of the best ($59.95 -79.95 for two). Save room for their hot fresh Granny Smith apple tart, NY cheesecakes made by Sansei and coffee served in a French press. *Comments:* Sushi and sashimi, as well as a selection of traditional Japanese and innovative Pacific Rim dishes, are made to share family-style with everyone at the table at this comfortable and inviting eatery. The small plates and small portions of these Asian tapas create a friendly, fun atmosphere. But as much as I love this innovative and original new dining concept, it's the food that's the ultimate test. Owner D.K's Spam roll (at $500 with 24-hour notice) gives insight to his wit. D.K. is such a nice guy that I'm really pleased his success has expanded to O'ahu. As I said before, if you don't like sushi bars, you'll like this one. And if you *love* them, this will probably be your favorite. If I had to pick half a dozen of my favorite restaurants on Maui, this would be at the top, even without an ocean view. Reservations strongly suggested.

★ **Sea House** *(American)*
Napili Kai Beach Resort, 5900 Lower Honoapi'ilani Road, beachfront; 808-669-1500.

Hours: Breakfast 8-10:30 a.m. Lunch 11:30 a.m.-2 p.m. Dinner 6-9 p.m. *Sampling:* Omelets, Hawaiian sweet bread French toast, banana macadamia pancakes, Belgian waffle, or poached eggs Napili Kai ($5.95-$10.95). Luncheon sandwiches include a crab croissant, shrimp BLT, chicken quesadilla and "Maui Cristo," or try the focaccia filet mignon or shrimp Greek salad ($5-$15). Begin your evening meal with a *pupu* of fresh steamed clams, ahi tempura, farm-raised Big Island abalone or Asian baby back ribs ($10-$14). They have a *keiki* menu for those 12 and under with favorites such as fish and chips, hamburgers, chicken nuggets, pasta or three-cheese pizza ($5-$8). Dinner entrees include fresh island fish, seafood pasta, grilled pork chops, veal piccata, or free-range chicken ($2-$27). Their Polynesian dinner show has been a favorite for years ($50 adults, $25 children) and is performed by the Children of the Napili Kai Foundation each Friday evening; seating at 6-6:30 p.m., show at 7:30 p.m. Your dinner includes a salad, prime rib, chicken breast or macadamia nut–crusted mahimahi, dessert and coffee. *Comments:* This is one of only a handful of island restaurants that looks right onto the beach and ocean. Their Whale Watcher's bar serves cocktails, lunches and *pupus*.

★ **Tiki Terrace** *(American/Hawaiian)*
Ka'anapali Beach Hotel, 2525 Ka'anapali Parkway; 808-661-0011.

Hours: Breakfast 7-11 a.m. (Sunday breakfast menu is served 7-8:45 a.m. followed by Sunday brunch 9 a.m.-2 p.m.). Dinner 6-9 p.m. *Sampling:* Best deal for breakfast in Ka'anapali is their continental breakfast. Choice of three baked goods from their bread selection and coffee or tea ($8.95). Their light buffet ($9.95) includes fruits, pastries, assorted cheese and sausage and their famous buttermilk pancakes with coconut and maple syrup. Or try their all-you-can-eat buffet for $11.95. In addition to the light buffet you also get poached, scrambled or boiled eggs plus omelets made to order, breakfast meats (including fresh catch) and potatoes ($11.95). Or order a la carte meals ($6.25-$14.95). On Sunday they serve champagne brunch ($28.95 adults; $14.50 children). The Tiki Terrace has some interesting appetizers. Pig in a Pareo is Hawaiian-style smoked pork with Maui onions wrapped in egg rolls, or crispy *opae* (shrimp) served with aioli, as well as their sweet Maui onion soup, spinach or Caesar salad. Entrees range from clam linguini to stuffed shrimp and for the land lover there is *kiawe*-roasted duck, barbecued pork ribs or grilled teriyaki chicken ($16.95-$36.95). Dessert offers a Napili lime tart, pineapple cheesecake or Banana Caramel Eruption, which is warm, gooey and wonderful. *Comments:* Before becoming Westernized, Hawaiians consumed less than 20 percent fat in their diet. If you'd like to sample a native Hawaiian diet they have a multicourse meal starting with a *pohole* fern salad and a choice of chicken or fish for your entree and culminating with chilled Hana papaya for dessert ($21.95). *Keiki* prices available.

★ **Va Bene Italian Beachside Grill** *(Italian)*
Maui Marriott Resort & Ocean Club, 100 Nohea Kai Drive, Ka'anapali; 808-667-8290.

Hours: Breakfast 6:30-11:30 a.m. Dinner 5-10 p.m. *Sampling & Comments:* Two daily breakfast buffets with a "Healthy Start" featuring oatmeal, cold cereals, fresh fruits, yogurt, breakfast breads and juices ($13 adults, $7 kids 7-12 years), or a full buffet that adds eggs cooked to order and breakfast meals to the "Healthy Start" option ($18 adults, $9 kids 7-12 years). Lighter options include Danish, oatmeal or yogurt, or choose an egg entree (which includes coffee or juice) such as NY steak and eggs, Va Bene Benedicts, Va Bene frittata or the "All American Breakfast" ($5-$16). From the griddle enjoy waffles, pancakes and French toast ($6-$13). The dinner menu is a fun one. They have fish and seafood selections such as tiger prawns, seafood stew or seafood pasta ($21-$28) and vegetable side dishes including wild mushrooms and asparagus ($7-$8). The pastas are available in *picollo* and *grande* sizes and include gnocchi, risotto *alla Monzese* and hand-pulled pizzas in *picollo* and *grande* sizes as well ($5-$13). But my recommendation is the chef's prix-fixe menu. They have two options. One includes a starter, pasta, entree (three choices) and a *dolci* for $29 ($39 with wine) and a lighter version with a starter and entree ($22, $30 with wine). As your dedicated consumer advocate I went with the larger prix-fixe menu served with wine. The wines are all red and a different 3 oz. glass is served with each course. The pasta course was made with grilled wild mushrooms and parmigiano reggiano cheese and I would have been delighted to have just this course for dinner. The smoked pork chop entree was huge and served with a sauce rich with roasted shallots and figs. The other entree was the beef tenderloin served with an herb and bread compound butter. This was the best beef I can remember enjoying in a very long time. While the sauces were very rich, they were served on the bottom so you could enjoy the flavor of the meat and as little, or as much, as you'd like. Many might expect resort-style dining at a hotel restaurant, but this is truly a step above. One of the best meals I had on a recent two-week trip to the island and a value that you don't want to miss.

Expensive-priced Dining

Banyan Tree *(Asian/Hawaiian)*
The Ritz-Carlton, 1 Ritz Carlton Drive, Kapalua; 808-669-6200.

Hours: Lunch 11:30 a.m.-3:30 p.m. Dinner 5:30-9:30 p.m. *Sampling:* Tropical libations and non-alcoholic fruit smoothies. Afternoon "starters" range from grilled globe tomato bruschetta or peppered Parker Ranch beef tenderloin salad to hibachi-grilled chicken and lemongrass brochette ($8-$12). Lunch entrees offer grilled Turkish flatbread ahi and herb-marinated eggplant panini, seared coriander-seed mahimahi sandwich, grilled New York steak sandwich, house-made udon noodles or a Big Island spiny lobster salad ($15-$24). The Banyan dinner menu changes seasonally but the last one we reviewed provided their signature coconut, sweet corn and lemongrass soup garnished with crabmeat, warm asparagus and crab salad, seared tuna Nicoise salad and Kobe beef carpaccio. Dinner entrees offer bouillabaisse, herb-crusted *onaga*, almond and pistachio–crusted salmon and ahi tuna with seared foie gras ($24-$34). *Comments:* This is an attractive island restaurant with Ritz-worthy dining and a great ocean view.

The Bay Club *(Island Continental)*
In Kapalua just before the entrance to the Kapalua Bay Hotel & Ocean Villas; 808-669-8008.

Hours: 6-9 p.m. *Sampling:* Appetizers include seared tiger prawns with watercress bruchette and pinenut brown butter, or a Kona Maine lobster salad ($9-$16). Entrees include macadamia nut–crusted mahimahi, seared ahi saltimbocca, pan-seared king prawns or a three-course lobster sampler. Not to be forgotten is the Basque-style rack of lamb, grilled veal chop, or seafood paella ($32-$60). Save room for one of their fabulous desserts: Kula lime pie or a warm apple crumb pie with vanilla ice cream and butterscotch caramel are divine. *Comments:* This Kapalua Hotel restaurant is housed in a separate building on a promontory that overlooks the ocean (and its own pool!) and offers a scenic panorama. It is fine island dining in a sophisticated setting. In the evening, a pianist in the adjoining lounge adds to the idyllic location with romantic music. Extensive wine list.

★ **Cascades Grille & Sushi Bar** *(American/Sushi)*
Hyatt Regency Maui Resort and Spa, 200 Nohea Kai Drive; 808-661-1234.
Hours: Lunch 11:30 a.m.-2 p.m. Dinner 6-10 p.m. Sushi bar 5-11 p.m. *Sampling:* Lunch selections include grilled chicken teriyaki or crab cake sandwich, or salads such as shrimp *poke*, island fruit *anuenue*, "Cobb" or seared ahi ($9-$15.95). Dinner options start with soups and salads ($5.50-$7.50), with entrees from the lava rock grill like rib-eye steak or filet mignon ($27-$29). Specialty entrees include seafood mixed grill, *huluhuli* chicken, five-spice pork chop ($24-$33) and island fish selections (market price). The sushi bar offers *maki* and *nigiri* sushi and sashimi ($7.50 and up) and sushi samplers ($18-$34). *Comments:* Perched above the pool and on the edge of one of the Hyatt's waterfalls, patio seating extends over the landscaped cliff, providing an ocean vista. Children can order most entrees on the menu at half price for half size. The dessert menu gets thumbs up for artistic presentation: coconut creme brulee is served in a partially edible fresh coconut shell; the chocolate mousse in a *totally* edible marbled white chocolate conch shell. The sushi bar is intimate yet spacious, with attractive wood, pleasant lighting, and Japanese artifacts.

★ **Gardenia Court Restaurant** *(Island Continental)*
Kapalua Bay Hotel & Ocean Villas; 808-669-5656.
Hours: Breakfast Monday-Saturday 6:30 a.m.-11 a.m. Sunday brunch 9:30 a.m.-1:30 p.m. Dinner Tuesday, Thursday and Saturday 6-9 p.m. *Sampling:* Gardenia Court features a lovely daily breakfast buffet but they enhance it for the fabulous Sunday brunch. A la carte is also offered for breakfast during the week. The daily breakfast buffet ($21.95) is a much better value than the a la carte menu if you choose to add orange juice or fruit and coffee to your breakfast fare. The Sunday brunch is $32 without champagne (half price for kids 6-12) and with champagne it's $37. Your dinner might begin with crispy Thai calamari with volcanic remoulade or rock shrimp and Kona crab cake ($10-$15). Soups and salads can precede your entree of tiger prawns with asparagus on angelhair pasta, Atlantic salmon, sea scallops, macadamia nut–crusted mahimahi, or a Kapalua club sandwich or burger ($14-$29). The seafood buffet is a best bet on the island with a lavish array of your favorite foods from the sea ($38, half price for kids 6-12). Prime rib all-you-can-eat special for $24 on Wednesday. Friday seafood buffet. *Comments:* The Sunday brunch and Friday-night seafood buffet are both very popular so reservations are highly recommended. This informal restaurant is open to gentle breezes and panoramic ocean views.

★ **Plantation House** *(Seafood/Continental)*
2000 Plantation Club Drive, Kapalua; 808-669-6299.

Hours: Breakfast/lunch 8 a.m.-3 p.m. Sunday Brunch 8 a.m.-3 p.m. Dinner 5:30-9:30 p.m. *Sampling:* The breakfast/lunch menu available until 3 p.m. Enjoy crab cake or salmon lox Benedict, omelets, or Rancher's breakfast ($8-$11); on Sundays indulge in Chef Alex's special brunch menu. Try his signature potato pancakes or omelets with local asparagus and goat cheese and the heart-healthy veggie omelet with steamed vegetables. Moloka'i sweet bread French toast with bananas or strawberries ($6-$18). Brunch can be complemented with Bellini (an Italian sparkling wine) or French-press house coffee. On other days you can sup on a lunch of fresh Hawaiian-catch sandwich, rosemary-garlic chicken breast sandwich or a Greek chicken salad with baby romaine. They also have daily lunch specials ($7-$15). Watch the sun set and start with spicy seared sashimi, crispy crab-stuffed ahi, or Maui onions and seasonal mushrooms with creamy polenta ($6-$10). Continue your dining pleasure with Plantation Pasta (penne tossed with Maui tomato and served with chicken or shrimp), Pacific prawns, oven-roasted Moloka'i pork tenderloin or oven-seared filet mignon. There are plenty of fish cooked up in delightful ways. Alex's signature dish is "A Taste of the Rich Forest" with wild mushrooms pressed and roasted and served with garlic mashed potatoes, or "Plantation Oscar" with your fish served with butter-braised asparagus and Alaskan snow crab meat ($16-$30). Each week there are special fish entrees to keep it interesting. They also have weekly wine specials where a nice bottle of wine runs in the $30 range. If you have a sweet tooth, don't miss the Bananas Foster for two people; my favorite "Brownie to Da Max" is served warm in a huge brandy snifter with lots of ice cream, whipped cream and macadamia nuts. *Comments:* Their location—in the clubhouse of the Plantation Golf Course—provides what is probably the best oceanview dining in West Maui. (Plan to arrive a half-hour or so before sunset for the full experience.) Just a short drive from Lahaina and Ka'anapali and worth it.

★ **Roy's Kahana Bar & Grill** *(Hawaiian Regional)*
Kahana Gateway, 4405 Honoapi'ilani Highway; 808-669-6999. Also Roy's Kihei Bar & Grill at Pi'ilani Shopping Village, 303 Pi'ikea Avenue; 808-891-1120.

Hours: 5:30-10 p.m. *Sampling:* Roy's offers a menu that changes nightly, which means you'll have the freshest foods available. Appetizers ($8-$13) might include Roy's original blackened rare ahi, seared shrimp on a stick with spicy wasabi cocktail sauce, or Hawai'i Kai–style crispy crab cakes. With an ever-changing menu, Roy's offers you plenty to choose from with entrees ($16-$28) such as Japanese style *misoyaki* butterfish, jade pesto–steamed Hawaiian white fish, or "Yama Mama's" meatloaf served with crispy onion rings and natural mushroom gravy or honey-mustard beef short ribs served with scalloped potatoes, poi and *lomi lomi* tomatoes. *Comments:* The trend these days is comfort food and Roy has certainly combined some of his talents to create comfort foods that are exciting and interesting. The food is as good as you've heard and Roy's is certainly deserving of its many rave reviews and dozens of national and local awards. Roy is one of the top chefs in the islands that have made Hawaiian Regional cuisine renown. Unfortunately, the noise from the kitchen combined with the high ceilings make it difficult to carry on a conversation. (But, hey—with its consistently good cuisine, it's worth it to just "shut up and eat" and keep an eye out for celebrity diners who might drop by.) Roy's Nicolina restaurant is connected next door.

★ **Roy's Nicolina** *(Hawaiian Regional)*
Kahana Gateway, 4405 Honoapi'ilani Highway; 808-669-5000.
   Hours: 5:30-9:30 p.m. *Sampling:* The menu changes nightly so it is always interesting. You might find appetizers like curried butternut squash soup, wok-seared ahi *poke*, or duck confit salad ($6-$12), to be followed up with grilled meats and pastas including herb chicken and goat cheese ravioli, or creamy wild mushroom linguine. For seafood aficionados there is *kiawe*-grilled *opah*, *shichimi*-seared sea scallops or try one of Roy's Hawaiian-style "Mixed Plates" ($16-$29) if you can't decide. And of course, there is dessert. *Comments:* Named after Roy and Janne Yamaguchi's daughter, Nicole, Roy's Nicolina is located right next door to Roy's and has become just as popular in its own right. It's a bit quieter than Roy's but the same great food. Lanai seating affords diners a view of the West Maui Mountains (and an occasional rainbow or two).

★ **Spats Trattoria** *(Northern Italian)*
Hyatt Regency Maui Resort and Spa, 200 Nohea Kai Drive; 808-661-1234.
   Hours: 6-10 p.m. *Sampling:* A hearty assortment of traditional Italian dishes. Antipasti selections include Manila clams, grilled prawns with polenta, or gnocchi *con prosciutto* ($7.75-$12.75). *Zuppe e insalate* offers a Tuscan salad with warm goat cheese or a classic minestrone soup ($6.25-$9.75). *Pesce* and *carne* selections range from veal marsala or piccata to scampi *con pancetta* and pan-seared local snapper. Pasta selections offer linguine *con frutta di mare*, penne *con funghi* (roasted chicken with mushrooms and a marsala sauce) or fettuccine carbona ($17.50-$32.50). Tiramisu, amaretto cheesecake, ganache or choco-

late silk torte may be among the evening selections for dessert ($6-$7). *Comments:* The atmosphere is comfortable and homey, yet very classy a la a parlor or drawing room of an old Italian mansion. Brass candelabras, sleek wood, beveled-glass partitions, and plush booths add to the distinctive ambiance. Focaccia, topped with cheese and herbs, arrives with a side of fresh pesto along with olive oil, balsamic vinegar, and herbs for dipping. Kids' menu available.

★ **Swan Court** *(Island Continental)*
Hyatt Regency Maui Resort and Spa, 200 Nohea Kai Drive; 808-661-1234.

Hours: Breakfast buffet 6:30-11:30 a.m., Sunday until noon. Dinner 6-10 p.m. *Sampling:* Breakfast buffet ($20.95, $10.95 children 5-12). Continental buffet includes fruits, pastries, cereal, plus juice, coffee or tea ($13.95 adults, $7.95 kids). Also breakfast a la carte. Their menu changes every month, but here is a sample of what you might enjoy. Dinner appetizers include lobster, crab and shrimp spring roll, seared forest mushroom potsticker or guava-painted baby back ribs ($8-$15). Featured entrees are Maui sugar cane–skewered ahi with tempura sushi roll and Asian greens, lemongrass chicken with *pancit* noodles, hibachi pork tenderloin with Moloka'i sweet potato or a vegetarian sampler with exotic mushrooms, truffled asparagus and almond-crusted tofu ($30-$36). They have plenty of tempting desserts so save room. *Comments:* A pond of graceful swans, cascading waterfalls and a landscape of oriental gardens create the atmosphere; view of the Swan Court. The ambiance alone is well worth the splurge for breakfast, a "best bet" for a daily breakfast buffet. The dinners are excellent and many unusual preparations are offered. Reservations are recommended.

Teppan Yaki Dan *(Japanese/Teppanyaki)*
Sheraton Maui, 2605 Ka'anapali Parkway; 808-661-0031.

Hours: 6-9 p.m. Closed Sunday and Monday. *Sampling:* Oriental duck salad and oyster Dan appetizer (fresh oysters seared with white wine and lemon juice on a bed of spinach leaves with chili pepper wasabi) ($5-$10) accompany entrees, which include shrimp with pineapple, lobster *batayaki* (chunks of lobster rolled in seasoned tempura flour), NY steak or hibachi teriyaki salmon ($22-$42). Finish up with a Polynesian coconut cream–filled donut or Grandma's hot apple pie. Seasonally they may offer an early-bird special at the first seating.

★ **The Terrace** *(Pacific Rim)*
The Ritz-Carlton, 1 Ritz Carlton Drive, Kapalua; 808-669-6200.

Hours: Breakfast 6:30-11:30 a.m. Dinner 5:30-10 p.m. *Sampling:* The Plantation Breakfast Buffet offers a great selection of freshly squeezed juices or fresh fruit, buttermilk waffles, French toast or pancakes, plus hot entrees such as eggs Benedict, Portuguese sausage or breakfast meats, and even Japanese breakfast selections ($24). A la carte breakfast entrees ($8-$18). *Comments:* Overlooking the courtyard and pool area with great sunset views. The pleasant, informal atmosphere is enhanced by an extended patio with awning that makes it look like a conservatory or the garden room of an elegant stately home.

tropica *(Pacific Rim)*
Westin Maui, 2365 Kaʻanapali Parkway, Kaʻanapali; 808-667-2525.

Hours: Sunday brunch 9:30 a.m.-1 p.m. Dinner daily until 9 p.m. Late-night snacks and drinks until midnight. *Sampling:* A fun and spicy menu. For starters you have volcanic crab and rock shrimp cake, *kalua* pork quesadilla, and tangled coconut prawns, to name only a few ($7-$14). Their icy-fresh island fish is served a number of ways including baked in a ti leaf with crabmeat stuffing. Chef's specialties include volcanic pepper prime rib, roasted salmon, crusted lamb and a tantalizing selection of sizzling flame-grilled steaks ($18-$38). The Sunday champagne brunch ($32.95 adults, $16 children 4-12, free children under 4) includes a Keiki Corner with cereals, milk and cookies and even chicken nuggets and french fries. Also Japanese specialties as well as fire-inspired seafood selections such as house-smoked peppered salmon, smoked mussels and spiced shrimp. Local favorites and classic brunch selections offer omelets made to order, fiery eggs Benedict, ahi *poke*, oriental chicken salad, or enjoy their wok-fired Thai snapper with tofu, beef sirloin with shiitake mushrooms and herbs, rotisserie-roasted chicken or their volcanic crusted lamb. Grand finales include warm chocolate and banana bread pudding, mango-lime pie or island cheesecake. If you leave hungry it will be your own fault. *Comments:* Dine outside, just off the beach, between the waterfalls, or inside a soaring space with glowing towers amid an array of vivid, fiery colors and textures. The restaurant and bar seats 200 guests and boasts a "hip island dining experience." This is certainly one of the "hottest" nightspots in Kaʻanapali, with ponds, wildlife, karaoke in the Lava lounge, and live nightly entertainment.

Maʻalaea-Kihei-Wailea-Makena Area

Inexpensive-priced Dining

Alexander's Fish, Chicken and Chips *(American)*
1913 South Kihei Road, Kihei; 808-874-0788; www.alexandersfishandchips.com.

Hours: 11 a.m.-9 p.m. *Sampling:* Meals ($7.25-$9.70) include shrimp, mahi, *ono*, ahi, calamari, ribs and chicken. Or go with a combo meal ($7.45-$9.75). A la carte items include onion rings, hushpuppies, zucchini, rice or barbecue beans. Just want a snack? Then get chicken, mahi, *ono*, ahi, ribs and clams by the piece. Sandwiches of fish, chicken or shrimp ($6.50-$7.75). *Comments:* I feel the food can be inconsistent. Sometimes good, sometimes mediocre, although this remains my friend Jody's favorite restaurant on Maui. They have limited seating at the counter or at a few patio tables.

★ **Annie's Deli & Catering** *(American)*
Nani Kai Village, 2511 South Kihei Road, Kihei; 808-875-8647.

Hours: 8 a.m.-4 p.m. *Sampling:* Breakfast featuring pancakes, French toast, lox and bagel, fresh fruit plate, breakfast croissant ($3.95-$6.59). Annie's Aloha Breakfast (2 eggs with toast, taters or rice, ham, sausage, bacon or cheese, and iced tea or coffee; $5.99). Sandwiches with choice of bread and cheese. Then select a side salad (potato, pasta, bean, or red slaw) to accompany your selection of turkey, ham, tuna, chicken salad, roast beef, French dip, Reuben, pastrami, corned beef, veggie or BLT with avocado, and pita melts ($4.95-$6.49). Daily specials (with entree, rice and salad). Smoothies and shakes, too. *Comments:* Small café with indoor and outdoor seating. Across from Kama'ole Beach II.

★ **Aroma D'italia Ristorante** *(Italian)*
Kihei Town Center, 1881 South Kihei Road, Kihei, next to Foodland; 808-879-0133.

Hours: Monday-Saturday 5-9 p.m. Closed Sunday. *Sampling:* Antipasto and salads ($4.95-$8.95). Spaghetti with meat or meatless sauce, spinach lasagna with homemade Italian sausage, chicken parmigiana, grilled marinated shrimp, eggplant parmigiana, veal marsala, piccata or parmigiana ($8-$18). For dessert try a spumoni wedge, gelato truffle turtle, freshly made cannoli, or "Tira Mesu" ($5-$6). *Keiki* menu. Wine list, too. *Comments:* Owner Marie Akina began with a small restaurant and expanded to this location a couple of years ago, but she hasn't gotten too big. This means you'll enjoy a casual, homey atmosphere with some of the best food and most affordable prices to be found for Italian dining anywhere on the island. Dishes are made from scratch using family recipes. Ample portions, flavorful sauces. Save room for their wonderful spumoni wedge. Layers and layers of cake and ice cream that I couldn't resist. We were all too stuffed to have dessert, but Marie put it on the table and it was gone. It's a charming, old-fashioned homestyle restaurant that has a lot of aloha—even if it *is* Italian.

Bocalino Bistro & Bar *(Mediterranean)*
Azeka Place Mauka, 1279 South Kihei Road, Kihei; 808-874-9299; www.bocalino.com.

Hours: 4 p.m.-1:30 a.m. Happy hour 4-6 p.m. Closed Sunday. *Sampling:* A lengthy *pupu* menu and plenty of appetizers and salads

($6.50-$12.95). Italian-style entrees include farfalle mamarosa, pork loin, linguini primavera or nettuna, chicken saltimbocca, chicken vodka with a tomato cream sauce ($13.95-$21.95). *Comments:* Entertainment 10 p.m.-1 a.m. No cover charge. Didn't get a chance to dine here yet, but have heard good things from friends about the food.

Café Kiowai *(Island)*
Maui Prince Hotel, 5400 Makena Alanui, Makena; 808-874-1111.

Hours: Breakfast 6-11 a.m. (breakfast buffet 6 a.m.-10:30 a.m.). Lunch 11 a.m.-3 p.m. *Sampling:* Hot breakfast buffet ($18.75) or a continental buffet ($13.95) are available as well as breakfast entrees ($10-$16.75) such as Prince corned beef hash with poached eggs, Portuguese sweet bread French toast or smoked salmon on toasted bagel. Begin your luncheon journey with *kalua* pork and Maui onion quesadilla, Thai crab summer rolls or Kula onion rings ($5.50-$9). From the garden enjoy Chinese chicken salad, Dungeness crab Caesar salad or five-pepper spice ahi salad ($6-$12). Main choices include Pulehu teriyaki short ribs, café saimin noodles, Molokini club sandwich or Hawaiian taro burger ($9.50-$14). *Comments:* Kiowai means "fresh flowing water." A casual, open patio atmosphere. The passion fruit iced tea is a wonderful accompaniment. *Keiki* menu available.

Café Kula *(Light Meals)*
Grand Wailea Resort Hotel & Spa, 3850 Wailea Alanui, Wailea; 808-875-1234.

Hours: Early-bird breakfast 6-7 a.m. (with coffees and bakery items); breakfast 7 a.m.-11 p.m. (a limited hot and cold menu). Hot sandwich selection 11:30 a.m.-2 p.m.; cold sandwiches and salads 11:30 a.m.-6 p.m. *Sampling:* Breakfast a la carte entrees include Portuguese sausage burrito, macadamia nut waffles or housemade granola with skim milk and dried fruit ($3.50-$7.50). Hot sandwiches offered are a lemon curry broiled chicken breast or Kula hamburger and cold sandwiches. Salad selections range from Kula pasta salad or chilled grilled ahi fillet to a New York peppered pastrami with smoked gouda ($6.95-$12.95). *Comments:* Open patio setting above flowering gardens with a panoramic view of the ocean. Fresh and healthy fast food. Kids' menu for breakfast includes cereal and lunch offers hot dogs, burgers, grilled cheese and of course PB&J ($3-$6.50). A good value for resort dining.

Da Kitchen Express *(Local)*
Rainbow Mall, 2439 South Kihei Road, Kihei; 808-875-7782.

Hours: 9 a.m.-9 p.m. *Sampling:* Breakfast served 9-11 a.m. includes *loco moco*, Maui-style French toast, or omelets ($5.25-$6.25). Plate lunches include two scoops of rice and mac salad with entrees of hamburger steak, lemon chicken, fish tempura or a *laulau* or Hawaiian plate ($5.25-$8.50), and oodles of noodles ($3-$5.75). Sandwiches or salads, local style ($4.85-$5.89). *Comments:* Good value, large portions, good grinds.

Deano's Maui Pizza Café *(Italian)*
Rainbow Mall, 2439 South Kihei Road, Kihei; 808-891-2200.
   Hours: 11:30 a.m.-8:45 p.m. Light later-night fare 8:45-10 p.m. *Sampling:* For appetizers enjoy *kalua* potstickers, seafood cocktail or crabby boboli ($6.95-$9.95). From the main course choose from plenty of interesting pizzas. There is Popeye pesto, local boy (with *kalua* pig), or goat cheese and roasted peppers ($12.50-$15.95). Pasta selections include fusilli Lana'i (corkscrew pasta with veggies), Thai chicken linguini, creamy garlic fettuccine or shrimp scampi ($12-$19). They also offer a selection of sandwiches in small or large sizes. *Comments:* Most of the dishes are available in small portions, great for the light dinner or for a lunch entree, as well as larger servings. Very attractively furnished and more a restaurant than a pizza parlor or café. Live entertainment Wednesday and Friday nights.

Fernando's *(Mexican)*
Lipoa Shopping Center, 41 East Lipoa Street, Kihei; 808-879-9972.
   Hours: Monday-Saturday 10:30 a.m.-9 p.m. Sunday 10:30 a.m.-7 p.m. *Sampling:* Combination plates ($5.75-$6.99) or hard and soft-shell tacos, burritos, enchiladas, tortas and quesadillas ($2-$6.75). *Comments:* Didn't try it but the food coming out to folks looked good.

Hanafuda Saimin *(Local/Asian)*
Azeka Place Mauka, 1279 South Kihei Road, Kihei; 808-879-9033.
   Hours: Monday-Thursday 6 a.m.-9 p.m. Friday-Saturday 6 a.m. to 3 a.m. *Sampling:* Breakfast meats and egg dishes served all day. Plate lunches include fried saimin with teri beef, roast pork, teri burger, curry or beef stew, chicken *katsu*, *kalbi* and *loco moco* ($3.75-$9). Sandwiches ($2.75-$3.75). Create your own saimin or chow fun by adding a variety of ingredients like *char siu* pork, sprouts, *kim chee*, or *won bok* ($4.95-$6.95). *Comments:* In the tradition of saimin houses, they are open until 3 a.m. on the weekends so you have someplace to go aftah da movie, da show or even aftah da midnight snack.

Hawaiian Moons Salad Bar & Deli *(Healthy/Vegetarian)*
2411 South Kihei Road, Kihei; 808-875-4356.
   Hours: 11 a.m.-7 p.m. Friday-Saturday until 9 p.m. Store open 8 a.m.-9 p.m.; Sunday until 6 p.m. *Sampling:* Salad bar offers organic greens and veggies plus rice and pasta salads all priced per pound. Hot entree selections include Third World macaroni and cheese, tofu enchi-

ladas, African black-eyed peas, *ulu* stew, and curried potatoes, also per pound. Lasagna, homemade soup, and free-range turkey, turkey Reuben, and roasted veggie sandwiches are available. *Comments:* The Hawaiian Moons Natural Food Store offers vitamins, herbs, and natural grocery items like fresh organic produce. The juice bar also serves espresso, smoothies, soft serve, and fruit cups.

★ **Hirohachi** *(Japanese)*
Kihei Town Center, 1881 South Kihei Road, Kihei; 808-875-7474.

Hours: Lunch Wednesday-Friday noon-2 p.m. Dinner 5:30-10:15 p.m. *Sampling:* Lunches include chicken *katsu*, soba and udon noodles, or tempura *teishoku* ($9-$17). "Roll" into dinner with a Bamboo Roll, Banzai Roll, California Roll or Rock'n Roll sushi combination ($6-$15). Sushi dinner combination ($23-$28.50) or dinner dishes such as *una don*, *ten don*, tempura *zen* (seafood with vegetables) or chicken *katsu zen* ($15-$20), or noodle dishes ($15.50). *Comments:* A large selection of sushi and sashimi. I stopped in for lunch and was *very* impressed. A cute local restaurant.

Home Maid Bakery & Deli *(Bakery)*
Azeka Place Makai, 1280 South Kihei Road, Kihei; 808-874-6035.

Hours: 6:30 a.m.-6:30 p.m. *Sampling:* Sandwiches, soups, turkey, lasagna and local plates mostly under $5. *Comments:* Wonderful *empanadas*, *manju* and bread pudding. (Original bakery is in Wailuku.)

Jawz Fish Tacos *(Mexican)*
Azeka Place Mauka, 1279 South Kihei Road, Kihei; 808-874-8226.

Hours: 11 a.m.-9 p.m. *Sampling:* The menu is basically $4-$9 and mahimahi or *ono* are the fish selections, shrimp, chicken and steak fill your taco, taco salad, burritos or kabobs. *Comments:* Opened in summer 2003, you'll recognize the menu and crew from the "Taco Van" that has been down at Makena Beach for years. *Keiki* menu, too.

Kaiona Café *(Gourmet Deli)*
Kihei Kalama Village, 1913-D South Kihei Road, Kihei; 808-891-2828.

Hours: 6 a.m.-8 p.m. *Sampling:* French toast, omelets, ratatouille, crepes and a variety of eggs Benedict ($4.75-$6.25). Deli sandwiches (grilled shrimp, salmon and spinach, roast beef with broccoli, crab meat and tropical fruit), paninis and fresh organic salads ($5.95-6.50). Gourmet desserts range from crepes to creme brulee along with gourmet cakes and cream puffs. *Comments:* Kaiona means "ocean fragrance," but Kaiona Café means yummy bakery aromas. Everything is baked fresh daily and is good to go or enjoy on the patio. Cream puffs are filled to order and they make their own crepes. Order your sandwich on freshly baked European bread or in a wrap. Picnics, coffee drinks and fresh pastries to go. They also sell their own blend of packaged gourmet coffee.

★ **Kihei Caffe** *(Continental)*
1945 South Kihei Road, Kihei; 808-879-2230.

Hours: Breakfast 5 a.m.-1:30 p.m. Lunch 11 a.m.-3 p.m. Dinner 5:30-8:30 p.m. *Sampling:* Breakfast includes huevos rancheros, biscuits and gravy, veggie scramble, French toast, flavored pancakes, Mueslix and omelets ($4.95-6.95). Burgers, and sandwiches ranging from grilled Reubens and Rachels to pastrami, roast beef, turkey and tuna ($6.95). Caesar, grilled chicken or fish, and honey cashew chicken salads ($6.50). *Comments:* A popular local hang-out that visitors have discovered as well. Coffee drinks plus fresh baked goods made daily. Picnic baskets with sandwiches, drinks, chips, fruit and cookies from $9. Really yummy breakfasts—not a steal, but a good value. Plan on a bit of a wait as there seems to be plenty of early-to-rise locals and jet-lagged visitors who take advantage of the 5 a.m. opening. The French toast (made with Portuguese sweet bread) was light and fluffy. Huevos rancheros were wonderful, as were the omelets. Heading out to the beach or on a road trip? Pick up a sandwich or roast chicken "Island Picnic Basket" to go ($9-$12). But don't overlook their expanding dinner menu. Inexpensive prices and food prepared by the talented owner Barry Allison. I appreciate their *keiki* breakfast and lunch menu with nothing over $2.75.

Life's a Beach *(American/Mexican)*
Kihei Kalama Village, 1913 South Kihei Road, Kihei; 808-891-8010.

Hours: 11 a.m.-10 p.m. Bar & selected *pupu* menu until 2 a.m. *Sampling:* Salads, burrito, soft tacos, burgers, hot dogs, nachos, quesadillas and sandwiches ($6.95-$9.95). *Comments:* There's real sand at the front entrance with tall tables and beach umbrellas for outdoor seating. Inside there's a wraparound bar with several TVs, lots of surfing and sports mementos, and bright yellow-and-white-striped tablecloths. Live entertainment on weekends along with karaoke. Mucho cheapo margaritas and mai tais. More bar than restaurant.

Makena Clubhouse *(American)*
5415 Makena Alanui, at the golf course, beyond Wailea and just past the Maui Prince Hotel, Makena; 808-879-1154.

Hours: Lunch 10:30 a.m.-4 p.m. *Pupus* and beverages 4-6 p.m. *Sampling:* Garlic french fries smothered in cheddar and pepper Jack cheese and served with dipping sauce, Thai summer rolls or ahi sashimi ($6-$11.75). Salads include bay shrimp and chicken Cobb or grilled ginger beef. Sandwiches run the board from hamburgers to pastrami Reuben or Maui cheesesteak ($6.75-$12.75). *Comments:* This open-air restaurant features an outstanding golf course view and one of the few ocean views where you can see Pu'u Ola'i (the rounded hill at the end of the island) up close.

Maui Onion *(American)*
Renaissance Wailea Beach Resort, 3550 Wailea Alanui, Wailea (poolside); 808-879-4900.

Hours: 11 a.m.-6 p.m. *Sampling:* Start with Maui onion rings or Maui onion soup ($6-$7). Salads ($10-$13.50) include tropical fruit boat with macadamia nut bread or traditional Cobb. Sandwiches ($8-$13) range from classic Reuben to vegetarian with portobellos, eggplant and avocado, or their hearty half-pound Black Angus burger with cheese. Daily lunch specials. Ice cream treats, too! Smoothies, tropicals, beer and wine by the glass. *Comments:* The onion rings have long been a huge hit and some say these are Maui's best burgers.

Maui Thai Kitchen *(Thai)*
Rainbow Mall, 2439 South Kihei Road, Kihei; 808-874-5605.

Hours: Lunch Monday-Saturday 11 a.m.-2 p.m. Dinner nightly from 5 p.m. *Sampling:* Thai crisp noodles, Thai toast, green papaya salad, long rice chicken soup, and chicken, beef, pork or shrimp served with Thai oyster sauce, Thai basil sauce, Thai ginger and more. Sample crab with yellow curry or sauteed mussels with chile sauce ($6.95-$13.95). Combination dinners ($35.95-$61.95). *Comments:* A very lengthy menu ranging from noodle dishes to salads, seafoods, vegetarian fare, and curry dishes. Chef's suggestions offer combinations for 2, 3 or 4 people. Entrees available in mild, medium or hot. Attractive eatery with white tablecloths tucked in the back of the mall.

Panda Express *(Mandarin Chinese)*
Azeka Place Mauka, 1279 South Kihei Road, Kihei; 808-879-0883.

Hours: 10:30 a.m.-9 p.m. *Sampling:* Combination plates with your choice of entrees. *Comments:* A chain of restaurants started in California.

Peggy Sue's *(Diner)*
Azeka Place Mauka, 1279 South Kihei Road, Kihei; 808-875-8944.

Hours: 11 a.m.-10 p.m. *Sampling:* The menu reflects the '50s diner/malt shop theme with sandwiches, burgers and hot dogs served with "the works" and a side of fries. Go for a Good Golly Miss Molly (teriyaki burger with pineapple), Earth Angel (garden burger) or Blue Moon (bacon and blue cheese) ($7.75-$9.25). Try a Sea Cruise (tuna), Splish Splash (mahi) or Funky Chicken sandwich ($8.25-$9.25). Plate lunches range from chili and rice to NY strip steak ($4.25-$12.95). *Comments:* They feature an original 1954 Seeburg jukebox that operates from the box or by remote from the dining table. The pink-and-blue decor gives the malt shop a suitable "Peggy Sue" look and the waitstaff is dressed to match. There are plenty of cool, creamy selections including malts, milkshakes, egg creams, phosphates, sundaes and banana splits to keep the '50s tradition alive in the new millennium. I thought they did a better job with the chicken dishes and sandwiches than with the burgers, and the french "fries" were oven baked, which took away from their, well, "authenticity" (too healthy?). Cute place—the atmosphere is fun and friendly, but the food wouldn't bring me back.

★ Pita Paradise *(Greek)*
Kihei Kalama Village, 1913 South Kihei Road, Kihei; 808-875-7679.

Hours: Lunch Monday-Saturday 11 a.m.-3 p.m. Dinner 5-9 p.m. *Sampling:* The pita sandwiches include lamb, veggie, Mediterranean chicken, steak and Kula onions, teriyaki chicken, chicken Caesar or fresh catch ($6.95-$11.95). Kabobs are served with grilled veggies and sautéed new potatoes ($12.95-$13.95). For dinner they have 5 pastas, from Australian range lamb to ultimate veggie or seafood pasta. Dinner prices slightly high but portions are bigger ($8.95-$18.95). Be sure to save room for the baklava ice cream cake. *Comments:* Following in his father's footsteps, John Arabatzis (son of Ioannis "Yanni" Arabatzizs of the Greek Bistro) and Christine Graham started this small, casual eatery. I loved the flavorful pita sandwiches. They serve wine and beer. Casual dining at patio tables on the deck or dine inside.

Royal Thai Cuisine *(Thai)*
Azeka Place Makai, 1280 South Kihei Road, Kihei; 808-874-0813.

Hours: Lunch Monday-Friday 11-3 p.m. Dinner nightly 5-9:30 p.m. *Sampling:* Traditional Thai appetizers, soups, salads plus entrees such as Evil Prince, lemon beef, Thai garlic or Thai ginger dishes ($6.95-$13.95). Complete dinners ($12.95-$13.95). *Comments:* The prices are pretty decent, but the portions are a little small. I prefer the Thai food down the road and across the street.

Seascape Ma'alaea Restaurant *(American)*
Maui Ocean Center, 192 Ma'alaea Road, Ma'alaea; 808-270-7043.

Hours: 11 a.m.-3 p.m. *Sampling: Pupus* include crisp onion rings, coconut shrimp with mango chutney or a pound of steamers ($6.75-$10.50). Pineapple fruit bowl and Chinese chicken salad are among the salad selections, or enjoy the "Local Boy Favorite," a sandwich filled with lobster salad and layers of shrimp with fresh dill aioli. Sautéed mahimahi or grilled ahi as well as a Cajun chicken sandwich ($12.50-$15.95). Entrees include clams and pasta, fish and chips, teriyaki platters or tofu chow mein ($12.50-$15.95). Finish it up with something sinfully sweet such as Chocolate Lovers Only, Strawberry Dream or Cookie Monster. Tropical drinks and wine and beer available. *Comments:* Open to the public without admission to the ocean center. Separate entrance on Lahaina side or up from the harbor. Overlooks the Ma'alaea Harbor with large viewing windows into the "Edge of the Reef" tank to watch the tropical fish and reef sharks.

★ **Senor Taco** *(Mexican)*
Dolphin Plaza, 2395 South Kihei Road, Kihei; 808-875-2901.
   Hours: 10 a.m.-9 p.m. Closed Sunday. *Sampling:* Tacos, enchiladas, tamales ($1.90-$2.25) or tostadas, quesadilla, chile relleno, taco salad, flautas, chimichangas, chilaquiles, *sopas*, nachos, burritos and *huevos* ($3.50-$6.50). Combination dishes run $6-$7. *Comments:* The usual beef and chicken varieties, with some surprises: mushroom quesadilla, potato chimichanga, or chorizo and egg burrito. Home-cooked "fast food" using authentic spices with many ingredients imported from Mexico. Small eatery with limited dining in front of the restaurant. Very good Mexican fare for your peso.

★ **Shaka Sandwich and Pizza** *(Sandwiches/Pizza)*
Paradise Plaza, 1295 South Kihei Road behind Jack-in-the-Box across from Star Market, Kihei; 808-874-0331.
   Hours: 10:30 a.m.-9 p.m. Friday-Saturday until 10 p.m. *Sampling:* Hot sandwiches in 7" (small) or 14" (large) sizes include chicken cheese steak, pizza steak, or supreme steak, as well as grilled turkey and cheese, grilled veggie, or homemade meatball and cheese (small $4.61-$5.81; large $9.22-$11.62). Assorted cold hoagies (small $4.85-$5.14; large $9.70-$10.28). Authentic NY-style pizzas are made with Shaka's homemade sauce and are available in thin crust or Sicilian thick crust. Choose their combos or make up your own ($13.97-$26.98). Also calzone and stromboli ($11.96-$14.93). *Comments:* If you like New York subway-style pizza you're in for a real treat. If you have no idea what New York subway-style pizza is, you're also in for a real treat! I've always been partial to their gourmet white cheese pizza with garlic and broccoli. They also have soft pretzels, Caesar salads, fresh-cut fries, homemade garlic bread, and cheesecake.

Smooth Moves *(Hawaiian/Local)*
2349 South Kihei Road, across from Kama'ole I, next to the ABC store, Kihei; 808-874-1221.
   Hours: Monday-Friday 6:30 a.m.-8 p.m. Saturday 8 a.m.-6 p.m. Sunday 9 a.m.-4 p.m. *Sampling:* Breakfast sandwich, omelets, egg dishes, *loco moco*, and "Spanish loco" ($3.50-$5.25). Fish sandwiches, hamburgers, chicken *katsu* or stir fry, teri beef and plate lunches

($6.95). Smoothies, shakes, shave ice and slushies ($2.75-$5.75). *Comments:* Daily lunch ($6.95) and dinner ($7.25) plates: Monday-Korean, Tuesday-Filipino, Wednesday-Chinese, Thursday-Whatevah!, Friday/Saturday-Hawaiian/Laulau.

Suda Snack Shop *(Local)*
61 South Kihei Road, by the gas station along South Kihei Road, Kihei; 808-879-2668.

Hours: 6 a.m.-12:30 p.m. Closed Sunday. *Sampling:* Burgers, hot dogs, bentos, saimin, chow fun (from $2.50). *Comments:* I was disappointed that this little "dive" really wasn't one of the island's best-kept secrets. The burgers were so-so, the french fries were pricey for the portion and the chow fun wasn't a meal, it was snack size. See you in Wailuku for better local grinds.

★ **Waterfront Deli** *(Deli)*
Shops at Wailea, inside the Whalers General Store, Wailea; 808-891-2039.

Hours: 7 a.m.-9 p.m. *Sampling:* Classic NY deli sandwiches or try a combination sandwich like Benny's Heaven with smoked turkey Jack cheese and hot peppers or an Empire State Monster with hot steamed corned beef, or roasted turkey breast and cheddar. From the grill there is a Maui taro burger, cheese dog, garden or chicken burger ($3.95-$9.95). Pizza available by the slice or whole ($2.95-$11). Salads, too. *Comments:* This is a nice addition to the Shops at Wailea and the surrounding hotels. A very nice deli and hearty sandwiches all reasonably priced. Some patio seating.

Young's Kitchen *(Korean/Local)*
1215 South Kihei Road, near Longs Drugs, Kihei; 808-874-8454.

Hours: 10 a.m.-9:30 p.m. *Sampling:* Same menu for lunch and dinner with slightly lower lunch prices. Plate-lunch special ($6.50) served until 2 p.m. House special $9.50. Meat dishes are barbecue Korean style, *katsu* (flake battered/deep fried) or teriyaki. Also seafood, vegetarian, stews, noodles and soups, and mixed plates ($5.95-$11.95). Or be adventurous and try *bi bim bap* or *pam bulgogi* cooked at your table for two. *Comments:* Private booths and attractive lace ruffles on the tables. Owner is Young Shishido.

Moderate-priced Dining

Antonio's *(Italian)*
Longs Center, 1215 South Kihei Road, Kihei; 808-875-8800.

Hours: Tuesday-Sunday 5-9 p.m. *Sampling:* Antipasti choices include homemade soup, sautéed calamari, and mozzarella, tomato and eggplant salad ($5.75-$7.95). Pasta with seafood, meatballs, smoked salmon or vegetarian style ($9.95-$16.95), or *rissotta* ($16.95-$17.55) and osso buco ($23.95). *Comments:* You'll enter a little piece of Antonio's homeland when you walk through the door. Decor is simple, with bright checkered tablecloths and some amusing memorabilia along the walls. And Antonio makes his own bread (baked on the premises) and a to-die-for tiramisu. The food is excellent (the fourth-generation recipes are all made from scratch) and Antonio's enthusiasm for cooking and sharing his food really shines through. (Eating a great tiramisu still makes his knees shake, but don't tell his mama that he has created some Sicilian recipes besides hers!)

Blue Marlin Harborfront Grill & Bar *(Seafood)*
Harbor Shops at Ma'alaea, 300 Ma'alaea Road #220 (harborfront, lower level), Ma'alaea; 808-244-8844.

Hours: 10 a.m.-10 p.m. *Sampling:* A la carte items include crab and shrimp–stuffed mushrooms, fish and chips, summer rolls and ahi *poke* ($6-$13) and sandwiches ($7-$10). Entrees include seafood platter, plenty of fresh fish selections, and "real food" like pork ribs, roast chicken, burgers ($11.95-$18.95). But there is still plenty of worldly fare on the menu like veggie focaccia sandwich and saimin. *Comments:* This is a very cute eatery—it looks like you're outside when you're in! Or sit at one of the tables on the boardwalk and really be outside if you choose. This could be another great reason to dine in Ma'alaea.

Buzz's Wharf *(American/Seafood)*
Harbor Shops at Ma'alaea, 300 Ma'alaea Road, Ma'alaea; 808-244-5426.

Hours: Lunch 11 a.m.-3 p.m. Dinner 5-9 p.m. *Sampling:* All-day *pupu* menu ($7.95-$12.95). Lunches offer fresh-catch sandwich, fish and chips, burgers or lunch entrees ($6.95-$15.95). Dinners range from Buzz's special prawns Tahitian to coconut milk shrimp curry, chicken marsala or prime rib ($17.95-$26.95). Entrees are served with salad, vegetables and fresh baked rolls. *Comments:* Offers a scenic view of the Ma'alaea Harbor activities. Bar/lounge. Vegetarian entrees and a full-page *keiki* menu. The food isn't as good as it used to be, in my opinion. The award-winning prawns Tahitian are more shrimp than prawn size.

★ **Caffe Ciao** *(Italian)*
Fairmont Kea Lani Hotel, 4100 Wailea Alanui, Wailea; 808-875-4100.

Hours: Deli 6:30 a.m.-10 p.m. Restaurant 11 a.m.-10 p.m. *Sampling:* Full bakery and deli serves coffee drinks, salads, sandwiches, homemade sausages, antipasto items, Italian gelatos, breads, pastries and desserts. Salads, minestrone or gazpacho, homemade linguine or angel-hair, panini, and fried calamari are on the lunch menu ($8-$20). All pizzas are baked in the outdoor brick oven, as are many of the lunch and dinner entrees. Pizzas are also available for dinner along with *bisteca* Toscana (grilled rib-eye with rosemary), lamb chops (with rosemary, mint and garlic) or *pollo all fiorentina* (roasted chicken breast with fresh artichoke, Maui onions, baby spinach and fontina cheese) ($26-$32). Accent your dinner with an assortment of "Gli Antipasti," "Le Zuppe" or "L'Insalate" ($10-$13). *Comments:* High ceilings, arches and stone inlays in this sleek black and gold deli that offers antipasti, focaccia sandwiches, gourmet condiments and food products—even fresh produce and an imported olive bar. While dining you can relax by reading one of a variety of complimentary international newspapers either indoors in the Art Deco ambiance or on the outside patio. They cure their own meats and produce their own private label of products to sell: macadamia blossom honey, Maui onion jelly, *poha* berry butter, pineapple mustard, and mango barbecue sauce. They also have full picnic and gift baskets and a variety of cheeses and other items imported from Italy. You can shop and eat at the same time—the best of both worlds!

Canton Chef *(Cantonese-Szechuan)*
Kama'ole Shopping Center, 2463 South Kihei Road, Kihei; 808-879-1988.

   Hours: Lunch 11 a.m.-1:30 p.m. Dinner 5-9 p.m. *Sampling:* Same menu for lunch and dinner. Choose from sizzling platters, chicken and duck dishes, earthen pot course, Szechuan selections, seafood, noodles or pre-set dinners. A la carte items $6 for hot and sour soup up to $37 for a Peking duck (advance notice required). Most items $7-$12 range. Combination dinners for two or four people are available ($13.75-$34).

★ **Greek Bistro** *(Greek/Mediterranean/Italian)*
Kai Nani Shopping Center, 2511 South Kihei Road, Kihei; 808-879-9330.

   Hours: 5-10 p.m. *Sampling:* From Greece sample moussaka, seafood souvlaki, sliced leg of lamb, or homemade spanakopita ($18-50-$25). From the Mediterranean regions selections include jumbo shrimp *santorini*, shish kabob (lamb and chicken), rack of lamb, Lebanese *oreganato* or fresh fish (but only when their boat "The Greek Bistro" catches one!) ($21-$25). Appetizers include traditional dolmathes, feta with kalamata olives, or bistro pita bread ($4-$9). *Comments:* Original owners are back at the helm and reported to me they are considering opening for lunch. They have, however, started some evening entertainment. Check out the belly dancing. Excellent Greek food and be sure also try out Pita Paradise at Kalama Village. Johnny's son runs that one.

Harry's Sushi and Pupu Bar *(Japanese)*
See Lobster Cove in "Expensive," below

★ **Hula Moons Restaurant** *(Contemporary Hawaiian-American)*
Wailea Marriott, an Outrigger Resort, 3700 Wailea Alanui, Wailea; 808-879-1922.

Hours: Breakfast 6-11 a.m. Dinner 5:30-10 p.m. *Sampling:* For breakfast try their Aloha Kahahiaka Buffet ($17.95 adults, $8.75 kids under 12) or order off the menu with a selection including fruit plate, French toast, or Ulupalakua steak and eggs ($9.95-$14.95). Dinners highlight seafood with grilled ahi and jumbo tiger shrimp, Hula's "Moonfish" (*opah*) served with a *laulau* of mahimahi, a seafood duo with mahimahi and *opakapaka* or sautéed jumbo shrimp. From the land enjoy grilled guava-glazed chicken breast, *lilikoi* lamb chops or braised barbecue short ribs ($19.95-$27.95). They also offer a Wednesday prime-rib and mahimahi buffet and a Friday-night seafood buffet. *Comments:* A lofty open-air dining room with plenty of ocean breezes. The bright tropical colors of the decor do not outshine the incredible ocean view, which every table seems to have. Bob Puccini, restaurateur and designer out of San Francisco, was the creative genius behind the restaurant and lounge. Hula Moons Restaurant has a great trendy, upbeat and fun look; the adjoining Mele Mele Lounge also has a bright colorful motif and allows an opportunity for a beautiful sunset or late-night relaxation and a *pupu* menu.

Isana *(Korean/Yakiniku/Sushi)*
Maui Beach Resort, 515 South Kihei Road, Kihei; 808-874-5700.

Hours: 11 a.m.-10 p.m. Sushi bar 5-10 p.m. *Sampling:* Select from their Korean barbecue offerings ($12.95-$17.50) or *kalbi* ribs, beef loin, chicken or seafood ($13.95-$21.95). *Kalbi tang*, oxtail soup or bean paste stew are some of the more exotic selections ($9.50-$15.50). Full sushi bar. *Comments:* Cocktails upstairs at the Karaoke Lounge.

★ **Kai Ku Ono Bar & Grill** *(Sandwiches and Pupus)*
Kai Nani Shopping Center, 2511 South Kihei Road, Kihei; 808-879-1954.

Hours: 8 a.m.-midnight. *Sampling:* Breakfast menu is one of the best Kihei/Wailea values. Half eggs Benedict, two-egg omelets, egg-white scramble with potato and bacon, French toast, and even Spam with eggs ($3.25-$6.25.) Lunchtime sandwiches include their yummy barbecue *kalua* pig sandwich, French dip or KKO "killa" burger with Maui onions, mushrooms, bacon, barbecue sauce and cheddar ($7.95-$14.95). Evening selections served 5-10 p.m. offer macadamia nut chicken, mango barbecue rib, peppered NY steak, fish and chips ($11.95-$18.95). Their seafood bar, available from 5 p.m., has a tantalizing array of the best from the sea: Thai grilled calamari, oysters on the half shell, spicy tuna roll, steams and even ceviche. Ahi selections available, too ($6.95-$12.95). There's also Ono Kai Sushi bar. Late-night menu selections available from 10-midnight includes burgers, fish and chips *pupu*, Greek, Kula or Caesar salad, vegetable spring rolls, assorted quesadillas and a chicken, fresh catch or Maui Taro burger sandwich ($5.25-$8.25). *Comments:* Kai Ku Ono means the "Good Bay" in Hawaiian, but they call it KKO for short. Breakfasts tend to be a little expensive on Maui, but KKO offers a great way to enjoy a good and affordable meal. Get a table that is oceanfront and enjoy some people watching and even a sunset. All around good fare and great prices. Good to have a late-night dining option in Kihei other than Denny's! Kids' menu (under age 12) only $4.95 for cheese quesadilla, grilled cheese, chicken dinosaurs or pasta. Live music 6-9 p.m.

Kumu Bar & Grill *(Pacific Rim)*
Wailea Marriott, an Outrigger Resort, 3700 Wailea Alanui, Wailea; 808-879-1922.
    Hours: Lunch 11 a.m.-5 p.m. Happy Hour 3-5 p.m. Dinner 5-9 p.m. Cocktails 11 a.m.-9 p.m. *Sampling:* Appetizers are a nice selection of Maui onion soup, shrimp cocktail, smoked, seared or traditional ahi, or *kalua* pork spring rolls ($4.95-$11.95). Dinners include combo specials with a house salad or Maui onion soup with fries and a burger, turkey BLT or grilled chicken sandwich for $14.95. Entree selections include miso garlic scampi, tofu stir-fry, barbecue baby back ribs or beer batter shrimp and fish ($13.95-$26.95). *Comments:* Hawaiian entertainment and hula from 6:30-9 p.m.

Lu Lu's *(Eclectic)*
Kihei Kalama Village, 1913 South Kihei Road, behind Bada Bing, Kihei; 808-879-9944.
    Hours: 11 a.m.-midnight, bar until 2 a.m. *Sampling:* Roast pork, meat loaf, steak, barbecue chicken, spare ribs or fresh catch ($13.95-$20.95). Burgers and sandwiches ($5.95-$9.95); spicy chicken wings, nachos, popcorn shrimp, quesadillas, island *poke*, crab cakes or steamers ($7.95-$10.95). *Comments:* An open, airy, upstairs "deck"' with a surprisingly great ocean view from this building in the rear of Kihei Kalama Village. Count up from 2 pool tables to 21 TVs, to 40 seats at the central bar. Bottle and draft beers. Fun, casual dining with live entertainment, and when the stage is not in use, it becomes a comfortable lounge area with leopard skin couches.

★ **Ma'alaea Grill** *(Hawaiian Regional)*
Harbor Shops at Ma'alaea, 300 Ma'alaea Road, Ma'alaea; 808-243-2206; www.maalaeagrill.com.
    Hours: Lunch 10:30 a.m.-3 p.m. Café menu 3-5 p.m. Dinner 5:30-9 p.m. *Sampling:* Lunch options include curry chicken, quinoa

or taro salads and sandwiches such as crab club, seared ahi sandwich, or entree such as creamy chicken fettuccini or tempura mahi and chips ($7.95-$9.95). Dinners offer appetizers such as Manoa lettuce wraps, tempura potato cakes or lemongrass chicken lumpia ($6.95-$11.95) and entrees range from rotisserie curry chicken to Thai coconut lobster with shrimp and calamari or *kiawe*-grilled NY steak ($14.95-$19.95). *Comments:* A great harborfront location. Owned and operated by chefs Dana and Michael Pastula, this is one of their five restaurants (and the largest). These folks have the Café O'Lei restaurants and give a great quality meal for a good price. Worth driving down for lunch or dinner from Wailea or Lahaina and a perfect stop after a trip to the aquarium or a boating excursion from the harbor. *Keiki* menu available ($2.95-$4.95).

Marco's Southside Grill *(Italian)*
1445 South Kihei Road, Kihei; 808-874-4041.

Hours: Breakfast Monday-Friday 7:30 a.m.-noon, Saturday/Sunday 7:30 a.m.-2 p.m. Lunch daily 10 a.m.-5 p.m. Dinner 7:30 a.m.-10 p.m. *Sampling:* Breakfast fare includes their special chocolate cinnamon French toast, create-your-own omelet, or flavored pancakes ($5.95-$14.95). Sandwiches and more sandwiches for lunch or dinner, from deli style to a huge selection of hot-off-the-grill choices: homemade Italian sausage, veggie burger, chicken parmigiano, tuna melt with tomatoes ($6.95-$11.95). Salads ($8.95-$10.95) include blue cheese, Oriental chicken, or stuffed tomato. For dinner appetizers enjoy mozzarella marinara, gnocchi, buffalo wings or bruschette ($5.95-$12.95); entrees such as cioppino, baked *opakapaka*, roasted chicken breast or clams and linguini, along with just about any other pasta dish you can imagine ($18.95-$28.95), with dinner salad an additional $3.95. For kids 12 and under they offer grilled cheese, pasta with marinara and chicken fingers ($7.95-$9.95). *Comments:* You won't miss Marco's. A white Mediterranean villa set along South Kihei Road looks a bit out of place. A wraparound patio lanai has seating along the Kihei Road side of the restaurant.

Margarita's Beach Cantina *(Mexican)*
Kealia Village, 101 North Kihei Road, Kihei; 808-879-5275.

Hours: 11 a.m.-10 p.m. Bar open until midnight. *Sampling:* Burgers, spicy fish sandwich, charboiled chicken sandwich, *ensaladas* are among the options, or choose seafood selections such as grilled mahi, fish tacos or seafood enchiladas. Specialties of the house range from sizzling fajitas to prime rib and lobster specials ($8.95-$19.95). *Comments:* Outdoor dining on their oceanview deck. Margaritas come in tropical flavors like mango, pineapple, guava, banana and coconut. Bar features satellite TV and electronic dart boards.

Mulligan's on the Blue *(American/Continental)*
100 Kaukahi Street, at the Wailea (Blue) Golf Course, Wailea; 808-874-1131; www.mulligansontheblue.com.

Hours: 8 a.m.-1:30 a.m. *Sampling:* Breakfasts include home fries or steamed rice and toast along with *loco moco,* an Irish breakfast (includes grilled tomato and baked beans), or steak and eggs ($7-$11). The lunch menu offers fish and chips, lamb stew, traditional shepherd's pie, Irish bangers and mash, a turkey jalapeno melt, and barbecue chicken and cheddar sandwich. Golfers can also pick up a quick fix: a ready-made cold sandwich ($5-$10). Dinner has many of the same lunch entrees but also a Guinness-marinated rack of lamb, corned beef and cabbage, roast pork chop or chicken curry ($11-$18). Their *keiki* menu for wee lads and lasses age 12 and under is $7.

Polo Beach Grille and Bar *(Island)*
Fairmont Kea Lani Hotel, 4100 Wailea Alanui, Wailea; 808-875-4100.

Hours: 11 a.m.-5 p.m. *Sampling:* Plenty of starters from crab cakes and potstickers to grilled and chilled shrimp cocktails ($8-$15). Salads offer a Chinese chicken salad, grilled Hawaiian fish Caesar or seared volcano spiced ahi ($11-$17). Garden burger, chicken breast sandwich or turkey croissant are available, or for a heartier appetite try their grilled chicken entree, NY steak or ahi tuna. *Comments:* A number of the items are highlighted as part of their lifestyle cuisine, which complements Fairmont's "Willow Stream" spas. The ingredients are unprocessed and naturally healthy and directed toward health and wellness. This café is situated amid the pools.

Spices *(Seafood/American)*
Maui Coast Hotel, 2259 South Kihei Road, Kihei; 808-874-6284.

Hours: Breakfast 7-11:30 a.m. Lunch 11:30 a.m.-2 p.m. Dinner 5-10 p.m. Tradewinds Poolside Café 5:30 p.m. with entertainment. *Sampling:* Breakfast omelets, crepes, island pancakes ($5.95-$10.95). Lunches include plenty of hearty soups and salads, house specials such as grilled fish taco or spicy wok vegetables and a selection of burgers and sandwiches ($6.95-$12.95). Dinners include roasted vegetable pasta, shrimp and chicken tortellini, peanut and miso chicken, or duck breast ($14.95-$24.95). Salads include strawberry, Athena, Kula house, and Zach's seafood salad ($8.25-$17.50). Fresh fish priced daily.

★ **Stella Blues Cafe & Deli** *(Eclectic)*
Azeka Place Mauka, 1279 South Kihei Road, Kihei; 808-874-3779.

Hours: Breakfast 7:30-11 a.m., Sunday until 2 p.m. Lunch to 5 p.m. Dinner 5-10 p.m. Late-night menu until midnight. *Sampling:* Egg dishes, French toast and flavored pancakes ($5.95-$8.95). Salads include Asian chicken, Kula green, Cobb, and several Caesars ($7.50-

$10.95). Homemade chicken chili and sandwiches such as chicken salad croissant, BLT, turkey, French dip, and fresh fish ($7.95-$10.95) and from Stella's grill there are burgers, pastrami or tuna melts, Reubens and quesadillas ($6.95-$9.95). Select for your dinner pasta, *kiawe*-oven pizza, fresh fish, jambalaya, miso shrimp, baby back ribs, or tofu red curry ($13.95-$18.95). *Comments:* Indoor dining space as well as patio seating and a sleek, curved bar. The modern decor is tailored with open-beamed ceilings and wood accents.

★ **Thailand Cuisine** *(Thai)*
Kukui Mall, 1819 South Kihei Road, Kihei; 808-875-0839.

Hours: Lunch Monday-Saturday 11 a.m.-2:30 p.m. Dinner nightly 5-10 p.m. *Sampling:* Noodles, curries or salads Thai style. Menu runs for lunch or dinner with the same prices. Pad Thai green curry, ginger coconut soup, pineapple fried rice ($8.95-$11.95). *Comments:* I tried the pad Thai and the pineapple fried rice for lunch. Both portions were very generous and the fried rice was attractively served in a scooped-out half-pineapple. Large dining facility and our hostess/waitress was garbed in authentic costume. Food was quickly prepared and came to the table steaming hot.

Tony Roma's *(American/Ribs)*
Kukui Mall, 1819 South Kihei Road, Kihei; 808-875-1104.

Hours: 11 a.m.-11 p.m., Friday-Saturday until midnight. *Sampling:* Ribs, ribs and more ribs. Beef ribs, pork ribs and, if you can't decide, the rib sampler ($15.99). Combo dinners ($13.99-$26) or chicken and seafood dishes ($9.99-$15.99). Caesar or Oriental chicken salads, potato skins, fried cheese, and chicken strips ($3.99-$7.99). *Comments:* Open 365 days a year. Lunch items until 4 p.m. All barbecue rib and grill entrees come with coleslaw and choice of baked potato, rice, french fries, or ranch beans. This chain is famous for its ribs, but shrimp and chicken dishes are just as good. *Keiki* menu available. Separate bar with a piano as a focal point.

Vietnamese Cuisine Restaurant & Bar *(Vietnamese)*
Azeka Place Makai, 1280 South Kihei Road, Kihei; 808-875-2088.

Hours: 11 a.m.-10 p.m. *Sampling:* Noodle specialties such as crispy egg noodle with seafood, rice plates, Vietnamese burritos (*banh hoi*), vermicelli noodles, and Chinese wok dishes filled with steamy vegetables and your choice of chicken, beef or seafood ($6.95-$10.95). *Comments:* The owner of this restaurant is the sister of Jennifer at A Saigon Café in Wailuku. It's all in the family!

Expensive-priced Dining

★ **Bistro Molokini** *(California Island)*
Grand Wailea Resort Hotel & Spa, 3850 Wailea Alanui, Wailea; 808-875-1234.
  Hours: 11:30 a.m.-9:30 p.m. *Sampling:* Enjoy bistro specialties, pastas and pizza from their *kiawe* wood-burning oven. Lunches include soups and salads as well as sandwiches and wraps such as *paniolo* burger, pizzas and bistro club ($8.50-$15). Evening entrees continue with pizza and salads with other entrees of penne pasta, braised chicken breast, oven-roasted filet mignon, or fresh catch ($22-$29). *Keiki* menu features spaghetti with tomato sauce, pizza, chicken fingers and burgers ($9.50). Smoothies, too. *Comments:* An open-air bistro overlooking the formal pool and the Pacific Ocean (pool service 11 a.m.-4:30 p.m.). Exhibition kitchen and wood-burning oven. Shorts and shoes are acceptable. The menu is light and innovative. Extensive wine list, beer, coffee drinks, tropicals, smoothies and Italian sodas.

★ **Capische?** *(Italian)*
Diamond Resort, 555 Kaukahi Street, Wailea; 808-879-2224.
  Hours: 6-10 p.m. summer, 5:30-10 p.m. winter. *Sampling:* Appetizers include lobster ravioli, sautéed calamari, portobello mushroom or antipasti selections ($10-$14), and soups and salads include roasted tomato soup or peppercress salad with pancetta, Asian pears and toasted almonds ($8-$12). Dinner selections include pasta and risotto dishes featuring Manila clams, shrimp or vegetables, or savory braised diver scallops, roasted rack of lamb with candied fig *jus*, quail saltimbocca or crispy Pacific snapper ($26-$34). *Comments:* Capische? has cozy dining environs on the hillside of Wailea with a panoramic view. The restaurant states that "Capische? captures the essence of Italian cooking with multi-regional influences." Chef Brian Etheredge has an innovative style and I've heard rave reviews about this restaurant. Lovely panoramic views from the lanai seating. Haven't had a chance to dine here, but based on reader feedback they earn a star!

Ferraro's *(Italian)*
Four Seasons Resort, 3900 Wailea Alanui, Wailea; 808-874-8000.
  Hours: Lunch 11:30 a.m.-4 p.m. Light lunch 4-6 p.m. Dinner 6-9 p.m. *Sampling:* For lunch enjoy a salmon and spinach burger, Maine lobster sandwich, chilled watercress vichyssoise soup or a turkey club sandwich along with an assortment of intriguing pizzas ($16-$20). Dinners might begin with an *insalata di campo* (mescalun greens with currant tomatoes), or fried calamari and jumbo shrimp in a spicy Calabrain chili sauce ($11-$16). For your first course there is slow-braised

lamb shank with toscanelle olives, angelhair pasta with pan-fried garlic, potato gnocchi or wood fire oven–baked wild mushroom cannelloni ($19-$39). For a main course there is fire-baked long tail red snapper on portobello mushrooms, grilled filet mignon with gorgonzola mashed potato or pan-seared swordfish with cannellini beans ($28-$42). And if you dare, there is lemon-lime sorbet or strawberries with mascarpone for dessert ($8). *Comments:* There is nothing to block the ocean view from this cliffside restaurant located right over the water. (Get there early and you'll be surrounded by the sunset!)

★ *Five Palms Beach Grill* (Pacific Rim)
Mana Kai Resort, 2960 South Kihei Road, Kihei; 808-879-2607.

Hours: Breakfast 8 a.m.-2:30 p.m. Dinner 5-9:30 p.m. *Sampling:* A very nice breakfast menu with prices 20-25 percent less than the resort dining rooms for an a la carte item. *Loco moco,* Portuguese omelet and, my personal favorite, plantation apple banana and cinnamon baked pancake with macadamia nut butter (although sometimes I do opt for the Hawaiian sweet bread French toast with grilled banana and crystallized sugar). Daily special features half-off on *pupus* from 3-6 p.m. in both the bar and open-air patio. *Pupu* menu includes baked artichoke, braised short ribs, lobster roll, calamari, spinach salad and seared ahi ($8-$12). For lunch enjoy a lobster BLT, Hawaiian-style Reuben (*kim chee* instead of cabbage), grilled chicken, hibachi ahi sandwich or a Caesar salad with chicken, calamari or shrimp ($6.95-$13.95). Sunset dinner specials are for 5 and 5:30 p.m. seatings only and are a prix-fixe meal started with a tossed green salad, a choice of macadamia-crusted mahi, prime rib or chicken, and *lilikoi* cheesecake for dessert ($19.95). Dinner specialties include star anise–scented braised short ribs, Szechuan glazed roast rack of lamb, porcini-dusted ahi steak, Hawaiian bouillabaisse or pan-seared salmon and baby spinach ($21.95-$32.95). *Keiki* menu offers French toast, buttered noodles, cheeseburger and fries or cheese pizza ($5.95-$8.95). *Comments:* Morning and afternoon meals are served out on the open-air patio, which is a lovely setting with views of Keawakapu Beach. Evenings dine inside, where you'll find rich wood and chandeliers, with booths in brown and cream-colored brocades that are accented by Hawaiian paintings. It has a very warm Hawaiian feeling. This is one of Kihei's nicest beachfront dining locations and the food is consistent and excellent.

★ *Grand Dining Room* (Breakfast)
Grand Wailea Resort Hotel & Spa, 3850 Wailea Alanui, Wailea; 808-875-1234.

Hours: Breakfast only 6:30-11 a.m. *Sampling:* Grand Breakfast Buffet ($22.50), continental buffet ($18). A la carte menu offers tropical fruits, a basket of pastries, omelets, eggs Benedict, banana mac-nut waffles, pancakes with berries, turkey or corned beef hash, homemade granola, Swiss Birchermuesli, sweet bread French toast, and a variety of breakfast meats ($5.50-$21). Grand Dining Room *keiki* breakfast includes the breakfast buffet ($11.25), and French toast, eggs or pancakes ($7). *Comments:* Great buffet and a lovely terraced seating area.

★ **Hakone** *(Japanese)*
Maui Prince Hotel, 5400 Makena Alanui, Makena; 808-874-1111.

Hours: Monday-night Japanese buffet 6-9 p.m. Tuesday through Saturday a la carte and sushi bar 6-9 p.m. *Sampling:* The Monday-evening buffet features more than two dozen specially prepared Japanese delicacies ($21 adults, $23 children) and is served buffet style. Dine on miso garlic chicken, breaded pork tenderloin, tuna sashimi, steamed crab, and a bountiful selection of sushi and salads. Dinners might begin with a steak and lobster roll or a cooked lobster salad ($8-$15). Their a la carte dinners offer mango mac teriyaki chicken, udon a la Moana or NY steak. Their *kaiseki* course dinner is available for the vegetarian ($38) or with steak and seafood ($58) and both run the gamut from appetizer to dessert. Their ice creams are freshly made and wonderful. Green tea (my favorite) or white chocolate ginger, azuki bean, or Tahitian vanilla. Or sample their green tea creme brulee with mango puree. Hot and cold *sake*, too. *Comments:* Authenticity is the key to this wonderful Japanese restaurant, from its construction (the wood, furnishings and even small nails were imported from Japan) to its food (the rice is flown in, as well). The food and atmosphere are both wonderful here and, of course, the presentation of the food is artistic. *Keiki* menu available. There is also a sushi bar but with only 11 seats, it is definitely on a first-come basis.

Hana Gion ★ *(Japanese)*
Renaissance Wailea Beach Resort, 3550 Wailea Alanui, Wailea; 808-879-4900.

Hours: 5-9:30 p.m. Teppanyaki reservations at 5:30 p.m., 7 p.m. and 8:30 p.m. *Sampling:* Teppanyaki dinners begin with a shrimp appetizer, pickled vegetables, miso soup and sautéed vegetables. Additional appetizers ($5-$12) include shrimp and vegetable tempura or aged dashi tofu. Adventure into entrees with a choice of scallops, teriyaki chicken, fresh island fish, tiger prawns, NY steak, steak and lobster, tofu steak, or a combination dinner ($24-$45). *Keiki* teppanyaki dinners are available for $9.95. Non-teppanyaki dinners are available as well. Hot and cold appetizers ($9-$18) or sushi and sashimi selections can precede your Japanese meal. Sukiyaki, salmon *shioyaki*, grilled cod, NY steak, or chicken teriyaki ($26-$30) are options, or choose the "Hana Gozan" ($37), which includes sashimi, shrimp and vegetable tempura, choice of beef or chicken teriyaki, "wafu" steak, and salmon. *Comments:* The decor is as authentic as its cuisine. Woodwork, screens, stone flooring, bamboo trim, and decorative artifacts were all produced in Japan to exacting standards. In fact, parts of the dining area were actually constructed in Japan before being dismantled for shipment to the Renaissance Wailea. Traditional Japanese fare emphasizes freshness, subtle flavors, and delicate preparations. The restaurant is designed to promote the feeling of privacy and intimacy. The main dining area has private dining rooms for 4-6 guests each. The sushi bar accommodates ten.

★ **Harlow's** *(American)*
Kai Nani Shopping Center, 2511 South Kihei Road, Kihei; 808-879-1954.

Hours: 5-10 p.m. Early-bird specials 5-6 p.m. *Sampling:* Appetizers include spicy garlic baked shrimp, smokey filet tidbits and lobster and crab cake ($10-$12). Entree "favorites" are served with vegetable, starch and rolls and include teriyaki grilled pork loin or braised brisket of beef. From the *makai* (the sea) section of the menu choose an entree such as Hawaiian seafood casserole, giant Thai scallops or *opakapaka* mac nut ($22-$36); from the *mauka* (the land) enjoy their famous prime rib, filet mignon, rack of lamb or surf and turf ($21-$37). *Comments:* Keiki menu, too. They also offer free shuttle service in South Maui. Second-floor location gives it a good ocean and sunset view. A long-time Kihei favorite.

★ **Humuhumunukunukua'pua'a** *(Island/Seafood)*
Grand Wailea Resort Hotel & Spa, 3850 Wailea Alanui, Wailea; 808-875-1234.

Hours: 5:30-9:30 p.m. *Sampling:* Starters include *kalua* pork potstickers, coconut prawns, or ahi lemongrass traps ($9-$16). Soup and salad choices ($8-$10) offer lobster tarragon soup or warm spinach salad. With a focus on foods from the sea you can enjoy seven spiced *hapu'upu'u* (island sea bass), seared fresh ahi, garlic and herb grilled prawns or lemongrass and ginger Hawaiian snapper. For the land lovers there is herb-roasted chicken breast, grilled NY sirloin or crispy duck breast ($22-$34). Humu specialties include a mixed grill plate, grilled spiny lobster with filet mignon ($39-$48, with lobster entrees priced by the pound). You can catch or choose your own lobster from the Humu Lobster Lagoon. Save room for your dining finale with warm chocolate lava cake, warm Hawaiian sweet bread pineapple cake or, if you can't decide, their *humu* sampler ($9-$13). *Comments:* If you're curious about the restaurant's name, it is the Hawai'i state fish, the trigger fish. Since the Hawaiian name is rather a mouthful, the eatery is affectionately and briefly referred to as Humuhumu. Tucked in the front grounds of the resort, it is situated on top of a saltwater pond filled with aquatic life. The huge saltwater tank that divides the bar area is worth stopping by to just admire. The restaurant floats on the lagoon and the thatched roof and bamboo railings inspire exotic Robinson Crusoe fantasies. They have a full-bar service and some wonderfully different tropical libations. (Skip the mai tai and try an exotic champagne cocktail!) Plus a nice *keiki* menu with meals at $9.50. Nightly entertainment 6-9 p.m.

Joe's *(Gourmet American)*
131 Wailea Ike Place, above the Wailea Tennis Club, Wailea; 808-875-7767.

Hours: 5:30-10 p.m. *Sampling:* Dinners start with Bev's famous crab dip, barbecue chicken quesadilla, ahi carpaccio, or assorted salads ($8-$14) and continue with an applewood-smoked bacon wrapped pork chop, Joe's favorite meatloaf with garlic mashed potatoes, black market ribs (stolen from the Hali'imaile General Store), grilled rack of lamb with rosemary demi glaze or farfalle pasta, jumbo stuffed prawns ($24-$38). *Comments:* From those folks who brought you Hali'imaile General Store, Joe and (Chef) Beverly Gannon. Bev's food is as good as it reads, but nothing is overly trendy. Joe's background as a Hollywood producer-director and lighting designer sets the tone with the shiny hardwood floors, 43-foot copper bar and individual geometric designs on the tables. The theater lighting is soft, yet strong enough to highlight the wall of show-biz memorabilia from Joe's days working with film, TV and music celebrities. All this and an ocean view, too!

★ Kea Lani Restaurant *(Breakfast)*
Fairmont Kea Lani Hotel, 4100 Wailea Alanui, Wailea; 808-875-4100.

Hours: Breakfast buffet and a la carte 6:30-11 a.m. *Sampling:* Continental breakfast buffet includes juice, pastries, and coffee or tea ($17), or my recommendation is to enjoy the works with their fabulous breakfast buffet ($23 adults, *keiki* discounts). Fresh seasonal and organic tropical fruits, smoked Scottish salmon, Japanese station, eggs Benedict, omelets made-to-order, pancakes, potatoes and rice, bacon and sausage, assorted hot and cold cereals. Cereals including granola and oatmeal with a choice of toppings—from walnuts to wheat germ, pumpkin seeds to pecans and pastries, muffins and nut breads. A la carte items include poached eggs with corned beef hash ($16.50), classic omelet ($17) or poached eggs with spicy papaya salsa and grilled ahi steak ($18). There is a bagel and bread station plus plenty of fresh fruits and yogurts along with hot breakfast entrees. *Comments:* Fairmont Kea Lani hosts "Grand Chefs on Tour," a weekend culinary experience pairing a "grand" chef from the mainland with a Hawaiian chef of equal prominence.

Kincha *(Japanese)*
Grand Wailea Resort Hotel & Spa, 3850 Wailea Alanui, Wailea;
808-875-1234.

Hours: Dinner only Saturday, Sunday, Monday 6-9 p.m. *Sampling:* Traditional Japanese cuisine with an American-style menu. Appetizers and salads ($3-$18) are followed by traditional main courses including a sashimi dinner, tempura dinner *sake* (broiled salmon) or *wafu* steak (grilled filet mignon ($25-$39) or try their *wakadori* (boneless breast of chicken with a light teriyaki sauce), *hotategai* (broiled sea scallops), *yaki kani* (broiled Alaskan king crab legs) ($28-$52) or the traditional dining experience of Japan *omakase* with multiple courses for $65. Desserts include an Asian pear crisp or try their tropical fruit sushi. Kincha's *keiki* menu offers the kids in your group teriyaki steak or chicken or tempura dinners ($9.50). Lots of fun *keiki* cocktails, too. They also have a sushi bar, which fills up fast, with sushi specialties along with the traditional sashimi and sushi selections. *Comments:* This tranquil Japanese restaurant was created from 350 tons of rock from Mount Fuji. The lush gardens and peaceful lagoons are an exquisite backdrop to contemporary Japanese cuisine.

★ **Le Gunji** *(French-style Teppanyaki)*
Diamond Resort, 555 Kaukahi Street, Wailea; 808-874-0500.

Hours: Dinner only with two seatings, 6 and 8 p.m. Closed Wednesday. *Sampling:* A gourmet teppanyaki restaurant offering set meals. The Diamond course is $70 and includes appetizer, soup, fresh catch, Hawaiian lobster, wine sherbet, steak, salad, rice, dessert and coffee; Mini-Diamond courses are the same except for the choice of either fish ($55) or lobster ($60). The Beef course ($50) substitutes a sirloin or tenderloin steak in place of the lobster and fresh catch. *Comments:* The prices may sound steep, but if you figure a dinner at most of the fine resorts in the mid-thirties and add appetizer, soup and dessert it will easily match this price. The dining room is small and intimate with a beautiful garden courtyard located behind where the chef cooks. This teppanyaki is a bit different in that it is cooked with a French flair, a style that was introduced to the restaurant by the original chef, Gunji Ito (from Osaka), who had previously cooked French cuisine. After the 6 p.m. seating diners can retire to a dessert room to relax and chat. Reservations required. Shorts and sandals not permitted.

Lobster Cove–Harry's Sushi Bar *(Seafood/Japanese)*
100 Wailea Ike Drive, Wailea; 808-879-7677.

Hours: Lobster Cove 5:30-10 p.m. Harry's Sushi Bar until midnight. *Sampling:* Begin your meal with seared island ahi, chardonnay garlic clams, sweet and sour crispy shrimp, or soft shell crab ($6.95-$11.95). Dinner salad, lobster salad, or a rock shrimp salad ($5-

$9.50) and sushi, of course. Selections of fresh island fish are priced daily with preparations such as poached in chardonnay sauce, sautéed Cajun barbecue, grilled miso marinade, or poached with lobster Creole sauce. Live Maine lobster, live Dungeness crab (no doubt the best type of crab in the world but then I'm an Oregonian!) or Alaskan king crab legs available by the pound. Entrees ($21.95-$44.50) offer filet mignon, lobster and shrimp, roast breast of chicken, seafood penne pasta, or spicy barbecue tiger prawns. Desserts ($6) include green tea ice cream, chocolate mousse, or coconut creme caramel. *Comments:* Harry's Sushi and Pupu Bar is at the entrance to Lobster Cove.

★ **Nick's Fishmarket Maui** *(Seafood)*
Fairmont Kea Lani Hotel, 4100 Wailea Alanui, Wailea; 808-875-4100.
    Hours: 5:30-10 p.m. *Sampling:* Begin your evening with a sampling of Alaskan crab, which comes with a spicy avocado remoulade, escargot, a carpaccio of yellowfin tuna with Alaskan King crab and wasabi aioli, Malaysian tiger shrimp or firecracker salmon roll ($10.95-$20). Ahi Nicoise or hand-picked baby greens can precede a selection from their interesting seafood menu. Roasted salmon with ahi *poke* pot stickers, potato "scaled" mahimahi with truffle potatoes, cabernet-pepper sauce and white truffle oil, seared Hawaiian swordfish with candied peanut crust or farmed baby abalone with crushed kukui nuts and buckwheat pasta. Those preferring "Not Seafood" can select from Mongolian-style rack of lamb, herb-roasted chicken with feta cheese stuffing, and quinoa salad or grilled beef filet ($27.95-$49.95). *Comments:* The fine-dining restaurant features 40-foot vaulted ceilings designed in a southern Mediterranean style and offers great ocean views. Shell-design lighting fixtures, fish-shaped chairs, wave-patterned mosaic tabletops, and an 800-gallon aquarium are all part of the blue and white aquatic theme. Private booths, indoor and outdoor seating, plus a glass mosaic bar for cocktails and *pupus. Keiki* menu features fresh island fish, barbecue beef, chicken or pasta along with dessert plus juice or milk for $13.95.

★ **Pacific Grill** *(American/Pacific Rim)*
Four Seasons Resort, 3900 Wailea Alanui, Wailea; 808-874-8000.
    Hours: Breakfast 6-11:30 a.m. (buffet 6:30-11 a.m., until noon on Sunday). Dinner 5:30-9:30 p.m. *Sampling:* The Wailea Buffet ($10.50) features fruits, cereals, assorted breads, and juices; the Full Island Buffet ($24.75) adds to that with French toast, pancakes, waffles, eggs and omelets along with breakfast meats and starches. A la carte breakfasts ($12.50-$18). Their egg-white omelet with baby spinach and grilled pita bread is one of their "alternative cuisine" selections and is so good you won't miss the fat or cholesterol. Dinners begin with Pacific Grill

spring rolls (rock shrimp, mango relish and chili garlic sauce), tempura tiger prawns, ahi *poke* with sevruga caviar or udon noodle soup ($10-$25). Dinners include a whole *moi* (fish) tempura with chow mein noodles, grilled swordfish with island vegetables, or from the rotisserie enjoy chicken with Yukon gold mashed potatoes or beef tenderloin with braised taro leaves and fingerling potatoes ($29-$49). On Friday nights they have a seafood buffet, but with a twist. Enjoy all the appetizers and salads you'd like and then choose your seafood entree. The seafood display includes oyster on the half shell, jumbo shrimp, marinated mussels, ahi and *tako poke* as well as crab claws. There are several *maki* sushi selections as well as salads like scallops, rock shrimp and pearl couscous or *togarashi*-crusted seared ahi with mango relish. The Asian charred duck breast was fabulous. Main courses include chicken or seafood stir-fry, Colorado lamb chops, grilled swordfish, chili-crusted *onaga* or beef tenderloin. If you'd like just an entree without the buffet they are priced individually ($21-$34). Desserts are also buffet style ($45 adults, children $21). *Comments:* A pleasant dining environment with indoor or lanai seating overlooking the pool and the ocean. Great seafood and a *keiki* menu is available.

The Palm at Elleair *(Seafood)*
Elleair Golf Course, 1345 Pi'ilani Hwy at Lipoa on the mauka side, Kihei; 808-879-5100.

Hours: Tuesday-Sunday 5-10 p.m. *Sampling:* Begin with an appetizer such as "Wave Runner," deep-fried oysters on the shell served with a spicy cocktail sauce, or "Surf's Up," with seared scallops with chilled melon and poached Maui onions served with an orange and lime vinaigrette ($7-$9), and move on to an entree of fresh island paprika *opakapaka* served with roasted red pepper and cilantro coulis or garlic, ginger and citrus herbed butter. Fresh island seared ahi or *ono* as well as filet mignon and grilled whole rack of lamb ($24-$28). *Comments:* Chef Paul Lynch was formerly of Tavern on the Green and The Russian Tea Room in New York City. Haven't gotten to try this one. Let me know if you do.

★ **Palm Court** *(International/Buffet)*
Renaissance Wailea Beach Resort, 3550 Wailea Alanui, Wailea; 808-879-4900.

Hours: Breakfast 6 a.m.-11 a.m. Dinner 5:30-9:30 p.m. *Sampling:* A salad bar alone is $13.50 (not available on Tuesdays and Fridays), or with your entree for an additional $8. Salads and sandwiches ($7-$13) such as island mahi with lemon-dill aioli or Chinese chicken salad will please those with a light appetite, or create your own pizza. Pasta selections ($15-$26) include smoked chicken tortelloni or seafood cioppino with angelhair pasta. Dinner entrees ($22-$32) range from braised veal chop with wild mushroom ragout, herb-crusted Hawaiian snapper, or jumbo scampi with wild mushroom risotto. The Palm Court dinner buffets, however, are a great dinner option. Tuesday and Fridays they feature a seafood buffet with a rotating menu that might include ahi Nicoise, sautéed mahi, grilled swordfish, and prime rib ($35). Mondays and Saturdays play host to the Prime Rib Buffet ($32), which also offers a selection of vegetarian, chicken and seafood entrees. Wednesdays takes you to the Mediterranean for pastas cooked to order, osso buco, eggplant parmigiano or risotto ($32). Thursdays and Sundays features the Pacific Rim with *gado gado* salad, minted couscous with shrimp salad, and the action station offering a featured item such as shrimp and vegetable tempura. Woodplank salmon, pork *tonkatsu*, or macadamia nut mahi might be among the other selections on this hearty buffet. *Comments:* This open-air dining hall offers evening breezes and an ocean view.

★ **Prince Court** *(Contemporary Island)*
Maui Prince Hotel, 5400 Makena Alanui, Makena; 808-874-1111.

Hours: Dinner 6-9 p.m. Sunday Champagne Brunch 9 a.m.-1:30 p.m. *Sampling:* Friday night they offer a prime rib and seafood buffet as well as the regular nightly dinner menu. The buffet is a feast for the eyes and palate ($40 adults, $25 children 6-12). Sample their seafood on ice, selecting from steamed Manila clams, snap-and-eat Dungeness crab legs, or fresh sashimi. Specialty salads range from baby artichoke salad with bay shrimp to ceviche of scallops with Maui onion. Plenty of salad selections and an impressive international cheese and bread display. The action and carving station features roasted herb-crusted prime rib or fresh fish served in a variety of styles. The chef's buffet selections might include herb-crusted chicken breast or seafood paella. Don't forget to start eyeing the desserts before you're too full! The dessert table is a sumptuous fantasy that tastes as extravagant as it looks. A worthy indulgence (which is actually very reasonable considering you won't eat again until Tuesday!). The standard dinner menu begins with appetizers including ginger duck potstickers, chilled seafood on ice, or crispy Dungeness crab cakes ($7-$14). Follow that up with an asparagus bisque, or a grilled shrimp and mango salad ($6-$9). Entrees include beef tenderloin and half-stuffed lobster, trio of fresh Hawaiian fish, spring vegetable stew, or Asian seafood house of noodles ($21-$32). *Comments:* Prince Court is a lovely spot for a great evening. The cuisine is an incredible blend of flavors that highlights the best and freshest Hawaiian produce, meats and fish. Beautifully situated, the dining room offers a splendid view of both the ocean and landscaped hotel grounds. They have an excellent wine list with particularly good prices on champagne and wine selections. The Sunday champagne brunch is one of the island's best ($39 adults, $25 children 6-12).

★ **Restaurant Taiko** *(Japanese with a French flair)*
Diamond Resort, 555 Kaukahi Street, Wailea; 808-874-0500.

Hours: Breakfast 7-11 a.m. Lunch 11 a.m.-2 p.m. Dinner 6-9 p.m. (no dinner on Tuesday). *Sampling:* Choose a traditional breakfast with eggs, breakfast meats, potatoes and juice or a Japanese breakfast with broiled fish, egg, *kobachi*, *nori taukemono*, miso soup, rice and Japanese tea; also a la carte French toast, Belgian waffle, fresh fruit. Lunches feature sandwiches and burgers along with Japanese specialties including *tenazru don*, *unatama don*, *zaru soba* or *wakadori teriyaki don* (an assortment of hot and cold noodle or rice dishes; $8-$16). For dinner ($21-$36) you can choose sushi or sashimi, but I recommend that you jump to the appetizer menu and sample some extraordinary flavor combinations. The foie gras and scallops sauté is simply fabulous. The Boursin garlic and fine herb- stuffed duck cotelette won the '99 Boursin Chef of the year contest for *katsu*. There are eight complete Japanese-style meals so sample black cod with orange miso sauce, fresh *onaga* salted and broiled, or *panko*-crusted chicken, seafood and vegetables fried until golden brown. The tempura is light and fluffy. You can sear your own meal on a cast-iron hibachi. The sukiyaki is a classic with beef, tofu, vegetables and udon in a huge pot. Dessert selection changes, but they are all great. The ice creams are specially made in Japan! *Comments:* Diamond Resort is a gem—if you haven't discovered this fine restaurant, then it is time. Very simple, yet elegant in decor and almost cathedral in style. Executive Chef Katsuyuki Ishikawa spearheads a menu that is "innovatively French Japanese cuisine." My friend Kathi and I dined here a few years ago and now it is her family's favorite restaurant for any family occasion.

★ **Sarento's on the Beach** *(Italian)*
2980 South Kihei Road, Kihei; 808-875-7555.

Hours: First seating 5:30 p.m., second seating 9:30 p.m. *Sampling:* Enjoy your evening meal with a first course of portobello Napoleon (a tower of prosciutto, eggplant, mozzarella and tomato with arugula pesto), smoked salmon Italiano, or calamari fritta ($10.95-$13.95). Entrees range from double pork chop with a Chianti dried-cherry sauce to penne *calabrese* (with homemade Italian sauce, eggplant with tomato, garlic and goat cheese) and lobster cannelloni with braised greens and grilled mushroom. We tried the baked potato ravioli and it was a carbo lover's dream come true. We finished off our meal sharing profiteroles, a puff pastry filled with espresso gelato. Other dessert selections included tiramisu, citrus pannecotta and a chocolate cream brulee. *Comments:* In my opinion this is one of the most outstanding dining vistas on Maui. You're right on the beach! Reminiscent of elegant dining in the 1940s, the style was perhaps emphasized by the Frank Sinatra tunes playing in the background. As the sun goes down the overhead lights continue to light up the beach. Not only is the setting divine but the service is the best I can remember in years of dining on Maui. It was attentive but not intrusive and the wait help worked in teams to make the system run very smoothly. We barely noticed water glasses being replaced when they had dipped down below the edge and they were continually replacing silverware with what was appropriate for the next course. I'd thought table service like this was extinct. The prices were no more than the fine resort hotels but the ambiance of being right on the beach made this truly a fabulous evening of dining. Reservations highly recommended. They also have a small bar and a private vintners dining area.

★ *Sea Watch Restaurant* (Island)
100 Wailea Golf Club Drive, Wailea; 808-875-8080; www.seawatchrestaurant.com.

   Hours: Breakfast and lunch 8 a.m.-3 p.m. Grill menu 3-10 p.m. Dinner 6-10 p.m. *Sampling:* Breakfasts offer *moki* special (an omelet with *kalua* pork, Maui onion, potato and spinach) or try crab cake Benedict with roasted pepper hollandaise. More conventional breakfast fare as well. Plenty of salads and sandwiches ($8-$14) for those appetites worked up from a round of golf. Dinners start with macadamia nut–crusted brie, ahi sashimi, tiger prawns, crab cakes, porcini seared sea scallops, or Manila clams ($6-$12). Entrees include miso-glazed tiger prawns, rack of lamb with garlic mashed potatoes, parmesan-crusted chicken breast, or a selection of fresh island fish ($23-$29). *Comments:* You can get lunch for breakfast or have breakfast for lunch. An elegant "grand hall" entrance with tall ceilings leads to the restaurant and several distinctive dining areas. The wide lanais offer the best views of Molokini, Kahoʻolawe, Makena and Maʻalaea and the grill room is highlighted by giant glass doors and artwork from Arthur Johnson, a Big Island muralist. The lounge has a white baby grand piano as its centerpiece. Spacious seating; descriptive wine list.

★ *Spago* (Contemporary American-Hawaiian)
Four Seasons Resort, 3900 Wailea Alanui, Wailea; 808-879-2999.

   Hours: 6-9:30 p.m. *Sampling:* Where to begin! You absolutely have to try the Thai coconut-galangal soup. It has always been one of my favorite Thai dishes but I've never tasted one like this! The tempura Kauaʻi prawns with island-grown vegetables had an amazingly light batter. Other starters include stir-fried *onaga* lettuce wraps or island seafood risotto ($11-$17). The menu changes seasonally but you might enjoy big-eye tuna grilled rare with wasabi butter, baked *opakapaka* with macadamia nut crust and Moloka'i yams or free-range chicken with Yukon gold potato puree. I tried the fabulous pan-seared *onaga* with Kula corn, asparagus succotash and lobster *nage*. The caramelized pork chop with *lomi lomi* tomatoes and creamy sage polenta was a huge portion—more like a pork roast. *Comments:* One of the few fine-dining experiences to be enjoyed on Maui, this romantic indulgence offers tranquil elegance indoors or on the terrace—both with an ocean view. The service is, of course, exemplary and the waiter was extremely knowledgeable about their extensive wine selection. Just an all-around wonderful addition to the Maui fine-dining scene. And there's a kids' menu: Chicken fingers, mac and cheese, spaghetti or cheese pizza; includes special kids' dessert for $15.

Tommy Bahamas Tropical Cafe and Emporium *(Caribbean)*
Shops at Wailea, 3750 Wailea Alanui, Wailea; 808-875-9983.

Hours: Sunday-Thursday 11 a.m.-11 p.m. Friday-Saturday 11 a.m.-midnight. *Sampling:* Select an appetizer for lunch or dinner such as Big Island goat cheese with warmed cheese rolled in macadamia nuts and garnished with balsamic rum syrup, mango salsa and served with a toasted baguette, or Tommy's famous coconut shrimp, Cayman Island clams or blacked ahi ($9-$15). Soups, salads and sandwiches ($7-$15) include a shrimp BLT, the Habana Cabana pork sandwich, or Cooper Island crab bisque. Entree-size salads offer the rum-runners fruit salad, classic Caesar salad, *saba* steak salad with marinated flank steak or a fandango mango chicken salad with char-grilled chicken, mango, hearts of palm, pecans and baby greens ($13-17). Dinner entrees for the land lover include hot Jamaican spiced pork tenderloin, Tommy's Papa's Pasta with jumbo shrimp, or Boca Chica Chicken with the chicken breast lightly breaded and sautéed in a tropical tequila lime sauce. From the sea you can select Martinique mahi served with a chipotle butter sauce or Salmon Street Croix with the salmon char-grilled and garnished with a Malibu rum salsa ($21-$28). *Comments:* This is a fun-filled menu with some very fresh flavor combinations. Festive atmosphere and pleasant open-air dining. The portions are enormous! I tried goat fish, which was a nightly special. I'd never seen it offered in a restaurant and it was pretty tasty.

★ **The Waterfront Restaurant** *(Seafood)*
Milowai Condo, Ma'alaea; 808-244-9028; www.waterfrontrestaurant.net.

Hours: Dinner nightly from 5 p.m. *Sampling:* For dinner you'll find a rotating menu with whatever freshest foods are available. They are renowned for their fresh island fish and you can choose 9 preparations including baked in papillote, Hawaiian salsa, Southwestern, and Sicilian-style *provencale* ($29-$32). Or choose vegetarian *ahu*, chicken parmesan, or center-cut pork chop from $19. *Comments:* A family operation, the Smith's have done a consistently excellent job ever since they opened, winning a number of well-deserved awards and accolades. Fish preparations are particularly innovative and are offered with shrimp, ginger and coconut milk; salsa, avocado and cilantro butter or "En Bastille": imprisoned in angelhair potato with scallions, mushrooms and tomatoes. Dinner entrees all start with a loaf of onion bread and beer cheese along with a garden salad with choice of four homemade dressings. They have a great location to get their fish right off the boat at the Ma'alaea Harbor. Can't get it much fresher!

Kahului– Wailuku Area

Along Lower Main Street in Wailuku are a number of local restaurants that are not often frequented by tourists and may well be one of the island's best-kept secrets! Don't expect to find polished silver or extravagant decor, but do expect to find reasonable prices for large portions of food in a comfortable atmosphere. Note that many of these local restaurants may not accept credit cards. Dairy Queen, Pizza Hut, McDonald's, Burger King and Jack-in-the-Box are a few of the fast-food restaurants in and around Kahului and the Maui Mall. These don't require elaboration.

Inexpensive-priced Dining

★ *A Saigon Café* (Vietnamese)
1792 Main Street, Wailuku; 808-243-9560.
   Hours: 10 a.m.-9:30 p.m. Sunday until 8:30 p.m. *Sampling:* Spring or summer rolls, shrimp pops marinated and grilled on a sugar cane stick ($4.25-$8.25), rare lemon beef or shrimps, chicken and green papaya salads, saimin, chow fun, or hot-and-sour soup. Sample entrees include catfish or mahi in clay pot, wok "wonders" served with jasmine rice, sautéed dishes, sweet-and-sour meals, or their Saigon classic fondue where you cook your meal at your table. Most dishes $6-$10, with a few seafood selections that are under $20. *Comments:* If you haven't tried Vietnamese food, now is the time and this is the place! It's all fresh, fresh, fresh—right out of owner Jennifer Nguyen's own garden. Lemongrass, cucumbers, sour garlic sauce, daikon pickles, fresh island basil, and mint leaves are among the many distinctive ingredients used for seasoning dishes

> While not restaurants, two of my favorite haunts are worthy of mention. The **Home Maid Bakery**, open 5:30 a.m.-9 p.m. daily, is an island institution. It has more than just donuts: you'll find unusual specialties such as *empanadas, manju* and bread pudding. They began almost 40 years ago on Maui and do not add any preservatives to their made-from-scratch formulas. They are the home of the original Maui Crispy Manju and noted for their Maui Crunch bread. Some items available at island groceries. 1005 Lower Main Street, Wailuku; 808-244-7015.
>
> Nearby is the **Four Sisters Bakery**, open daily 5 a.m.-8 p.m. It is run by Melen, Mila, Beth and Bobbie, who arrived from the Philippines after helping their father run a Spanish bakery in Manila for 15 years. Not a large selection, but delicious and different items. They offer a sweet bread filled with a cinnamon pudding, a sponge cake "sandwich," as well as cinnamon rolls and butter rolls. The only place you can purchase these goodies is at the bakery or the Kahului Swap Meet. Vineyard and Hinano, Wailuku; 808-244-9333.

such as *ga xao xa ot* (curried chicken with lemongrass) or *bo lui* (grilled beef sirloin rolls). The most fun is *banh hoi*: Fill rice paper with a variety of meats or seafood (along with bean sprouts and vermicelli cake noodle) then dip in hot water and wrap. Located in the old Naokee Steak House location, they still serve steaks on the menu in homage to the former tenant. Try the tapioca for dessert or bring your ID for a piece of homemade Kahlua cake. A little hard to find (easiest way is from the road behind Ooka's) but well worth it. They are so popular they don't even need a sign! Look for the big stars that are lit on the roof. Simple atmosphere, great food, ample portions, prompt and friendly service—they deserve all their accolades and awards. A definite best bet! Don't miss this one.

Ale House *(Steaks/American/Sports Bar)*
355 East Kamehameha Highway, Kahului; 808-877-9001.

Hours: 11 a.m.-midnight. *Sampling:* Same menu for lunch/dinner offers a basic burger you can top with onion, melted blue cheese or bacon, or garden burgers. Roll-up sandwiches are shrimp, ahi, chicken or steak in a soft tortilla. Specialty salads, gourmet pizza, calzones or sandwiches along with a large *pupu* appetizer selection ($6-$11). *Comments:* Pool tables, dart boards, video games and over two dozen TVs. Karaoke. Late-night entertainment.

Aloha Grill *(Diner)*
Maui Marketplace, 270 Dairy Road, Kahului; 808-893-0263.

Hours: 8 a.m.-9 p.m. Sunday until 6 p.m. *Sampling:* Regular and large hot dogs (Moon Doggie, Hound Dog). Burgers with bacon, teriyaki, ham, chiles, chili and names like Buddy Holly and Gidget plus a good variety of vegetarian burgers. Surfer (sloppy) Joe and other sandwiches plus fountain treats like sundaes, shakes, malts, floats—even flavored colas and banana splits. Prices are very affordable ($2-$7). *Comments:* Small (one counter) '50s-style soda fountain with stools in the Kau Kau Food Court.

★ **Asian Star** *(Vietnamese)*
Millyard Industrial Park, 1764 Wili Pa Loop, Wailuku; 808-244-1833.
Hours: 10 a.m.-10 p.m. Sunday until 9 p.m. *Sampling:* Fresh island fish (market price). Plenty of authentic Vietnamese fare including *pho* (beef noodle soup), *goi* (salads) and *con dia* (rice plates). Wok dishes are vegetarian or with beef, chicken, seafood or pork. Make your own Vietnamese burritos with boneless chicken breast, shrimp or beef sirloin rolls. Vietnamese fondue with beef, shrimp or calamari cooked at the table. A huge menu and we've heard some very good things about this restaurant. Dishes are $5.95-$12.95. *Comments:* Current owner Jason formerly worked at A Saigon Café so he learned from the best. Don't think you'll go wrong dining here.

Biwon Restaurant *(Korean)*
752 Lower Main Street, Wailuku; 808-244-7788.
Hours: 10:30 a.m.-8:30 p.m. *Sampling:* Local favorites (served with *kim chee*, vegetables and rice) include barbecue dishes, shrimp fried rice, pan-fried chicken, shrimp or beef, or mixed plates such as barbecue beef and *mandoo* ($6.95-$8.95). Soup and noodle dishes ($6.25-$9.50) include *mandoo* soup, *duk kook* or *bi bim kook soo*.

★ **Brigit and Bernard's Garden Café** *(German/Italian)*
335 Hoohana Street, Kahului; 808-877-6000.
Hours: Lunch Monday-Friday 10:30 a.m.-2:30 p.m. Dinner Wednesday-Friday 5-9 p.m. *Sampling:* The lunch menu offers grilled burgers (including a pork "schnitzelburger"), fresh sandwiches and six daily specials ($5-$9). Begin your dinner with signature starters like "East meets West" sushi rolls, black and blue ahi, creamed mushroom, and shrimp Dijon ($6-$7.50). Dinners ($8-$15) feature a variety of salads, pastas, gourmet entrees (chicken pizzaiola, peppersteak, shrimp fettuccine, and fresh catch), and Bernard's own creation of "Potizza"—pizza toppings served on shredded, sauteed potatoes. Specialties like wienerschnitzel, coq au vin, rack of lamb, and sauerbraten. Yum! *Comments:* Good food. Select indoor or a cute outdoor patio for dining. Worth the search to find.

Café Marc Aurel (Coffee/Internet Café)
28 North Market, Wailuku; 808-244-0852.

Hours: Monday-Friday 7 a.m.-6 p.m. Saturday 7 a.m.-1 p.m. Closed Sunday. *Sampling & Comments:* Cute European-style café with great espresso drinks (they have soy milk) along with *tramezzimo* sandwiches. These are small square, crust-free sandwiches with interesting combinations like pastrami with artichoke. Other light lunches include quiche or cold-cut plates. *Comments:* Afternoon teas 3-5 p.m. each Monday through Friday with sweets and savories served on a silver platter. Also internet access—only $8 an hour when I last checked.

★ **Café O'Lei** (Healthy Salads & Sandwiches)
Hawaii Nature Center, 875 Iao Valley Road.

Hours: 10:30 a.m.-3 p.m. *Sampling:* Changing menu with interesting taste treats ($5.95-$8.95). You might find creamy chicken fettuccine or blackened mahi or sandwich selections that include fresh Maui vegetables, crab club, Italian prosciutto with an Asian salad, hot chicken salad or curry chicken salad. *Comments:* Pick up a great lunch to take on your hike. One of a small chain of Maui restaurants popular with residents and tourists alike.

Cupie's (American/Local)
134 West Kamehameha Avenue, Kahului; 808-877-3055.

Hours: Monday-Saturday 9 a.m.-9 p.m. *Sampling:* Breakfast served until 10:30 a.m. ($4.25-$6). Plate lunches of chopsteak, *kalbi* bentos ($5.75), burgers or a bacon deluxe cheeseburger ($2.29-$4.50). Soup of the day, hot dogs, BLT, tuna or fried ahi sandwiches ($1.50-$3.50). *Comments:* This used to be one of those places where you sat in your car with the trays on your window, now it is a drive up with orders to go or limited seating. It really is an old-fashioned place—you can still get a grilled cheese sandwich or a 32-ounce soda for 99 cents! (As we go to press Cupie's has a new owner. Hope they don't get rid of the grilled cheese!)

Curry in a Hurry (Vegetarian)
Located between Down to Earth and Wowwee's Café, 333 Dairy Road, Kahului; 808-877-3328.

Hours: Lunch 11 a.m.-2 p.m. Dinner 6-9 p.m. *Sampling & Comments:* Owners Hans and Lori Lee Mayne who own Simple Pleasures operate this newcomer. Food only "to go." They specialize in Ayurveda cooking which they describe as "matching your diet to your *dosha*, or mind-body type, to insure your health and well being. The three body types or *doshas* are Vata, Pitta and Kapha and have corresponding physical and emotional elements that are aggravated or pacified by different foods." Interesting stuff and good eats. Hans and Lori are very talented cooks.

Da Kitchen Express *(Local)*
Triangle Square, Kahului; 808-871-7782.

Hours: 9 a.m.-9 p.m. *Sampling:* Breakfast, served 9 a.m.-11 a.m., includes *loco moco*, Maui-style French toast and omelets ($5.25-$6.25). Plate lunches include two scoops of rice and mac salad with entrees of hamburger steak, lemon chicken, fish tempura or a *laulau* or Hawaiian plate ($5.25-$8.50) and oodles of noodles ($3-$5.75). Sandwiches or salads, local style ($4.85-$5.89). *Comments:* Good value, large portions, good grinds.

Down to Earth Natural Foods & Café *(Vegetarian)*
305 Dairy Road, Kahului; 808-877-7548. Another location at 1169 Makawao Avenue, Makawao; 808-572-1488.

Hours: 8 a.m.-7:30 p.m. Store open 7 a.m.-9 p.m., Sunday until 7 p.m. *Sampling:* Soups and hot vegetarian entrees like bell pepper with couscous, "to fu young," enchilada pie, lasagna and mock chicken tofu plus freshly made sandwiches, burritos, spring rolls, quesadillas and wraps ($5). Salad bar $5.99 lb. Low-fat, whole-grain bakery items include streusel, carrot cake, toffee bars, muffins, baklava, almond walnut and tea cookies, and date bars; also tofu cheesecake and vegan carob chip cookies. *Comments:* The mock chicken is tasty by itself or with added stir-fry vegetables. Fruit compote made with blueberries or peaches and coconut baked with crumble topping—yummy! Pleasant seating area upstairs. Retail store has fresh organic produce, bulk items, and packaged vegetarian food products.

Dragon Dragon *(Chinese)*
Maui Mall, 70 East Ka'ahumanu Avenue, Kahului; 808-893-1628.

Hours: Lunch 10:30 a.m.-2 p.m. Dinner 5-9 p.m. *Sampling & Comments:* You can tell right away from the honey walnut stir-fried prawns or the drunken clams with Chinese wine offered as appetizers that this will be an innovative menu. Seasonal live lobster and crab are served with black bean, ginger and green onion, or supreme sauce, or try the fried pepper salt pork chops, five-flavored roast duck, stir-fried ong choy with shredded pepper and preserved bean curd, or beef fried rice with lettuce. There are 56 dishes to choose from and all served daily. Most dishes under $12. They also serve dim sum for lunch Monday through Friday, the only restaurant I know of that does.

Eddie's Fast Food *(Local/Filipino)*
230 Hana Highway, Suite 2-B, Wailuku; 808-871-8821.

Hours: Monday-Friday 10 a.m.-8 p.m. Saturday 10 a.m.-3 p.m. Closed Sunday. *Sampling:* Daily buffets ($7.95) feature different selections during the week. Monday: creamed chicken, beef tomato, mussels. Tuesday: chicken with mushroom, beef with black beans, tempura. Wednesday: fried chicken, squid. Thursday: orange chicken, long beans with shrimp. Friday: teriyaki chicken, seafood medley and *kalua* pig or *laulau*. *Comments:* Yet another fabulous local eatery where you get a bang for your vacation buck. In addition to the buffets you can also sample authentic Filipino dishes like chicken *adobo*, mango beans, pork and peas, or *pansit* (a combination of zucchini, green beans and eggplant). They have *dinardaaran*, blood pork, which is a dark purple sauce—I tried it once and once was enough!

★ **Fiesta Time** *(Mexican)*
1132 Lower Main Street, Wailuku; 808-249-8463.

Hours: 11 a.m.-8 p.m. *Sampling:* Great tostados, burritos, enchiladas all a la carte. Most items $5-$6, with steak or shrimp at $10.95. *Comments:* A hole-in-the-wall with very little counter seating. Food is excellent, fresh and inexpensive.

Fujiya's *(Japanese)*
133 Market Street, Wailuku; 808-244-0206.

Hours: 5-9 p.m. Closed Sunday. *Sampling:* Dinners of tempura, teriyaki, *donburi*, curry, chicken or pork tofu ($5.95-$11.95). Sushi, too. Five combination dinner choices such as tempura with *yakitori*, *shumai*, *tsukemono*, miso soup and rice. Beer and *sake* available. *Comments:* A best bet for Japanese food. Sushi lovers will appreciate their sushi bar, where a large variety of selections are available at half the usual resort area price.

Hale Imua *(Internet Café/Coffee)*
1980 Main Street, Wailuku; 808-242-1896.

Hours: Monday-Friday 9 a.m.-5:30 p.m. Saturday 9 a.m.-4 p.m. Closed Sunday. *Sampling:* Full espresso bar and smoothies. Deli sandwiches, green salads, desserts ($4.25-$6.50). *Comments:* Cost for internet is $2 for first 10 minutes then 10¢ a minute.

International House of Pancakes *(American)*
Maui Mall, 70 East Ka'ahumanu Avenue, Kahului; 808-871-4000.

Hours: Sunday-Thursday 6 a.m.-midnight. Friday and Saturday until 2 a.m. *Comments:* A very large facility with a menu that is popular with all family members. Something for everyone at reasonable prices. Breakfasts begin in the $5 range, dinners from $12.

★ **Koho Grill and Bar** *(American)*
Queen Ka'ahumanu Center, 275 Ka'ahumanu Avenue, Kahului; 808-877-5588.

Hours: Breakfast 7-11 a.m. Lunch 11 a.m.-5 p.m. Dinner 5 p.m.-midnight. *Sampling:* This location opens early for breakfast. Plate lunches, burgers, sandwiches, salads ($6.75-$9.45). Dinner entrees include your choice of soup or Kula salad. Rib plate, chicken stir fry, top sirloin, or catch of the day prepared five different ways ($9-$16). *Comments:* A diverse menu and affordable prices, which boils down to good family dining. They also have a great *keiki* menu. Sports bar and large-screen TV.

★ **Las Pinatas of Maui** *(Mexican)*
395 Dairy Road, Kahului; 808-877-8707.

Hours: Monday-Saturday 10:30 a.m.-8 p.m. Sunday 11 a.m.-8 p.m. *Sampling:* Nachos, tostadas, hard and soft-shell tacos, enchiladas, burritos, quesadillas, Mexican salads ($2.45-$8). Combination plates ($6.75-$8.25). Plus daily specials. *Comments:* A family operation with affordable prices. Everything is made from scratch, from the beans to the salsa, and they use only 100 percent cholesterol-free oils. Dine in or take out. A small, fast food–sized place; very convenient to the airport.

★ **Mama Ding's Pasteles Restaurant** *(Puerto Rican/Local)*
255 East Alamaha Street, Kahului; 808-877-5796.

Hours: Monday-Friday 6:30 a.m.-2:30 p.m. *Sampling:* Eggs Bermuda (2 eggs scrambled with cream cheese and onion) served with potatoes or rice and toast, French toast (choice of cinnamon or sweet bread), or Puerto Rican breakfast with eggs, meat, half *pastele*, and *gandule* rice. My favorite is the big pancake with peaches ($4-$6). The plate lunch comes with *pastele*, *gandule* rice, *empanadilla*, choice of meat, *bacalao* salad, and dessert ($6-$7). Other lunches include teri beef or fried rice plate, saimin, sandwiches and a homemade chorizo burger ($3.25-$5.75). *Comments:* Ready for a different breakfast? Skip IHOP and Denny's and try this cozy restaurant tucked away in the Kahului Industrial Area. Try a *pastele*, which has an exterior of grated green banana and a filling of pork, vegetables and spices that is then steamed. Delicious! I've tried several of their breakfasts, all were good. No credit cards. They also sell specialty breads in flavors like coconut-papaya-pineapple, strawberry guava, and Portuguese sweetbread as well as cinnamon, apple-cinnamon or potato bread.

Marco's Grill & Deli *(Italian)*
444 Hana Highway, Kahului; 808-877-4446.

Hours: 7:30 a.m.-10 p.m. *Sampling:* Large selection of omelets and breakfast sandwiches plus chocolate cinnamon French toast. Enjoy granola with strawberries and bananas or chocolate chips, banana nut, strawberry or apple cinnamon pancakes ($5.95-$9.95). Lots of deli sandwiches or choose hot-off-the-grill pastrami, grilled *ono*, meatball parmigiano, or chicken breast sandwiches ($8.95-$11.95). Salads and pizzas from $6.95. Entree selections include vodka rigatoni, mushroom chicken, pasta penne, grilled salmon, and NY steak

($10.95-$15.95). *Comments:* They feature a cocktail lounge with big-screen TV.

★ Maui Bake Shop & Deli *(European Pastries/Deli)*
2092 Vineyard Street, Wailuku; 808-242-0064.

Hours: Monday-Friday 6 a.m.-4 p.m. Saturday 7 a.m.-1 p.m. *Sampling:* Everything is on a readerboard and updated daily. Sample one of their ready-made salads, homemade soups, and sandwiches ($4-$6.50); the breads are all freshly homemade. They have a full bakery with lots of delicious sweets and coffee or espresso drinks. *Comments:* An early-morning arrival assures a greater selection from the goodies like handmade puff pastry or fresh fruit tarts. This European-style bakery is the combined effort of French chef Jose and his wife, Claire Fjuii Krall. The big stone oven is left over from the Yokouchi family that was in this location in the 1930s. Yum! A few tables inside or get your lunch and head to the beach.

Maui Coffee Roasters *(Light Meals)*
444 Hana Highway, Kahului; 808-877-CUPS.

Hours: Monday-Friday 7 a.m.-6 p.m. (kitchen closes 4:30 p.m.). Saturday 8 a.m.-5 p.m. (kitchen closes 4 p.m.). Sunday 9 a.m.-2:30 p.m. *Sampling:* They specialize in the "ultimate veggie burger" made of low-fat grains and vegetables with green chile pesto, or try a veggie melt or veggie wrap. Also plenty for meat eaters with roast beef, ham and cheese, or tuna caper. Bagel sandwiches, wraps and "eggs with" ($4.95-$6.95). And pastries, of course, to accompany your coffee drinks. *Comments:* Brightly and whimsically decorated with counter and table seating. Hawaiian, imported and flavored coffees, freshly roasted for retail sale or to order off the menu. Specialty drinks include granitas, rice milk, Maui juices, flavored teas, espressos, lattes and cappuccinos.

Maui Mall
70 East Ka'ahumanu Avenue, Kahului; 808-872-4320; www.mauimall.com.

Not a food court, but there are several small food outlets here. Among them are *Siu's Chinese Kitchen, Maui's Mixed Grill* and *Tasaka Guri Guri* for a local type of creamy sherbet you can order with or without beans. *IHOP* and *Dragon Dragon* are listed individually.

Maui Marketplace *(Food Court)*
270 Dairy Road, Kahului; 808-873-0400.

The Kau Kau Food Court offers some small food outlets including *Ba-Le Sandwiches* (tasty Vietnamese sandwiches), *Aloha Grill* (see individual listing), *L&L Drive-Inn* (generous plate lunches) and *Chopsticks Express* (Chinese plate lunches).

Maui Tropical Plantation Café *(Salads/Sandwiches)*
Maui Tropical Plantation, 1670 Honoapi'ilani Highway, Waikapu; 808-244-7643.

Hours: 10 a.m.-3 p.m. *Sampling:* Sandwiches and burgers, as well as stuffed mahimahi, fish tacos and lunch-size salads ($7.50-$13.50). *Comments:* Pleasant view of the grounds; many of the fruits are plantation-grown. Beer, wine and tropical drinks available.

Mike's Restaurant *(Local)*
1900 Main Street, Wailuku; 808-244-7888.

Hours: Monday-Thursday 9:30 a.m.-9 p.m. Friday and Saturday 8:30 a.m.-10 p.m. Sunday 8:30 a.m.-9 p.m. *Sampling:* Try their island breakfast combo ($3.25) with a choice of three items; omelets, too ($5.50). Plate lunches include rice and macaroni salad with options such as pork *katsu*, teri beef or house specialties such as sesame chicken, NY steak or grilled mahi. Lots of burgers, noodle dishes and combination plates ($4.95-$9.50). *Comments:* Yet another restaurant I haven't had a chance to try.

Nazo's *(Local)*
Puuone Plaza, 1063 Lower Main Street, Wailuku; 808-244-0529.

Hours: Lunch 10 a.m.-2 p.m. Dinner 5-9 p.m. Closed Sunday. *Sampling:* Mini-plates include one scoop rice and one scoop mac salad with entrees of chicken cutlet, breaded teri beef, chop steak or oxtail soup ($4.50-$8.50). They offer more diverse selections such as salmon steak, shrimp tempura, and liver with bacon and onions. Noodle dishes (pigs feet on Thursdays and Saturdays), saimin, dry mein, and won ton ($4.25-$6.75); salads, too, with tuna-stuffed tomato, chicken Caesar, or Chinese chicken ($4.25-$4.95). A variety of burgers and sandwiches including ham, tuna, BLT, club and egg combos ($2.50-$4.95). *Comments:* A small, family-owned restaurant. Very affordable.

Pizza in Paradise *(Pizza)*
60 Wakea Avenue, Kahului; 808-871-8188.

Hours: Sunday-Thursday 11 a.m.-9 p.m. Friday-Saturday until 10 p.m. *Sampling:* Pizza and more pizza ($10.47-$18.97) including local specials like *kalua*, Portuguese, or ranch classic chicken. Traditional calzone, a wide selection of tossed salads as well as a 15-item salad bar ($2.97-$6.50). *Comments:* All their dough and sauces are made fresh with olive oil right in the store. They have chessboard tables and every Friday is Chess Day. Wednesday is Family Feast night ($7.97 adults, $4.47 kids under 12), which is sure to fill up the family.

Queen Ka'ahumanu Center *(Food Court)*
275 Ka'ahumanu Avenue, Kahului; 808-877-3369; www.kaahumanu.net.

The Queen's Market Food Court features seven upstairs restaurants near the main entrance. *Edo Japan* has teppanyaki plate dinners, rice bowls, saimin and sushi. *Yummy Korean BBQ* offers *kalbi* and barbecued meats, noodle and dumpling soups, plus curries. Head to *Athens* for Greek cuisine or *Sbarro* for Italian. *Maui's Mixed Plate* has local food. Prices $4-$8. *Sushi Go!* serves sushi fast with a popular Japanese food service system called *kaiten*, which uses a conveyor belt that passes dishes around the counter in front of customers. About 20 different types of sushi ($1.50-$2.25 per plate; $22.99 for all-you-can-eat sushi Wednesday 4-8 p.m.). *Koho Grill and Bar, Maui Tacos* and *Ruby's Diner* are listed individually.

Ruby's Diner *(Diner)*
Queen Ka'ahumanu Center, 275 Ka'ahumanu Avenue, Kahului; 808-248-7829.

Hours: Monday-Friday 7 a.m.-9:30 p.m. Saturday-Sunday 7 a.m.-11 p.m. *Sampling:* Nothing on the menu over $9. Try Ruby's special cinnamon roll French toast for breakfast, an array of omelets or huevos rancheros. Try a Ruby Burger with an old-fashioned shake or a malt. Healthy food alternatives include vegetarian specialties, lots of salads and even "lite fries." Dinner specialties include meatloaf, turkey and stuffing, shrimp and chips or country fried steak. Plenty of burgers served with cheese, chiles, mushrooms, bleu cheese, bacon or guacamole. Salads include Cobb, chicken Caesar or Chinese chicken. Save room for a classic hot fudge sundae, banana split, or fresh-baked apple pie. A fun kids' menu with breakfast and lunch/dinner favorites like grilled cheese, chicken fingers and PB&J. *Comments:* Back in 1962 Ruby visited Hawai'i about the famous Lurline cruise ship. Discovering that Maui was *no ka oi*, she returned with her friends and family for many years. In 2002 her son Doug (who lives part-time in Hana) brought one of the Ruby restaurants to Maui. Ruby's features airplane models that were a part of Hawai'i's aviation history. Turn back time to the days of the Clipper ship, when the 16-hour flight aboard a giant Boeing 314 left San Francisco at 4 p.m. and arrived at 8 a.m. the next morning. Plenty of comfort food and a broad menu. Seniors will find Ruby's "Jitterbug Club" a swinging place. For "friends" 55 and older you'll receive 10 percent off your entire check. And yes—that is the check of your entire party!

★ **Saeng's Thai** *(Thai)*
2119 Vineyard Street, Wailuku; 808-244-1567.

Hours: Lunch Monday-Friday 11 a.m.-2:30 p.m. Dinner 5-9:30 p.m. *Sampling:* Bean cake, stuffed chicken wings, broccoli satay, and other appetizers ($4.95-$7.50). Entrees of assorted curry dishes, barbecue dancing prawns, cornish game hen, seafood sauté, and lots of vegetarian selections ($7.50-$12.95). *Comments:* A little Eden with lots of plants providing privacy between tables. This is one of the most attractive local restaurants in Wailuku and one of the best restaurants on Maui for Thai cuisine. Not only is the service attentive, but the portions are generous. (I'm especially partial to their peanut sauce.) Don't miss this one.

Sam Sato's *(Local)*
1750 Wili Pa Loop, Wailuku; 808-244-7124.

Hours: Breakfast and lunch 7 a.m.-2 p.m., *manju* and pastries pick-up until 4 p.m. *Sampling:* Omelets, hot cakes, or set breakfast ($2.50-$5). Plate lunches include teriyaki beef, stew, chop steak, spare ribs ($5.50-$6.25). Sandwiches and burgers ($2.35-$2.65). But what you really come to Sam's for is the saimin. Dry noodles, saimin, chow fun, won ton ($3.75-$5) are available in small or large sizes. Take-out noodles available for $14-$26-$46 (to feed 10-15, 25 or 50 people). *Comments:* The homemade pastries are wonderful; peach, apple and coconut turnovers are fragrant and fresh and they also specialize in *manju*, a Japanese tea cake. These tasty morsels are filled with a mashed version of lima beans.

Siam Thai *(Thai)*
123 North Market Street, Wailuku; 808-244-3817.

Hours: Lunch Monday-Friday 11 a.m.-2 p.m. Dinner nightly 5-9 p.m. *Sampling:* Appetizers include fresh (or fried) spring rolls, green papaya salad, coconut or spicy soup ($5.50-$7.95). Garlic mahimahi, ahi with ginger sauce, eggplant tofu, Siam omelet, honey chicken, and Evil Jungle Prince ($7.50-$10.95). *Comments:* The white tablecloths give this local restaurant an elegant air. You can't go wrong with any of the curries (just pick your favorite color!) or the Thai tapioca with coconut milk. Good food and friendly service.

★ **Simple Pleasures Café/Café Romantica** *(Gourmet Vegetarian)*
2103 Vineyard Street, Wailuku; 808-249-0697.

Hours: Tuesday-Thursday 11 a.m.-3 p.m. *Sampling:* Homemade soups from coconut curry to carrot bisque; Hawaiian focaccia with macadamia nut pesto, falafel, tofu tandoori, Indian samosas with peanut sauce, and *timbales*. Vegetarian crepes, lasagna, cordon bleu and veggie burger Wellington in puff pastry plus assorted salads: green bean and potato, chick pea and spinach, black bean and rice, and pasta with raisins, carrots and almonds—all in $4 and $8 sizes. Specialty breads, pastries and their signature Hawaiian-style desserts: apple streudel, tangy lemon tart, chocolate truffle, coconut *haupia* pie, Kona coffee tiramisu, and mango-lime cheesecake—all in a macadamia nut crust. *Comments:* Owned and operated by Hans and Lori Lee Mayne, Hans is of British descent, was born in India, and lived in Sweden. Hence the eclectic flair to their tasty and innovative options. In the evening the restaurant becomes Café Romantica with lots of fabulous Indian dishes on the menu as well as tofu dishes. Evening entertainment, too.

Simply Healthy *(Healthy)*
Cameron Center, Mahalani Road (near the hospital), Wailuku; 808-249-8955.

Hours: Monday-Friday 11 a.m.-2 p.m. *Sampling:* Lunch plate ($4.50), veggie plate or sandwich ($3.50), chef salad ($4), soup or soup and half sandwich ($3-$4). *Comments:* No salt, no sugar and minimal fat with a menu that changes daily. Take out or dine in.

Stillwells Bakery & Cafe *(Bakery/Deli)*
1740 Ka'ahumanu Avenue, Wailuku; 808-243-2243.

Hours: Monday-Friday 9 a.m.-3 p.m. Saturday 9:30 a.m.-2 p.m. *Sampling:* Awesome sandwiches including pastrami with sauerkraut, ham and cheese, tofu burger, garden burger, vegetarian, or try a crab cake sandwich with or without soup. Once you've selected the filling, the bread is the hard part: wheat or white? Rye, croissant, focaccia? Salads include chicken Caesar, tofu, crab, and chef's or noodle dishes like chow fun, dry men, saimin and pasta. Menu items run $4.95-$8.25.

Stinger Ray *(Light Meals)*
Kahului Airport across from Gate 23; 808-877-5858 ext. 29.

Hours: 10 a.m.-9:30 p.m. *Sampling: Kakahiaka* breakfasts served until 11 a.m. ($5.29-$6.99). Appetizers include coconut shrimp, Stinger wings, macho nachos or island chowder ($6-$11) plus salads and sandwiches ($5.29-$9.99). *Comments:* Cute, bright eatery offers dining fare while you wait for your plane. Full bar service, too.

★ Sub Paradise *(Sandwiches)*
395-E Dairy Road, Kahului; 808-877-8779.

Hours: 7 a.m.-7 p.m. Sunday until 2 p.m. *Sampling:* Caesar, Greek and chef's salads and over two dozen varieties of subs in 6" or 12" sizes: ham, turkey, pastrami, salami, roast beef, meatball, chicken, vegetarian, egg salad, cheese and combinations; if you're really hungry check out the Big Kahuna with eight meats and four cheeses. Nothing on the menu over $9. *Comments:* Specials include turkey, bacon and avocado or Chinese chicken salad. Hana picnic lunch includes 6-inch sub, soda, chips, cookie, candy or orange with cooler (refundable deposit). Very good sandwiches—the bread is freshly baked and tastes it.

★ Tasty Crust Restaurant *(Local)*
1770 Mill Street, Wailuku; 808-244-0845.

Hours: 5:30 a.m.-10 p.m. *Sampling:* Delicious crusty hotcakes are their specialty, two are a meal for $3. Waffles $2.75. Omelets and egg dishes ($3.60-$4.95). Lunch and dinner feature plate lunches of *loco moco, kalbi* ribs, teri meat, chop steak, chicken *katsu,* all with steamed rice and macaroni salad ($5.85-$6.75). Saimin, sandwiches and salads ($3.95 and up). *Comments:* Local atmosphere and no frills, just good food at great prices. (Actually, the pancakes are good; the coffee is bad.) They've been here since 1943, and I keep hearing a buzz about retirement for the owners—I'm still hoping to get the secret of those legendary pancakes before they go.

Tokyo Tei *(Japanese)*
1063 East Lower Main Street, Wailuku; 808-242-9630.

    Hours: Lunch 11 a.m.-1:30 p.m. Dinner 5-8:30 p.m. Sunday 5-8 p.m. *Sampling:* Lunch specials include beef cutlet, sweet-and-sour pork, teriyaki meat, omelets and noodles ($6.75-$7). Saimin or fried noodles ($3.75-$4). *Teishoku* trays for lunch or dinner include shrimp tempura, sashimi, fried fish, teriyaki pork or steak ($10-$11). Dinner selections offer *hakata* chicken, seafood platter, calamari *katsu*, *yakitori*, tempura, teriyaki steak, broiled salmon, sukiyaki and *donburi* dishes that include rice, miso soup, *ko-ko* and hot tea ($8-$11.25). *Comments:* Small and cozy. Take-out also available. Cocktails. Popular with both visitors and residents and deservedly so. (I'd probably eat here at least once a week if it wasn't such a long drive from Portland!) A winner for local dining at its best; don't miss this one.

Wowwee—Maui's Café *(Sandwiches)*
333 Dairy Road, Kahului; 808-871-1414.

    Hours: 5 a.m.-11 p.m. *Sampling:* Breakfast sandwiches, bagels with toppers, soups, salads and pizza ($5.95-$7.95). Boxed lunches to go ($6.95). Coffee drinks, homemade ice cream, desserts and their own line of candy bars (also available at stores around the island). *Comments:* All freshly made, great stop en route to the airport, Hana or Haleakala—and they'll give you a crater weather report!

Moderate-priced Dining

★ ***Cary & Eddie's Hideaway*** *(American/Seafood)*
500 North Pu'unene Avenue, Kahului; 808-873-6555.

    Hours: 11 a.m.-9:30 p.m. Sunday 8 a.m.-2 p.m. *Sampling:* Sunday breakfast buffet includes pancakes, potatoes, breakfast meats and fruit and salad bar ($10.99) or other breakfast entrees ($5.99-$6.99). Daily lunch specials and plate lunches ($6.99-$12.99). A nightly Hawaiian dinner buffet includes barbecued pork ribs, *kalua* pig and cabbage, chicken long rice and the works for $18.99. Other "ribstickin'" *paniolo* entrees include barbecued shrimp stir-fry, ribs and combination plates. Sample teriyaki NY strip, T-Bone steak or fresh fish ($17.99-$22.99) Or how about the family feast? Two halves of barbecue chicken, two slabs of pork ribs, four barbecue beef prime rib bones, barbecue *kalua* pork, all served with *paniolo* ranch beans, rice and vegetables. Fitting for a family of four, or even more ($51.99).

★ ***The Class Act*** *(International)*
Maui Community College Campus, Kahului; 808-984-3280.

    Hours: Wednesday and Friday 11 a.m.-12:15 p.m. *Comments:* This is one of Maui's best little finds. Insiders know they are in for a treat when they stop by for a four-course gourmet lunch prepared by the Food Service students of the Maui Community College. At $15 (plus tip) it's become a bit expensive, but not when you know you're supporting such a worthwhile student program. Students shop, serve, clean and wait on tables and a different menu is offered each week. Each meal represents a different country or region like Italy, New Orleans, France, California or the Pacific Rim. A heart-healthy alternative, low in sodium and cholesterol, is available at each meal. The program is only offered during the school year, so call ahead. Reservations suggested. At press time, The Class Act was still located on the MCC campus adjacent to the upstairs Cafeteria, but both will be moving to the brand-new Pa'ina Culinary Arts Center building by fall 2003. Enjoy outdoor or air-conditioned dining (as well as a north shore ocean view) at The Class Act or visit the new downstairs cafeteria (open to the public, 11 a.m.-2:30 p.m.) that will be set up as a food court with a bakery along with outlets for sushi, pizza and hamburgers, hot lunches, and local plates for less than $6.

★ **Mañana Garage** (Latin American/Cuban)
Lono Building, 33 Lono Avenue, Kahului; 808-871-2074.

Hours: Lunch 11 a.m.-2:30 p.m. Midday menu 2:30-5 p.m. Dinner 5-9 p.m. Tapas Wednesday-Saturday 9-10:30 p.m. *Sampling:* Mañana Garage offer an opportunity to sample some authentic Latin American cuisine. *Adobo* barbecue duck with sweet potato quesadilla, or chicken tortilla *epozote* soup ($7-$13). For dinner begin with a fried green tomato salad, ahi ceviche or smoked salmon pastrami ($5-$13). Entrees such as lamb sirloin, pumpkin seed–crusted garlic shrimp, or roasted vegetable enchilada ($13-$25). Lunch or dinner desserts include coconut rum raisin rice pudding, sweet potato praline pound cake and ice cream sandwich ($4-$6). *Comments:* This place has some outstanding fare, different from the run-of-the-mill. Bar open from 11 a.m.

Upcountry

Inexpensive-priced Dining

Café Del Sol *(Deli)*
3620 Baldwin Avenue, Makawao; 808-572-4877.

Hours: 8 a.m.-5 p.m. Closed Sunday. *Sampling:* A variety of egg dishes including eggs Benedict as well as other breakfast favorites. For lunch enjoy salads, hamburgers and sandwiches ($4.75-$10.50). *Comments:* Chefs and owners Lisa Wise and Tami Ritchey of Key West have brought a Caribbean influence to their food. Eat indoors or in the patio garden. Tucked back in the shops.

★ **Café O'Lei** (Healthy Salads & Sandwiches)
Paniolo Courtyard, 3673 Baldwin Avenue, Makawao; 808-573-9065.

Hours: 11 a.m.-4 p.m. Closed Sunday. *Sampling:* Gourmet sandwiches such as snowcrab and avocado and warm camembert and bacon or grilled eggplant and roast breast of chicken. Sample taro salad, curry chicken, and quinoa salads ($4.95-$6.95). Soup of the day by the cup ($1.95) or bowl ($3.90) along with a selection of coffees and espresso. *Comments:* Good, healthy food with fresh, organic ingredients in a charming setting. The European-style courtyard is lined with flowers and foliage; tables along the brick pathway make this a "real" sidewalk café. The menu is simple, but extra touches make it special: fresh herbs from the garden, lots of garlic in the creamy Caesar dressing, pungent lemongrass in the Asian salad—they even use "real" china and pottery—no paper plates or cups here!

Duncan's Coffee Company/Duncan's Rockin' Sushi (Pastries/Sushi)
3645 Baldwin Avenue, Makawao; 808-573-9075.

Hours: Coffee: Monday-Saturday 6:30 a.m.-5:30 p.m. Sunday 8:30 a.m.-3:30 p.m. Sushi: Monday-Saturday lunch 11 a.m.-3 p.m. Dinner 5-9 p.m. (Saturday until 10 p.m.). Sunday 11 a.m.-9 p.m. *Sampling:* Duncan's features a full espresso bar along with teas, non-coffee beverages such as smoothies, Lappert's Hawaiian ice cream, fresh pastries, and a lunch menu that varies daily. Homemade soups, salads (their specialty is carrot/orzo) and sandwiches grilled on their panini machine. Also quiches and vegetarian lasagna. Lunch items are priced $5.95-$6.25. At Duncan's Rockin' Sushi, get a combo platter if you're undecided ($15-$34), by the piece ($2-$3.50) or by the roll ($5-$7). *Comments:* Margot, Duncan and their two girls relocated from Canada after spending time as Maui visitors. They offer indoor seating and an outdoor bamboo garden deck.

★ **Grandma's Coffee House** (Local)
Located in Keokea, just five miles before the Tedeschi Winery; 808-878-2140.

Hours: 7 a.m.-5 p.m. *Sampling & Comments:* This coffee house is run by Alfred Franco, who is encouraging the return of the coffee industry in Upcountry Maui. Born and raised in Upcountry, his grandmother taught him how to roast the coffee beans to perfection. He does this several times a day in his century-plus-old coffee roasting machine that was brought from Philadelphia by his great-grandmother. The coffee is sold by the pound. Some of the beans used are grown on Moloka'i, which is part of Maui

County. A few tables invite visitors to sit down, enjoy a cup of coffee, espresso, cappuccino or fresh fruit juice along with cinnamon rolls (get there early!), muffins and more, all fresh from the oven. A bit more of an appetite might require one of their fresh avocado sandwiches, deli salads, or a bowl of chili and rice, pasta ($5-$8). They also sell their own chocolates, made from Grandma's recipe, of course. With the popularity of this place, it is tough for them to keep up with the demand for these goodies. There's a deck for outdoor seating with a great view.

Kitada's Kau Kau Corner *(Local)*
3617 Baldwin Avenue, Makawao; 808-572-7241.

Hours: 6 a.m.-1:30 p.m. Closed Sunday. *Sampling:* French toast, eggs and omelets ($2.75-$6.50). Small or large portions of beef teriyaki, hamburger steak, beef or pork tofu, chopsteak, beef stew, pork chops, and spare ribs served with rice, macaroni salad, and salted cabbage ($4.25-$5.25). Sandwiches and burgers ($1.50-$3), saimin from $3. *Comments:* Owned and operated by the same family for over 50 years! It is a popular local eatery and, with these prices and the variety of plate lunches, you can see why.

Mixed Plate *(Local)*
Pukalani Terrace Center, 55 Pukalani Street, Pukalani; 808-572-8258.

Hours: 6 a.m.-1 p.m. Closed Sunday. *Sampling:* Four breakfast specials; plate lunch of chopsteak, *loco moco*, saimin, chicken *hekka*, or hamburger ($3-$7). Daily specials, too.

Pizza Fresh *(Italian)*
1043 Makawao Avenue, Unit 103, Makawao; 808-572-2000.

Hours: 10 a.m.-9 p.m. *Sampling:* Lunch menu available only from 10 a.m.-2:30 p.m. Monday-Friday and is a selection of sandwiches and salads ($4-$8). Pizza varieties include eggplant gouda, portobello, scampi, Thai chicken, or alfredo vegetarian, or create your own. Start with the basic cheese $6.95 for 9" up to $18.95 for 18" and add toppings for $.80-$1.60 each. You even have a selection of sauces from sun-dried tomato pesto to marinara, basil pesto or alfredo. Choose between traditional or wheat crust (all made fresh daily). Caesar, garden or Greek salads also available as well as calzones. *Comments:* Delivery in the area available after 4 p.m.

Polli's *(Mexican)*
1202 Makawao Avenue, Makawao; 808-572-7808.

Hours: 11 a.m.-10 p.m. *Sampling:* Mexican pizza, taquitos, jalapeno poppers, tacos, tostadas, nachos, chili, steak *pupu* ($6-$11). Chile relleno or tamale plate, stuffed quesadilla, seafood enchilada, chimichanga, sizzling fajitas, burritos supreme, vegetarian chile ($6.95-

$17.95). Choose from burritos, Mexican chicken or fish dinners, or Mexican *especialidades* such as carnitas or baked bajas. Also offered is barbecue chicken, ribs, steak and burgers ($7.50-$14.95). *Comments:* Black beans and chile verde sauce are two alternative menu options, and vegetarians can request any menu item made with tofu or vegetarian taco mix. Children's plates available—children's night is Tuesday, with meals only $1 for kids under 12. An extra charge to refill your basket of chips seems a little chintzy, though.

Pukalani Country Club Restaurant *(American/Hawaiian)*
360 Pukalani Road (turn right just before the shopping center at Pukalani and continue until the road ends), Pukalani; 808-572-1325.

Hours: 7:30 a.m.-2 p.m. *Sampling:* Hearty breakfasts such as omelets, pancakes, French toast, Belgian waffles, egg dishes ($4-$7). Popular for their local foods. For lunch you might choose between *kalua* pig, tripe stew, or *laulau* offered as Hawaiian plates (under $10), or you can get them a la carte along with *lomi* salmon, *pipi kalua*, squid or *pulehu* ribs. More traditional fare includes a tuna melt, jumbo hot dog, burger, club or egg salad sandwich ($5-$7). Similar offerings at dinner along with steaks, breaded mahi or shrimp, fried chicken, and teriyaki beef ($9-$16). *Comments:* Lunch reservations are a must as this is a popular place with the tour groups. Or eat lunch elsewhere and stop back on the way down from Upcountry for a drink, the tropical sunset, and a wonderful view. In addition to their authentic Hawaiian menu, they also have nightly specials and a salad bar at dinner. *Keiki* menu available.

Royal King's Garden *(Chinese)*
Pukalani Terrace Center, 55 Pukalani Street, Pukalani; 808-572-7027.

Hours: Tuesday-Sunday 11 a.m.-2 p.m. and 4-9 p.m. *Sampling:* Lunch specials include two entrees plus rice or chow mein and soda or barbecue teri beef or chicken with rice and salad (served all day). Dinners offer potstickers or *char siu* to start and with entrees such as beef with broccoli, shrimp with ginger and onion, sliced fish with oyster sauce, chicken with eggplant, egg foo yong, crispy duck, pork hash, steamed mahimahi, mu shu chicken, vegetarian chow mein, pork cake noodle, or won ton mein ($5.25-$9.95). Oysters ($12.50), and abalone or lobster entrees ($24.95). *Comments:* No MSG is used in the dishes here.

Stopwatch Sports Bar *(Italian/American)*
1127 Makawao Avenue, Makawao; 808-572-1380.

Hours: 11 a.m.-2 a.m. *Sampling:* Sandwiches include burgers, roast beef, grilled mahi or chicken breast ($6-$8). Entrees include fish and chips or fried shrimp ($8-$12).

Moderate-priced Dining

Casanova Italian Restaurant and Deli *(Italian)*
1188 Makawao Avenue, Makawao; 808-572-0220.

Hours: Lunch Monday-Saturday 11:30 a.m.-2 p.m. Dinner nightly 5:30-9:15 p.m. (pizza until midnight Wednesday, Friday, Saturday). Deli daily 7:30 a.m.-6 p.m. *Sampling:* The deli offers sandwiches with interesting combinations of lemon chicken, smoked salmon, roast peppers, mozzarella, eggplant, smoked ham, brie and pastrami plus Caesar, Greek and pasta salads ($5-$9). Breakfast pastries (*lilikoi* poppy-seed cake, corn bread, blueberry scones), waffles, French toast, and omelets are served until 11:30. Lunch includes soups, salads, sandwiches, pizza and plenty of great pasta selections ($8-$12). The dinner menu offers antipasti with an Italian flair including cioppino, *insalata di* tofu and deep-fried calamari. Salads include Mediterranean or Caesar ($5-$9). Pizzas baked in their authentic wood-fired oven are in the tradition of Napoli, "where pizza was born." All pizzas are 12" ($10 and up). The pasta selection nears almost a dozen, with every shape and size served with seafood and chicken breast, or stuffed with ricotta ($12-$14). Entrees include fresh fish of the day, filet of ahi, filet mignon, New York steak, or grilled lamb chops ($22-$24). *Comments:* One of a few places left to go for dining and dancing. Good food and a variety of entertainment (including special celebrity concerts) have won them accolades. Each night you'll find something different.

Kula Lodge *(American-Hawaiian)*
Five miles past Pukalani on Haleakala Highway; 808-878-1535.

Hours: Breakfast Monday-Saturday 6:30-11 a.m. Lunch Monday-Saturday 11:30 a.m.-3:30 p.m. Appetizers daily 3:30-5 p.m. Dinner daily 5-8:30 p.m. *Sampling:* Warm up from your early-morning visit to Haleakala with a cappuccino, latte, mocha or perhaps a Bloody Mary or mimosa. A hearty breakfast at this must-stop might require some tough decisions. Everything sounds good: vegetarian Benedict (with sliced tomatoes, artichoke crowns and mushrooms), Sunrise Classic (eggs plus applewood smoked bacon, ham or Portuguese sausage), Cajun fish eggs Benedict, *loco moco.* Select a tofu stir-fry or create your own omelet. And from the grill there is apple cinnamon French toast, malted Belgian waffle, Bananas Foster pancakes, or griddle cakes ($8-$16). The lunch menu offers a huge selection of soups, salads and appetizers, a great option if you'd just like a break and don't have a huge appetite. Papaya shrimp salad, "broke da mouth" potstickers, "crabby crab cake," or three-cheese quesadilla ($6-$12). Sandwiches and plenty of burgers, or a main course of brick oven–roasted free-range chicken or grilled eggplant and portobello mushroom on polenta cake ($8-$13). Soups, salads and appetizers are the same as those offered for lunch; follow it up with dinner entree of prime aged NY steak, rosemary chicken, zebra *panzotti* (with Caribbean seared salmon and rock shrimp in a tomato basil butter sauce), or spinach fettuccine with stir-fry vegetables and grilled tofu ($17-$29). *Comments:* Chef Domenico Garfola was previously with Carelli's in Kihei. Breakfast, the most popular meal of the day, has the added benefit of the fireplace (a warming delight after a cold trip to the mountain top) and a spectacular panoramic view. A combined breakfast/lunch menu is served on Sunday.

Kula Sandalwoods Restaurant *(American)*
15427 Haleakala Highway, Kula; 808-878-3523
 Hours: Monday-Friday 6:30 a.m.-2:30 p.m. Sunday 6:30 a.m.-noon. Closed Saturday. *Sampling:* Sunrise breakfast and lunch and Sunday brunch. Breakfast menu is broad. For lunch enjoy a grilled chicken breast sandwich, grilled turkey and jack, or a chicken Caesar salad ($5-$9.50).

★ **Makawao Steak House** *(American)*
3612 Baldwin Avenue, Makawao; 808-572-8711.
 Hours: 5:30-9 p.m. *Sampling:* Sample their popular chicken Zoie (stuffed breasts with creamed spinach filling), teriyaki pork tenderloin, Kalaheo shrimp or calamari steak. But if you're hankering for beef don't miss their prime rib. Served while supply lasts. They also have great steaks: pepper steak, teriyaki top sirloin, beef tenderloin ($17.95-$27.95). Dinners come with potato or rice and breads. They have a small all-you-can-eat salad bar for an additional $3.95. *Comments:* This family-owned Makawao landmark has attractive *paniolo* artwork, wood floors and paneling, and a cozy ambiance with a stately fireplace that glows on those chilly Upcountry evenings. Great kids' menu ($2.50-$3.75), too.

Expensive-priced Dining

★ **Hali'imaile General Store** *(Hawaiian Regional/Continental)*
Hali'imaile Road, Hali'imaile; 808-572-2666.
 Hours: Lunch Monday-Friday 11 a.m.-2:30 p.m. Dinner 5:30-9:30 p.m. *Sampling:* The menu changes seasonally, but always features an innovative selection of dishes. Lunch includes their popular Nicoise with a toss, Upcountry-style Caesar, or baby back ribs ($7-$14). For dinner begin with Bev's Boboli (crab dip served on a 6" Boboli), sashimi Napoleon, Asian pear and duck taco, or brie and grape quesadilla topped with sweet pea guacamole ($8-$17). Entrees ($20-$28) include *kalua* pork enchiladas, Hunan-

style rack of lamb, Szechuan barbecued salmon and crispy lacquered half-duck. Desserts tempt you from the display case and it is definitely worth saving room. *Comments:* This restaurant (and Chef Beverly Gannon) has put Hali'imaile on the map, collecting rave reviews and top ratings since it opened in 1988. The original structure dates back to the 1920s when it served as the general store and hub of this community. The 5,000-square-foot wood building maintains its original high ceiling; the floors are refurbished hardwood. The intricately designed bar in the front dining room is surrounded by tall pine shelves and an exhibition kitchen. The admirable wine list includes some nice port, sherry and cognac. The food is exquisite and it's well worth the drive across the island. They periodically feature specials and take 50 percent off your meal ticket on Aloha Mondays. A great deal for diners. Look for Beverly Gannon's cookbook and take a little of the island home with you, and enjoy her food service if you fly on Hawaiian Airlines.

Hana Highway

Inexpensive-priced Dining
Anthony's Coffee Co. *(Coffee/Light Meals)*
90 Hana Highway, Paia; 808-579-8340.

Hours: 5:30 a.m.-6 p.m. *Sampling:* Belgian waffle, French toast plain or with "fruit and whip," eggs Benedict regular style or with lox or *kalua* pork, breakfast croissant with a choice of meat, bagels plain or with toppings, catch of the day with toast, rice or potatoes ($4.50-$6.50). Add a breakfast meat with your meal for an extra dollar. Cold sandwiches include pastrami, salami, roast beef, or veggie ($4.25) or try a hot one such as tuna melt or a burger ($5.25) served with chips and a pickle. Side salads of pasta or potato, or green $1 more. Large salads include Cobb or chicken Caesar ($5.95). They feature made-on-Maui ice cream in their cones, shakes, sundaes, floats and smoothies ($2-$3.50). *Comments:* Counter and table seating with plenty of newspapers and magazines to read while you enjoy a variety of hot coffee drinks. They roast their own coffees and sell more than 20 international varieties. The roaster is in the shop, so if you time it right you can watch and smell as they toast up their beans. Cozy place and good prices.

Café Des Amis *(Creperie)*
42 Baldwin Avenue, Paia; 808-579-6232.

Hours: 8:30 a.m.-8:30 p.m. Closed Sunday. *Sampling:* Assorted crepes include spinach with feta, brie with avocado, apple and black pepper, mahimahi with shrimp in a creamy wine sauce, or shrimp curry with coconut milk and rice all accompanied with house salad ($5.90-$9.80). Salads include Nicoise, Greek, shrimp Caesar, or seafood ($7.95-$10.95). For dessert enjoy a sweet crepe made with bananas and chocolate, strawberries and cream, peaches with raspberry sauce, or caramelized apples with rum ($1.75-$3.80). *Comments:* Owners Bob and Tina serve up more than a small traditional crepe, it's a large, hearty, stuffed rectangular portion. Breakfast crepes are available all day. Daily specials, too!

★ *Café Mambo* (American/Healthy)
30 Baldwin Avenue, Paia; 808-579-8021.

Hours: 7 a.m.-7 p.m. *Sampling:* Hawaiian pancakes or egg dishes ($4.25-$5.75). Lunch fare offerings include hot and cold sandwiches and burgers or salads ($5-$8). Plate lunches are served 11 a.m.-5 p.m. with two scoops of rice, Haiku greens, tropical fruit, or potato salad with selections ranging from teri beef or chicken to half herb-roasted chicken or catch of the day ($7-$9). A little tired? Try one of their power smoothies. Excursion box lunch meals (picnics!) include sandwich, fresh fruit, homemade cookie and beverage or a Hana Bay Picnic for two. Plenty of espresso and cappuccino if you're in need of an eye opener. *Comments:* Coffee drinks and fresh baked pastries plus soft-serve ice cream and sundaes. A very popular place to pick up some lunch goodies for the road to Hana or Haleakala. Their newsprint menu contains a map and a guide to Hana with information about Hana's parks, bridges and points of interest. Anything on their menu is available to go and everything is ready from 7 a.m.

Charley's (American/Italian)
142 Hana Highway, Paia; 808-579-9453.

Hours: Breakfast 7 a.m.-1 p.m., Sunday until 2:30 p.m. Lunch 11:30 a.m.-2:30 p.m. *Pupus*/burgers 2:30-5 p.m. Dinner 5-10 p.m. *Sampling:* Buttermilk, Hawaiian macadamia, whole wheat, or blueberry pancakes, or enjoy Charley's steak and eggs, huevos rancheros, or a vegetarian breakfast taco ($4-$12). Lunches include their popular one-third pound burgers ($7-$9) or choose from grilled fish, turkey, avocado or Charley's chicken sandwich ($7-$8). Lunch entrees include *ono* pan fry, fish and chips, or cashew chicken ($8-$10). Dinners of chicken marsala, seafood fettuccine, scampi, lasagna, barbecue ribs, hand-tossed pizza, calzone, *kiawe*-smoked ribs or marlin, and nightly fish specials ($8-$23). *Comments:* This is a Paia landmark. Big-screen TV for satellite sporting events. Charley's was named for the owner's black-and-white Great Dane (named for the movie *Goodbye, Charley* in which Debbie Reynolds was reincarnated as a Great Dane), which

> ### SUNSET-WATCHING SUGGESTIONS
>
> Because the sun goes down over Lana'i in the winter if you're in Lahaina, sunsets in Wailea are better in winter and best in West Maui in the summer. Here are my suggestions:
> - Settling down to dinner at The Plantation House in Kapalua
> - Enjoying *pupus* from the lobby bar of the Kapalua Bay Resort
> - On the promontory at the Bay Club, Kapalua
> - Torchlighting, cliff diving and music nightly at sunset at the Sheraton Lagoon Bar
> - Sitting at a lanai table at the Sea Watch Restaurant in Wailea
> - From the lanai at Capische? at the Diamond Resort
> - Relaxing in the lobby bar at the Renaissance Wailea Beach Resort
> - From the sea wall on Front Street
> - Nalu's Sunset Bar & Sushi at Maui Marriott
> - On a sunset cruise as you sail back into Ma'alaea or Lahaina Harbor
> - Overlooking the valley from Kula Lodge
> - En route down from Haleakala, at the Pukalani Country Club

roamed freely around Front Street when the restaurant began as a small fruit juice stand in Lahaina. Charley the dog and Charley's moved to Paia in 1971 and Charley P. Woofer Restaurant and Saloon was born. Today, the original dog has been "reincarnated" several times, and the most recent one is "C.W."

★ Haiku Gourmet Take-out & Deli *(Deli)*
771 Haiku Road, Haiku; 808-575-5404.

Hours: 6 a.m.-8 p.m. *Sampling:* Caesar, Chinese chicken, or Greek salads along with chicken walnut, blackened ahi, or French dip sandwiches ($5.95-$7.95). A limited variety of entrees include barbecue ribs, herb-roasted chicken, prime rib (Friday and Saturday only) or daily specials ($8.99-$15.99). *Comments:* Deli salads and other goodies to go. A nice espresso bar. Cozy indoor dining.

Hokus Pokus *(Vegan/Vegetarian)*
115 Baldwin Avenue, Paia; 808-579-9144.

Hours: 3-9 p.m. *Sampling:* Vegetarian cuisine. Tempeh burger, grilled veggie sandwich or "Hokus Wrap," a tortilla filled with hummus, veggie pate, avocado delight or spicy tofu. Tofu or bean tacos and appetizers like potato knish and *saganaki*. Full dinners include garlic or ginger veggies, curry veggies, pad Thai, polenta au gratin, vegetable kebab or quiche lorraine ($4.25-$10.95). Desserts include *fugelhopf*, vegan cake, Thai tapioca or schoggi mousse ($2.50-$2.95). *Comments:* Owners Thomas and Edith Stiglmayer are from Austria. Indoor and outdoor seating for a dozen people. You're welcome to bring your own wine or beer to accompany you meal.

Lynne's Café *(Local)*
810 Kokomo Road, Haiku; 808-575-9363.

Hours: 5 a.m.-6 p.m. *Sampling:* Breakfast, sandwiches, salads and bentos along with plate lunches like pork *laulau*, beef or chicken *hekka* ($3.50-$5.50). *Comments:* Very small, local-style operation.

Milagros Food Co. *(Tex-Mex)*
3 Baldwin Avenue on the corner of Hana Highway, Paia; 808-579-8755.

Hours: Breakfast 8-11 a.m. Lunch 11:30 a.m.-5 p.m. Dinner 5:30-9:30 p.m. *Sampling & Comments:* Outside veranda; coffee drinks and a full bar with margaritas and micro beers. I'm told this is the only Maui restaurant with Santa Fe–style Mexican food. Huge chicken burritos, but mostly filled with beans and rice. Haven't eaten here recently, last time it was pretty mediocre. Sitting outside was good for people watching, but a bit too noisy with the busy road right in front. They always look busy, so maybe the margaritas are better than the food! Prices $8-$12.

Paia Fish Market Restaurant *(Seafood)*
101 Hana Highway, on the corner of Baldwin Avenue and Hana Highway, Paia; 808-579-8030.

Hours: 11 a.m.-9 p.m. *Sampling:* Charbroiled burgers, fish and chips, and lunch- or dinner-size portions of quesadillas or teriyaki chicken. They offer a variety of seafood prepared Cajun style, blackened, sautéed or charbroiled ($6.50-$13.95). A blackboard slate details the fresh fish offerings. Beer and wine. *Comments:* Place your order at the counter then pick up your meal and seat yourself at a half-dozen oversized picnic tables. Humorous artifacts lining the walls make for interesting topics of conversation.

★ **Pauwela Café** *(Healthy)*
Pauwela Cannery, 375 West Kuiaha Road, Haiku; 808-575-9242.

Hours: Monday-Friday 7 a.m.-3 p.m. Sunday 8 a.m.-2 p.m. *Sampling:* Breakfast is served throughout the day and includes hot-out-of-the-oven coffeecake, muffins, scones breakfast breads ($1.75-$2.25). *Pain perdu* (French bread baked in orange custard) is a must-try for breakfast or as dessert; get there early because it often sells out quickly! Belgian waffles (served until 10:30 a.m.) or homemade English muffins topped with scrambled eggs, turkey ham, tomato and cheese ($4-$5.75). Lunch selections include green leaf, Greek and Caesar salads. A little bigger appetite will enjoy the *kalua* turkey sandwich (yum!), the Very Veggie (eggplant and red pepper), or veggie burrito or with *kalua* turkey ($6-$7.50). The *chilaquile* is excellent (an innovative alternative to huevos rancheros). Their cheesecake is also one of a kind, made with ricotta, golden raisins, and pinenuts. Daily specials. Coffees, fresh orange or carrot juice, fruit and yogurt and (non-dairy) smoothies. *Comments:* The lively artwork of Nancy Hoke dresses the walls of this cannery café, located on Highway 36 in the old Libby Pineapple Cannery, about 15 miles from Kahului. Built in 1918, it now houses many famous manufacturers of windsurf and surfing gear. *Keiki* menu and take out available. Everything is made fresh with unbleached flour and raw sugar in all the baked goods.

Hana Ranch Store
Hana Highway; 808-248-8261.

Hours: Open daily. *Sampling:* Ready-made sandwiches and hot dogs.

Hasegawa General Store
5165 Hana Highway, Hana; 808-248-8231.

Hours: Open daily. *Sampling:* You'll find a little bit of everything.

Tutu's *(Local/Sandwiches)*
174 Hana Bay, Hana; 808-248-8224.

Hours: 8:30 a.m.-4 p.m. *Sampling:* Sandwiches, plate lunches. *Comments:* People have been known to drive for miles for their *haupia* ice cream.

Moderate-priced Dining

★ Hana Hou *(Local)*
Haiku Marketplace, 810 Haiku Road, Haiku; 808-575-2661.

Hours: 10 a.m.-10 p.m. *Sampling:* Saimin ($4.50-$5.95), burgers and plate lunches ($6.95-$9.65), Hawaiian plates such as *kalua* pork and cabbage or chicken long rice, NY steak, *paniolo* ribs, shrimp curry or pastas such as wild mushroom or Kula garden pasta. Hana Hou dinners ($12.95-$16.95). *Comments:* A great local diner in the old plantation home next to Haiku Cannery. There is a to-go window, or sit inside and enjoy. Thursday through Saturday they have entertainment 7-9:30 p.m.

★ Jacques' North Shore Restaurant and Sushi Bar *(Seafood/Sushi)*
120 Hana Highway Paia; 808-579-8844.

Hours: 5-10 p.m. *Sampling:* Appetizers include chicken martini, coconut shrimp ravioli with spinach and shiitake mushrooms, mini pesto caper pancakes, soup Pauvert (Jacques' special pumpkin coconut soup) or sushi from the sushi bar ($4.25-$9.95). Salads include spinach and shrimp with a citrus vinaigrette, salad Nicoise, lobster brochette with salad greens or a fried tofu salad ($4.25-$12.95). Vegans enjoy an entree of vegetable tofu curry or a tofu stir-fry ($11.95). Fish is a specialty here and the preparations are all fabulous. All are served with seasonal vegetables and rice. North Shore Pumpkin Fish with fish, bananas and oranges served with a ginger pumpkin sauce and miso butter. Pacific free-range salmon or try pickled salmon (broiled in a unique marinade then poached medium rare and seared before serving on angelhair pasta), macadamia nut–crusted fish, or fish dynamite (with a portobello mushroom, havarti cheese, and spicy mayo) ($14.95-$19.95). For pasta you can try pork spare rib pasta, seafood linguini, or smoked chicken pasta ($10.95-$16.95). The meat lover can be satisfied with an entree of chicken piccata, spicy peanut chicken, pork on a sugar cane, beef sauteed in a peppercorn brandy cream sauce, or roast duckling ($10.95-$21.95). *Comments:* Jacques' has been in a few different locations on Maui. In Paia, they continue to have exciting and innovative preparations and did you get a load of those prices? Their most expensive appetizer would be the bottom of the rung price-wise at any of the resorts. It's definitely worth the drive to Paia for some top-notch cuisine.

★ **Moana Bakery & Café** *(Bakery)*
71 Baldwin Avenue, Paia; 808-579-9999.

Hours: Breakfast 8 a.m.-11 a.m. Lunch 11 a.m.-3 p.m. Dinner 3-9 p.m. *Sampling:* For breakfast sample a surfer's omelet, malted Belgian waffles or tropical pancakes plus quiche, saimin, frittata or *loco moco* ($4.95-$7.95). For lunch try their Caesar with creamy roasted garlic (served in an edible bread basket) or the crispy Thai chicken salad with colorful Asian veggies. Sandwiches range from grilled mahi or roasted vegetable to breast of chicken or gourmet burger. But don't expect the usual; everything seems to come with a little something extra and different. For dinner starters try their roasted vegetable Napoleon or begin with a Hana Bay crab cake, chile seared ahi with Moloka'i sweet potatoes, taro leaves and mango salsa, or medallions of filet mignon. Dinner prices top out at just about $21.95 for the rack of lamb. *Comments:* The innovative chef is Don Ritchey. Evening entertainment three nights a week, ranging from blues, flamenco and even vintage Hawaiian.

Expensive-priced Dining

Hana Ranch Restaurant *(American)*
5031 Hana Highway, Hana; 808-248-8255.

Hours: Lunch buffet 11 a.m.-3 p.m. Dinner Wednesday, Friday and Saturday 5:30-8:30 p.m. *Sampling:* On Wednesday you can enjoy Pizza Night and there is an a la carte menu for dinner on Friday and Saturday. Dinners include seared ahi, grilled rib eye, barbecue baby back ribs, sweet chili glazed roasted chicken or grilled salmon ($17.95-$22.95). Appetizers, soups and salads ($5.75-$10.95) and salad bar is all-you-can-eat for $11.95, or with dinner an additional $4.95. *Comments:* Buffet lunch has full bar service. On dinner nights they also offer *pupus* and drinks throughout the evening. *Keiki* dinner menu. A to-go window is also available and serves hamburgers some evenings when the restaurant is closed.

Hotel Hana-Maui Dining Room *(Continental)*
Hotel Hana-Maui, Hana; 808-248-8211.
   Hours: Breakfast 7:30-10 a.m. Lunch 11:30 a.m.-2 p.m. Dinner 6:15-9 p.m. Paniolo Bar 11:30 a.m.-10:30 p.m. *Sampling:* Breakfasts ($11-$14) include rainforest omelet (three eggs with local fern shoots), mushroom, tomato and cheese), eggs Benedict, banana pancakes and apple pie French toast. Lunches ($12.50-$16) offer light selections on their starter menu such as ahi sashimi tempura roll or Hana-style Nicoise salad. Sandwiches and burgers feature smoked turkey, avocado and havarti sandwich grilled, vegetable and mozzarella open-faced sandwich or teriyaki burger. Dinner menus may change seasonally but you could begin your meal with Manila clams, Hana breadfruit cake served with green apple–pineapple chutney and curry aioli or a shiitake mushroom soup ($8-$13.50), then enjoy an entree of tofu Napoleon, roast Colorado rack of lamb, pan-seared sea scallops (in truffled shellfish cream), roasted lemongrass-ginger chicken with Moloka'i sweet potato cake and red Thai curry sauce ($24-$37). Daily desserts selections. *Comments:* Hawaiian shows are Thursdays and Sundays. On Thursdays there is a Hawaiian buffet and Sundays it is a prime rib buffet for $37. Overall, good food and very friendly waitstaff. Prices are actually less than the high-end restaurants in Ka'anapali and Wailea. In-room dining is available 7:30 a.m.-9 p.m.

★ **Mama's Fish House** *(Continental/Seafood)*
On Highway 36 just 1.5 miles past Paia at Kuau, look for the ship's flagpole and the angel fish sign; 808-579-8488.
   Hours: Lunch 11 a.m.-2:30 p.m. *Pupus* 2:30-5 p.m. Dinner 5-9:30 p.m. *Sampling:* You may mistake the prices on the lunch menus as dinner fare, but people from far and wide come to enjoy the island's very best seafood and an excellent oceanfront location. Lunch appetizers, soups and salads range from macadamia nut crab cake and fire and ice relish to Chef Martin's classic fish chowder. There are oysters fresh from Fanny Bay, Pacific Northwest butter clams, or Polynesian lobster soup with coconut, fresh spinach, and Hana breadfruit crisps ($10-$14). Both lunch and dinner offer a twist that really personalizes the menu. You might enjoy *ono* caught by Matt Moser trolling offshore from Hana Bay, mahimahi caught by Mark Hobson along the north shore of Maui or *shutome* caught in local waters aboard the *Kawika*. Any fish may be served grilled with pineapple salsa, sautéed Mama's style, or with a bit more Pacific-Rim flair you could have your ahi seared in *nori* and roasted *kukui* nut

with wasabi beurre blanc and soba noodles. Entrees $24 and up. Luncheon salads ($17-$25) available and sandwiches include fresh fish or perhaps *kalua* pig with Asian pear chutney ($15-$22). Since Mama has her own fishing fleet you can expect the best and freshest. There are also other seafood selections or select from sugar cane grilled chicken salad with mac nut mustard dressing, or pork tenderloin. But you really shouldn't come to Mama's without a hankering for fish because the land-lover selections definitely take a back seat to seafood. The menu changes daily. *Comments:* Mama's opened in 1973, making it one of the island's oldest restaurants and one of the few that consistently offers an outstanding variety of excellently prepared foods. And how inviting is a restaurant named "Mama's?" It's a beach house, right on the ocean, with just the kind of atmosphere you'd expect to find in Hawai'i. Mama's mission was "to serve creative seafood dishes with that elusive taste of Maui island cooking." And it appears she has accomplished her mission. Expensive, but a must-do if you're looking for great Hawaiian seafood and an only-in-Hawai'i splurge. And nothing beats a sunny afternoon here as you gaze onto the beach with the palm trees swaying! Valet parking. Reservations, especially for dinner, strongly recommended. Full bar service.

Luaus and Dinner Shows

Most of the luaus are large, with an average of 400-600 guests. Most serve traditional Hawaiian foods. The entertainment ranges from splashy Broadway-style productions to more subtle offerings of authentic Hawaiian dance and song. In general there are a few standard things to be expected at luaus. These are an *imu* ceremony (to uncover the cooked pig that will be served that night), the Hawaiian wedding song, poi, *haupia* (coconut pudding) and mai tais. Upon arrival there may or may not be some waiting in line before it's your turn to be greeted with a shell or flower lei; a snapshot of your group (available for purchase after the show) is a sure bet.

It is very difficult to judge these luaus due to their diversity. While one reader raves about a particular show, another reader will announce disappointment with the same event. Read the information provided, carefully keeping in mind that performers do come and go. Luau prices run $68-$89 for adults; youth prices are discounted by about half.

Feast of Lele
505 Front Street, Lahaina; 800-248-5828; 808-667-LELE.

This luau celebrates the cuisine and culture of Polynesia. A five-course dinner is served at this oceanfront location. Each course cor-

Text continued on page 296.

NIGHTLIFE

With so many activity options during the day, by nightfall you're likely to be ready to unwind (if not head straight for bed). But if you still have energy left, here are a few suggestions for after the sun goes down. The following spots generally offer entertainment, but as everything else, things change very quickly. Call to see what's on on which nights. Check the "Scene" section of the Thursday edition of the *Maui News,* which lists current late-night happenings.

LAHAINA **Paradice Bluz Nightclub/Lounge** at the Lahaina Store on Front Street is open until 2 a.m. with jazz, blues and comedy. Lots of couches and a cross between the old Blue Max and a Starbucks internet café. **Moose McGillycuddy's** is always hopping for the young crowd. **Kobe Japanese Steakhouse** offers karaoke on Friday and Saturdays. **Kimo's** has entertainment on different nights of the week. **Lahaina Coolers** has live music one night a week (currently Wednesday). **Longhi's** at the Old Lahaina Center has entertainment Friday nights. **BJ's Chicago Pizzeria** has lots happening on a variety of evenings. **Bubba Gump Shrimp** has music on Saturday. **Cheeseburger in Paradise** offers music almost every night and has an early (4:30-7:30 p.m.) and late (8-11 p.m.) set. **Compadres** at Lahaina Cannery Mall features salsa dancing from 10 p.m. to closing on Saturday. Check **Pioneer Inn** for music a few nights each week 6-9 p.m. There's weekend entertainment at **Pacific 'O's** at 505 Front Street. Visit **Warren & Annabelle's** for magic shows at 6 and 8 p.m.

KA'ANAPALI-KAPALUA AREA Most of the resorts have live music in their lounges. At Kapalua Bay Hotel and Ocean Villas, the elegant **Bay Club** is situated on a promontory overlooking the ocean, boasting an idyllic setting from which to enjoy the scenic panorama along with *pupus* and tropical drinks; **Lehua Lounge** serves cocktails from 4:30-11 p.m. and has a panoramic ocean view from their comfortable open-air living room setting. Both **Hula Grill** and **Leilani's** offer live Hawaiian music at Whalers Village. **Fish & Game Brewing Company** in Kahana offers jazz on Sunday. **Kahana Terrace** has music three nights a week 6-9 p.m. **Sea House Restaurant** has a Polynesian dinner show on Friday and other Hawaiian music throughout the week. **Sansei** at Kapalua has karaoke several nights a week.

MA'ALAEA-KIHEI-WAILEA-MAKENA AREA Most resorts have great soft jazz or Hawaiian music in their lobby lounges. The **Botero Lounge** at the Grand Wailea Resort Hotel & Spa is open until midnight and offers Hawaiian musical entertainment nightly from 6-9 p.m. The 10,000-square-foot **Tsunami Night Club** is the only true nightclub on Maui and operates Fridays and Saturdays 9:30 p.m.-1:30 a.m. for dancing to R&B, hip-hop, Top-40 and house music; evening resort wear and proper footwear required, no beachwear; $10 cover. At the Four Season Resort, the **Games Room** (open until 11 p.m.) is fun for families with big-screen TVs, video games, table shuffleboard, pool tables, and jukebox; alcohol and smoke-free area on lower level. The **Lobby Lounge**, open until midnight, offers entertainment; the terrace adjoining the lobby overlooks the ocean and West Maui Mountains. The Fairmont Kea Lani's **Lobby Lounge**, which specializes in martinis, overlooks the ocean and tropical gardens and features a cozy "living room" atmosphere with couches and overstuffed chairs; entertainment from 8-11 p.m. Entertainment is frequently available in the **Molokini Lounge** or in the lovely outdoor courtyard at Maui Prince Hotel.

Sansei in Kihei has karaoke several nights a week. **Bocalino Bistro** has deejays and dancing almost every night. **Capische?** at the Diamond Resort in Wailea has live piano music nightly. **Lulu's**, located behind Bada Bing's, has 22 televisions and a pool table room. **DeanO's Maui Pizza Café** has music, a comedy and magic show, open-mic night and karaoke, some with cover charge. **El Restaurante Pasatiempo** has music Wednesday-Saturday. **Hapa*s Nightclub** has something happening most nights of the week from 9 p.m.-1:30 a.m. **La Creperie** is the place to be if you like jazz; in the evening it becomes "La Jazzerie." Check out classical Thai dance at **Thailand Cuisine**.

Other spots to check out are **Kai Ku' Ono**, **Life's a Beach** (young bar scene), **Ma'alaea Grill** at Marco's Southside Grill, **Margarita's Beach Cantina**, **Mulligan's on the Blue** at the Wailea Blue Course, and **Tommy Bahama's** at the Shops at Wailea.

KAHULUI-WAILUKU AREA **Moana Café** has a mix of salsa, jazz and Hawaiian music three nights a week. Jerome E. Metcalfe's **Kahului Ale House Sports Bar & Restaurant** has music with deejays as well as karaoke. **Manana Garage** and **Wow-Wee Maui's Café** are other spots to check out.

UPCOUNTRY **Casanova's** in Makawao has a dance floor and features blues, jazz, Western, disco and a bit of everything else. **The Stopwatch** in Makawao has live music primarily on weekends.

HANA HIGHWAY **Hana Hou** in Haiku has entertainment. Down in Paia check out **Charley's** and **Jacques**.

responds to a specific region of Polynesia, which is depicted in a segment of the show. The meal begins with traditional Polynesian staples of green banana, sweet potato and taro to sample throughout your meal. This is followed by native Hawaiian dishes of pohole ferns, steamed *moi*, *imu kalua* pig and poi. From Tonga there is octopus, lobster and *ogo* salad along with *tunu pulu* (grilled strip steak) and roasted squash. From Tahiti you'll be served *poisson cru* (marinated fish), scallop on the shell and *fafa* (steamed chicken and taro leaf in coconut milk). The Samoan course brings you grilled fish in banana leaf and *palusami* (breadfruit with taro leaf and coconut cream) along with shrimp and avocado with *lilikoi*. Dessert includes banana coconut bundles, tropical fruits, and Hawaiian chocolate truffles. Tropical drinks, cocktails and wine are included. The entire program is a little too lethargic with too much time between the dinner course, the segment of the show, and then another dinner course. For these prices, you don't want to be disappointed. $89 adults, $59 child (infants in stroller or on lap free).

Hotel Hana-Maui
Hana; 808-248-8211.

The hotel dining room offers a dinner buffet (with prime rib) on Fridays 6-9 p.m. There is a Hawaiian music and hula show at 7 p.m. Many of the performers are hotel employees or their family members, so it is an authentic and charming musical production. $45 adults, $31 children.

Hyatt Regency Maui Resort and Spa ("Drums of the Pacific")
200 Nohea Kai Drive, Ka'anapali; 808-667-4420.

"Drums of the Pacific" is more a dinner show than a luau. The performance is on the grounds of the Hyatt (Lahaina side) but there is no ocean view. The show is from 5-8 p.m. and there is usually a bit of a line. Pictures are taken while waiting prior to admission to the grounds, where you are greeted with a lei and taken to a table by your server. The dinner buffet I experienced featured mahimahi, *shoyu* chicken, *kalua* pork, and steaks cooked on the grill. Baked potatoes, roasted sweet potatoes with pineapple glaze, Upcountry vegetable stir-fry, and island-style fried rice complete the dinner offerings. The desserts were a cut above: the *haupia* had good texture and coconut flavor, and the hot bread pudding was baked with

> **LUAU VALUE**
>
> Check the *Maui News* for advertisements listing local luaus that might be held by churches or other community organizations as fundraisers. The public is welcome and the prices are usually half that of the commercial ventures. A terrific value and you're sure to enjoy some great "local" food.

a meringue topping. They also had chocolate macadamia nut pie and pineapple upside-down cake. The show starts off with the blowing of the conch and the beating of the drums. The *kahiko* hula followed the chant and had a very effective smoke-like mist surrounding the dancers. The *imu* ceremony was short and nondescript, but did have the "Pig Procession," carrying his piggly majesty through the center aisle of the audience. A separate side stage for solo dances made things visually interesting. Perhaps the best number was the Maui Waltz, a pretty song with girls in high-collared white Victorian blouses and colored skirts. Chief Fa'a, the fire dancer, continues to be one of the best. A good, professional and fast-paced production. All in all, a show worth seeing. Adults $75 ($65 for Hyatt guests), teens $49, children $34.

Kupanaha: Maui Magic for All Ages
Ka'anapali Beach Hotel, 2525 Ka'anapali Parkway, Kanahele Room Theater; 808-667-0128; 800-262-8450.

Kupanaha is the Hawaiian word for "amazing" and "marvelous" and Kupanaha: Maui Magic for All Ages is just that—an evening of cutting-edge illusions and sleight-of-hand magic tricks along with legends of Hawaiian demigods illustrated through hula and chant. The sit-down, three-course meal, held Tuesday-Saturday from 5:15-8 p.m. (check in 4:30 p.m.), begins with pig in a *pareo* (the KBH signature appetizer) or roasted vegetable bruschetta, then choose your entree of snapper, roasted stuffed chicken breast, steak and shrimp, or vegetarian. Finish with pina colada cheesecake served in a fresh Ka'anapali pineapple. *Keikis* can choose from hamburger and cheesy fries, breaded chicken nuggets, or spaghetti with meat sauce. Enjoy complimentary beer and wine or indulge in an exotic tropical drink like a Tropical Storm, Lava Flow or Magic Tiki Tai (a mai tai in a souvenir tiki mug). Or try a Flashing Mojito, a fresh blend of lime and mint with rum and club soda served with a flashing ice cube that you take home. There are also Harry Potter smoothies for the kids. Adults $69-$79, teens (ages 13-20) $49, children (ages 6-12) $29. Reservations required for confirmed seating; complimentary validated self-parking.

Maui Marriott Resort & Ocean Club ("Marriott Luau Review")
100 Nohea Kai Drive, Ka'anapali; 808-661-5828; 800-745-6997.

Offered nightly (except Monday), the evening begins with a 4:30 p.m. arrival with greeting and optional photo. They have open seating, so an early arrival affords the best seats. At 5 p.m. there are demonstrations of coconut husking, lei making, basket weaving and other Hawaiian arts and crafts. Dinner is a traditional luau buffet featuring *kalua* pig, *hulihuli* chicken, fresh mahimahi, grilled teriyaki steak, poi and assorted vegetables and salads followed by chocolate cake, coconut cake, and *haupia* for dessert. The open bar includes pina coladas and strawberry daiquiris. The Hawaiian/Polynesian show begins at 7 p.m. and lasts approximately one hour. Adults $75, children 3-12 years $35. If you are a Marriott Resort guest call direct and inquire about "in-house" specials.

★ Old Lahaina Luau
1251 Front Street, Lahaina; 808-667-1998; 800-248-5828.

Start your luau evening with reserved seating, which means no need to stand in line for an hour or more before they open! You can choose cushioned seating on the ground or table seating (I'd recommend this). You'll be greeted with a fresh flower lei and a cool beverage and then visit the bar or have your waiter supply you with refills. The theater is in the round with buffet dining. Before the meal they have the traditional *imu* ceremony, then you're called by tables to the buffet line. With plenty of buffets, there are no long lines while you wait for your food. The taro salad with spinach was creamy and wonderful and the island crab salad was interestingly different. The *kalua* pork wasn't soaked with fat (hence a bit dryer) but excellent flavor. Chicken, fish and lots of good taro rolls. An excellent selection of items. At the end of your meal, waiters bring a miniature guava cake and a pineapple upside-down cake for each table to slice up and serve. Macadamia bars, too. Entertainment begins with a few casual hula dances during the dinner; the show follows the dining. Table service for beverages continues throughout the show so you don't have to miss anything. This isn't the usual luau show. It actually has a story line, following the immigration of the Polynesians to Hawai'i from the days of the Kahiko (ancient hula) to the 'Auana, modern hula. The raised levels around the stage means every seat has a good view at this fast-paced show. The oceanfront location is a big plus. All in all if you're looking for a luau, you can't go wrong with this one. Nightly 5:30-8:30 p.m. Adults $75, children under 12 $45.

Royal Lahaina Resort In Ka'anapali
2780 Keka'a Drive, Ka'anapali; 808-661-9119.

Get ready for mai tais, fruit punch, open bar, and shell leis as the first order of business, with the photographs following. They take two of them, one of your party with male and female greeters, the other a circle inset in a picture of the luau performers on stage, making it an effective souvenir. The luau grounds are near the ocean, but without an ocean view (unless you peek over the hedge). Seating is at padded picnic table benches. The *imu* ceremony was the shortest I've seen

> Luaus are definitely not low-calorie dining options. So eat and enjoy, but just in case you're interested: • *kalua* pig: 1/2 cup 150 calories; • *lomi lomi* salmon: 1/2 cup 87 calories; • poi: 1 cup 161 calories; • fried rice: 1 cup 200 calories; • fish (depending on type served): 150-250 calories; • chicken long rice: 283 calories; • *haupia*: 128 calories; • coconut cake: 200-350 calories; • mai tai: 302 calories; • piña colada: 252 calories; • fruit punch: 140 calories: • Blue Hawai'i: 260 calories; • chi chi: 190 calories.

and some people hadn't even reached the pit before it was over! While people are settling in, the host/hostess welcomes guests. Dinner begins around 6:15 p.m., with four tables and eight lines allowing people to flow quickly through. Large wooden trays are offered in lieu of standard plates, so there is plenty of room to pile on the teri chicken, *kalua* pig and turkey, grilled steaks, mahimahi, Hawaiian sweet potatoes, corn on the cob, *lomi lomi* salmon, poi, fresh fruit, taro bread, and an interesting selections of salads. The desserts included *haupia*, chocolate cake and a coconut cream cake. They also feature a *keiki* buffet with chicken nuggets, hot dogs, potato chips, macaroni and cheese, and more. Following the meal, the Polynesian revue features songs and dance that retell the story of Hawai'i, Tahiti and Samoa. The fire-knife dance highlights the close of the show. Drawbacks at this luau included the gravel-covered dirt ground that made annoying crunching sounds as people got up throughout the show to pick up a drink at the bar, which remained open during the show. This is a good but not great luau. A nice touch is the original music and choreography along with some of the old familiar favorites. Nightly at 5 p.m. $67 adults, $32 children.

Sea House

Napili Kai Beach Resort, 5900 Lower Honoapi'ilani Road, beachfront, Lahaina; 808-669-1500.

Open daily for breakfast, lunch and dinner but for years they have had a popular Polynesian dinner show that they do each Friday. Entertainment is performed by the Children of the Napili Kai Foundation. Seating at 6-6:30 p.m., and show at 7:30 p.m. Your dinner includes salad, prime rib, chicken breast or macadamia nut–crusted mahimahi, dessert and coffee. A big plus is that this restaurant looks right out onto the beach and ocean. You won't get the free mai tai or the group photo shot nor will you have a glitzy

Broadway-type performance, but you'll get very simple hula entertainment. $50 adults, $25 children.

Tony 'N Tina's Wedding
Hyatt Regency Resort and Spa, Ka'anapali; 808-661-1234; www.tonyandtinamaui.com.

The wedding happens several nights a week at Swan Court or the Pavillion dining area. The wedding has been celebrated in more than 40 American cities and the Hawaiian production has some aloha twists. The wedding takes place either overlooking the beach or up in the Banyan Lounge, where you're warmly greeted by the bride and groom's families and members of the wedding party. The minister, the nun and the party planner are among the characters and you'll be selected to be a member of the Vitale family (bride Valentina's relatives) or the Nunzio family (groom's). Following the ceremony you and the other guests are ushered to dinner. The buffet has vegetarian penne pasta, beef lasagna, roast chicken, Caesar salad and great focaccia. The play continues in an interactive format with the member of the wedding party (a.k.a. cast) coming to chat at your table. Play along and introduce yourself as the long lost rich aunt as you converse with the pregnant bridesmaid. And enjoy the champagne toast to the happy couple. There are different plot lines if you sit on the bride's or groom's side of the dinner theater. Bar service available. Play and dinner 6:30-8:45 p.m. Adults $76.50. This is an adult-oriented show. A refreshing addition to the Maui theater scene. Call for weekly schedule.

★ Wailea Marriott, an Outrigger Resort
3700 Wailea Alanui, Wailea; 808-874-7831.

The Wailea Marriott refers to their luau as "Wailea's Finest Luau" and I'd have to agree. The fabulous outdoor setting in their luau garden is both beautiful and spacious with a sublime ocean view. The stage is set up to offer the ocean and sunset as backdrop. An open bar is available. Dinner moves swiftly through several buffet lines serving sautéed fish with lemon macadamia nut butter, teriyaki steak and *kalua* pig (which was the best of all the luaus). *Laulau*, Hawaiian sweet potatoes, chicken long rice, taro rolls, and a variety of salads are just a few of the other offerings. The dessert table has a huge selection of cream pies and cakes, tropical fruit cobbler, macadamia nut cake, and coconut macaroons. The show begins just as the sun is setting with the music of Ka Poe o Hawai'i and Paradyse. First is a *kahiko* hula, which is followed by a *paniolo* number, traditional love songs, Tahitian number and finally the fire-knife dancer, Ifi So'o, who proved to be the best out of all the luaus. He did stunts, somersaults across the stage, and even seemed to twirl much faster than the others. After almost a dozen luaus, it is pretty hard to be impressed, but this guy was impressive. (And, by the way, he has won the World Championship Fire-Knife Dancer competition an unprecedented three times and remains the first and only one in the world to do so!) The show features a good range and quality of entertainment with one of the best outdoor settings. For overall food, entertainment and setting, this is a great luau that continues to rate in this book as the best overall. And at $68 adults ($29 children 6-12), it is also one of the least expensive. 5-8 p.m. Monday, Tuesday, Thursday and Friday.

Wailea Sunset Luau
Renaissance Wailea Beach Resort, Wailea; 808-891-7811.

This luau is held on Tuesday, Thursday and Saturday in the Luau Gardens and the adjoining Makena Lawn, both of which offer an ocean view and pleasant sunset. The luau showcases the unique traditions and stories of Maui's ancient past. It begins with the blowing of the conch and the lighting of the resort's 37 torches. After feasting on the Hawaiian buffet, complete with favorites such as *kalua* pork, grilled fish, *lomi lomi* salmon and *hulihuli* chicken, guests enjoy a Polynesian revue produced by Tihati Productions. The show includes dances that focus on the legends of old Hawai'i and popular favorites such as a unique version of the Hawaiian Wedding song. Rounding out the evening is a performance by master fire dancer, Kikipi. $69 adults, $33 children 5-12, free children under 4.

Warren & Annabelle's
900 Front Street, Lahaina; 808-667-6244.

Warren and Annabelle open their enchanted parlor each evening for two intimate magic club shows (6 and 8 p.m.), serving close-up magic along with a menu of *pupus* and desserts. The title characters are Magician Warren Gibson and Annabelle, the Ghost—or is it the other way around? Annabelle is a piano that plays requests as if by magic, and Warren's expert sleight-of-hand involves the audience with card, coin and telepathy tricks that you can't "see" no matter how hard you look. Annabelle's parlor is elegant and sophisticated, a perfect spot to enjoy a menu of "spirits" and gourmet appetizers like stuffed mushrooms, chicken satay, crab cakes and coconut shrimp. For the sweet tooth there is creme brulee, chocolate truffle cake, rum cake, apple pie and cheesecake. Admission to the parlor and the one-hour magic show is $39.95; food/drink/show packages $70.20-$77.95 per person. They offer a seasonal family show Monday-Friday (children must be at least 6 years old) at 4:30 p.m. ($36 adults, $26 juniors 13-17, $20 children 6-12). Open Monday-Saturday for "prestidigitaddicts" over age 21.

CHAPTER 5

Beaches

If you are looking for a variety of beautiful, uncrowded tropical beaches, nearly perfect weather year-round and sparkling clear waters at enjoyable temperatures, Maui will not disappoint you.

Maui's beaches are special for good reason. If you check out a map of the Hawaiian islands you'll quickly notice that Maui is situated with its south shore flanked by Lana'i, Moloka'i and Kaho'olawe. Millions of years ago, during the Ice Age, the seas were much lower than they are now. The water between these islands was obviously much shallower than it is today. This area became almost an inland sea and today remains more protected than the shores of the other islands. Hence, its beaches are actually safer (with regard to rip currents and shorebreaks) than those on other islands.

The beaches range from small to long, and sand can be white, black, rock or more exotic shades like green or salt-and-pepper. Many are well developed, a few (at least for a little longer) remain remote and unspoiled. There is something for everyone, from the lie-on-the-beach-under-a-palm-tree type to the explorer-adventurer. The Maui Visitors Bureau reports that there are 81 accessible beaches, 30 with public facilities, around an island that spans 120 linear miles.

Maui's beaches are publicly owned and most have right-of-way access. However, the access is sometimes tricky to find and parking may be a problem. Parking areas are provided at most developed beaches, but are generally limited to 30 cars or less, making an early arrival at the more popular beaches a good idea. In the undeveloped areas you will have to wedge along the roadside.

You can check with the Office of Economic Development, County of Maui, 200 South High Street, Wailuku, HI 96793, to see if they have any current shoreline-access maps. They don't seem to have them in stock regularly, but if they do, the maps nicely outline the facilities and accesses for each beach.

Pick up a copy of a free snorkel guide from Maui Dive Shop in Lahaina or Kihei. Any of the dive shops can assist you in choosing a beach that is the best and safest for your snorkeling ability.

At the larger developed beaches, a variety of facilities are provided. Many have convenient rinse-off showers, drinking water, restrooms and picnic areas. A few have children's play or swim areas. The beaches near the major resorts often have rental equipment available for snorkeling, sailing and boogie boarding, and even have underwater cameras. These beaches are generally clean and well maintained. Above Kapalua and below Wailea, where the beaches are undeveloped, expect to find limited signage to mark the location, no facilities and sometimes less cleanliness.

Since virtually all of Maui's good beaches are located on the leeward side of East and West Maui, you can expect sunny weather most of the time. This is because the mountains trap the moisture in the almost-constant trade winds. Truly cloudy or bad weather in these areas is rare but when the weather is poor in one area, a short drive may put you back into the sun again. Swells from all directions reach Maui's shores. The three basic swell sources are the east and northeast trade winds, the North Pacific lows and the South Pacific lows. The trades cause easterly swells of relatively low heights (2 to 6 feet) throughout most of the year. A stormy, persistent trade wind episode may cause swells of 8 to 12 feet and occasionally 10 to 15 feet on exposed eastern shores. Since the main resort areas are on leeward West and East Maui, they are protected.

THEFT DOES HAPPEN

It is vital that you leave nothing of importance in your car because theft, especially at some of the remoter locations, is high. And be careful of watchful eyes if you stow your valuables in your trunk. There are some unscrupulous folks who may be looking for visitors to do just that. Car-rental companies often advise customers to leave nothing in the car and keep the vehicle unlocked to minimize damage in a break-in.

North Maui and Hana are exposed to these conditions, however, along with strong ocean currents. Therefore very few beaches in these areas are considered safe for casual swimming.

Winter North Pacific storms generate high surf along the northwestern and northern shores of Maui. This is the source of the winter surf in Mokule'ia Bay (Slaughterhouse), renowned for body surfing, and in Honolua Bay, which is internationally known for surfing.

Land and sea breezes are local winds blowing from opposite directions at different times, depending on the temperature difference between land and sea. The interaction of daytime sea breezes and trade winds, in the Wailea–Makena area particularly, produces almost-daily light cloudiness in the afternoon and may bring showers. This is also somewhat true of the Honokowai-to-Kapalua region.

Oceanic tidal and trade wind currents are not a problem for the swimmer or snorkeler in the main resort areas from Makena to Kapalua except under unusual conditions such as Kona storms. Beaches outside of the resort areas should be treated with due caution since there are very few considered safe for casual swimming and snorkeling except by knowledgeable, experienced persons.

Maui's ocean playgrounds are probably the most benign in the world. There is no fire coral, jellyfish are rare and sharks are well fed by the abundant marine life so encounters are rare. However, you should always exercise good judgment and reasonable caution when at the beach.

Especially with little ones, be sure to pack plenty of water on your trip to the beach. With all the sun and surf it is easy to get dehydrated. Same for you parents, too. And don't forget the sunscreen.

Beach Precautions

WATER SAFETY

Maui's beaches are far safer than those on, say, Kaua'i. The islands of Lana'i, Moloka'i and Kaho'olawe form an inland sea that makes for calmer shores. The southern shore of Maui has an extensive reef system that affords additional protection.

Most of the north shore beaches of Maui do not have the coral reefs or other barriers that are found on the south and west shores. I cannot recommend any water activities at north shore beaches. These wide expansive beaches pose greater risks for swimmers, with their strong currents and dangerous shorebreaks. You may see surfers at some of the beaches where we recommend that you enjoy the view and stay out of the water. Keep in mind that just because there is someone else in the water, it doesn't mean it's safe. Do not take undue risks. Others might be visitors just like you, but not as well informed. Common sense needs to be employed at all beaches.

We don't want to be alarmists, but we'd prefer to report the beaches conservatively. Always, always use good judgment. Here are some basic water safety tips and terms.

A **shorebreak** is when the waves break directly on the beach. Small shorebreaks may not be a problem, but waves that are more than a foot or two high may create undertows and hazardous conditions. Conditions are generally worse in the winter months. Even venturing too close to a shorebreak could be hazardous, as standing on the beachfront you may encounter a stronger, higher wave that could catch you off guard and sweep you into the water.

A **rip current** can often be seen from the shore. They are fast-moving river-like currents that sometimes can be seen carrying sand or sediment. A rip current can pull an unsuspecting swimmer quickly out to sea, and swimming against a strong rip current may be impossible. They are common in reef areas that have open channels to the sea.

Undertows happen when a rip current runs into incoming surf. This accounts for the feeling that you are being pulled down. They are more common on beaches that have steep slopes.

Kona winds generated by southern-hemisphere storms cause southerly swells that affect leeward Maui. This usually happens in the summer and lasts several days. Surf heights over 8 feet are not common, but many of the resort areas have beaches with fairly steep drop-offs that cause rather sharp shore breaks. Although it may appear fun to play in these waves, many minor to moderate injuries are recorded at these times. Resorts will post red warning flags along the beach during times of unsafe surf conditions. Most beaches are affected during this time with water turbidity and poor snorkeling conditions. At a few places, such as Lahaina, Olowalu and Ma'alaea, these conditions create good surfing.

Northerly swells caused by winter storms northeast of the island are not common but can cause large surf, particularly on the northern beaches, such as Baldwin, Kanaha and Ho'okipa beach parks.

All beaches located along the north shore road to Hana are dangerous so please stay onshore. The beaches beyond Kapalua (D. T. Fleming, Mokule'ia, Honolua) can be dangerous at anytime, so leave them to the experienced surfers when high winter surf arrives. These beaches share such cautionary features as a lack of a protective reef, a large channel in a reef where a strong current forms during high surf, and a river emptying into the sea. Most of them are also fairly remote and response times are prolonged.

Please, treat Maui's wild beaches with respect. Since many have no restroom facilities, try to use the bathroom before you head to the beach. If you must relieve yourself, go well away from the waterline and bury your deposit and any tissue you used. Also, pack out your trash and bring out a little bit that someone else left, too.

LIFEGUARDS ON DUTY

For families concerned about water safety, the following beaches feature lifeguards: Hanaka'o'o Beach in Ka'anapali; Kahana Beach in Kahului; D. T. Fleming Beach in Kapalua; and Kama'ole Beaches I, II and III in Kihei. The Ocean Safety phone line is 808-270-6136.

OCEAN MENACES

Maui's ocean playgrounds are among the most benign in the world. There are, however, a few ocean creatures that you should be aware of. We will attempt to include some basic first-aid tips should you encounter one of these. Since some people might have a resulting allergic reaction, we suggest you contact a local physician or medical center should you have an unplanned encounter with one of them.

Portuguese Man-of-War are sea animals seen only rarely but caution is in order. It's one of those ocean critters to be avoided. These very small creatures are related to the jellyfish and are adrift in the ocean via the currents and the wind. These unique sea creatures are sometimes blown on shore by unusual winds and can cover the beach with their glistening crystal orbs filled with deep blue filament. If they are on the beach, treat them as if they were still in the water—stay away. On rare occasions they will be seen drifting in the ocean during a snorkeling cruise or sea excursion and the cruiseboat staff may change snorkeling destinations if this is the case. The animal has long filaments that can cause painful stings. If you are stung, rinse the affected area with sea water or fresh water to remove any tentacles. If you need to pick out the tentacles, do not use your bare fingers; use gloves, a towel or whatever is available to protect yourself. Vinegar, isopropyl alcohol and human urine, once considered effective remedies, are no longer recommended treatments.

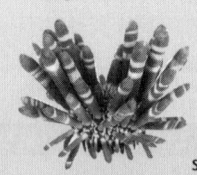

In the water, avoid touching **sea urchins**: the pricking by one of the spines can be painful. And if you do encounter one, be sure the entire spine has been removed. Soaking the wound in vinegar helps to dissolve the spine; for pain, soak the puncture in hot water for 30 to 90 minutes.

Coral is made up of many tiny living organisms. Coral cuts require thorough disinfecting and can take a long time to heal. If an inflamed wound's redness begins to spread, it suggests an infection and requires medical attention. So stay off the coral—and don't touch it!

TIPS

Here are some additional beach safety and etiquette tips:
- "Never turn your back to the sea" is an old Hawaiian saying. Don't be caught off-guard; waves come in sets, with spells of calm in between.

Cone shells look harmless enough, are conical and come in colors of brown or black. The snails that inhabit these shells have a defense mechanism that they use to protect themselves—and to kill their prey. Their stinger does have venom so it is suggested that you just enjoy looking at them. Cleaning the wound and soaking it in hot water for 30 to 90 minutes will provide relief if you're stung.

Eels live among the coral and are generally not aggressive. You may have heard of divers who have "trained" an eel to come out, greet them and then take some food from their hands. We don't recommend you try to make an eel your pal. While usually non-aggressive, their jaws are extremely powerful and their teeth are sharp. And as divers know, sea animals could mistake any approach or movement as an aggressive or provoking act. Just keep a comfortable distance—for you and the eel. Also, should you poke around with your hands in the coral, they might inadvertently think your finger is food. This is another reason you shouldn't handle the coral. Eels are generally not out of their homes during the day, but a close examination of the coral might reveal a head of one of these fellows sticking out and watching you! At night during low tide at beaches with a protective reef, you might try taking a flashlight and scanning the water. A chance look at one of these enormous creatures out searching for its dinner is most impressive.

Sharks? Yes, there are many varied types of sharks. However, there are more shark attacks off the Oregon coastline than in Hawai'i. In the many years of snorkeling and diving, we have only seen one small reef shark, and it was happy to get out of our way. If you should see one, don't move quickly, but rather swim slowly away while you keep an eye on it. Avoid swimming in murky waters near river mouths after it rains.

Also, stay out of the water if you have open cuts and remember, urine might attract sharks, so don't urinate in the water. Some Maui beaches are year-round shark breeding grounds; please heed the posted signs and stay out of the water.

- Use the buddy system, never swim or snorkel alone.
- If you are unsure of your abilities, use flotation devices attached to your body, such as a life vest or inflatable vest. Never rely on an air mattress or similar device from which you may become separated.

- Study the ocean before you enter; look for rocks, shorebreak and rip currents.
- Duck or dive beneath breaking waves before they reach you.
- Never swim against a strong current, swim across it.
- Know your limits.
- Small children should be allowed to play near or in the surf *only* with close supervision and should wear flotation devices. And even then, only under extremely calm conditions. Pu'unoa in Lahaina is a quiet saltwater area ideal for kids, especially beginner snorkelers.
- When exploring tidepools or reefs, always wear protective footwear and keep an eye on the ocean. Also, protect your hands.
- When swimming around coral, be careful where you put your hands and feet. Urchin stings can be painful and coral cuts can be dangerous. You can also damage or injure the coral. Yes! Coral is living and it grows very slowly so don't knock into it or stand on it while snorkeling.
- Respect the yellow and red flag warnings when placed on the developed beaches. They are there to advise you of unsafe conditions.
- After heavy rains, stay out of the ocean until the water clears.
- Avoid swimming in the mouths of rivers or streams or in any areas of murky water.

A good place and a "secret find" for small children is the park at the end of Hauoli Street in Ma'alaea, just past the Makani A Kai condos. There are two small, sandy-bottomed pools protected by reefs on either side of the small rock jetty.

Another great place for very young kids to learn to snorkel is at "Baby Beach," or Pu'unoa, located north of Lahaina. There is limited parking and no facilities but the offshore reef affords a chance to enjoy the water without currents or surf conditions. Wearing watershoes here is a great idea as there is coral rubble in the water and on the shore. At age 3 my son started snorkeling here, where the water is even warmer because of the reef conditions. He also discovered he could easily relay his excitement at the sights below the surface, being very adept at talking through the snorkel. What a delight to hear his little voice coming out of the top of the snorkel. He's now scuba certified.

Quiet waters for young beginning snorkelers are available in front of the Lahaina Shores Resort as well.

- Always use fins when boogie boarding.
- Don't feed the fish.
- Keep your distance from pole and net fishermen.
- Remember, it's illegal to do *anything* that causes a dolphin, monk seal, turtle or whale to change its behavior, so stay away from them.

Surface **water temperature** varies little with a mean temperature of 73 degrees Fahrenheit in January and 80.2 degrees in August. Minimum and maximum range from 68 to 84 degrees. This is an almost ideal temperature (refreshing, but not cold) for swimming and you'll find most resort pools cooler than the ocean. Of course, if it's windy, it may feel chilly when you get out of the water.

Note: Ulysses Press, Paradise Publications and the authors of this guide have endeavored to provide current and accurate information on Maui's beautiful beaches. However, remember that nature is unpredictable and weather, beach and current conditions can change. Enjoy your day at the beach, but utilize good judgment. Ulysses Press, Paradise Publications and the authors of this guide cannot be held responsible for accidents or injuries incurred.

Best Bets

Lahaina: Olowalu has easy access and excellent snorkeling.

Ma'alaea–Kihei–Wailea–Makena Area: On South Maui, our favorite beaches are Makena for its unspoiled beauty, Malu'aka for its deep fine sand and beautiful coral, Wailea and Ulua–Mokapu for their great beaches, good snorkeling and beautiful resorts, and Keawakapu and Kama'ole II for gentler offshore slopes and excellent swimming.

Ka'anapali–Kapalua Area: Kapalua offers a well-protected bay with very good swimming and snorkeling. Hanaka'o'o Beach, next to the Hyatt, has a gentle offshore slope and a park with lots of parking, good facilities and numerous activities.

Using This Chapter

The following listings refer to a variety of beaches and beach parks. However, you'll find that some are not true beaches. For example, Spouting Horn is a beautiful beach location, but only for viewing and not good for aquatic activities.

The pail and shovel icon indicates beaches that are recommended for family activities. They are more protected and most likely have lifeguards on duty.

Lahaina

These beaches are described in order from Ma'alaea through Lahaina and are easy to spot from Honoapi'ilani Highway. They are all narrow and usually lined with *kiawe* trees. However, they have gentle slopes to deeper water and the ocean is generally calmer and warmer than in other areas. The offshore coral reefs offer excellent snorkeling in calm weather, which is most of the time. These beaches are popular because of their convenient access and facilities as well as good swimming and snorkeling conditions.

Papalaua State Wayside Park

As you descend from the sea cliffs on your way from Ma'alaea you will see an undeveloped tropical shoreline stretch before you. At the foot of the cliffs at mile-marker 11, Papalaua State Wayside Park is marked by an easily seen sign. There are picnic tables, barbecue grills and portable restrooms. The beach is long (about .5 mile), narrow and lined with *kiawe* trees that almost reach the water's edge in places. The trees provide plenty of shady areas for this beautiful beach. Good swimming and fair snorkeling; popular picnicking area.

Ukumehame Beach Park

The entrance to the park is near mile-marker 12, but there is no identifying sign. There is paved off-street parking for about 12 cars. Five concrete picnic tables. This is also a narrow .5-mile-long sand beach with lots of *kiawe* trees providing shade. Good swimming, fair snorkeling.

★ Olowalu Beach

About two-tenth's of a mile before and after mile-marker 14 you will see a large but narrow stand of *kiawe* trees between the road and the beach, followed by a few palm trees, then a few more scattered *kiawe* trees. Parking is alongside the road. No facilities. This narrow sand beach slopes gently out to water four or five feet deep, making it good for swimming and beach playing. There are extensive coral formations starting right offshore and continuing out a quarter mile or more, and a fair amount of fish expecting handouts. The ocean is generally warmer and calmer than elsewhere, making it a popular snorkeling spot. In 2002 they posted shark warning signs for this beach, but it does not seem to be deterring snorkelers. At this or any beach there may, of course, be sharks.

Awalua Beach

The beach at mile-marker 16 may be cobblestone or sand depending on the time of year and the prevailing conditions. No facilities. At

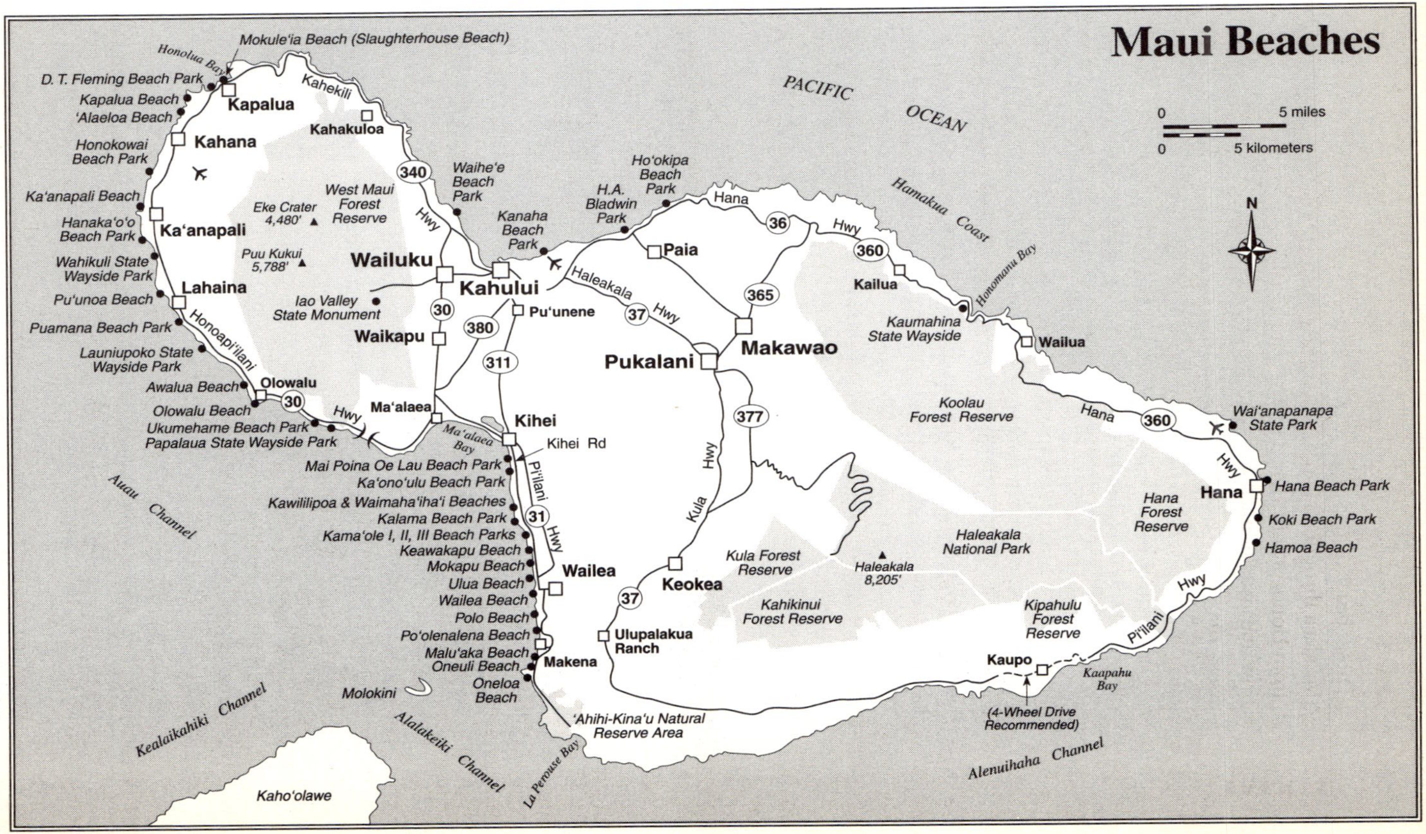
Maui Beaches
PACIFIC OCEAN
0 5 miles
0 5 kilometers
N
Mokule'ia Beach (Slaughterhouse Beach)
Honolua Bay
D. T. Fleming Beach Park
Kapalua Beach
'Alaeloa Beach
Honokowai Beach Park
Ka'anapali Beach
Hanaka'o'o Beach Park
Wahikuli State Wayside Park
Pu'unoa Beach
Puamana Beach Park
Launiupoko State Wayside Park
Awalua Beach
Olowalu Beach
Ukumehame Beach Park
Papalaua State Wayside Park
Kapalua
Kahekili
Kahakuloa
Kahana
Ka'anapali
Lahaina
Honoapi'ilani
Olowalu
30
Hwy
Eke Crater 4,480'
Puu Kukui 5,788'
West Maui Forest Reserve
340
Hwy
Waihe'e Beach Park
Wailuku
Kahului
Iao Valley State Monument
Waikapu
30
380
311
Ma'alaea
Ma'alaea Bay
Kanaha Beach Park
H.A. Bladwin Park
Ho'okipa Beach Park
Paia
Pu'unene
Kihei
Kihei Rd
Pi'ilani
31
Hwy
Mai Poina Oe Lau Beach Park
Ka'ono'ulu Beach Park
Kawililipoa & Waimaha'iha'i Beaches
Kalama Beach Park
Kama'ole I, II, III Beach Parks
Keawakapu Beach
Mokapu Beach
Ulua Beach
Wailea Beach
Polo Beach
Po'olenalena Beach
Malu'aka Beach
Oneuli Beach
Oneloa Beach
Wailea
Makena
Molokini
Auau Channel
Kealaikahiki Channel
Alalakeiki Channel
La Perouse Bay
Kaho'olawe
'Ahihi-Kina'u Natural Reserve Area
Haleakala
37
Hwy
Hana
36
Hwy
360
365
Makawao
Pukalani
377
Kula
Hwy
Keokea
37
Ulupalakua Ranch
Kula Forest Reserve
Kahikinui Forest Reserve
Haleakala 8,205'
Haleakala National Park
Kailua
Hamakua Coast
Honomanu Bay
Kaumahina State Wayside
Wailua
Koolau Forest Reserve
Hana
360
Wai'anapanapa State Park
Hwy
Hana
Hana Beach Park
Koki Beach Park
Hamoa Beach
Hana Forest Reserve
Hwy
Pi'ilani
Kipahulu Forest Reserve
Kaupo
Kaapahu Bay
(4-Wheel Drive Recommended)
Alenuihaha Channel

times when Kona storms create a good southern swell, this becomes a very popular surfing spot until the swells subside.

Launiupoko State Wayside Park
This well-marked beach park near mile-marker 18 offers a large paved parking area, restrooms, many picnic tables, barbecue grills, rinse-off showers, drinking water, a pay phone and a large grassy area with trees, all of which make for a good picnic spot. There is a large man-made wading pool constructed of large boulders centered in the park; this is child-friendly. (Sand has accumulated to the extent that even at high tide there is no water in the pool.) To the right is a rocky beach and to the left is a 200-yard dark-sand beach with a fairly gentle slope. It looks nice, but posted signs warn "Sharks have been seen in the shallow water off this beach. Entry into the water is discouraged." This area is rumored to be a shark breeding ground with shark fishing done here in the past: There is also a "No alcohol" sign posted. For some reason the beach does not seem to be used for much besides picnicking. However, a couple hundred yards offshore is good snorkeling and you may see snorkel excursions visit this shoreline when the weather prohibits a trip to Molokini or Lana'i.

Puamana Beach Park
This well-marked beach park is near mile-marker 19, just south of the Puamana Resort complex. Parking for 20 cars in paved parking area, with additional parking along the highway. Nice grassy park with seven picnic tables and plenty of shade trees. At the park itself there is no sandy beach, only a large pebble beach. The only beach is a narrow 200-yard-long white-sand beach just north of the park and fronting Puamana Resort. Fairly gentle slope to shallow water.

Lahaina Beach
This narrow sand beach fronts the Lahaina Shores and 505 Front Street and is protected by a reef 30 to 50 yards out. The beach is generally sandy offshore with a gentle slope. The water stays fairly shallow out to the reef and contains some interesting coral formations. The area offers fair snorkeling in clear water on calm days. A good place for beginning snorkelers and children, but not good for swimming due to shallow water and abundant coral. There is a large public parking lot across from the 505 Front Street shopping center with easy access to the beach through the mall. There is also on-street parking near the Lahaina Shores with public

right-of-way to the beach by the south end of the complex. Public restrooms and showers at 505.

★ Pu'unoa Beach

The beach, at the north end of Lahaina between Kai Pali Road and the old Mala Wharf, can be seen as you leave Lahaina on Front Street. This narrow, dense, dark-sand beach is about 300 yards long and well protected by a reef approximately 100 to 150 yards offshore. The beach slopes gently to water only 3 to 4 feet deep. Unfortunately, rock and coral near the surface make swimming unadvised. There are areas of the beach clear of coral 10 to 15 feet out where children can play safely in the calm, shallow water. At high tide there are more fish to see while snorkeling. This continues to be a favorite with our children because of the calm, warm water. Southern access: Take Kai Pali Road off Front Street. Parking for about 20 cars along the road, which is the entrance for the Pu'unoa Beach Estates. Public Beach access sign with concrete sidewalk to the beach. Mid-beach access: Take Pu'unoa Place off Front Street at the Public Beach access sign. Parking for about four cars at the end of the road that ends at the beach. A rinse-off hose here is the only facility for the beach. North access: Take Mala Wharf off Front Street. Parking for approximately 20 cars along the road just before the entrance to the Mala boat-launching parking area.

Wahikuli State Wayside Park

There are three paved off-street parking areas between Lahaina and Ka'anapali. Many covered picnic tables, restrooms, showers and barbecue grills are provided. The first and third parking areas are marked but have no beach. The second unmarked area has an excellent dark-sand beach with a gentle slope to deeper water. There is some shelf rock in places but it's rounded and smooth and not a problem. With handy facilities, trees for shade and the nice beach, this is a good (and popular) spot for sunning, swimming and picnicking.

★ Hanaka'o'o Beach Park (Canoe Beach)

Off Honoapi'ilani Highway, immediately south of the Hyatt Regency, there is a large, well-marked, off-street parking area. The park has rinse-off showers, restrooms and picnic tables. Wide, dark-sand beach with gentle slope to deeper water. This is a popular area because of the easy parking, facilities, good beach, shallow water and good swimming, and proximity to the Hyatt Regency.

Ka'anapali-Kapalua Area

★ *Ka'anapali Beach (Hanaka'o'o Beach)*
The beach fronts the Hyatt Regency, Maui Marriott, Ka'anapali Alii, Westin Maui, Whalers Village shopping center, The Whaler, Ka'anapali Beach Hotel and Sheraton Maui, and is known as Ka'anapali Beach. Access is through the Ka'anapali Resort area. Turn off Honoapi'ilani Highway at either of the first two entrances. Parking is definitely a problem.

- The Hyatt end of the beach is only a short walk from the large parking area of Hanaka'o'o Beach Park.
- Public right-of-way with parking for 10 cars at the left of the Hyatt's lower parking lot.
- Public right-of-way between the Hyatt and Marriott, no parking.
- Public right-of-way between Marriott and Ka'anapali Alii with parking for 11 cars only.
- Public right-of-way between Ka'anapali Alii and Westin, no parking.
- Public right-of-way between Ka'anapali Beach Resort and the Sheraton with parking for 11 cars only.
- Whalers Village shopping center has a three-story pay parking lot, but with beach access only through the complex.
- There is no on-street parking anywhere in the Ka'anapali Resort complex.

The Hyatt Regency, Maui Marriott, Westin Maui and Sheraton Maui all have restrooms, showers, bars and rental equipment. There is a beautiful, long, wide, white-sand beach with an abrupt drop-off to deep water. There are small areas of offshore coral from the Hyatt to the Westin Maui at times, but no true offshore reef. Great swimming and good wave-playing with the exception of two or three points along the beach where the waves consistently break fairly hard. In the winter, snorkeling can be fair off the Westin when the coral is exposed underwater. The best snorkeling is at Black Rock, fronting the Sheraton. The water is almost always clear and fairly calm, with many types of nearly tame fish due to the popularity of hand-feeding by snorkelers. (Bread, frozen peas and packaged dry noodles seem popular.) Not much colorful coral. The best entrance to the water is from the beach alongside Black Rock.

★ *Alii Kahekili Nui 'Ahumahi Beach Park*
This beach, usually referred to as Ka'anapali Beach—South End, begins at the north side of Black Rock and runs for over a mile to the north, fronting the Royal Lahaina Resort and the Maui Ka'anapali

Villas. This beach park has been developed just north of these two resorts. Turn off Honoapi'ilani Road at the last Ka'anapali exit at the stoplight by the Maui Ka'anapali Villas. The beach park is open 6 a.m. to 6:30 p.m. with plenty of paved parking spaces. There are pavilions with dining tables and a very pleasant grassy lawn area dotted with barbecues and more tables. A rinse-off shower is available. There is a gate that is locked nightly. This area was formerly the Ka'anapali Airport. This wide, (usually) white-sand beach has a steep drop-off to deep water and is usually calm—a good place to swim. Snorkeling around Black Rock is almost always good. Kahekili was the last ruler of Maui. This park, which pays tribute to him, is lovely. The park's name, which is quite a mouthful, translates to "Feather Cloaked Nightly Thunderer." Kahekili ruled 1766–1793.

Ka'anapali Beach (North End)
This section of beach fronts the Mahana Resort, Maui Kai, Embassy Vacation Resort, Ka'anapali Shores, Papakea, Maui Sands and Paki Maui from south to north, and ends at the Honokowai Beach Park. Access is generally only through the resorts. Most of the resorts have rinse-off showers convenient to the beach; however, no other facilities are available. This is a long, narrow, white-sand beach that is fronted by a close-in reef. All the resorts except the Ka'anapali Shores and Embassy Vacation Resort have retaining walls along the beach. The Ka'anapali Shores has, over the last couple of years, suffered considerable erosion of its once-wide beach and has built an expensive under-the-sand retaining wall in an effort to stabilize and restore it. There is also a cleared area through the coral in front of the resort. This is the only good swimming area on the north section of the beach and is the only good access through the reef for snorkeling. The reef comes into shore at the south end of Papakea and again at the Honokowai Beach Park. At low tide the reef fronting Papakea can be walked on like a wide sidewalk. (See "Traveling with Children" in Chapter 1 for night walking on the reef.) The reef is generally only 10 to 20 yards offshore and the area between is very shallow, with much coral and rock making it undesirable for swimming and snorkeling. The middle section of beach, fronting the old Ka'anapali Airport, is slated for future development.

Honokowai Beach Park
Turn off the Honoapi'ilani Highway on the first side street past the airport (at the Honokowai sign) and get onto Lower Honoapi'ilani Highway, which parallels the ocean. The park is across the street from the Food Pantry (a pay phone is available there, as is water sport equipment). There is paved off-street parking

for 30 cars. There are 11 picnic tables, five barbecue pits, restrooms, showers and a grassy park with shade trees. The white-sand beach is lined by a wide shelf of beach rock. Between the shelf rock and reef there is a narrow, shallow pool with a sandy bottom that is a good swimming area for small children. There is a break in the reef at the north end of the beach where you can get snorkeling access to the outside reef.

Kahana Beach

Kahana Beach is in front of the Kahana Beach Condominiums, Sands of Kahana, Royal Kahana, Valley Isle Resort and Hololani from south to north on Lower Honoapi'ilani Highway. There is limited off-road parking at the south end of the beach. Another access is through the condos. The only facilities available are at the condos, usually rinse-off showers. Kahana Manor Grocery is across the street from Valley Isle Resort and a Whalers General Store is at the nearby Kahana Gateway shopping center. This white-sand beach varies from narrow to wide and its offshore area is shallow with rock and sand, semi-protected by reef. Good swimming, fair snorkeling. The beach may be cool and windy in the afternoons. Since 1989, this area has been particularly plagued by an unexplained green algae bloom that tends to concentrate here due to the wind, current and shoreline conditions. The beach is frequently unappealing for swimming and beach use due to the amount of slimy green algae on the beach and in the water. One possible cause of this unsightly mess may be nitrates and other chemicals used for agriculture and golf-course maintenance flowing into the ocean. The county is continuing to investigate and may find it necessary to institute some controls.

★ Keonenui Beach

The beach is in front of and surrounded by the Kahana Sunset with no convenient public access. A lovely wide crescent of white sand with a fairly gentle slope to water's edge, then a fairly steep slope to deeper water, the beach is set in a small shallow cove about 150 yards wide, which affords some protection. At times, especially in winter, rough seas come into the beach. When calm (most of the time), this is an excellent swimming and play area with fair snorkeling.

'Alaeloa Beach ("The Cove")

This miniature jewel-like cove is surrounded by low sea cliffs. The small (approximately 25 to 30 yards long) white-sand beach has a gentle slope with scattered rocks leading into sparkling clear waters. Pavilion and lounge chair area for use by 'Alaeloa guests. Good swimming and snorkeling with very clear and calm waters except when storm-generated waves come in. Fortunately, or unfortunately, depending on your point of view, this small cove is surrounded by the 'Alaeloa residential area, which has no on- or off-street public parking. Thus, public access to this beach is very difficult.

★ Napili Bay

There are two public accesses to this beautiful beach. There is a small, easily missed public right-of-way and Napili Beach sign just past the Napili Shores at Napili Place Street. On-street parking at sign for Napili Surf Beach Resort. The public beach right-of-way sign shows the entrance to the beach. Public phone in parking lot of Napili Surf. The second entrance is at the public beach right-of-way and Napili Sunset, Hale Napili and Napili Bay signs on Hui Street. On-street parking and pay phone at entrance to beach walk. This is a long, wide crescent of white sand between two rocky points. The offshore slope is moderately steep. Usually very safe for swimming and snorkeling except during winter storms when large waves occasionally come into the bay. At the south end of the beach are a series of shallow, sandy tidepools that are excellent for children, but only under close supervision. Coral formations 30 to 40 yards offshore can provide fair snorkeling on calm days, especially at the northern end of the beach, and decent boogie boarding with mild swells. No public facilities along the beach. A grocery store is past the second entrance at the Napili Village Hotel.

★ Kapalua Beach

Just past the Napili Kai Beach Resort you will see a public beach right-of-way sign. Off-street parking area for about 30 to 40 cars. Showers and restrooms. A beautiful crescent of white sand between two rocky points. The beach has a gentle slope to deeper water, maximum about 15 feet. From the left point, a reef arcs toward the long right point, creating a very sheltered bay, probably the nicest and safest swimming beach on Maui. Shade is provided by numerous palm trees lining the back shore area. Above the beach are the lovely grounds of the Kapalua Bay Resort. Swimming is almost always excellent with plenty of play area for children. Snorkeling is usually good with many different kinds of fish and interesting coral. It is no surprise that this beach has been selected as one of the top ten beaches in the world. Remember: Parking is limited, so arrive early.

★ Namalu Bay

Park at Kapalua Beach and take the concrete path along the beach, up through the hotel's grounds and out to the point of land separating Kapalua Bay from Namalu Bay. This small bay has a shoreline of large lava boulders, no beaches. On calm days snorkeling is very good and entry and exit over the rocks is easy. This little-known spot is definitely worth the short walk down the trail.

Oneloa Beach
Enter at the public right-of-way sign just past the Kapalua Bay Resort. Paved off-street parking for 12 to 15 cars only, no other facilities. Long, straight, white-sand beach with a shallow sand bar that extends to the surf line. The beach is posted with a sign warning "No swimming at time of high surf due to dangerous currents." This area tends to get windy and cloudy in the afternoons, especially in the winter months. I have usually found this beach deserted.

D. T. Fleming Beach Park
The County maintains a lifeguard on this beach. The Ritz-Carlton operates The Beach House restaurant. Off-street parking for 70 cars. Public showers. Private restrooms by The Beach House. The long white-sand beach is steep with an offshore sand bar that may cause dangerous water conditions when swells hit the beach. This beach was named for David Thomas Fleming (1881–1955), who became manager of the Honolua Ranch in 1912. Under his guidance, the Baldwin cattle ranch was converted into a pineapple plantation. Once called "Stables Beach" because the Fleming family kept their horses at this site into the 1950s.

★ Mokuleʻia Beach (Slaughterhouse Beach)
On Highway 30, past D. T. Fleming Beach Park, look for cars parked along the roadside and the Mokuleʻia–Honolua Marine Reserve sign. Park your car and hike down one of the steep dirt and rock trails—they're not difficult. There are no facilities. The wide white-sand beach has a gentle slope to deep water and is bordered by two rocky points; it is situated at the foot of steep cliffs. The left middle part of the beach is usually clear of coral and rocks even in winter, when the beach is subject to erosion. During the winter this is *the* bodysurfing spot, especially when the surf is heavy; however, dangerous water conditions also exist. This area is only for the strong, experienced swimmer. The summer is generally much better for swimming and snorkeling at this very popular beach. Snorkeling is fair to good, especially around the left rocky point where there is a reef. Okay in winter when the ocean is calm and visibility good.

Note: The beach is known as Slaughterhouse because of the once-existing slaughterhouse on the cliffs above the beach, not because of what the ocean can do to body surfers in the winter when the big ones are coming in. Remember: This is part of the Mokuleʻia–Honolua Bay Marine Life Conservation District—look, but don't disturb or take.

★ Honolua Bay
The next bay past Mokuleʻia is Honolua Bay. Watch for a dirt side road on the left. Park here and walk in along the road. There is no

beach, just cobblestone with irregular patches of sand and an old concrete boat ramp in the middle. Excellent snorkeling in summer, spring and fall, especially in the morning, but in winter only on the calmest days. In summer, on calm days the bay resembles a large glassy pond and in our opinion, this is the best snorkeling on Maui. *Note:* After a heavy rainfall, the water may be turbid for several days before it returns to its sparkling clear condition again. You can enter at the boat ramp or over the rocks and follow the reefs either left or right. Remember, this is a Marine Life Conservation area, so look but don't disturb. There is an interesting phenomenon affecting the bay. As freshwater runoff percolates into the bay, a shimmering boundary layer (usually about three feet below the surface) is created between the fresh and salt waters. Depending on the amount of runoff it may be very apparent or not. It is less prevalent on the right side of the bay. Honolua Bay is also an internationally known winter surfing spot. Storm-generated waves come thundering in around the right point, creating perfect waves and tubes. A good vantage point to watch the action is the cliffs at the right point of the bay, accessible by car via a short dirt road off the main highway.

Ma'alaea-Kihei-Wailea-Makena Area

The Kihei beaches aren't quite as beautiful as Wailea's. They don't have the nicely landscaped parking areas or the large, beautiful resort complexes (this is condo country). They do, however, offer increased facilities such as barbecues, picnic tables, drinking water and grassy play areas. The Kama'ole I, II and III beaches even have lifeguards. The beaches are listed in order from Ma'alaea Bay to Wailea.

Ma'alaea Bay Beach

This gently curving white-sand beach stretches three miles from the Ma'alaea boat harbor to Kihei. For the most part, the beach is backed by low sand dunes and large, generally wet, sand flats. Public access is from many areas along South Kihei Road. There are no facilities. Casual beach activities are best early in the morning before the strong, prevailing, mid-morning winds begin to sweep across the isthmus. Due to the length of the beach and the hard-packed sand near the water, this has become a popular place to jog. Windsurfing is popular in the afternoons.

The beach begins in front of the last three condominiums in Ma'alaea, the Kana'i A Nalu, Hono Kai and the Makani A Kai. Just past the Makani A Kai on Hauoli Street is a public park and beach access. There is a good section of beach here with a fairly gentle drop-off.

Also there are two small, sandy-bottomed pools, protected by the reef on either side of the small man-made rock jetty. These are good play areas for kids. The waves remain fairly calm, except at high tide or high surf conditions. The best snorkeling is out from the beach here, but the conditions are extremely variable, from fairly clear to fairly murky, depending on the time of year and prevailing conditions. Snorkeling is usually better in the winter months. The beach from this point to North Kihei is generally fronted by shelf rock or reef and is not good for swimming but excellent for a lengthy beach walk! The beach becomes excellent for swimming and other beach activities in front of the North Kihei condos. Snorkeling is fair. A beach activity center is located on the beach at the Kealia Beach Center.

Mai Poina Oe Lau Beach Park
On South Kihei Road, fronting Maui Lu Resort. Paved parking for eight cars at the Pavilion (numerous other areas to park are along the road). Five picnic tables, restrooms, showers. This is actually part of the previous beach. In-shore bottom generally sandy with patches of rock, fronted by shallow reef. Swimming and snorkeling are best in the morning before the early afternoon winds come up. Popular windsurfing area in the afternoon.

Ka'ono'ulu Beach Park
Located across the street from the Kihei Bay Surf. Off-road parking for 20 cars, restrooms, drinking water, rinse-off showers, picnic tables and four barbecue grills. Very small beach, well protected by close-in reef.

Kawiliki Pou Park
Located at the end of Waipulani Street. Paved off-street parking for 30 cars, restrooms, large grassy area and public tennis courts. Fronts Laule'a, Luana Kai and the Maui Sunset Hotel. Tall, graceful palms line the shoreline. Narrow sandy beach generally strewn with seaweed and coral rubble. (See "Traveling with Children" in Chapter 1 for frog hunting information.)

Kawililipoa and Waimaha'iha'i Areas
Any of the cross streets off South Kihei Road will take you down toward the beach where public right-of-ways are marked. Limited parking, usually on the street. No facilities. The whole shoreline from Kalama Park to Waipulani Street (3 to 4 miles) is an area of uninterrupted beaches lined by residential housing and small condo complexes. Narrow sandy beaches with lots of coral rubble from the fronting reefs.

Kalama Beach Park
Well-marked, 36-acre park with 12 pavilions, three restrooms, showers, picnic tables, barbecue grills, playground apparatus, roller rink, soc-

cer field, baseball field, tennis courts and volleyball and basketball courts. Lots of grassy areas. There is no beach (in winter), only a large boulder breakwater. Good view of the cinder cone in Makena as well as Molokini, Kahoʻolawe, Lanaʻi and West Maui.

Kamaʻole I
Well-marked beach across from the Kamaʻole Beach Club. Off-street parking for 30 cars. Facilities include picnic tables, restrooms, rinse-off showers, rental equipment, children's swimming area and lifeguard. Long, white, sandy beach offering good swimming, poor to fair snorkeling. The small pocket of sand between rock outcroppings at the right end of the beach is known as Young's Beach. It is also accessible from Kaiau Street with parking for about 20 cars. Public right-of-way sign at end of Kaiau Street.

★ Kamaʻole II
Located across from the Kai Nani shopping and restaurant complex. On-street parking, restrooms, rinse-off showers, rental equipment and lifeguard. White-sand beach between two rocky points with sharp drop-off to overhead depths. Good swimming, poor to fair snorkeling.

★ Kamaʻole III
Well-marked beach across from the Kamaʻole Sands Condominiums. Off-street parking, picnic tables, barbecues, restrooms, rinse-off showers, drinking water, playground equipment, a grassy play area and a lifeguard. This 200-yard-long, narrow (in winter) white-sand beach has some rocky areas along the beach and a few submerged rocks. Good swimming, fair snorkeling around rocks at south end of the beach. Kamaʻole II and III are very popular beaches with locals and tourists because of the nice beaches and easy access.

The Wailea area generally has small, lovely, white-sand beaches that have marked public access. Parking is off-street in well-maintained parking areas, and restrooms as well as rinse-off showers are provided. Several major resorts have transformed this area into a world-class resort destination rivaling Kaʻanapali, and even surpassing it in some ways.

★ Keawakapu Beach
There are two convenient public accesses to this very nice and generally under-used beach. There is paved parking for 50 cars across the street from the beach, about .2 mile south of Mana Kai Resort. Look for

the beach access sign on the left as you travel south. There are two small crescent-shaped, white-sand beaches separated by a small rocky point. Good swimming, offshore sandy bottom, fair snorkeling around rocks at far north end. There are rinse-off showers and a restaurant at the Mana Kai, which is right on the beach. Access to southern end of beach: go straight at left turnoff to Wailea, road says "Dead End." Parking for about 30 cars. Rinse-off showers. Beautiful, very gently sloping white-sand beach with good swimming. Snorkeling off rocks on left. Popular scuba-diving spot. Four hundred yards offshore in 80 to 85 feet of water there is supposedly an artificial reef of 150 car bodies.

★ Mokapu Beach

A public access sign (Ulua/Mokapu Beaches) is near the Renaissance Wailea Beach Resort. Small parking area, restrooms and showers. Rental equipment at nearby Wailea Resort Activities Center at Renaissance. Beautiful white-sand beach. Excellent swimming. Good snorkeling in mornings around the rocks that divide the two beaches. The best snorkeling is on the Ulua beach side.

★ Ulua Beach

A public access sign is located near the Renaissance Wailea Beach Resort. Small paved parking area with a short walk to beach. Showers and restrooms. Rental equipment is only a short walk away at the Wailea Resort Activities Center. Beautiful white-sand beach fronting the Ulua Resort complex. Ulua and Mokapu beaches are separated by a narrow point of rocks. The area around the beaches is beautifully landscaped because of the resorts. The beach is semi-protected and has a sandy offshore bottom. Good swimming, usually very good snorkeling in the mornings around the lava flow between the beaches. Parking is limited.

★ Wailea Beach

One half mile south of the Wailea Marriott, an Outrigger Resort, there is a public beach access sign and a paved road down to a landscaped parking area for about 40 cars. Restrooms and rinse-off showers. Rental sailboats and windsurfing boards are available. Beautiful wide crescent of gently sloping white sand. Gentle offshore slope. Good swimming. Snorkeling is only fair to the left (south) around the rocks (moderate currents and not much coral or many fish). The Grand Wailea and Four Seasons are situated on this beachfront.

Polo Beach

Just past the Kea Lani Hotel, turn right at the lava-rock wall sign (Wailea Golf Club—Blue Course—Restaurant) toward the Polo Beach Resort condominiums. The public access sign is easy to spot. Paved parking area for 40 cars. Showers and restrooms. The beaches are a short walk on a paved sidewalk and down a short flight of stairs. There are actually two beaches, 400-foot-long north beach and 200-foot-long south beach, separated by 150 feet of large rocks. The beaches' slope begins gently, then continues more steeply offshore. It is not well protected. This combination can cause swift beach backwash that is particularly concentrated at two or three points with a rough shorebreak, especially in the afternoons. The beach is dotted with large rocks. Fair swimming, generally poor snorkeling.

The Makena area includes the beaches south of Polo Beach, out to La Perouse Bay (past this point, you either hike or need to have a four-wheel drive). The Makena beaches are relatively undeveloped and relatively unspoiled, and not always easy to find. There are few signs and confusing roads, and some beaches are not visible from the road. Generally, no facilities, and parking where you can find it. I hope our directions will help you find these sometimes hard-to-find, but very lovely, nearly pristine beaches.

Palauea Beach

Palauea Beach lays along Makena Alanui road, which is reached via Old Makena Road, but is not visible through the trees. There is a break in the fence .35 mile from Polo Beach with a well-worn path to the beach. Although this is all private and posted land, the path and the number of cars parked alongside the road seem to indicate that this beautiful white-sand beach is getting much more public use than in the past. Good swimming. No facilities. Both Palauea and Po'olenalena beaches have the same conditions as Polo Beach, with shallow offshore slope then a steep drop-off that causes fairly strong backwash in places and tends to cause a strong shorebreak in the afternoon.

Po'olenalena Beach

As you leave Wailea, there is a four-corner intersection with a sign on the left for the Wailea Golf Club and one on the right for the Polo Beach Condos. About .8 mile past here turn onto the second right turnoff at the small "Paipu Beach" sign. At road's end (about .1 mile), park under the trees. Po'olenalena Beach lies in front of you. Walk several hundred feet back towards Polo Beach over a small hill (Haloa Point) and you will see Palauea Beach stretching out before you. A beautiful beach, largely unknown to tourists. The area above the beach at the south end has been developed with pricey residential homes.

This is a lovely wide, white-sand beach with a gentle slope offering good swimming. This used to be a popular local camping spot; however "No Camping" signs are now posted. There is another section of this beach sometimes referred to as **Paipu Beach**, but it is a continuation of Poʻolenalena. Continue another .2 to .3 miles on Makena Alanui, past Poʻolenalena and you will come to Makena Surf (about 1.2 miles from the Wailea Golf Club sign). This development surrounds **Chang's Beach**; there is a public beach access sign and paved parking for about 20 cars. It's a short walk down a concrete path to the beach. A rinse-off shower is provided. There is a small sandy beach used mostly by guests of the Makena Surf, but there is another public beach access there as well.

Ulupikunui Beach
Turn right just past the Makena Surf and immediately park off the road. Walk down to the beach at the left end of the complex. The beach is 75 to 100 feet of rock-strewn sand and not too attractive, but is well protected.

Five Graves
From the Makena Surf, continue down Old Makena Road another two-tenths of a mile to the entrance of Five Graves. Limited parking. The 19th-century graves are visible from Makena Road just a few hundred feet past the entrance. There is no beach, but this is a good scuba and snorkeling site. Follow the trail down to the shore where you'll see a rocky entrance to the water.

★ Makena Landing—Papipi Beach
This beach is about 75 to 100 feet long with a gentle slope, sometimes rock strewn. Not very attractive and used mostly for fishing, but snorkeling can be good if you enter at the beach and follow the shore to the right. Restrooms and showers available. Instead of turning right onto Old Makena Road at the Makena Surf, continue straight and follow the signs to the Makena Golf Course. About .9 mile past the Makena Surf there is another turnoff onto Old Makena Road. At the stop sign at the bottom of the hill, you can turn right and end up back at Makena Landing or turn left and head for Maluʻaka Beach. About .2 mile past the stop sign you will see the old Keawalai Church U.C.C. (Sunday services continue to be held here) and cemetery. Along the road is a pay phone.

★ Maluʻaka Beach
Past the Maui Prince Resort you'll turn right at the first paved dead-end road and find a beach park development created by the resort. This public access has plenty of paved parking. The 200-yard beach is set between a couple of rock promontories. The very fine white-sand beach is wide with a gentle slope to deeper water. Snorkeling

can be good in the morning until about noon when the wind picks up. There are interesting coral formations at the south end with unusual abstract shapes, and large coral heads of different sizes. Coral in shades of pink, blue, green, purple and lavender can be spotted. There are enough fish to make it interesting, but not an abundance. In the afternoon when the wind comes up, so do the swells, providing good boogie boarding and wave-playing.

Oneuli Beach
The entrance is a non-paved dirt road. The beach is composed of black lava, white cinder and coral combining to form a greyish-colored sandy beach. Just past the Maui Prince Resort is a dirt-road turnoff. A four-wheel-drive or high-ground-clearance vehicle is a good idea because the road can be a rutted, non-paved .3 mile to the beach. The beach is lined by an exposed reef. No facilities.

★ Oneloa Beach (Makena Beach, "Big Beach")
The entrance for Oneloa is the next paved dead-end road. On weekends, particularly Sundays, parking may be almost impossible. There is a second parking area a little farther. Makena's very lovely white-sand beach is long (.75 mile) and wide and is the last major undeveloped beach on the leeward side of the island. Community effort is continuing in its attempt to prevent further development of this beach. The 360-foot cinder cone (Pu'u Ola'i) at the north end of the beach separates Oneloa from Pu'u Ola'i Beach. The beach has a quick, sharp drop-off and rough shorebreak particularly in the afternoon. Body surfing is sometimes good. Snorkeling around the rocky point at the cinder cone is only poor to fair with not much to see, and not for beginners due to the usually strong north-to-south current. Following years of car break-ins, there is now a citizens patrol. Be sure you thank these people for their time and efforts. But still, don't leave any valuables in your car at any beach.

Pu'u Ola'i Beach (Little Makena)
Park at Oneloa Beach. From the beach (Big Beach) to your right you will see a cinder cone. You can hike uphill over the very sharp, steep and craggy cinder cone and down the other side to reach a flat, white-sand beach with a shallow sandy bottom that is semi-protected by a shallow cove. The shorebreak is usually gentle and swimming is good. Bodysurfing sometimes. Snorkeling is only poor to fair around the point on the left. Watch for strong currents. Although illegal, beach activities here tend to be *au naturel*.

★ 'Ahihi-Kina'u Natural Reserve Area
Past Makena Beach, a sign indicates the reserve, and a short distance past the sign there is a small, six-foot-wide, rocky and sandy beach alongside the remnants of an old concrete boat ramp in the water.

Although the beach and cove are well protected, the water is shallow and the shoreline is rocky. Not good for swimming, mostly used for snorkeling and scuba. There is also very limited parking here. Up around the curve in the road is a large parking area. It's a short walk to the shore on a crushed lava-rock trail that leads to a large "pebble" beach. At the end of this beach you'll find a better entrance than over the slippery rocks. Remember, this is a marine reserve—look, but don't disturb. No facilities.

La Perouse Bay

Past 'Ahihi-Kina'u, over a road carved through Maui's most recent lava flow, is the end of the road unless you have a four-wheel drive. It is about 1.5 miles to the La Perouse Memorial Plaque. From here, if you choose, you can hike. Wear good hiking shoes as you'll be walking over stretches of sharp lava rock. There are a series of small beaches, actually only pockets of sand of various compositions, with fairly deep offshore waters and strong currents.

Kahului-Wailuku Area

Beaches along this whole side of the island are usually poor for swimming and snorkeling. The weather is generally windy or cloudy in winter and very hot in summer. Due to the weather, type of beach, and distance from the major tourist areas on the other side of the island, these beaches don't attract many tourists (except Ho'okipa, which is internationally known for windsurfing).

Waihe'e Beach Park

From Wailuku take Kahekili Highway about three miles to Waihe'e and turn right onto Halewaiu Road, then proceed about .5 mile to the Waihe'e Municipal Golf Course. From there, a park access road takes you into the park. Paved off-street parking, restrooms, showers and picnic tables. This is a long, narrow, brown-sand beach strewn with coral rubble from Waihe'e Reef. This is one of the longest and widest reefs on Maui and is about 1000 feet wide. The area between the beach and reef is moderately shallow with good areas for swimming and snorkeling when the ocean is calm. Winter surf or storm conditions can produce strong alongshore currents. Do not swim or snorkel at the left end of the beach because there is a large channel through the reef that usually produces a very strong rip current. This area is generally windy.

Kanaha Beach Park

Just before reaching the Kahului Airport, turn left, then right onto Ahahao Street. The far south area of the park has been landscaped and includes barbecues, picnic tables, restrooms and showers. Paved off-street parking is provided. The beach is long (about one mile) and wide with a shallow offshore bottom composed of sand and rock. Plenty of thorny *kiawe* trees in the area make footwear essential. The main attraction of the park is its peaceful setting and view, so picnicking and sunbathing are the primary activities. Swimming would appeal mainly to children. Windsurfing and surfing can be good here. Weekend camping with county permit.

Hana Highway

H. A. Baldwin Park
The park is located about 1.5 miles past Spreckelsville on the Hana Highway. There is a large off-street parking area, a large pavilion with kitchen facilities, picnic tables, barbecues and a tent camping area. There are also restrooms, showers and a baseball and a soccer field. The beach is long and wide with a steep slope to overhead depths. This is a very popular park because of the facilities. The very consistent, although usually small, shorebreak is good for bodysurfing. Swimming is poor. There are two areas where exposed beach rock provide a relatively calm place for children to play.

Hoʻokipa Beach Park
Located about two miles past Lower Paia on the Hana Highway. Restrooms, showers, four pavilions with barbecues and picnic tables, paved off-street parking and a tent camping area. Small, white-sand beach fronted by a wide shelf of beach rock. The offshore bottom is a mixture of reef and patches of sand. Swimming is not advised. The area is popular for the generally good and, at times (during winter), very good surfing. Hoʻokipa is internationally known for its excellent windsurfing conditions. This is also a good place to come and watch both of these water sports.

Waiʻanapanapa State Park
About four miles before you reach Hana on the Hana Highway is Waiʻanapanapa State Park. There is a trail from the parking lot down to the ocean. The beach is not made of sand but of millions of small, smooth, black volcanic stones. Ocean activities are generally unsafe. There is a lava tunnel at the end of the beach that runs about 50 feet and opens into the ocean. Other

well-marked paths in the park lead to more caves and freshwater pools. An abundance of mosquitos breed in the grotto area so bug repellent is strongly advised.

Hana Beach Park

If you make it to Hana, you will have no difficulty finding this beach on the shoreline of Hana Bay. Facilities include a pavilion with picnic tables, restrooms and showers, and also Tutu's snack bar. A 200-yard beach lies between old concrete pilings on the left and the wharf on the right. Gentle offshore slope and gentle shorebreak even during heavy outer surf. This is the safest swimming beach on this end of the island. Snorkeling is fair to good on calm days between the pier and the lighthouse. Staying inshore is a must because beyond the lighthouse the currents are very strong and flow seaward.

Kaihalulu Beach (Red Sand Beach)

This reddish-sand beach is in a small cove on the other side of Kauiki Hill from Hana Bay and is accessible by trail. At the Hana Bay intersection follow the road up to the school. A dirt path leads past the school and disappears into the jungle, almost vanishes as it goes through an old cemetery, then continues out onto a scenic promontory. The ground here is covered with marble-sized pine cones that make for slippery footing. As the trail leads to the left and over the edge of the cliff, it changes to a very crumbly rock/dirt mixture that is unstable at best. This trail becomes two feet wide and slopes to the edge of a 60-foot cliff in one place. The trail down to the beach can be quite hazardous. Visitors and Hana residents alike have been injured seriously and fatally. *Hence, we cannot recommend this beach due to the dangerous access.* This cove is bordered by high cliffs and almost enclosed by a natural lava barrier seaward. The beach is formed primarily from red volcanic cinder, hence its name. There is also danger here of rip currents. And although illegal, beach activities here may be *au naturel* at times.

Koki Beach Park

This beach is reached by traveling 1.5 miles past the Hasegawa Store toward 'Ohe'o Gulch. Look for Haneo'o Road, where the sign will read "Koki Park—Hamoa Beach—Hamoa Village." This beach is unsafe for swimming and the signs posted warn "Dangerous Current."

★ Hamoa Beach

This gorgeous beach has been very attractively landscaped and developed by the Hotel Hana-Maui in a way that adds to the surrounding lushness. The long white-sand beach is in a very tropical setting and is hugged by a low sea cliff. To reach it, travel toward 'Ohe'o Gulch after passing through Hana. Look for the sign 1.5 miles past the Hasegawa Store that says "Koki Park—Hamoa Beach—Hamoa Village." There are two entrances down steps from the road. Parking is limited to along the roadside. The left side of the beach is calmer, and offers the best snorkeling. Because it is unprotected from the open ocean, there is good surfing and bodysurfing, but also strong currents alongshore and rip currents are created at times of heavy seas. The Hotel Hana-Maui maintains the grounds and offers restrooms, a changing area and beach paraphernalia for their guests. There is an outdoor rinse-off shower for non-hotel guests.

CHAPTER 6

Recreation and Tours

Maui's ideal climate, diverse land environments and benign leeward ocean have led to an astounding range of land, sea and air activities. With such a variety of things to do during your limited vacation time, I suggest browsing through this chapter and choosing those activities that sound most enjoyable. The following suggestions should get you started.

Remember: If you are making your vacation recreation plans from the mainland or another island you'll need to use the 808 area code. Toll-free numbers begin with 800 or 888. If you are a person with a disability, see "Travel Tips for the Physically Impaired" in Chapter 1 for more information.

Maui is abloom with street corner hawkers selling any and every form of recreational activity. In fact, we find it quite unpleasant that every nook has been filled with an activity booth. You should be aware that there are several kinds of activity vendors. Some activity booths are what they appear to be. They explain the various activities and can book you on your choice. Be aware that they may have favorites. This is fine—recommendations are helpful—but if this is based on how much commission they receive from a certain tour operator, then they may not be giving you the full picture. Concierge desks at the major hotels and resort can also book your activities. Most of these (although I'd guess probably all of them) also receive commissions. Those affiliated with the resort will no doubt give you the best service since they are a reflection of the resort. However, some activity desks at hotels, condos and the like are merely a concession. They rent the space, just like the activity booths on Front Street do, hence, the educated and informed visitor is ahead of the game in any case. The prices will be about the same, although there are those like Tom Barefoot's Cashback Tours who offer a 10 percent discount on every tour. (Barefoot's not only offers some great deals, they are also the only activity outlet I know of that *does not* sell timeshare. Read on.)

The other kind of tour activity broker is the one that *appears* to have the best deal: half price on a helicopter trip; $50 off on a luau. These are the folks that are using the activity as "bait." The "catch" is that you must attend some sort of breakfast meeting or tour of a property. Their aim is to sell you a timeshare unit on Maui. A timeshare is a week of time that you purchase once each year at a specific property. In a sense, you own 1/52 of a condominium. The cost is in the thousands of dollars. You can put your week into a pool by joining one of several organizations and trade with someone else; this way you could get a week at some other location around the world. In addition to the purchase price you pay a yearly or monthly maintenance fee. It appears to us that this is a great deal for the condo owner/developer. For example, they charge you $15,000 a week for your one-bedroom oceanview condo. Then they find another 51 folks to do the same and *voila*, they have just made $780,000 for a condo that would sell for perhaps $210,000. A lot of people own timeshares and love them. You may be interested in learning more about them, so you could take advantage of one of these opportunities and have a free meal or save on an activity. If you have plenty of time and more patience than I do, then attending one of these sessions (even if you aren't interested in a timeshare) may be worth your while to save money on an excursion. However, the timeshare programs I have attended were full of very high pressure sales tactics. The Activity Owners Association of Hawai'i regulates these booths. For information contact them at 800-398-9698 or check out www.maui.org. It also offers a "Gold Card" for $30 that entitles you to 10 to 25 percent discounts on recreational discounts and restaurants.

The final option is to book the tour yourself by calling one of the numbers listed in this chapter. Ask your questions and inquire if they have any specials or discounts. Since there is not a middle man to take a commission, you might be pleasantly surprised. In any case, it certainly won't hurt to ask. And inquire if they have a website and internet specials. Enough of our editorial comments, now on to the rest of this chapter. (P.S. I do not get commissions, nor do I sell timeshares!)

Best Bets

Experience the real Maui by taking a hike with guide Ken Schmitt and crew.

Enjoy a guided walk through a lava cave located along the Hana Highway. (See "Spelunking.")

On an overcast day, make the drive up to Makawao and enjoy a massage at the Maui School of Therapeutic Massage.

For great snorkeling try Honolua Bay, Namalu Bay, 'Ahihi-Kina'u or Olowalu.

Enjoy a romantic sunset sail on a Trilogy catamaran.

Take a helicopter tour and get a super-spectacular view of Maui.

Golf one of Maui's excellent courses.

Sail to Lana'i and snorkel Hulopo'e Beach on a Trilogy cruise.

Outrigger canoeing with the Kihei Canoe Club.

If the whales are in residence, take advantage of a whale-watching excursion to view these beautiful mammals a bit more closely. An estimated 1,500 whales winter each year in the waters surrounding Maui.

For an underwater thrill consider an introductory scuba adventure, no experience necessary. Or there is Snuba or the helmet dive.

For those who like to stay dry in the water, take a submarine trip to view the underwater sights off Lahaina.

For a wet and wild water tour—plus snorkeling—try a raft trip.

If you're really adventurous, consider parasailing (during the summer when the whales have gone back north) or sea kayaking, or try scuba kayaking at Kapalua.

For great scenery at a great price, drive yourself to Hana and visit the Pools of 'Ohe'o at Haleakala National Park or to Upcountry and Haleakala.

Check out kiteboarding.

Adventures and Tours

AIRPLANE TOURS

"Flightseeing" trips are generally available via small plane. Trips are arranged by customer request and could include Hana and Haleakala, as well as island flights to Mauna Loa on the Big Island, O'ahu, Kaho'olawe, Lana'i or Moloka'i. Small plane trips are less expensive than a helicopter tour, but you won't get as close to the scenery. There are several charter companies.

Pacific Wings This company provides scheduled flights, charter service and scenic air tours. They service Kahului to Hana (Maui), Moloka'i and Kamuela (Big Island) in their 8-passenger, twin-engine

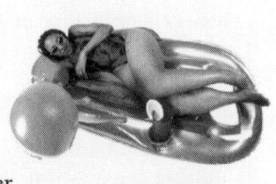

Cessna 402C. 888-575-4546; 808-873-0877; e-mail: info@pacificwings.com; www.pacificwings.com.

Paragon Air Paragon has 24-hour charter service to all islands in five- and nine-passenger planes. Excursions are quite different than helicopter tours. Their Kilauea volcano trip is a 2.5-hour narrated flight that travels to Hana along the picturesque coastline before traveling the 33 miles across the Alenuihaha Channel to the Big Island of Hawai'i. Departs from Kahului, Kapalua and Hana. Combine this with a helicopter tour over Kilauea before returning by charter flight to Maui. Or plan a trip to Moloka'i with a tour of the Kalaupapa Peninsula or fly to Lana'i for a round of golf. P.O. Box 575 Kahului, HI 96732. 800-428-1231; 808-244-3356; e-mail: wings@maui.net; www.paragon-air.com.

Volcano Air Tours To date, Volcano Air Tours has a perfect safety record. Log on to their website to read about the unique ways to see the "fire in the sky" of a Maui sunset and the "fire down below" created by miles and miles of lava flow from the active volcano areas of the Big Island. There is no other way to see the lava so close or to see land actually forming and being created as you watch. The Big Island Volcano Tour ($259) takes you over the Parker Ranch and Mauna Kea before flying over the active volcano area of Kilauea and the cooling waterfalls of Kohala, before viewing Hana and the north shore back on Maui. Departures are from Kapalua at 8 and 11:30 a.m. or from Kahului at 7:30 and 11 a.m. The Sunset Volcano Tour ($239) departs two hours prior to sunset and also explores the active volcano areas and the sites above Maui and the Big Island. 808-877-5500; e-mail: info@volcanoairtours.com; www.volcanoairtours.com.

ALL-TERRAIN VEHICLES

Haleakala ATV Tours Their tour starts you off at the 4,000-foot elevation and you'll travel 14 miles over upcountry terrain. The 3.5-hour tours include a picnic lunch in 'Ukulele Forest. The two-hour tour is available with no lunch stop. Guests 5 to 15 years old can ride along in the amphibious vehicle. They are located 2.5 miles up Crater Road. Bring lots of clothing layers to accommodate the changing weather conditions; closed-toe shoes and long pants are recommended. They provide helmets and rain gear, as well as warm clothing if necessary. 808-661-0288; www.atvmaui.com.

Maui ATV Tours Kick up some Maui dirt with Maui ATV Tours, which operates next to the Tedeschi Winery Tasting Room. The ATV vehicle allows you more involvement on the tour. For those who prefer to let someone else do the driving you can ride along in their nine-passenger "Extreme Machine," a big, bright yellow Pinzgauer that would be at home on Maui or on the African Safari. The 7:30 a.m. tour is 4 hour and is $130.21 per adult. A 2-hour trip leaves at 1:30

p.m. and is $93.70 per adult. Kids age 5 and older may also take the trip. The 3.5-hour Pinzgauer trip checks in at 8 a.m. or 12:30 p.m. and is $114.50 per adult. The tour route depends on the weather conditions. A variety of tours that climb up to 5,200 or down to the coastal King's Highway are available. Helmets and eye protection provided; long pants and closed-toed shoes are required. Riders must be 16 years or older to ride alone on an ATV. Customers 7 years old and older may ride along as a passenger in the 3-passenger ATV. Long pants and T-shirts available for rent. *808-878-2889; www.mauiatvtours.com.*

AQUARIUM (See "Museums/Gardens: Maui Ocean Center" later in this chapter)

ARCHERY (See "Lana'i Pine Sporting Clays" in Chapter 7)

ART CLASSES AND ART TOURS

Wailea Marriott, an Outrigger Resort   The Marriott Wailea's **Ho'olokahi Hawaiian Cultural Program** includes lectures and workshops on Hawaiian culture that vary throughout the year. Classes, available to guests and non-guests, run $5 to $20 each and include fiber basket weaving, Hawaiian quilting, feather-lei making and other crafts rich with Hawaiian heritage. Lectures and demonstrations are also offered (reservations required; small fee). *Ho'olokahi* ("to create unity") strives to preserve and perpetuate the Hawaiian culture. The *Hana Ka Lima* is a free arts-and-crafts exhibition, held every Friday at the resort from 9 a.m. to 2 p.m. and open to the public. The exhibition features Maui artisans displaying, demonstrating and selling their creations throughout the lobby of the resort. *808-874-7822.*

> Enjoy a self-guided tour of the wonderful art galleries in Lahaina. "Friday Night Is Art Night" has many free activities and a chance to meet some of the artists in person. The Lahaina Arts Society is a non-profit organization that features work by local Maui artists. They hold arts-and-craft shows under the Banyan Tree on Saturdays.

Hui No'eau Visual Arts Center   This center near Makawao offers art classes. The three-hour session every Tuesday explores the ancient art forms of Hawaii. Advanced registration required, $35. *808-572-6560.*

Art School of Kapalua   This school offers visual and performing-arts classes and workshops. Also an art gallery featuring local artists. Summer programs for kids available. *808-665-0007; www.kapaluaart.com.*

ASTRONOMY

Tour of the Stars   The rooftop of the Hyatt Regency is home to Big Blue, the 16-inch recreational telescope. Three times each evening, a maximum of ten people head to the hotel's rooftop for a guided "Tour of the Stars" with the Hyatt's own Director of Astronomy; seating is limited to 10 persons per show. For Hyatt guests the cost is $20 adults, $10 children 12 and under. Non-resort guests pay $25 adults, $15 children. *808-661-1234 ext. 4727.*

Star Party   In south Maui join the "Star Party" twice each week (Tuesday and Friday) at the Maui Prince Hotel. The party lasts 60 minutes and is conducted by an on-site astronomer using two large computer-guided telescopes. Adults $20, children 6 to 15 $15. *808-875-5888; www.starparty.net.*

Star Party on the Volcano   "Star Party on the Volcano" provides ski jackets and hot chocolate for an evening trip to the top. Watch the sun go down and then use a computer-guided telescope to see the stars in the clear Haleakala skies. The trip includes a picnic meal, volcano crater viewing and geology lecture. *808-281-0949.*

BIKING

The Hawaiian islands offer an endless array of spectacular air, sea and land tours, but only on Maui is there an experience quite like the bicycle ride down from the 10,000-foot summit of the world's largest dormant volcano. Bob Kiger, better known as Cruiser Bob, was the originator of the Haleakala downhill.

Cruiser Bob is reported to have made 96 individual bike runs himself to thoroughly test all aspects of the route before the first paying customers attempted the trip. Cruiser Bob's operations are now *pau*, but there are a number of companies still operating Haleakala downhill and upcountry trips.

Each downhill bike tour company differs slightly in its adaptation of the trip, but the principal is the same: to provide the ultimate in biking experiences. For the very early riser (2-3 a.m.) you can see the sunrise from the crater before biking down. Later-morning expeditions are available as well. Your day will begin with a van pickup at your hotel for a narrated trip to the Haleakala summit along with safety information for the trip down. The temperature at the summit can be as much as 30 degrees cooler than sea level, so appropriate clothing would include a sweater or sweatshirt.

General requirements are for riders to wear closed-toe rubber-soled shoes and sunglasses or prescription lenses (not all helmets have visors). A height requirement of about 5 feet is requested by some and no pregnant women are allowed on the trip. Bikers must also sign an acknowledgment of risk and safety consideration form. For the descent, riders are equipped with windbreaker jackets, gloves, helmets and specially designed bicycles with heavy-duty brakes. Dress in layers as the temperature change can be dramatic.

> If you are interested in doing some self-exploration on bikes, please use caution on the roadways. There are far too many accidents involving bicyclists and motorists. Remember that a good percentage of those behind the wheel of a car are island visitors who aren't familiar with the area, which perhaps is a contributing factor in these roadway accidents. There is a Maui County Bicycle Map that might assist you in your pursuits. It highlights all the major roads and rates them according to their suitability or unsuitability. It describes terrain features, elevation and even tradewind directions, and contains a distance guide. The map is available from Maui bike shops or from the **Maui Visitors Bureau**, 1727 Wili Pa Loop, Wailuku, HI 96793. 808-244-3530

A leader will escort you down the mountain curves with the van providing a rear escort. Somewhere along the way will be a meal break. Some tours provide picnics, others include a sit-down meal at the lodge in Kula or elsewhere. Actual biking time will run about 3 hours for the 38-mile downhill trip. The additional time (about 5 hours for the entire trip) is spent commuting to the summit, meals and the trip from the volcano's base back to your hotel. Prices for the various tours are competitive and reservations should be made in advance.

A few years ago I biked down with Maui Downhill and opted for the "late" 7 a.m. trip. I found them to be very careful, courteous and professional. Unfortunately they don't have control over the weather and the day I chose was clear on the drive up, fogged in and misty at the summit, and there was a torrential downpour for more than half of the 38 miles down. Due to the weather, I couldn't enjoy much of the scenery going down. The leader set a fairly slow pace, not much of a thrill for the biking speedster, but safe and comfortable for most. Riders were invited to hop in the van at any time, but ours was a hearty group and after a stop to gear up in rain slickers, we all continued on. Our leader also advised that if the weather posed any kind of risk, he would load us on the van. The weather broke just long enough for us to enjoy sandwiches or salads at the Sunrise Market and to bask in the sun's momentary warmth. In radio contact with the group just ahead of us we were advised that the rain promised to await us just a little farther down the volcanic slope. As predicted, the drizzle continued as we biked down through the cowboy town of Makawao. We arrived in Paia only a little wetter for the experience.

Aloha Bicycle Tours This volcano bike adventure begins at Rice Park in Kula with a continental breakfast before boarding the tour van to the starting area at Haleakala National Park's entrance. Outfitted with safety gear you begin your descent with a stop at the Sunrise Market and Protea Flower Farm. Other stops at Kokea and the final descent to Tedeschi Winery for a deli-style lunch and time to tour the winery and tasting room. The distance is 33 to 40 miles. Minimum age is 14 years, height is 4'10". Cost is $99 per person with a 7 a.m. departure and return by 1:30 p.m. Groups are small and they promise that what sets this tour apart is their relaxed pace, stunningly beautiful route and personal service. 800-749-1564; 808-249-0911; e-mail: marc@mauibike.com; www.mauibike.com.

Bike It Maui   What makes this company unique is that they offer a radio communication system for each rider. Safety and fun are their main concerns. They also offer Helly Hansen cold-weather gear. There's a sunrise tour and a midday tour. Sunrise includes a continental breakfast and a sit-down breakfast at the finish of the ride. The sunrise tour is $99 if you call them directly. Must be 12 years of age and 5 feet tall. 866-766-2453; 808-878-3364.

Cruiser Phil's   Chances are if you call it'll be Phil answering the phone at this owner-operated company. His sons and girlfriend are also on staff. They offer three tours daily: sunrise (pickup about 2 a.m.; $119), morning (pickup at 7:30 a.m.; $99) and day trip (a civilized noon pickup; $99). They do a nice sit-down meal in Paia. Riders must be at least 12 years of age. Unable to ride? You can come along and enjoy the scenic van ride at a special price. 877-764-2453; 808-893-2332; e-mail: mauibikeman@aol.com; www.cruiserphil.com.

Haleakala Bike Co.   They have a sunrise special ($84.99) and Summit Deluxe ($74.99); both include a tour of the park. The Express trip is $64.99 but does not include a tour of Haleakala Park. These are unguided tours; a van takes you up and you bike down at your own pace. *1043 Makawao Avenue, Makawao, HI 96768. 888-922-2453; 808-572-2200; www.bikemaui.com.*

Maui Downhill   Their 22- and 38-mile trips include a sunrise tours and midday tours. They offer a half-day trip ($79), Super Sunrise excursion ($150) and day tour ($120). The day and sunrise trips include a meal. All trips begin with a stop at their base-yard before your departure up the mountain. Must be over 12 years. Transportation from your hotel/condo. 800-535-2453; 808-871-2155; www.mauidownhill.com.

Maui Eco-Adventures   They have the only off-road Haleakala mountain biking trip as well as helicopter/biking combination tours. This trip is for experienced mountain bikers only and travels 4 to 6 miles depending on the group. Plan on a total of six hours for the trip to Upcountry, the biking and return to your hotel. Transportation,

BIKE SALES AND RENTALS

Bikes and mopeds are an ambitious and fun way to get around the resort areas, although you can rent a car for less than a moped. Available by the hour, day or week, they can be rented at several convenient locations.

A & B Rentals—They have bicycles in addition to beach equipment, surf and boogie boards, snorkel gear, fishing poles and underwater cameras. 3481 Honoapi'ilani Highway at the ABC store in Honokowai. 808-669-0027.

Kukui Activity Center—Bicycles $12.50/day, $65/week. Kukui Mall, 1819 South Kihei Road. 808-875-1151.

South Maui Bicycles—Bikes for cruising around Kihei run $19-22 per day/$89-99 per week. Road bikes $30 day/$130 week. 1993 South Kihei Road #5. 808-874-0068.

---

continental breakfast and a full lunch are provided. The trek is mostly downhill through private pastureland. $165 per person. *808-661-7720; www.ecomaui.com.*

Maui Mountain Cruisers Pickup provided from Kapalua, Ka'anapali, Lahaina, Kahului, Kihei and Wailea. Minimum age is 12 years, minimum height is 4'10". Closed-toe shoes and protective eyewear (sunglasses or prescription glasses) are required. Sunrise tour ($130) includes a continental breakfast prior to the tour and a sit-down stop for breakfast after the tour. Hotel pickup is 2:15 a.m. to 2:45 a.m. with a return about noon. The midday tour ($125) includes a continental breakfast and a lunch stop. Pickup time is 7 a.m. to 7:15 a.m., returning at 2:30 p.m. to 3:30 p.m. They also rent Big Dog and Harley motorcycles. *800-232-MAUI; 808-871-6014; fax 808-871-5791; www.mauimountaincruisers.com.*

Mountain Riders They offer a guided sunrise Haleakala tour ($125) that includes a breakfast stop and a day tour ($120) with lunch included. Hotel pickup available. *800-706-7700; 808-242-9739; e-mail: mtriders@maui.net.*

BODY SURFING

A number of beaches have good body surfing, depending on the season and daily weather conditions. One of the most popular is **Moku-le'ia (Slaughterhouse) Beach**. This is not a place for inexperienced or weak swimmers. When the surf is up, it can be downright dangerous. The high surf after a Kona storm brings fair body surfing conditions (better boogie boarding) to some beaches on leeward Maui. Inquire at local surfing shops where the safest conditions are during your visit.

BOWLING

Maui Bowling Center   This is Maui's only alley; ten lanes. Open Monday to Thursday from 10 a.m. to 10 p.m., Friday and Saturday until midnight, and Sunday from 9 a.m. to 10 p.m. Rates are $2 per person per game; shoe rental 50 cents. *1976 Vineyard, Wailuku. 808-244-4596.*

CAMPING

Safe and healthy camping is what it is all about. The Maui Department of Health in Wailuku has a wonderful free booklet called *Healthy Camping in Hawai'i* that outlines some safety tips you should know while enjoying the island's outdoors: surf and currents, flash floods, heat stroke, fungal and bacterial infections, pesky critters, as well as diseases such as leptospirosis and giardiasis.

Camp Pecusa   Located six miles southeast of Lahaina, it's halfway between the 14 and 15 mile-markers (behind the sugar cane fields). On the beach tent sites, $6 per person per night. No reservations. Maximum stay 7 nights per month. Toilets, showers, picnic tables, campfire pits, shade trees. No electricity. Managers-in-residence Norman and Linda Nelson advise us that the area is very safe and secure. Camp Pecusa also has cabins for groups. *808-661-4303; e-mail: norm@maui.net, linda@maui.net; www.maui.net/~norm/pecusa.html.*

Maui County Parks

County camping permits are available for H.A. Baldwin and Kanaha beach parks. The fee is $3 per night (children 50 cents) and camping is allowed seven days a week with a maximum of three nights. Camping is limited to weekends only at Kanaha Beach Park. Permits can be obtained by writing the Department of Parks and Recreation, County of Maui, 1580 Ka'ahumanu Avenue, Wailuku, HI 96793. *808-270-7230, 808-270-7389 (county-wide permits), 808-661-4685 (West Maui permits); www.co.maui.hi.us/departments/Parks.*

H.A. Baldwin Park   This county park is a grassy fenced area near the roadside. It is located near Lower Paia on the Hana Highway and has tent camping space, restrooms and outdoor showers.

Kanaha Beach Park   Located near the Kahului airport, this park has picnic tables, restrooms, barbecues, showers. Open seven days a week, but closed the last Tuesday, Wednesday and Thursday of each month.

State Parks

There are several state parks on Maui where camping is allowed. There is a small fee for overnight camping at all state campgrounds including Polipoli Springs and Wai'anapanapa. The cost is $5 per family campsite (up to 10 people) per night. The revenues fund park maintenance and interpretive programs. For staying in the cabins at Polipoli and Wai'anapanapa, see "Upcountry" section in Chapter 3. For information on day-use of state parks, see Chapter 5. For permits and additional information, contact Department of Land and Natural Resources, Division of State Parks: P.O. Box 621, Honolulu, HI 96809. 808-587-0300; www.hawaii.gov/dlnr/dsp/dsp.html.

Polipoli Springs State Recreation Area Located in Upcountry, this park has one cabin (see "Upcountry" in Chapter 3) and offers tent camping. This is a wooded, two-acre area at the 6,200-foot elevation on Haleakala's west slope. The road has been improved, but check to see if a four-wheel-drive vehicle may be required to reach the park. Extensive hiking trails offer sweeping views of Maui and the other islands in clear weather. Seasonal bird and pig hunting. Nights are cold and can be near freezing in winter. Toilets, picnic tables. No showers.

Wai'anapanapa State Park Located near Hana, the park covers 120 acres. Tent camping and cabins (see "Upcountry" in Chapter 3). Restrooms, picnic tables, outdoor showers. This is a remote volcanic coastline. Shore fishing, hiking, marine study, forests, caves, blow holes, black-sand beach and a *heiau*. Bring mosquito repellent.

Haleakala National Park

A permit is currently not required to camp at either Hosmer Grove or 'Ohe'o (called "drive-in" campgrounds). A maximum stay of three nights is allowed; first-come, first-served. Wilderness campgrounds at Paliku and Holua require a permit. Permit camping is allowed on a first-come, first-served basis in designated areas only. There is no fee. Permits must be obtained the day of the trip at Park Headquarters between 8 a.m. and 3 p.m. 'Ohe'o Headquarters Ranger Station, open 10 a.m. to 4 p.m., has information for 'Ohe'o campgrounds. For Haleakala Crater camping information write to the park or call the recorded information line. For information on use of one of the three cabins located in the Haleakala Crater, please refer to the "Upcountry" section in Chapter 3. P.O. Box 369, Makawao, HI 96768; 808-572-4400 (recorded information); 808-248-7375 ('Ohe'o station); 808-871-5054 (weather); www.haleakalanationalpark.com/camping.html#camp.

Hosmer Grove Located at the 7,000-foot elevation on the slope of Haleakala in Haleakala National Park. Tent camping in this wooded area. Cooking area with grill, pit toilets, potable water, picnic tables. Hosmer Grove Campground is often cool, windy or rainy. Maximum 50 people.

'Ohe'o Located in Haleakala National Park, Kipahulu District, just outside of Hana. Tent camping. Chemical toilets, picnic tables, barbecue grills; bring your own water. No open fires allowed. Maximum 25 people.

Holua Located near the Holua cabin on the northwest side of the crater, about 4 miles down Halemau'u Trail (from the 8,000-foot level). It is the most accessible site and sits in a shrubland at the top of Ko'olau Gap. It has pit toilets, and a limited non-potable water supply. Water must be treated before drinking. You will have to carry your water in times of drought. No open fires are permitted. Maximum occupancy is 25 people in each campground.

Paliku Located on the southeast side, 6 miles down the Sliding Sands Trail (from the 9,740-foot level) at the base of a rainforest cliff. Paliku is reached via a strenuous 10-mile hike from Sliding Sands trailhead. It has pit toilets and limited non-potable water.

Kapalaoa Kapalaoa is isolated in the cinder desert, six miles down Sliding Sands Trail. Pit toilets only.

CANOEING (OUTRIGGER)

Kihei Canoe Club They are open to recreational (as opposed to competitive) members (both resident and non-resident). The 30-day visitor fee is $25 and allows you to canoe twice a week at 8 a.m. If you fall in love with the sport and want to become a full member, you pay $125 a year, which allows access Monday, Wednesday and Friday at 6 a.m. and Saturday at 8 a.m. They also have some competitive events and social activities such as potlucks. They paddle from across the street from the Suda Store up in North Kihei with a small sign that appropriately enough reads, "Kihei Canoe Club." There is something about the stillness of the ocean and the camaraderie of paddling with five other folks to commands called out in Hawaiian. I'm not terribly athletic but had no trouble paddling. (You use your leg and stomach muscles as much as your upper body.) The day I went out I was told to take a spot on the canoe and I was paddling before I had any instruction. The steerswoman explained things as we headed out into the ocean (it did take a little time to get the motions and hand-holds down). We headed out to a buoy where there are plenty of green sea turtles. You can jump overboard for a swim if you choose. We were given additional instruction and some were asked to swim to different positions in different canoes. Two of us in my canoe were novices, but the remaining paddlers were local residents who were more experienced and very welcoming. I was happy to keep my spot. Ladies' attire should be swimsuits but shorts over the top prevent chaffing from the seats. P.O. Box 1131, Kihei, HI 96753. 808-879-5505.

Fairmont Kea Lani This resort in sunny Wailea welcomes resort guests and non-resort guests for complimentary outrigger canoeing.

They go out Tuesdays and Thursdays at 7 a.m., 7:45 a.m., 8:30 a.m. and 9:15 a.m. with four people plus two instructors. And yes, you *do* get to paddle. Call to confirm times and to reserve your paddle. *808-875-4100.*

CRUISES

Sunset cruises are quite popular on Maui with their free-flowing mai tais, congenial passengers, tropical nights and Hawaiian music that entertains while the boat cruises along the coastline. They are especially rewarding during whale season when you are likely to see some of these handsome mammals frolicking during your trip. The sunset cruises are far more numerous than dinner cruises and are a pleasant way to enjoy a Maui evening on the water in the $30 to $40 range. In the past couple of years, most of the dinner cruises seem to have sunk. In my opinion, this is just as well. Dinner aboard the smaller catamarans is most definitely not *haute cuisine*. The food is generally prepared ahead of time and often tepid by the time it is served. Balancing a plate on your lap is anything but leisurely dining. Several dinner cruises serve a sit-down meal on a larger vessel. I didn't personally review all the dinner cruises so your appraisal (as always) is appreciated. Dinner cruises last about two hours and run $60 to $85. Dinners may vary. All in all, don't expect the kind of food quality you'd experience at one of the island's land-locked restaurants, but private dinner charters are the most elegant way to enjoy a dining experience.

Dinner Cruises

Island Star Aboard this 57-foot Columbia sailboat you can enjoy a sit-down dinner for 8 on the aft deck or up to 28 if you arrange for *pupus* and buffet-style dining. They can work with any resort chef as well as Chez Paul so dine on steak and lobster or hamburgers. They can arrange to depart from either Lahaina or Ma'alaea. *808-669-STAR; www.islandstarsailing.com.*

Manate'a This 50-foot sailing catamaran offers a relaxed dinner cruise. Sample teriyaki chicken, volcano beef and broccoli stir-fry, vegetable chow fun and pineapple fried rice. Sail and sunset with musical accompaniment. Departs Lahaina Harbor. Adults $53.02, kids 4 to 12 $15.92. *808-249-8811.*

Maui Princess Dine and cruise aboard the 118-foot *Maui Princess*. A tour of the west Maui coastline departs at 5:15 p.m. and returns at 7:45 p.m. The dinner menu features roasted chicken or prime rib, salads, vegetable, breads, desserts and beverage of your choice. Open bar and live music complements the dancefloor. This is an attractive, upscale yacht with a good menu. Adults $79, children

12 and under $59. *800-275-6969; 808-667-6165; e-mail: ismarine@maui.net; www.maui.net/~ismarine.*

Shangri-La Aboard the 65-foot *Shangri-La* catamaran you can accommodate 2 to 49 guests for your dinner party. The *koa* dining table seats 10 passengers or buffet service is also available. They work with a number of chefs, and for groups of 12 or under they can arrange for an onboard chef to customize your dinner. Entertainment can be arranged. *Departure off Ka'anapali Beach. 888-855-9977; 808-665-0077; www.sailingmaui.com.*

Spirit of Lahaina The 65-foot *Spirit of Lahaina* is Maui's newest and largest catamaran. They feature a buffet dinner menu that offers a selection of scampi, island fish, teriyaki chicken and *kalbi* ribs along with potatoes, rice, salad and desserts plus open bar. Cost is $70 for adults, half-price for kids. *800-531-5262; 808-667-9595; e-mail: club@mauigateway.com; www.clublanai.net.*

Spirit of Windjammer A 70-foot three-masted schooner offers an evening of fine dining, romance and South Seas entertainment. As you cruise with the Hawaiian sunset as your backdrop, you are served an all-you-can-eat buffet dinner that includes prime rib, Alaskan salmon, rice pilaf, green salad, green beans and fresh Hawaiian pineapple with cheesecake and brownies for dessert. Music and hula. An open bar serves unlimited sodas, juice, cocktails, beer or wine. Adults $75.35, children $37.62. A Champagne Brunch Cruise is featured May through November on Fridays and Sundays for $37.10 adults, child under 12 with paying adult are free. Check for online discounts. Menu includes prime rib, ham, Portuguese sausage, rice, eggs, potatoes, French toast, fresh fruit muffins and pastry. Cocktails, juices and other beverages. *Departs Lahaina Harbor. 800-SEA-HULA; 808-661-8600; www.windjammercruisesmaui.com.*

Teralani They offer a sunset dinner and seasonal sunset/whale-watching excursion aboard their two catamarans, *Teralani I* and *Teralani II*. The dinner sunset whale-watching cruise is $69 adults, $65 teens and $55 children. The meal has an Italian flair with antipasto, Caesar salad and Giovanni's mahimahi or chicken marsala. *Passengers from the beaches of the Sheraton and Royal Lahaina as well as Dig Me Beach in Ka'anapali. 808-661-5500; fax 808-661-0448; www.teralani.net.*

Sunset Cruises

Gemini This 64-foot glass-bottom catamaran is used by the Westin and departs from Ka'anapali Beach. They offer a champagne sunset sail nightly from 5 to 7 p.m. that includes *pupus*, champagne, mai tais, beer and wine, and non-alcoholic beverages; $55 adults and $35 kids 2 to 12. This catamaran has long tables and padded seats inside. A wide passage area, accessible steps and ample headroom make it a comfortable boat. There are viewports on each side and big side windows. No music or entertainment, just a good chance to wind down on a pleasant sail. The *Gemini* also does snorkel sails. 808-669-0508; 808-669-1700.

Kaulana More than your average cocktail cruise, this is with entertainment and even dancing on deck if you'd like from 4 p.m. to midnight. Cost is $49 adults and half-price for kids. They feature hot and cold hors d'oeuvres, an open bar and, at no extra charge, that magical Maui sunset. 800-531-5262; 808-667-9595; e-mail: club@maui gateway.com; www.clublanai.net.

King Kamehameha This 40-foot Woody Brown catamaran was built in and for the waters of the Hawaiian islands. Two-hour sunset trips depart around 4:30 p.m. (depending on the season) and run $50 per person. No children discounts. They can also be privately chartered. Tom Warren has been sailing on various charter boats since 1969 and purchased the *Kamehameha* in 1977. BYOB with limited snacks provided. An intimate cruise if you're seeking a smaller boat. 808-661-4522.

Paragon Their sunset sail departs at 5 p.m. from Lahaina and is a two-hour trip with an open bar and appetizers. The vessel is licensed for 49 passengers but they only take 24 max. $51 adults, $34 12 and under. Book online and save 15 percent. 808-244-2087; e-mail: paragon@maui.net; www.sailmaui.com.

Scotch Mist Champagne and chocolate sunset sail, 2 hours, $40 adults, children 5 to 12 $20; no children under five permitted. 23 passenger max. Private charter available. *Departs Lahaina Harbor.* 808-661-0386; www.scotchmistsailingcharters.com.

Teralani They offer a sunset and seasonal sunset/whale-watching excursion aboard their two catamarans, *Teralani I* and *Teralani II*. Cost for the "Original Sunset Sail" is $52 adults, $45 teens and $35 kids. They also have a sunset dinner cruise. *Passengers depart from the beaches of the Sheraton and Royal Lahaina as well as Dig Me Beach in Ka'anapali.* 808-661-5500; fax 808-661-0448; www.teralani.net.

Trilogy Trilogy offers the fabulous Ka'anapali Sunset Sail three times each week. Departs along the beach, in front of the Ka'anapali Beach Hotel, for the two-hour trip. Departures change seasonally but plan on about 4 p.m. Enjoy an assortment of hot and cold appetizers that are heartier than average. The captain throws a flank steak on the grill and there is an impressive cheese tray. Staff move around the deck delivering beverages, sushi rolls and other goodies. This is a lovely sail with an amazing Maui sunset as a backdrop (weather permitting) and a fabulous way to spend an evening. If you want to spread out the sunset experience head out of Lahaina Harbor for a popular 10 a.m.-to-7 p.m. sail to Lana'i plus a sunset sail home (see "Sea Excursions, Sailing" later in this chapter). Cost is $169 adults; half-price children 3 to 15. Book online for discount. 800-732-4852; www.sailtrilogy.com.

DANCE

The **Hawaiian Ballroom Dance Association** lists some contacts for dancing on their website. *www.maui.net/~mpda/hbda.html.*

Paniolo Dance Association meets Mondays at Lahaina Civic Center for line-dance lessons and open dance and Thursdays at Bada Bing in Kihei from 7 to 9 p.m. for an informal get-together for those who want to practice West Coast swing. Fridays they meet at 7 p.m. at Bocalinos in Kihei for an informal get-together. *Miki, 808-669-8343; e-mail: mpda@maui.net; www.maui.net/~mpda.*

Everyone is welcome to the **MCC** (**Maui Community College**) ballroom dance practice parties. Held at the MCC Student Lounge the music ranges from Latin to rock-and-roll, country, swing and ballroom. Bring your dance shoes. *808-579-9755; www.maui.net/~mpda/mcc.html.*

The **Maui Dance Council** has more options. *808-575-5227.*

Also see "Nightlife" in Chapter 4 for more ideas.

FISHING

Deep-sea fishing off Maui is among the finest in the world and no licenses are required for either trolling or bottom fishing. Fish that might be lured to your bait include the Pacific blue, black or striped marlin (*a'u*) weighing up to 2,000 pounds, yellowfin tuna (ahi) up to 300 pounds, Jack Crevalle (*ulua*) to 100 pounds, bonita-skipjack (*aku*) to 40 pounds, dolphin fish (mahimahi) to 90 pounds, wahoo (*ono*) to 90 pounds, mackerel (*opelu*), amberjack (*kahala*), grey snapper (*uku*), red snapper (*onaga*) and pink snapper (*opakapaka*). Boats generally offer half- or full-day fishing trips on a shared or private basis. Some are willing to take non-fishing passengers along at half-price. Most boats take 4 to 6 on a shared basis, but several can handle larger groups. All gear is provided.

Finding a charter: Your local activity center can direct you to a particular boat that they favor, or you could go down to the docks at the Lahaina or Ma'alaea harbors in the afternoon and browse around. There are also a number of activity booths at both harbors that can be consulted. When reserving a spot, be aware that some boats will give full refunds only if a 48-hour notice is given for cancellation. If you want to take children fishing, many have restrictions for those under age 12. If you are a serious fisherman, you might consider entering one of the numerous tournaments. Some charters offer tournament packages. Following are a list of just some of the charter fishing boats. **Finest Kind** for years has been ranked the #1 fishing boat on Maui.

A word of advice: The young man had a grin that reached from ear to ear as he stood on the pier in Ma'alaea, holding up his small ahi for a snapshot of his catch. The surprise came when the deck hand returned the fish to the ice chest and continued on with his work. The family all stood on the dock, unsure of what to do. It appeared that the fish was to remain on board, though the family had envisioned a nice fresh fish dinner. One family member spoke up and a very unhappy crew member sliced a small filet, tossed it into a sack and handed it to the young man. Unlike sportfishing charters in some parts of the country, the fish caught on board generally remain the property of the boat. The pay to captain and crew is minimal and it is the selling of the boat's catch that subsidizes their income. Many vacationers booking a fishing excursion are unaware of this fact. There seems to be no written law for how fishing charters in Hawai'i handle this, at least everyone I talked to had different answers. Many of the brochures lead one to believe that you keep your fish, but they neglect to mention that it may be only a filet of fish. Occasionally you may find a head boat that operates under a different sort of guideline. In this situation, you pay for your bait, gear and boat time and then keep the fish. In any case, be sure you check when you book your trip about just how much fish will be yours to keep. If the person at the activity desk assures you that you keep your catch, don't leave it there. Also check with the captain when you board. (I checked with Carol Ann of Carol Ann Charters and was told on board her vessel, you *do* get to keep your fish.) Communication is the key word—and have an *ono* day!

Aerial Sportfishing   *No Problem*, 37' Merritt, Criss-craft Charters: 8-hour $850 full-day private, $750 6 hours and $650 for 4 hours. *Aerial III*, 36', is $750/$650/$550. Shared boat is $165 full day, $140 6-hour and $110 four-hour. *Departs from Lahaina Harbor.* 808-667-9089.

Carol Ann Charters   33' Bertram, max. 6. Private charters only. Departs from Ma'alaea Harbor. 808-877-2181.

Extreme Sport Fishing   39' custom force; 8-hour trip $180, $160 for six-hour excursion. The newest fishing option at Lahaina Harbor. 808-878-2362.

Finest Kind, Inc.   *Exact*, 31' Bertram; *Finest Kind*, 37' Merritt; *Reel Hooker*, 35' Bertram. Charters: 8-hour $175, 6-hour $160, 4-hour $140. Maximum 6 people. Private charters available. P.O. Box 10481, Lahaina, HI 96761. 808-661-0338.

Hinatea Sportfishing   *Hinatea*, 41' Hataras. Shared rates: Full-day $160, 6-hour $145, 4-hour $130. *Slip #27, Lahaina Harbor.* 808-667-7548.

Ka'anapali Sportfishing   *Desperado* 31' Bertram. 8-hour $150, 6-hour $135. Shared-boat and private charters available. *Departs Ka'anapali.* P.O. Box 11208, Lahaina, HI 96761. 808-667-5792.

Lahaina Charters *Judy Ann II,* 43' Delta (max 20). 8 hours $125, 6 hours $100, 4 hours $75. The *Alohilani,* 28' Topaz (max 6). Private charters available. P.O. Box 12, Lahaina, HI 96761. 808-667-6672.

Luckey Strike Charters *Kanoa,* 31' Uniflite, max. 6, *Luckey Strike II,* 50' Delta. Four-, six- or eight-hour trips. Shared-boat rates $115, $150, $175. Private charters available. P.O. Box 1502, Lahaina, HI 96767. 808-661-4606; www.luckeystrike.com.

Marlin Mischief *Marlin Mischief,* 47' Buddy Davis. Fish in luxury on this boat. It even has air conditioning. Shared 6 hours $165/8 hours $185. *Departs Lahaina slip #63.* 808-662-3474.

Rascal Sportfishing Charters 40' Hatéras *Rascal.* $155 for 6-hour shared, $170 for 8-hour shared charter. Private charters $650 for 4 hours, $750 for 6 hours and $850 for 8 hours. *Departs slip #13 at Ma'alaea.* 808-874-8633.

Start Me Up 42 ft. Bertram sportfisher is just one of several boats they offer. It is air-conditioned, and has TV/VCR, microwave, live bait and lures. Family-owned and -operated. 6 passengers maximum. *Departs from Lahaina Harbor.* 808-268-2449; 808-667-2774.

Unreel Sport Fishing 42' Ditmar & Donaldson. $115 4 hours; $135 6 hours; $163 8 hours. Private charters available. *Departs Ka'anapali.* 808-244-2123; www.sportfishing-maui.com.

GOLF

Maui's golf courses have set a high standard of excellence for themselves. Many are consistently ranked among the top in the United States and the world by prominent golf magazines. Not only do they provide some very challenging play, but they also offer distractingly beautiful scenery. Most of the major resorts have golf packages; for the avid player, this may be an economical plan.

If you are a real golf enthusiast, consider subscribing to *Hawaii Golf.* It details lots of upcoming golf events throughout the islands. P.O. Box 6107, Honolulu, HI 96818. There is also a very good and free magazine, *Maui Golf Review,* available around the island at various brochure racks.

The Dunes at Maui Lani The newest course on Maui, this 18-hole, links-style golf course was designed by Robin Nelson (who also designed Maui's Sandalwood course and the Mauna Lani course on the Big Island) and winds from Wailuku through Kahului. The par-72 course measures 6,841 yards. There are four sets of tees from which to choose from. Rates are $95 and twilight (after 2 p.m.) is $45. Club ($30) and shoe ($10) rentals are also available. *Take the Maui Lani Parkway (near the Maui Memorial Hospital) from Wailuku. Another option*

STAND-BY GOLF

Stand-by Golf is a great option for golfers interested in some serious savings. They feature discounted rates at public and private courses. They sell unsold tee times beginning around 6 p.m. until 11 p.m. for the next day of play and after 7 a.m. for the same day. They book your game at a guaranteed price and time. Discounts range from 10 percent on the lowest priced courses up to 33 percent. Prices always include the cart. They cannot book municipal golf courses. Bookings are handled by telephone and you pay with a credit card. 888-645-BOOK.

is to look for the sign on Kuihelani Highway, several miles before you approach Kahului at the First Assembly of God on Dairy Road. 808-873-0422; www.mauilani.com.

Elleair Golf Course This non-resort course in Kihei offers a par-71, 6,800-yard, 18-hole course located off Pi'ilani Highway near Lipoa Street. The course was designed by Bill Newis. Green fees $90 for morning play. Ask about seasonal golf specials, twilight play ($70 after 1 p.m.) and discounts for reply on the same day. Rental clubs $30. The company also owns the Maui Beach and Maui Palms hotels in Kahului. 808-874-0777.

Ka'anapali Golf College This college at Ka'anapali Golf Course offers golf instruction for the beginner or advanced golfer. Their "curriculum" includes video analysis, half- and all-day schools, beginner clinics, private lessons and any of the above paired with 9 or 18 holes of play on the Ka'anapali Golf Course. 808-661-0488; www.rodgerfredericks.com.

Ka'anapali Resort There are two championship courses here. The Royal Ka'anapali driving range is located at the southern entrance to the Ka'anapali resort area. Club rental $30. You can set up your tee time online. 808-661-3691; www.kaanapalibeachhotel.com.

Ka'anapali North Course—Designed by Robert Trent Jones, this 6,305-yard course places heavy emphasis on putting skills. It has been attracting celebrities since its inauguration when Bing Crosby played in the opening of the first nine holes. At par 72, it is rated 70 for men and 71.4 for women. Green fees are $130 (morning), non-resort guests $150. Twilight discount (2 to 6 p.m.) $77.

Ka'anapali South Course—This course first opened in 1970 as an executive course and was reopened in 1977 as a regular championship course after revisions by golf architect Arthur Snyder. At 6,205 yards and par 72 it requires accuracy as opposed to distance, with narrower fairways and more small, hilly greens than the North Course.

As an added attraction, the Sugar Cane Train passes by the 4th hole. Green fees are $117, non-resort guests 142. Twilight discount (2 to 6 p.m.) $74. Kama'aina discounts.

Kapalua Golf Academy   Located in the Village Course clubhouse, this academy offers individual lessons, including junior instruction, on-course playing lessons or half-day, 2-day and 3-day "schools." Indoor instruction utilizes digital video for swing and short game analysis. 808-669-6500; e-mail: info@kapaluagolfacademy.com; www.kapaluagolfacademy.com.

Kapalua Resort   Kapalua has demonstrated its dedication to the land. All three of its golf courses are Certified Audubon Cooperative Sanctuaries. Kapalua's courses received this Sanctuary designation by meeting the stringent environmental standards set forth by the New York Audubon Cooperative Sanctuary System for water conservation, habitat enhancement, public involvement, integrated pest management and more. An environmental awareness program, "Eagles and Birdies at Kapalua," encourages players to identify the many birds (23 varieties) they encounter during their rounds at Kapalua. Discounts for registered guests of Kapalua Bay Hotel and Ocean Villas, The Kapalua Villas and The Ritz-Carlton, Kapalua; twilight play (2 p.m. to 6 p.m.) is $80 to $85. Replay on any of the courses the same day is available, as are club and shoe rentals. Guests may reserve tee times up to 7 days in advance; non-guest reservations 4 days in advance. Special golf events held at various times throughout the year. 808-669-8044; www.kapaluagolfacademy.com.

Bay Course—This beautiful and scenic 6,600-yard, par-72 course has a distinctly Hawaiian flavor. Under the design of Arnold Palmer, it opened in 1975 and sprawls from sea level to the mountain's edge. With its picturesque signature hole extending onto an ocean-framed black lava peninsula, the Bay Course is an excellent example of a premier resort golf course. It has plenty of hilly terrain, and you'll be challenged by eight water hazards as it meanders through the West Maui Mountains and down to the surf. The fourth hole is a par 4 and play is along the water, but it is the signature fifth hole that is impressive as it shoots out over the Pacific. The Bay Course has been host to a number of PGA tours and other national championships. Green fees $180 including cart; $125 discounted fee.

Village Course—At par 71 and 6,632 yards, designer Arnold Palmer and course architect Ed Seay are reported to have given this course a European flavor. It opened in 1981 and sweeps inland along the pineapple fields and statuesque pine trees. Resembling the mountainous countryside of Scotland, it rises from sea level to over 800 feet—and this is over just the first six holes. By the last hole you've returned back down to sea level. The course is reputed to be the most difficult and demanding in Hawai'i and one of the most challenging in the world. With narrow fairways a player can enjoy 57 bunkers and the wind can play a factor on this course. The Village Course has a clubhouse; Fleming's on the Green offers dining and a golf school/clinic. Green fees $180 including cart; $125 discounted fee.

Plantation Course—This lengthy 18-hole championship course opened in 1991 and was designed by Coore and Crenshaw of Austin, Texas. It's situated on 240 acres and is north of the Village Course. The 7,263-yard course has a par 73 and features expansive greens, deep valleys and expansive fairways. If you can afford it, I'm told you get better the second round of play at this course. Green fees $225; $135 discounted fee.

Lana'i Two 18-hole courses are available on Lana'i, **The Challenge at Manele** (808-565-2222) and **The Experience at Koele** (808-565-4653). Reservations can be made from the mainland by calling 800-321-4666. A day package that includes round-trip transportation via the Expeditions ferry boat out of Lahaina, green fees and Lana'i island transfers available. See "Recreation and Tours: Golf" in Chapter 7 for more details.

Makena This area offers two courses designed by Robert Trent Jones, Jr. The original 18-hole course opened at the same time as the Maui Prince resort in the early 1990s. In 1993, the course was divided in half, and each half was combined with nine new holes to create the North and South Courses. *808-879-3344.*

South Course—This classic open-style course leads to the ocean. The large cacti which abound in this area were imported to feed the cattle that were once ranched here. This course is 6,168 yards from the resort tee with a par 72. Makena guest rate $105, non-guest rate $175, twilight play (after 2 p.m.) $100.

North Course—This narrower course travels along the slopes of Haleakala, offering some spectacular panoramic views. It's a par 72 and is 6,151 yards from the resort tee. Makena guest rate $90, non-guest rate $155, twilight play (after 2 p.m.) $90.

Maui Country Club This private course in Spreckelsville, originally opened in 1925, invites visitors to play on Mondays only. The course is fairly flat, especially when compared to many of the other island courses. The narrow fairways are lined with *kiawe* and banyan trees. Call Sunday after 9 a.m. to schedule Monday tee times. If you choose to play 18 holes, you'll be playing the 9-hole course twice for a total of 6,546 yards and a par 74. Green fees are $45 for 9 holes, $65 includes cart. *808-877-0616.*

Pukalani Country Club and Golf Course This semiprivate course nestled along the Upcountry slopes of Haleakala affords a tremendous panoramic view of Central Maui and the ocean from every hole. The course designed by Bob Baldock covers 160 acres. The first nine holes opened in 1978, with nine additional holes added, making the course 6,962 yards (par 72). Green fees are $60 up to 11 a.m., $50 up to 2 p.m.; twilight play is $40. Cart fee is $16. *808-572-1314; www.pukalanigolf.com.*

Sandalwood Golf Course Located at Waikapu is a par-72 course of 5,162 to 6,469 yards—depending on your choice of the blue, white or red tee-offs. The course was designed by Robin Nelson and Rodney Wright and constructed in 1992 along the side of the West Maui Mountains. Mandatory cart fee is included. Regular rate $80; twilight is $50 and starts at noon. Club and shoe rentals are available. Check website for specials and unlimited playtime by the month. *808-242-4653; www.sandalwoodgolf.com.*

Waiehu Municipal Course Located north of Wailuku on the windward side of the island, this course opened with nine holes in 1929; an additional nine holes were added in 1966. The course was constructed by Maui civil engineers. The 18 holes measure 6,330 yards with a par of 37-35-72. The front nine are at sea level along the beach with *kiawe* and ironwood trees framing this section of the course. The back nine are on an old sand dune above the shoreline. Green fees are $25 weekdays and slightly higher fees may prevail on weekends and holidays. A cart is optional at $15. Inexpensive food and drink at the Waiehu Inn located on the course. *808-243-7400 or 808-244-5934; www.gvhawaii.com.*

Wailea Resort Wailea Resort offers three courses: the challenging Emerald, Blue and Gold. There are junior rates for children up to 17 years of age and is $60 anytime of the day from May to late December; otherwise, a noon tee time restriction applies. There are sometimes seasonal specials and these might include the Wailea Triple Play Pass, good for 3 rounds at Wailea. *888-328-MAUI (tee-time reservations); 800-332-1614; 808-879-7450; e-mail: info@wailea-resort.com; www.waileagolf.com.*

Emerald Course—*Golf Digest* and *Golf Magazine* have both ranked the Emerald in their top courses. This par-72, 6,825-yard course was designed by Robert Trent Jones, Jr., to provide a tropical garden experience. It also boasts spectacular scenery with an outstanding ocean view on the fourth hole. Definitely worth packing a camera along with your clubs. Green fees $135; $160 non-resort guests.

Blue Course—A creation of Arthur Jack Snyder, this par-72, 6,758-yard course opened in 1972. Four lakes and 74 bunkers provide hazards along with the exceptional scenery. The 16th hole is particularly lovely with numerous people stopping to snap a picture from this magnificent vantage point. Green fees $120; $145 non-resort guests. This is also the only Wailea course to offer twilight play (after 2 p.m.), $80; $95 non-resort guests.

Gold Course—Designed by golf course architect Robert Trent Jones, Jr., it opened January 1, 1994. Jones' design concept was to create a classical, rugged style of golf that takes advantage of the natural sloping terrain. The course is par 72 and stretches 7,070 yards across the lower slopes of Haleakala, affording exquisite views of the Pacific Ocean. Green fees $135; $160 non-resort guests.

GOLF—MINIATURE

There's an 18-hole miniature golf course on the roof of the **Embassy Vacation Resort** in Honokowai. Open from 11 a.m. to 9 p.m. daily. Adults $5; 12 and under $2.50. *808-661-2000.*

HANG GLIDING

Hang Gliding Maui   Motorized flights out of Hana over the coastline and pristine waterfalls. Not offered everyday, so call ahead for reservations. Cost is $115 for half hour and $190 for full hour. Weight maximum is 240 pounds. *808-572-6557; fax 808-873-8960; e-mail: info@hangglidingmaui.com; www.hangglidingmaui.com.*

Proflyght   No experience? That's okay. Tandem flights or solo flights fly mornings over Upcountry in the Polipoli area. Groups up to 6. $175 for 15-minute 3,000-foot jump. $75 for lower flights. $125-$275 for higher-elevation flights. *808-874-5433; e-mail: gliding@maui.net; www.paraglidehawaii.com.*

HELICOPTER TOURS

The price of an hour-long helicopter excursion may make you think twice. After all, it could be a week's worth of groceries at home. I had visited Maui for 7 years before I finally decided to see what everyone else was raving about. It proved to be the ultimate island excursion. When choosing a special activity for your Maui holiday, I'd suggest putting a helicopter flight at the top of the list. (When you get home you can eat beans for a month.) Adjectives cannot describe the thrill of a helicopter flight above majestic Maui. A tour of the islands from the air is truly an unforgettable experience. Among the most popular tours is the Haleakala Crater/Hana trip, which contrasts the desolate volcanic crater with the lush vegetation of the Hana area. Maui's innermost secrets unfold as the camera's shutter works frantically to capture the memories (one roll is simply not enough) and pilots narrate as you pass by waterfalls cascading into cool mountain pools. Virtually all the tour companies provide headsets for two-way communications between the pilot and passengers during the flight. Another option is the West Maui to Moloka'i, which affords an incredible opportunity to see the whales from a bird's-eye view between November and April. Keeping up with the prices is impossible. Listed are standard fares, and I hope you'll be delighted to learn of special discount rates if you call the helicopter company directly for reservations. Currently all helicopters depart from the Kahului heliport. Most companies include a video of your trip, though some are now charging an additional fee for this service. In choosing a helicopter tour, you should know that there are several different types of helicopters with different seating configurations. The four-passenger Bell Jet Ranger seats one passenger in front next to the pilot and three in the back seat. The AStar has two passengers in the front and four passengers in the rear seat. The ECO-Star is perhaps the most quiet and advanced avionic helicopter, offering unparalleled passenger comfort and cockpit design for fantastic sweeping views. Interested in helicopter flight training while on Maui? Contact **D&H Hawaii, Inc.** 808-875-8998. Or if you just want to go along for the ride, there are plenty of companies to accommodate you:

Air Maui Owner Steven Egger offers flights aboard a six-passenger AStar aircraft. Steve has been flying for 30 years and Air Maui is a family operation. The office staff and crew range from brothers and mothers to best friends. The 45-minute tour of Haleakala and Hana is $180; Circle the Island, one-hour, is $230. The West-Maui and Moloka'i tour is $225; West Maui, 30 minutes, $115. Online discounts are available. *877-238-4942; 808-877-7005; www.airmaui.com.*

Alexair They feature two six-passenger AStar helicopters. West Maui specials begin at $79. A variety of trips are available and include the Deluxe West Maui tour $125, East Maui $150, Circle the Island $205. Deluxe Circle Island is $230 and includes flight video. *888-418-8455; 808-871-0792; e-mail: alexair@mauigateway.com; www.helitour.com.*

Blue Hawaiian Dave and Patti Chevalier began their operation on Maui in 1985 and offer a variety of aerial and air/ground tour combinations in either the ECO-Star or AStar aircraft. The West Maui tour, 30 minutes, is $150 (this is ECO-Star price; AStar slightly less); Hana/Haleakala is 45 minutes, $215. A complete island tour, 65 minutes, is $275. Moloka'i/West Maui, 65 minutes, is $275. The Sky Trek is a six-hour event with a 36-minute flight and a landing and tour in Hana, $280. The Maui Spectacular is a complete island flight with a 20-minute landing at the Ulupalakua Ranch, on the slope of the Haleakala volcano. Their multimillion dollar terminal encompasses 9,600 square feet and includes a customer lounge area with an atrium, waterfalls and a 1,000-gallon reef aquarium. Group rates are also available. Blue Hawaiian was chosen to help shoot the aerial photography on such Hawai'i-based films as *Jurassic Park, The Lost World, George of the Jungle, Honeymoon in Las Vegas, Crimson Tide, Flight of* the Intruder and Six Days Seven Nights. 800-745-BLUE; 808-871-8844; fax 808-871-6971; e-mail: info@bluehawaiian.com; www.bluehawaiian.com.

Sunshine Helicopters Inc. Maui's most experienced pilots fly you in their comfortable "Black Beauties." Sunshine offers AStar helicopters featuring state-of-the-art audio and video systems. Three external cameras and one cockpit camera capture live video of your actual flight including passenger reactions. Air-conditioned comfort and recordable CD players on board make for a pleasurable ride into our nation's largest rainforest. The five-hour Paniolo Horseback Combination ($260) includes a 30-minute flight with lunch and a horseback ride. Journey into an actual working cattle ranch in the heart of West Maui and then enjoy a Western-style open-pit barbecue lunch followed by a take-off for a full helicopter tour of West Maui. The West Maui Deluxe tour is $125. The Hana/Haleakala special is $189. The Circle Island Explorer tour is $209. The Circle Island Special tour with a stop at Kaupo is $275. West Maui/Moloka'i Tour is $245. Ask Sunshine about their helicopter and submarine adventures. I've flown with Sunshine on a number of occasions and can recommend their courteous ground crew along with their engaging and informative pilots. 800-469-3000; 808-871-5600; e-mail: reservations@sunshinehelicopters.com, sales@sunshinehelicopters.com (group sales); www.sunshinehelicopters.com.

Windward Aviation Sightseeing available on charter basis only. 808-877-3368.

HIKING

Maui offers many excellent hiking opportunities for the experienced hiker or for a family outing. Comprehensive hiking information is available from several excellent references. Craig Chisholm and his wife Eila were the pioneers in the field of Hawaiian hiking information with the first edition (1975) of *Hawaiian Hiking Trails*, which is continually updated. This book describes six Maui trails. The Chisholms' books are attractively done with beautiful color photographs in the frontpiece and easy-to-follow U.S. geological maps for each of the hikes. Throughout the text are black-and-white photos. These books are thoroughly researched by the authors and very accurate.

Robert Smith's *Hiking Maui* was first published in 1977. He continues to update his book every couple of years, the latest in 1999. The book is compact in size with a color cover and a scattering of black-and-white photographs and maps. The Maui edition covers 27 trails. Kathy Morey writes *Maui Trails*, which is published by Wilderness Press. There are over 50 trails listed in the hiking table of contents; however, some are really more walks than hikes. It has plenty of easy-to-use maps.

Hiking Trails

There are many interesting and diverse hiking opportunities on Maui. They vary from hiking in a volcanic crater, strolling among a grove of eucalyptus, exploring a rocky shoreline, or walking through a tropical rainforest. I'm not going to even attempt to cover the many hiking trails available on Maui, but would like to share with you several guided and non-guided hiking experiences that I have enjoyed.

Haleakala National Park   At Park Headquarters (open 7:30 a.m. to 4 p.m.; 808-572-4400), you can obtain hiking information and permits. Day-hike permits are not required. Keep in mind that the increased elevation may affect your endurance. Short walks include the .5-mile loop trail to **Hosmer Grove Nature Trail Lookout**, the .25-mile trek to the **Leleiwi Overlook**, the .5-mile hike to **White Hill** and a .67-mile hike to the first switchback on the Sliding Sands Trail. Day hikes include the 2.2-mile hike from **Halemau'u to the valley rim** and **Sliding Sands to Ka Lu'u o ka 'o'o**, a distance of 5 miles with a 1,400-foot change in elevation each way. For the hiker with more stamina, there is the 10-mile **Halemau'u to Silversword Loop** and the **Sliding Sands to Halemau'u Trailhead** that traverses 11 miles. *Caution:* The thin air and steep inclines may be especially tiring.

Hoapili Trail   Referred to as the King's Highway, this trail starts just beyond La Perouse Bay. It is believed that at one time the early Hawaiians made use of a trail that circled the entire island and this is a remnant of that ancient route. The State Forestry and Wildlife Division and volunteers worked together putting in place stone barricades to keep the four-wheel-drive vehicles and motorcycles from destroying any more of the trail.

Lahaina Pali Trail   This trail was originally built as a foot trail and later used as a horse trail. (While horses were introduced to the islands in 1803, their use was restricted to chiefs or *ali'i* until the middle of the century.) It traverses from sea level to an elevation of 1,600 feet on the Kealaloloa Ridge. Portions of the old trail were well preserved. Today, access to the trailhead is possible through the courtesy of the Wailuku Agribusiness Company. An interesting and informative guide for the trail and the area is provided by the Na Ala Hele Statewide Trail and Access Program, a Division of Forestry and Wildlife. It corresponds to markers along the trail and provides some fascinating historical narratives. For example, in bygone days robbers would wait along the trail, ready to pounce on unsuspecting travelers. If you'd like information on the trail call 808-871-2521.

Polipoli Springs State Recreation Area   This park is ideally situated on the leeward slopes of Haleakala. Cool crisp mountain air provides a temperate climate for hiking and the trails are suitable for the entire family. Since the weather can be cool, warm attire and rain apparel should be included in your day or night pack. The clouds often clear, however, and treat visitors to a sunny and very mild afternoon. To get to the turnoff, go just past the Kula Botanical Gardens and turn on Waipoli Road, or go .3 mile past the junction of Highways 37 and 277. Follow the steep and windy paved road approximately eight miles. The last portion is graded, but rain quickly makes the roads impassable for all but 4-wheel-drive vehicles. *Warning*: Rental car agencies are not responsible for damage done to cars that travel this road. I have found it passable in a car with high clearance only if the road has been recently graded and is dry. Once you reach the park there is a gravel parking area and a grassy camping area. There are two barbecues and a flush toilet in a small outhouse. Drinking water is available. Trail options include a .8-mile trek to the Redwood Forest, a 6-mile Haleakala Trail, 4.8-mile loop trail, 1 mile to the cave shelter and 1.5 miles to Plum Trail.

The 4.8-mile loop is a very easy trail and, with frequent snack stops, even my (then) three-year-old was able to make it the entire distance. There is an array of lush foliage and plums may be ripe if you arrive during June and July. The clouds can roll in quickly, causing it to be pleasant and warm one minute and cool the next. The cave shelter, however, is a bit of a disappointment. It is a shallow cavern and reaching it meant a descent down a steep incline of loose gravel that was too difficult for my young ones. The eucalyptus was especially fragrant as the fallen leaves crunched underneath our tennis shoes. An area along the trail that had been freshly rutted by wild boars demonstrated the incredible power of these animals. On one trip I heard a rustling in the bushes nearby followed by grunting sounds. While you definitely want to avoid the wild boars, they are accustomed to being hunted and will also choose to avoid you. Apparently my family was downwind of them and since they have poor eyesight we passed by quietly without them noticing us and without us seeing them.

Pu'u Ola'i cinder cone   This red-earth hillock juts out to the sea just beyond the cover fronting Wailea's Maui Prince Hotel. It is one of Haleakala's craters (under which is a large cave), and is said to be the sacred dwelling place of Mano, the ancestral shark deity. To reach the top of the cinder cone, turn right on the first dirt path after the hotel, then pass giant cacti and dry brush to reach the hiking trail. The short 15-minute hike uphill offers a rewarding sight of the coast—a black-sand beach just below the hill, and broad white beaches and black lava contrasting with the lush greens of the Makena Golf Course.

Hiking Groups
Big Kahuna Adventures Maui   In addition to surfing and kayaking, they also do rainforest hikes. *808-875-6395; e-mail bka@lava.net; www.bigkahunaadventures.com.*

Among the most incredible adventures to be experienced on Maui is one or more of the hikes your personal guide **Ken Schmitt** and his staff have available. (Ken has expanded from a one-man operation to a number of experienced guides, with specialties including archaeology, anthropology, botany, marine biology and Hawaiian history.) These hikes (for 4 to 8 people only) can encompass waterfalls and pools, ridges with panoramic views, rock formations, spectacular redwood forests, the incomparable Haleakala Crater or ancient structures found in East Maui. Arriving on Maui in 1979, Ken has spent much of that time living, exploring and subsisting out-of-doors, experiencing the natural energy of this island. This soft-spoken man offers a wealth of detailed knowledge on the legends, flora, fauna and geography of Maui's many diverse areas. Ken has traversed the island nearly 400 times and established his eight day-hikes after considerable exploration. His favorites are the 4- and 8-mile crater hikes that, he says, offer unique, incredible beauty and magic unlike anywhere else in the world. The early Hawaiians considered Haleakala to be the vortex of one of the strongest natural power points on earth.

A Haleakala hike with Ken or his crew is a thrill for all the senses. Not only does he pack a great lunch and yummy snacks, the hike provides beauty for the eyes; cool, fresh air for the lungs; tantalizing scents for the nose; peace and serenity for the ears; and an opportunity to touch and get in touch with Maui's natural beauty. The four-mile Crater Sampler tour is a hike partway down both the switchback trail at 8,000 feet and the summit trail at 10,000 feet. They don't reach the crater floor, but you will get an opportunity to experience the volcano's power and its silence, plus those magnificent vistas from the vantage point up high. This is an excellent hike because it provides a true feeling of the crater without being overly strenuous. (Keep in mind the elevation adds tremendously to the level of exertion you will feel.) This moderate hike takes about seven hours. Cost is $106 for adults, children are approximately 20 percent less. The more adventurous and strenuous 11-hour, eight-mile hike will take you to the crater floor and is $135.

Hikes are tailored to the desires and capabilities of the individual or group (5 to 12 hours, $75 to $135, children less). Hikers are supplied with waterproof daypacks, picnic lunch, specially designed Japanese fishing shoes, wild fruit and, of course, the incredible knowledge of Ken. Tours include transportation to the trails from the meeting spots in air-conditioned tour vans. Ken and his staff can be reached at Hike Maui, P.O. Box 330969, Kahului, HI 96733; 808-879-5200, fax 808-893-2515; www.hikemaui.com; e-mail: hike maui@hikemaui.com.

Haleakala National Park Haleakala National Park offers guided hikes and tours. The hikes are free of charge, but admission to the park is $10. *808-572-4400; weather and viewing information 808-871-5054.*

A reminder: Hiking off established trails without a knowledgeable guide is definitely not advised.

Hawai'i Nature Center A super option with fairly light exertion is a guided rainforest walk through the **Iao Valley**. Follow ancient footpaths, explore rock terraces and settlement sites, see forest birds, groves of *kukui*, guava and coffee trees. Vegetation types range from dense rainforests to open shrub and grasslands to introduced pine tree plantations. The area is remote and very rugged with many steep gulches. The area is named after a stream that runs through the property. Along with a waiver and release form, they will provide you with an information sheet on hiking dates and work party dates, as well as background on the native and introduced birds of the area, and a brochure on the many island areas throughout the Hawaiian chain that are under their protection. Lead by naturalists, this walk is appropriate for adults and children over eight years of age. Cost is $24.95 adults, $22.95 children; includes admission into the Hawai'i Nature Center (see "Museums/Gardens" later in this chapter). Reservations suggested, as are closed-toe shoes. See "Traveling with Children: Excursions and Adventures" in Chapter 1 for information on their hiking adventures for families. Open 10 a.m. to 4 p.m. Admission $6 adults, $4 children. *875 Iao Valley Road. 808-244-6500; e-mail: hinature@maui.net.*

Maui Cave Adventures Interested in hiking in a cave? See "Spelunking" later in this chapter. *P.O. Box 40, Hana, HI 96713. 808-248-7308; e-mail: info@mauicave.com; www.mauicave.com.*

Maui Eco-Adventures Maui Eco-Adventures tell us they are an "ecologically minded company dedicated to the education, exercise and entertainment of our visitors." They feature hiking excursions to waterfalls and ancient Hawaiian villages. The Maunalei Arboretum tour is a 4-hour trip to the arboretum established more than 70 years ago by D.T. Fleming. Cost is $80 for 4 to 12 guests. Their Kahakuloa Cultural Tour travels to Nakalele Point, the northernmost point of Maui, to see ancient lava formations and tour where the *ahupua'a* system of farming is still in practice. $100 per person. The Hike/Kayak trip is a six-hour adventure through tropical rainforests with time for ocean kayaking in West Maui. $160 per person for 4 to 12 guests. The Rainforest Waterfall Hike is a six-hour tour that includes a continental breakfast and a deli-style lunch. $115 for 4 to 12 guests. Haleakala Crater Cloud Forest Hike is over private property on the slopes of Haleakala. $125 per person. Add on a helicopter trip to any of these tours. Located just 15 minutes from Kapalua. *1087 Limahana Place # 2, Lahaina. 877-661-7720; 808-661-7720; e-mail: ashlee@ecomaui.com; www.ecomaui.com.*

Nature Conservancy of Hawaii   The Nature Conservancy of Hawaii is an international nonprofit organization dedicated to protecting Hawai'i's native forests and wildlife. Nature Conservancy preserves on Maui include Maui Lava Tubes, Kapunakea and Waikamoi, and, on the island of Lana'i, Kanepu'u. The Waikamoi Preserve is 5,230 acres and takes its name from a stream that runs through it; elevation ranges from 4,400 to 8,000 feet with annual rainfall between 50 and 200 inches and temperatures ranging from 35-70 degrees. This is a sanctuary for hundreds of native Hawaiian species, many of them endangered or rare. You might catch sight of the rare 'akohehekohe, or Maui parrotbill, which exists nowhere else on earth. Much of the original forest on Maui has been lost or damaged but what remains is a vital watershed. Haleakala Ranch Company owned the lands since 1888 and conveyed it to the Conservancy for management in 1983. The ranch and the Conservancy work together to preserve the area. To reach Waikamoi Preserve travel to Haleakala National Park via Highways 377 and 378. Public hikes usually begin outside the Hosmer Grove campground. Access to the preserve is limited. The National Park Service conducts hikes at Waikamoi Preserve Monday, Thursday and Friday mornings (call for details and schedule; 808-572-9306). Hikes are also available for Conservancy members on the second Sunday of each month with reservations via the preserve manager (808-572-7849). Access to Waikamoi Preserve is by permit only and guests can enjoy the preserve by joining a guided hike or a volunteer project. Permits for other access must be made through the preserve manager. *Honolulu office: 922 Nuuanu Avenue, Honolulu; 808-537-4508.*

Sierra Club Maui Group of the Hawaii Chapter   The Sierra Club invites the public to join their guided hikes. This is a wonderful and affordable way to enjoy Maui with a knowledgeable group of people. There are several weekend outings every month. They offer a variety of hikes: introductory, youth and educational. Donations are accepted. *808-573-4147; www.hi.sierraclub.org.*

HORSEBACK RIDING

Historically, the first six horses arrived on the islands in 1803 from Baja California. These wild mustangs were named *lio* by the Hawaiians, which means "open eyes wide in terror." They roamed and multiplied along the volcanic slopes of Maui and the Big Island until they numbered 11,000. They adjusted quickly to the rough terrain and had a reputation for terrific stamina. Today these ponies, also known as Kanaka ponies or Mauna Loa ponies, are all but extinct, with fewer than a dozen purebreds still in existence.

Lush waterfalls, pineapple fields stretching up the mountain's flanks, cane fields, *kukui* nut forests, and Haleakala's huge crater are all scenic environs that can be enjoyed on horseback. Beginner, intermediate or experienced rides can last from 1 to 2 hours up to three days. Most stables have age and weight restrictions.

Adventures on Horseback A 6-hour "Waterfall Adventure Ride" outside Haiku includes lunch and gear. Enjoy the cliffs of North Maui, the slopes of Haleakala, the old Hana Highway, rainforest streams and secluded waterfalls. Breakfast, picnic lunch and swimming. Maximum 6 riders; $185. Children 16 years of age or older are welcome provided they have prior riding experience. (Same folks that do the Horse Whisperer, below.) *Reservations 808-242-7445; ranch 808-572-6211; fax 808-572-4996.*

The **Maui Horse Whisperer** is Franklin Levinson, who told us that most visitors to his ranch have some fear of horses. Whether you own a horse or just want to understand these majestic animals, consider a day in Huelo. Franklin has for many years operated Adventures on Horseback. Now he has expanded into a new arena and has added a Ranch Hale. For the Maui Horse Whisperer Experience your full day begins with a discussion, followed by hands-on experience. The day ends with an optional trail ride. A friend and I had a private mini-lesson and discovered something magical. Not only did we learn to be comfortable dealing with a 1200-pound black beauty named Zip, we gained a sense of confidence, strength, well being and respect for building a relationship. Franklin promised us more than just a horsemanship class and we were pleasantly rewarded. If you think you've done and seen everything on Maui, this is something new and wonderful to try. 808-572-6211; www.wayofthehorse.org.

> **RIDING LESSONS**
>
> Hobby Horse provides riding lessons in Olinda. They specialize in kids, but adults are welcome. Half-hour lessons $25, 1 hour $40. Horse camps are held twice a year (March and August) for 4 days from 9 a.m. to 4 p.m.; $250. They also have pony parties. 808-572-8725.

Hotel Hana-Maui Guided trail rides around the 3,000-acre working cattle ranch on open range, shoreline, rainforest and mountains. Maximum 5 riders. One-hour ride $50. Monday through Saturday: 9:30 a.m. and 1:30 p.m. for the coastline; 10:30 a.m. for the mountain ride. *808-248-8211.*

Ironwood Ranch Located at the West Maui foothills. Follow Honoapi'ilani Highway 11 miles north of Lahaina, entrance near exit for Napili where a van picks you up. Trips are available for beginning, intermediate or advanced riders. Western-style rides tour lush tropical valleys through the Honolua Pineapple Plantation. $55 for one hour,

$80 for 1.5 hours, $110 for two hours. Advanced ride $150. They also offer weddings on horseback and/or rental of their oceanview gazebo through Royal Hawaiian Carriages. *808-669-4991; fax 808-669-4702; www.ironwoodranch.com.*

Makena Stables   Operating since 1983, Patrick and Helaine Borge match each person to their horse by ability and offer help and lessons as needed. Their horses were personally raised and trained. All of their rides are on Ulupalakua Ranch, a 20,000-acre open-range ranch that overlooks the Ahihi-Kinau Reserve, La Perouse Bay and the lava flows. A two-hour introductory ride, at $130 per person, goes out in the morning. This ride climbs to Kalua O Lapa, the vent that was the last eruption of Haleakala. It offers panoramic views of the south slopes of Haleakala, La Perouse Bay and the islands of Kahoʻolawe, Molokini, Lanaʻi and Molokaʻi. Three-hour rides are designed for the intermediate to experienced rider; $145. These trips continue up the slopes of Ulupalakua Ranch to the cinder hills overlooking La Perouse Bay. The variety and terrain of the trails are more challenging. Sunset and morning rides include a break for beverages and snacks. Their La Perouse Bay Lunch Ride leaves in the morning and tours the south slope of Haleakala through Ulupalakua Ranch. A leisurely picnic lunch at La Perouse Bay is offered for advanced riders. The sunset ride is by special request: Friday and Saturday for parties of 4 or more; 2 hours $150, 3 hours $185. La Perouse or all-day rides also by special request, $195. All rides are guided and done Western style. They are all physically strenuous and it is recommended that all riders be in good physical condition. Weight limit is 205 pounds. Maximum of six riders. Children 13 and over are welcome when accompanied by an adult. Reservations required for all rides. *8299 South Makena Road, located at La Perouse Bay. 808-879-0244; www.makenastables.com.*

Mendez Ranch   Journey onto an actual working cattle ranch in the heart of West Maui. After a Western-style open-pit barbecue lunch, take off with Sunshine Helicopters for a full tour of West Maui. $130 for the Paniolo Horseback Adventure, which includes lunch but no helicopter tour ($85 without lunch). With helicopter tour $250. Weight limit 250 pounds, minimum age 7 years, Western saddle. *808-871-5222.* Call Sunshine Helicopters to book the helicopter/horseback experience. *808-871-0722.*

ʻOheʻo Stables   Travel around the backslope of Haleakala in the Kipahulu District. Two rides daily at 10:30 or 11 a.m.: $129 including gourmet snacks and beverage. *Stables located 25 minutes past Hana on County Road 31. 808-667-2222.*

Piiholo Ranch   True *paniolo*-style hospitality from Maui's Baldwin family. The ranch is named for the cinder cone hill that is a predominant feature in upcountry Maui. Henry Perrine Baldwin and some Honolulu businessmen began Haleakala Ranch back in 1888. Five generations of the Baldwin family have continued ranching operations and Peter Baldwin owns and operates Piiholo Ranch. I haven't done this trip but it sounds like it is far more than a horseback trail ride. The history of the *paniolo* and stories and legends along with cultural information make this a tantalizing trip for those of us who love Hawaiian legend, lore and history. *For more information call Moani Pao 808-357-5544; e-mail: info@piiholo.com; www.piiholo.com.*

Pony Express Tours Trips across Haleakala Ranch and into Haleakala Crater. Haleakala Ranch treks: one-hour introductory ride $55; two-hour intermediate $85; 3-hour picnic ride $105. Trips available Monday through Saturday. Haleakala Crater trips include lunch: 5-hour, 7.5-mile junction ride $155; full-day, 7.5-hour, 12-mile cabin rides $190. *808-667-2200; www.ponyexpresstours.com.*

Thompson Riding Stables Located at 3,700 feet, the Thompson Ranch was established in 1902. They offer 1.5- and 2-hour trail rides ($60 to $70) with snack and beverage. Sunset rides available by special request. *Thompson Road in Kula. 808-878-1910 or 808-244-7412; www.thompsonranchridingstables.com.*

Royal Hawaiian Carriages If you prefer a little something between you and the horse, Royal Hawaiian Carriages offers romantic excursions and sunset tours as well as wedding transportation by horse-drawn carriage. The carriage (and driver) rent for $300 per hour for a tour of Kapalua. (Additional time at $175 per hour). Ka'anapali and Wailea/Makena tours are available by special request at substantially higher rates. The narrated tour goes from the Bay Club restaurant to D. T. Fleming Beach Park, from the ocean to the top of Pineapple Hill, and through historic Cook Pine Drive. Pickup at The Ritz-Carlton or in the Kapalua Resort. Hay rides are offered seasonally for large groups, parties, Christmas caroling and other functions. No alcoholic beverages allowed. 24-hour advance booking suggested. *808-669-1100; fax 808-669-4702.*

HUNTING/SPORTING CLAYS

Hunting Adventures of Maui, Inc. Owner/guide Bob Caires offers year-round hunting options. Game includes Spanish goat (*kao*) and wild boar (*pua'a*). Hunting on 100,000 acres of privately owned ranches with all equipment provided. Rates: Goat $500 one person, $350 second and third person each. Boar $500 one person, $250 second and third person each. Non-hunters $100. Three-person maximum. Includes sunrise-sunset hunt, food, beverages, four-wheel-drive transportation, clothing, boots, packs, meat storage and packing for home shipment and Kahului airport pickup. Rifle rentals and taxidermy available. Sightseeing safaris also available. A non-resident hunting license is required ($100) and you must provide your hunter safety card to purchase the license. Trips scheduled weekdays only. *1745 Kapakalua Road, Haiku, HI 96708. 808-572-8214.*

Papaka Sporting Clays The 12.5-acre range is inside a small volcanic crater on the slopes of Haleakala, at Ulupalakua at a private ranch operated by Dave Barnes. Shotguns available at Papaka are 12-gauge, 20- and 28-gauge and 410s. They are open daily 8:30 a.m. to dusk. Since they are at a 1,000-foot elevation there is no scuba diving at least 12 hours before coming up to the ranch. There are no live birds or rabbits, just clay targets used to mimic the flights of different game birds. Their program is designed for any ability ages 12 and up. Their "Birdbrain" computerized 5-stand course has five levels of difficulty and consists of 25 randomly selected targets to challenge the best marksman. Customers can be met at the Maui Prince Hotel in Makena for a shorter trip up the private road to upcountry. Two trips per day, one at 8:30 a.m. and the other at 1 p.m. Pickups available from the west side for an extra fee. Cost is $125 for 100 targets, $88 for 75 targets and $69 for 50 targets. *808-879-5649.*

JET SKIING

Thrillcraft activities, which include parasailing and jetskiing, are banned during whale season. The "open season" for jet-skiing recreation is May 16 to December 14. **Pacific Jet Sports** is at the south end of Ka'anapali Beach at Hanaka'o'o Beach Park. Their Waverunners are for 1 to 3 people. Rental prices are per person, per jet ski, with an additional charge of $15 per person for more than one. (Three people max.) Half hour $55, 1 hour $90. Hawaiian law requires a person be 18 years old to operate a machine alone. Younger persons can ride as a passenger on the Waverunner with someone who is at least 18 years of age. All renters are fitted with a life vest. Daily 9 a.m. to 4 p.m. (weather permitting). *808-667-2066.*

KAYAKING

Big Kahuna Adventures Maui Kayak rentals (from $30) and tours. Kayak/snorkel from Makena or La Perouse $59.95 for 2.5 to 3 hours; lunch tour $84.95 for 4 hours. The Lanai Kayak tour includes a catamaran excursion to Lana'i, guided kayaking on the coastline, snorkel gear, continental breakfast, deli lunch and no-host bar for $120; children 12 and under $60. Monday, Wednesday and Saturday, 8 a.m. to 1:30 p.m. Check in at 7:30 a.m. at Lahaina Harbor for the 5.5-hour trip. You don't have to kayak, so the whole family can go along and kids or others who choose to can stay aboard the boat. They also have rainforest hikes, a surfing school, and surf and boogieboard rentals. *808-875-6395; e-mail: bka@lava.net; www.bigkahunaadventures.com.*

Hawaiian Ultimate Adventures Eco-kayak and snorkel treks $79 for 3 hours; whale watching in season $49 for 2 hours. Design your own trek. Snacks or lunch and beverage included. They also offer hiking and surfing tours. *877-247-3198; 808-669-3720.*

Kelii's Kayak Tours Environmentally friendly tours with experienced guides. Small groups. Makena or Olowalu $59/2.5 hours; $85/4.5 hours. Honolua or La Perouse Bay $69/3 hours; $99/5 hours. Departures at 7:30 and 11 a.m. Lunch and/or refreshments included. Lahaina sunset tour at 4 p.m. $59/2.5 hours. *888-874-7652; 808-874-7652; e-mail: info@keliiskayak.com; www.keliiskayak.com.*

Lahaina Center The Lahaina Center has a shop that rents clear kayaks (how cool is that?); $69 for a single. If you inquire with some of the operators listed below, I'm sure they have or will be adding them to their rental line. *808-661-1970.*

Makena Kayak Tours Your local guide is Robert "Dino" Ventura, who operates "family-style" tours limited to small groups. He offers 2.5-hour ($55) or 4-hour ($85) tours that depart from Makena Landing, La Perouse Bay or ʻAhihi-Kinaʻu Natural Marine Reserve. He shares his knowledge of the island and its history. *808-879-8426.*

Maui Eco-Adventures Hiking/kayaking combination tours twice daily at 8 a.m. and 2 p.m. Coastal kayaking through the caves of West Maui with exclusive access to the Maunalei Arboretum and a private tropical rainforest. $160 includes continental breakfast, lunch and snacks. *808-661-7720; www.ecomaui.com.*

Maui Eco-Tours Swim with dolphins and/or turtles with kayak/snorkel or hiking combo adventures to the Ahihi-Kinau Natural Marine Reserve or La Perouse Bay. $59 for 2 to 2.5 hours, $79 for 4 to 5 hours, $99 for 6 to 7 hours. Sunset tour $59 for 2.5 hours. Free trip if no dolphins are seen. Kayak rentals from $25 a day. *808-891-2223; www.mauiecotours.com.*

Maui Kayaks Kayak/snorkel with state-of-the art equipment. Small groups with personalized service and attention to detail. Snacks and refreshments included on all tours. Kaʻanapali or Olowalu $59/2.5 hours; Turtle Town & Makena $69/3 hours; Honolua Bay (April through October) $79/3 hours; and La Perouse Marine Reserve $99/5 hours with lunch included. Unique four-hour adventures at Hana ($109) and "extreme" Molokini ($129). *866-771-MAUI; 808-874-4000; www.mauikayaks.com.*

Private Kayak Tours Enjoy their 2.5-hour La Perouse Dolphin Search. Departing La Perouse Bay at 7 a.m. $59 per person. ʻAhihi-Kinaʻu Reserve Kayak/Snorkel Adventure is a 4.5-hour trip starting at La Perouse and paddling along the ʻAhihi-Kinaʻu reserve with three stops and snorkeling; $79 per person. Makena Landing Turtle/Whale Watch is recommended for first-time kayakers; the 2.5-hour trip is perfect for families with kids. Paddling along the Makena coast you're sure to spot turtles. $59 per person. Sunset Whale Paddle departs before sunset from either Makena Landing or Olowalu for a 1.5-hour sunset excursion; $59 per person. For the extreme kayaker try the Molokini Express, approximately 3.6 miles of ocean magic; $110 per person. Also available are private tours at $150 per person or $200 for a couple, kayak rentals with delivery and pickup included. 808-875-7098; www.privatekayaktours.com.

Ron Bass This independent tour guide specializes in kayaking and snorkeling for the disabled. His special equipment includes three-person kayaks, view boards and beach-access wheelchairs. Ron also operates "Wilderness Wish," a non-profit organization that assists disabled folks in experiencing new adventures by discovering and exploring out-of-the-way places. P.O. Box 106, Pu'unene, HI 96784. 808-572-6299; fax 808-572-6151; www.maui.net/~kayaking.

South Pacific Kayaks & Outfitters They offer introductory paddle and snorkel excursions in south and west Maui. Short paddling distances combined with offshore snorkeling: 2.5 to 3 hrs from $59. Marine Reserve Explorer trip searches for turtles, dolphins and whales as it travels along the southern coast, with time for snorkeling and a deli lunch, $89 for 6 hours. Kayak dives for certified divers $125. Also available are single and double kayaks as well as car racks, life vests, snorkel gear and more. *Rainbow Mall, 2439 South Kihei Road. 800-776-2326; 808-875-4848.*

Tradewind Kayaks "Wet Your Okole" is a 2.5-hour introductory shoreline kayak and snorkel trip $55. The "Marine Reserve Experience" is a trip to La Perouse along the Kinao lava flow. This 4.5-hour excursion runs $75. Both tours depart at 7 a.m. *808-879-2247.*

KITEBOARDING

This sport might appeal mostly to windsurfers who are looking for another challenge. Although the sport has been around for about 20 years in Europe and parts of the U.S., it didn't reach Maui until 1999 with the opening of the **Kiteboarding School of Maui**. The basic premise is that you take a board, not unlike a snowboard, and add a kite and wind. Check it out at "Kite Beach" at the lower end of Kahana Beach Park and then call for lessons. There are three beginning-level class that run $90 for one hour; the three-hour package is $240. Intermediate levels are a 2-hour minimum at $75 an hour and advanced class are $90 an hour with two-hour minimum. *808-873-0015; e-mail: martin@kasmaui.com; www.ksmaui.com.*

LAND TOURS

Land excursions on Maui are centered upon two major attractions, Hana/'Ohe'o Valley and Haleakala Crater. Lesser attractions are trips to the Iao Valley or around West Maui. You can do all of this in your rental car. However, with a tour and tour guide you can sit back and enjoy the scenery while a professional guide discourses on the history, flora, fauna and geography of the area. The single most important item on any tour is a good guide/driver and, unfortunately, the luck of the draw prevails here. Another (somewhat expensive) option is a personalized custom tour. A local resident will join you, in your car, for a tour of whatever or wherever you choose. You can choose to do the driving or sign on a guide with your rental car company to do the driving. This may allow you the opportunity to linger at those places you enjoy the most, without following the pace of a group. Your guide may also be able to take you to locations the tour vans don't include.

Driving to Hana and back requires a full day and can be very grueling, so this is one trip I recommend you consider taking a tour. A Haleakala Crater tour spans 5 to 6 hours and can be enjoyed at sunrise (2 a.m. departure), midday or sunset. The West Maui and Iao Valley trips are half-day ventures. Only vans travel the road to Hana, although large buses as well as vans are available for other trips. Prices are competitive and those listed here are correct at the time of publication. Some trips include the cost of meals, others do not. Also available are one-day tours to the outer islands. The day begins with an early-morning departure to the Big Island, O'ahu or Kaua'i. Some excursions provide a guided ground tour; others offer a rental car to explore the island on your own.

Carey Hawaii/Town & Country Limousine   Enjoy a private Hana "Navigator Tour." Daily tours begin with hotel pickup, a continental breakfast and lunch at the Hotel Hana-Maui, returning at around 5 p.m. Price is $219 per person for 2 people/$189 for 3/$149 for 4. Also airport limousine service. 808-572-3400, 808-661-9788.

Ekahi Tours   Van tours of Hana include hotel pickup, continental breakfast, deli-style box lunch, national park fees. $88.50 adult, $62.50 child (0-11 years). Wheelchair guests must give advance notice and have assistance with collapsible wheelchair. Sunrise Haleakala $67.50 adult, $52.50 child (0-11) includes national park fees, full breakfast at Pukalani Country Club. Some restrictions to guests with heart or breathing problems. Hidden Valley Tour to Kahakuloa $67.50 adults, $52.50 children, includes hotel pickup, light snacks and refreshments; since this is a hiking tour, no wheelchair guests. The Kahakuloa Valley tour is an opportunity to enjoy a cultural experience at a Hawaiian *kuleana* (parcel of land) that is part of an *ahupua'a* (land division extending from the uplands to the oceans) located along the northwest coast of Maui. According to background information provided to us from Ekahi Tours, "The Kahakuloa Valley is inhabited by some of the same families of past generations of Hawaiians who were the original settlers 1,500 years ago and is the only village in existence that still has a working Konohiki." A Konohiki is the caretaker of the *ahupua'a* and oversees the land and fishing rights. Guides provide guests with background on the plants, taro farming and Hawaiian lifestyle. Other areas may be arranged by charter at $75.50 per hour. 532 Keolani Place, Kahului, HI 96732. 888-292-2422; 808-877-9775; *fax* 808-877-9776; *e-mail: fun@ekahi.com; www.ekahi.com.*

Guides of Maui Discover Maui in your car with an island resident as your guide. Explore the destinations of your choice. $235 per car for up to four people, 8 hours (plus your own gas in your own car). *800-231-8022; 808-877-4060; e-mail: info@guidesofmaui.com; www.guidesofmaui.com.*

Polynesian Adventure Haleakala Crater & Iao Valley $58 adult/$35 child; Haleakala Sunrise $56 adult/$35 child; Hana $75 adult/$45 child. They also offer one-day trips to O'ahu to see the *Arizona* or the Polynesian Cultural Center ($208). *800-622-3011; 808-877-4242; www.polyad.com.*

Robert's Hawaii Tours Offers land tours in their big air-conditioned buses or vans. They depart to all scenic areas from Kahului, Kihei, Wailea and the West Maui hotels. Tours include Iao Valley/Lahaina ($40 adults/$28 child); Haleakala/Iao Valley/Lahaina ($55 adults/$38.50 child); Heavenly Hana ($79 adult/$45 child); Haleakala Crater ($40 adult/$28 child). *From Maui 800-831-5541; 808-871-6226 (dispatch); www.robertshawaii.com.*

Temptation Tours With a maximum of 8 passengers, this is a very comfortable way to explore Maui—and what a treat to get to travel the Hana Highway and not drive it. If you'd really like to pamper yourself, then enjoy the luxury of a tour by these folks. The Hana picnic ($134/9 to 10 hours) is a round trip in their limo van that includes a continental breakfast and a beachside picnic lunch. Working in conjunction with a local helicopter company, they provide a unique option to Hana with the Hana Sky-Trek ($239), available mornings or afternoons with guests checking in at the Kahului Airport. You travel either to or from Hana by helicopter and do the opposite direction on a 3.5-hour limo van tour. The Summit Safari ($184/9 to 10 hours)

> **Hapa Papa's** supply an island guide on van and private tours who can share with you their *mana'o* (knowledge) and aloha (love) for the *aina* (land) they call home. 808-242-8500; e-mail: hapa@lava.net.

begins with a continental breakfast in Paia and then an ascent up Haleakala in their luxury limo van to the eucalyptus forests and pastureland of the Thompson Ranch. An hour and a half to enjoy the view on horseback is followed by an elegant picnic lunch at the Silver Cloud Ranch. Or choose the Haleakala Rain Forest excursion ($149/9 to 10 hours) that includes a continental breakfast in Paia and then a scenic drive to the top of Haleakala volcano. You'll descend through Hosmer's Grove, a conifer forest and then stop at a protea farm. Have lunch Upcountry before heading east to Haiku to visit rainforests and

SUGAR CANE TRAIN

The Lahaina Ka'anapali and Pacific Railroad is affectionately referred to as the **Sugar Cane Train**. In Lahaina in 1862, the harvesting of sugar cane was one of the island's biggest industries. More than 45,000 tons were produced from 5,000 acres. The Lahaina Ka'anapali & Pacific Railroad began in 1882, replacing the slower method (mules and steers) of hauling sugar cane between the harvest area and the Pioneer Sugar Mill. This allowed a greater area of cane to be planted as well. By the 1900s the railroad was also transporting an ever-increasing number of workers to their jobs. In 1970, the Sugar Cane Train was once again restored, but financial difficulties silenced the train whistle once more. In 1973, Mr. Willes B. Kyele purchased the railroad and brought life back to its engines. Currently two trains operate on a three-foot narrow-gauge railroad with eight departures daily between 10:15 a.m. and 4 p.m. The trains are pulled by two steam locomotives, "Anaka" and "Myrtle." The locomotives were built in 1943 and were restored to resemble those that were used in Hawai'i at the beginning of the 20th century. The singing conductor will guide you through history as you wind through the cane fields of Lahaina. Their main depot is located just outside of Lahaina (turn at the Pizza Hut sign). The Ka'anapali Station is located across the highway from the resort area. The Pu'ukoli'i boarding platform and parking lot are located on the Kapalua side of Ka'anapali. Round-trip $15.95; children 3 to 12 $9.95. Reservations needed for groups of 12 or more. There is also an evening activity. Board the Paniolo Express Thursdays at 5 p.m. for a train ride to Lahaina just in time for sunset and then back to the Ka'anapali Station in time for the dinner bell. The kids will love the hearty dinner of chicken, ribs, hot dogs, hamburgers and a salad bar, topped off with smoothies to drink and a little cowboy-hula entertainment. Reservations required for the Paniolo Express $65 adult, $39 children 3-12. 808-661-0080, 808-667-6851; 800-499-2307; www.sugarcanetrain.com.

waterfalls. A drive out to Ke'anae will give you a piece of what the Hana Highway is like. The Ke'anae Peninsula is still a traditional Hawaiian farming community with a rugged shoreline and some spectacular scenery. They also offer a Haleakala Sunrise Tour ($139/7 to 8 hours) that begins with a 3 to 4 a.m. pickup. A breakfast at Kula Lodge follows your sunrise experience at the Haleakala visitor center.

Interested in spelunking? Here's what you can expect when you combine a Temptation Tours luxury motorcoach trip from with one of Maui's most interesting activities. After an early-morning pickup, a van transports up to eight guests to Paia Plantation for a continental breakfast. Then everyone assembles into their respective vans and you are off. The comfy vans have nice views and our driver was both funny and informative and easy to hear with his microphone headset. There are many opportunities to take scenic photos. One of the stops includes a flower farm where a tour is given; a small bouquet of flowers is a pleasant tour souvenir. Once in the lava cave, you are outfitted with a hardhat, gloves and flashlight. You'll spend a couple of hours at Ka'eleku Caverns, with a full 1.25 to 1.5 hours underground. The leisurely walk through the winding trails of the cave is safe and easy. Trails consist mostly of cinder with flat lava rocks constructing stairs over any obstructions. This Cave Quest tour is $169/9 to 10 hours. There are several small optional crawling spaces that the more adventurous can try out. The lava caves are far more interesting than one might expect, with dozens of various lava formations never seen on the surface. Light and sound are both quickly absorbed by the cave and somewhere along the way your knowledgeable guide usually stops for "Lights Out!" To experience a complete absence of light is really amazing. At one point on the walk you'll pass under a volcanic vent, a chimney hole 30 feet to the surface, from which the lava spewed high in the air 25,000 years ago. The passages of the cave are large, open and spacious with millions of stalactites adorning the ceiling and beautiful lava flowstone running down the walls appearing as melted chocolate. You'll definitely want to bring your camera, although the low light doesn't afford great photo opportunities. After the hike the group all had a hearty appetite. We loaded up again in the luxury van and drove to Hana (we stopped at Wai'anapanapa Beach) for a delicious picnic lunch. There was also time to explore either this beach or the Hana Bay, another picnic location option, before driving through Hana town to see all the sights. Unfortunately, heavy rains made the surf high and the rushing waterfalls caused the freshwater pools to swell dangerously. The afternoon swim, which is usually included in this Temptation Tours outing, had to be excluded from this day of adventures. All too soon we returned to the van for the trip back to Paia. Check out the Hana Cave or other luxury trips available from Temptation Tours. *800-817-1234; 808-877-8888; fax 808-876-0155; e-mail: tmptour@aloha.net; www.temptationtours.com.*

Valley Isle Excursions Tour Hana in a 12-passenger motorcoach van. A Hana picnic trip includes continental breakfast and a picnic lunch with barbecue chicken, macaroni and green salads with dinner rolls. These trips go around the island. Special surround sound makes it accessible for the hearing impaired. $109 adults; $99 seniors; $79 children. *877-871-5224; 808-661-8687; www.tourmaui.com.*

MUSEUMS/GARDENS

Alexander and Baldwin Sugar Museum Located on Highway 35 between Kahului and Kihei, the museum is housed in a 1902 plantation home that was once occupied by the sugar mill's superintendent. Memorabilia includes the strongbox of Samuel Thomas Alexander and an actual working scale model of a sugar mill. The displays are well done and very informative. Open Monday through Saturday 9:30 a.m. to 4:30 p.m. Admission $5 adult, $2 children. *3957 Hansen Road, Puʻunene. 808-871-8058.*

Bailey House Museum To reach the circa 1834 Bailey House Museum, follow the signs to Iao Valley and you will see the historical landmark sign on the left side of the road. Open Monday through Friday. Admission $5 adults, $4 seniors and $1 children. *808-244-3326.*

Baldwin Home This was the home of Dwight Baldwin from the 1830s to the mid-1800s. The residence of this medical missionary has been restored and contains many original pieces of furniture. Tours available. Open 10 a.m. to 4 p.m. daily with $3 admission per person or $5 per family. *695 Front Street, Lahaina. 808-661-3262.*

Brig Carthaginian Built in 1920, this steel-hulled freighter is restored to the likeness of a whaler. It is the only authentically restored brig in the world and you can enjoy her onboard whale displays. This is a reincarnation of the first Brig, built in Sweden, originally used as a navy trainer. It made the big screen when it was used in the filming of the movie, *Hawaii*. Then en route to dry-dock in the 1970s, it met with disaster on the reef. As we go to press the current vessel can be viewed from the dock but is no longer open to the public. Its future or a possible replacement is yet unknown. *Lahaina. 808-661-3262.*

Enchanting Floral Gardens A self-guided botanical tour. Open 9 a.m. to 5 p.m. daily. Admission $5 adults, $1 children. *Highway 37, Kula. 808-878-2531.*

Hale Kohola Hale Kohola (House of the Whale) is located on the upper level of the Whale Center of the Pacific. They feature a wonderful exhibition of the great whales with special emphasis on the humpback whale. There are also short films on whales and whaling, and tours can be arranged. Open 9:30 a.m. to 10 p.m. daily. Free admission, but donations appreciated. *Whalers Village, Ka'anapali. 808-661-5992.*

Hale Paahao Lahaina's prison from the 19th-century whaling days, Hale Paahao was built from coral taken from the old waterfront fort. Open weekdays 10 a.m. to 4 p.m. Free admission. *Prison Street, Lahaina.*

Hale Pa'i This former printing house is located at Lahainaluna, the oldest school west of the Rockies. An exact replica of an original Ramage Press is on display along with facsimiles of old books, manuscripts and copies of Hawaiian newspapers. The campus is located *makai* of Lahaina. Open 10 a.m. to 4 p.m. Monday through Friday. Free admission. To reach the museum travel up Lahainaluna Road toward the mountain (and the high school). It's about two miles up; watch out for signs that will direct you to Hale Pa'i. *Located on the campus of Lahainaluna school, Lahaina. 808-667-7040.*

Hale Piula Down near what is now 505 Front Street was a two-story stone building used as a palace for Kamehameha III called Hale Piula, or "iron-roofed house." The home was little used and never even completed. After a storm in 1858 caused damage, the stones were used to build the current courthouse. *Front Street, Lahaina.*

Haleakala National Park Visitor Center Haleakala's visitor center features displays about the wildlife, flora and geology of this massive dormant volcano. Located one parking lot below the summit. Open from sunrise to 3 p.m. daily. Admission is $10 per car.

Hana Cultural Center Opened in 1983, this contains a collection of relics of Hana's past in the old courthouse building and a museum. The museum houses thousands of photographs, along with hundreds of old artifacts of early Hawaiian life. Tour the Kauhale O Hana, a complex of four authentic Hawaiian *hales*, as well as the restored Hana Courthouse and jail. Open daily 10 a.m. to 4 p.m. Admission $2 for those over age 12. *Located on Uakea Road Street near Hana Bay, watch for signs. 808-248-8622.*

Hana Gardenland The private five-acre Hana Gardenland estate has walking paths winding through the palm trees and botanical gardens. Hana Gardenland is 3.5

> The Lahaina Restoration Foundation has saved many buildings and artifacts for our enjoyment today and in the future. They offer a free "Maui Historical Walking Guide," which is published three times a year. Pick one up at the local publication racks around town. In addition to the main landmarks, they discuss the many churches and cemeteries around town and there is a handy little map that makes finding the locations easy.

miles before you reach the town of Hana (driving from Kahului). Look for mile-marker 31 and turn right on Kalo Road. You will see the Garden Café sign on the corner. *808-248-8610; www.hanapalms retreat.com.*

Hui No'eau Visual Arts Center Located in the Baldwin plantation home (built in 1917), this center offers historical tours and art exhibits. Open 10 a.m. to 4 p.m. Monday through Saturday. Free admission, but donations welcome. *2841 Baldwin Avenue, Makawao. 808-572-6560; e-mail: hui@maui.net; www.maui.net/~hui.*

Kahanu Garden The National Tropical Botanical Garden operates the Kahanu Garden. The headquarters of the non-profit NTBG is on Kaua'i, where they operate three gardens with another garden in Florida. The 126-acre gardens are located at Kalahu Point, which is also the location of Hawai'i's largest *heiau*. The Pi'ilanihale Heiau is six centuries old and was constructed by the sons of Maui chief Pi'ilani in his honor. Restoration of the *heiau* is ongoing and they have two gardens: the Canoe Gardens (plants that were brought to the islands in canoes) and the Coastal Gardens (indigenous plants grown next to the shoreline). Open Monday through Friday 10 a.m. to 2 p.m. Self-guided tours $10. *The Kahanu Garden is reached by turning makai on Ulaino Road, just past mile-marker 31; it is 1.5 miles to the entrance of the garden. 808-248-8912.*

Kula Botanical Gardens This 6-acre facility with over 2,000 plants (including native Hawaiian plants like the sandalwood tree) is available to tour. Open 9 a.m. to 4 p.m. Admission $5 adults, $1 children 6 to 12 years. *Upper Kula Road. 808-878-1715.*

Kapalua Discovery Center Learn about Maui's culture, environment and history here. Begin with a display of ancient Hawaiian tools, learn more about the Pu'u Kukui Preserve as well as Kapalua's plantation history on a self-guided tour. Free admission. *In the Kapalua Shops.*

Kealia Pond National Wildlife Refuge Take a self-guided tour of the coastal wetlands and sand dunes of the Kealia Pond National Wildlife Refuge in North Kihei. You'll see turtles and whales from the elevated vantage point—with the aid of interpretive signs along the .75-mile boardwalk on the tour trail.

Lahaina Courthouse Museum The old courthouse has seen much activity over its many years standing sentry over the Lahaina Harbor. Its birth began when a storm destroyed Hale Piula and the stones were used to construct the courthouse. During the days of whaling it was a custom house. In the later part of the 19th century it was damaged by an earthquake but rebuilt and used by the county as the courthouse. The museum is located upstairs in the old courtroom. Docents explain the courthouse's history. Open 10 a.m. to 4 p.m. *Lahaina.*

Lahaina Lighthouse Built in 1840 as an aid for navigation for the whale boats, the old Lahaina Lighthouse was originally a mere 9-foot wooden tower. In 1866 its size increased to 26 feet and the light was kept burning by the use of whale oil. The present concrete version was built in 1916.

Lahaina Jodo Mission This mission is a bit farther toward Ka'anapali. The huge Buddha arrived from Kyoto, Japan, to celebrate the 100th anniversary of the Japanese arrival to the islands in 1868. Open to the public. *Ala Moana Street near Mala Wharf, Lahaina.*

Maui Botanical Gardens They no longer have a zoo, but it's still a great stop-off so bring along a picnic lunch! *150 Kanaloa Avenue, Kahului. 808-249-2798; e-mail: mnbg@maui.net.*

Maui Ocean Center In 1998 Coral World International opened Maui Ocean Center. The aquarium is the only one of its kind in Hawai'i, but it is the sixth project developed worldwide by Coral World International. Their aim is to inspire appreciation for the ocean's environment and ecology and to provide education regarding the need for reef conservation. Part of the center has been set aside as an educational and research center. This non-profit arm presents tours, films and classes for groups, schools and the public. Upon entry to the Reef Building you will view a reef pool with seawater surge that replicates the coastal surf off Maui. The walkway descends and exhibits can be viewed from different levels. There are fascinating turtle and ray pools as well as an outdoor Touch Pool. The Whale Discovery Center fea-

---

Little-known to most visitors is that back in the early 19th century, Lahaina had a series of canals that were used for crop irrigation. Lahaina was dubbed "Venice of the Pacific." For a fee you could travel the canal to reach the Government Market. Here, trade (but not always fair trade) was carried between visiting ships and the native people. The area was nicknamed "Rotten Row." Malu'ulu-o-lele will someday be fully restored as a historic site. This was one of Lahaina's earliest sites, but when the canals and the pond were filled in 1918 it became just a memory. At the south end of Lahaina is a baseball field. This used to be a large pond called Mokuhinia. Legend has it that a giant lizard lived on the island, called Moku'ula, and in the pond. The island was shared by Maui chiefs and later served as the palace for Kamehameha I, II and III. Records hold that there was a royal tomb here with an elaborate crypt. Friends of Moku'ula, a non-profit native Hawaiian organization, are working to unearth the secrets of this extraordinary site and restore it. They have an office at 505 Front Street, Lahaina.

> **The Hawai'i Nature Center** at Iao Valley has an interactive nature museum that houses a towering glass solarium and offers more than 30 hands-on exhibits and experiences focusing on Hawai'i's natural history. Rainforest explorations, dispersal arcade games, live insects and stream animal exhibits along with a dragonfly ride make this a unique, adventuresome and educational attraction. There is nothing like hands-on exploration for learning and there is plenty of that here. They also offer an "Iao Valley Rainforest Walk" geared for kids 5 and older. The walk and talk is $24.95 adults, $22.95 kids (includes admission to the center). Reservations recommended. Currently they do the trip twice daily with Monday through Friday departures at 11:30 a.m. and 1:30 p.m., Saturday and Sunday at 11 a.m. and 2 p.m. Call to confirm times. Environmental walks, weekend programs and a fun gift shop. Great stop for the whole family. Open daily 10 a.m. to 4 p.m. Admission $6 adults, $4 children. 808-244-6500; fax 808-244-6525; e-mail: hinature@maui.net

tures life-sized humpback models and displays focusing on their feeding, migrating and mating habits. A 600,000-gallon tank in the Pelagic Building is home to tiger sharks, mahimahi and tuna. An acrylic tunnel allows visitors to walk through the tank with a 240-degree view of marine life. One portion of the floor is transparent, affording a very realistic in-the-ocean experience. By the time you have toured the facility, you may have worked up an appetite. The oceanview Seascape Ma'alaea Restaurant offers California and Pacific Rim items for lunch; a kiosk features fast food and snacks. Plan on spending at least two hours to enjoy all the exhibits. Audio headset recorded tours are available in several languages. The Maui Ocean Center has also partnered up with the Kahului Airport to present a 1200-gallon aquarium that showcases Hawai'i's beautiful fish, living coral and other marine life in their natural habitat. A great way to welcome guests to the island and a place to pause and reflect on all the great times of your vacation. Open 9 a.m. to 5 p.m. everyday of the year. Hours extend to 6 p.m. in July and August. Tickets are $19 adults, $13 children 3 to 12. *Harbor Shops at Ma'alaea. 808-270-7000.*

Maui Pineapple Company This 1,000-square-foot shop is Maui Pineapple Company's retail outlet. A 40-pound box of the hybrid Hawaiian Gold extra sweet pineapple is only $25. They also box up already inspected "jet-fresh" as well as hybrid organic pineapples for take home. This enjoyable store is also a museum with a wonderful collection of plantation artifacts accumulated throughout the Pineapple Company's near-century-old history. Historical pictures decorate the walls and Neida Cahoj, the store manager, is in the process of creating a pineapple garden and picnic area. The garden will feature the fruits in their various stages of development. She has her eye on an old harvester and fire truck she found in the plantation "bone yard" and hopes to make these items part of the picnic area as well. Open 10 a.m. to 6 p.m. Monday through Saturday. *Located in Hali'imaile, about 15 minutes from Kahului. 808-573-5129.*

Maui Tropical Plantation   Maui Tropical Plantation operates a 40-minute narrated tram ride ($9.50 adults, $3.50 children) through their tropical plantation. Open daily 9 a.m. to 5 p.m. Admission to the grounds is free. For more information see Chapter 2. *808-244-7643.*

Paper Airplane Museum   This museum features the one-of-a-kind juice-can creations of the Tin Can Man; model exhibits and pictures depict the history of aviation in the Hawaiian islands. Tin can and paper airplane demonstrations, too. Open 9 a.m. to 5 p.m. Monday through Saturday, 11 a.m. to 5 p.m. Sunday. *In the Maui Mall. 808-877-8916.*

Sunrise Protea Farm   This farm has a small but diverse variety of protea growing adjacent to their market and flower stand for shipment home. Picnic tables available and no charge just for looking. Open daily 8 a.m. to 4 p.m. *416A Haleakala Crater Road, Kula. 808-876-0200.*

Wo Hing Temple Museum   Built in 1912, this temple now houses a museum that depicts the history of the Chinese immigrants and their influence on the island. This museum is affiliated with the Chee Kung Tong, a Chinese fraternal organization. Open daily 10 a.m. to 4:30 p.m. $1 admission. *Front Street, Lahaina. 808-661-5553.*

PARASAILING

The parasail "season" on Maui is May 16 to December 14 due to the restrictions during whale season. For those that aren't familiar with this aquatic experience, parasailing is a skyward adventure in which you are hooked to a parachute and attached to a tow line behind a boat. Before you know it you are floating high in the air with a bird's-eye view of Maui. The flight lasts 8 to 10 minutes, which may be either too long or too short for some. Prices $40 and up. Some allow an "observer" (friend) to go along on the boat for an extra fee.

UFO Parasail   They use a new wrinkle, a self-contained "winch" boat. You get started standing on the boat and as your parachute fills, you are reeled out 400-800 feet. When it comes time to descend, you're simply reeled back in. $42 standard, $52 deluxe, $37-$47 for early bird (before 8:30 a.m.). Observers can go for $17. *Departs Whalers*

Village. 800-FLY-4UFO; 808-661-7836; fax 808-667-0373; e-mail: ufomaui@mauigateway.com; www.ufoparasail.net.

West Maui Para-sail   Uses "Skyrider" harness flights. Dry take-off and landing. Boat departs every 30 minutes with six passengers. A choice of 400' line ($45) or 800' ($53). First flight of the day (early bird) is $9 off. Kids under 75 pounds are $40. Observer $17. The crew is helpful and patient and gives plenty of instructions. They take a roll of pictures for you that you can purchase and develop yourself. *Lahaina Harbor, Slip #15. 808-661-4060.*

POLO

Polo season on Maui is April, May and June and again in October and November. **Maui Polo Club** events every Sunday (during season) in Makawao at the polo field on Haleakala Highway #377 near the junction with Kula Highway #37. Gates open at noon, games start at 1 p.m. Tickets are $3 adults, free kids under 12. Weekly activities may include practice, a club game or events such as the Oski Rice Memorial Polo Cup or the Annual Rocking Kapalaia Ranch Cup. *808-877-5544.*

RUNNING

Maui is a scenic delight for runners. **Valley Isle Road Runners** can provide up-to-date information on island running events. *808-871-6441.*

SCUBA DIVING

Diving the waters of Maui and Lana'i is truly exciting and spellbinding for both the experienced diver as well as for those who have always desired to explore the mysteries and wonders of a whole new world below the surface. Virtually all dive operators offer boat excursions, beach dives, instruction and certification, and rental equipment. Your scuba endeavors can be arranged through many of the resorts and hotels or directly through the many dive operators on the island.

Approximately 21 percent of all Hawaiian marine life is unique such as the bandit angelfish, belted wrasse and the burnt murex. Humpback whales make Hawai'i their summer home from late November through April. And if you are fortunate, you may have a once-in-a-lifetime encounter with the largest fish on the planet, the whale shark. Spinner dolphins are also plentiful if not playful. And you will most probably see the enchanting green sea turtles. An encounter with a manta ray is always thrilling. In any case, Hawaiian waters showcase a spectacular variety of marine life.

Water temperatures average around 82 degrees during the summer and 72 degrees in the winter. A wetsuit is always recommended. It is much better to be warm and comfortable during your dive experience than be distracted by a chill. Average depth for most dive sites is 30 to 60 feet, while the backside of Molokini provides diving to a depth of 130 feet, which is the limit for recreational purposes. Visibility is generally very good at all sites and especially the backside of Molokini, where the visibility is at least 100 feet or greater.

Introductory dives provide the first-time diver a chance to savor the wonders of scuba. If the bug should bite or already has bitten and your time on the island is sufficient, you can take your first step and become open-water certified. Open-water courses are widely available and usually require four days. If you already are open-water certified and wish to improve you scuba skills and knowledge, an advanced open-water certification will require three days. Since your vacation time is always too limited, the most popular option to become open-water certified is through the referral program. Basically, you complete your open-water course work and pool work at home. You then arrange with a dive operator on Maui who participates in the referral program and you present your PADI paperwork upon arrival. And in two days you can be open-water certified and maximize your vacation time.

Please note: Prices for introductory dives run roughly around $85. However, pricing for open water, advanced open water and referrals vary significantly. If cost is of concern to you, you would be well advised to consult several dive operators and compare prices. Pricing information is generally posted on each operator's website or call directly.

Although many dive operators are listed here, this is by no means a complete list of diving services on Maui. If you so desire, you may visit the following websites for additional sources of fun and adventure: www.maui.net, www.mauigateway.com, www.padi.com.

B & B Scuba   Offers introductory dives for the beginning diver as well as shore and 12-passenger boat dives to sites off South Maui and Molokini. Extensive PADI instruction is available through Dive Master and specialty courses. Retail store is available for accessories and equipment rentals. *1280 South Kihei Road, Shop #129, Kihei. 808-875-2861; e-mail: bvarney@aol.com; www.bbscuba.com.*

Boss Frog's Dive and Surf Shop   Since they cater to snorkeling and other beach and surf activities, scuba is not their primary focus. However, Boss Frog's does offer charters and will accommodate snorkel, Snuba and scuba divers as a group. All scuba divers must be certified. The primary destination is Molokini with several other alternate sites on the schedule. Scuba gear is included in the price. *Boss Frog's has five locations throughout Maui: 156 Lahainaluna Road, Lahaina, 808-661-3333; Napili Plaza, 808-669-4949; Kahana Manor Shops, 808-669-6700; Kihei at Dolphin Plaza, 808-875-4377; Honokowai, 808-665-1200; www.bossfrog.com or www.maui.net.*

Dive & Sea Maui   For those folks looking for the intimate and relaxed dive experience, the *Sundance II* is a 26-foot boat for six passengers. Viewing sea life is the prime objective at dive sites off South Maui and Molokini. Open-water and advanced open-water certifications are offered. Complete your open-water book and pool work at home and become certified with Dive & Sea Maui. *1975 South Kihei Road, Kihei. 800-526-9915; 808-874-1952; e-mail: captron@maui.net; www. diveandseamaui.com.*

Dive Maui, Inc. Offers a variety of dive sites around Maui including Molokini, Lana'i and occasionally Moloka'i. Dive instruction available for introductory dives, open water and advanced open water. Divers can chose between shore and boat excursions, and those who prefer to snorkel can join in as well. *900 Front Street, Suite J6, Lahaina. 866-821-7450; 808-667-2080; fax 808-667-2351; e-mail: info@divemauiscuba.com; www.divemauiscuba.com.*

Ed Robinson's Diving Adventures Caters to certified divers although introductory shore dives are available for those who have never dove before. More experienced divers will enjoy the diverse array of dive sites including wreck dives off Maui, Lana'i and Molokini. Open-water and advanced open-water instruction is offered. Ed deploys two dive boats, each with a capacity for 12 divers. Underwater photographers are welcome. Don't forget to enjoy a night dive as well. *800-635-1273; 808-879-3584; e-mail: info@mauiscuba.com; www.mauiscuba.com.*

Extended Horizons Caters mainly to certified and advanced divers. Introductory dives for the beginner diver are also available either from shore or boat. Open-water certification is also available. Extended Horizons offers a large variety of dive sites around Maui and particularly off the shores of Lana'i as well as Moloka'i, weather permitting. Equipment rentals and night dives, too. The 36-foot dive boat accommodates 13 divers in two groups. Rated #1 in 2002 by the Maui Concierge. *94 Kupuohi #A-1, Lahaina. 888-348-3628; 808-667-0611; e-mail: info@scubadivemaui.com; www.scubadivemaui.com.*

Happy Maui Diving & Tours Dives mostly limited to the shores of Maui; however, boat dives are available to Molokini and Lana'i. Caters to beginning divers and as well as introductory dives. Night dives and rental gear, too. *840 Wainee Street, Suite 106, Lahaina. 808-669-0123; fax 808-669-7800; e-mail: mmiller@maui.net.*

Island Scuba Perfect for both certified and novice divers to share the experience with introductory dives for the beginner. Advanced instruction is also offered. Beach dives possible at Black Rock or Turtle Reef as well as charters. Boat destinations include extensive sites off Lana'i and Molokini. Go night diving or rent a scooter. *Lahaina. 888-606-4608; e-mail: island@maui.net; www.scubadivingmaui.com.*

Lahaina Divers PADI 5-star dive center. Addresses the needs of experienced or advanced divers and can provide a full range of services to all levels of divers including introductory dives for the beginner.

Advanced instruction offered for Dive Master, Nitrox and Rebreathers. Charter boats include the 43-foot Reliant to accommodate 22 divers and the 50-foot Endeavor to accommodate 24 divers. Dive sites include Lana'i, Molokini and locations off Maui. Underwater photographers welcome. Check website for dive packages. *143 Dickenson Street, Lahaina.* 800-998-3483; 808-667-7496; e-mail: *lahdiver@maui.net*; *www.lahainadivers.com*.

Makena Coast Charters   Offers adventures for the certified diver as wells as introductory dives for the beginner. Dive sites are located off South Maui and Molokini. Private chartered excursions to Lana'i are also an option. Engaged to be married? Why not tie the knot at Makena Coast Charters for a truly memorable occasion? Underwater photographers and cinematographers are welcome. 800-833-6483; 808-874-1273; e-mail: *diving@maui.net*.

Maui Diamond II   Environmentally conscious divers will be happy to learn the *Maui Diamond II* is powered by recycled vegetable oil. This 40-foot vessel will accommodate up to 15 passengers. Caters to certified divers; however, introductory dives are available for the beginner with open-water and advance open-water instruction and certification offered. Dive sites include South Maui and Molokini. Private scuba and snorkel charters to Molokini are also an option. *Departs daily from Slip #23, Ma'alaea Harbor.* 866-879-9119; e-mail: *mauidiamond@maui.net*; *www.mauiscubatours.com*.

Maui Dive Shop   Two dive boat charters depart from Ma'alaea Harbor. The 45-foot *Maka Koa* accommodates up to 18 divers while the *Ala Kai II* will take up to 12 divers. Dive destinations include Molokini and Lana'i, with night dives off South Maui. Caters to certified divers; however, introductory dives are available for the beginner. 800-542-DIVE; e-mail: *sylvia@mauidiveshop.com*; *www.mauidiveshop.com*.

Maui Diving Scuba Center   Caters to beginning divers and is a full-service scuba center. Shore and boat dives are available. Strong emphasis on safety and personal attention. Visit their website for dive package information. *222 Papalaua Street, Suite 112, Lahaina.* 800-959-7319; 808-667-0263; e-mail: *john@mauidiving.com*; *www.mauidiving.com*.

Maui Scuba Diving   A PADI International Resort Center. Caters to beginning and novice divers. Open-water and advanced open-water certifications are offered. Dive boats depart daily from Lahaina Harbor, Ma'alaea Harbor and Kihei to sites off West Maui, Lana'i and Molokini. Visit their website for scuba packages. *P.O. Box 13085, Lahaina, HI 96761.* 877-873-4837; e-mail: *info@mauiscubadiving.cc*; *www.mauiscubadiving.cc*.

Maui Sun Divers   Caters exclusively to beginning divers and referral programs as well as those who are in need of a refresher course. 877-879-3337; e-mail: *sundiver@maui.net*; *www.mauisundivers.com* or *www.maui.net*.

Mike Severns Diving Provides a unique experience for certified divers. The 38-foot dive boat *Pilikai* accommodates up to 12 divers split into two groups, with excursions to dive sites off Maui and Molokini. Caters to underwater photographers and offers a relaxed approach to the dive experience. For those folks who embrace a keen interest in marine life, you will find yourselves in good company with Mike Severns. My experienced dive friends have had very good things to say about Mike and his crew. *808-879-6596; e-mail: severns@mauigateway.com; www.mikeseversdiving.com.*

Pacific Dive Maui PADI 5-star dive center. Full-service facility for all levels of divers and offers experienced and advanced divers many options to satisfy their needs and desires. Instruction offered for all levels of divers. Shore and boat charters are available for access to a full range of dive sites. *150 Dickenson Street, Lahaina. 877-667-7331; 808-667-5331; e-mail: pacificdive@tiki.net; www.pacificdive.com.*

Scuba Gods Offers services to both certified and non-certified divers. Shore dives available off South Maui as well as boat dives to Molokini aboard a 40-foot vessel, which will accommodate 12 divers split into two groups. Introductory dives available for the beginning diver as well as advanced instruction up to Dive Master and specialty courses. *2130 South Kihei Road, Kihei. 866-224-4159; 808-879-3066; e-mail: thescubagod@hotmail.com; www.scubagods.com.*

Scuba Shack Certified divers as well as new divers will enjoy the services of Scuba Shack. Dive sites include locations around Maui and Molokini. Dive instruction available up to Dive Master, and specialty courses are offered as well as referral programs. Their 40-foot dive boat will accommodate 12 divers split into two groups. Snorkel enthusiasts are invited as well so that divers and non-divers can enjoy the experience together. Scuba Shack also offers programs especially for kids 5 and up. Underwater photographers welcome. Rated #1 in 2002 for best staff by *Scuba Diving Magazine*. *2349 South Kihei Road, Kihei. 877-213-4488; 808-879-DIVE; e-mail: wetanku@scubashack.com; www.scubashack.com.*

Trilogy With an impressive fleet of catamarans, Trilogy offers snorkel and scuba excursions to Lana'i, Molokini and sites off West and South Maui. Caters to certified divers and offers introductory dives for the beginner. Beach dives are also provided. Open-water and advanced open-water instruction is also available. A good company for the family interested in learning to dive. They have lots of experience with introductory divers. Introductory scuba $59, certified one-tank scuba dive $49, two-tank Lana'i dive $139. *Excursions depart Lahaina and Ma'alaea harbors. 888-225-MAUI; 808-661-4743; e-mail: carey@sailtrilogy.com; www.sailtrilogy.com.*

Tropical Divers Caters primarily to the beginning and novice divers with introductory dives and certification instruction. More experienced divers will benefit as well with charter boats to the back wall of Molokini and Lana'i. Specialty instruction is also available such as night diving, multilevel diving, underwater photography, nitrox and others. 800-994-MAUI; 808-667-5309; 808-669-6284; e-mail: getwet@scubamaui.com; www.scubamaui.com.

SEA EXCURSIONS, SAILING
(*See also* Cruises; Snorkeling)

Maui offers a bounty of choices for those desiring to spend some time in and on the ocean. Boats available for sea expeditions range from a three-masted schooner to spacious trimarans and large motor yachts to the zodiac-type rafts for the more adventurous. Or, if you prefer, there are small boat rentals (Hobie Cats) available at many of the beachside cabanas at major resorts. Excursion boats seem to have a way of sailing off into the sunset. The number of new ones is as startling as the number of operations that have disappeared since the last edition. Many boat companies now promote dolphin-watching trips.

You can choose a large-group trip or a more pampered small-group excursion with a maximum of six people. Two of the most popular snorkeling excursions are to Molokini and Lana'i. Competition to Molokini has become fierce; 20 to 30 boats a day now arrive to snorkel in this area. Many more boats now take trips to Lana'i as well. Most sailboats motor to these islands and, depending on wind conditions, sail at least part of the return trip. All provide snorkel equipment. One of the nicest amenities on a number of boats is the option of a freshwater shower. Some of them even solar-heat their water, which provides a

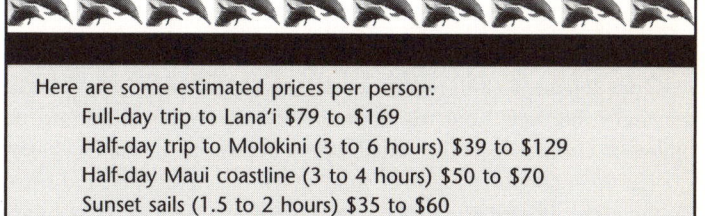

Here are some estimated prices per person:
   Full-day trip to Lana'i $79 to $169
   Half-day trip to Molokini (3 to 6 hours) $39 to $129
   Half-day Maui coastline (3 to 4 hours) $50 to $70
   Sunset sails (1.5 to 2 hours) $35 to $60
   Whale watching (2 to 3 hours/seasonal) $30 to $40
   Scuba introduction from $80 beach/$90 boat
   Private charters $100 per hour and up, $400 per day and up
   Dinner cruise from $75

MOLOKINI

Molokini is a distinctive landmark off the South Maui coastline and one of the most popular sea excursion destinations. It is located 8 miles off the Ma'alaea Harbor and most of the tours depart from that port. Most trips are taken in the morning. There are some afternoon trips, but expect rougher ocean conditions. On occasion even the morning trips are forced to snorkel at an alternative site, usually La Perouse or another spot off the South Maui coastline.

The remnant of a 10,000-year-old dormant volcano reveals only one crescent-shaped portion of the crater rim and serves as a sanctuary for marine and bird life. The inside of the crater offers a water depth of 10 to 50 feet; a 76-degree temperature and visibility sometimes as much as 150 feet on the outer perimeter creates a fish bowl effect. According to legend, the atoll of Molokini was created as the result of a jealous rage. Pele had a dream lover, Lohiau, who lived in Ma'alaea, located north of Makena. Lohiau married a *mo'o* (lizard) and Pele was so angry she bisected the lizard. The head became Molokini islet and the tail became Pu'u Ola'i, the rounded hill at the end of Makena.

Molokini has had some turbulent years. Long before tourist boats frequented this sight, it was used by the Navy as a bombing target. My first snorkeling trip to the crescent-shaped crater was in the days when only two or three boats operated trips. But with undetonated bombs an obvious danger, the Navy went ahead and detonated them. Obviously, the aquatic life and the reef system was decimated. The many tour boats dropping anchors further damaged and destroyed the reef. While it hasn't been restored to the way it was during my first excursions and likely will never be, it is still a popular snorkeling location. Fortunately, concerned boat operators were granted semi-permanent concrete mooring anchors, thereby preventing further reef damage.

---

refreshing rinse-off after your saltwater snorkel/swim. Food and beverage service varies and is reflected in the price. Many sailboats are available for hourly, full-day or longer private charters. *Note:* Due to weather conditions, your trip to Molokini may, at the last minute, be altered to another location, usually along the southern shore of Maui.

In the following list, phone numbers of the excursion companies are included; however, most activity desks can also book your reservation. Unless you have a lot of extra time, avoid the timeshare offers; you may get a discount on an activity, but you'll end up spending at least a portion of a day hearing their sales pitch. The best deal with an activity operator is **Tom Barefoot's Cashback Tours**, who can book most boats and offers a 10 percent refund (and no timeshare!). *Located* in Lahaina at 834 Front Street and in Kihei at 2395 South Kihei Road. 888-222-3601; 808-661-8889; *www.maui.net/~barefoot.*

America II This unique sailing vessel was built to compete in the 1987 America's Cup races in Fremantle, Australia; *America II* was skippered by John Kollius but lost to Dennis Connor of the *Stars & Stripes*. Enjoy a snorkeling and sailing experience on this 65-foot (12-meter) class yacht. Morning and afternoon sails as well as sunset sails are $40 for adults, children half-price. Two-hour seasonal whale watching, too. Excursions include soda, juice, water and snacks; beer and wine may be brought on board. Private charter is also available at $500 for the first two hours, $100 for each additional half-hour. *Departs Lahaina Harbor. 888-667-2133; 808-667-2133; www.galaxymall.com/stores/americaII.*

Atlantis (Submarine) The *Atlantis* submarine tours the underwater world beyond Lahaina Harbor. The underwater submarine tour lasts about 45 minutes, except the Discover Dive, which is about 30 minutes. Child rates apply to kids 12 and younger, but they must be at least 36 inches tall to ride aboard *Atlantis*. The *Atlantis* adventures include an ocean cruise out to the dive site (whale watching in season) and complimentary beverages. The dive descends to a depth of 120 feet. The fully submersible submarine is an 80-ton, 65-foot touring vessel that accommodates 46 passengers. They operate eight dives daily, beginning at their Pioneer Inn shop. There is a short boat ride to reach the submarine and it is quite surprising to watch it suddenly emerge out of the middle of the depths of the Pacific. Then you step across from the tender and load onto the submarine. The seats are lined up on both sides in front of half a porthole. The area is a little close, but the temperature is kept cool and comfortable. There are plenty of fish, and fish cards at each station help you identify them. Rocks and coral formations resemble an environ that is somehow extraterrestrial. The Maui Discover is a 45-minute submarine ride plus a 15-minute shoreline excursion to and from the sub, $79.99 adults, $39.99 children. Inquire about their combination packages that include the submarine trip combined with a luau, Maui Tropical Plantation Tram ride or admission to Maui Ocean Center and/or Sugar Cane Train ride. *808-667-2224.*

Blue Water Rafting These folks were among the first to initiate ocean rafting on Maui back in 1985. They operate a 6-passenger, 19' *Norvuania* and two 24-passenger high-powered rigid-hulled inflatable. This is for those die-hard snorkelers who enjoy an early-bird arrival to the crater to explore up to three different sites. It isn't always a gentle trip, so definitely for the adventurer. Trip includes a lunch and beverages. Snorkel Molokini or the Kanaio Sea Cave Adventure, where you can explore the caves and lava arches on the remote Kanaio coastline. Snorkeling tours range from $45 to $110 for adults and $39 to $95 for children. Two-and-a-half-hour seasonal whale watching is also offered. Also inquire about private charters. *Trips depart Kihei Boat Ramp. 808-879-RAFT; www.bluewaterrafting.com.*

Captain Steve's Take a trip aboard their rigid-hull raft to do some snorkeling and see whales and dolphins. One of the last owner-operated companies, Captain Steve really is your captain. He's been doing it for nearly 20 years and offers 6-hour winter and summer snorkel trips to Lana'i; $130 adults, $95 children 12 and under. Two-hour seasonal whale watching is also offered at $45 adults, $35 kids 12 and under. Maximum 20 passengers aboard his 32-foot, high-tech raft. *Departs Mala Wharf. 808-667-5565; www.captainsteves.com.*

Dive Maui Visit Lana'i or Molokini and enjoy a snorkel or scuba excursion with the folks of Dive Maui. Dive Maui primarily caters to scuba divers and offers snorkel adventures along the way. Dive Maui can also arrange packages such as whale watching, snorkeling and luau or dinner cruises. *866-821-7450; 808-667-2080; www.divemauiscuba.com.*

Expeditions Ferry service from Lahaina to Lana'i five times daily (currently 6:45 a.m., 9:15 a.m., 12:45 p.m., 3:15 p.m., 5:45 p.m.) and equal returns from Manele Bay (8 a.m., 10:30 a.m., 2 p.m., 4:30 p.m., 6:45 p.m.); $50 round-trip adult, $40 child. If you'd like to explore Lana'i on your own, you can take the early-morning ferryboat over and return on the late-afternoon trip. From the dock it is a moderate but easy walk to Manele Bay and the adjacent Manele Bay Resort. Once you arrive on Lana'i there is a shuttle that runs between the dock and the two resorts that charges $15 round-trip to Manele Bay and $25 round-trip to the Lodge at Koele. Expeditions can combine your boat trip with golf, a round of play at Lana'i Pines (a sporting clay course), or a night at Manele Bay Hotel or Lodge at Koele. *800-695-2624; 808-661-3756; www.go-lanai.com.*

Friendly Charters Friendly Charters has been operating on Maui since 1983. Your trip will be aboard the *Lani Kai*, a 53-foot double-deck catamaran that was launched in 1997. Two heads, two freshwater showers, water slide, snorkel staircase and trampoline. Protected cabin area. Continental breakfast and deli lunch. Adults $79.95, children 3 to 12 $49.95. Underwater cameras and Snuba are optional. Book online and save 20 percent. *Departs Ma'alaea Harbor at 6:45 a.m. for Molokini (weather permitting) and Turtle Town; return at noon. 888-893-8080; 808-244-1979; www.mauisnorkeling.com.*

Frogman Charters Frogman has been in operation since 1986 and offers snorkel and scuba adventures plus seasonal whale watching on their two catamarans, *Frogman II* and *Blue Dolphin*. They depart Ma'alaea Harbor twice daily. Frogman morning snorkel is $73.95 adults/$53.95 kids, one-tank scuba $99, two-tank $119. Frogman afternoon scuba is $63.95 and snorkeling is $32.95 adults/$24.95 kids. Blue Dolphin is $79.95 for a morning trip and $59.95 for afternoon. *Locations at 150 Lahainaluna Road, Lahaina; Dolphin Plaza at 2395 South Kihei Road, Kihei; and Napili Plaza. 888-700-FROG ext. 3; 808-661-3333; www.bossfrog.com.*

Gemini Charters   The *Gemini* is a 64-foot catamaran with glass-bottom view ports that departs daily from Ka'anapali Beach in front of the Westin Maui. Year-round picnic snorkel sails departing at 11 a.m. provide snorkel equipment including prescription masks, flotation devices, snorkel instruction, a freshwater shower and a hot buffet lunch. The picnic/snorkel cruise is $85 for adults, $70 teens and $50 children 2 to 12. Enjoy the summer champagne Sunset Sail (April through December) with champagne, beer, wine, mai tais and non-alcoholic beverages; $55 adults, $45 teens and $35 kids 2 to 12. Seasonal morning and afternoon whale watching with a marine naturalist on board and an underwater hydrophone to listen to the whales singing. Private charters are available for groups, weddings or special occasions. *800-820-7245; 808-669-0508.*

Hawaii Ocean Rafting   This family-owned and -operated business takes 14 passengers aboard their raft for half-day adventures ($69.95 adults, $49.95 children) or a full-day Lana'i trip ($109.95 adults, $79.95 children). Full-day trip includes continental breakfast and deli lunch. Half-day tour visits three snorkel sites and includes continental breakfast. Private whale watching charters are also available. 15 percent discount by booking online. *888-677-RAFT; 808-661-RAFT; www.hawaiioceanrafting.com.*

Hawaiian Rafting Adventures   In their RAIV (Rigid Aluminum Inflatable Vessels) you can enjoy a full-day expedition circumnavigating the island of Lana'i for snorkeling and diving, including a continental breakfast and deli-style lunch; adults $130, children 5 to 12 $100. Their half-day snorkel expedition crosses the 'Au'au Channel and includes continental breakfast, snacks and beverages; adults $65, $45 children 5 to 12. Two-tank scuba dive for certified divers is $120. An introduction for non-certified divers is $110. Private whale-watching charters are also offered. *Departs from Lahaina. Discount for booking online. 808-661-7333; www.hawaiianrafting.com.*

Island Marine   Depart from Lahaina Harbor, slip #3, aboard the *Lahaina Princess* for Molokini and Olowalu snorkel excursions (May through December), $73.14 for adults and $41.34 for children. The 65-foot touring yacht takes up to 149 passengers. Includes continental breakfast, buffet deli lunch with barbecue chicken. This is the only Molokini tour that currently departs from West Maui. (They are also the only vessel that has a 15-foot "water trampoline" that deploys on the water for you to jump on, jump from or just lie around on top of.)

The *Maui Princess*, a 150-passenger 118-foot touring yacht, offers fine-dining cruises with stunning views of the island sunsets and the night lights of the islands when the stars come out. The menu includes roasted chicken or prime rib, salads, vegetable *du jour*, breads, desserts and beverages of your choice. Departs at 5:30 p.m. and returns at 8 p.m.; $79 for adults and $59 for kids. The *Moloka'i Princess* offers one-day package excursions to the island of Moloka'i as well as one-way passage to the island, seven days a week. The 100-foot interisland yacht is state-of-the-art and will take you there in style. Look for whales along the way. Call or check the website for departure times. One-way tickets are $40 for adults and $20 for children. Children 2 and under are free. These vessels are also available for private charters. Seasonal whale watching is available on all their vessels with prices starting at $20 for adults and $13 for kids, depending on the time of day. Save 10 percent by booking online; AAA members receive a 15 percent discount. *800-275-6969; 808-667-6165; www.mauiprincess.com.*

Island Star   Offers customer charters only. Choose from a variety of tours ranging from the three-hour sunset sail or a week of sailing around the islands aboard the 57-foot *Island Star*. Master stateroom with deluxe king bed, forward cabin with four berths and a private port cabin. Two heads, plus hot and cold water pressure are amenities. Your crew includes a scuba instructor, marine naturalist and chef. USCG certified for 28 passengers but will comfortably sleep 10. Ask about snorkeling and whale-watching tours on their ocean-going rafts or private sightseeing on a sleek, high-speed Scarab. *888-677-7238; 808-669-STAR; www.islandstarsailing.com.*

Kamehameha Sails, Inc.   *King Kamehameha*, a 40-foot Woody Brown catamaran built in Hawai'i for Hawaiian waters. Snorkel excursions, sunset sails or whale watching depart from Lahaina Harbor, slip #17. Although the vessel is rather large, the *Kamehameha* ensures a personalized cruise with a maximum 6 passengers, with padded seating around the wheel area and a big net out front. You may recognize it by the big picture of King Kamehameha on the sail. Owner Tom Warren has been sailing on various charter boats since 1969 and purchased the *Kamehameha* in 1977. A congenial captain, fun casual atmosphere and small passenger manifest allows for a pleasantly intimate sailing experience. Minimal snacks provided or bring your own. The two-hour seasonal whale excursion departing at 9 a.m. and the sunset cruise departing at 4:30 p.m. is $50 per person (no child discounts due to the small manifest). The 12-to-3-p.m. snorkel and whale tour is $75 per person. The *King Kamehameha* can also be privately chartered for $200 per hour. *808-661-4522.*

Kapalua Kai   Their 53-foot wing-mast, 49-passenger catamaran offers plenty of shaded area in their open-air salon embellished in teak and state-of-the-art sound system. Snorkel trip includes equipment, a buffet lunch catered by Hula Grill that includes smoked turkey and a salad bar featuring Kula greens. Departs 10 a.m. Adults $85, children 2 to 12 $55. The Sunset Sail offers finger sandwiches, veggie platter and fresh fruit platter with sails hoisted through the sunset. $50 adults, $35 children. Departure times vary depending upon the time of year, between 4 and 5 p.m. Both tours have a premium bar and the food is about the best you'll find. Private charters are also available upon request with a two-hour minimum. *They operate out of Whalers Village in Ka'anapali. 808-665-0344, 808-667-5980; www.sailingmaui.com.*

Kaulana Club Lanai is long gone, but the name lives on with activities aboard the *Kaulana* and the 65-foot catamaran *Spirit of Lahaina*. Board the *Kaulana* for a cruise with "heavy *pupus*" and an open bar to enjoy Maui sunsets with live music. Snorkel Lanai at Manele Bay aboard the *Spirit of Lahaina*; includes continental breakfast, "build your own sandwiches" for lunch and poundcake and juice for morning refreshments. Price is $69 adults, children half-price. Enjoy a dinner cruise on the *Spirit of Lahaina*. *800-531-5262; 808-667-9595; e-mail: club@mauigateway.com; www.clublanai.net.*

Kiele V A 55-foot catamaran that departs from the beach of the Hyatt Regency, Ka'anapali. Snorkel excursions daily, 10 a.m. to 2 p.m., $85 for adults, $70 for teens and $50 for children under 12. Seasonal whale watching is offered from 3:30 p.m. to 5:30 p.m., $55 for adults, $45 for teens and $35 for children under 12. *808-661-1234.*

Lahaina Princess—*See* Island Marine.

Makena Boat Partners *Kai Kanani*, 46-foot catamaran, departs from the Maui Prince Hotel. Molokini picnic/snorkel cruise offered Tuesday through Saturday is $75 for adults, $45 children 11 and under. Afternoon seasonal whale watching offered Tuesday, Thursday and Saturday, $35 adults and $25 kids. *808-879-7218; www.makenaboat.com.*

Maui Classic Charters The *Four Winds* departs daily from Ma'alaea to Molokini with a maximum of 112 passengers. *Four Winds II* is a 55-foot glass-bottom catamaran that offers a morning half-day snorkel sail, $79 for adults, $49 for children 3 to 12. Breakfast is a varied selection of fresh bagels and cream cheese with jellies and fresh pineapple and orange slices and barbecue lunch. An afternoon snorkel cruise, departing at 1:30 p.m., is offered at $39.95 for adults and $29.95 for children. Beer, wine and soda included as well. Freshwater showers and an on-board waterslide add to the day's fun. There are two decks, one covered and one uncovered, and those of you who prefer to stay dry can sample the scenic underwater delights through their submarine-style glass-bottom hull. An optional activity is Snuba ($45 extra), which takes six people at a time with air tanks carried on rafts that float at the surface, as well as underwater video and cameras. Snorkel excursions are also available on the 54' catamaran, *Maui Magic*, departing at 7 a.m. Seasonal whale watching is also offered, starting at $39.95 for adults, discounts for children. *800-736-5740; 808-879-8188; www.mauicharters.com.*

Maui Dive Shop Besides selling scuba and snorkel gear, they also offer boating activities and combination packages. Molokini or La Perouse snorkel from $49 per person, $39 for children 4 to 12. Scuba Introduction $79.95 beach/$89.95 boat. Scuba Scooter Dive $99.95. "Fire & Water"—Luau and Molokini snorkel cruise, $99. "Sun to Sea"—Bike downhill and a Molokini snorkel cruise, $139. "Inside & Out"—Snorkel Molokini and visit the Maui Ocean Center, $54. "Above & Below"—A Molokini snorkel trip and a 45-minute helicopter trip, $194. "Night & Day"—A Molokini snorkel and dinner and dancing on the *Maui Princess*, $119. Stop by and pick up a copy of their free dive guide. *They have a number of shops around the island: Kihei Town Center, 808-879-1919; Azeka II, 808-879-3388; and Lahaina, 808-661-5388. 800-542-3483 ext. 5; www.mauidiveshop.com.*

Maui-Moloka'i Sea Cruises The *Prince Kuhio* is a 92-foot motor yacht. Whale watching, private charters, half-day snorkel to Molokini/Kalaeloa (a.k.a. Turtle Town), departs Ma'alaea at 12:30 p.m. This boat has the benefits of a larger vessel with more comforts, but with a bigger capacity, there are a lot more people. Rates are $86.63 for adults and $47.77 for children 12 and under. Children under 5 sail free. Their snorkel trips include continental breakfast, deli lunch and beverages. You and your family can also enjoy Snuba for an extra fee of $45. Seasonal whale watching departs daily with a field naturalist onboard, $31.84 for adults and $21.23 for kids under 12. *800-468-1287; 808-242-8777; www.mvprince.com.*

Maui Princess—*See* Island Marine.

Moloka'i Princess—*See* Island Marine.

Ocean Activities Departures from Ma'alaea aboard the 37-foot Tolleycraft *No Ka Oi III* for deep-sea sport fishing. Sail aboard the 65-foot catamaran *Wailea Kai* or power cat *Maka Kai* for Molokini picnic snorkel, $60 per person. *Wailea Kai* does sunset cruises, $45 on Wednesdays only. *808-879-4485; 800-798-0652.*

Ocean Riders "Adventure rafting" on one of their rigid-hull, 28' inflatable rafts with a maximum capacity of 18. They feature unusual snorkel and dive destinations (depending on daily weather conditions). Reefs of Kaho'olawe, Moloka'i's cliffs or Lana'i. Seasonal whale watching. $135 per adult, $95 children. Continental breakfast included and snacks throughout the day. Check in at 6:30 a.m. *Departs Mala Wharf in Lahaina. 808-661-3586; e-mail: oriders@maui.net.*

Pacific Whale Foundation Cruises A variety of adventures await you aboard their 54-foot power catamaran *Ocean Explorer* or their graceful 50-foot sailing catamaran *Manute'a*, both departing out of Lahaina Harbor. Its fleet at Ma'alaea Harbor includes the *Ocean Odyssey*, a state-of-the-art 149-passenger power catamaran with all of the luxurious amenities, as well as the 65-foot *Ocean Spirit*, which can accommodate a manifest of 142 passengers. Whale watching December 1–May 15 with prices varying, they offer special kid and family rates. The Molokini and Turtle Arches excursion (7 a.m. to noon) departs Ma'alaea, $55.95 for adults, kids six and under free with each paying adult. Kids 6-12 are $15. Board the *Manute'a* for a Lana'i Wild Dolphin Eco-adventure, 7 a.m. to 12:30 p.m., $74.95 for adults and discount for kids. May 1–November 30 they also offer an Oceanic Dolphin Encounter and Snorkel Eco-Adventure aboard the *Ocean Explorer*, 7 a.m. to 1 p.m. Cost is $74.95 for adults, $37.48 for kids 4 to 12, under four free. Their Lana'i Afternoon Snorkel and Eco-Adventure aboard the *Manute'a* departs May 1–November 20 for their 1 to 4 p.m. excursion. Price is $36.50 for adults, half-off kids 4 to 12, kids under four free. Book online for a 10 percent discount. Proceeds from tours benefit aquatic wildlife. 800-942-5311; 808-879-8811; www.pacificwhale.org.

Paragon Sailing Charters They have two 47-foot catamarans, *Paragon I* and *II*, built in California with state-of-the-art rotating carbon fiber masts. The Cabin House offers shade and shelter, and trampolines offer outside lounging. Their five-hour Molokini Sail & Snorkel departs from Ma'alaea Harbor, offering a morning snorkel-sail that begins with a 7:30 a.m. departure and a continental breakfast as you head toward Molokini. Snorkel gear is provided and they have small-size gear for children. A fresh hot/cold-water shower is located on top of the swim ladder for after your swim and before a buffet lunch with refreshments. Maximum of 49 passengers. $84.15 for adults, children 12 and under half price. Children three and under sail free. Their afternoon 3-hour Speed Sail & Snorkel Coral Gardens trip includes snorkeling followed by a speedrun back; $51 for adults, children under 12 half price. Trip includes appetizers and beverages. Depart aboard their second vessel from the Lahaina Harbor at 8:30 a.m. for an all-day Lana'i trip that includes a deluxe continental breakfast. Unloading is done at Manele Bay on Lana'i and guests are provided with snorkel gear, picnic baskets, beach mats and umbrellas for 2.5 hours of dining and ocean fun before re-boarding the boat. En route back, while catching the afternoon tradewinds, they serve desserts, champagne and have an open bar. Halfway back, the captain stops for a deep-water swim before returning to the Lahaina Harbor at 4 p.m. Cost is $149 adults, $99 children. Limited to 24 passengers per trip. Their Sunset Sail trip departs Lahaina at 5 p.m. with an open bar and appetizers. The vessel is licensed for 49 passengers, but they take a maximum of 24. $51 for adults, $34 12 and under. Save 15 percent by booking online. *800-441-2087; 808-244-2087; fax 808-878-3933; www. sailmaui.com.*

Pier 1   At Lahaina Harbor representing 37 excursions companies, you'll get the real scoop here. Friendly folks with good information. From scuba diving to rafting adventures, dinner cruises, snorkeling, sailing or fishing. Other activities include Lana'i Golf and Jeep Excursions or Weddings on the Water. *808-667-0680; www.pier1lahaina.com.*

The Pride of Maui   A 65-foot Maxi catamaran featuring a spacious indoor sundeck, barbecue grills, hot showers, water slide, glass-bottom view port and handicap access. Daily departures begin at 8 a.m. from the Ma'alaea Harbor. Their morning trip includes a continental breakfast and a hot barbecue lunch with beer and mai tais. This trip includes a 5-hour cruise to Molokini and Turtle Town (Pu'u Ola'i). Depending on weather conditions, other snorkel locations may be Olowalu or Coral Gardens. The afternoon cruise offers snacks and beverages (mai tais and beer at an additional cost) and an optional lunch. This trip lasts three hours and goes to two snorkel sites (Molokini if weather permits). Whale watching seasonally aboard their 45-foot monohull luxury yacht, *The Leilana*. Rates are $26 for adults and $17 for kids 3 to 12. Underwater video cameras are also available for rent. The boat accommodates up to 149 passengers but the crew intentionally limits the number of passengers to ensure a quality experience. Morning snorkel $86 adults, $51 children. Afternoon snorkel $35 adults, $22 children. Scuba is $40 for one tank and $60 for two. Snuba for an additional $49. (Note: The afternoon sails, on any excursion, can be a rougher and windier trip.) *877-867-7433; 808-244-2100; fax 808-244-7555; www.prideofmaui.com.*

Rainbow Chaser   Given the name the Honeymoon Boat, it is for adults only or for private family charter. There is a maximum of six passengers for this all-day Lana'i excursion featuring the finest cuisine for breakfast, lunch and dessert. Relax, snorkel or enjoy a bluewater swim adventure aboard the catamaran *Rainbow Chaser. Departs from Lahaina. 800-667-2270; 808-667-2270; www.rainbowchasermaui.com.*

Reef Dancer   For a truly unique viewing experience of Maui's mystical underwater world, board the exclusive semi-submersible *Reef Dancer*. Get close and personal with Hawai'i's unique marine life. This is a semi-submersible, meaning it only partially submerges, so anytime you feel a bit claustrophobic, you can go up on top for some fresh air. The glass-paneled hull allows viewing on both port and starboard sides so you don't miss any of the action. The bottom is six feet below the surface and they cruise around the ocean floor off of Puamana. *Reef Dancer* divers will be in the water to bring the most interesting sea creatures right up to your window while the adventure is videotaped. Be sure to bring your camera as well; 400 ASA films works best. *Reef Dancer* departs five times daily from Lahaina Harbor and has a maximum capacity of 34. The one-hour trip runs $32.95 for adults, $18.95 for children 6 to 12 years, free for 5 and under. Their 90-minute tour includes a second turtle site, $4.95 adults, $24.95 children. If you have enjoyed snorkeling on Maui, you won't see much more through the viewing windows. But if you are unable or unwilling to get wet, this is a trip worth considering. 888-667-2133; 808-667-2133; www.galaxymall.com/stores/reefdancer.

Scotch Mist Charters *Scotch Mist II* is a Santa Cruz 50-foot sailboat that took first place in the 1984 Victoria-Maui International. Take an afternoon "Fast is Fun" sail along the West Maui coast from May to December; $35 for adults, $17.50 for kids 5 to 12. Or enjoy a 4-hour sail and snorkel excursion to the best sites along the coast. Gear, snacks and beverage provided. Available May through December and departs 8 a.m.; adults $60, kids 5 to 12 $30. Savor a two-hour champagne and chocolate sunset sail year-round; $40 adults, $20 kids 5 to 12. Sorry, no children under five permitted on this cruise. Seasonal whale-watching excursions are offered four times daily starting at $35 for adults and $12.50 for kids. Private charters are also available. *Departs Slip #2 at Lahaina Harbor. 808-661-0386; fax 808-667-2113; www.scotchmistsailingcharters.com.*

Sea Escape Boat Rentals Rent the 26-foot *Shamrock* or the 24-foot *Splendor*. *Splendor* rents for $125, minimum three hours; *Shamrock* rents for $125, minimum of four hours, $75 each additional hour. 808-879-3721; www.seaescapeboat.com.

Seaview Adventure Cruises *Seaview* offers two high-speed vessels to accommodate smaller crowds and will whisk you to Lana'i in a hurry for their six-hour snorkel excursion with a stop in Manele. Includes equipment, breakfast, picnic lunch and beverages; $99 for adults and $74 for kids 5 to 12. The coastline cruise is offered three days a week for a three-hour snorkeling tour along Maui's western shore; $49 for adults and $29 for kids. A two-hour, narrated seasonal whale watching is also available with several daily departure times; the cost is $35 for adults and $20 for kids. All excursions depart from Lahaina Harbor. Freshwater shower and on-board restrooms are a nice plus. Private charters can also be arranged. *808-661-5550; www.seaview-maui.com.*

Shangri-La This sleek, high-performance, custom 65-foot catamaran offers private charters by the hour only. The vessel was custom built by owner/operators Peter Wood and Inca Robbin with a dream of yacht retirement and the South Pacific in mind. The vessel is tastefully decorated and spacious, with guest comfort in mind. Day charters are available for $1,000 per hour with space for 49 guests. Specialty cruises include wine-tasting dinners, candlelight dinners, weddings, eco tours and scuba diving. Price includes a USCG-certified captain and crew. Catering from the Hula Grill Restaurant, open bar, along with snorkeling and flotation equipment available. Extended charters are available for a maximum of six guests. On-board gourmet chef and meals, hostess, kayaks, snacks, fuel and bar are provided according to your desires and added to the final billing. *Depart from Lahaina. 888-855-9977; 808-665-0077; www.sailingmaui.com.*

Teralani They offer snorkel, sunset and whale-watching excursions aboard their two catamarans, *Teralani I* and *Teralani II*. The Lana'i barbecue picnic snorkel and dolphin search is $135 for adults, $99 for teens and $79 for children. The dinner sunset whale-watching cruise is $69 for adults, $65 for teens and $55 for children. Morning whale-watching cruises depart at 8 a.m. and are $52 for adults, $45 for teens and $35 for children. The *Teralani I* and *II* board passengers from the beaches of the Sheraton and Royal Lahaina as well as Dig Me Beach in Ka'anapali. Private charters are also available. *808-661-5500; fax 808-661-0448; www.teralani.net.*

Trilogy Trilogy's impressive fleet includes the *Trilogy I*, 64-foot cutter-rigged catamaran with maximum capacity of 55 passengers; *Trilogy II*, 55-foot sloop-rigged catamaran, maximum of 44 passengers; *Trilogy III*, 51-foot sloop-rigged with a maximum of 36 passengers; *Trilogy IV*, a 50-foot sloop-rigged with a maximum of 49; *Trilogy V* and *VI* are 54-foot. The *Manele Kai* is a 32-foot rigid aluminum, high-

TRILOGY: A BEST BET

The Coon family knows better than to mess with a good thing. The morning boat trip over to Lana'i still starts earlier than most would like, but once underway with warm (yes, still homemade by the Coons) cinnamon rolls and a mug (the ceramic kind, no Styrofoam here!) of hot chocolate or coffee, it seems all worth the effort. Don't forget to bring the camera. Trilogy boats now take guests Monday through Friday for snorkeling, sun and fun at Manele Bay. (On Saturdays, snorkeling is off the boat, not at the beach.) Beginning snorkelers are carefully instructed before entering the ocean. And they also have an eco-enrichment summer camp program for kids. If you would prefer, you can skip the tour of Lana'i City and snorkel even longer (but only on weekday trips). The chicken is cooked on the grill by the ship's captain and served on china-type plates. The chicken is accompanied by a delicious stir-fry, fresh rolls and salad (but Mrs. Coon still isn't giving out the secret ingredients for her salad dressing to anyone). The eating area has a series of picnic tables and is pleasantly shaded by an awning. *808-661-4743; 800-874-2666; www.sailtrilogy.com.*

speed, inflatable zodiac. Children ages 3 to 15 are half-price off adult fare on all tours. There are numerous tour options.

Their Discover Lana'i excursion is offered Monday through Friday and begins at 6:15 a.m., when you'll meet a Trilogy First Mate at the Trilogy parking lot on Dickenson Street. Enjoy hot chocolate, coffee, fresh fruit and those very special homemade cinnamon rolls en route. Trilogy arrives at Manele Harbor on Lana'i by 8:30 a.m., which leaves plenty of time for a guided van tour of Lana'i City, snorkeling and scuba at Hulopo'e Bay Marine Sanctuary before a hot barbecue lunch at their private picnic area. The afternoon affords another opportunity to snorkel and swim or the option of a guided tour of Lana'i City. It is approximately 2 p.m. when you depart Manele Harbor, arriving at Lahaina Harbor between 3:30 and 4 p.m. Discover Lana'i Sail and Discover Lana'i Sunset are each $169, discounts for children. Scuba is an additional fee. Discover Lana'i with Kayaking, $199.

On Saturday their Ultimate Adventure in Paradise differs in that you snorkel from the vessel off the coast of Lana'i and enjoy a "Jeep Safari" of the island. They also offer Lana'i Overnight packages Monday through Friday with a stay at the Manele Bay Hotel or Lodge at Koele. Cost is $239. Discover Molokini Sunrise Sail is aboard *Trilogy V.* Breakfast is the same as on the Lana'i excursion; lunch consists of hot barbecue teriyaki chicken, green salad, corn on the cob and dinner rolls. Vegetarian selection also available. Price is $95 for adults.

Board on Ka'anapali Beach for a *pupu* and sunset sail. This is an outstanding opportunity to see the beautiful coastline of Maui from the ocean. Beer, wine and soft drinks are available as well as a very impressive selection of appetizers including flank steak grilled up for you by the captain. So leave the kids at the condo and enjoy a special evening. The sunset sails are a far better value than a dinner cruise and the *pupus* on this trip were hearty. Deluxe Ka'anapali Sunset Sail, $59.

The Trilogy Excursions Ka'anapali Snorkel Sail meets in front of Ka'anapali Beach Hotel for beach-loading aboard the *Trilogy IV* at 8:45 a.m.—a good choice for those of you who aren't early risers. Their continental breakfast is followed by snorkeling at Honolua Bay (weather permitting) and a second site of the Captain's choice. Lunch fare is the same as above and you'll arrive back at Ka'anapali Beach at 2:30 p.m. Discover Ka'anapali Snorkel Sail, $95. Seasonal whale watching from Ka'anapali aboard *Trilogy III* or *IV* is $39. Summer program for kids, Camp Trilogy offers an eco-enrichment opportunity for the whole family between June through August, as well as during major holidays. The program begins with a snorkel lesson with Camp Trilogy's counselors and then a guided reef tour. Organized beach games and activities teach team-building skills as well as respect for the environment. Camp Trilogy kids receive special T-shirts, eco-coloring books and their own barbecue. Cost is $152.71 ($63 per child in addition to the regular fare of $89.71). *180 Lahainaluna Road, P.O. Box 1119, Lahaina, HI 96767-1119. 888-225-MAUI; 808-661-4743; fax 808-667-7766; www.sailtrilogy.com.*

Ultimate Rafting Departs Lahaina Harbor, slip #17, aboard their rigid "V" hull high-speed inflatable with awning for shade and swim ladder for easy ocean entry. All tours are catered with local fruit, sweet breads, fresh vegetables and dips and a deli-style lunch. Half- and full-day trips to Lanai (April–November) are offered with wildlife viewing (including seasonal whale watching) tours (December–April). Full-day Lana'i snorkel trips depart 8:45 a.m. and return about 3 p.m.; $135 adults, $115 kids 4 to 12. Half-day trips depart 8:45 a.m.; $89 adults, $79 kids. During the December–April whale season they have an early-bird special (7:30 to 9:30 a.m.); $39 adults, $29 kids 4 to 12. A picnic snorkel and whale-watching trip departs at 9:30 a.m., returning at 1:30 p.m.; $89 adults, $79 kids 4 to 12. A two-hour afternoon whale-watching tour departs 1 p.m. and sightings are guaranteed; $45 adults, $29 kids. Check their website for specials. *808-667-5678; fax 808-667-7611; www.ultimatewhalewatch.com.*

Windjammer Cruises Maui *Spirit of Windjammer*, a 70-foot, three-mast schooner, offers 2-hour dinner cruise along the West Maui coastline. Along with breathtaking sunsets, enjoy a buffet-style prime rib and salmon dinner. Price is $74.95 for adults and $37.48 for children. Children 12 and under are free with each paying adult. On Sundays and special charters, May through October, a Champagne Brunch Cruise is offered at $38.95 for adults, and free children under 12. Seasonal whale-watching cruises offered three times daily range from $19.95 to $34.95. Children under 12 free. Transportation is available from West Maui and South Maui for an additional fee. Departs Lahaina Harbor, slip # 1. Book online and save 15 percent. *800-732-4852; www.windjammercruisesmaui.com.*

SNORKELING (*See also* Scuba Diving; Sea Excursions, Sailing)

The coastlines of Maui offer exceptionally clear waters, warm ocean temperatures and abundant sea life with safe areas (no adverse water conditions) for snorkeling. If you are a complete novice, most of the resorts and excursion boats offer snorkeling lessons. From the youngest to the oldest, everyone can enjoy this sport that needs little experience and does not necessitate diving to see all the splendors of the sea. If you are unsure of your snorkeling abilities, the use of a flotation device may be of assistance. Be forewarned that the combination of tropical sun and the refreshing coolness of the ocean can deceive those paddling blissfully on the surface and result in a badly burned backside. Water-resistant sunscreens are available locally and are recommended.

UNDERWATER PHOTOGRAPHY

You may feel the urge to rent an underwater camera to photograph some of the unusual and beautiful fish you've seen. By all means try it, but remember, underwater fish photography is a real art. The disposable underwater cameras are fun and inexpensive and available everywhere, but your resulting photos may be disappointing. There are several videotapes of Maui's marine life available at the island bookstores if you want a permanent record of the fish you've seen. Several of the sea excursions offer video camera rentals.

All snorkeling boat trips provide equipment as a part of their package. Some offer prescription masks. It is convenient but expensive to rent snorkel (and any other) equipment at the beachside activity booths. You can get gear at a dive shop for a week or pay the same for a one-day beachside rental. Rental prices at the shops are very competitive, running about $2.50 per day and as little as $10 a week. Children's equipment is less at $1.49. Prescription masks will be slightly higher. If you plan on doing a lot of snorkeling, the purchase of your own equipment should be considered. Good quality gear is available at all the dive shops. Less expensive sets can be purchased at Longs or Costco. Most major dive shops can fit you with a prescription mask, as long as your vision impairment is not too severe. As a contact wearer with a strong prescription, I wear my soft lenses and have no problem with a good-fitting mask. Most dive shops rent snorkel equipment. Here are a just a few options.

Mask-Fins-Snorkel Rentals

Auntie Snorkel in Kihei (Rainbow Mall) charges $9.95 to $14.95 per week (808-879-6263)

Maui Dive Shop at Kamaole Shopping Center, Lahaina Cannery Mall, Honokowai Market Place, Whalers Village and Harbor Shops at Ma'alaea (808-661-5388 is their Lahaina shop)

Snorkel Bob's in Kihei (808-875-7449), Lahaina (808-661-4421), Napili (808-669-9603)

Snorkel's -n- More in Lahaina (808-665-0804)

Snorkeling Spots

Good snorkeling spots, if not right in front of your hotel or condo, are only a few minutes' drive away. Generally, the best snorkeling at all locations is in the morning until about 1 p.m., before the wind picks up. For more information on each area and other locations, see Chapter 5. The following are my favorites, each for a special reason.

'Ahihi-Kina'u Natural Reserve   Approximately five miles past Wailea. No facilities. This is not a very crowded spot and you may feel

a little alone here, but the snorkeling is great with lots of coral and a good variety of fish.

Black Rock   At the Sheraton in the Ka'anapali Resort. Pay for parking at Whalers Village and walk down the beach. Clear water and a variety of tame fish that expects handouts.

Honolua Bay   No facilities, park alongside the road and walk a .25 mile to the bay. This is possibly the best snorkeling on Maui, anytime but winter.

Kapalua Bay   Public park with off-street parking, restrooms and showers. A well-protected bay and beautiful beach amid the grounds of the Kapalua Resort. Limited coral and some large coral heads, fair for fish watching. Arrive early as parking is very limited.

Maluaka Beach   Located in Makena, no facilities and roadside parking. Good coral formations and a fair amount of fish at the left end of the beach.

Molokini Crater   This volcanic remnant affords good snorkeling. See " Scuba Diving" above for additional information.

Namalu Bay   Park at Kapalua Bay, walk over from Kapalua Bay to the bay that fronts the grounds of the resort. Difficult entry, very good on calm days.

Olowalu   At mile-marker 14, about 5 miles south of Lahaina. Generally calm and warmer waters with ample parking along the roadside. Very good snorkeling. If you find a pearl earring, let me know, I *still* have the match.

Ulua-Mokapu Beach   Well-marked public beach park in Wailea with restrooms and showers. Good snorkeling on the Ulua side of the rocky point separating these two picturesque and beautiful beaches.

Suzzy's Shoreline Snorkel Tours   Suzzy Robinson and her associates share their love of the ocean with beginning, intermediate or advanced snorkelers. They promise there is something for everyone.

A good way to become acquainted with Maui's sea life is a guided snorkeling adventure with **Ann Fielding**, marine biologist and author of *Hawaiian Reefs and Tidepools* and *Underwater Guide to Hawai'i*. She takes small groups (minimum 2, maximum 6) to the best location, generally Honolua Bay in summer and Ahihi Kinau in winter. These excursions begin with an introductory discussion on Hawaiian marine life, identification and ecology, followed by snorkeling. Flotation devices, snorkel gear and lunch are included. A great educational experience for the kids and parents. 808-572-8437

A pre-snorkel briefing is followed by snorkel instruction and a narrative tour. 8 a.m. to noon. 808-879-4528.

SNUBA (*See also* Scuba Diving; Sea Excursions, Sailing)
One of the newer water recreations available is Snuba, a combination of snorkeling and scuba diving. It allows the freedom of underwater exploration without the heavy equipment of scuba diving. In brief, the Snuba diver has a mask and an air hose that is connected to the surface. Some of those currently offering Snuba are *The Pride of Maui, Prince Kuhio* and *The Four Winds.* (Fee in addition to cruise fee: $40 to $50).

SPAS/FITNESS CENTERS/HEALTH RETREATS

If you are interested in keeping in shape and you have no fitness center at your resort, here are several that welcome drop-in guests.

Gold's Gym   *Lahaina Square, 808-667-7474; Wailuku Industrial Park, 808-242-6851; Lipoa Shopping Center, Kihei, 808-874-2844; 8 1 Kolu Street, Wailuku, 808-242-5773.*

Sports Club Kahana   These folks have a lot of extras with Kahana Care (for kids), a boxing ring, a climbing wall and the Kahana Grill (juice and healthy food bar) located inside. *At the Kahana Villas Condominium. 808-669-3539; www.sportsclubkahana.*

24-Hour Fitness   *150 Hana Highway, Kahului. 808-877-7474.*

Many of the resorts have wonderful fitness centers. Some resorts charge resort guests a usage fee, others give complimentary guest privileges. A number of them allow non-resort guests for a day-use fee. A spa is a great way for moms and daughters to enjoy a day of pampering. Teenage girls may love getting a facial and it is great for their complexion as well.

Hotel Hana-Maui   Their fitness and wellness center offers exercise equipment, aerobic, yoga and aquacise classes, nature walks, recreational excursions and body treatments. If you need more pampering, a new spa is underway in what was the old Hawaiian Court cottages; it should be completed in late 2003. They'll offer natural practitioners with eight treatment rooms. *808-248-8211.*

Maui School of Therapeutic Massage   Whether venturing to Haleakala for an early-morning sunrise or visiting the Tedeschi Wineries, be sure to include a stop in Makawao at the Maui School of Therapeutic Massage. This is one of the best deals on the island and I make a stop every time I'm on the island. Appointments are required. The cost for a one-hour massage is an unbelievable $25. My friends and I have no complaints. Current clinic hours are Monday, Wednesday and Friday 5 p.m. to 9 p.m., Tuesday, Thursday 1 p.m. to 5 p.m. and Saturday (call for hours). There are other massage schools on Maui but I haven't tried them all; check the phone book for other listings. *1043 Makawao Avenue (upstairs). 808-572-2277.*

The Ritz-Carlton, Kapalua Spa services and a fitness center. The fitness center is complimentary for hotel guests, visiting guests are $25 per day, but the fee is waived if you purchase a 60-minute spa service. Personal training, body composition analysis, sports massage, *lomi lomi*, reflexology, oceanside massage or even in-room massage are available. *808-669-6200.*

Spa Grande Grand Wailea Resort Hotel & Spa invites non-guests to their luxurious spa for $85 (use of fitness facilities and specialty baths). Added fees for massage and extras $145 to $445 for a full-day program. Designed with Italian marble, original artwork, Venetian chandeliers, mahogany millwork and inlaid gold, this spa (Hawai'i's largest) offers two full floors of invigorating fitness, rich luxury, soothing relaxation and stimulating rejuvenation. Whether you need your rusty joints oiled and massaged, your body reshaped and freshened with a honey steam wrap, or you just want to come out with your mane washed and conditioned with the essence of Maui Mist, Spa Grande is the place to point your ruby slippers. This magical city takes you around the globe with a blend of European, Indian, Oriental and American spa philosophies and treatments, but it's the Hawaiian Regional regime that makes this spa unique. Cleanse with the Hawaiian Salt Glo Scrub, relax with the healing *lomi lomi* massage or Hawaiian Limu Rejuvenator body masque and soak in a soothing bath of seaweed or fragrant tropical enzymes. Then sit under an indoor waterfall to massage and relieve tired back muscles or refresh under an "ordinary" shower with extraordinary Honey Mango Bath Gel. The fitness center offers daily fitness classes, weight room, cardiovascular equipment and personalized instruction; there's also an aerobics studio and racquetball and squash court (the only ones on Maui). And what's the password to enter this jewel-like kingdom and enjoy such a multifaceted experience? Why,"Pamper me," of course! As soon as you arrive at the magical, underground, autonomous "city" of the "Ahhhs," you'll know you're not in Kansas anymore. *808-875-1234.*

Spa Kea Lani The spa facility at Fairmont Kea Lani Hotel, Suites & Villas in Wailea. Experience a variety of massage techniques with their Massage Combo or try a synchronized "double massage"—the ultimate in relaxing massage therapy. Refreshing body treatments, rejuvenating wraps, facials and waxing services are available individually ($70-$195) or as part of a treatment package (couples package up to $440). I have to tell you: the hot-rock massage is simply too divine for words. The technique apparently began in the Midwest, but here on Maui they use palm-size warmed beach rocks to massage the body. They also offer a special facial for teens at the spa. Or focus on fitness with a personal training session in their workout facilities. 808-875-4100 ext. 229.

Spa Moana The 9,000-square-foot, full-service oceanfront spa at the Hyatt Regency in Ka'anapali offers an exercise floor with ocean view, 11 treatment rooms, a full-service beauty salon, a relaxation lounge, sauna and steam rooms, and a spa suite for couples. Spa guests also have the option of massages, manicures and pedicures in oceanfront cabanas. A signature of the spa is its exfoliating body treatment that uses sugar, coffee and honey as well as macadamia nut oils from the island. Other treatments inspired by Hawaiian traditions include *lomi lomi* or hot stone massages and ti leaf body wraps. In addition, the spa menu offers traditional favorites like shiatsu, deep-tissue massage, Swedish massage, aromatherapy facial massage, enzyme facial peels and even couples' massage lessons. Wet treatment services include vichy showers, mud packs and "soft" scrubs like passion fruit and lime. Non-hotel guests may use the facilities for $25 a day; treatments from $65-$210. Reservations required. 808-661-1234 ext. 4500.

Seaside Salon and Day Spa This spa at the Sheraton Maui offers oceanside massages, body treatments, facials, and nail and hair care. The salon has just completed a 1,000-square-foot expansion to the 7th floor of the resort's Hale Nalu Tower. This area offers 4 massage rooms, a single shower and a double shower, as well as a terrace massage area. 808-661-0031.

SPELUNKING

★ ***Maui Cave Adventures*** All that is missing is Willie Wonka and the oompa-loompas on this cave adventure. The Scenic Walking Tour takes you to a wondrous world of lava, with oozing brown formations that look like rich, dark chocolate. The name of this region in Hana is Ka'eleku, or "standing in a dark hollow cavity." Obviously, the early Hawaiians felt that this cave was a prominent landmark in the area. Interestingly enough, however, the early history of these caves is unclear. Chuck has traversed miles of the underground passages and has yet to find any evidence of petroglyphs. He believes that during times of war the women and children may have been kept safely underground in these caverns while the men fought off attacks from neighboring island chiefs. It was also a safe haven in modern times. Chuck's backyard caves were identified as a bomb shelter during the Cold War. There is room for 14 folks, so that'll be Chuck and 13 ladies. (We had at least one lady volunteer during my cave tour.) The caves are unique and exciting. The scenic walking tour is very easy and necessitates ducking slightly in only one area. With plenty of fresh air and large caverns there isn't even a claustrophobic feeling to the tour. (The Wild Adventure Tour, however, takes you to more small caverns.) Chuck explains his quest to reach the end of the lava tube. He's explored the shore from the ocean (he's also an experienced scuba diver with a book on the subject) and has yet to find an entrance. Judging by the air flow the caves definitely go somewhere. He's managed, a rock at a time, to open up new sections of the lava tube and there is still a lifetime's worth to be explored. Chuck points out interesting lava phenomena and if you have any interest in geology you'll find it fascinating. Don't let the scattered bones around the floor concern you—at one time a huge hole to the surface was used as a dumping ground for a cattle slaughterhouse. Almost any day you have the opportunity to trek on an underground adventure. This is the only Hawaiian cave open to such an activity. The 1- to 1.25-hour Scenic Walking Tour is $29 (kids or adults); the 2- to 3-hour Wild Adventure Tour is $69 and requires a little more agility. The minimum age is 15 years. Closed-toe shoes, long pants and T-shirts are suggested. Hip packs with water and snacks are provided on their 2-hour tour. Call 8 a.m. to 8 p.m. P.O. Box 40, Hana, HI 96713. 808-248-7308; e-mail: info@mauicave.com; www.mauicave.com.

SURFING (*See also* Body Surfing)

Honolua Bay is one of the best surfing spots in Hawai'i, and undoubtedly the best on Maui, with waves up to 15 feet on a good winter day and perfect tubes. A spectacular vantage point is on the cliffs above the bay. In the summer this bay is calm and, since it is a marine reserve, offers excellent snorkeling. Also in this area is Punalau Beach (just past Honolua) and Honokeana Bay off Ka'eleki'i Point (just north of the Alaeloa residential area). In the Lahaina area there are breaks north and south of the harbor and periodically good waves at Awalua Beach (mile-marker 16). On the north shore, Ho'okipa Beach Park, Kanaha Beach and Baldwin all have good surfing at times. In the Hana area there is Hamoa Beach. There are a couple of good spots in Ma'alaea Bay and at Kalama Beach Park. Conditions change daily—even from morning to afternoon—around the island. Check with local board rental outlets for current daily conditions.

Alan Cadiz' Hawaiian Sailboarding Techniques HST goes "surf-surfari" to wherever the best place for learning happens to be that particular day. Small groups and private instruction available for beginners wanting to cruise the waves their first time out; also intermediate and advanced lessons. Longboard surfing classes ($69) are two hours, five people per class maximum, includes surfboard for beginner and intermediate lessons. *425 Koloa Street, Kahului; P.O. Box 1199 Paia, HI 96779. 800-968-5423; 808-871-5423; fax 808-871-6943.*

Goofy Foot Surf School   Ever see the old Disney cartoon where Goofy is surfing? Well, standard surfing position is left foot forward, but Goofy has his right forward. (Guess the artists weren't surfers.) The resulting term "Goofy Foot" applies to those folks who surf Goofy-style. Tim Sherer, "Board Director," guarantees you'll stand in your first two-hour lesson or the experience is on Goofy Foot. Class sizes are kept small, not more than five students. He promises to make the seemingly difficult task remarkably easy. Tim and associates begin your 2-hour introduction to surfing at the beach in front of 505 Front Street. The boards are marked with lines to help you position your feet. The first 30 minutes or so are spent learning the different body and foot positions for surfing and the transitions between. After that, it's out to the harbor, where the waves break small but are long and consistent. We discovered that surfing isn't the hard part, it's the paddling. But if they called it paddling, rather than surfing, who'd want to do it? Everyone in the class got up at least once or twice. If there are 5 or more in a class, Tim calls in for reinforcements so the classes are always very personal. Two-hour lessons (daily at 8 a.m., 11 a.m. or 2 p.m.) are $55 per person with a guarantee that you'll be able to stand and ride at least one wave or your money back. Surfboard rentals are $20 for 2 hours/$30 a day (subsequent rentals $15/$25), but if you rent during one of their scheduled classes, you'll have the added benefit of surfing under semi-supervised conditions with an instructor nearby. Private lessons are $125. The six-hour Day Camps are like "instructional beach parties" that include an extended three-hour introductory surfing lesson, lunch, discussions about surfing and its history ,with additional tips, advice and instruction to take you to the next level. Great for the kids. From $250 per person to $850 for groups of five. *Office and surf shop: 505 Front Street #123, Lahaina. 808-244-WAVE; www.goofyfootsurfschool.com.*

Nancy Emerson School of Surfing   "Learn to Surf in One Lesson." Group, private and semiprivate lessons from $75 for a two-hour clinic to $265 for the group Day Camp (breakfast and lunch included). *358 Papa Place, Suite F, Kahului, HI 96732. 808-244-SURF; e-mail: nancy@surfclinics.com; www.surfclinics.com.*

Outrageous Adventures   Learn from the Locals with their team of instructors. Three classes daily (8 a.m., 11 a.m. and 2 p.m.) with free hotel pickups available. You'll surf off the beach in Lahaina. *808-669-1400; www.youcansurf.com.*

Surf Dog Maui   Private and small groups learn surfing from their mobile surf clinic. Lessons based on wherever surf and weather conditions are the best. Lessons by appointment. Board rentals available. *Lessons at Puamana Park. 808-250-SURF; 808-242-5582; e-mail: surf dog@maui.net; www.surfdogmaui.com.*

SWIMMING

Kihei Aquatic Center The Kihei Aquatic Center is located just below the highway near Safeway. This is a community center with free use of all facilities. Open 9 a.m. to 4:30 p.m. Monday, Tuesday, Thursday, Friday and Saturday. On Wednesday they are open 10 a.m. to 4:30 p.m. and Sunday from noon to 4:30 p.m. *808-874-8137.*

Lahaina Aquatic Center On the Westside there is the Lahaina Aquatic Center above the highway at Shaw Street. No charge for use of the facility or services including water aerobics and swimming lessons. Open daily 9 a.m. to 4:30 p.m. Monday, Wednesday, Saturday; 9:30 a.m. to 4:30 p.m. Tuesday and Friday; 10 a.m. to 4:30 p.m. Thursday; 12 to 4:30 p.m. Sunday. *808-661-7611.*

TENNIS

Tennis facilities abound on Maui. Many condos and major hotels offer tennis facilities. Also, there are quite a few very well-kept public courts. They are, of course, most popular during the cooler early morning and early evening hours.

Public Courts

Hali'imaile One court by the baseball park.

Hana Hana Ball Park, one double lighted court.

Kahului Maui Community College (Ka'ahumanu and Wakea Avenue) has four unlighted courts. Kahului Community Center (Onehe'e and Uhu Street) has four lighted courts. The Kahului War Memorial Complex has four lighted courts plus a practice area, located at Ka'ahumanu and Kanaloa Avenue. *808-270-7389.*

Wailuku Wellspark has six courts, five are lighted. South Market Street and Wells Street. *808-270-7389.*

Kihei Kalama Park has four lighted courts. Six unlighted courts in park fronting Maui Sunset condos. *808-879-4364.*

Lahaina Lahaina Civic Center has five lighted courts. There are four lighted courts at Malu-ulu-olele Park. *808-661-4685.*

Makawao Eddie Tam Memorial Center has two lighted courts. *808-572-8122.*

Pukalani Pukalani Community Center has two lighted courts, located across from the Pukalani Shopping Center. *808-572-8122.*

Kula There are two lighted courts at Kula Community Center. *808-572-8122.*

Private Courts

These private courts have facilities open to the public.

Hyatt Regency, Ka'anapali   Six unlighted courts. 7 a.m. to dusk. Guest and non-guest rates. *808-661-1234 ext. 3174.*

Kapalua Bay Hotel, Kapalua   Guest and non-guest rates. The Tennis Garden has 10 courts, 4 are lighted. Tennis attire required at all times. *808-669-5677.* The Village Tennis Center also has 10 courts, 4 lighted. *808-665-0112.*

Makena Tennis Club   Two lighted courts. Guest and non-guest rates. 5415 Makena Alanui, Makena Resort. *808-879-8777.*

Maui Marriott Beach & Tennis Club   Pro shop, fitness center and tennis courts open daily from 7 a.m. to 8 p.m. Court fees $10 per person. Racquets and tennis shoes available for rent. Lessons available. Marriott tennis passes can also be used at the Royal Lahaina and Sheraton Maui. *808-661-6200.*

Royal Lahaina Tennis Ranch, Ka'anapali   The largest facility in West Maui with 11 courts, 5 lighted including 1 stadium court. Pro shop and snack bar open 8 a.m. to noon and 2 to 7 p.m. Courts available until 8:30 p.m. (See also "Maui Marriott Beach & Tennis Club" listing above.) *808-667-5200 or 808-661-3511 ext. 2296.*

Sheraton Maui Tennis Club, Ka'anapali   Three lighted courts and pro shop open daily from 8 a.m. to noon and 2 to 8 p.m. (See also "Maui Marriott Beach & Tennis Club" listing above.) *808-667-92008 or 808-661-0031 ext. 8208.*

Wailea Tennis Club, Wailea   Has 11 courts, 3 lighted. 7 a.m. to 7 p.m. Resort guests $30 per hour/day; non-guests $35 per hour/day. (Your first hour is guaranteed with your reservation and you can play anytime during the rest of the day that the courts are free.) Year-round program for "juniors." *808-879-1958.*

Resort Courts for Guests Only

Hale Kamaole, Hotel Hana-Maui, Ka'anapali Alii, Ka'anapali Plantation, Ka'anapali Royal, Ka'anapali Shores, Kahana Villa, Kamaole Sands, Kihei Akahi, Kihei Alii Kai, Kihei Bay Surf, Kuleana, Ma'alaea Surf, Mahana, Makena Surf, Maui Hill, Maui Islander Hotel, Maui Lu Resort, Maui Vista, Papakea, Puamana, Royal Kahana, Sands of Kahana, Shores of Maui, The Whaler.

THEATER, MOVIES AND THE ARTS

There is a six-plex cinema at the Ka'ahumanu Center and a four-plex in Kihei's Kukui Mall. In Lahaina, there is a tri-cinema at The Wharf Cinema Shopping Center and another set of four theaters at the Lahaina Center. The Maui Mall offers their twelve theaters with stadium seating.

The Front Street Cinemas at Lahaina Center and the Wharf Cinemas both offer a matinee rate of $5 (before 6 p.m. weekdays and before 3:30 p.m. on weekends and holidays). Senior and children rates are $4.25. The same rates and times apply for the Wallace Theater at

Maui Mall. The Kaʻahumanu Center Theaters and the Kukui Theaters are owned by Consolidated and their matinees cost $5.50 before 4 p.m. All of the theaters have all-day matinee prices on Tuesdays.

Film buffs will enjoy the **Maui Film Festival**, a weekly series of award-winning, critically acclaimed films shown every Wednesday in the state-of-the-art Castle Theater at Maui Arts & Cultural Center. Admission is $10, or purchase a passport for $35 good for five films. The festival expands to Wailea in June, offering two weeks of premiere films and entertainment under the stars during the "Celestial Cinema." In December, the premiere series becomes "First Light" and runs for two weeks over the holidays at the Maui Arts & Cultural Center. And for films particular to the Pacific/Asian culture, don't miss the **Hawaii International Film Festival** at MACC in November. *808-572-FILM.*

The Maui Arts & Cultural Center offers everything from local community events to concert performances by internationally known performers. Entertainers as diverse as Tony Bennett, Pearl Jam, Tibetan monks, the Lakota Sioux Indian Dance Theatre, Harry Belafonte, the Doobie Brothers, Santana and the Vienna Boys Choir have performed at the center. It has also featured the ballet, symphony, multicultural music and dance presentations, and art gallery exhibits. Weekly tours of the center 11 a.m. every Wednesday. *808-242-SHOW.*

Maui On Stage produces a full season of professional-quality plays and musicals, performed almost every weekend from October through June. Comedies, musicals and dramas are balanced with classic and contemporary theater. In existence since the 1920s when two theater groups (the Maui Players and Little Theatre of Maui) joined forces, they have continued in varying forms and locations (interrupted only by World War II in the '40s and a fire in the '80s) until settling into their present home at the renovated Historic Iao Theatre on Market Street in Wailuku. *808-242-6969.*

The Maui Academy of Performing Arts clearly has it all when it comes to entertainment. An educational and performing-arts organization for kids and adults, the Academy is located at the old National Dollar Store on Main Street in Wailuku. They offer community theater performances, special events, ongoing dance and drama classes, and special drama and dance workshops for kids and adults. Visitors welcome. Larger productions are currently held at the Maui Arts & Cultural Center, but they hope to have additional theater space in the Main Street building by 2004. *808-244-8760.*

The Maui Theatre presents *'Ulalena* (which means "Wind from the North"), one of the most exciting theatrical presentations on the island. Picture a Hawaiian hologram, shadow poetry, a waterfall of illusion, virtual rain showers created from pure imagination, and a liquid stage that goes from the drama of hot lava to the lilt of cool ocean waves. This is just part of the experience that is 'Ulalena. I recommend this for the discerning visitor who appreciates a little provocative thought and educational culture along with their entertainment. They provide you with a flyer upon entrance, and I highly recommend you read it before the show starts. You'll understand the experience far better. Shows are Tuesday through Saturday at 6 p.m., with an additional 8:30 show on Tuesday. Ticket prices are $48; premium seats $58; and $68 for the backstage package. Refreshments are available for purchase. *808-661-9913.*

The dinner theater **Tony 'n Tina's Wedding** takes place several nights a week at Swan Court or the Pavilion dining area at the Hyatt Regency Maui. See "Luaus and Dinner Shows" in Chapter 4 for more information. *808-661-1234; www.tonyandtinamaui.com.*

Warren & Annabelle entertain each evening with two intimate magic club shows (6 and 8 p.m.), serving close-up magic along with a menu of *pupus* and desserts. See "Luaus and Dinner Shows" in Chapter 4 for more information. *900 Front Street, Lahaina. 808-667-MAGIC.*

Looking for something a little different? Check out ★ **Moonlight Mo'olelo** (moonlight storytelling) held on the first of each month nearest the full-moon date. The presentations have proved popular with a variety of programs including Chicken Skin Stories, Fishing Tales and Hawai'i's Young Chiefs. The two-hour monthly events are held at the amphitheater at The Ritz-Carlton, Kapalua. *808-669-6200.*

WATERSKIING

Hawaii Island Watercraft, Inc. dba Ka'anapali Waterski   Located at Whalers Village on Ka'anapali Beach. Waterskiing runs $50 for 30 minutes, $100 for one hour. Also available are the aqua sled (banana boat), which runs $20 for 10 to 15 minutes, along with private coastal tours and seasonal whale watching. *Call Maui Ocean Activities, the booking agent, at 808-667-1964.*

WHALE WATCHING (*See also* Scuba Diving; Sea Excursions)

Every year beginning December 15 and continuing through May 15 (official whale season—but peak sightings are January through March), the humpback whales arrive in the warm waters off the Hawaiian islands for breeding and their own sort of vacation. The sighting of a whale can be an awesome and memorable experience with the humpbacks (small as whales go) measuring some 40 to 50 feet and weighing in at 30 tons. The panoramic vistas as you drive over the Pali and down the beachfront road to Lahaina afford some excellent opportunities to catch sight of one of these splendid marine mammals. However, *please* pull off the road and enjoy the view. Many accidents are caused by distracted drivers.

For an even closer view, there are plenty of boat trips—from large vessels to rigid-haul rafts and kayaks. Almost every boat operator does whale-watching tours in season. Many of the tour boats have a marine biologist onboard to offer insight during your whale-watching excursion.

WINDSURFING

Windsurfing is a sport that is increasing (astronomically!) in popularity. Ho'okipa Beach Park on Maui is one of the best windsurfing sites in the world. This is due to the consistently ideal wind and surf conditions; however, this is definitely *not* the spot for beginners. For the novice, boardsailing beginner group lessons run around $80 and generally involve instruction on a dry-land simulator before you get wet with easy-to-use beginners equipment. Some resorts offer their guests free clinics. Rental by the hour can get expensive so inquire about full-day rental rates. Equipment and/or lessons are available from the following.

Alan Cadiz' Hawaiian Sailboarding Techniques Alan Cadiz and his staff of professional instructors offer a full range of small group and private lessons for beginner or expert. They specialize in one-on-one instruction tailored to each person's ability, travel schedule, budget and goals. Beginning group 2.5 hours or private 1 hour $79; three-day lesson package $219, four-day $288. *425 Koloa Street, Kahului. 808-871-5423; 800-968-5423; fax 808-871-6943.*

Aloha Windsurf Vans Call them for van rentals. You can get rental equipment via Maui Windsurf Co. (see below). *22 Hana Highway; 808-893-2111.*

Al West's Maui Windsurfing Vans They offer vans with racks and hangers for boards and equipment. *180 East Wakea, Kahului. 808-877-0090; 800-870-4084.*

Hawaiian Island Surf and Sport Sales, service, rentals, instruction and travel (condo and car packages). Three-hour windsurfing group (up to 3 students), beginner lessons or advanced water start at $79 for level 1 and level 2 surfers. *415 Dairy Road, Kahului. 800-231-6958; 808-871-4981; fax 808-871-4624;* e-mail: paradise@hawaiianisland.com; www.hawaiianisland.com.

Hi-Tech Surf Sports Equipment Sales and rentals; they also have lessons. *425 Koloa, Kahului, 808-877-2111; Paia, 808-579-9297;Wind & Surf Report 808-877-3611.*

Maui Sports Unlimited Windsurfing classes $70 for 2.5 hours. Kid's (ages 6 to 12) windsurf sessions offered Saturdays (January–April) from 9 to 11 a.m. at Kanaha Beach Park; $25 fee includes coaching and equipment. Three-day Kid's Windsurfing Camps ($150) offered

Wednesday to Friday, June to August. *1001 Kauhikoa Road, Haiku. 808-575-2266; e-mail: stottie@maui.net.*

Maui Windsurfari   Vacation rental agency offering private homes, cottages and condos from $50 up. Many of their vacation rentals are unusual due to close proximity to windsurfing locations. Packages include accommodations, rental car, windsurfing equipment and excursions. *808-871-7766; 800-736-6284; e-mail: info@windsurfari.com; www.windsurfari.com.*

Second Wind   Pro shop rental as well as used and new sales. Also surfing and kite boarding. Their travel desk assists with accommodation and car rental plans. *808-877-746; 800-936-7787; e-mail: secwind@maui.net; www.maui.net/~secwind.*

CHAPTER 7

Lana'i

Lana'i Best Bets

- A round of golf at the Lodge at Koele (for non-golfers, Koele or Manele guests can enjoy a complimentary nine holes at the lodge. It is loads of fun!)
- A scuba dive to Arches with Trilogy
- An evening just sitting in the lobby of the Lodge at Koele
- A Saturday-morning trip to Lana'i City for an island-style Saturday Market
- A meal at the Lodge at Koele
- Getting a Jeep and heading off to explore the island
- Take your walking stick out of the closet (there is one in every room at the lodge) and stroll the nearby trails
- Snorkeling at Manele Bay
- A kayak/snorkel trip with Lana'i Ecoadventure
- Mountain biking
- Lunch or dinner at the affordable Café 565

The Pineapple Isle

The meaning of the name Lana'i seems to be steeped in mystery, at least this was our experience. Several guidebooks report that it means "swelling" or "hump." In discussions with local residents I was told it meant the obvious interpretation of "porch" or "balcony," perhaps because Lana'i, in a rather nebulous fashion, is the balcony of Maui. So, with no definitive answer I continue the search, but in the meantime, come enjoy this piece of paradise.

Just before and immediately following the turn of the 20th century, Lana'i was a bustling sheep-and-cattle ranch. Beginning in the

FACTS & FIGURES

A few brief island facts and figures:
- Lana'i has a population of approximately 3,000 and its major industries are tourism and agriculture.
- Dole Park in Lana'i City forms the center of the town and the other Lana'i park is Hulopo'e Beach Park.
- The island plays host to three golf courses.
- The highest peak is Lana'ihale at 3,370 feet.
- The most popular visitor attractions are Kanepu'u (Garden of the Gods), Hulopo'e Beach, Lana'ihale and Kaiolohia Bay (Shipwreck Beach).
- There are three hotels with a total of 363 rooms, a few bed-and-breakfast accommodations and no vacation condominiums.
- Lana'i has four beaches (with only one accessible via paved road), and 47 miles of shoreline that surround the 141-square-mile island.

1920s, Dole transformed Lana'i into the largest single pineapple plantation in the world. The 1990s brought Lana'i into the visitor industry with the opening of two elegant and classy resorts, the country-style Lodge at Koele in Lana'i City and the seashore resort at Manele Bay. Under the helm of David Murdock, the metamorphosis was a positive one, with young people returning to the island to work in the tourism industry. Pineapple fields are now a memory, and cattle again dot the landscape as the silver-blue fields of pineapple have faded into extinction.

While each isle has its own nickname, it appears that Lana'i has outgrown hers. "The Pineapple Isle" no longer bears much symbolism for an island that has transformed from an agricultural setting to "an oasis within an oasis" for the lucky tourist. In the past it had been a wonderful retreat and happily much of what was good about Lana'i has not changed. The slow pace of the isle has not been as significantly altered by the arrival of the mega-resort as one might imagine. What new term of endearment will be vested upon the isle? The Isle of Relaxation? Pine Isle? The Island Less Traveled? The Isle of Enchantment? Hawai'i's Most Secluded Island? Time will tell, or perhaps the tourist bureau will. With the continuing construction of luxury homes in the Koele district on 68 acres, and plans for 350 homes at Manele, the rich and famous will very shortly (if not already) be anteing up to purchase a vacation home on Lana'i. As with each Hawaiian island, Lana'i is unique. The price for a stay at the two resorts may be steep, but if you want to really indulge, read on. A truly luxurious and relaxing island getaway that is only eight miles (but in many ways, 30 years removed) from Maui, Lana'i will simply enchant you. If you'd like a glimpse of Lana'i via cyberspace, visit www.lanai-resorts.com.

History

The historical tales of the island of Lana'i are intriguing, filled with darkness and evil. As legend has it, in ancient times the island of Lana'i was uninhabited except for evil spirits. It is said that in the olden days, those who went to Lana'i never returned and that the island was *kapu* (taboo). Hawaiians banished wrong-doers to Lana'i as punishment for their crimes. The story continues that around the 16th century on West Maui there was a chief named Kaka'alanaeo. He had a son named Kaulula'au who was willful and spoiled. The people became furious with his many misdeeds and finally rebelled and demanded that Kaulula'au be put on trial by the ancient laws. The verdict was guilty and, according to the ancient laws, his punishment was death. His father begged for his life and it was agreed that Kaulula'au would be banished to the island of Lana'i. He was set ashore near the Maunalei Gulch, the only source of potable water on the island. His father promised him that if he could banish the evil spirits from Lana'i, he could then set a bonfire as a signal and his father and the warriors would return for him. And, as luck would have it, Kaulula'au managed to trick the evil spirits and send them over to Kaho'olawe. He signaled his father and returned to Maui, heralded as a hero.

During the 16th and 17th centuries, Maui was reaching its population zenith and Hawaiians relocated to Lana'i with settlements near Keomuku and inland as well. The first archaeological studies of Lana'i were done in 1921 by Kenneth Emory from the anthropology department of the Bishop Museum. He published his work in 1923. Emory found many ancient villages and artifacts that had been, for the most part, undisturbed for hundreds of years. He found the area of Kaunolu to be Lana'i's richest archaeological region, filled with house sites and remnants of a successful fishing village. Ashes from old fires at the village sites were analyzed. The findings showed that the ashes dated from 900 A.D., much later than the other islands, which were inhabited as early as 40 or 50 B.C. He also ventured to the eastern coastline and explored Naha and Keomuku. He noted 11 *heiaus*, found relics including old stone game boards, and discovered a network of trails and petroglyphs. One of the earliest *heiaus*, the Halulu Heiau, is in the Kaunolu area, and it is thought that this region may have been one of the earliest Hawaiian settlements.

> Be sure you take time to view the beautiful, large murals on either side of the entrance at the Manele Bay Hotel. One depicts Kaulula'au, the fallen son being taken by canoe to Lana'i. The other shows Kaulula'au, head held high in victory, standing over his signal bonfire.

While the Hawaiian population increased throughout the archipelago, Lana'i was left largely uninhabited until the 1500s. In the late 1700s, two of Captain Cook's ships, the *Discovery* and the *Resolution*, reported a visit to Lana'i. They found the Hawaiians friendly along the windward coastal area where they replenished their supplies of food and water. In talking with the islanders, they estimated that the population was approximately 10,000. They observed and noted that the island was a dry dustbowl and that the people fished and grew some taro. It was about at this same time chiefs of Maui became worried that the people on Lana'i might become too powerful. So they divided Lana'i into 13 *ohanas* (*ohana* means family, but this refers more to regions) and put a *konahiki* in charge of each. This insured that no one chief would be too powerful. These district names are still used today: Kaa, Paomai, Mahana, Maunalei, Kamoku, Kaunolu, Kalulu, Kealiakapu, Kealiaaupuni, Palawai, Kamao, Pawili and Kaohai.

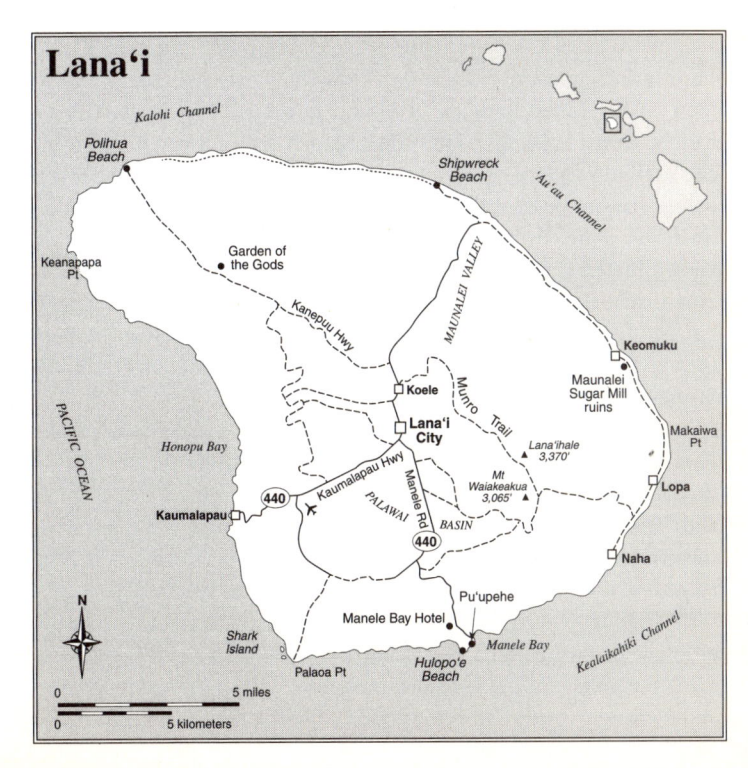

Six months after the island was visited by Cook's vessels a tragic event happened that would change life on Lana'i forever. Interisland battles among the island chiefs were not uncommon, but until this time Lana'i had remained unaffected. In 1778 Kalaniopu'u, the chief on the Big Island, launched an unsuccessful attack on Lahaina, Maui. He retreated, then turned and attacked central Maui. Here again his warriors were overcome. As they returned to the Big Island in great anger he passed the island of Kahoʻolawe, which was loyal to the Maui chieftains. In retaliation, Kalaniopuʻuʻs warriors massacred the entire population on Kahoʻolawe. Bolstered by his victory, Kalaniopuʻu turned once again to assault Lahaina and again was defeated. Now enraged, Kalaniopuʻu and his warriors chose to strike the leeward coastal villages of Lanaʻi. Lanaʻiʻs warriors were unprepared and retreated to the Hoʻokia Ridge, a better location from which to launch their counterattack. However, without access to food and water, the Lanaʻi warriors soon weakened and Kalanaiopuʻu moved quickly to crush them. The Big Island warriors continued their path of destruction around Lanaʻi and systematically destroyed all the villages. Kalaniopuʻu returned to the Big Island of Hawaiʻi and there, seven months later, died. His lieutenant, Kamehameha, came to rule.

During the rule of Kamehameha the population of Lanaʻi once again increased. King Kamehameha and his warriors visited Kaunolu Bay on Lanaʻiʻs southwestern coastline. Here Kahekili, a brave warrior, is said to have leapt from a cliff above the sea into the Pacific waters, proving his loyalty to the king. Other warriors were then challenged to follow his example. (The area continues to be referred to as Kahekiliʻs Leap.)

The elders from the Church of Jesus Christ of Latter-day Saints acquired land on Lanaʻi from one of the chiefs in 1855. In 1860 Walter Murray Gibson came to Lanaʻi with the intent of establishing a Mormon colony called the City of Joseph in the Palawai basin. Gibson had been instrumental in assisting Kamehameha. He served on his cabinet and was among the advisors for the construction of the Iolani Palace. He purchased 20,000 acres of land on Lanaʻi and obtained leases on more. By 1863 there were about 600 Mormons living on Lanaʻi. In 1864, when the church elders arrived to visit they discovered that Walter had purchased additional lands with church money, but had listed ownership under his own name, and he wasn't willing to release them. He was quickly expelled from the church and the Mormons went on to develop their church on Oʻahu.

As owner of 26,000 acres, Gibson first established the Lanaʻi Sheep Ranch, which later became the Lanaʻi Ranch. In 1867 the population was 394 people (the 600 Mormons had departed earlier), 18,000 goats and 10,000 sheep. In 1870 Gibson attempted a cooperative farm, but this operation soon proved unsuccessful. By 1875 Gibson controlled 90 percent of the island for ranching or farming operations. In 1874, Gibson's daughter, Talula, married Frederick Harrison Hayselden, formerly of England and Australia, and by the early 1880s Hayselden was managing the ranch. Walter Gibson passed away in San Francisco in 1888 and ownership of the land transferred to his daughter and son-in-law.

In 1894 the Lana'i Ranch ran 40,000 sheep, 200 horses and 600 head of cattle in addition to large herds of goats, hogs and wild turkeys. By 1898 the ranch was in debt, but the sugar industry looked promising. The Hayseldens established the Maunalei Sugar Company on the island's windward coast. They began by building three wells and a wharf at Kahalepalaoa for shipment of the cane to Olowalu on Maui for grinding. A railroad was also built between the wharf and Keomuku, along with a two-story building, a store, a boarding house, camp houses and barracks.

In 1802, a Chinese entrepreneur spent one season attempting sugar cultivation in Naha from wild sugar cane. The Maunalei Sugar Company in nearby Keomuku did little better, lasting only a little more than two years. The Hayseldens constructed a six-mile train track for transporting their sugar cane. However, they failed to respect the local culture and custom. Stones from an ancient *heiau* were used to build part of the railroad bed and then the disasters began. Their Japanese workers fell sick and many died. The ever-important supply of drinking water went brackish and rain did not fall. Company records show the closure was due to lack of labor and water. The local population knew otherwise. Fred and Talula Hayselden soon left Lana'i.

In 1902 Charles Gay (a member of the Robinson family from Ni'ihau) and George Munro visited the island and Gay acquired the island at public auction for $108,000. He enlarged his holdings further through various land leases. Gay began making major improvements and brought cattle from Kaua'i and Ni'ihau to his new ranch on Lana'i. In 1903 Gay purchased the remaining holdings from the Hayseldens and through land leases and other avenues became the sole owner of the entire island. By 1909 financial difficulties forced Charles Gay to lose all but 600 acres of his farmland. On the remaining acres he planted pineapples and operated a piggery while moving his family from Koele to Keomuku. In 1909 a group of businessmen that included Robert Shingle, Cecil Brown and Frank Thompson purchased most of the island from Charles Gay for $375,000 and formed the Lana'i Ranch Company. At that time there were 22,500 sheep, 250 head of cattle and 150 horses. They changed the emphasis from sheep to cattle and spent $200,000 on ranch improvements. However, because the large herds were allowed to graze the entire island, destroying what vegetation was available, the cattle in-

The building in the middle of Dole Park was once a bowling alley, pool hall and restaurant until the late 1970s, when it was made into a meeting hall. As a part of the development of Lana'i, David Murdock had a large new community center built, complete with swimming pool. It's located a block away from the park.

dustry soon floundered. The island population had dwindled to only 102 at the turn of the 20th century, with 50 people living in Koele (which, by the way, means "farming") and the rest residing along the windward coastline in Keomuku. There were only 13 men to work the entire cattle ranch, an insufficient number to manage the 40,000 head of beef on land which was overgrazed by the cattle, pigs and goats that roamed freely.

George Munro, a New Zealander by birth who had visited the island in 1902, was asked to return to Lana'i by the new owners to manage the ranch. Soon after arrival he began instituting much-needed changes. He ordered sections of the range fenced and restricted the cattle to certain areas, allowing other areas to re-grow. He also ordered the wild pigs and goats to be rounded up and destroyed. In 1911 a large three-million-gallon stormwater reservoir—now a beautiful reflecting pond—was built. In 1912 an effort to destroy the goat population began in earnest. The first year 5,000 goats were killed and an additional 3,300 more were destroyed by 1916. (It wasn't until the 1940s, however, that the last pigs and goats were captured.) In addition, sheep dogs were introduced to assist the cowboys.

> Today, as in the days of Munro, there is only one Norfolk pine tree on the island. The tree, planted in 1875 by Frederick Hayselden, is the same one that stood outside Munro's home and has become a noted Lana'i landmark. It remains a stately sight right outside the Lodge at Koele.

Water continued to be a major concern. An amateur naturalist, Munro noted that the Norfolk pine tree outside his home seemed to capture the mist that traveled past the island. From that pine an idea was born, and Munro ordered the *paniolos* to carry a bag of Cook Island Pine seeds with them. They poked a small hole in the sack and, as they traveled the island on horseback, left a trail of seeds. The result is an island of more pines than palms. In 1914 the automobile age arrived on Lana'i in the form of a single 1910 Model T owned by George Munro. By 1917 there were 4,000 head of cattle and 2,600 sheep, but profits were slim and the Lana'i Ranch Company sold its land to the Baldwin family for $588,000. George Munro remained as foreman and the ranch slowly became more profitable. In 1920, axis deer were introduced on Lana'i from Moloka'i and a pipeline was constructed from Maunalei Gulch to provide fresh water.

James Dole came to Lana'i, liked what he saw and purchased the island in 1922 for $1.1 million from Alexander & Baldwin. George Munro was retained as manager. The Kaumalapua Harbor was dredged and a breakwater constructed in preparation for shipment of pineapple to O'ahu for processing. Lana'i developed into the single largest pineapple plantation in the world, which produced 90 percent of the United States' total pineapples. The company was called Hawaiian Pineapple Company until 1960, when the name was changed to the Dole Corporation. (Today it is called the Dole Company Foods.) Castle & Cooke acquired one-third ownership in the Hawaiian Pineapple Company soon after its purchase by Dole.

The community of Lana'i City also began in the 1920s. The houses were very small because families were discouraged. The workers arrived from Japan, Korea and the Philippines. The last residents left the Palawai and moved to Lana'i City between 1917 and 1929. The population of Lana'i soared to 3,000 by 1930. In 1923 Dole realized the need to provide a center for entertaining island guests and had "The Clubhouse" constructed. (Today it is known as Hotel Lana'i.) The dining room provided meals for guests as well as for the nurses and patients from the plantation hospital. Also constructed in the center of town was Dole Park. In the 1950s larger homes, located below Fraser Avenue, were built to accommodate the workers and their families, and employees were given the option of purchasing their homes fee simple. Today less than 100 Lana'ians are part- or full-blooded Hawaiian.

An excellent account of the history of the island is *True Stories of the Island of Lana'i* by Lawrence Kainoahou Gay, the son of Charles Gay. First published in 1965 and reprinted in 1981 it is available for $12 at the resort gift shops on Lana'i.

Geography and Climate

Lana'i is the sixth largest of the eight major Hawaiian islands. It is situated eight miles west of Maui and seven miles south of Moloka'i. It is likely that millions of years ago (when the glaciers were larger and the seas much lower), Maui, Lana'i, Moloka'i and Kaho'olawe comprised one enormous island. This is further substantiated by the fact that the channels between the islands are more shallow and the slopes of the islands visibly more gradual than on the outer coastlines of the islands.

The island of Lana'i was formed by a single shield volcano. A ridge runs along the eastern half of the island and forms its most notable feature. This large, raised hump is dotted with majestic Cook Island pines. The summit of the island is Lana'ihale, located at an elevation of 3,370 feet. A rather strenuous hike along the Munro Trail provides access to this summit, where you will be treated to the only location in Hawai'i where you can view (on a clear day) five other Hawaiian islands.

> The word *manele* means "soap berry plant" or is the word used for a hand-carried chair, a "sedan." The Manele boat harbor was once a small black-sand beach and a fishing shrine found here indicates it was used by the early Hawaiians. You can spot the old *pepe* (cattle) ramp that Charles Gay used for loading his steers onto freighters.
>
> In the 1970s E.E. Black was contracted to build the breakwater. It is traditional for any new project in Hawai'i to be blessed at the onset, but E.E. Black chose to forego the blessing. After only 20 feet of breakwater were constructed, the huge crane fell into the ocean and the people then refused to work. After great effort, another crane was brought over to lift the first from the ocean, but by the time it was recovered, the saltwater had taken its toll and it was worthless. Before resuming construction, E.E. Black held a blessing ceremony, the people returned to work, and the breakwater was completed without further incident.

Maunalei and Hauola are Lana'i's two deepest gulches. Today the Maunalei Gulch continues to supply the island with its water. The center of the island, once a caldera, is the Palawai basin, which has been used as both farm and ranch land. Lana'i has one city, cleverly dubbed Lana'i City. Located at an elevation of about 1,700 feet, it can be much cooler—and wetter—than the coastline. It is the hub of the island, or what hub there is, and visitors soon learn that all roads lead to Lana'i City, where almost everyone resides. The houses are generally small, mostly roofed with tin, and the yards are abloom with fruits and flowers.

Rainfall along the coastline is limited to only 4 or 5 inches a year. The heart of the island and Lana'i City, however, may have rainfall of 20 inches or more, and the higher slopes receive 45 to 60 inches annually. The weather in Lana'i City might range from 80-degree days in September (with lows in the mid-60s) to cooler low-70s temperatures in January, dropping an additional 10 degrees at night. The coastline can be warmer by 10 degrees or more.

Pineapples and pines, not palms, were the predominant vegetation on the island. At its peak in the 1970s, there were 15,000 acres of pineapple in cultivation. Castle & Cook made the decision in the 1980s to diversify the island and enter the tourist industry in a big way. The pineapple fields have been reduced to only about 120 acres, just enough for local consumption. The production of hay and alfalfa is underway, and some fields are spotted with Black Angus cattle. Other acreage has been converted to an organic garden for use by the Manele and Koele restaurants.

The island flower is very unusual. The kaunaoa is more a vine in appearance than a flower and there are two varieties. One grows in the uplands and the other near the ocean. The ocean species has a softer vine with more vivid hues of yellow and orange than its mountainous counterpart. Strands of the vine are twisted and adorned with local greens and flowers to make beautiful and unusual leis. The mountain vines make a stiffer lei and, I was told, are used as leis for decorating animals. One of the best places to spot this plant is along the drive down to Keomuku and Shipwreck Beach or along the shoreline.

You will note that it is a very arid island. Water supply has always been a problem and most of the greenery is supplied by the Cook Island pines that dot the landscape.

Island Ecology

You'll notice very quickly that there are many birds on Lana'i, a far greater number than on Maui. Fortunately for the birds, Lana'i does not have the mongoose as a predator. Wild turkeys, the last non-native animal to be introduced to Lana'i, are hunted in early November for about two weeks. They are easily spotted, but we understand that as soon as the 1st of November appears (the turkeys must have calendars) they disappear until after Thanksgiving. These wild birds look very lean and don't appear to make a very succulent Thanksgiving dinner. The easiest place to spot them is down near the Manele boat harbor, where a group of turkeys and a pack of wild cats together enjoy the leftovers from the *Trilogy* boat's daily picnics.

Pheasant are also hunted seasonally. Wild goats were rounded up and captured years ago. The only island pigs are in the piggery, where they are raised for island consumption. Pronghorn antelope, introduced in 1959, have now been hunted to extinction. Twelve axis deer were introduced by George Munro and have adapted well to Lana'i. It is estimated that there are some 3,000 to 6,000 animals and, given the fact that they produce offspring twice yearly, the number is ever-growing. In fact, deer far outnumber Lana'i's human population. The deer run a mere 110 to 160 pounds and are hunted almost year-round. It is easiest to spot these lean, quick deer in the early mornings or late evenings bounding across fields; during the day they seek sheltered, shaded areas. There are still a few remaining mouflon sheep, which have distinctive and beautiful curved horns. You'll note many of the houses in Lana'i City are decorated with arrays of horns and antlers across their porch or on a garage wall.

Traveling with Children

Kids of any age will love Lana'i. There are plenty of activities from beach-going to horseback riding. Older kids can take a sea kayak trip, hike, golf, or try their hand at archery or shooting at the sporting clay facility.

There are many activities your child can enjoy on Lana'i. A Pilialoha staff member can accompany your child during any of the following activities for an additional $20 fee. Activities include tennis lessons, half- or full-hour for youths 12 and younger; golf lessons at the Challenge of Manele (private or semi-private). Children 5 and up can enjoy a pony ride ($10), children 9 and up are invited on the one-hour Plantation horseback excursion ($35), and youth 12 and up can have private horseback riding lessons or take the two-hour Paniolo ride. A five-hour excursion on *Trilogy* is offered for $42.50 (ages 11 and younger), $85 (12 and older). Spinning Dolphin Fishing Charter has half-day excursions for children 12 and up, $85. Scuba and snorkeling lessons at the Manele Bay Pool for those 8 years and up. Hiking, biking and sporting clays activities also available.

The Manele Bay Hotel and the Lodge at Koele offer the **Pilialoha Adventure Program** for youth 5 to 12 years. (*Pilialoha* means close friendship and beloved companionship.) The program believes in a multi-age approach where older and younger children share, interact and have fun. Group sizes are small, allowing close attention to the interest of each child. They require a minimum of two children to operate the day and night programs and require 24-hour advance reservations. In the event your child must arrive earlier or depart later than the session, a fee of $10 per child per half-hour will be charged. The half-day, full-day or evening (Tuesday and Friday) programs are full of great adventures: full-day program (9 a.m. to 3 p.m.) $60, morning session (9 a.m. to 12:30 p.m.) $40, afternoon session (11:30 a.m. to 3 p.m.) $40, evening session (5 p.m. to 10 p.m.) $55. Daily activities vary, but might include a chance to meet the horses and ride ponies, play tennis, trek through the Manele Bay Gardens in search of fish, creeping crawlers and waterfalls, or build a volcano at Hulopo'e Beach.

Babysitting is available for $12 per hour with each additional child at $7 per hour and a three-hour minimum. Also available for parents are baby joggers, umbrella strollers, cribs, childproofing of guest rooms, car seats and playpens.

Weddings & Honeymoons

Lana'i may well be one of the most romantic places on earth. A Lana'i wedding can be arranged through the resorts. The various wedding packages includes a garden setting at Manele Bay Hotel or a gazebo at the Lodge at Koele, minister, bouquet, bridal leis and much more. Or you can choose your special wedding day à la carte. Specialized wedding packages start at $4,200. Contact Dena Galiza at Castle & Cooke Resorts Wedding Services. 808-565-2426.

Getting There

To reach Lana'i you may travel by air or sea. The Lana'i Airport is serviced by **Island Air** and **Hawaiian Airlines** (see "Transportation" in Chapter 1). Airfare can run $79 to $140 one way from O'ahu or Maui to Lana'i when you use one of their Bank of Hawaii ATM machines to buy your ticket.

By boat you can travel a cool and comfortable 45 minutes from the Lahaina harbor aboard **Expeditions**. For a $25 one-way ticket (children $20), you can have a scenic tour spotting dolphins, flying fish and whales during the winter season. It is a pleasant way to travel, and much more affordable for a family than air transportation. The boat travels round-trip five times daily to Manele Small Boat Harbor, where a shuttle van will pick you up for transport to the Manele Bay Hotel and from there up to the Lodge at Koele. Reservations are advised as space is limited. They can also arrange a

On your return, you'll be happy to know that Lana'i Airport has a federal agricultural inspection station so you can check your luggage directly through to the mainland.

leisurely overnight stay, golf, jeep or guided-tour package. Overnight parking is provided in Lahaina. 808-661-3756; www.go-lanai.com.

Getting Around

Lana'i City Services offers scheduled transportation from the Manele Small Boat Harbor for a $10 fee each way to Koele and $5 to Manele. They shuttle between the dock and Manele Bay Resort, the Lodge at Koele, either golf course, and Lana'i City. (If you are a daytripper or don't have much luggage, you can walk from the harbor to Manele Bay Resort and catch the free resort shuttle up to Koele.)

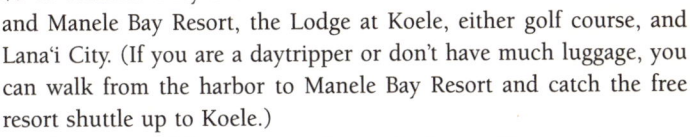

For guests of the resorts or those who have golf reservations, you can then take the complimentary shuttle every hour between Manele Bay Hotel and the Lodge at Koele; in the evenings and on weekends the schedule increases to every half hour.

For further independent exploration of the island check with **Dollar Rental Car**. Compact $59.99, midsize $79.99, mini-van $129, Jeep Wrangler $129. Rented on a 24-hour basis. (Major car repairs require that the unit be transferred by barge to Honolulu, hence the inflated rates.) The rental car company notes that given the unique terrain of the island, they are not able to obtain (and therefore cannot provide) insurance of any kind on rental vehicles. Renters take full responsibility for the vehicle, whether it is damaged by the renter or a second or third party. 800-JEEP-808.

Rabaca's Limousine Service offers hourly charter rates as well as airport transfers. Neal Rabaca provides 24-hour limousine service in his seven-passenger Mercury Grand Marquis. Call for hourly rates. Island tours are also available. P.O. Box 304, Lanai City, HI 96763. 808-565-6670; fax 808-565-6670; e-mail: rabaca@aloha.net.

Lana'i Ecoadventure Centre rents on- and offroad vehicles. All come with "fat" offroad mud tires, roof rack, towels, masks, fins, snorkel, ice chest and island map. A Jeep 4x4 for four persons is $104 daily. Suburban for 9 people is $129. 808-565-7373; www.adventurelanai.com.

What to See, Where to Shop

There are only three paved roads on Lana'i outside of Lana'i City, no stop lights and very few street signs once you leave town. After driving around on even a dry day, we assure you that they aren't kidding when they recommend a four-wheel drive. On rainy days, you can be fairly certain you'll get stuck in the mud and muck.

You can pretty much see all of Lana'i in a long day, but if you want to slow down, do some hiking or simply sit in the sun on a quiet beach, there is plenty to occupy you for days. Either of the resorts can provide you with a map and advice.

If you rent a car, you'll be limited to the paved roads on the island. A four-wheel-drive vehicle will get you out to more sights, as long as the roads are open. Be sure to bring along a picnic, and definitely some water. The car rental company will close roads that are impassable. You can check out the Dollar "accident" book and see why you need a four-wheel drive. The roads are a little better marked now than they were the first time I toured the island. The first part of the road to the Garden of the Gods was through pastures and rains had left it seriously rutted. A second road next to the first was only slightly less bumpy. (Kidney buster is what they called it at the car rental agency, and for good reason.) A lovely stand of ironwoods with pale green needles covering the ground almost looked like a recent snowfall. It now takes less than 30 minutes to travel east and reach the Garden of the Gods. Just before you reach the Garden you'll note a pullout to your right. This **self-guided trail** was installed by the Nature Conservancy. The five-minute walk takes you on a visual exploration of the plants which have been introduced over the past centuries that are threatening the native species. They hope to expand the trail to include an area with more native plants.

The **Garden of the Gods**, which was named in 1935, is perhaps viewed best in the early morning or late evening when the shadows cast bizarre light on this lunar-like and rather mystical place. In the early morning, on a clear day, you can see the faint outline of Honolulu's skyscrapers and a sharp eye can observe axis deer out foraging. The rays of the sun in the early evening cast strange shadows on the amber-baked earth and huge monolithic rocks and your imagination can do the rest as the wind whistles over the landscape and you hear the distant call of a bird. Interestingly enough here, in what seems to be the middle of nowhere, are street signs. One indicates Awalua Road, which is a very rugged and steep dirt path down to the ocean. Most of these roads are used by the local residents for fishing or hunting. Be advised, if you attempt to start down, there may be no place to turn around should you change your mind. Follow Polihua Road and you'll arrive at a stretch of white sandy beach with rolling sand dunes.

According to Lawrence Kainoahou Gay, in his account entitled "True Stories of the Island of Lana'i," *Polihua* means *poli* (cover or bay) and *hua* (eggs). He reported that in this area turtles would visit to lay their eggs above the high water mark. He had seen turtles, in days gone by, that were large enough to carry three people! This beach is not recommended for swimming or other water activities.

The Kaena Road winds down to a very isolated area called **Kaena Iki Point**, which is the site of one of Lana'i's largest *heiaus*.

Shipwreck Beach, or Kaiolohia, on Lana'i's northeast coast, is about a half-hour drive along a paved road from the Lodge at Koele. The road is lined with scrub brush, and as you begin the descent to the shoreline you catch a glimpse of the World War II liberty ship. Be sure to keep an eye out for pheasant, deer, turkeys and small Franklin partridges.

At the bottom of the road you can choose to go left to Shipwreck Beach or continue straight and follow the coastline on the unpaved, dusty and very rugged **Awalua Road** to the now defunct Club Lana'i. Club Lana'i was a day resort that shuttled visitors from Lahaina, Maui, to the leeward shores of Lana'i for a day of relaxation and recreation— sort of a Hawaiian version of Gilligan's Island. It's a bit of a drive and slow-going getting there; four-wheel-drive vehicles are advised. It is about five miles down the road to **Keomuku**, where there are still remnants of the failed Maunalei Sugar Company, and a Japanese cemetery, also a memento of the failed sugar company. The old **Kalanakila Church** (aka Malamalama Church), located near Keomuku, is in the process of being renovated.

The beaches along this coastline are wonderful for sunbathing or picnicking, but not advisable for swimming. If you keep driving south, you'll run into **Lopa** and **Naha**, two uninhabited old villages. There are also some ancient Hawaiian trails at Naha. The road ends at Naha and you'll have to drive back along the same route.

If you're headed for Shipwreck Beach, drive northwest. This is **Lapahiki Road**, and while dry and bumpy during our drive it could be impassable even in a four-wheel-drive vehicle during heavy rains. If you have a regular rental car, you can park here and walk down the road to the beach, but it is a bit of a trek. The dirt road is lined by *kiawe* trees and deserted shacks. This is a getaway spot for the local residents, although there is no fresh water. The reef along **Kaiolohia Beach** is very wide, but the surf can be high and treacherous.

There is a remnant of an old lighthouse and also some old petroglyph sites near Shipwreck Beach. The concierge desk can give you a list of petroglyphs around the island. Please respect these sights. The beach is unsafe for swimming, but you might see some people shorefishing. Sometimes after storms, interesting shells, old bottles and assorted artifacts are washed up along the shoreline.

SHIPWRECKS AND GROUNDINGS

During a storm, waves come crashing down over the liberty ship that sits beached on the reef. This was one of three Navy L.C.M. ships that were not shipwrecked but purposely grounded here in 1941 and 1942. The other two have disappeared after losing their battle with the ocean. Barges are also towed here, anchored and left to rot. The channel between here and Moloka'i is called *Kolohi*, which means mischievous and unpredictable. The channel between Lana'i and Maui is the *'Au'au* ("to bathe") channel. There were several other ships that were wrecked here or on other parts of the island. In the 1820s the British ship *Alderman Wood* went aground and in 1826 the American ship *London* was wrecked off Lana'i. In 1931, George A. Crozier's *Charlotte C.* foundered somewhere along the beach. A 34-foot yawl called *Tradewind* was wrecked off the mouth of the Maunalei Valley on August 6, 1834, while cruising from Honolulu to Lahaina.

Pohaku'O, which roughly translates to mean "rock," is located in the Mahana region on Lana'i's leeward side. The rocks here resemble tombstones and were avoided by the early Hawaiians as a place of evil. If the breezes are favorable, the wind blowing by the rock creates an "O" sound that changes with the wind, which is the reason this rock received its evil connotations.

For another adventure, leave Lana'i City and follow Kaumalapau Highway past the small airport and continue on another five minutes toward **Kaumalapau Harbor**. It's paved all the way. The harbor isn't much to see, but the drive down to the water shows the dramatically different landscape of Lana'i's windward coastline. Here you can see the sharply cut rocky shoreline that drops steeply into the ocean, in some places more than 1,500 feet.

Kaunolu Bay can be accessed from the Kaumalapau Highway along a very rugged road. Follow the road just a bit farther and you'll reach Kaumalapau Harbor.

Hulopo'e Beach, along a crescent of white sandy beach, is a splendid marine reserve. It is in front of the Manele resort and Lana'i's best swimming beach. As with all beaches, be aware of surf conditions. There are attendants at the beach kiosk who can provide beach safety information. Although netting and spearfishing are not allowed, shorefishing is permitted. The best snorkeling is in the morning before the surf picks up. Across the bay from the Manele Bay Hotel are a series of tidal pools. When the tide drifts down, sea creatures emerge, making this a great spot for exploration.

The Lodge at Koele and Manele Bay Hotel offer a handy *Tide Pool Guide*, prepared by Kathleen Kapalka. It notes that the Hulopo'e Bay and tidepool areas are both part of a marine-life conservation district that was set up in 1976. Also included in the conservation district are Manele Bay and Pu'upehe Cove, and as such, all animals and plants (dead or alive) are protected from collection or harm. The color brochure is an easy-to-follow guide to these wonderful tidal areas. Mollusks, arthropods, marine vertebrates, annelids, echinoderms, marine invertebrates and marine plants are described and illustrated. Safety and conservation tips include the fact that suntanning oils are detrimental and should be cleansed from the hands before reaching into the pools. This is an excellent brochure, which will make your tidal pool adventure a valuable learning experience. *Note*: Reef shoes are available at the hotel's beach kiosk for resort guests, a recommended protection when prowling around the rocky shoreline.

Climb up the bluff above the beach and you will be rewarded with a great view of Maui and Kaho'olawe. A large monolithic rock sits off the bluff. This is **Pu'upehe** (often referred to as Sweetheart Rock), which carries a poignant local legend. As with most oral history, legends tend to take on the special character of the storyteller. Such is the story of Pu'upehe. We asked people about the legend and heard different versions. One made the hero into a jealous lover, the other a thoughtful one. So here is our interpretation. There was a strong handsome young Hawaiian man whose true love was a beautiful Hawaiian woman. They made a sea cave near Pu'upehe rock their lover's retreat. One day the man journeyed inland to replenish their supplies, leaving his love in the sea cave. He had gone some distance when he sensed an impending storm. He hurriedly returned to the sea cave, but the storm preceded him and his love had drowned in the cave. He was devastated. Using superhuman strength he carried her to the top of the monolithic rock called Pu'upehe and buried her there before jumping to his death. Whether there is truth to this legend is uncertain, but some years back a scientist did scale the top of the peak, which was no easy task, to investigate. No bones or other evidence were found. However, we were told that in ancient times, the bones were removed and hidden away. And so ends this sad tale of lost love.

Manele Bay is a quaint boat port that offers excellent snorkeling just beyond the breakwater. When the surf at Hulopo'e is too strong, Lana'i tour boats often anchor here for snorkeling.

Gifts with Aloha, owned and operated by Kim and Phoenix Dupree, offers jewelry, *koa* products, quilts, candles and books as well as clothing and footwear. They feature *raku* pieces, ceramic ornaments, fusible glass, handmade beads and island wood creations made by Lana'i artists and crafts people. Open Monday to Saturday, 9:30 a.m. to 6 p.m. 808-565-6589.

Local Gentry is located behind Gifts with Aloha and offers some great clothes as well as swimsuits and even shoes.

Just like the big city you can stop by Coffee Works for a cup of java, and combine local shopping with local dining on Saturday mornings at Dole Park. Beginning around 8 a.m. local residents set up shop at long tables with hot plates. I visited Magdelena's booth and sampled some *ono* Filipino cuisine. She and her daughter both work at Richard's grocery store, too. The vendors stay all day—that is, unless they sell out and call it quits early. Stop by and talk story! The folks on Lana'i are all warm and welcoming. (Plate lunches in general run about $6.)

The **Lodge at Koele** and the **Manele Bay Hotel** both have small sundry gift shops. You can arrange for a day of shopping in Lahaina town from Manele Harbor aboard Expeditions. Cost is $25 per person one way.

Where to Stay

There are currently three choices for hotel accommodations: Lana'i's original Hotel Lana'i, and two luxury hotels, Manele Bay Hotel and the Lodge at Koele.

CAMPING ON LANA'I

Tent camping is available at **Hulopo'e Bay Beach Park**, which has six sites. Permits are issued by the administrative office of the Castle & Cooke Resorts company. They can be reached at 808-565-3982. The cost is $5 for the permit and $5 per day per person, with a maximum stay of three nights. Advanced reservations are encouraged.

PRIVATE HOMES

Kay Okamoto of **Okamoto Realty** offers single family homes in Lana'i City for short-term vacation rentals. 808-565-7519.

BED AND BREAKFASTS

Lana'i Plantation Home
1168 Lana'i Avenue. 800-566-6961; www.dreamscometruelanai.com.
Michael and Susan Hunter operate this B&B, also known as "Dreams Come True." The Plantation Home offers four rooms, each with a private bathroom embellished in fine Italian marble, with whirlpool tubs and ventilation skylights. Three of the bedrooms have queen beds and the other consists of two single beds. All come with hardwood floors, a built-in chest of drawers, reading lights and other amenities. A full kitchen and laundry room is also available. Primarily a B&B, the entire house can be rented and weekly rates are available. It will sleep up to ten people with two additional couch beds in the living room. B&B rates per night are $98.50 plus 11.4 percent tax and includes an island breakfast for two. Call for rate information if you're interested in renting the entire house. Also ask Susan or Michael about Lana'i adventure packages.

HOTELS AND RESORTS

Hotel Lana'i
828 Lanai Avenue (P.O. Box 630520, Lana'i City, HI 96763). 808-565-7211; 800-795-7211; fax 808-565-6450 from 7 a.m. to 8 p.m Hawaiian time; www.hotellanai.com; e-mail: hotellanai@wave.hicv.net.

Hotel Lana'i was built in 1923 by James D. Dole as a retreat for Dole Company executives and other important guests. Before the opening of the luxury resorts, this ten-room hotel had the only accommodations on the island. You'll still find it quiet and comfortable, with rooms located in two wings of the original building and connected by a glass-enclosed veranda. All rooms have private tiled bathroom facilities, with pedestal sinks, hardwood floors, ceiling fans, country quilts and original pictures of Lana'i's old plantation days. The hotel and restaurant are owned and operated by the Richardson family. Rooms range from twins to kings, and don't plan on watching TV because there isn't any. Ask for a room on the back side if you want to go to bed early. The original caretakers' cottage is also available for rent. Rooms are standard: two double beds, two twin beds or one double bed ($105); king rooms ($115); Lana'i rooms with queen bed, two twin beds and view of Lana'i City ($135); cottage with queen four-poster bed, TV, tub and private entrance ($175). Children under 10 are free in a room with parents, and teens are an additional $10 per night. Hotel Lana'i offers a complimentary shuttle between Manele Bay Hotel and the Lodge at Koele. Transportation to and from the Manele Boat Harbor and the Lanai Airport are provided for an extra charge. You'll want to book as far in advance as possible.

The Hotel Lana'i staff (family!) can provide you with complimentary inter-resort shuttle service and can arrange a variety of island activities, often with discounted rates. (The hotel works closely with Dollar Rental and Lana'i Ecoadventure Centre.)

Manele Bay Hotel

Castle & Cooke Resorts, P.O. Box 630310, Lana'i City, HI 96763. 800-321-4666; fax 808-565-3868; www.manelebayhotel.com or www.islandoflanai.com.

The Manele Bay Hotel is spread across the cliffside of Hulopo'e Beach like an enormous Mediterranean villa. It is a strikingly beautiful building with a pale blue–tile roof. There are four buildings in the east wing and five in the west wing; each is slightly different. The rooms line sprawling walkways that meander through five lush courtyard gardens, each with a unique theme. The gardens include the Hawaiian, the Bromeliad, the Chinese, the Japanese and the Kama'aina Gardens. The original resort plan called for a 450-room hotel directly on the beach, but was revised to the current structure with 250 rooms on the cliff alongside the beach. Behind the resort is the 18-hole golf course, the Challenge at Manele, which encompasses 138 acres along the ocean.

In many of the public areas the ceilings have been given special attention. In the main dining room are huge floral paintings; in the Hale AheAhe lounge you'll see fish and starfish. The resort took advantage of the undiscovered talent of island residents and much of the artwork is done by locals.

We enjoyed the proximity to the beachfront. The pool water is slightly warm, yet delightfully refreshing. It seems here on Lana'i, there is no reason to hurry. Attendants from the adjoining restaurant circulate, taking drink and sandwich orders. The poolside restaurant was a little pricey, but the portions were large. We noted with appreciation that they provided a more economical children's menu here as well as in their main dining rooms.

If you're thinking that too much lying in the sun and fine food will affect your waistline, the fitness studio is open from 6 a.m. to 8 p.m. There is plenty of equipment for working out, then treat yourself to a steam room, massage, pedicure or facial.

This place is truly an island getaway. If our stay was any indication, then celebrities have quickly found Lana'i to be a convenient and luxurious retreat. Both Kevin Costner and Billy Crystal were guests during our brief stay. The Manele Bay Hotel has ranked in the top ten in *Condé Nast Traveler*'s Readers' Choice Awards for a number of years. The rooms are spacious, a bit larger than the standard rooms at the Lodge, and each wing differs slightly in decor. Our wing had bright, bold yellow wall coverings and bedspreads accented with very traditional furniture. The bathroom amenities thoughtfully included suntan lotion and moisturizer in a little net bag to take along to the pool or beach. Some rooms have private butler service and all have mini-bars and mini-refrigerators.

Deluxe Ocean Front $795, Garden Room $375, Partial Ocean View $500, Ocean View $625, Ocean Front $695, Mauka Mini-Suite $750, Mauka Suite $800, Ocean Mini Suite $1,100, Ocean Front Suite $1,200, Mauka Corner Suite $1,250, Makai Suite $1,850, Center Makai Suite $1,800, Makai Corner Suite $2,500, Presidential Suite $3,000.

A third person age 18 or older is charged an additional $75 per night. Maximum occupancy is three adults or four persons, including children. Meal plans are available including the modified American Plan (breakfast and dinner) $100, or Full American Plan (breakfast, lunch and dinner) $125.

Lodge at Koele

Castle & Cooke Resorts. P.O. Box 630310, Lana'i City, HI 96763. 800-321-4666; fax 808-565-3868; www.lodgeatkoele.com or www.islandoflanai.com.

The Lodge at Koele is not what a visitor might expect to find in Hawai'i. Guests arrive via a stately drive lined with Cook Island pines to this Victorian/Plantation–era resort that typifies turn-of-the-20th-century elegance. The inscription on the ceiling of the entry was painted by artist John Wullbrandt and translates: *In the center of the Pacific is Hawai'i. In the center of Hawai'i is Lana'i. In the heart of Lana'i is Koele and it may quickly find its way into your heart as well.*

The Lodge at Koele continues to receive top accolades in *Condé Nast Traveler*'s "Gold List of World's Best Places to Stay." This award is voted upon by some 26,000 subscribers.

When the Lodge at Koele was built in 1989, 35 local artists from the island of Lana'i were hired to contribute to the aesthetic design of the property. The island's unique art program was intended to introduce and integrate the small, closely knit and very talented community on Lana'i with the Lodge. The results were more extraordinary than anyone had imagined.

The 102 guest rooms at the Lodge are artistically decorated in three different fresh, bright color schemes. The artwork that lines the corridors was done by Lana'i residents and each floor has a different theme. The beds feature a pineapple motif and were custom-made in Italy, then handpainted by Lana'i artisans. The floral pictures on each door were painted by the postmaster's wife.

The rug in the entry is circa 1880, made of Tibetan wool. The Great Hall features enormous natural stone fireplaces that hint at the cooler evening temperatures here in upcountry Lana'i. The twin fireplaces on either side of the lobby are the largest in the state of Hawai'i and the Lodge itself sets the record for being Hawai'i's biggest wooden structure. The high-beamed ceilings give the room a spacious character, yet the atmosphere is welcoming and the comfortable furnishings invite you to sit and linger. Designer Joszi Meskan of San Francisco spent more than two years securing the many beautiful artifacts from around the world. A descriptive list is available from the concierge. The Great Hall's rug was handmade in Thailand for the resort and utilizes 75 different colors. Some of the furniture are replicas, but many pieces are antiques, including the huge altar desk where steaming morning coffee awaits the guests. Be sure to notice the two exotic chandeliers, with playful carved monkeys amid the leaves, designed by Joszi Meskan. The large portrait on one end of the Great Hall is of Madame Yerken, painted by Belgian artist Jan Van Born in 1852. An intricately stenciled border with antelope, deer and wild turkeys runs around the perimeter of the ceiling. Another more subtle stenciling is done around the floors. The skylights are beautiful etched glass. The furnishings are covered in lush brocade tapestries and suede upholstery in hues of burgundy, blue and green. The room is accented with fresh flowers, many of them orchids grown in the greenhouse located beyond the reflecting pool. The woodwork is finely carved, with pineapples often featured. At the end of an exhausting day of vacationing, there is nothing like curling up in the big overstuffed armchair next to a crackling fire with an after-dinner drink to enjoy the evening entertainment, play a game of checkers or visit with local women as they demonstrate Hawaiian quilting. The bellman, concierge and front desk staff are all crisply attired in pine green suits.

Several public rooms surround the Great Hall. The library overlooks spacious lawns and offers newspapers from around the world as well as books, backgammon and chess. The Trophy Room also has an assortment of board games and an interesting, but very uncomfortable, English horn chair. Both of these rooms have fireplaces that can be lit at the request of the guest. A grounds tour is offered daily. Each afternoon there is "Tea-Time" on the Terrace and includes a high caliber of loose-leaf and rare teas: Jasmine Dragon Phoenix Pearls, Single-estate Darjeeling and Yinzhen Silver Needles, to name a few. An assortment of tea sandwiches, warm English scones with Devonshire cream, tropical butter and fruit preserves along with cakes and pastries complement the service. Offered daily from 3 p.m. to 5 p.m. Service for the "specialty teas" is $20 and premium teas are available for $18. Reservations are recommended.

Surrounding the main building is a wonderful veranda with comfortable rattan furniture accented by Hawaiian quilted pillows. Huge trees hug the building and the view of the horses and fields beyond has a tranquilizing effect. The setting is truly picture perfect. Adjoining the Great Hall is the Terrace Dining Room, open for breakfast, lunch and dinner. The food is excellent and the service outstanding. (In fact, the restaurants at the Lodge at Koele could very possibly be the best in all of Hawai'i.)

The hotel is located on the site of the farming community known as Koele. The pine-lined driveway was planted in the 1920s and led to the 20 or 30 homes in this area. Only two remain on the property and are owned by the Richardson family, descendants of the early Lana'i *paniolos*. The church was moved to the front grounds of the Lodge and a small schoolhouse is being restored and converted into a museum. The grounds of this country manor are sprawling and exquisitely landscaped. More than a mile of lush garden pathways and an orchid house can be enjoyed while strolling the grounds. The large reflecting pond was once the reservoir for the town of Koele.

There are plenty of activities to be enjoyed—from strolling the grounds to swimming or just relaxing in the jacuzzi. In fact, it is so relaxing and so lovely that we didn't even miss the beach. But if you're hankering for some sand and sun, it is only a 25-minute shuttle trip to the shore. The elegant, uniformed staff are efficient, very friendly and courteous. We were impressed with the quality of service at the Lodge. It is also pleasing to know that the development of the tourist industry on Lana'i has meant a return of many of the island's young people.

Guest bathrooms have Italian tile floors and vivid blue marble countertops. Room amenities are thoughtfully packaged and include an array of fine toiletries. There are in-room televisions with video recorders and a couple of beautifully carved walking sticks in the closet to tempt you to enjoy one of the leisurely walks around the grounds or along the Munro Trail that is accessible from the Lodge.

The workout facility by the pool provides free weights and aerobic machines.

Garden Koele Room ($375), Koele Deluxe Room ($525), Norfolk Suite ($725), Terrace Suite ($725), Banyan Suite ($900), Koele Suite ($1,200), Fireplace Entrance Suite ($1,500), Fireplace Garden Suite ($2,200). The Koele Suites have a wraparound lanai and a separate living and sleeping area with a Murphy bed in the living room. The Garden Koele Room and Koele Deluxe Room can be combined into one large living area. The Norfolk, Terrace, Banyan or Fireplace Garden suites provide separate living room and sleeping areas, and an oversized lanai. Located along the balcony above the Great Hall, these are the only guest rooms that are air conditioned. The Fireplace suites are slightly larger than the standard rooms and just as beautifully decorated. Packages such as Tee Time Golf, 4x4 Adventure, Romance/Honeymoon and 5th Night Free are some of the available options for extra value and amenities.

As much as we enjoyed the Manele Bay Hotel, we found something very appealing about the Lodge in upcountry. Perhaps it was because the service was so superb, perhaps it was because the air was so fresh, perhaps it was the comfortable and homey quality of the Great Hall, or perhaps it was because we truly were in the heart of Lana'i. This resort had a special quality, and both the kids and adults in our group were enchanted. Our visit will long be a fond memory—that is, until we visit once again. Given the many awards and accolades they have received, we're not alone in our impressions.

Where to Dine

There are three grocery stores from which to choose. **Richard's**, which has the honor of being on Lana'i since 1946, the small **Pine Isle Market**, and **International Food & Clothing**. Since everything must be brought in by barge, prices are steep. Don't be surprised if they are closed for noontime siesta and closed for the day by 6 p.m. Pineapples are available for sale at all three groceries. We suggest you purchase one and sample the difference between the mainland version of this fruit and the field-ripened variety.

Tanigawa's
419 7th Street, Lana'i City.

One of the limited local-style fast-food restaurants is Tanigawa's. Open daily for breakfast, lunch and dinner. You can select from sandwiches or burgers $2 to $4, plate lunches and breakfasts $4 to $6. The fare is filling and the atmosphere charmingly rustic.

Blue Ginger Cafe
7th Street, Lana'i City. 808-565-6363.

Next door to Tanigawa's is the Blue Ginger Cafe, which serves up some of the best freshly made pastries in town. Blue Ginger opens at 6 a.m. for breakfast, which is surprisingly diverse for such an early hour. They serve breakfast, lunch and dinner. Start your day with eggs, pancakes or waffles with blueberries, strawberries or macadamia nuts. The French toast is divine. Lunches include sandwiches, local-style plate lunches and saimin; dinners include steak, seafood and pizza. Most meals are under $15. They have really great T-shirts for sale, too. Hours are 9:30 a.m. to 3 p.m. and 5 p.m. to 9 p.m.

Henry Clay Rotisserie
Hotel Lana'i. 828 Lanai Avenue, Lana'i City. 808-565-7211; 800-795-7211; www.hotellanai.com; e-mail: hotellanai@wave.hicv.net.

Henry Clay Rotisserie features the Cajun-influenced cuisine of its talented chef, who held executive chef positions at some of Maui's most prestigious hotels and restaurants before he and his family moved to Lana'i. Always a popular place for island residents, this Hotel Lana'i dining room has become the island's first "signature" restaurant and a definite must-do on your Lana'i dining schedule. Henry Clay Richardson is a native of New Orleans and his heritage is reflected in his menu selections. Starter selections range from Henry Clay's pate, applewood-smoked salmon and Pacific oyster shooters to warm dishes such as ragout of wild mushrooms pot pie, tangy rotisserie ribs and Penn Cove mussels with a spicy saffron sauce ($6.75 to $12.95). Entrees are diverse, with a toasted butternut squash ravioli with tomato fondue, an eggplant Creole with angelhair pasta, free-range Lana'i axis deer and "almost grandma's" gumbo as choices ($16.95 to $36.95). The bar closes at 9 p.m.

Pele's Other Garden
811 Houston Street, Lana'i City. 808-565-9628.

Pele's Other Garden is a deli operated by Mark Zigmond. He offers wonderful New York–style deli (hot and cold) sandwiches featuring a variety of lunch meats and cheeses. You'll also find pizzas, salads and quesadillas, too ($6 to $7.99). Picnic lunches for two available. The dinner menu includes such appetizers as shrimp cocktail, garlic bread and teri ribs ($3.50 to $9). Entrees ($13 to $20) range from butterfly pasta in creamy pesto with prosciutto and garlic shrimp to teriyaki ribs and rice, cheese ravioli with marinara, or beef and vegetable stew ($10 to $17). Pizzas ($6 to $8) are also available for dinner. Open Monday through Saturday 9:30 a.m. to 3 p.m., dinner 5 p.m. to 9 p.m. They have opened another location down at the Manele Bay Small Boat Harbor where they serve pizzas by the slice, sandwiches, salads and assorted beverages. Breakfast selections include cereals and pastries. It's a cool place to rest and enjoy a smoothie or shave ice while you wait for the interisland ferry. Open 7:30 a.m. to 4:30 p.m.

Café 565
408 8th Street, Lana'i City. 808-565-6622.

New, wonderful *and* inexpensive. Can it be? Café 565 features a blend of local and ethnic cuisines with daily specials. Hours currently are only Monday through Friday for lunch and dinner but once they catch on that is likely to change. There are hot and cold sub sandwiches ($3.95-$4.95 junior size and $6.95-$8.95 full size). Specialty pizzas include tomato basil, wild garden, Greek or spicy chicken ($15.95-$19.95). Try a wild garden, Caesar, oriental chicken or tuna salad ($5.25-$8.95) and check out their daily soup and plate lunch specials (with two scoops of rice). Closed Saturday-Sunday.

Hulopo'e Court
Manele Bay Hotel. 800-321-4666; www.manelebayhotel.com.

The Hulopo'e Court in the Manele Bay Hotel is the more casual of two dining rooms at the resort and serves breakfast and dinner, with a children's menu available. Breakfasts entrees include brioche French toast with tropical *lilikoi* butter and cracked macadamia nuts, Hawaiian coconut and tapioca waffle with roasted island bananas, roasted vegetable frittata with island herbs and shaved parmesan, or a "Feast of Island Inspired Hash" that includes Hawaiian seafood with sweet peppers and sun-dried tomatoes and *imu*-roasted pork with Maui onions and Finnish potatoes ($10 to $15). Side orders are also available as well as a bounty of fresh fruit juices, cereals and bakery items. The dinner menu is tropical American cuisine, using ingredients and flavors "from sun-drenched regions around the world." Cilantro hummus or guava-glazed baby back ribs might warm those tastebuds up for an entrée of chilled lobster, prawn and scallop salad, spice-rubbed chicken, Hawaiian *moi* in a lemongrass ginger broth, "boneless" Dungeness crab or seared pork tenderloin with a cashew coconut crust ($17 to $29).

Ihilani
Manele Bay Hotel. 800-321-4666; www.manelebayhotel.com.

Ihilani is the Manele Bay Hotel's elegant formal dining room. The menu is contemporary Mediterranean cuisine, or you can choose a five-course food-and-wine pairing for $85 (meal only) or $125 (wine inclusive). A sample dinner might be summer gazpacho or Ihilani salad followed by braised deep-sea snapper with Charmoula, grilled filet mignon, a selection of gourmet cheeses and walnut bread. A

"Symphony of Desserts" serenades the conclusion. I haven't had the opportunity to dine here, so let me know if you do.

Hale AheAhe
Manele Bay Hotel. 800-321-4666; www.manelebayhotel.com.

Hale AheAhe (House of Gentle Breezes) is an indoor lounge located off the upper main lobby that offers nightly entertainment on its outdoor veranda. They feature a full bar as well as an appetizer menu ($8 to $22).

Pool Grille
Manele Bay Hotel. 800-321-4666; www.manelebayhotel.com.

The Pool Grille is open 11 a.m. until 5 p.m. and serves lunch only. They offer light fare and local favorites including grilled Black Angus beef burger, a smoked turkey "Manele Club" sandwich, or a Lana'i venison "ham and cheese" sandwich. You can also try the chicken and mushroom pizza, spicy chicken breast salad, Cobb salad or grilled tiger prawns ($13 to $15) and follow that with a brownie à la mode for dessert.

Challenge at Manele Clubhouse
Manele Bay Hotel. 800-321-4666; www.manelebayhotel.com.

The Challenge at Manele Clubhouse offers a lunch (11 a.m. to 5 p.m.) and evening (5:30 p.m. to 9 p.m.) menu. On the midday meal menu you'll find sandwiches ($10 to $12), salads, appetizers, soups ($7 to $15) or island favorites such as battered fish with fries, a grilled fresh-catch sandwich or stir-fried chicken with chow mein noodles ($11 to $13). The evening menu is *pupu* style so you can sample a variety of smaller dishes to make a complete meal. Chilled and warm *pupus* are smaller than "meal-size portions," and include oxtail soup, sun-dried tomato and mushroom ravioli, steamed Chinese dim sum, shrimp tacos or Chinese barbecue chicken salad ($7.50 to $12). My friends and I were not terribly impressed by our eight selections, although the portions for most were quite large. Our recommendation is the stir-fry vegetables, not exotic, but good and hearty. Follow it up with one of their tropical desserts.

The Terrace
Lodge at Koele. 800-321-4666; www.lodgeatkoele.com.

The Terrace at the Lodge at Koele's breakfast features island smoothies, warm cinnamon bread pudding with cinnamon-berry sauce (yum!), poached eggs on blue crab cakes with citrus-chive hollandaise, blood orange and honey waffles, or brioche French toast with vanilla bean sauce, caramelized sliced apples and almonds ($7.25 to $15). Dinner is served from 6 p.m. to 9:30 p.m. with an equally tantalizing but less expensive menu than the Lodge's formal dining room.

Starters include fried calamari tossed with radicchio, frisée and *ver jus* vinaigrette, smoked chicken and corn cake salad or a Koele Caesar ($11 to $12.50). Entrees offer chef's seafood selection of the day, little pot of Maine lobster and tiger shrimp with spring vegetables, braised vegetable and pumpkin tart with roasted garlic and spinach coulis, or roasted half chicken on toasted fennel seed and mashed potatoes ($17 to $27.50). Dinner reservations are recommended and evening attire is requested.

Formal Dining Room
Lodge at Koele. 800-321-4666; www.lodgeatkoele.com.

The Formal Dining Room at Koele is open for dinner only (6:30 to 9:30 p.m) and makes excellent use of their five-acre organic farm to ensure the freshest ingredients in their meal preparations. As you might expect, prices are a bit higher on Lana'i, but not much more than Maui's signature restaurants. For starters try the sumptuous seared diver scallops on braised vegetables and spinach with a saffron broth, or semi-smoked pineapple salmon on tomato tartar ($12 to $19). Soups include Kona crab and lobster bisque with cognac essence and grilled asparagus and spring pea soup ($9 to $10). A roasted baby beet and orange salad with toasted hazelnuts or a carpaccio of heirloom tomato salad with warm basil gnocchi sound enticing ($11). Evening features might include pancetta-wrapped roast loin of Lana'i venison with baby carrot puree, seared Hawaiian snapper on braised greens, shrimp ravioli and spring peas coulis; or seared Hawaiian ahi with foie gras and portobello mushroom relish ($32 to $42). Jackets are required for men and you will need reservations.

Clubhouse Bar & Grill
Lodge at Koele. 800-321-4666; www.lodgeatkoele.com.

Another dining option is at the Experience at Koele golf clubhouse. The Clubhouse Bar & Grill offers a lunch menu with plenty of sandwich selections, from shaved roast beef with roasted peppers, onions and jack cheese to a smoked turkey club, shredded BBQ chicken or Mediterranean-style fresh grilled catch ($7 to $14.50). Or try some venison chili ($6).

Beaches

Along Lana'i's northern shore is **Polihua**. There is an interesting stretch of long sand dunes. This coast is often very windy, and some days the blowing sand is intense. The surf conditions are dangerous and swimming should never be attempted. Also along the northern shore is the area from **Awalua to Naha**. The beaches are narrow and the offshore waters are shallow with a wide reef.

However, the water is often murky. Swimming and snorkeling are not recommended. **Lopa**, on the eastern shore, is a narrow white-sand beach that can be enjoyed for picnicking and sunbathing. Surf conditions, however, can be dangerous.

Along the western coastline is **Kaunola**, a rocky shore with no sandy beach and no safe entry or exit. Conditions can be dangerous. Swimming is not advised at any time. Also on the western shore is **Kaumalapau Harbor**, the deep-water harbor used for shipping. Water activities are not recommended at any time.

The southern coastline affords the safest ocean conditions. Manele Bay is the small boat harbor, but water activity is not recommended due to heavy boat traffic. **Hulopoʻe Bay** is the island's best and most beautiful white-sand beach. It is located in front of the Manele Bay Hotel. It is popular for swimming, surfing, boogie boarding and snorkeling. The tidepools make for fun exploration and, although a marine preserve, shore fishing is permitted. On summer weekends the camping area is often filled with local residents. However, large swells and high surf conditions can exist. During times of high surf, undertows become very strong. During these times it is not safe to stand or play even in the shore break, as severe injury can occur. Be aware of water safety signs. There are no lifeguards on duty; however, there are attendants at the resort's beach kiosk who might be able to answer questions you have. Never swim alone and always exercise good water safety judgement.

Recreation and Tours

Lanaʻi offers a wealth of interesting activities for children of all ages. In 2002, readers of *Condé Nast Traveler* magazine ranked activities on Lanaʻi as #3 for all of the United States. There are short as well as ambitious hikes, and plenty of fun can be enjoyed off-roading to beaches and geological formations in a Jeep. You can spot axis deer, wild turkeys and perhaps even a mouflon sheep. Ocean activities include kayaking, scuba diving and snorkeling.

If exploring the island's beauty is not enough, kids might like trying their hand at the Lanaʻi Pine Sporting Clays (adjacent to the Lodge at Koele), where they provide youth-level target shooting. The pools at the Lodge at Koele and Manele Bay Resort both offer cool diversion, and those kids who hope to be a future Tiger Woods might enjoy the recreational nine-hole putting green behind the Lodge at Koele. Feel like a *paniolo*? Then sign up for a horseback trail ride; kiddie rides are also available. Or grab a mountain bike and take off on the roads, trails and golf cart paths (after golf-course hours, of course). Read on to select your perfect Lana'i activities.

If you would like some company on your island tour, contact **Lana'i Ecoadventure Centre**, which offers guide service for $25 per hour. They also offer guided hikes. Try their 4x4 adventure trek ($99 per person), which is a four-hour beginning-level island trek available in the morning or afternoon. They stop at Lana'i's Cook Island pine forest on the Munro Trail and explore ridges and gorges, viewing ferns and tropical plants. On to the Garden of the Gods and a stop at Shipwreck Beach. Their kayak snorkel adventure ($99 each morning) provides novice-level sea kayaking and snorkeling eco-adventures. View green sea turtles, dolphins and even whales. Trips include basic kayak and snorkel instruction, single or double kayaks, and snorkel gear. Snacks included. They also offer full-day combo trips so you can enjoy a snorkeling or sea kayaking adventure in the morning. 808-565-7373; www.adventurelanai.com.

ARCHERY

Lana'i offers a modern archery range at the **Lana'i Pine Sporting Clays** complex. The 12-station range is set up for 5, 10, 15 and 20 yards, for the novice, intermediate or advanced archer. Recurve, compound and youth bows are available for rent at the pro shop. Private and group lessons are offered. The range is located on the north side on the plains of Mahana. There is complimentary transportation from the Lodge at Koele. Hours are 8:15 a.m. to 2:30 p.m. daily. Introductory lessons are $45 per hour (including equipment). Maximum of six per group. Range use for experienced archers is $35 per hour, including equipment, or $25 if you bring your own equipment (crossbows are not allowed). Arrangements can be made through the concierge at all Lana'i resorts.

ART & CULTURE

Lana'i Art Program If you're a resident or a visitor and interested in pursuing your artistic talents, you can register for the Lana'i Art Program. Classes are taught by local and visiting artists and might include a variety of paint medias or craft classes. *Raku* (Japanese pottery), silk screening, herbal wreaths, *gyotaku* (Japanese art using real fish to imprint a design on T-shirts). It is also a great place to purchase artwork done by local artists. The shop is open whenever they have volunteers. Weekends you can count on Mrs. Fujie being behind the counter. She does calligraphy, knits caps and has even written some stories for the book *Spookey Tales. 339 7th Street, Lana'i City. 808-565-7503.*

Lana'i Visiting Artist Program Lana'i is abloom with artistic opportunities. The island's Lana'i Visiting Artist Program was initiated in 1992 to provide the Lana'i community and visitors an opportunity to interact with distinguished artisans from varying fields. Chefs, authors and artists are among the guests to visit the island each year. The program is co-sponsored by Creative Leisure International. For additional information you can contact them at Creative Leisure 800-413-1000, fax 707-778-1223, or e-mail: res@creativeleisure.com. Check the website for the island and you will be directed to upcoming Artists in Residence events; www.lanai-resorts.com. All events (except dinners) are free of charge. For further information about the Visiting Artist Program, contact Castle & Cooke Resorts at 800-321-4666.

Lana'i Conference Center For history buffs, there is a permanent exhibit of Lana'i artifacts on display at the Lana'i Conference Center, the meeting and convention facility perched on a seaside knoll just above the Manele Bay Hotel. These items were returned "home" after their initial discovery and display at Honolulu's Bishop Museum.

Kaupe Culture & Heritage Center Kaupe Culture & Heritage Center also has frequent cultural exhibits in town.

BIKING

Lodge at Koele Mountain bikes can be obtained at the Lodge at Koele Activity Desk. Rates are $8 per hour or $40 for a full day. You can enjoy Lana'i's scenic pathways or tour around town at your own pace.

Lana'i Ecoadventure Centre Lana'i Ecoadventure Centre offers mountain bike rentals. The 24-speed aluminum-frame bikes run $25 per day. Or for $99, beginning bicyclists can enjoy a van-supported downhill tour. You bike down the Keamoku switchbacks and then head down to the beach road to Federation Camp for refreshments, some short hikes to the petroglyphs and time for hunting shells and spotting humpback whales (seasonally). 808-565-7373; www.adventurelanai.com.

FISHING

Deep-sea fishing excursions are available. Check with the concierge at any of the resorts or hotels. **Spinning Dolphin Charters** offers sport-fishing and seasonal whale watching. Seasonal whale-watching trips last about three hours. Deep-sea fishing charters are four, six or eight hours aboard a 28-foot Sport Omega. The maximum capacity is six persons per trip. 808-565-6613.

GOLF

There are a number of selections for the golfer on Lana'i. At Koele there is the 18-hole Experience at Koele course, the older community 9-hole course, and one stupendous 18-hole putting course adjacent the Lodge. The Challenge at Manele is near the Manele Resort. Golfers and non-golfers of all ages will delight in the executive 18-hole putting green at Koele, a beautifully manicured course with assorted sand traps and pools lined with tropical flowers and sculptures. No charge. (Putt-putt will never be the same again!)

Challenge at Manele   The Challenge at Manele, designed by Jack Nicklaus, opened on December 25, 1993. Built on several hundred acres of lava out-croppings among natural *kiawe* and *ilima* trees, this links-style golf course features three holes constructed on the cliffs of Hulopoʻe Bay, using the Pacific Ocean as a dramatic water hazard. *808-565-2222.*

Experience at Koele   This 18-hole course was designed by Greg Norman and Ted Robinson. From a golfer's standpoint, Greg Norman assures the golfing guest that this course will require both skill and strategy, and adds that it is the only course in Hawaiʻi with bent-grass greens. He also noted that the beauty of the course, with its lush natural terrain marked by thick stands of Cook Island pines and panoramic views, make concentrating on the game difficult for even the most expert golfer. The signature eighth hole of the Experience at Koele has a truly inspired setting. This is a 390-yard par 4 with a dramatic 200-foot drop in elevation from tee to green. The course is laid out on a multitiered plan. The upper seven holes meet the lower eleven at this sublime tee. From the top of the bluff at the eighth tee is a view so stunning that our first thought was that this could be right out of Shangri-la. The mist floats by this enchanted valley filled with lush vegetation, and there's a lovely lagoon. The lagoon at one time had served as a back-up reservoir for the old cattle ranch. Now, while we are not golf aficionados, this single hole was enough to at least consider taking up the sport! The Experience at Koele was rated in the world's top ten in the 2002 Readers' Poll of the World's Best Golf Courses in *Condé Nast Traveler*. A restaurant at the golf clubhouse offers some good lunch selections. *808-565-4653.*

> Course rates for the 18-hole Challenge at Manele or Experience at Koele is $185 for non-guests and $135 for hotel guests. Reservations for either course can be made from the mainland via their toll-free number 800-321-4666. www.lanairesorts.com.

Cavendish Golf Course   The Cavendish, a 9-hole, 36-par, 3,071-yard course, is located at the front of the Lodge at Koele and was the island's first golf course. It is a community course and there is no phone, no clubhouse and no charge. (Donations are suggested to help with upkeep.)

HIKING

Walking sticks are provided in all the rooms at the Lodge at Koele for guest usage. It's almost impossible to resist strolling around the pastoral grounds. Near the Lodge at Koele are two small houses. These were originally located where the orchid house is now. The Richardson families live here and their ancestors were among the early Lana'i *paniolos*. You can stroll around the front grounds to view the enormous Norfolk pine or watch guests try their hand at lawn bowling, croquet or miniature golf. Walk down to the horse stables or peek inside the old church. The stables are new, but the church was relocated due to the construction of the Lodge. A small school was also moved and it is currently being restored and perhaps will one day house Lana'i's first museum.

The **Munro Trail** is a nine-mile arc trek along the ridge of Lana'i. The view from the 3,370-foot summit of Lana'ihale can be spectacular on a clear day. (This route can also be tackled by four-wheel-drive vehicles, but only during very dry conditions.) For the adventurous, there is also the **High Pasture Loop**, the **Old Cowboy Trail**, **Eucalyptus Ladder** or **Beyond the Blue Screen**. A light- to moderate-weight raincoat might be a good idea to take along if you're planning on hiking. The concierge can provide you with a map showing the various routes. Picnics can be provided by the hotel. A guided five-mile hike is available daily up to the Koloiki Ridge. The five-mile hike includes snacks and drinks and departs at 11 a.m., returning at 1:30 p.m. This is arranged through the hotel concierge. The fee is $15 per person. Private hikes can also be arranged through your resort concierge. If you'd like to learn more about the flora of Hawai'i and the plight of the native species, contact Brian Valley and The Nature Conservancy, 730 Lanai Avenue, 808-565-7430. Guided hikes can be arranged or you can enjoy a self-guided walk in the preserve.

Lana'i Ecoadventure Centre also offers some guided day hikes. 808-565-7373; www.adventurelanai.com.

HORSEBACK RIDING

Lodge at Koele   The Lodge at Koele has an impressive stable. A variety of rides are available, from a ten-minute children's ride to one- or two-hour treks through the plantation along wooded trails (trail availability changes from year to year). More experienced riders can enjoy longer trips with a stop for lunch. Riding lessons (a two-rider limit per lesson) are also available. Riders must wear long pants and sports shoes and children must be at least nine years of age and four feet, six inches in height to ride. Maximum weight of riders is 200 pounds. Safety helmets are provided for all riders. Prices begin at $10 for the children's introductory experience and $85 per person for the group ride on the Mahana trail. Private trail rides start at $75 per person for the first hour, $130 for two hours. Riding lessons start at $50 per hour. Reservations can be made through the concierge at all of the hotels.

Lana'i Ecoadventure Centre Lana'i Ecoadventure Centre offers some guided day hikes. *808-565-7373; www.adventurelanai.com.*

HUNTING

Axis deer (chital) and mouflon sheep hunting is available year-round on the island of Lana'i and is managed by Castle & Cooke Game Management. Hunting excursions are a three-day guided affair with one full day devoted to the hunt itself. Gary Onuma has served as a Lana'i hunting guide for over 20 years. Gary and his colleagues provide not only a spectacular hunting trip but serve as expert guides to the island's geological features. The cost of the hunt is $1,000 plus a $105 fee for a non-resident license. A hunter safety card or certificate is required. Hunting clothes and gear can be provided. If you decide to bring you own firearm, it must be a flat shooter and must be registered with the State. *Contact Game Management, P.O. Box 630310, Lana'i City, HI 96763. 808-565-3981.*

Lana'i Pines Sporting Clays An unusual recreational option is the target range on the hillside just behind the Lodge at Koele. There is a free shuttle from the lodge. The 14-station solar-powered traps are designed to entice beginners and challenge experts. Choose packages with 50 ($85) or 100 ($145) targets. Packages include gun and cartridges, vest, eye protection and foam ear protection. After 100 targets the charge is $.80 per target and $8 per box of shells. À la carte pricing for cartridges and targets is available, as are gun rentals. Introductory instruction is $75 per person; private lessons are offered upon request. The complex also has six air rifle stations for novices and youngsters. Price is $36.75 for 204 shots.

Lawn bowling and both English and American croquet fields surround the Lodge at Koele.

Should you bring your own shotgun, gun lockers are available at both the Lodge at Koele and the Manele Bay Resort. (Be aware that any firearm brought into the state of Hawai'i longer than three days must be registered with the State. Contact Castle & Cooke Resorts at 800-321-4666 or the concierge at any of the Lana'i resorts.)

KAYAKING

Lana'i Ecoadventure Centre has kayak rentals ($49 a day or $10 for an hour), which include towels, snorkel gear, paddles, life jackets and dry bags. They also offer a half-day snorkel/kayak adventure ($69 per person); full-day and overnight excursions can be arranged. 808-565-7373; www.adventurelanai.com.

OFF ROADING

See "Getting Around" above for information on Jeep rentals.

SCUBA DIVING

Diving the waters of Lana'i is guaranteed to instill awe in both the beginning and advanced diver. The island's volcanic origin has created spectacular lava arches, tubes and pinnacles, with **Cathedrals** being the most popular dive site. But it doesn't stop there. Lana'i offers an impressive array of dive sites along the eastern shore, down around the southern shore, and up the west coast of the island. In typical Hawaiian fashion, you won't be disappointed with the myriad colorful varieties of marine life. Many of the dive sites are open to blue water, which means that if you keep a sharp eye out you may encounter whales, whale sharks, sharks and manta rays. To learn more about Lana'i dive sites, you can browse the web pages of Maui dive operators. We have found Maui Scuba Dive's web page to be very detailed and informative: www.scubadivemaui.com.

Trilogy Lana'i Ocean Sports Most scuba-diving excursions originate from Maui but if you are enjoying a pleasant stay on Lana'i, Trilogy Ocean Sports on Lana'i offers scuba boat trips from Manele Harbor or beach dives in Hulopo'e Bay. One of the most exciting dives offered by Trilogy is the Cathedral Sunrise Special. This dive location is reportedly one of the premier dive sites in the Pacific. The majority of Cathedrals stand 80 feet below the surface, but one can still manage to see it at 50 to 60 feet. The main entrance is approximately 60 feet under and the back entrance lies at approximately 90 feet. Usually there is very little current and visibility is excellent, with at least 120 feet distance. Upon descending with your Trilogy guide, the Cathedral arches emerge from the blue—these arches mark the main entrance and are large enough to drive a bus through! The entire channel is riddled with old lava tubes that create an early-Gothic ambience. Cathedrals is actually one big lava tube with many small openings that allow for beams of light. This one-tank certification dive meets at Manele Harbor at 6:30 a.m. and returns by 8 a.m., leaving the rest

RESORT TOURS

Both Manele and Koele offer daily complimentary tours of their resorts. Just sign up at the concierge desk. The tour of Koele is especially informative and discusses the many unique pieces of art gracing the lobby, making it a worthwhile 30 minutes.

Guests and non-guests can rent a mountain bike at the Lodge at Koele ($8/hour, $40/day) and ride into town or around the resort paths. In the early morning or early evening, they are allowed to ride along the golf course paths. One evening we followed one of the garden paths behind the putting green that led to a very steep golf cart track from the lower nine holes to the upper nine. It was so steep, in fact, that it proved quite a challenge to just walk the bikes up. After the journey up, we were delighted to find an ample supply of water and cups that reappeared every couple of holes on the golf course. Once on top, we biked around a few holes of the golf course that were fairly level. We were pleasantly surprised to find ourselves at the tee off for the eighth hole of the golf course and, as previously described, it was an inspired location. We then attempted to ride down from the tee to the green. The path down was so steep that it required our brakes on full force to go slow enough to maintain control. Beyond is another picturesque lagoon and more golf cart trails to follow on flat ground. The walk into town takes about 15 minutes at a fairly brisk pace, but only about 5 minutes by bike. Biking is a good option for seeing Lana'i City or if you just want to sample some of Lana'i's local eateries.

Both resorts have wonderful swimming pools. The Koele pool, flanked by two bubbling jacuzzis, was seldom busy during our stay. The Manele pool is slightly larger and, at a lower elevation than Koele, became quite hot during the afternoon. The adjacent pool-

of the day open for golf, horseback riding or the spa. The Cathedral Sunrise Special is $95 plus tax and only for certified divers. You can combine this dive with Trilogy's Lana'i Adventure Scuba. *Contact Trilogy through the concierge of the Hotel Lana'i, the Manele Bay Hotel or the Lodge at Koele. If you prefer, call Trilogy direct at 888-MAUI-800; www.visit lanai.com or www.sailtrilogy.com.*

Lana'i Ecoadventure Centre   Lana'i Ecoadventure Centre offers private scuba dives and rents equipment. *808-565-7373; www.adventure lanai.com.*

SNORKELING

Lana'i Ecoadventure Centre   Snorkel sets from Lana'i Ecoadventure Centre rent for $10 a day (includes towel). *808-565-7373; www.adven turelanai.com.*

side restaurant provided refreshing drinks and light fare. Guests at the resorts have pool privileges at both facilities.

Scuba diving, fishing expeditions, raft trips and other ocean excursions can be arranged through the concierge at either resort. Half-day raft trips (two and a half hours) run $40 to $60. Half-day sailing and snorkeling trips are run by Trilogy Excursions. At both resorts, a sheet describing the activities for the next day is left in the room with the evening maid service.

Lodge at Koele Complimentary coffee and tea are available in the lobby and each of the accommodation wings each morning. The Music Room has an array of interesting musical instruments lining the walls, and the grand piano may be used by guests. This is also where you'll find a delightful afternoon tea. In the Trophy Room are board games, or sit back and relax with a book in The Library. Complimentary video tapes are available at the concierge for guests to view in their rooms. A grounds tour is offered daily and at night there is varied musical entertainment in the Great Hall. The twin fireplaces are ablaze and the overstuffed chairs invite you to slow down and relax. The fireplaces are lit, upon request, in the Library, Music or Trophy rooms. This may be as close to heaven on earth as you can get.

Manele Bay Hotel Manele also has varied daily activities. A tour of the resort is available and in the evening there is entertainment and complimentary *pupus* (5 to 6 p.m.) at Hale AheAhe. Complimentary video tapes are available for guest use in their rooms and complimentary morning coffee is a pleasurable experience in the Orchid Lounge or Coral Lounge.

SPAS & FITNESS CENTERS

Lodge at Koele A fitness center and spa, complimentary for resort guests, is located at the Lodge at Koele and is open from 6 a.m. to 7 p.m. Massages and specialty treatments are available between 10 a.m. and 5 p.m. and include masks, foot treatments, scrubs and a variety of massage styles. Yoga classes are $10 per person and are offered twice weekly.

Manele Bay Resort The Spa at Manele is described as having an elegant yet simple tone, a place where guests will be pampered. Features include His-and-Hers red cedar sauna and granite steam rooms. Treatments include hot stone massage and hot stone facials. There are six indoor private massage rooms and four outdoor garden and ocean-view private massage areas, as well as facial rooms, manicure stations, pedicure thrones and a salon.

SURFING

Lana'i Ecoadventure Centre Surfboards and boogieboards are available at Lana'i Ecoadventure Centre; boards run $39 daily and boogie boards are $10. Or try out their novice surf safaris for *keikis* or Big Kahunas. Local surf instructors demonstrate techniques, etiquette and all basic skills on lightweight wooden longboards. Safari includes snacks and sodas. *808-565-7373; www.adventurelanai.com.*

TENNIS

There are plexi-pave courts at both Koele and Manele Bay. These are complimentary for use by hotel guests. Lessons are available at an extra charge. There is also a public court at Lana'i School in Lana'i City.

THEATER

The refurbished **Lana'i Playhouse** has been Lana'i's movie theater since 1993.

SWEET MAUI MOON

Now after the sun goes to sleep,
My Sweet Maui Moon will whisper to me
'cause now that you've gone and said "goodbye,"
My Sweet Maui Moon sings a lullaby

And finding her way to the sea,
She never fails to look down on me
'cause now that you've gone and said "goodbye,"
My Sweet Maui Moon sings a lullaby

CHORUS
And it doesn't matter what mood I am in
Or whether I'm feeling down
'cause sometimes I'm losin' and sometimes I win
And She never lets me down

And rising up into the sky,
My Sweet Maui Moon will kiss me goodnight
'cause now that you've gone and said "goodbye,"
My Sweet Maui Moon sings a lullaby

And it doesn't matter what mood I am in
Or whether I'm feeling down
'cause sometimes I'm losin' and sometimes I win
And She never lets me down
Now that you've gone and said "goodbye,"
My Sweet Maui Moon sings a lullaby....

Copyright 1987 Starscape Music.
Our thanks to Keola Beamer for permission to reprint these lyrics.

Recommended Reading

Allen, Gwenfread. *Hawaiian Monarchy Kings and Queens*. Pacific Monograph. 1999.

Barnes, Phil. *A Concise History of the Hawaiian Islands*. Hilo, Hawai'i: Petrogylph Press. 1999.

Bartholomew, Gail and Bren Bailey. *Maui Remembers*. Mutual Publishing. 1994.

Beamer, Nona. *Na Mele Hula*. Honolulu: University of Hawaii Press. 1998.

Bird, Isabella. *Six Months in the Sandwich Islands*. Honolulu: Booklines. 1998.

Chisholm, Craig. *Hawaiian Hiking Trails*. Lake Oswego, Oregon: Fernglen Press. 1994.

Clark, John. *Beaches of Maui County*. Honolulu: University Press of Hawaii. 1989.

Cook, James, et al. *The Explorations of Captain James Cook in the Pacific, as told by his own Journals*. Dover Publishing. 1971.

Daws, Gavan. *Shoal of Time*. Honolulu: University of Hawaii Press. 1989.

Fielding, Ann. *Hawaiian Reefs and Tidepools*. Honolulu: Island Explorations. 1998.

Grant, Glen. *Glen Grant's Chicken Skin Tales*. Honolulu: Mutual Publishing. 1998.

Kane, Herb Kauainui. *Ancient Hawaii*. Kawainui Press. 1998.

Kepler, Angela. *Maui's Hana Highway*. Honolulu: Mutual Publishing. 1995.

Kyselka, Will and Ray Lanterman. *Maui, How It Came to Be*. Honolulu: The University Press of Hawaii. 1980.

Malinowski, Mel. *Snorkel Maui and Lanai*. Indigo Publications. 2000.

Malo, David. *Hawaiian Antiquities*. Honolulu: Bishop Museum Press. 1903/1951/1987.

Palancy, Tom. *So You Want to Live in Hawaii*. Maui: Barefoot Publications. 1999.

Pukui, Mary K., et al. *The New Pocket Hawaiian Dictionary*. Honolulu: The University of Hawaii Press. 1998.

Reece, Kim Taylor. *Hula Kahiko: Images of Hawaii's Ancient Hula*. Gecko Stufs. 1999.

Smith, Robert. *Hiking Maui*. Maui: Hawaiian Outdoor Adventure. 1999.

Sterling, Elspeth. *Sites of Maui*. Honolulu: Bishop Museum Press. 1998.

Stevenson, Robert Louis. *Travels in Hawaii*. Honolulu: University of Hawaii Press. 1991.

Titcomb, M. *Native Use of Fish in Hawaii*. Honolulu: University of Hawaii Press. 1982.

Twain, Mark. *Letters from Mark Twain*. Honolulu: University of Hawaii Press. 1989.

Westervelt, H. *Myths and Legends of Hawaii*. Honolulu: Mutual Publishing. 1989.

Whitman, John. *An Account of the Sandwich Islands*. Salem, Oregon: Topgallant Publishing. 1979.

One cannot determine in advance to love a particular woman,
nor can one so determine to love Hawaii.
One sees, and one loves or does not love.
With Hawaii it seems always to be love at first sight.
Those for whom the islands were made,
or who were made for the islands,
are swept off their feet in the first moments of meeting embrace
and are embraced.

Jack London

Index

Accommodations. *See* Lodging
Agricultural inspection, 41
'Ahihi-Kina'u Natural Reserve Area, 325–26
Airlines, 40–45, 419
Airplane tours, 332–33
'Alaeloa Beach ("The Cove"), 316–17
Alexander and Baldwin Sugar Museum, 95, 370
Alii Kahekili Nui 'Ahumahi Beach Park, 314–15
All-terrain vehicles, 333–34
Animals: Lana'i, 417; Maui, 13–14
Archery (Lana'i), 436
Armory Park (Kamehameha Iki Park), 73
Art & culture: Lana'i, 436–37, 444; Maui, 403–405
Art classes and tours, 334
Astronomy, 334–35
ATVs, 333–34
Awalua Beach, 310, 312
Awalua Road (Lana'i), 421–22

Bailey House Museum, 92, 370
Baldwin Home, 68, 370
Banyan Tree (Lahaina), 64
Beaches and beach activities (Lana'i), 434–35
Beaches and beach activities (Maui), 302–29; best bets, 309; and children, 16–17; Hana Highway area, 327–29; Lahaina, 310, 312–13; Ka'anapali–Kapalua area, 314–19; Kahului–Wailuku area, 326–27; Ma'alaea–Kihei–Wailea–Makena area, 319–26; map, 311; safety, 303, 304–309
Bed & breakfast rental agencies, 186
Best bets (Lana'i), 408
Best bets (Maui), 1–6; beaches, 309; dining, 197–200; lodging, 124–27; recreation and tours, 332
Biking: Lana'i, 437; Maui, 335–38
Black Rock, 78
Body surfing, 338
Bowling, 339
Brick Palace, 68
Brig *Carthaginian*, 67, 370
Bufo (frog), 13
Buses, 47

Calendar of annual events, 54–58
Camp Pecusa, 339
Camping: Lana'i, 425; Maui, 339–41
Canoe Beach, 313
Canoeing, 341–42
Car and truck rentals: Lana'i, 420; Maui, 48–51
Carriage rides, 362

INDEX

Carthaginian, 67, 370
Cave adventures, 399–400
Chang's Beach, 324
Childcare programs: Lana'i, 418; Maui, 17–20
Children, traveling with: Lana'i, 417–18; Maui, 14–26
Clothing to bring, 29–30, 58
Communications, 36–39
Condominiums. *See* Lodging
Cone shells, 307
Coral, 306
Cottages. *See* Lodging
County parks, and camping, 339
Cruises and cruise lines, 46–47, 342–44

D. T. Fleming Beach Park, 318
Dancing, 345
Dining (Lana'i), 430–34
Dining (Maui), 191–301; best bets, 197–200; and children, 16; ethnic foods, 193–97; Hana Highway area, 286–93; Lahaina, 200–18; Ka'anapali–Kapalua area, 218–38; Kahului–Wailuku area, 267–80; Ma'alaea–Kihei–Wailea–Makena area, 238–67; Upcountry, 280–86. *See also* Dining Indexes
Dinner cruises. *See* Cruises and cruise lines
Dinner shows, 293, 296–301
Disabled travelers, 27–29
Diving: Lana'i, 441–42; Maui, 376–81, 394–97

Ecology: Lana'i, 417; Maui, 13–14
Eels, 307
Emergencies, 39
Enchanting Floral Gardens, 102, 370
Events, annual, 54–58

Fish, 196–97
Fishing: Lana'i, 437; Maui, 345–47

Fitness centers: Lana'i, 443; Maui, 397–99
Five Graves, 324
Food festivals, 200

Garden of Eden, 109
Garden of the Gods, 421
Gardens, 370–75
Geckos, 13
Golf: Lana'i, 437–38; Maui, 347–52
Gorilla Foundation, 82
Grand Wailea Resort Hotel & Spa, 89–90
Grocery shopping: Lana'i, 420; Maui, 52–54

H. A. Baldwin Park, 327, 339
Haiku, 108
Hale Kahiko, 74–75
Hale Kohola (House of the Whale), 78, 370–71
Hale Pa'i, 70, 371
Hale Paahao (Old Prison), 68–69, 371
Hale Piula, 371
Haleakala National Park, 98, 100, 114, 355, 371; camping, 340–41; map, 101
Haleakala Observatories, 100
Halekii State Monument, 92
Hamoa Beach, 114, 328–29
Hana. *See* Hana Highway area
Hana Bay, 113
Hana Beach Park, 326
Hana Cultural Center, 113, 371
Hana Gardenland, 371–72
Hana Highway area: beaches, 327–29; dining, 286–93; lodging, 181–86; map, 107; sights and shops, 104–18
Hana Ranch, 113
Hanaka'o'o Beach (Ka'anapali Beach), 314
Hanaka'o'o Beach Park (Canoe Beach), 313
Hang gliding, 352
Hauola Stone, 68
Hawai'i Nature Center, 92, 374

Hawaiian islands: map, xiv
Hawaiian language, 11–12
Hazards, 39
Health retreats, 397–99
Helicopter tours, 352–54
Heritage Garden—Kepaniwai Park, 94
Hiking: Lana'i, 439; Maui, 354–59
History: Lana'i, 410–15; Maui, 6–11
Ho'okipa, 108
Ho'okipa Beach Park, 327
Hoapili Trail, 90, 355
Holidays, 36
Holua, 341
Honeymoons. *See* Weddings and honeymoons
Honokahua Burial Grounds, 81
Honokowai, 79
Honokowai Beach Park, 315–16
Honolua Bay and Beach, 83, 318–19
Honomanu Bay, 109
Horseback riding: Lana'i, 439–40; Maui, 359–62
Hosmer Grove, 340
Hostels, 176–77
Hotel rentals. *See* Lodging
Huelo, 109
Hui Aloha Church, 117
Hui No'eau Visual Arts Center, 103, 372
Hulopo'e Beach, 423
Hunting: Lana'i, 440; Maui, 362–63
Hurricanes, 59–60
Hyatt Regency Maui Resort and Spa, 77–78

Iao Valley, 94
Interisland flights, 44–45
Internet access, 38–39

Jet skiing, 363

Ka'ahumanu Church, 92
Ka'anapali Beach (Hanaka'o'o Beach), 314
Ka'anapali Beach (North End), 315
Ka'anapali–Kapalua area: beaches, 314–19; dining, 218–38; lodging, 132–52; map, 77; sights and shops, 76–84
Ka'ono'ulu Beach Park, 320
Kaena Iki Point, 421
Kahakuloa, 83
Kahana, 79–80
Kahana Beach, 316
Kahanu Garden, 111–12, 372
Kahului–Wailuku area: beaches, 326–27; dining, 267–80; lodging, 176–78; map, 93; sights and shops, 91–97
Kaihalulu Beach (Red Sand Beach), 114, 328
Kaiolohia (Shipwreck Beach), 421, 422
Kalama Beach Park, 320–21
Kalanakila Church, 422
Kama'ole I–III Beaches, 321
Kamehameha Iki Park, 73
Kanaha Beach Park, 326–27, 339
Kanaha Wildlife Sanctuary, 95
Kapalaoa, 341
Kapalua. *See* Ka'anapali–Kapalua area
Kapalua Beach, 317
Kapalua Discovery Center, 372
Kaumahina State Wayside, 109
Kaumalapau Harbor, 423
Kaupo Store, 118
Kawiliki Pou Park, 320
Kawililipoa area beaches, 320
Kayaking: Lana'i, 441; Maui, 363–65
Ke'anae Arboretum, 109–10
Ke'anae Congregational Church, 110
Ke'anae Peninsula, 110
Kealia Pond National Wildlife Refuge, 86–87, 372
Keawakapu Beach, 321–22
Keawala'i Church, 91
Keokea, 102
Keomuku, 422

Keonenui Beach, 316
Kihei. *See* Ma'alaea–Kihei–Wailea–Makena area
Kipahulu Hawaiian Church, 116
Kipahulu Valley, 114–16
Kiteboarding, 365
Koki Beach Park, 328
Kula, 100, 102
Kula Botanical Gardens, 102, 372

La Perouse Bay and Beaches, 326
Lahaina: beaches, 310, 312–13; dining, 200–18; lodging, 127–31; map, 65; sights and shops, 63–76. *See also nearby areas*
Lahaina Beach, 312–13
Lahaina Courthouse and Museum, 66–67, 372
Lahaina Harbor, 67
Lahaina Jodo Mission, 70, 373
Lahaina Ka'anapali & Pacific Railroad, 25, 75–76, 368
Lahaina Lighthouse, 67–68, 373
Lahaina Pali Trail, 355
Lahaina Reunion Time Capsule plaque, 64
Lana'i: beaches, 434–35; best bets, 408; dining, 430–34; ecology, 417; facts and figures, 409; history, 410–15; lodging, 425–30; map, 411; overview, 408–409; recreation and tours, 435–44; sights and shops, 420–24; transportation in, 419–20; transportation to, 419; weather, 415–17
Land tours, 366–70
Language, 11–12
Lapahiki Road (Lana'i), 422
Launiupoko State Wayside Park, 312
Limousine services: Lana'i, 420; Maui, 48
Lindbergh (Charles) gravesite, 116
Little Makena (Pu'u Ola'i Beach), 325

Lodging (Lana'i), 425–30
Lodging (Maui), 119–90; abbreviations in listings, 120; best bets, 124–27; Hana Highway area, 181–86; Lahaina, 127–31; Ka'anapali–Kapalua area, 132–52; Kahului–Wailuku area, 176–78; Ma'alaea–Kihei–Wailea–Makena area, 152–76; rental agents, 120, 186–90; Upcountry, 178–81
Lopa, 422
Luaus, 293, 296–301
Lyon's Hill, 114

Ma'alaea Bay Beach, 319–20
Ma'alaea–Kihei–Wailea–Makena area: beaches, 319–26; dining, 238–67; lodging, 152–76; map, 85; sights and shops, 84–91
Mai Poina Oe Lau Beach Park, 320
Makahiku Falls, 115–16
Makawao, 103–104
Makena. *See* Ma'alaea–Kihei–Wailea–Makena area
Makena Beach (Oneloa Beach), 325
Makena Landing—Papipi Beach, 324
Malamalama Church (Kalanakila Church), 422
Malu'aka Beach, 324–25
Manele Bay, 424
Maria Lanakila Church, 69
Masters' Reading Room, 68
Maui: annual events, 54–58; beaches, 302–29; best bets, 1–6; dining, 191–301; ecology, 13–14; history, 6–11; lodging, 119–90; map, 310; overview, 1–62; phone numbers, 61–62; recreation and tours, 330–407; sights and shops, 63–118; transportation

INDEX

in, 47–52; transportation to, 40–44; visitor info, 36; weather, 58–61
Maui Botanical Gardens, 94, 373
Maui Central Park, 94
Maui Jinsha Mission, 92
Maui Ocean Center, 86, 373
Maui Pineapple Company, 374–75
Maui Research & Technology Park, 87
Maui Swap Meet, 95
Maui Tropical Plantation and Country Store, 94, 375
Medical emergencies, 39
Miniature golf, 352
Miracle Church, 110
Mokapu Beach, 322
Moku'ula, 73–74
Mokule'ia Beach (Slaughterhouse Beach), 318
Mokumana Island, 110
Molokini, 382
Motorcycle rentals, 51–52
Movies, 22, 403–405
Museums, 370–75

Naha, 422
Namalu Bay and Beach, 317–18
Napili, 80
Napili Bay, 80
Napili Bay and Beach, 317
Nightlife, 294–95. *See also* Dinner shows; Luaus

'Ohe'o, 340–41
Old Fort (Lahaina), 64
Older travelers, 26–27
Olowalu Beach, 310
Oneloa Beach (Makena Beach), 318, 325
Our Lady of Fatima Shrine, 110
Outfitters. *See* Camping; Hiking
Outrigger canoeing, 341–42

Packing, 29–30
Paia, 108
Paipu Beach, 324
Palauea Beach, 323
Paliku, 341
Papalaua State Wayside Park, 310
Paper Airplane Museum, 97, 375
Papipi Beach (Makena Landing), 324
Parasailing, 375–76
Parking (Lahaina), 66
Periodicals, 37–38
Phone numbers, 61–62
Pihana State Monument, 92, 94
Pi'ilanihale Heiau, 112
Pineapples, 2
Pioneer Inn, 64, 66
Pohaku'O, 423
Polipoli Springs State Recreation Area, 102, 340, 355–56
Polo, 376
Polo Beach, 323
Po'olenalena Beach, 323–24
Pools of 'Ohe'o, 114–15
Portuguese man–of–war, 306
Price seasons, 122
Pua'a Kaa State Wayside, 111
Puamana Beach Park, 312
Public transportation, 47–48
Puohokamoa Falls, 109
Pu'u Ola'i Beach (Little Makena), 325
Pu'u Ola'i cinder cone, 90–91, 356
Pu'unoa Beach, 313
Pu'upehe, 423–24

Radio, 36–37
Rain: Lana'i, 416; Maui, 59
Recreation and tours: Lana'i, 435–44. *See also specific sports or activities*
Recreation and tours: Maui, 330–407; best bets, 332; booking services, 330–31; and children, 21, 23–26. *See also specific sports or activities*
Red Sand Beach, 328
Resort tours (Lana'i), 442–43
Restaurants. *See* Dining

Riding lessons, 360
Running, 376

Sailing, 381–94
St. Gabriel's Mission, 110
St. Joseph's Church, 118
Sales tax, 36
Scuba diving: Lana'i, 441–42; Maui, 376–81
Sea excursions, 381–94
Sea urchins, 306
Seamen's Cemetery, 69
Seamen's Hospital, 69–70
Seasons (high/low), 122
Senior travelers, 26–27
Seven Sacred Pools, 114–15
Sharks, 307
Shipwreck Beach (Kaiolohia Beach), 421, 422
Shipwrecks, 422
Shopping. *See* Sights and shops
Shuttles: Lana'i, 419; Maui, 48
Sights and shops (Lana'i), 420–24
Sights and shops (Maui), 63–118; and children, 21–26: Hana Highway area, 104–18; Lahaina, 63–76; Ka'anapali–Kapalua area, 76–84; Kahului–Wailuku area, 91–97; Ma'alaea–Kihei–Wailea–Makena area, 84–91; Upcountry, 98–104
Silversword, 100
Slaughterhouse (Mokule'ia) Beach, 83, 318
Sliding Sands Trail, 100
Snakes, 14
Snorkeling: Lana'i, 442; Maui, 394–97
Snuba, 397
Spas: Lana'i, 443; Maui, 397–99
Spelunking, 399–400
Sportfishing: Lana'i, 437; Maui, 345–47
Sporting clays: Lana'i, 440; Maui, 362–63
Spreckles Ditches, 111

State parks, and camping, 339–40
Sugar Cane Train, 25, 75–76, 368
Sun safety, 39
Sunrise and sunset, 61, 288
Sunrise Protea Farm, 375
Sunset cruises. *See* Cruises and cruise lines
Sunset watching, 288
Surfing: Lana'i, 444; Maui, 400–402
Sweetheart Rock (Pu'upehe), 423–24
Swimming, 402

Taxis, 48
Tedeschi Winery, 102
Television, 36
Temperatures: Lana'i, 416; Maui, 58
Tennis: Lana'i, 444; Maui, 402–403
Theater and the arts: Lana'i, 436–37, 444; Maui, 403–405
Tides, 61
Time zone, 37
Timeshares, 331
Totem pole (Kihei), 87
Trails. *See* Hiking
Transportation: in Lana'i, 419–20; in Maui, 47–52
Transportation: to Lana'i, 419; to Maui, 40–44
Travel wholesalers and packagers, 40–43
Tropical Gardens of Maui, 94
Tsunamis, 60–61
Twin Falls, 108

Ukumehame Beach Park, 310
Ulua Beach, 322
Ulupalakua Ranch, 102
Ulupikunui Beach, 324
Underwater photography, 395
Upcountry: dining, 280–86; lodging, 178–81; maps, 99, 101; sights and shops, 98–104

INDEX

Visitor info, 36

Wahikuli State Wayside Park, 313
Wai'anapanapa Caves, 112
Wai'anapanapa State Park, 112–13, 327–28, 340
Waihe'e Beach Park, 326
Waikamo Bridge, 109
Waikamoi Ridge Nature Trail, 109
Waikapu, 94
Wailea. *See* Ma'alaea–Kihei–Wailea–Makena area
Wailea Beach, 322
Wailua Wayside Lookout, 111
Waimaha'iha'i area beaches, 320
Waimoku Falls, 115–16
Waiola Church, 69
Water safety, 304–309
Waterskiing, 405
Weather: Lana'i, 415–17; Maui, 58–61
Websites, 38
Weddings and honeymoons: Lana'i, 418–19; Maui, 30–36
Westin Maui, 77–78
Whale watching, 405–406
Whaling Museum, 69
Windsurfing, 406–407
Wo Hing Temple and Museum, 69, 375

Lodging Index

Aloha Cottages, 181
Aston Ka'anapali Shores, 140
Aston Maui Banyan, 162

Banana Bungalow Maui—Hotel & International Hostel, 176–77
Banyan Tree Vacation Rentals, 178
Best Western Pioneer Inn, 127

Diamond Resort, 167

Ekahi Village, 174
Ekolu Village, 174
Elua Village, 174–75
Embassy Vacation Resort—Ka'anapali Beach, 138–39

Fairmont Kea Lani Hotel, Suites & Villas, 167–68
Four Seasons Resort Wailea, 168–70

Garden Gate Bed and Breakfast, 127–28
Grand Champion Villas, 175
Grand Wailea Resort Hotel & Spa, 170–71

Haiku Getaway, B&B Vacation Rentals, 178
Haiku Lani, 181–82
Hale Alana, 155

Hale Huelo Bed & Breakfast, 179
Hale Hui Kai, 155
Hale Kai, 139
Hale Kai O' Kihei, 156
Hale Kamaole, 156
Hale Mahina Beach Resort, 139
Hale Maui Apartment Hotel, 139
Hale Napili, 146–47
Hale Ono Loa, 139–40
Hale Pau Hana, 156
Haleakala National Park, 179
Haleakala Shores, 156
Halfway to Hana House, 182
Hamoa Bay Bungalow and Hamoa Bay House, 182
Hana Gardenland, 183
Hana Kai-Maui, 182
Heavenly Hana Inn, 182
Hololani, 144
Hono Kai, 152–53
Honokeana Cove, 147
Hotel Hana-Maui at Hana Ranch, 183–84
Hotel Lana'i (Lana'i), 425–26
House of Fountains, 128
Hoyochi Nikko, 140
Huelo Point Lookout, 184–85
Hyatt Regency Maui Resort and Spa, 132

Inn at Mama's Fish House, 185
Island Sands, 153

Ka'anapali Alii, 133
Ka'anapali Beach Hotel, 133–34
Ka'anapali Plantation, 134
Ka'anapali Royal, 134
Kahana Beach Resort, 144
Kahana Outrigger, 144
Kahana Reef, 144–45
Kahana Sunset, 145
Kahana Villa, 145
Kahana Village, 145
Kaleialoha, 140
Kamaole Beach Royale, 156–57
Kamaole Nalu, 157
Kamaole Sands, 157
Kana'i a Nalu, 153
Kapalua Bay Hotel and Ocean Villas, 150–51
Kapalua Villas, 151
Kathy Scheper's Maui Accommodations, 157
Kauhale Makai (Village by the Sea), 157–58
Kealia, 158
Kihei Akahi, 158
Kihei Alii Kai, 158
Kihei Bay Surf, 158
Kihei Bay Vista, 159
Kihei Beach Resort Vacation Condominiums, 159
Kihei Garden Estates, 159
Kihei Holiday, 159
Kihei Kai, 159
Kihei Kai Nani, 160
Kihei Resort, 160
Kihei Sands, 160
Kihei Surfside, 160
Koa Lagoon, 160
Koa Resort, 161
Kula Cottage, 179–80
Kula Lodge, 180
Kula Lynn Farm, 180
Kulakane, 140–41
Kuleana, 141

Lahaina Inn, 128–29
Lahaina Roads, 129
Lahaina Shores Beach Resort, 129

Lana'i Plantation Home (Lana'i), 425
Lauloa, 153–54
Leilani Kai, 161
Leinaala, 161
Lodge at Koele (Lana'i), 427–30
Lokelani, 141
Luana Kai, 161

Ma'alaea Banyans, 154
Ma'alaea Kai, 154
Ma'alaea Surf, 161–62
Ma'alaea Yacht Marina, 154
Mahana, 141
Mahina Surf, 141–42
Makani a Kai, 154–55
Makani Sands, 142
Makena Surf, 175–76
Maluhia Hale, 180
Mana Kai, 162
Manele Bay Hotel (Lana'i), 426–27
Maui Beach Hotel, 177
Maui Coast Hotel, 162–63
Maui Dream Cottages, 180
Maui Eldorado, 134
Maui Hill, 163
Maui Islander Hotel, 130
Maui Ka'anapali Villas, 134–35
Maui Kai, 142
Maui Kamaole, 163
Maui Lu Resort, 163
Maui Marriott Resort & Ocean Club, 135
Maui Oceanfront Inn, 164
Maui Palms, 177
Maui Parkshore, 164
Maui Prince Hotel, 176
Maui Sands, 142
Maui Sunset, 164
Maui Vista, 164–65
Mauian, 147
Menehune Shores, 165
Milowai, 155
My Waii Beach Cottage, 165

Nani Kai Hale, 165
Napili Bay Resort, 147

Napili Gardens, 148
Napili Kai Beach Resort, 148
Napili Point, 148
Napili Shores, 148–49
Napili Sunset, 149
Napili Surf, 149
Napili Village Suites, 149
Noelani, 142–43
Nohonani, 143
Nona Lani, 165–66

Old Lahaina House Bed & Breakfast, 130
Old Wailuku Inn at Ulupono, 177–78
One Napili Way, 149

Paki Maui, 143
The Palms at Wailea, 171–72
Papakea, 143
Pikake, 143–44
Pilialoha Bed & Breakfast Cottage, 185
Plantation Inn, 130–31
Polipoli Springs State Recreation Area, 180–81
Polo Beach Club, 172
Polynesian Shores, 144
Puamana, 131
Punahoa, 166
Puunoa Beach Estates, 131

Renaissance Wailea Beach Resort, 172–73
Ritz-Carlton, Kapalua, 151–52
Royal Kahana, 146
Royal Lahaina Resort, 135–36
Royal Mauian, 166

Sands of Kahana, 146
Sheraton Maui, 136–37
Shores of Maui, 166
Silver Cloud Upcountry Guest Ranch, 181
Sugar Beach Resort, 166
Sunseeker Resort, 167

Valley Isle Resort, 146

Wai Ola, 131
Wai'anapanapa State Park, 185
Wailana Inn, 167
Wailana Kai, 167
Wailea Marriott, an Outrigger Resort, 173–74
Wailea Villas, 174–75
Westin Maui, 137–38
The Whaler, 138

YMCA Camp Ke'anae, 186

Dining Index

A & J Kitchen Deli & Bakery, 200–201
Ale House, 268
Alexander's Fish, Chicken and Chips, 238–39
Aloha Grill, 268–69
Aloha Mixed Plate, 201
Annie's Deli & Catering, 239
Anthony's Coffee Co., 286
Antonio's, 247–48
Aroma D'italia Ristorante, 239
Ashley's Internet Cafe, 218
Asian Star, 269
Athens (Kahului), 275
Athens Greek Restaurant (Lahaina), 205

The Bakery, 201
Ba-Le Sandwiches (Kahului), 274
Ba-Le Sandwiches (Lahaina), 205
Bamboo Bar & Grill, 201
Banyan Tree, 233
Basil Tomatoes, 223
Bay Club, 233
Beach Club, 218
Beach House, 223
Bistro Molokini, 255
Biwon Restaurant, 269
BJ's Chicago Pizzeria, 201–202
Blue Ginger Cafe (Lana'i), 431
Blue Lagoon Tropical Bar and Grill, 202

Blue Marlin Harborfront Grill & Bar, 248
Bocalino Bistro & Bar, 239–40
Brigit and Bernard's Garden Café, 269
Bubba Gump Shrimp Company Restaurant & Market, 209
Buzz's Wharf, 248

C.J.'s Deli & Diner, 219
Café Del Sol, 280
Café Des Amis, 286–87
Café 565 (Lana'i), 432
Café Kiowai, 241
Café Kula, 241
Café Mambo, 287
Café Marc Aurel, 270
Café O'Lei (Iao Valley), 270
Café O'Lei (Lahaina), 209–10
Café O'Lei (Makawao), 281
Café Romantica, 277
Café Sauvage, 210
Caffe Ciao, 248–49
Canoes, 210
Canton Chef, 249
Capische?, 255
Captain Dave's Fish & Chips/Pipeline Pizza, 202
Cary & Eddie's Hideaway, 279
Casanova Italian Restaurant and Deli, 284
Cascades Grille & Sushi Bar, 234

DINING INDEX

Castaway Café, 224
Challenge at Manele Clubhouse (Lana'i), 433
Charley's, 287–88
Cheeseburger in Paradise, 202–203
Chez Paul, 214–15
China Boat, 218
Chopsticks Express (Kahului), 274
Chopsticks Express (Lahaina), 205
Class Act, 279–80
Clubhouse Bar & Grill (Lana'i), 434
Coconut Grove, 210–11
Coffee Store, 219
Compadres, 211
Cool Cat Café, 203
Cupie's, 270
Curry in a Hurry, 270

Da Kitchen Express (Kahului), 271
Da Kitchen Express (Kihei), 240–41
David Paul's Lahaina Grill, 215
Deano's Maui Pizza Café, 241
Denny's, 203–204
Dollies, 219
Down to Earth Natural Foods & Café, 271
Dragon Dragon, 271
Duncan's Coffee Company, 281
Duncan's Rockin' Sushi, 281

Eddie's Fast Food, 271–72
Edo Japan (Kahului), 275
Edo Japan (Lahaina), 204–205
Erik's Seafood & Sushi, 211–12

Feast of Lele (luau), 293, 296
Fernando's, 241
Ferraro's, 255–56
Fiesta Time, 272
Fish and Games Brewing Company & Rotisserie, 224–25
Five Palms Beach Grill, 256

Four Sisters Bakery, 268
Fujiya's, 272

Gaby's Pizzeria & Deli, 204
Gardenia Court Restaurant, 234
Gazebo, 220
Gerard's, 215–16
Giovani's Tomato Pie Ristorante, 225
Grand Dining Room, 256–57
Grandma's Coffee House, 281–82
Greek Bistro, 249
Greenleaf's Grille, 205

Haiku Gourmet Take-out & Deli, 288
Hakone, 257
Hale AheAhe (Lana'i), 433
Hale Imua, 272
Hali'imaile General Store, 285–86
Hana Gion, 257–58
Hana Hou, 290
Hana Ranch Restaurant, 291–92
Hana Ranch Store, 290
Hanafuda Saimin, 241
Hard Rock Cafe, 212
Harlow's, 258
Harry's Sushi and Pupu Bar, 249
Hasegawa General Store, 290
Hawaiian Moons Salad Bar & Deli, 241–42
Hecocks, 212
Henry Clay Rotisserie (Lana'i), 431
Hirohachi, 242
Hokus Pokus, 288
Home Maid Bakery (Wailuku), 268
Home Maid Bakery & Deli (Kihei), 242
Honokowai Okazuya & Deli, 220
Honolua General Store, 220–21
Hotel Hana-Maui Dining Room, 292; dinner show, 296
House of Saimin, 204
Hula Grill, 225
Hula Moons Restaurant, 250

Hulopo'e Court (Lana'i), 432
Humuhumunukunukua'pua'a, 258–59
Hyatt Regency Maui Resort and Spa (luau), 296–97

Ihilani (Lana'i), 432–33
I'o, 216
International House of Pancakes, 272
Isana, 250

Jacques' North Shore Restaurant and Sushi Bar, 290–91
Jameson's Grill & Bar at Kapalua, 226
Java Jazz, 226
Jawz Fish Tacos, 242
Joe's, 259

Ka'anapali Mixed Plate, 221
Kahana Terrace Restaurant, 221
Kahuna Kabob, 204
Kai Ku Ono Bar & Grill, 250–51
Kaiona Café, 242–43
Kamaaina Kitchen, 204
Kea Lani Restaurant, 259
Keka'a Terrace, 226
Kihei Caffe, 243
Kimo's, 212–13
Kincha, 260
Kitada's Kau Kau Corner, 282
Kobe Japanese Steak House, 213
Koho Grill and Bar, 272–73
Kula Lodge, 284–85
Kula Sandalwoods Restaurant, 285
Kumu Bar & Grill, 251
Kupanaha: Maui Magic for All Ages (dinner show), 297

L&L Drive-Inn (Kahului), 274
L&L Drive-Inn (Lahaina), 205
Lahaina Cannery Mall, 204–205
Lahaina Coolers, 213
Lahaina Fish Company, 213–14
Las Pinatas of Maui, 273
Le Gunji, 260

Leilani's on the Beach, 227
Lemongrass, 205
Life's a Beach, 243
Lobster Cove–Harry's Sushi Bar, 260–61
Lodge at Koele's Formal Dining Room (Lana'i), 434
Longhi's, 216–17
Lu Lu's, 251
Lynne's Café, 289

Ma'alaea Grill, 251–52
Makawao Steak House, 285
Makena Clubhouse, 243–44
Mama Ding's Pasteles Restaurant, 273
Mama's Fish House, 292–93
Mama's Ribs -N- Rotisserie, 221–22
Mañana Garage, 280
Marco's Grill & Deli, 273–74
Marco's Southside Grill, 252
Margarita's Beach Cantina, 252
Maui Bake Shop & Deli, 274
Maui Coffee Roasters, 274
Maui Mall, 274
Maui Marketplace, 274
Maui Marriott Resort & Ocean Club (luau), 297–98
Maui Onion, 244
Maui Swiss Café, 205
Maui Tacos, 205
Maui Thai Kitchen, 244
Maui Tropical Plantation Café, 274–75
Maui's Mixed Grill, 274
Maui's Mixed Plate, 275–76
Mike's Restaurant, 275
Milagros Food Co., 289
Mr. Sub, 205–206
Mixed Plate, 282
Moana Bakery & Café, 291
Moose McGillycuddy's, 206
Mulligan's on the Blue, 253

Nachos Grande, 222
Nalu Sunset Bar & Sushi, 222
Nazo's, 275

Nick's Fishmarket Maui, 261
No Ka Oi Deli, 206
North Beach Grille, 227

Ohana Grill and Bar, 222
Old Lahaina Luau (luau), 298
'OnO Surf Bar & Grill, 227–28
Outback Steakhouse, 228

Pacific Grill, 261–62
Pacific 'O, 217
Paia Fish Market Restaurant, 289
The Palm at Elleair, 262
Palm Court, 262–63
Pancho and Lefty's, 206–207
Panda Express, 244
Pauwela Café, 289–90
Pavillion, 228
Peggy Sue's, 244–45
Pele's Other Garden (Lana'i), 431–32
Penne Pasta Café, 207
Pioneer Inn Bar & Grill, 214
Pipeline Pizza, 202
Pita Paradise, 245
Pizza Fresh, 282
Pizza in Paradise, 275
Pizza Paradiso, 222–23
Plantation House, 235
Plumeria Terrace Restaurant and Bar, 228–29
Polli's, 282–83
Polo Beach Grille and Bar, 253
Pool Grille (Lana'i), 433
Prince Court, 263–64
Pukalani Country Club Restaurant, 283

Queen Ka'ahumanu Center, 275–76

Reilley's, 229
Restaurant Taiko, 264
Roy's Kahana Bar & Grill, 235–36
Roy's Nicolina, 236
Royal King's Garden, 283
Royal Lahaina Resort In Ka'anapali (luau), 298–99

Royal Ocean Terrace Restaurant, 229
Royal Seafood Chinese Restaurant, 207
Royal Thai Cuisine, 245
Ruby's Diner, 276
Rusty Harpoon, 229–30
Ruth's Chris Steak House, 217–18

Saeng's Thai, 276
A Saigon Café, 267–68
Sam Sato's, 277
Sansei Restaurant and Sushi Bar, 230–31
Sarento's on the Beach, 264–65
Sbarro, 275
Sea House, 231; luau, 299–300
Sea Watch Restaurant, 265
Seascape Ma'alaea Restaurant, 245–46
Senor Taco, 246
Shaka Sandwich and Pizza, 246
Siam Thai, 277
Simple Pleasures Café/Café Romantica, 277
Simply Healthy, 277–78
Siu's Chinese Kitchen, 274
Smokehouse Bar & Grill, 214
Smooth Moves, 246–47
South Philly Steak & Fries, 205
Spago, 265–66
Spats Trattoria, 236–27
Spices, 253
Sports Club Kahana Grill, 223
Stella Blues Cafe & Deli, 253–54
Stillwells Bakery & Cafe, 278
Stinger Ray, 278
Stopwatch Sports Bar, 283
Sub Paradise, 278
Suda Snack Shop, 247
Sunrise Café, 207
Sushi Go!, 276
Sushiya, 207–208
Swan Court, 237

Take Home Maui, 208
Tanigawa's (Lana'i), 430

Tasaka Guri Guri, 274
Tasty Crust Restaurant, 278
Teppan Yaki Dan, 237
The Terrace (Kapalua), 237–38
The Terrace (Lana'i), 433–34
Thai Chef, 208
Thailand Cuisine, 254
Tiki Terrace, 231–32
Tokyo Tei, 279
Tommy Bahamas Tropical Cafe and Emporium, 266
Tony 'N Tina's Wedding (dinner show), 300
Tony Roma's, 254
tropica, 238
Tutu's, 290

Va Bene Italian Beachside Grill, 232–33
Vietnamese Cuisine Restaurant & Bar, 254

Wailea Marriott, an Outrigger Resort (luau), 300–301
Wailea Sunset Luau (luau), 301
Warren & Annabelle's (dinner show), 301
Waterfront Deli, 247
Waterfront Restaurant, 266–67
Whale's Tale, 208
Wowwee—Maui's Café, 279

Yama, 208
Young's Kitchen, 247
Yummy Korean BBQ, 275

Zushi, 208–209

Dining Index by Cuisine

American
Ale House, 268
Alexander's Fish, Chicken and Chips, 238–39
Aloha Grill, 268–69
Annie's Deli & Catering, 239
Beach Club, 218
Beach House, 223
Blue Lagoon Tropical Bar and Grill, 202
Buzz's Wharf, 248
Café Mambo, 287
Canoes, 210
Cary & Eddie's Hideaway, 279
Cascades Grille & Sushi Bar, 234
Castaway Café, 224
Charley's, 287–88
Cheeseburger in Paradise, 202–203
Cool Cat Café, 203
Cupie's, 270
Denny's, 203–204
Dollies, 219
Gazebo, 220
Hana Ranch Restaurant, 291–92
Hard Rock Cafe, 212
Harlow's, 258
Hecocks, 212
Honolua General Store, 220–21
Hula Moons Restaurant, 250
International House of Pancakes, 272
Jameson's Grill & Bar at Kapalua, 226
Java Jazz, 226
Joe's, 259
Ka'anapali Mixed Plate, 221
Kahana Terrace Restaurant, 221
Keka'a Terrace, 226
Kimo's, 212–13
Koho Grill and Bar, 272-73
Kula Lodge, 284–85
Kula Sandalwoods Restaurant, 285
Lahaina Coolers, 213
Lahaina Fish Company, 213–14
Leilani's on the Beach, 227
Life's a Beach, 243
Makawao Steak House, 285
Makena Clubhouse, 243–44
Maui Onion, 244
Moose McGillycuddy's, 206
Mulligan's on the Blue, 253
Ohana Grill and Bar, 222
Pacific Grill, 261–62
Pioneer Inn Bar & Grill, 214
Pukalani Country Club Restaurant, 283
Ruby's Diner, 276
Rusty Harpoon, 229–30
Sea House, 231

Seascape Ma'alaea Restaurant, 245–46
Spago, 265–66
Spices, 253
Stopwatch Sports Bar, 283
Take Home Maui, 208
Tiki Terrace, 231–32
Tony Roma's, 254
Whale's Tale, 208

Asian
Banyan Tree, 233
Hanafuda Saimin, 241
Nalu Sunset Bar & Sushi, 222
Royal Seafood Chinese Restaurant, 207

Bakery
The Bakery, 201
Four Sisters Bakery, 268
Home Maid Bakery (Wailuku), 268
Home Maid Bakery & Deli (Kihei), 242
Maui Bake Shop & Deli, 274
Moana Bakery & Café, 291
Stillwells Bakery & Cafe, 278

Barbecue
Mama's Ribs -N- Rotisserie, 221–22
Smokehouse Bar & Grill, 214
Tony Roma's, 254

Breakfast
Grand Dining Room, 256–57
Kea Lani Restaurant, 259

Buffet
'OnO Surf Bar & Grill, 227–28
Palm Court, 262–63
Royal Ocean Terrace Restaurant, 229

Caribbean
Mañana Garage, 280
Tommy Bahamas Tropical Cafe and Emporium, 266

Chinese
Canton Chef, 249
China Boat, 218
Chopsticks Express (Kahului), 274
Chopsticks Express (Lahaina), 205
Dragon Dragon, 271
Panda Express, 244
Royal King's Garden, 283
Royal Seafood Chinese Restaurant, 207
Siu's Chinese Kitchen, 274

Coffee
Anthony's Coffee Co., 286
Café Mambo, 287
Café Marc Aurel, 270
Coffee Store, 219
Duncan's Coffee Company, 281
Grandma's Coffee House, 281–82
Hale Imua, 272
Java Jazz, 226
Maui Bake Shop & Deli, 274
Maui Coffee Roasters, 274

Continental/Island Continental
Bay Club, 233
Gardenia Court Restaurant, 234
Hali'imaile General Store, 285–86
Hotel Hana-Maui Dining Room, 292
Kihei Caffe, 243
Longhi's, 216–17
Mama's Fish House, 292–93
Mulligan's on the Blue, 253
Plantation House, 235
Swan Court, 237

Crepes
Café Des Amis, 286–87

Cuban
Mañana Garage, 280

Deli
Café Del Sol, 280
C.J.'s Deli & Diner, 219
Haiku Gourmet Take-out & Deli, 288
Kaiona Café, 242–43
Maui Bake Shop & Deli, 274
Ohana Grill and Bar, 222

Peggy Sue's, 244–45
Waterfront Deli, 247

Diner
Aloha Grill, 268–69
Cool Cat Café, 203
Peggy Sue's, 244–45
Ruby's Diner, 276

Dinner Shows
Feast of Lele, 293, 296
Hotel Hana-Maui, 296
Hyatt Regency Maui Resort and Spa, 296–97
Kupanaha: Maui Magic for All Ages, 297
Maui Marriott Resort & Ocean Club, 297–98
Old Lahaina Luau, 298
Royal Lahaina Resort In Ka'anapali, 298–99
Sea House, 299–300
Tony 'N Tina's Wedding, 300
Wailea Marriott, an Outrigger Resort, 300–301
Wailea Sunset Luau, 301
Warren & Annabelle's, 301

Eclectic
Honokowai Okazuya & Deli, 220
Lu Lu's, 251
Maui Swiss Cafe, 205
Stella Blues Cafe & Deli, 253–54

Family Dining
Aroma D'italia Ristorante, 239
Asian Star, 269
Ashley's Internet Cafe, 218
BJ's Chicago Pizzeria, 201–202
Bubba Gump Shrimp Company Restaurant & Market, 209
Café Del Sol, 280
Café Mambo, 287
Café O'Lei, 209–10
Caffe Ciao, 248–49
Castaway Café, 224
Cheeseburger in Paradise, 202–203
C.J.'s Deli & Diner, 219
Coconut Grove, 210–11
Compadres, 211

Cupie's, 270
Dragon Dragon, 271
Erik's Seafood & Sushi, 211–12
Five Palms Beach Grill, 256
Gardenia Court Restaurant, 234
Gazebo, 220
Grandma's Coffee House, 281–82
Hali'imaile General Store, 285–86
Hanafuda Saimin, 241
Hard Rock Cafe, 212
Honokowai Okazuya & Deli, 220
Hula Grill, 225
Hula Moons Restaurant, 250
Jacques' North Shore Restaurant and Sushi Bar, 290–91
Jawz Fish Tacos, 242
Ka'anapali Mixed Plate, 221
Kaiona Café, 242–43
Kea Lani Restaurant, 259
Kihei Caffe, 243
Kimo's, 212–13
Kupanaha: Maui Magic for All Ages, 297
Leilani's on the Beach, 227
Makawao Steak House, 285
Mama Ding's Pasteles Restaurant, 273
Mama's Fish House, 292–93
Nick's Fishmarket Maui, 261
Old Lahaina Luau, 298
'OnO Surf Bar & Grill, 227–28
Outback Steakhouse, 228
Palm Court, 262–63
Pauwela Café, 289–90
Pavillion, 228
Pizza Paradiso, 222–23
Plantation House, 235
Restaurant Taiko, 264
Roy's Nicolina, 236
A Saigon Café, 267–68
Sam Sato's, 277
Sansei Restaurant and Sushi Bar, 230–31
Sea House, 299–300
Senor Taco, 246
Smooth Moves, 246–47
Stella Blues Cafe & Deli, 253–54
Tasty Crust Restaurant, 278

Tiki Terrace, 231–32
Tommy Bahamas Tropical Cafe and Emporium, 266
Tony Roma's, 254
Va Bene Italian Beachside Grill, 232–33
Wailea Marriott, an Outrigger Resort, 300–301
Warren & Annabelle's, 301
Waterfront Deli, 247

Filipino
Eddie's Fast Food, 271–72

Fish & Chips
Captain Dave's Fish & Chips/Pipeline Pizza, 202

Food Courts
Lahaina Cannery Mall, 204–205
Maui Mall, 274
Maui Marketplace, 274
Queen Ka'ahumanu Center, 275–76

French
Café Des Amis, 286–87
Chez Paul, 214–15
Gerard's, 215–16

German
Brigit and Bernard's Garden Café, 269

Greek
Athens (Kahului), 275
Athens Greek Restaurant (Lahaina), 205
Greek Bistro, 249
Pita Paradise, 245

Hawaiian
Aloha Mixed Plate, 201
Banyan Tree, 233
Coconut Grove, 210–11
Ka'anapali Mixed Plate, 221
Pukalani Country Club Restaurant, 283
Smooth Moves, 246–47
Tiki Terrace, 231–32

Hawaiian-American
Castaway Café, 224
Hula Moons Restaurant, 250

Kula Lodge, 284–85
Spago, 265–66

Hawaiian Regional
Hali'imaile General Store, 285–86
Hula Grill, 225
Ma'alaea Grill, 251–52
Roy's Kahana Bar & Grill, 235–36
Roy's Nicolina, 236

Healthy
Café Mambo, 287
Greenleaf's Grille, 205
Hawaiian Moons Salad Bar & Deli, 241–42
Kahuna Kabob, 204
Maui Tacos, 205
Pauwela Café, 289–90
Simply Healthy, 277–78

International
Class Act, 279–80
Palm Court, 262–63
Plumeria Terrace Restaurant and Bar, 228–29

Internet Café
Ashley's Internet Cafe, 218
Café Marc Aurel, 270
Hale Imua, 272
Maui Swiss Café, 205

Island Cuisine
Bay Club, 233
Bistro Molokini, 255
Café Kiowai, 240
Café Sauvage, 210
Gardenia Court Restaurant, 234
Humuhumunukunukua'pua'a, 258–59
Polo Beach Grille and Bar, 253
Prince Court, 263–64
Sea Watch Restaurant, 265
Swan Court, 237

Italian
Antonio's, 247–48
Aroma D'italia Ristorante, 239
Basil Tomatoes, 223
BJ's Chicago Pizzeria, 201–202
Brigit and Bernard's Garden Café, 269

Caffe Ciao, 248–49
Capische?, 255
Casanova Italian Restaurant and Deli, 284
Charley's, 287–88
Deano's Maui Pizza Café, 241
Dollies, 219
Ferraro's, 255–56
Gaby's Pizzeria & Deli, 204
Giovani's Tomato Pie Ristorante, 225
Greek Bistro, 249
Marco's Grill & Deli, 273–74
Marco's Southside Grill, 252
Penne Pasta Café, 207
Pizza Fresh, 282
Pizza Paradiso, 222–23
Sarento's on the Beach, 264–65
Sbarro, 275
Spats Trattoria, 236–27
Stopwatch Sports Bar, 283
Va Bene Italian Beachside Grill, 232–33

Japanese
Edo Japan (Kahului), 275
Edo Japan (Lahaina), 204–205
Fujiya's, 272
Hakone, 257
Hana Gion, 257–58
Harry's Sushi and Pupu Bar, 249
Hirohachi, 242
Kincha, 260
Kobe Japanese Steak House, 213
Le Gunji, 260
Restaurant Taiko, 264
Sansei Restaurant and Sushi Bar, 230–31
Teppan Yaki Dan, 237
Tokyo Tei, 279
Yama, 208
Zushi, 208–209

Korean
Biwon Restaurant, 269
Isana, 250
Kamaaina Kitchen, 204
Young's Kitchen, 247
Yummy Korean BBQ, 275

Latin American
Mañana Garage, 280

Light Meals
Anthony's Coffee Co., 286
Café Kula, 241
Maui Coffee Roasters, 274
Stinger Ray, 278
Sunrise Café, 207

Local
A & J Kitchen Deli & Bakery, 200–201
Aloha Mixed Plate, 201
Cupie's, 270
Da Kitchen Express (Kihei), 240–41
Da Kitchen Express (Kahului), 271
Eddie's Fast Food, 271–72
Grandma's Coffee House, 281–82
Hana Hou, 290
Hanafuda Saimin, 241
Honokowai Okazuya & Deli, 220
House of Saimin, 204
Kahuna Kabob, 204
Kamaaina Kitchen, 204
Kitada's Kau Kau Corner, 282
L&L Drive-Inn (Kahului), 274
L&L Drive-Inn (Lahaina), 205
Lynne's Café, 289
Mama Ding's Pasteles Restaurant, 273
Maui's Mixed Plate, 275–76
Mike's Restaurant, 275
Mixed Plate, 282
Nazo's, 275
No Ka Oi Deli, 206
Sam Sato's, 277
Smooth Moves, 246–47
Suda Snack Shop, 247
Sushiya, 207–208
Tasty Crust Restaurant, 278
Tutu's, 290
Young's Kitchen, 247

Luaus
Feast of Lele, 293, 296
Hyatt Regency Maui Resort and Spa, 296–97

Maui Marriott Resort & Ocean Club, 297–98
Old Lahaina Luau, 298
Royal Lahaina Resort In Ka'anapali, 298–99
Sea House, 299–300
Wailea Marriott, an Outrigger Resort, 300–301
Wailea Sunset Luau, 301

Mediterranean
Athens (Kahului), 275
Athens Greek Restaurant (Lahaina), 205
Bocalino Bistro & Bar, 239–40
Greek Bistro, 249
Pita Paradise, 245

Mexican
Compadres, 211
Fernando's, 241
Fiesta Time, 272
Jawz Fish Tacos, 242
Las Pinatas of Maui, 273
Life's a Beach, 243
Margarita's Beach Cantina, 252
Maui Tacos, 205
Nachos Grande, 222
Pancho and Lefty's, 206–207
Polli's, 282–83
Senor Taco, 246

New American
David Paul's Lahaina Grill, 215

Pacific Rim
Café O'Lei, 209–10
Canoes, 210
Five Palms Beach Grill, 256
I'o, 216
Kumu Bar & Grill, 251
North Beach Grille, 227
Pacific Grill, 261–62
Pacific 'O, 217
Pavillion, 228
Sansei Restaurant and Sushi Bar, 230–31
The Terrace, 237–38
tropica, 238

Pastries
The Bakery, 201
Café Mambo, 287
Coffee Store, 219
Down to Earth Natural Foods & Café, 271
Duncan's Coffee Company, 281
Four Sisters Bakery, 268
Home Maid Bakery (Wailuku), 268
Home Maid Bakery & Deli (Kihei), 242
Maui Bake Shop & Deli, 274
Moana Bakery & Café, 291
Stillwells Bakery & Cafe, 278

Pizza
BJ's Chicago Pizzeria, 201–202
Captain Dave's Fish & Chips/ Pipeline Pizza, 202
Casanova Italian Restaurant and Deli, 284
Deano's Maui Pizza Café, 241
Ferraro's, 255–56
Gaby's Pizzeria & Deli, 204
Giovani's Tomato Pie Ristorante, 225
Pizza Fresh, 282
Pizza in Paradise, 275
Pizza Paradiso, 222–23
Shaka Sandwich and Pizza, 246

Puerto Rican
Mama Ding's Pasteles Restaurant, 273

Salads
Café O'Lei (Iao Valley), 270
Café O'Lei (Makawao), 281
Maui Tropical Plantation Café, 274–75
No Ka Oi Deli, 206

Sandwiches
Ashley's Internet Cafe, 218
Ba-Le Sandwiches (Kahului), 274
Ba-Le Sandwiches (Lahaina), 205
Café O'Lei (Iao Valley), 270
Café O'Lei (Makawao), 281
Kai Ku Ono Bar & Grill, 250–51

Maui Swiss Café, 205
Maui Tropical Plantation Café, 274–75
Mr. Sub, 205–206
No Ka Oi Deli, 206
Shaka Sandwich and Pizza, 246
South Philly Steak & Fries, 205
Sports Club Kahana Grill, 223
Stillwells Bakery & Cafe, 278
Sub Paradise, 278
Sunrise Café, 207
Tutu's, 290
Wowwee—Maui's Café, 279

Seafood
Blue Marlin Harborfront Grill & Bar, 248
Bubba Gump Shrimp Company Restaurant & Market, 209
Buzz's Wharf, 248
Cary & Eddie's Hideaway, 279
Coconut Grove, 210–11
Erik's Seafood & Sushi, 211–12
Fish and Games Brewing Company & Rotisserie, 224–25
Hula Grill, 225
Humuhumunukunukua'pua'a, 258–59
Jacques' North Shore Restaurant and Sushi Bar, 290–91
Jameson's Grill & Bar at Kapalua, 226
Kimo's, 212–13
Lahaina Fish Company, 213–14
Leilani's on the Beach, 227
Lobster Cove–Harry's Sushi Bar, 260–61
Mama's Fish House, 292–93
Nick's Fishmarket Maui, 261
Paia Fish Market Restaurant, 289
The Palm at Elleair, 262
Plantation House, 235
Reilley's, 229
Spices, 253
Waterfront Restaurant, 266–67

Steakhouse
Ale House, 268
Makawao Steak House, 285

Outback Steakhouse, 228
Reilley's, 229
Ruth's Chris Steak House, 217–18

Sushi
Bamboo Bar & Grill, 201
Cascades Grille & Sushi Bar, 234
Duncan's Rockin' Sushi, 281
Edo Japan (Kahului), 275
Edo Japan (Lahaina), 204–205
Erik's Seafood & Sushi, 211–12
Fujiya's, 272
Hakone, 257
Harry's Sushi and Pupu Bar, 249
Hirohachi, 242
Isana, 250
Jacques' North Shore Restaurant and Sushi Bar, 290–91
Kincha, 260
Kobe Japanese Steak House, 213
Nalu Sunset Bar & Sushi, 222
Sansei Restaurant and Sushi Bar, 230–31
Sushi Go!, 276
Yama, 208

Teppanyaki
Edo Japan (Kahului), 274
Edo Japan (Lahaina), 204–205
Kobe Japanese Steak House, 213
Le Gunji, 260
Teppan Yaki Dan, 237

Tex-Mex
Milagros Food Co., 289

Thai
Bamboo Bar & Grill, 201
Maui Thai Kitchen, 244
Royal Thai Cuisine, 245
Saeng's Thai, 276
Siam Thai, 277
Thai Chef, 208
Thailand Cuisine, 254

Vegetarian/Vegan
Curry in a Hurry, 270
Down to Earth Natural Foods & Café, 271
Hawaiian Moons Salad Bar & Deli, 241–42

Hokus Pokus, 288
Simple Pleasures Café/Café Romantica, 277

Vietnamese
Asian Star, 269
Ba-Le Sandwiches (Kahului), 274
Ba-Le Sandwiches (Lahaina), 205
Bamboo Bar & Grill, 201
Lemongrass, 205
A Saigon Café, 267–68
Vietnamese Cuisine Restaurant & Bar, 254

Paradise Family Guides

Ideal for families traveling with kids of any age—toddlers to teenagers—Paradise Family Guides offer a blend of travel information unlike any other guides to the Hawaiian islands. With vacation ideas and tropical adventures that are sure to satisfy both action-hungry youngsters and relaxation-seeking parents, these guides meet the specific needs of each and every family member.

Hidden Guides

Adventure travel or a relaxing vacation?—"Hidden" guidebooks are the only travel books in the business to provide detailed information on both. Aimed at environmentally aware travelers, our motto is "Where Vacations Meet Adventures." These books combine details on unique hotels, restaurants and sightseeing with information on camping, sports and hiking for the outdoor enthusiast.

The New Key Guides

Based on the concept of ecotourism, The New Key Guides are dedicated to the preservation of Central America's rare and endangered species, architecture and archaeology. Filled with helpful tips, they give travelers everything they need to know about these exotic destinations.

Ulysses Press books are available at bookstores everywhere. If any of the following titles are unavailable at your local bookstore, ask the bookseller to order them.

You can also order books directly from Ulysses Press
P.O. Box 3440, Berkeley, CA 94703
800-377-2542 or 510-601-8301
fax: 510-601-8307
www.ulyssespress.com
e-mail: ulysses@ulyssespress.com

PARADISE FAMILY GUIDES

___ Paradise Family Guides: Kaua'i, $16.95
___ Paradise Family Guides: Maui, $16.95
___ Paradise Family Guides: Big Island of Hawai'i, $16.95

HIDDEN GUIDEBOOKS

___ Hidden Arizona, $16.95
___ Hidden Bahamas, $14.95
___ Hidden Baja, $14.95
___ Hidden Belize, $15.95
___ Hidden Big Island of Hawaii, $13.95
___ Hidden Boston & Cape Cod, $14.95
___ Hidden British Columbia, $18.95
___ Hidden Cancún & the Yucatán, $16.95
___ Hidden Carolinas, $17.95
___ Hidden Coast of California, $18.95
___ Hidden Colorado, $15.95
___ Hidden Disneyland, $13.95
___ Hidden Florida, $18.95
___ Hidden Florida Keys & Everglades, $12.95
___ Hidden Georgia, $16.95
___ Hidden Guatemala, $16.95
___ Hidden Hawaii, $18.95
___ Hidden Idaho, $14.95
___ Hidden Kauai, $13.95
___ Hidden Maui, $13.95
___ Hidden Montana, $15.95
___ Hidden New England, $18.95
___ Hidden New Mexico, $15.95
___ Hidden Oahu, $13.95
___ Hidden Oregon, $15.95
___ Hidden Pacific Northwest, $18.95
___ Hidden Salt Lake City, $14.95
___ Hidden San Francisco & Northern California, $18.95
___ Hidden Southern California, $18.95
___ Hidden Southwest, $19.95
___ Hidden Tahiti, $17.95
___ Hidden Tennessee, $16.95
___ Hidden Utah, $16.95
___ Hidden Walt Disney World, $13.95
___ Hidden Washington, $15.95
___ Hidden Wine Country, $13.95
___ Hidden Wyoming, $15.95

NEW KEY GUIDES

___ The New Key to Costa Rica, $18.95
___ The New Key to Ecuador and the Galápagos, $18.95

Mark the book(s) you're ordering and enter the total cost here ➡

California residents add 8.25% sales tax here ➡

Shipping, check box for preferred method and enter cost here ➡

❑ Book Rate (free) ❑ Priority Mail/UPS Ground (call for rates)
❑ UPS Overnight or 2-Day Air (call for rates)

Billing, enter total amt. due here and check payment method ➡

❑ CHECK   ❑ MONEY ORDER
❑ VISA/MASTERCARD_____ EXP. DATE _____

NAME_____ PHONE _____
ADDRESS_____
CITY _____ STATE_____ ZIP_____

MONEY-BACK GUARANTEE ON DIRECT ORDERS PLACED THROUGH ULYSSES PRESS.

About the Author

CHRISTIE STILSON, a native Oregonian, is also one of the original authors of *Paradise Family Guides: Kaua'i*. She first visited the Hawaiian islands in the late 1970s and loved Hawai'i so much, she began writing travel guides for the islands. Christie and her two children have been frequent visitors to the Aloha State ever since.